Auditing Theory and Practice

The Willard J. Graham Series in Accounting
Consulting Editor   Robert N. Anthony   *Harvard University*

Auditing Theory and Practice

Roger H. Hermanson, Ph.D., C.P.A.
Research Professor of Accounting
Georgia State University

Stephen E. Loeb, Ph.D., C.P.A.
Professor and Chairman of Accounting
University of Maryland

John M. Saada, M.B.A., C.P.A.
Partner, Ernst & Whinney

Robert H. Strawser, D.B.A., C.P.A.
Professor and Chairman of Accounting
University of Houston

1980   Revised Edition

 RICHARD D. IRWIN, INC.   Homewood, Illinois   60430

This book includes quotations and adaptations
from the Uniform CPA Examinations and Unofficial
Answers Copyright 1949, 1950, 1951, 1952, 1953, 1954,
1955, 1956, 1957, 1958, 1959, 1960, 1961, 1962, 1963,
1964, 1965, 1966, 1967, 1968, 1969, 1970, 1971, 1972,
1973, © 1974, © 1975, © 1976, © 1977, © 1978, ©
1979, by the American Institute of Certified Public
Accountants, Inc. Such passages have been reprinted or
adapted with permission of the AICPA.

ISBN 0-256-02330-1
Library of Congress Catalog Card No. 79-89468

Printed in the United States of America

4 5 6 7 8 9 0 MP 7 6 5 4 3 2

Preface

This Revised Edition continues to be the result of a unique marriage of academic and professional approaches to auditing. It was written by three academic accountants and a practitioner. As a result we believe it contains the best of theory and the best of practice.

This edition incorporates accounting and auditing pronouncements through late 1979. The new material has been integrated with the materials which appeared in the first edition.

Much of the content of the text is based on materials supplied by Ernst & Whinney from their professional training manuals which were based on actual auditing engagements. We believe this adds an element of realism which does not exist in many other auditing textbooks. Yet, the book is not based entirely on professional practice. It is a blending of the conceptual and procedural approaches to auditing. The book is designed for use in a one-semester or one-quarter undergraduate or graduate course in auditing.

Organization of the Contents

The material is divided into four categories or parts:

Part	Chapters	Coverage
One	1–4	The Auditing Environment
Two	5–8	The Audit Process
Three	9–13	Audit Procedures
Four	14–15	Auditors' Communications

Part One, contains an introductory chapter on the auditing environment, a chapter on professional ethics, and two chapters dealing with the auditor's legal liability. Chapter 1 describes the purposes of auditing, attributes of a profession, various professional organizations, organization of firms within public accounting, generally accepted auditing standards, the purpose of the accountant's report, and the steps in performing an audit. Chapter 2 is concerned with professional ethics, including why a code of ethics is necessary, the nature of the rules of conduct, the specific obligations, and how the code is enforced. An Appendix to the chapter contains the Code of Professional Ethics as revised through late 1979. Chapter 3 covers the accountants' legal liability under the common law; while Chapter 4 is concerned with the SEC and the accountants' liability under statute law. Many of the famous liability cases are covered in these two chapters.

Part Two covers the audit process. Chapter 5 deals with general aspects of internal control, the use of compliance tests, errors and irregularities, and illegal acts by clients. This chapter has four appendixes, the first showing a partial internal control questionnaire, the second illustrating the flowchart method of documenting the internal control system, the third giving an example of an audit program for selected compliance tests, and the fourth discussing the main features of the Foreign Corrupt Practices Act of 1977. Chapter 6 is concerned with evidence and working papers. The nature and use of evidence is described. The importance, nature, and purposes of working papers are also discussed. Chapter 7 deals with audit sampling, including the objectives of testing, statistical concepts used, estimation sampling for attributes and variables, and how sampling is applied in practice. The chapter has been divided into two reading parts for flexibility in assigning the chapter. Chapter 8 covers the audit aspects of systems which utilize electronic data processing. The chapter was written completely by Michael J. Jett, who at the time was a manager in the National Office of Ernst & Whinney. The chapter is a thorough and up-to-date coverage of the topic.

Part Three is concerned with specific auditing procedures for various types of accounts. The "march through the balance sheet" is somewhat more concise than that in many other texts. Each of these chapters discusses the auditor's objective in auditing the account(s). It also describes the essential features of internal control of the account(s) involved, gives the specific procedures to follow in the various audit tests, and illustrates the various schedules that may be utilized. Each of these chapters includes a description of the audit memorandum or memoranda which the auditor should prepare for inclusion in the working papers. The chapters and titles are: 9—Cash; 10—Receivables; 11—Inventories; 12—Other Types of Assets; and 13—Creditors' and Owners' Equities; Income Statement Accounts; and Other Matters. A discussion of the audit aspects of segment information, related party transactions, and the review of interim financial information has been added to Chapter 13. We view the condensing of the coverage of procedures as a principal advantage of the text. Some users may want to condense this coverage even further by not spending considerable class time covering each one of these chapters. Others may even choose to have their students cover some of these chapters on their own should time become a problem.

Part Four is concerned with communications of the auditor. Chapter 14 covers the auditor's report. The standard (short-form) report is discussed. The various opinions and the situations in which they should be used are described. Other topics covered include subsequent events, segment information, interim financial data, long-form reports, special reports, other reports, and the auditor's role and responsibilities when associated with unaudited financial statements. Chapter 15 deals with management letters. This form of communication, which the auditor has with the management of a client, is often not covered in detail in other texts. Our purposes in giving this topic a fuller coverage are to impress on the students the importance of being alert to identifying management problems while performing audit tests, to stress the auditor's responsibility for communicating problems to management, and to impress upon students the importance of being able to organize and express their thoughts in an effective and efficient manner. The instructor could assign students the task of preparing several management letters and spend class time on a critique of these letters.

Other Special Features

The inclusion of learning objectives at the beginning of each chapter is a unique feature. Their purpose is to direct the student's attention to the most important points in the chapter and to better prepare the student to receive and assimilate the new knowledge.

There are numerous questions and problems at the end of each chapter. New questions and problems have been added to many of the chapters. They can be utilized in the classroom or as outside assignments to assist the instructor in determining whether the student has understood each chapter. Many of these items have been taken or adapted from CPA examinations and give students experience in answering these types of questions. Additionally, a glossary has been added to each chapter.

Acknowledgments

The authors wish to thank Ernst & Whinney for granting permission to use materials from the firm's files. John A. Haga was particularly helpful in our preparation of the chapter on audit sampling. Various other Ernst & Whinney personnel provided valuable technical review assistance.

We thank both Arthur J. Francia of the University of Houston for writing Chapter 3 and parts of Chapter 4 and Michael J. Jett for his

x

development of Chapter 8. Harry Brown developed Chapter 8 in the original edition.

The authors appreciate the permissions given to use materials under copyright. Especially, we thank the American Institute of Certified Public Accountants for permission to use material from Uniform CPA examinations as well as from other AICPA sources. Throughout the text constant reference is made to current relevant AICPA pronouncements.

Several reviewers, including Robert N. Anthony of Harvard University, Charles G. Carpenter, Miami University of Ohio; Lewis Davidson, University of North Carolina at Chapel Hill; Paul E. Dascher, Drexel University; Frederick L. Neumann, University of Illinois at Urbana; James M. Lahey, Northern Illinois University; Joe R. Fritzemeyer, Arizona State University; Oscar J. Holzmann, University of South Carolina; Clair W. Janes, San Jose State University; and Johnny R. Johnson, University of Georgia provided helpful guidance. Other individuals including James P. Bedingfield, University of Maryland; Larry H. Beard, University of South Carolina; Gary A. Luoma, Georgia State University; Kathryn C. Buckner, Georgia State University; H. Frank Stabler, Georgia State University; Ronald M. Copeland, University of South Carolina; John H. McCray, College of William and Mary; E. Barry Rice, Loyola College (Baltimore); Carl Warren, University of Georgia; Lawrence Gramling, University of Maryland; Richard Leegant, University of Maryland; Teresa Iannaconi, University of Maryland; Christina McMullen, University of Maryland; and several Ernst & Whinney executives made helpful comments on various portions of the manuscript. Any shortcomings in the final version are, of course, the responsibility of the authors.

February 1980

Roger H. Hermanson
Stephen E. Loeb
John M. Saada
Robert H. Strawser

Contents

Extent of Confirmation. Recording Accounts Circularized. Controlling Customer Statements and Confirmation Requests. Investigating Exceptions to Confirmation Requests. Performing Alternative Procedures. Interim Transactions from Confirmation Date to Balance-Sheet Date. The Evaluation Procedures. Sales Cutoff. Accounts Sold or Assigned. Substantive Tests: Notes Receivable. Items for Letter of Representation. Audit Memorandum.

Methods of Determining Cost. Internal Control over Inventory: *Safeguarding Inventory. Accurate Accounting.* Compliance Testing: Inventory: Substantive Testing: Inventory: *Observations and Tests of Physical Inventories. Review of Company's Inventory Plans. Observation of the Taking of the Physical Inventory. Tracing Test Counts, Checking Cutoffs, and Testing Clerical Accuracy. Inventory Valuation. Physical Inventory Adjustments. Consignments, Purchase and Sales Commitments. Items for Letter of Representation.* Audit Memorandum.

Securities: *Internal Control over Securities. Audit Procedures.* Property, Plant, and Equipment: *Internal Control over Property, Plant, and Equipment. Auditing Property, Plant, and Equipment Accounts.* Prepaid Expenses and Deferred Charges. Intangible Assets. Miscellaneous Assets. Audit Memoranda.

13. Creditors' and Owners' Equities; Income Statement Accounts; and Other Matters **489**

Liabilities: *Internal Control over Liabilities. Audit Procedures for Liabilities.* Items for Letter of Representation. Stockholders' Equity: *Internal Control. Auditing Stockholders' Equity.* Operations: *Analysis of Operating Accounts. Recognizing Management Problems. Financial Reporting and Changing Prices.* Payrolls: *Payrolls—Plant. Payrolls—Office and Executive.* Audit Aspects of Segment Information: *Materiality. Modification of Regular Audit Procedures. Procedures Applied to Segment Information.* Related Party Transactions: *Audit Procedures. Disclosure.* Review of Interim Financial Information: *Objective of a Review. Nature of Procedures for a Review. Timing and Extent of Procedures.* Audit Memoranda.

part four
Auditors' Communications

The Standard Report: *Separate Financial Statements. Consolidated Statements. Parent Statements. Comparative Statements.* Qualifications, Adverse Opinions, and Disclaimers: *Middle Paragraphs. Qualified Opinion. Adverse Opinion. Disclaimer of Opinion.* Reasons for

Departure from the Wording of the Standard Report: *Limitations of Scope. Other Auditors. Lack of Conformity with GAAP. Departure from a Promulgated Principle. Consistency. Uncertainties. Emphasizing a Matter. Independence.* Subsequent Events: *Types of Subsequent Events. Auditing Procedures in the Subsequent Period. Subsequent Discovery of Facts.* Other Information and the Auditor. Reporting Segment Information: *Misstatement or Omission. Consistency. Scope. Reporting Separately.* Long-Form Reports: *Report on Additional Financial Information. Comments. A Proposed Revision.* Special Reports: *Basis Other Than GAAP. Reports on Specific Elements, Accounts or Items. Reports on Compliance. Prescribed Forms.* Other Types of Reports: *Reports on Interim Financial Information Presented Other Than in a Note to Audited Financial Statements. Reporting on Interim Financial Information Presented in a Note to Audited Financial Statements. Forecasts. Reports on Internal Control. Reporting on Required Supplemental Information.* Unaudited Statements: Public Entities: *When an Accountant Is Associated with Financial Statements. Disclaimer of Opinion. Modified Disclaimer.* Unaudited Statements; Nonpublic Entities: *Reporting Obligation. Compilation. Review of Financial Statements. Departures form GAAP.*

part one

The Auditing Environment

Learning Objectives

Study of the material in this chapter is designed to achieve a number of learning objectives. These include an understanding of the:

1. Purpose of auditing.
2. Various functions performed by public accountants.
3. Categories of public accountants.
4. Attributes of a profession and the extent to which public accounting meets these attributes.
5. Names and purposes of professional organizations relating to certified public accountants.
6. Organization of firms within public accounting and the typical organization within a public accounting firm.
7. Consideration of the auditing standards and an introduction to the nature and purpose of the accountant's report.
8. Steps the certified public accountant takes in performing an audit.

1

The CPA and the Auditing Environment

THE PURPOSE OF AUDITING

Accounting is concerned with the collection, summarization, and communication of information regarding economic events, and the results thereof especially as these events relate to business entities. Various groups, such as investors, stockholders, creditors, labor unions, government, and investment bankers have an interest in the economic affairs of business entities. Auditing is an integral part of the communication process.

The American Accounting Association's Committee on Basic Auditing Concepts has broadly defined auditing as

> . . . a systematic process of objectively obtaining and evaluating evidence regarding assertions about economic actions and events to ascertain the degree of correspondence between those assertions and established criteria and communicating the results to interested users.[1]

The communication of accounting information to interested users is depicted in Figure 1-1.

Users of accounting information are concerned with both the information content of the subject matter and the quality of the information received. Auditing (the attest function) assists users in evaluating the quality of the accounting information communicated to them.[2]

In our society independent public accountants act as outside auditors. These are professional accountants who are engaged by the stockholders, board of directors (or its audit committee), and/or management to evaluate the fairness of the presentation of financial state-

---

[1] Joseph A. Silvoso et al., "Report of the Committee on Basic Auditing Concepts," Supplement to vol. 47 of *The Accounting Review*, 1972, p. 18.

[2] Ibid., p. 25.

FIGURE 1-1
The communication of
accounting information

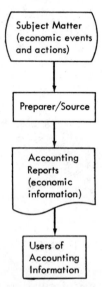

Source: Joseph A. Silvoso et al., "Report of the Committee on Basic Auditing Concepts," Supplement to vol. 47 of *The Accounting Review*, 1972, p. 25.

ments (reports of economic events) issued by management. After conducting an audit of the accounting system of a business, the independent auditor issues an opinion on the financial statements (this is an evaluation of the quality of the information). This is called "attestation." Specifically, the American Accounting Association's Committee on Basic Auditing Concepts defined attestation as

> . . . a communicated statement of opinion (judgment), based upon convincing evidence, by an independent, competent, authoritative person, concerning the degree of correspondence in all material respects of accounting information communicated by an entity (individual, firm, or governmental unit) with established criteria.[3]

The auditor attests to the fairness of the presentation of financial statements. In our society various outside groups rely on this attestation by independent auditors when they use financial statements.

Conditions Creating a Demand for Auditing

Four conditions in our business environment create a demand for an independent audit.[4] They are:

---

[3] Ibid., p. 22.

[4] This discussion and the discussion in the next section are based on Silvoso et al., "Report of the Committee," pp. 21 and 25–28.

Conflict of Interest. Users are concerned with the possibility of bias in the information provided them when there is an actual or potential conflict of interest between the user and the provider of the information.

Consequence. When information is used as input for decisions of significant consequence, users are concerned with the possibility of biased, misleading, irrelevant, or incomplete information.

Complexity. As information communicated has become more complex, users of information have found it more difficult or even impossible to obtain direct assurance as to the quality of the information received.

Remoteness. Remoteness is caused by the separation of the user of the information and the information source and prevents the user from directly assessing the quality of the information received.

Value Added by the Audit Function

While auditing does not alter the primary communication process between subject matter and users of financial statements, it adds a secondary communication process between the auditor and users (indicated by the broken lines in Figure 1–2). The purpose of the auditor's communication of the audit report is to assist users in determining the quality of information as defined in terms of established criteria based on evidence obtained by the auditor during the course of the examination.

The Committee on Basic Auditing Concepts believed that the auditor derives the criteria from users of accounting information (Figure 1–2). This process may be quite indirect in that users are a large and heterogeneous group. The Committee seems to be implying that users inform the auditor of the criteria to be used by making the actual criteria establishers (the SEC, FASB, AICPA, and so on) aware of user needs and expectations.

The entire process (Figure 1–2) applied to financial statement audits will be discussed throughout the remainder of this text.

THE GROWTH IN PUBLIC ACCOUNTING PRACTICE

At the beginning of the 20th century, there were very few certified public accountants in the United States. Today there are over 140,000 CPAs, and the accounting profession continues to grow. Some of the reasons for this growth are discussed in the following paragraphs.

Corporate Form of Organization

At the turn of the century, most American businesses were small and were managed by their owners. Since these owner-managers had

FIGURE 1-2

The communication of accounting information and role of audit function

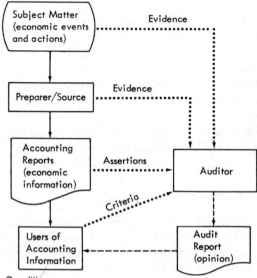

Conditions:
Conflict of interest between preparer and users.
Consequence of information to users.
Complexity of subject matter and audit process.
Remoteness of users from subject matter and preparer.

Source: Joseph A. Silvoso et al., "Report of the Committee on Basic Auditing Concepts," Supplement to vol. 47 of *The Accounting Review*, 1972, p. 27.

extensive firsthand knowledge of the business and its operations, they had little need for independent public accountants except to have them extensively check records for possible employee fraud. As businesses increased both in size and complexity, owners found it more difficult to maintain complete knowledge of all aspects of their businesses. More sophisticated means of obtaining information were needed. The tremendous business expansion which followed World War I required large-scale financing, and more and more companies met this need through the sale of stock to the public. There was thus a marked shift toward outside ownership.

The new groups of public stockholders and creditors frequently found many companies' financial reports not only uninformative but, in some cases, actually misleading. The accounting principles used by companies varied, and even those used by the same company varied from one time to another. This situation was aggravated by the prevalence of such abuses as inadequate disclosure and inaccurate statement balances. Consequently, there arose a demand for independent public accountants to examine companies' financial statements and to report on them. Thus, the work of independent public accountants switched in emphasis from searching for fraud to judging the fair presentation of financial statements.

The independent public accountant attests to (gives an opinion on) the fairness of the presentation of the financial statements of clients. In performing this function, CPAs are in a unique position in that they are responsible both to the client who pays their fee and to any third party who relies on their audit reports. In a special sense, then, any user of financial statements is also the CPA's client.

Functions Other Than Auditing

Independent public accountants also render services other than auditing. They do tax work, act as management consultants, prepare reports for government agencies, and serve as expert witnesses.

Tax Work. In 1913, Congress enacted the federal income tax law. Because the tax was based on accounting information, an added burden was placed on companies to perform these additional accounting responsibilities. However, independent accountants were well equipped to assist their clients by virtue of their special knowledge of accounting and of their clients' financial affairs. Today, tax services are an important aspect of the practice of most independent public accountants.

Reports for Government Agencies. The Securities Act of 1933 and the Securities Exchange Act of 1934 require that many businesses supply the government and various other parties with certain information including financial statements. Independent public accountants attest to the financial statements presented to the SEC. (The SEC Acts are discussed in detail in Chapter 4.) CPAs also assist their clients in preparing reports for other governmental agencies.

Management Services. From the earliest days of the profession, most practitioners perceived the responsibility of independent accountants as going beyond the process of auditing and the rendering of tax services. The auditors' position as observers who were both knowledgeable and independent provided them with a unique opportunity to serve as advisors on many matters (e.g., systems design, budgeting, and so on). Today, management services comprise an important portion of the practices of many accounting firms. Many CPA firms, in fact, have separate management services departments. The range of management services offered by CPA firms includes such diverse activities as budgeting, systems design and installation, and operations research.

Expert Witness. Independent public accountants may be called upon to testify in court as expert witnesses. CPAs have specialized knowledge and thus may serve in court as experts in areas that involve accounting expertise.

PUBLIC ACCOUNTANTS AND CPAs

Public accountants operate as independent individuals or firms of individuals who hold themselves out to the public as being qualified to render services such as auditing, taxes, and management services. Furthermore, public accountants themselves may be categorized into two broad types: certified public accountants (CPAs) and public accountants who are not certified (PAs).

An individual designated as a CPA is recognized by at least one state government (or the District of Columbia or a U.S. territory) as possessing at least a minimum level of competence in certain designated areas. The criterion used to measure this competence is an examination administered by each state but prepared and graded nationally by the American Institute of Certified Public Accountants (AICPA), the national professional association of CPAs.

Each jurisdiction has enacted public accounting legislation which is administered by a board of accountancy. It is within the province of each board to determine, within the standards set by law, who is qualified to sit for the national CPA examination. The results of the CPA examination are communicated to the boards of accountancy which award the designation of CPA to the successful candidates. The advantage of becoming a CPA is that the CPA is generally recognized as being the most qualified of accounting practitioners.

There are three classifications of non-certified public accountants. These categories vary according to the applicable state law. And there are two classes of legislation, depending on the jurisdiction. "Non-continuing laws" permit non-certified public accountants, who were practicing prior to or during the time the laws were passed, to be licensed. They are usually identified as Public Accountants and are permitted to perform the same services as CPAs. But these laws prohibit further licensing of Public Accountants. Certain jurisdictions have "continuing laws." These states allow additional public accountants (non-CPAs) to be licensed. Requirements for such licensing vary from state to state. A third type exists in a few jurisdictions which have no regulation regarding non-certified public accountants. In these jurisdictions anyone is permitted to practice as a public accountant without restriction.[5]

---

[5] John L. Carey, *The CPA Plans for the Future* (New York: American Institute of Certified Public Accountants, 1965), pp. 475–77.

PUBLIC ACCOUNTING AS A PROFESSION

Professions generally are recognized in our society as elite occupational classifications. Recognition as a profession is a goal toward which many occupations strive. The social science literature reveals that there is no general agreement on any single definition of a profession.

One approach used by social scientists to determine whether or not a particular occupation is a profession is to identify the characteristics of a profession and then to ascertain if that occupation has these characteristics. Some authorities hold the view that professional attributes are not the exclusive domain of a few elite occupations. This approach regards all occupations as possessing most of the attributes ascribed to professionalism. At any moment in time, then, an occupation will have developed to a varying degree in terms of each characteristic.[6]

One often-used group of professional characteristics has been defined by Ernest Greenwood. In positing what he considers an ideal profession Greenwood sets forth five major characteristics: ". . . (1) systematic theory, (2) authority, (3) community sanction, (4) ethical codes, and (5) a culture."[7]

Systematic Body of Theory[8]

Greenwood suggests that a profession has a body of theory that is internally consistent. The accounting principles that have evolved over the years have not always been a model of consistency. However, both practicing and academic accountants are working to develop a more consistent system of both accounting and auditing theory.

Greenwood also suggests that a profession requires the mastery of an existing body of theory as a prerequisite to the acquisition of professional skill. Certainly the mastery of accounting theory is necessary for auditing. Auditors (as will shortly be explained in more detail) must determine whether their client's financial statements are prepared and presented in accordance with generally accepted accounting principles.

---

[6] Ernest Greenwood, "Attributes of a Profession," *Social Work* (July 1957), p. 46. Also, Archie Kleingartner, "Professionalism and Salaried Worker Organization," *Industrial Relations Research Institute*, University of Wisconsin, 1967, p. 8.

[7] Greenwood, "Attributes of a Profession," p. 45. Reprinted with permission of the National Association of Social Workers, from *Social Work*, vol. 2, no. 3 (July 1957).

[8] This section and the following four sections are based on ibid., pp. 46-52. Paraphrased with permission of the National Association of Social Workers, from *Social Work*, vol. 2, no. 3 (July 1957), pp. 46-52.

Professional Authority

Clients who use the services of a professional often do not really understand their own needs. The professional thus determines what is good or bad for the client, and the client accedes to this professional judgment. In many instances companies turn to the CPA for advice on accounting and related matters. Also, as previously mentioned, financial statement users are, in essence, also the clients of independent CPAs since they often rely heavily on their judgment.

A profession is functionally specific. In other words, professionals' authority is limited to the area in which they have competence. In auditing, independent CPAs are performing their traditional function. All CPAs should have competence in auditing since it is such an important portion of their work. This competence is gained through a combination of education and supervised experience. The accounting curriculum at most universities includes at least one course devoted exclusively to auditing.

Taxation is an area in which both CPAs and attorneys have contended for a number of years. A review of the uniform CPA examination for the past ten years reveals that there often have been at least two fairly extensive questions on taxation included in each examination. Also, most university accounting curricula contain one or more courses in taxation which are taken by accounting majors.

In the past, CPAs typically have not been educated in some of the areas related to management services (exceptions include areas such as budgeting and systems). However, many business curricula now include courses which are directly related to the broader areas of management consulting.

Sanction of the Community

Greenwood asserts that each profession attempts ". . . to persuade the community to sanction its authority within certain spheres by conferring . . . a series of powers and privileges."[9] Professions generally wish to: (1) control training centers; (2) control admission; (3) have privileged communication; (4) have autonomy on technical matters.[10]

Control of Training Centers. Presently the accounting profession has little *direct* influence on accounting programs in colleges and universities. One authority noted that "it is probably fair to say that in no country where the profession has reached a position of comparable

---

[9] Ibid., p. 48. Reprinted with permission of the National Association of Social Workers, from *Social Work*, vol. 2, no. 3 (July 1957).

[10] Ibid., p. 49.

importance has the accounting profession less control over the basic education of its candidates than in the United States."[11]

At present, the primary means used by practitioners to influence the accounting curricula of colleges and universities are by suggestions made through the professional associations, the rules of the boards of accountancy, and by the structure of the CPA examination. As of this writing, accreditation of university accounting programs seems to be a distinct possibility. The practicing profession will likely have a "voice" in this process.

Admission. Professions obtain from the larger community a licensing system for admission to the profession. In the United States, the licensing system for CPAs is controlled by the states and territories. All jurisdictions require, as a minimum, the successful completion of the Uniform CPA Examination before awarding a CPA certificate.

Privileged Communication. Generally, society has not granted privileged communication (the privilege of not having to reveal a client's confidence in a court of law) to CPAs, and the federal government generally does not recognize privileged communication for CPAs. In the few jurisdictions which have granted CPAs privileged communication it is sometimes granted only under certain limited circumstances.

Technical Autonomy. A profession is granted autonomy on technical matters. The general public does not fully understand technical matters; therefore, the work of the practicing professionals must be evaluated by their colleague-group. Generally, CPAs have been granted a fairly high degree of (but not complete) autonomy in their practice.

Code of Ethics

In order to maintain its autonomy, a profession must have a self-regulative code of ethics which it voluntarily adopts. The American Institute of Certified Public Accountants (AICPA) code of ethics is discussed in Chapter 2. This code has been in the process of development since the beginning of the current century.

Professional Culture

A professional culture is the social pattern generated by the interaction of the social roles which are required by the network of informal and formal groups through which a profession operates. In

---

[11] Carey, *The CPA Plans for the Future*, p. 262.

studying the culture of a profession, it is necessary to examine its values, norms, and symbols. Accounting has developed a professional culture. This is evidenced by such factors as the formal norms of the code of ethics, the informal rules that guide relationships among practitioners, and the traditions and myths that have arisen concerning the CPA examination.

PROFESSIONAL ORGANIZATIONS

American Institute of Certified Public Accountants (AICPA)

The American Institute of Certified Public Accountants is the national professional association of CPAs. The Institute is a voluntary professional association; consequently, not all CPAs are members.

Headquartered in New York City, the AICPA has a large full-time staff which performs such functions as: (1) providing members with advice on technical matters, (2) performing research, (3) publishing various items relating to accounting, (4) providing a national political lobby for the profession, and (5) generally administering the national affairs of the profession. It accomplishes much of its work through committees composed of its members. One of the publications of the AICPA—*The Journal of Accountancy*—is a leading accounting journal. Over the years it has contained many important articles on accounting and auditing. A board of the AICPA issues Statements on Auditing Standards (SAS) that are authoritative statements on auditing matters.[12]

In September 1977, the AICPA established a division within the Institute which firms may join. The division is called the AICPA Division of CPA Firms and consists of two sections: (1) the SEC Practice Section and (2) the Private Companies Practice Section.

SEC Practice Section.[13]   Any CPA firm may join the SEC Practice Section. The firm must apply and agree to abide by the rules for members. Some of these requirements include: (1) ensuring that all U.S. partners or shareholders (when the firm is organized as a profes-

---

[12] *Statement on Auditing Standards (SAS) No. 1*, entitled "Codification of Auditing Standards and Procedures" was issued in 1972 (first available in March 1973) by the AICPA. *SAS No. 1* is a codification of and supersedes Statements on Auditing Procedure Nos. 33 through 54 previously issued by the AICPA.

[13] Information for the next two sections of the chapter is taken from: "The AICPA Division of CPA Firms," *The Journal of Accountancy*, November 1977, pp. 113–120; "Organization Structure and Functions of the SEC Practice Section of the AICPA Division for CPA Firms," American Institute of Certified Public Accountants, 1978; and "Organization Structure and Functions of the Private Companies Practice Section of the AICPA Division for CPA Firms including Revisions through October 31, 1978," American Institute of Certified Public Accountants, 1978.

sional corporation), who are eligible to join the AICPA, are members of the Institute; (2) adhering to certain quality control standards; (3) at selected times submitting to peer review (peer review is discussed later); (4) ensuring that professional staff residing in the United States participates in at least 120 hours of continuing education over a three-year period (with not less than 20 hours in any given year); (5) filing certain information with the section each year (e.g., number of firm offices and their location, total number of CPAs with the firm); and (6) maintaining certain minimum amounts and types of liability insurance.

The objectives of the section include: (1) the improvement of the quality of practice by CPA firms before the SEC; (2) self-regulation of firms that are members of the section; and (3) provision of a forum for information relating to practice before the SEC. To help achieve these objectives, the section is administered by an Executive Committee. Furthermore, the activities of the section are subject to the oversight and public reporting by a Public Oversight Board.

The Executive Committee is composed of individuals from at least 21 firms that are members of the section. They are appointed by the Chairman of the Board of the AICPA (from a list provided by the section's nominating committee) subject to the approval of the AICPA Board and (after the appointment of the initial Executive Committee) the section's Executive Committee. This Executive Committee establishes the policies of the section and oversees the activities of the section. Subject to the approval of the AICPA's Board of Directors, the Executive Committee appointed the first five members of the Public Oversight Board. Thereafter, appointment to the Board is done by the Board itself (subject to the approval of the AICPA Board of Directors).

The Public Oversight Board consists of five members drawn from such areas as business, education, banking, law, economics, and government. They monitor and evaluate the regulatory, sanctioning, and other activities of the section.

Private Companies Practice Section. Any CPA firm, a majority of whose partners, shareholders, or proprietors are AICPA members, may join the Private Companies Practice Section. The firm must apply and agree to abide by the rules for members. Some of these rules include: (1) ensuring that all partners and shareholders, who are U.S. residents and are eligible for AICPA membership, are members of the Institute; (2) adhering to quality control standards; (3) at selected times submitting to peer review; (4) ensuring that all professional staff members residing in the U.S. participate in at least 120 hours of continuing education every three years with at least 20 hours every year; and (5) maintaining certain minimum amounts and types of liability insurance.

The objectives of the section include: (1) the improvement of the quality of practice to private companies; (2) self-regulation of member firms; and (3) providing a forum for member firms on professional matters. This section is governed by an Executive Committee consisting of representatives of 21 member firms. The Executive Committee at its discretion may appoint a Public Oversight Board. As of this writing, it had not done so.

State Societies

CPAs in the various states and other jurisdictions have organized CPA societies. Like the AICPA, these societies are voluntary professional associations. They generally hold monthly dinner meetings and other professional development meetings for their members. In many states the state societies are organized on a local chapter basis, with each chapter holding its own meetings. The societies provide various informational services to members and generally administer the affairs of the accounting profession within each state. Like the AICPA, much of their work is accomplished through committees composed of their members. These societies sometimes act as a lobbying force to the state legislatures within each state. State societies are autonomous and have no direct affiliation with the AICPA. However, the AICPA and the state societies cooperate on various matters.

Boards of Accountancy

As was noted previously, a board of accountancy is the agency of a state or territory government that is empowered to administer that jurisdiction's accounting law. There are 54 such boards (one in each state, the District of Columbia, and each U.S. territory). As a licensing agency of the state, the board is usually the only body that may issue and revoke CPA certificates and grant licenses to practice. Thus, a board has much influence over the practices of certified public accountants within its jurisdiction.

ORGANIZATION OF FIRMS

Certified Public Accountants conduct their practice as individual practitioners or in firms. It is possible to classify CPA firms in the United States into three general categories: (1) national firms; (2) regional firms; and (3) local firms.

The national firms typically have offices in most major cities of the United States, and in many instances, cities around the world. Traditionally, the "Big Eight"—Arthur Andersen & Co.; Arthur Young &

Company; Coopers & Lybrand; Ernst & Whinney; Deloitte Haskins & Sells; Peat, Marwick, Mitchell & Co.; Price Waterhouse & Co.; and Touche Ross & Co. have been considered the national firms. In recent years, other firms (e.g., Alexander Grant & Co.; Elmer Fox, Westheimer & Company; Laventhol & Horwath; Main Hurdman and Cranstoun; and Seidman & Seidman) have also attained national stature.

Regional firms usually have offices in one or two geographical regions. Local firms are usually in one town or city.

ORGANIZATION WITHIN A FIRM

A public accounting firm may consist of a sole practitioner, a partnership, or a professional corporation. Most CPA firms are organized as partnerships. In a partnership the professional staff consists of partners, managers and supervisors, seniors, and staff accountants. The exact titles and different levels vary from firm to firm. Also, the organization of tax and management service departments usually differs somewhat from the organization of the audit staff.

When a firm is organized as a professional corporation it is generally required that shareholders be public accountants. Also, the shareholders, directors, officers, and employees still have the same professional obligations as those in a firm organized as either a proprietorship or a partnership. Lay (non-CPA) directors or officers should not have any influence on professional matters.[14]

In addition to the professional staff, there usually are various types of support personnel such as typists, clerks, secretaries, messengers, and receptionists. Additionally, some firms are beginning to use paraprofessional personnel in some situations. These individuals perform certain of the functions formerly performed by the professional staff.

Partners

In a firm organized as a partnership the partners own and administer their firm. They maintain the primary contact with clients. Generally, partners review and approve the work of subordinates. Only partners may sign the audit report that results from the audit engagement.

Managers and Supervisors

Managers usually manage the *entire scope* of several engagements that may be conducted simultaneously. Supervisors, depending upon

[14]AICPA Professional Standards, Volume 2, American Institute of Certified Public Accountants.

the firm, often manage the *field work* of several engagements that may be running simultaneously. Generally, managers and supervisors prepare, review, and approve drafts of audit reports and other communications.

Senior Accountants

Senior accountants supervise the work and activity of the staff accountants assigned to them on field engagements. They also draft audit programs, audit reports, tax returns, and other communications to clients. In many instances, seniors will perform or direct the performance of the review of internal control, and perform certain research projects related to the engagement.

Staff Accountants

Staff accountants (sometimes called junior accountants) participate in engagements under the supervision of more experienced accountants. Staff accountants obtain evidence to substantiate the fairness of clients' financial statements. They prepare schedules and reports of findings, work on tax returns, and sometimes assist in proofreading and checking.

AUDITING STANDARDS

In the early history of public accounting, the quality of audit examinations often varied widely depending on the skill, understanding, and judgment of the particular auditor involved. Even at this early stage in its development, the profession quickly recognized that standards clearly were needed. Accordingly, the profession began drawing up a number of authoritative statements which have now undergone several decades of refinement and interpretation.

A set of "generally accepted auditing standards"—to use their official designation—was issued by the AICPA. It is essential that every auditor have a thorough understanding of these standards. The auditor's report refers directly to generally accepted auditing standards. Also, as will be noted in Chapter 2, the lack of compliance with generally accepted auditing standards is a violation of the AICPA's code of professional ethics. The importance of these standards to the auditor is signified by the following statement from *Statement on Auditing Standards (SAS) No. 4:* "Complying with generally accepted auditing standards is a basic objective of every firm conducting an audit practice."[15]

---

[15] *Statement on Auditing Standards No. 4,* "Quality Control Considerations for a Firm of Independent Auditors," American Institute of Certified Public Accountants, 1974, p. 1.

At the outset, a clear distinction must be made between *auditing standards* and *auditing procedures*. The term *procedures* in auditing refers to the methods and techniques used by the auditor in the conduct of the examination. The audit procedures used will vary according to the particular circumstances of the individual audit examination. On the other hand, auditing *standards* deal with measures of the quality of the performance of the procedures used by the auditor and the objectives to be obtained by the use of the procedures undertaken. Auditing standards change only rarely and then only by official decree. Generally accepted auditing standards are important for several reasons: they define the broad objectives for every independent audit; they provide a gauge for judging an auditor's performance; and they are recognized throughout the business and legal world as the standards of the profession.

There are ten generally accepted auditing standards which are divided into three broad classes or categories: *general standards, standards of field work,* and *standards of reporting.* These standards, as approved and adopted by the members of the American Institute of Certified Public Accountants, are as follows:

General Standards

1. The examination is to be performed by a person or persons having adequate technical training and proficiency as an auditor.
2. In all matters relating to the assignment, an independence in mental attitude is to be maintained by the auditor or auditors.
3. Due professional care is to be exercised in the performance of the examination and the preparation of the report.

Standards of Field Work

1. The work is to be adequately planned and assistants, if any, are to be properly supervised.
2. There is to be a proper study and evaluation of the existing internal control as a basis for reliance thereon and for the determination of the resultant extent of the tests to which auditing procedures are to be restricted.
3. Sufficient competent evidential matter is to be obtained through inspection, observation, inquiries, and confirmations to afford a reasonable basis for an opinion regarding the financial statements under examination.

Standards of Reporting

1. The report shall state whether the financial statements are presented in accordance with generally accepted accounting principles.
2. The report shall state whether such principles have been consistently observed in the current period in relation to the preceding period.

Full disclosure

3. Informative disclosures in the financial statements are to be regarded as reasonably adequate unless otherwise stated in the report.
4. The report shall either contain an expression of opinion regarding the financial statements, taken as a whole, or an assertion to the effect that an opinion cannot be expressed. When an overall opinion cannot be expressed, the reasons therefor should be stated. In all cases where an auditor's name is associated with financial statements the report should contain a clear-cut indication of the character of the auditor's examination, if any, and the degree of responsibility he is taking.[16]

Auditing standards require an accountant to make sound judgments in a wide variety of circumstances, a skill which is mastered only with experience.

AUDITING STANDARDS AND THE CPA

The standards and their implications for the accountant will now be explained in detail.

General Standards

1. The examination is to be performed by a person or persons having adequate technical training and proficiency as an auditor.

Auditors are expected to have adequate academic training in accounting, taxation, auditing, and other areas that relate to their profession. In addition, they should receive further training, both formal and informal, throughout their careers. This standard has several long-range implications for accountants who wish to grow within the profession. They should pass the CPA examination. They should stay abreast of current developments in accounting, auditing, and tax matters. In fact, an increasing number of jurisdictions now require CPAs to engage in continuing education to maintain their right to practice. Finally, the CPA should be willing to acquire technical knowledge in new subject areas.

SAS No. 4 discusses the responsibility of CPA firms for the professional development and training of their personnel. Firms are admonished to establish policy and procedures for the professional development of firm personnel. Personnel should be trained for the work and responsibilities to which they are assigned.

To become proficient, auditors need a combination of practical experience and academic training. Auditors must understand the ac-

---

[16] *Statement on Auditing Standards No. 1*, Section 150.02. Copyright © 1973 by the American Institute of Certified Public Accountants, Inc.

counting and auditing problems which are involved in every assignment they undertake. In addition, before beginning an engagement it
is important that they become familiar with the nature of the company,
its size, its products or services; and previous years' financial statements, accountants' reports, working papers, tax returns, and other
documents relating to special accounting problems.

SAS No. 4 also suggests that CPA firms establish other policies to
provide reasonable assurance that the audit work is performed by
individuals with proper training and proficiency. These include:

1. *Assignment policies.* It is suggested that policies be established
   to help assure that individuals assigned to an engagement have
   the proper training to handle the engagement. This requires
   careful planning.
2. *Consultation policies.* It is suggested that policies be established to help assure that individuals assigned to an engagement
   seek appropriate assistance when they are confronted with a
   problem which is beyond their expertise.
3. *Hiring policies.* It is suggested that firms establish policy standards to be used when hiring personnel. Firms should consider
   creating policies concerning investigating the backgrounds of new
   employees.
4. *Advancement policies.* It is suggested that firms establish
   policies to help assure that individuals promoted are qualified for
   their new responsibilities.

**2. In all matters relating to the assignment, an independence in
mental attitude is to be maintained by the auditor or auditors.**

The importance of the auditor's independence is further reflected
in Rule 101 of the *Code of Professional Ethics* of the AICPA, which
states:

> A member or a firm of which he is a partner or shareholder shall not
> express an opinion on financial statements of an enterprise unless he
> and his firm are independent with respect to such enterprise. . . .

Auditors must be independent in both fact and appearance. To be
independent in fact, auditors must be intellectually honest; to be recognized as independent, however, they must not have any financial
interest in the company they are auditing. Other factors are also important. For example, auditors should not have a close relative in an
important position within the company they are auditing. Since it is
impossible to provide rules for every situation in which independence
may be an issue, auditors are expected to use good common sense at
all times.

SAS No. 4 suggests that CPA firms establish policies and procedures to help assure that all firm personnel are independent in both fact and appearance. Such policies and procedures might include keeping records of which firm personnel were employed in the past by a client and where relatives of firm personnel have important positions with clients. Also, firm personnel might be informed of the names of all clients of the firms whose securities are publicly held and traded.

The concept of audit independence is discussed further in Chapter 2.

3. Due professional care is to be exercised in the performance of the examination and the preparation of the report.

"Due care" requires several important things of accountants. First, and most obvious, they should understand what they are doing and why they are doing it. If they are uncertain about any phase of the assignment, it is their responsibility to seek the guidance of their superior. "Due care" requires that accountants prepare working papers that are both accurate and complete. Working papers prepared in a careless and incomplete fashion bring into question the "evidential matter" that has been gathered by the auditor. The typical audit involves the use of tests and samples. Thus, each item selected for testing must be carefully examined to ensure that due professional care has been followed.

Standards of Field Work

1. The work is to be adequately planned and assistants, if any, are to be properly supervised.

Adequate planning of the audit field work is extremely important. Since the audit plans for field work are always subject to modification as the examination progresses, the work of auditors often leads to changes in the initial plans. Auditors may find in some instances that not all of their instructions will be completely detailed; often it will be necessary for them to plan the details of their own work within the framework of the general engagement. For example, an instruction may require that the auditor observe and test the taking of a physical inventory at a plant. It may be the auditor's responsibility to make decisions on such matters as the extent of observation to be made in each department, how much observation should be made of the various segments of the inventory, and how the performance of the inventory crews should be checked.

SAS No. 4 suggests that CPA firms establish policies and procedures for the performance and supervision of audit work. Furthermore, as part of supervision, SAS No. 4 suggests that policies might be established as to: preparation of working papers; content of audit programs; use of standardized forms and questionnaires; and review of working papers. *SAS No. 4* notes that "the responsibility of a firm for establishing procedures for supervision is distinct from the responsibility of an auditor to comply with the first standard of field work when he is in charge of the work on a particular engagement."

SAS No. 22[17] notes that "supervision involves directing the efforts of assistants who are involved in accomplishing the objectives of the examination and determining whether those objectives were accomplished. . . . The extent of supervision appropriate in a given instance depends on many factors, including the complexity of the subject matter and the qualifications of persons performing the work." Some of the factors that *SAS No. 22* suggests are related to proper supervision of subordinates include:

1. Informing subordinates of their responsibilities and the objectives of the audit procedure that they will be performing.
2. Informing subordinates of their responsibility to bring to the attention of their supervisor any important questions raised during their work.
3. Reviewing the work of subordinates.
4. Establishing a system so that subordinates may document any disagreement with the final conclusions of the examination.

2.   There is to be a proper study and evaluation of the existing internal control as a basis for reliance thereon and for the determination of the resultant extent of the tests to which auditing procedures are to be restricted.

Internal control will be discussed in Chapter 5. Briefly, from the perspective of the auditor, internal control is concerned with the plans and procedures used by a business entity to assure that transactions are recorded accurately and that assets are safeguarded properly. It is also concerned with administrative control (the decision process that leads to the authorization of a transaction—see Chapter 5).

This standard is of the utmost importance because of the nature of the typical audit examination. The audit procedures used will not be the same for the companies with good internal control as for those with poor internal control. It should be noted that much of the work of the auditor involves testing the effectiveness of internal controls (see Chapter 5). Accordingly, the need for constant care and alertness in detecting weaknesses and breakdowns in the system of internal control is important.

---

[17] *Statement on Auditing Standards No. 22*, "Planning and Supervision," American Institute of Certified Public Accountants, 1978.

3. Sufficient competent evidential matter is to be obtained through inspection, observation, inquiries, and confirmations to afford a reasonable basis for an opinion regarding the financial statements under examination.

To comply with this standard, the auditor should: (1) understand the assignment completely; (2) follow instructions; (3) use "due care" in the performance of the work; (4) note errors and unusual or questionable items; (5) prepare complete and self-explanatory working papers.

Evidence is discussed in detail in Chapter 6 and will not be further discussed at this point.

Standards of Reporting

The four reporting standards were listed earlier in this chapter. Accountants who prepare auditors' reports need to be thoroughly aware of the meaning and implications of generally accepted standards of reporting. In addition, they will draw heavily on their knowledge of generally accepted accounting principles. The section which follows provides valuable background for the reader in understanding the standards of reporting.

THE AUDITOR'S REPORT

The financial statements of an entity belong to and are the responsibility of the management of the entity. It is the responsibility of the independent auditor who is evaluating these statements to render a professional opinion as to the fair presentation of the statements. The auditor reports on the fair presentation in what is known as an auditor's report. (See Figure 1–3.)

Auditors' reports are addressed to the group or individuals that engaged them—including the stockholders and/or the board of directors. In their reports auditors discuss the scope of their examination (usually referred to as the scope paragraph) and their opinion as to the fair presentation of the financial statements (usually referred to as the opinion paragraph). Such reports are then signed by a partner of the CPA firm involved. These reports are dated as of the date the audit work was completed so as to indicate to the reader the point at which the auditor was in a position to render an opinion.

Relationship of Standards to the Auditor's Report

The report in Figure 1–3 is an example of the standard (short-form) report which has been adopted by the AICPA and therefore used by

FIGURE 1-3
Example of auditors' report

To the Stockholders of
ABC Company:

We have examined the balance sheet of ABC Company as of December 31, 1980, and the related statements of income, retained earnings and changes in financial position for the year then ended. Our examination was made in accordance with generally accepted auditing standards and, accordingly, included such tests of the accounting records and such other auditing procedures as we considered necessary in the circumstances.

In our opinion, the financial statements referred to above present fairly the financial position of ABC Company as of December 31, 1980, and the results of its operations and the changes in its financial position for the year then ended, in conformity with generally accepted accounting principles applied on a basis consistent with that of the preceding year.

Hamilton & Co.

Boston, Massachusetts
February 20, 1981

auditors. This report is a carefully considered reflection of the reporting standards. Its two paragraphs comprise two distinct sections. The first paragraph or "scope" section describes the extent of the examination; while the second paragraph, the "opinion" section, sets forth the conclusions reached as a result of the audit examination. Five key phrases in the report relate to auditing standards. Two are included in the scope paragraph, and three are in the opinion paragraph.

Scope Paragraph

In the scope paragraph, the statement "Our examination was made in accordance with generally accepted auditing standards" relates to both the general standards and the standards of field work. Although it contains only 11 words, its implications for both the auditor and the user of the financial statements are most important and wide-ranging. In the area of general standards, this statement implies that the examination was performed by adequately trained, proficient auditors who maintained an independent mental attitude and who used due professional care. As for field standards, the statement implies that the work was properly planned; that assistants, if any, were properly supervised; that a proper study and evaluation of internal control was made; and that sufficient competent evidential matter was obtained. These important considerations are discussed in detail throughout this text.

Another important phrase included in the scope paragraph states that the examination "accordingly, included such tests of the accounting records and such other auditing procedures as we considered necessary in the circumstances." This statement relates principally to the standards of field work. The auditor's use of tests must be based on a proper study and evaluation of the client's system of internal control. Sufficient competent evidential matter must be obtained to justify an opinion on the financial statements. The discussion of the auditor's evaluation of internal control is included in Chapter 5, while evidence is discussed in Chapter 6.

Opinion Paragraph

Adequate Disclosure. In the opinion paragraph the phrase "the financial statements referred to above present fairly" relates to the third standard of reporting which states that informative disclosures in the financial statements are to be considered reasonably adequate unless the report includes a statement to the contrary. This standard emphasizes the auditor's responsibility for determining that adequate disclosure has, in fact, been made in the financial statements. It requires the disclosure of any important fact needed to ensure that the financial statements are not misleading. Auditors must exercise their professional judgment in determining which matters require disclosure.

Statement on Auditing Standards (SAS) No. 5[18] suggests that "... 'fairness' of the overall presentation of financial statements should be applied within the framework of generally accepted accounting principles." It also suggests that the auditor's opinion should be based on his or her judgment as to whether the accounting princi-

---

[18] *Statement on Auditing Standards No. 5*, "The Meaning of 'Present Fairly in Conformity with Generally Accepted Accounting Principles' in the Independent Auditor's Report," American Institute of Certified Public Acountants, 1975.

ples applied have general acceptance and are appropriate in the circumstances and whether the financial statements (including the related notes) contain adequate disclosures involving all important matters. Such matters may relate to both form and content of the financial statements, terminology, the detail given, and classification. If adequate disclosure is not made in the financial statements, the accountant should appropriately qualify the opinion, as described later in this chapter.

Generally Accepted Accounting Principles. The phrase "in conformity with generally accepted accounting principles" complies with the first standard of reporting. It is, of course, left to independent accountants to judge whether the principles used in the statements are, in fact, generally accepted, and they must know what other principles, if any, might be acceptable in the circumstances.

Consistency. The phrase "applied on a basis consistent with that of the preceding year" relates to the second standard of reporting. According to *SAS No. 1*, section 420.02:

> The objective of the consistency standard is
>
> a. to give assurance that the comparability of financial statements between periods has not been materially affected by changes in the accounting principles, which include not only accounting principles and practices, but also methods of applying them, or
>
> b. if comparability has been materially affected by such changes, to require appropriate reporting by the independent auditor regarding such changes. It is implicit in the objective that such principles have been consistently observed within each period.

Expression of Opinion. The opinion paragraph of the accountant's report gives general recognition to still another standard of reporting. This standard requires auditors to express an opinion on audited financial statements; or, if they cannot express an opinion, to so indicate and to state clearly all the reasons.

If auditors' examinations are made in accordance with generally accepted auditing standards, and if they are satisfied that the financial statements are presented fairly in conformity with generally accepted accounting principles, applied on a consistent basis, and include all necessary disclosures, they give a "clean" (i.e., unqualified) opinion. This opinion means that the statements present fairly the financial position, results of operations, and changes in financial position. Otherwise they must give a qualified opinion, an adverse opinion, or disclaim an opinion. In a *qualified* opinion the auditors express certain reservations in the report concerning the scope of the audit and/or the statements. When the auditors' reservations are more serious a disclaimer of opinion or an adverse opinion may be given. In an *adverse* opinion the auditors state that the financial statements do *not* present fairly the financial position of the company, the results of its operations, and the changes in its financial position. In *disclaimers of opinion* auditors are stating that they cannot give an opinion because of scope limitations or some other reason (e.g., the auditor is not independent). These opinions are discussed in much greater detail in Chapter 14.

The auditors' report in Figure 1–3 is an unqualified (clean) opinion. This opinion indicates that the auditor is not taking any exceptions or is not in any way qualifying the opinion as to the fairness of the presentation of the financial statements.

When auditors find a departure from generally accepted accounting principles, they may not be able to give an unqualified opinion. More specifically, when in their judgment the departure is very material or significant, they may be required to issue an adverse opinion. In contrast, when in their judgment the departure is not extremely material, a qualified opinion may be possible. Moreover, when in their judgment the exception is not material an unqualified opinion would be in order. (An item is "material" if its omission or misstatement would affect a decision of a knowledgeable user. Materiality is a matter of professional judgment.)

On certain engagements there may be an uncertainty affecting the client that the CPA was unable to evaluate (e.g., pending litigation). When the uncertainty is judged to be very significant (or material) a disclaimer may be in order. In contrast, when the uncertainty is judged to be material, but an opinion can be given, a qualified opinion may be in order. When the uncertainty is judged to be not material an unqualified opinion is possible.

When the scope of the auditors' examination is limited, an exception is needed in the report. Auditors should disclaim an opinion when they believe that the limitation will have an important effect on their being able to form an opinion on the financial statements. Likewise, when they judge the limitation not to be extremely important in forming an opinion, they may give a qualified opinion. If the limitation is judged not to be important an unqualified opinion is possible.

It is important to understand that while auditors are responsible for their own audit reports, it is management (and not the auditor) that is responsible for both the accuracy and adequacy of the financial statements. Although the accountant may have assisted in preparing the statements, or suggested changes in their form, this in no way absolves management from its responsibility.

STEPS IN AN AUDIT

Every audit includes three principal steps: (1) preliminary planning; (2) performing the audit work; and (3) reporting the findings. The separation of these steps is not always apparent.

Preliminary Planning

Preliminary planning is defined as an important audit element in the first standard of field work. Such planning may be categorized into three distinct but closely related segments: (1) the preliminary study of the company's business; (2) the preparation of the audit program; and (3) the assignment of staff members. The steps will be discussed in this order, which is their normal order of occurrence.

At the start of the field work, auditors make a preliminary study of the company's business and the industry in which it operates. The auditor should understand industry accounting practices, competitive trends and, if possible, financial trends and ratios (*SAS No. 22*, paragraph 7). They must obtain detailed information concerning the company's operations to decide on the detailed procedures that will be included in the audit program (an outline of the audit procedures to be used in the performance of the audit). This information is obtained and documented for the working papers. The broad classes of information that auditors obtain or review in their preliminary study may include: the history of the business, organization data, product lines, processes, plant locations, branches, and similar items of general information; the functional organization and internal control of the company; preliminary estimates of materiality levels; accounts that may require adjustments; conditions that may require changes in audit tests; reports to be rendered; and the accounting policies and procedures used by the business (*SAS No. 22*, paragraph 3).

An extremely important part of the preliminary study is identifying the apparent strengths and weaknesses in the client's system of internal control (as discussed in Chapter 5.)

The second element in the preliminary planning step of the audit is the preparation of the audit program. Briefly stated, an audit program is a plan for the engagement. It is designed initially to meet the conditions disclosed in the preliminary study. A typical audit program outlines the nature of the engagement and the procedures to be followed in all of the important areas of the examination. The original audit program may be modified during the examination, as the auditor's tests disclose the effectiveness or weakness of internal controls. On each repeat engagement, the audit program is reviewed prior to the field work to determine whether it should be modified in view of known changes in the company's business, internal controls, or accounting methods. Revisions in the program are also made in view of the experience gained in previous examinations.

The third element in the preliminary planning stage is the assignment of staff members to the audit team. Staff assignments should be made only after careful consideration of the circumstances surrounding each engagement. The CPA firm should attempt to match the skills required with the experience and demonstrated abilities of the staff. The auditing standards which apply here are those requiring that all engagements receive "adequate supervision," that they be staffed by individuals possessing "adequate training and proficiency," and that the personal situation of the auditors assigned to the client would not raise a question of lack of independence.

Performing the Audit Work

The second step in an audit is the actual performance of the audit work. This step consists of applying the audit procedures as outlined in the audit program and any modifications thereto and reviewing the work performed. Due care is very important in both of these phases of the examination. The audit procedures must be performed by the auditor before an opinion may be expressed on the financial statements. Audit procedures may be performed: (1) at one time, near the year-end; (2) in several stages, including some work at a time prior to the company's year-end (referred to as "preliminary," "interim," or "bring up" work); or (3) on a continuous basis throughout the year. As a matter of good practice auditors normally attempt to transfer as much audit work as possible from the busy year-end period to an interim period. This transfer of work also permits auditors to study internal controls at an earlier date; enables them to consider in advance the nature of any changes in the company's business or accounting procedures which may require modifications in the audit program; and may make it possible for them to issue their reports earlier.

The review of the work performed is made as a check that audit *procedures* have been properly applied, that the work of the staff is satisfactory, that working papers are complete and adequate, and that all procedures necessary to form an opinion have been completed. It is conducted by senior personnel of the firm.

Reporting the Findings

The third principal step in an audit examination is reporting the findings. This step involves: (1) management preparing the financial statements and the auditor preparing the accountant's (or audit) report; and (2) the auditor processing and issuing the audit report. It should be remembered that the financial statements, including footnotes, are presentations made by, and the primary responsibility of, the management of the business entity and not the auditor. As stated earlier, this principle remains unchanged even though the auditor sometimes assists in or supervises the preparation of the statements. On the other hand, with respect to the opinion expressed by the auditor and the comments relating to the scope of his or her examination, the responsibility is entirely the auditor's.

Each time a CPA signs an accountant's report, it is done with a keen awareness of the professional and legal responsibilities involved. Each audit examination presents the auditor with an entirely new set of circumstances and findings. Before signing the report the auditor must be fully satisfied that the work of everyone involved in the engagement conforms to generally accepted auditing standards.

QUALITY REVIEW

CPA firms always should be concerned with the quality of their audit work. As will be noted in Chapters 3 and 4, substandard work may lead to legal problems. In order to assure high-quality audit work, a CPA firm periodically should reevaluate its practices. *SAS No. 4* suggests that "policies and procedures for inspection should be established to provide reasonable assurance that the other procedures designed to maintain the quality of the firm's auditing practice are being effectively applied."

Some firms, especially those with more than one office, have had programs of self-evaluation and inspection for many years. Such programs were often in the form of interoffice reviews. Some firms are engaging other CPA firms to perform quality (peer) reviews for them. In addition, one national CPA firm has established its own public review board to continually review the operations of the firm.

The AICPA and some state societies have had various quality review programs for a number of years. The two new AICPA sections require that member firms undergo a quality review usually every three years.

APPENDIX
GAO AUDIT STANDARDS[19]

The U.S. General Accounting Office (GAO) is the audit agency of the legislative branch of the federal government. The GAO audits

---

[19] This appendix is adapted from (1) *Auditing Standards Established by the GAO— Their Meaning and Significance for CPAs,* American Institute of Certified Public Accountants, 1973 (prepared by the AICPA Committee on Relations with the General Accounting Office). Copyright © 1973 by the American Institute of Certified Public Accountants, Inc. and (2) *Standards for Audit of Government Organizations, Programs, Activities & Functions,* United States General Accounting Office, 1972 (1974 Reprint).

30

government agencies as well as other matters that involve public funds and is concerned with both financial matters and administrative practices.

In 1972, the GAO issued a publication entitled, *Standards for Audit of Government Organizations, Programs Activities & Functions.* The standards are concerned with (1) financial presentations, (2) compliance with laws and regulations, (3) operational efficiency and program results. Furthermore, the standards are applicable to audits of (1) governmental units, (2) contractors, (3) grantees, and (4) other external organizations (involving audits by or for a government unit). The standards apply to work done by government auditors or by independent public accountants.

The GAO considers an audit to consist of the following three elements:

1. *Financial and compliance*—determines (a) whether financial operations are properly conducted, (b) whether the financial reports of an audited entity are presented fairly, and (c) whether the enitity has complied with applicable laws and regulations.
2. *Economy and efficiency*—determines whether the entity is managing or utilizing its resources (personnel, property, space, and so forth) in an economical and efficient manner and the causes of any inefficiencies or uneconomical practices, including inadequacies in management information systems, administrative procedures, or organizational structure.
3. *Program results*—determines whether the desired results or benefits are being achieved, whether the objectives established by the legislature or other authorizing body are being met, and whether the agency has considered alternatives which might yield desired results at a lower cost.[20]

Thus, the GAO view of an audit is somewhat broader than the AICPA view. The GAO does not expect that all three aspects of their view of an audit will be included in every audit. However, it is expected that all three will be included in the audit of most government programs or activities. The GAO suggests that the engagement letters (see Chapter 3 for a discussion of engagement letters) between government entities and independent auditors clearly specify which of the three elements of an audit are to be performed.

The Standards

The GAO standards include general standards, examination and evaluation standards, and reporting standards. These standards are as follows:

---

[20] *Standards for Audit of Government Organizations, Programs, Activities & Functions*, p. 3.

General Standards

1. The full scope of an audit of a governmental program, function, activity, or organization should encompass:

    a. An examination of financial transactions, accounts, and reports, including an evaluation of compliance with applicable laws and regulations.
    b. A review of efficiency and economy in the use of resources.
    c. A review to determine whether desired results are effectively achieved.

    In determining the scope for a particular audit, responsible officials should give consideration to the needs of the potential users of the results of that audit.

2. The auditors assigned to perform the audit must collectively possess adequate professional proficiency for the tasks required.
3. In all matters relating to the audit work, the audit organization and the individual auditors shall maintain an independent attitude.
4. Due professional care is to be used in conducting the audit and in preparing related reports.

Examination and Evaluation Standards

1. Work is to be adequately planned.
2. Assistants are to be properly supervised.
3. A review is to be made of compliance with legal and regulatory requirements.
4. An evaluation is to be made of the system of internal control to assess the extent it can be relied upon to ensure accurate information, to ensure compliance with laws and regulations, and to provide for efficient and effective operations.
5. Sufficient, competent, and relevant evidence is to be obtained to afford a reasonable basis for the auditor's opinions, judgments, conclusions, and recommendations.

Reporting Standards

1. Written audit reports are to be submitted to the appropriate officials of the organizations requiring or arranging for the audits. Copies of the reports should be sent to other officials who may be responsible for taking action on audit findings and recommendations and to others responsible or authorized to receive such reports. Unless restricted by law or regulation, copies should also be made available for public inspection.
2. Reports are to be issued on or before the dates specified by law, regulation, or other arrangement and, in any event, as promptly as possible so as to make the information available for timely use by management and by legislative officials.

3. Each report shall:
   a. Be as concise as possible but, at the same time, clear and complete enough to be understood by the users.
   b. Present factual matter accurately, completely, and fairly.
   c. Present findings and conclusions objectively and in language as clear and simple as the subject matter permits.
   d. Include only factual information, findings, and conclusions that are adequately supported by enough evidence in the auditor's working papers to demonstrate or prove, when called upon, the bases for the matters reported and their correctness and reasonableness. Detailed supporting information should be included in the report to the extent necessary to make a convincing presentation.
   e. Include, when possible, the auditor's recommendations for actions to effect improvements in problem areas noted in his audit and to otherwise make improvements in operations. Information on underlying causes of problems reported should be included to assist in implementing or devising corrective actions.
   f. Place primary emphasis on improvement rather than on criticism of the past; critical comments should be presented in balanced perspective, recognizing any unusual difficulties or circumstances faced by the operating officials concerned.
   g. Identify and explain issues and questions needing further study and consideration by the auditor or others.
   h. Include recognition of noteworthy accomplishments, particularly when management improvements in one program or activity may be applicable elsewhere.
   i. Include recognition of the views of responsible officials of the organization, program, function, or activity audited on the auditor's findings, conclusions, and recommendations. Except where the possibility of fraud or other compelling reason may require different treatment, the auditor's tentative findings and conclusions should be reviewed with such officials. When possible, without undue delay, their views should be obtained in writing and objectively considered and presented in preparing the final report.
   j. Clearly explain the scope and objectives of the audit.
   k. State whether any significant pertinent information has been omitted because it is deemed privileged or confidential. The nature of such information should be described, and the law or other basis under which it is withheld should be stated.
4. Each audit report containing financial reports shall:
   a. Contain an expression of the auditor's opinion as to whether the information in the financial reports is presented fairly in accordance with generally accepted accounting principles (or with other specified accounting principles applicable to the organization, program, function, or activity audited), applied on a basis consistent with that of the preceding reporting period. If

the auditor cannot express an opinion, the reasons therefor
should be stated in the audit report.

b. Contain appropriate supplementary explanatory information
about the contents of the financial reports as may be necessary
for full and informative disclosure about the financial operations
of the organization, program, function, or activity audited. Violations of legal or other regulatory requirements, including instances of noncompliance, and material changes in accounting
policies and procedures, along with their effect on financial reports, shall be explained in the audit report.[21]

Further Comments

GAO standards do not contemplate a CPA expressing an audit
opinion on economy and efficiency of an entity or as to a program's
effectiveness. The CPA should express an opinion on financial information. In such instances the CPA may then comment on the fairness
of presentation in conformity with appropriate accounting principles.
However, the auditor may comment on lack of compliance with laws
or regulations. The auditor may also comment on potential areas for
improvement and make recommendations.

New Development

In March 1979 the GAO issued three supplemental standards relating to auditing computer-based systems. These standards are as
follows:

1. The auditor shall actively participate in reviewing the design and
   development of new data processing systems or applications, and
   significant modification thereto, as a normal part of the audit function.
2. The auditor shall review general controls in data processing systems
   to determine that (A) controls have been designed according to
   management direction and legal requirements, and (B) such controls
   are operating effectively to provide reliability of, and security over,
   the data being processed.
3. The auditor shall review application controls of installed data processing applications to assess their reliability in processing data in a
   timely, accurate, and complete manner.[22]

GLOSSARY

Adverse opinion An opinion in which the auditors state that the financial
statements do *not* present fairly the financial position, results of operations,
and changes in financial position.

---

[21] Ibid., pp. 6–9.

[22]*Additional GAO Audit Standards: Auditing Computer-Based Systems,* U.S. General Accounting Office, 1979, p. 2.

34

American Institute of Certified Public Accountants (AICPA)   A voluntary national professional association of CPAs headquartered in New York City. It provides members with advice on technical matters, performs research, publishes various items relating to accounting, provides a national political lobby for the profession, and administers the national affairs of the profession. It also publishes *The Journal of Accountancy.*

Attestation   The opinion issued by an independent auditor on the fairness of the presentation of financial statements.

Auditing   ". . . a systematic process of objectively obtaining and evaluating evidence regarding assertions about economic actions and events to ascertain the degree of correspondence between those assertions and established criteria and communicating the results to interested users." [Taken from Joseph A. Silvoso et al., "Report of the Committee on Basic Auditing Concepts," Supplement to vol. 47 of *The Accounting Review*, 1972, p. 18.]

Auditing procedures   The methods and techniques used by the auditor in the conduct of the audit examination.

Boards of accountancy   The entity within each jurisdiction which has the responsibility for administering that jurisdiction's public accounting legislation. They may issue and revoke CPA certificates and grant licenses to practice.

Certified Public Accountant (CPA)   An individual who is recognized by at least one state government, the District of Columbia, or a U.S. territory as possessing at least a minimum level of competence in certain designated areas of accounting. Competence is determined by the results of a rigorous examination called the CPA examination.

Disclaimer of opinion   When the auditors state that they cannot give an opinion because of scope limitations or some other reason.

Generally accepted auditing standards   Authoritative statements regarding the measures of quality of performance of the procedures used by the auditor and the objectives to be obtained by the use of the procedures undertaken. There are ten such standards which are divided into three categories: general standards, standards of field work, and standards of reporting. These standards change rarely and only by official decree.

Managment services   Advisory services performed for clients including services such as operations research, systems design and installation, and budgeting.

Managers   The level below partners who manage the entire scope of several professional engagements that may be running simultaneously.

Opinion paragraph   The paragraph of the auditor's report which gives the auditors' opinion as to the fairness of the presentation of the financial statements. For an example, see Figure 1–3, Chapter 1.

Partners   Owners and administrators of a CPA firm organized as a partnership.

Private Companies Practice Section   A section within the AICPA which any firm having an interest in private company practice may join.

Professional corporation (of CPAs)   A CPA firm organized as a corporation. It has shareholders, directors, officers, and employees.

Public accountants   Independent accountants or firms of individuals who hold themselves out to the public as being qualified to render services such as auditing, taxes, and management services. There are two types: certified public accountants (CPAs) and public accountants who are not certified (PAs)

Qualified opinion　An opinion in which the auditors express certain reservations concerning the scope of the audit and/or the financial statements.

Scope paragraph　The paragraph of the auditors' report which describes the scope of the examination. For an example, see Figure 1-3.

SEC Practice Section　A section within the AICPA which any CPA firm having an interest in SEC practice may join.

Senior accountants　Supervise the work and activity of the staff accountants assigned to them on field engagements (among other duties).

Staff accountants (sometimes called junior accountants)　Generally the entry level professional accountant in a public accounting firm. Their work is supervised by more experienced accountants.

State societies of CPAs　Voluntary professional associations in the various states and jurisdictions. They hold monthly dinner meetings and other professional development meetings for their members.

Supervisors　Usually manage the field work of several engagements that may be running simultaneously.

Unqualified opinion　A "clean" opinion, meaning that the auditors believe that the financial statements present fairly the financial position, results of operations, and changes in financial position.

QUESTIONS AND PROBLEMS

1-1.　What are some of the reasons for the rapid growth of the accounting profession in our modern economy?

1-2.　Define the term "auditing."

1-3.　What are the characteristics of a profession?

1-4.　Is public accounting a profession? Why?

1-5.　Are all CPAs required to join both the AICPA and their state society?

1-6.　Are the state societies directly under the AICPA in an organizational sense?

1-7.　Do boards of accountancy issue CPA certificates?

1-8.　What are the major services usually offered by a public accounting firm?

1-9.　What is the difference between auditing standards and auditing procedures?

1-10.　What is the objective of the consistency standard?

1-11.　List and discuss the three principal steps of an audit.

1-12.　What is attestation?

1-13.　Write the standard report.

1-14.　List and discuss the general standards, the standards of field work, and the reporting standards.

1-15. Who may join the AICPA's SEC Practice Section?

1-16. Discuss some of the "rules for members" of the AICPA's SEC Practice Section.

1-17. What are the objectives of *(a)* the AICPA's SEC Practice Section, and *(b)* the AICPA's Private Companies Practice Section?

1-18. Describe the Public Oversight Board of the AICPA's SEC Practice Section.

1-19. *a.* Discuss the concept of quality review in public accounting. Why is it needed?

    b. Describe some of the forms of quality review in public accounting.

1-20. Discuss the elements that are needed in the proper supervision of subordinates.

1-21. Select the *best* answer for each of the following items.

    a. Auditing standards differ from auditing procedures in that procedures relate to

      1. Measure of performance.
      2. Audit principles.
      3. Acts to be performed.
      4. Audit judgments.

    b. Independent auditing can *best* be described as

      1. A branch of accounting.
      2. A discipline which attests to the results of accounting and other functional operations and data.
      3. A professional activity that measures and communicates financial and business data.
      4. A regulatory function that prevents the issuance of improper financial information.

    c. The independent auditor of 1900 differs from the auditor of today in that the 1900 auditor was more concerned with the

      1. Validity of the income statement.
      2. Determination of fair presentation of financial statements.
      3. Improvement of accounting systems.
      4. Detection of irregularities.

    d. The primary reason why a CPA firm establishes quality control policies and procedures for professional development of staff accountants is to

      1. Comply with the continuing educational requirements imposed by various states for all staff accountants in CPA firms.
      2. Establish, in fact as well as in appearance, that staff accountants are increasing their knowledge of accounting and auditing matters.
      3. Provide a forum for staff accountants to exchange their experiences and views concerning firm policies and procedures.
      4. Provide reasonable assurance that staff personnel will have the knowledge required to enable them to fulfill responsibilities.

e. The fourth generally accepted auditing standard of reporting requires an auditor to render a report whenever an auditor's name is associated with financial statements. The overall purpose of the fourth standard of reporting is to require that reports
1. State that the examination of financial statements has been conducted in accordance with generally accepted auditing standards.
2. Indicate the character of the auditor's examination and the degree of responsibility assumed by the auditor.
3. Imply that the auditor is independent in fact as well as in appearance with respect to the financial statements under examination.
4. Express whether the accounting principles used in preparing the financial statements have been applied consistently in the period under examination.

f. The auditor's report makes reference to the basic financial statements, which are customarily considered to be the balance sheet and the statements of
1. Income and changes in financial position.
2. Income, changes in retained earnings, and changes in financial position.
3. Income, retained earnings, and changes in financial position.
4. Income and retained earnings.

g. The first general standard of generally accepted auditing standards which states in part that the examination is to be performed by a person or persons having adequate technical training, requires that an auditor have
1. Education and experience in the field of auditing.
2. Ability in the planning and supervision of the audit work.
3. Proficiency in business and financial matters.
4. Knowledge in the areas of financial accounting.

h. The first standard of field work, which states that the work is to be adequately planned, and assistants, if any, are to be properly supervised, recognizes that
1. Early appointment of the auditor is advantageous to the auditor and the client.
2. Acceptance of an audit engagement after the close of the client's fiscal year is generally *not* permissible.
3. Appointment of the auditor subsequent to the physical count of inventories requires a disclaimer of opinion.
4. Performance of substantial parts of the examination is necessary at interim dates.

i. Which of the following *best* describes why an independent auditor is asked to express an opinion on the fair presentation of financial statements?
1. It is difficult to prepare financial statements that fairly present a company's financial position and changes in financial posi-

tion and operations without the expertise of an independent auditor.

2. It is management's responsibility to seek available independent aid in the appraisal of the financial information shown in its financial statements.

3. The opinion of an independent party is needed because a company may *not* be objective with respect to its own financial statements.

4. It is a customary courtesy that all stockholders of a company receive an independent report on management's stewardship in managing the affairs of the business.

(AICPA, adapted)

1-22. CPA J, a staff accountant, is assigned to the audit of XYZ Co. Before the field work was started CPA J reviewed last year's working papers. When the field work began CPA J noted that XYZ Co. actually prepares and distributes 15 copies of each purchase order. CPA J feels that there is an unnecessary amount of paper work. What should CPA J do?

1-23. At a party which includes only some very close friends, a CPA is discussing an interesting assignment that involves the possible purchase of a company. She is very careful not to mention the company's name, referring to it only as a food supplier that is concerned with avoiding possible heavy estate taxes. Comment on this situation.

1-24. In April you are told that your next assignment will start May 15. This is a new client engaged in manufacturing work clothing. You are advised that the client has a standard cost system and prices a portion of his inventory on the last-in, first-out (LIFO) method. You have had no practical experience with either standard costs or LIFO inventories. Should you request another assignment since you lack experience in these matters? Alternatively, what might you do to prepare yourself for this assignment?

1-25. As a staff accountant, you ask the treasurer for copies of bank reconcilements and canceled checks for several months of the year under examination. The treasurer says he will get them for you. After several days you ask again and are informed that the checks and reconcilements have been accidentally lost, and it is suggested that you do your work for different months. What would you tell the treasurer? What other things might you do?

1-26. During the course of an audit the independently wealthy president of the company poses certain involved questions about estate and inheritance taxes. It appears to you that the president has explored the area thoroughly, but is in need of specific answers to a few questions which bear directly on her own personal situation. How should you handle this matter?

1-27. What are (1) the function and (2) the responsibilities of the independent auditor in the examination of financial statements?

1-28. How would you reply to the following questions?

    a. Since responsible financial reporting seems to be directed principally toward outside stockholders and creditors, to what extent do you suppose generally accepted auditing standards can be relaxed in the case of:

        1. A small corporation which has no creditors and is wholly owned by the chairman of the board who asks for an audit?

        2. A sole proprietorship with no creditors?

    b. Since the accountants' report is sometimes referred to as a "certificate," what do you think about changing the wording to:

        "We hereby certify that the . . . (financial statements) . . . are accurate . . . etc"?

    c. Generally accepted auditing standards state quite clearly that the auditor must disclose any exceptions that are taken to the financial statements. Rather than go through all the difficulties of qualifying the opinion, why doesn't the auditor simply change the statements to reflect an acceptable treatment?

1-29. "An audit by a CPA is essentially negative and contributes to neither the gross national product nor the general well-being of society. The auditor does not create; he or she merely checks what someone else has done." Comment on the statement.

                                  (AICPA, adapted)

1-30. The following statement is representative of attitudes and opinions sometimes encountered by CPAs in their professional practices:

    It is important to read the footnotes to financial statements, even though they often are presented in technical language and are incomprehensible. The auditor may reduce his exposure to third-party liability by stating something in the footnotes that contradicts completely what he has presented in the balance sheet or income statement.

Required:

Evaluate the above statement and indicate:

    a. Areas of agreement with the statement, if any.

    b. Areas of misconception, incompleteness or fallacious reasoning included in the statement, if any.

                                    (AICPA, adapted)

1-31. CPA X was faced with the following situations during the past year (1980):

    a. During the year ended December 31, 1980, Jolly Corporation (a client of CPA X) had its fixed assets appraised and found that they had substantially appreciated in value since the date of their purchase. The appraised values have been reported in the balance sheet as of December 31, 1980; the total appraisal increment has been included as an extraordinary item in the income statement for the year then ended; and the appraisal adjustment has been fully disclosed in the footnotes. CPA X believes that the values are reasonable. What opinion should he issue?

  b. CPA X accepted the audit engagement of Sad Mfg. Inc. During the audit, X became aware of the fact that he did not have the competence required for the engagement. What should X have done?

(AICPA, adapted)

1-32. Student A says that the primary responsibility for the adequacy of disclosure in the financial statements and footnotes rests with the auditor in charge of the audit field work. Student B says that the partner in charge of the engagement has the primary responsibility. Student C says that the staff person who drafts the statements and footnotes has the primary responsibility. Student D contends that it is the client's responsibility. Which student is correct?

(AICPA, adapted)

1-33. In late spring of 1980 you are advised of a new assignment as in-charge accountant of your CPA firm's recurring annual audit of a major client, the Prancer Company. You are given the terms of the engagement (contained in a letter) for the audit covering the calendar year December 31, 1980, and a list of personnel assigned to this engagement. It is your responsibility to plan and supervise the field work for the engagement.

Required:

Discuss the necessary preparation and planning for the Prancer Company annual audit *prior to* beginning field work at the client's office. In your discussion include the sources you should consult, the type of information you should seek, the preliminary plans and preparation you should make for the field work, and any actions you should take relative to the staff assigned to the engagement. *Do not write an audit program.*

(AICPA, adapted)

1-34. Feiler, the sole owner of a small hardware business, has been told that the business should have financial statements reported on by an independent CPA. Feiler, having some bookkeeping experience, has personally prepared the company's financial statements and does not understand why such statements should be examined by a CPA. Feiler discussed the matter with Farber, a CPA, and asked Farber to explain why an audit is considered important.

Required:

  a. Describe the objectives of an independent audit.
  b. Identify ten ways in which an independent audit may be beneficial to Feiler.

(AICPA)

1-35. Jones and Todd, a local CPA firm, received an invitation to bid for the audit of a local, federally assisted program. The audit is to be conducted in accordance with the audit standards published by the General Accounting Office (GAO), a federal auditing agency. Jones and Todd has become familiar with the GAO standards and recognizes that the GAO standards are not inconsistent with generally accepted auditing standards (GAAS). The GAO standards, unlike GAAS, are concerned with more than the financial aspects of an entity's operations. The GAO standards broaden the definition of auditing by establishing that the full scope of an audit should encompass the following elements:

1. An examination of **financial** transactions, accounts, and reports, including an evaluation of **compliance** with applicable laws and regulations.
2. A review of **efficiency** and **economy** in the use of resources, such as personnel and equipment.
3. A review to determine whether desired results are effectively achieved (**program results**).

Jones and Todd has been engaged to perform the audit of the program and the audit is to encompass all three elements.

Required:

a. Jones and Todd should perform sufficient audit work to satisfy the **financial** and **compliance** element of the GAO standards. What should such audit work determine?
b. After making appropriate review and inquiries, what uneconomical practices or inefficiencies should Jones and Todd be alert to, in satisfying the **efficiency** and **economy** element encompassed by the GAO standards?
c. After making appropriate review and inquiries, what should Jones and Todd consider to satisfy the **program results** element encompassed by the GAO standards?

(AICPA)

1-36. Ray, the owner of a small company, asked Holmes, CPA, to conduct an audit of the company's records. Ray told Holmes that an audit is to be completed in time to submit audited financial statements to a bank as part of a loan application. Holmes immediately accepted the engagement and agreed to provide an auditor's report within three weeks. Ray agreed to pay Holmes a fixed fee plus a bonus if the loan was granted.

Holmes hired two accounting students to conduct the audit and spent several hours telling them exactly what to do. Holmes told the students not to spend time reviewing the controls but instead to concentrate on proving the mathematical accuracy of the ledger accounts, and summarizing the data in the accounting records that support Ray's financial statements. The students followed Holmes's instructions and after two weeks gave Holmes the financial statements which did not include footnotes. Holmes reviewed the statements and prepared an unqualified auditor's report. The report, however, did not refer to generally accepted accounting principles nor to the year-to-year application of such principles.

Required:

Briefly describe each of the generally accepted auditing standards and indicate how the action(s) of Holmes resulted in a failure to comply with **each** standard.

(AICPA, adapted)

Learning Objectives

Study of the content of this chapter is designed to achieve several learning objectives. These include an understanding of:

1. Why a code of ethics is necessary to a profession.
2. The general nature of the rules of conduct which make up the CPA's code of ethics.
3. The specific obligations and accepted and prohibited actions under the code of ethics.
4. How the code of ethics is enforced and some of the problems associated with enforcement.
5. The fact that the code of ethics applies to tax practice and management services as well as to the attest function.

2

The Code of Professional Conduct

WHY A CODE OF ETHICS

The adoption of a code of ethics is an important milestone in the professionalization of any occupation. In order to obtain professional recognition, many occupations quickly adopt some type of formal code of ethics. The mere adoption of such a code is not enough, however. The individuals involved in the practice of the profession must actually guide their actions by both the prescriptions and proscriptions (prohibitions) of such a code. By embracing and living by their code, they enhance the respect that others hold both for them and for their profession.

One authority traces the origins of the AICPA's code of ethics back to the turn of the century.[1] Since that time the AICPA code has undergone many changes. In 1973, the membership of the Institute adopted a substantially revised version of the code. Then, in 1978 the AICPA's membership approved revisions relating to general standards, independence, advertising, solicitation, incompatible occupations, and staff recruiting. Again, in 1979 the Institute's membership approved revisions. These latest changes dealt with encroachment and direct uninvited solicitation. The purpose of this chapter is to communicate an appreciation and understanding of this code and its meaning for both CPAs and those who rely on their work.

Professions in our society generally are granted a great deal of autonomy. With such autonomy, professions are expected to regulate themselves. Failure of a profession to regulate and discipline its

---

[1] Darwin J. Casler, "The Evolution of CPA Ethics: A Profile of Professionalization," Occasional Paper No. 12, Bureau of Business and Economic Research, Graduate School of Business Administration, Michigan State University, East Lansing, Michigan, 1964, p. 5.

members may result in that profession losing some, or all, of its autonomy. At the heart of professional self-discipline is a code of ethics. The code defines acceptable and unacceptable professional behavior. Additionally, the code enhances the image of a profession in the eyes of society by attracting the confidence of the public it seeks to serve.[2]

Our society is ruled by law. As a citizen, a professional is expected to conform both to the written laws and the informal customs of society. But, above and beyond these requirements, professionals are proscribed from engaging in certain behavior that would otherwise be acceptable for the layperson. The professional has assumed obligations that are above and beyond those of a business executive, as will become evident from reading this chapter.

THE STRUCTURE OF ACCOUNTING ETHICS

The American Institute of Certified Public Accountants, the state societies of CPAs, and the various boards of accountancy each have adopted a code of professional ethics. In many instances, the state societies and the boards have adopted or at least modeled their own codes after the AICPA code. As a consequence, the discussion in this chapter will be limited to a consideration of the AICPA code.

Composition of the Code

The AICPA code consists of a set of rules of conduct that were adopted by a vote of the Institute's membership. These rules are supplemented by a somewhat philosophical essay approved by the Institute's Ethics Division and interpretations of the code which are issued by that division. The rules of conduct are contained in the appendix to this chapter. You are encouraged to read these before proceeding with the remainder of the chapter.

Discussion of the Code

CPAs have three categories of ethical responsibilities. First, they have a responsibility to society—the public in general. CPAs are in a unique position. They are hired by the client, but also serve creditors and stockholders, as well as any other group that relies on audited financial statements.

Second, CPAs have a responsibility to their clients. Carey and Doherty suggest that, since a fiduciary relationship exists between

---

[2] See William J. Goode, "Community within a Community: The Professions," *American Sociological Review* (April 1957), pp. 196–98.

CPAs and their clients, practitioners must be extremely careful in dealing with their clients' affairs. Specifically, "the CPA owes it to his client to be competent, honest, loyal, independent, and solicitous."[3] These authors suggest that "it is the accountant's duty to respect the confidential relationship with his clients."[4]

Finally, CPAs also have responsibilities to their fellow practitioners. Colleague norms help build and maintain internal cohesion within a profession. Carey and Doherty note that the advancement of the profession is dependent upon goodwill and mutual trust among practitioners.[5] As will be noted later in this chapter, the 1978 and 1979 amendments to the Rules of Conduct deleted or modified many of the formal proscriptions that were collegial in nature.

Matters Relating to Society and to the Client

Independence (Rule 101). CPAs should issue their opinion as to the fairness of presentation of financial statements only if they are independent both in fact and in appearance. Figure 2–1 gives examples of situations in which a CPA's independence might be questioned.

It is evident that, today, independence means not only independence in fact but also in appearance. Not only must auditors be independent of their clients, but CPAs must be perceived to be independent of their clients by third parties. Unless CPAs are regarded as independent, their opinions will be looked upon as being of little, if any, consequence to the users of the statements.

Integrity and Objectivity (Rule 102). The code prohibits the misrepresentation of facts. This, of course, holds true for any aspect of CPAs' work, whether they are engaged in performing audit work, tax work, or management services.

General Standards (Rule 201).[6] One of the 1978 modifications to the code relates to the establishment of general standards that are applicable to all areas of public accounting. Five general standards were established concerning (1) professional competence, (2) due professional care, (3) planning and supervision, (4) sufficient relevant data, and (5) forecasts.

Competence. CPAs should not attempt to undertake work for

---

[3] John L. Carey and William O. Doherty. *Ethical Standards of the Accounting Profession* (New York: AICPA, 1966), p. 129.

[4] Ibid., p. 131.

[5] Ibid., p. 147.

[6] This section is based in part on *Proposed Amendments to the Bylaws and Code of Professional Ethics: Referendum January 30, 1978,* American Institute of Certified Public Accountants, pp. 7-8. Copyright © 1978 by the American Institute of Certified Public Accountants, Inc.

FIGURE 2-1
Selected situations that may cause an auditor's independence to be impaired
(as defined by the AICPA)

1. CPA had or was committed to acquire any direct or material indirect financial interest in the client during the period of the professional engagement or at the time of expressing an opinion.
2. CPA had any joint closely held business investment with client or important client personnel that was material in relation to the CPA's net worth or the CPA's firm's net worth during the period of the professional engagement or at the time of expressing an opinion.
3. CPA had a loan to or from client or important client personnel during the period of the professional engagement or at the time of expressing an opinion. Loans from financial institutions under certain circumstances are excepted (see the appendix to this chapter).
4. CPA was a director, promoter, underwriter, voting trustee, executive, or employee of the client during the period covered by the financial statements, during the period of the professional engagement, or at the time of expressing an opinion.
5. The CPA was a trustee of any pension or profit sharing trust of the client during the period covered by the financial statements, during the period of the professional engagement, or at the time of expressing an opinion.
6. The CPA was a trustee of a trust or an administrator of an estate that had or was committed to acquire any direct or material indirect financial interest in the client during the period of his or her professional engagement or at the time of expressing an opinion.

Source: *AICPA Professional Standards,* Vol. 2 (New York: American Institute of Certified Public Accountants, 1978), pp. 4411–3.

which they are not competent. If they do, they may do unsatisfactory work which might bring discredit both to themselves and to the entire profession. CPAs initially may have, or feel they have, the competence to complete a particular engagement. However, during the course of their engagement they may find that they must do additional research in particular areas. In interpreting Rule 201, the AICPA notes that this is normal and does not signify any lack of competence (Interpretation 201-1).

Due Professional Care. A CPA should use due professional care in performing any engagement. To do otherwise would be a violation of the CPA's obligation as a professional.

Planning and Supervision. CPAs should adequately plan and supervise any engagement. A more thorough discussion of planning and supervision can be found in Chapter 1.

Sufficient Relevant Data. The conclusions and/or recommendations that result from any professional accounting engagement should be based on sufficient and relevant data.

Forecasts. Often CPAs are asked by clients to assist them in the preparation of forecasts. This is a legitimate request; auditors may prepare or assist clients in preparing forecasts. However, CPAs must not allow their names to be used in any way that would lead others to believe they are attesting to the accuracy of the forecasts. Chapter 14 contains a further discussion of forecasts.

Auditing Standards (Rule 202). CPAs should not issue their opinion as to the fairness of presentation of financial statements unless their audit examination was carried out in accordance with the ten generally accepted auditing standards that were discussed in Chapter 1. The *Statements on Auditing Standards* (SASs) are authoritative interpretations of these auditing standards and must also be considered and followed. Furthermore, Rule 202 requires CPAs to justify any departure from a SAS.

Accounting Principles (Rule 203). CPAs should not state that the financial statements they examined are in conformity with generally accepted accounting principles if the statements contain a material departure from an accounting principle which has been established by the Financial Accounting Standards Board or its predecessors. CPAs may accept a departure from such an accounting principle only if they are able to demonstrate clearly that following generally accepted accounting principles would result in misleading statements. Such a departure from accepted principles must always be explained clearly.

Other Technical Standards (Rule 204).[7] One of the 1978 modifications to the code was the addition of a new Rule 204 entitled "Other Technical Standards." This rule relates to technical standards other than those covered in Rules 201, 202, and 203. Under Rule 204, AICPA members are asked to comply with technical standards promulgated by appropriate bodies designated by the Council of the Institute to establish such standards. It would be up to a member to justify a departure from such standards.

A Comment on Rules 201 and 204. The new form of Rules 201 and 204 now enable anyone ". . . to look to the Code of Professional Ethics for a comprehensive statement of the standards that members must follow in performing any professional engagement."[8] The Council in October 1978 designated the Management Advisory Service Executive Committee to establish technical standards in the management services area. In May 1979, the Council designated the Accounting and Review Services Committee to establish standards for both unaudited financial statements and unaudited financial information for

---

[7] The next two sections are based in part on *Proposed Amendments to the Bylaws and Code of Professional Ethics: Referendum January 30, 1978*, pp. 7–9.

[8] *Proposed Amendments to Bylaws and Code of Professional Ethics: Referendum January 30, 1978*, p. 8.

nonpublic entities. Chapter 14 discusses unaudited financial statements in detail. It is expected that the Council will eventually instruct the Federal Taxation Executive Committee to establish standards in the tax area.

Confidential Information (Rule 301). Society has granted certain professions (e.g., medicine, law) the right of "privileged communication." This privilege means that professionals may never be required to reveal information given to them by a client, even in a court of law. Generally CPAs have *not* been granted this right of "privileged communication." The federal government, for example, does not extend this privilege to the CPA. CPAs are expected, however, not to voluntarily reveal information obtained by them in confidence from a client. As professionals, auditors are expected not to profit from information gained during the course of a professional engagement. The rule on confidential information generally does not prevent practitioners from revealing such information in a proper judicial proceeding if required to do so by the court.

Contingent Fees (Rule 302). CPAs' fees should not be based on any variables or contingencies related to the findings or results of the services rendered by them. If this practice were permitted, the objectivity and independence of their opinion would soon become questionable. The AICPA has included a rule prohibiting contingent fees in its code of professional ethics. If, however, CPAs' fees are based on the findings or results of the proceedings of a governmental body, then the AICPA would not consider these fees to be contingent. This is because the fees are fixed by the court or agency and not by the CPA.

Incompatible Occupations (Rule 504). The prohibition of incompatible occupation has been in existence for a number of years. In 1978, the membership of the AICPA voted to define an incompatible occupation as one that ". . . would create a conflict of interest in rendering professional services." Consequently, a CPA in public practice should not also engage in another business or activity that would create such a conflict and thus be incompatible with his or her public practice as a CPA. The rule prohibits other occupations that conflict with all of the tasks performed by CPAs in public practice (i.e., auditing, taxes, management services, reports for government agencies, and serving as an expert witness). This rule assures that in all areas of public practice the public practitioner objectively serves the best interest of his or her client as well as the general public. The rule does not prohibit a CPA from engaging in an occupation that might feed clients into the CPA's public practice.[9]

---

[9] *Proposed Amendments to the Bylaws and Code of Professional Ethics: Referendum January 30, 1978*, p. 15.

Matters Relating to Colleagues

Advertising and Other Forms of Solicitation–Arguments For and Against. For more than two generations the AICPA proscribed advertising and solicitation. Then in the mid-1970s, pressures to allow advertising and solicitation began to appear. Over the years many arguments against permitting advertising and solicitation by members of the accounting profession have been advanced. These arguments can perhaps best be divided into two basic categories. First, it has been observed that advertising and solicitation may easily become real threats to the internal cohesion of a profession. Intensive competition, brought about by advertising and solicitation of clients, easily could threaten the internal unity of the profession. It is therefore in the best interest of all CPAs as members of the accounting profession to present a united front in relations with competing professions (e.g., law, management consulting) and with society as a whole.[10]

Second, a profession serves clients, not customers, and there is an important distinction between the two. A nonprofessional usually serves customers rather than clients. Because a customer may be able to evaluate the performance of a craftsman, it is logical for the latter to advertise his or her qualifications.[11] Since the CPA's clients are usually not in a position to evaluate the services rendered, advertising and solicitation would serve only to commercialize the profession and might well create opportunities for increased client control over the practitioner. Finally, some argue that the more established firms are better able to afford to advertise. This might hurt smaller firms.

In 1977, the U.S. Supreme Court ruled in the *Bates decision* that certain forms of advertising were permissible in the legal profession.[12] The implications for the accounting profession were apparent. The AICPA moved to permit advertising and solicitation. In urging the membership to allow certain forms of advertising and solicitation the Institute advanced the following reasons for such a change:[13]

1. The complete proscription of advertising and solicitation is not consistent with the desire of the public for information about CPAs and the services they perform.
2. Complete prohibition of advertising and solicitation might be in violation of antitrust laws.

---

[10] Carey and Doherty, *Ethical Standards of the Accounting Profession,* p. 147.

[11] Ernest Greenwood, "Attributes of a Profession." Paraphrased with permission of the National Association of Social Workers, from *Social Work,* vol. 2., no. 3 (July 1957), pp. 47–48.

[12] *Bates et al* v. *State Bar of Arizona,* 97 S. Ct. 2691 (1977).

[13] The reasons are adapted from *Proposed Amendments to the Bylaws and Code of Professional Ethics: Referendum January 30, 1978,* American Institute of Certified Public Accountants, 1978, pp. 13–14. Copyright © 1978 by the American Institute of Certified Public Accountants, Inc.

FIGURE 2-2
A partial list of informative and objective content that may be used in advertising

1. Name of firm, address, telephone number.
2. Number of partners, shareholders, or employees.
3. Office hours.
4. Date firm was established.
5. Foreign language.
6. Services offered and corresponding fees (both hourly rates and fixed fees).
7. Educational and professional attainments including:
   a. Date and place of certifications.
   b. Schools attended and dates of graduation.
   c. Degrees received.
   d. Memberships in professional groups.
8. Policy or position statements relating to public accounting or a subject of public interest. Such a statement may be made by a firm or a member of the firm.

Source: Adapted from Interpretation 502-1 of the AICPA's Rules of Conduct.

3. Some form of advertising or solicitation would enable CPAs to inform the public of their services in areas in which non-CPA competitors are already advertising.
4. Some forms of advertising or solicitation might facilitate new CPAs making their services known to potential clients.

New rules.[14] In 1978, the AICPA's membership approved a change which allowed certain advertising and solicitation. Generally, advertising and solicitation were allowed if they were not "false, misleading, or deceptive." However, "a direct uninvited solicitation of a specific potential client [was] prohibited."

Even after this change, the Institute was still concerned with the legality of the proscription against "a direct uninvited solicitation of a specific potential client. . . ." There were serious questions as to whether such a proscription could be successfully defended.[15] Consequently, in 1979 the membership voted to eliminate this proscription. Currently, then, advertising and other types of solicitation are permitted if they are not "false, misleading, or deceptive."

Interpretation 502-1 of Rule 502 indicates that informative and objective advertising is allowed. Figure 2-2 contains a partial list of the

---

[14] This section is based in part on *Proposed Amendments to the Bylaws and Code of Professional Ethics: Referendum January 30, 1978*, pp. 11–13.

[15] *Referendum: Background Information on Proposed Amendments to the Code of Ethics*, January 30, 1979, American Institute of Certified Public Accountants, 1979, p. 8.

FIGURE 2-3
A partial list of activities that are considered to be false, misleading, or deceptive

1. An activity that would create a false or unjustified expectation of favorable results.
2. An activity that implies the ability to influence any court, tribunal, regulatory agency, or similar body or official.
3. An activity that consists of self-laudatory statements that are not based on verifiable facts.
4. An activity in which comparisons are made with other CPAs.
5. An activity that contains testimonials or endorsements.
6. An activity that contains any other representations that would be likely to cause a reasonable person to misunderstand or be deceived.
7. Self-designation as an expert or specialist.

Source: Adapted from Interpretations 502-2 and 502-4 of the AICPA's Rules of Conduct.

content such advertising might include. The Institute does not restrict the types of media that are used, the frequency of advertising, the size of the advertisements, nor the artwork or style (Interpretation 502-1). As is noted above, false, misleading, or deceptive advertising and other types of solicitation are proscribed. A partial list of such activities is contained in Figure 2-3.

Item number 7 in Figure 2-3 "self-designation as an expert or specialist" needs further clarification. Interpretation 502-4 notes in prohibiting such a designation that ". . . an AICPA program with methods for recognizing competence in specialized fields has not been developed and self-designation would be likely to cause misunderstanding or deception."

Guidelines for Advertising. Wood and Ball in an article in *The Journal of Accountancy* suggest the following three broad guidelines as elaborations on Rule 502:[16]

(1) Advertising should at all times be in good taste. "In good taste" means, simply that advertising should be fairly moderate and professional in tone. This requires prudence, which involves good judgment, caution, circumspection and the ability to discipline oneself. . . .

(2) Advertising should be consistent with the accountant's capabilities and limitations. . . .

* * * * *

---
[16] Thomas D. Wood and Donald A. Ball, "New Rule 502 and Effective Advertising by CPAs," *The Journal of Accountancy*, June 1978, pp. 65–66. Copyright © 1978 by the American Institute of Certified Public Accountants, Inc.

54

(3) Accountants should avoid overexposure through advertising, whatever the medium. . . .

Encroachment. In 1979, the Institute's membership voted to repeal Rule 401 that was concerned with encroachment. Under this now deleted provision of the code, practitioners who received a referral engagement from another practitioner were prohibited from extending their services beyond the original referral work without first contacting the referring CPA. In addition, Rule 401 had indicated that while a CPA should not endeavor to serve a client of another CPA, it was permissible to provide services if requested to do so by the client. Furthermore, Rule 401 indicated that a practitioner should not accept an audit engagement if the prospective client was already the client of another CPA without first consulting the other CPA ". . . to ascertain that the [practitioner was] aware of all the available relevant facts." (former Rule 401)

The Institute's legal counsel advised that Rule 401 ". . . seemed too broad a restraint to survive an antitrust attack. . . ."[17] Thus, in 1979, the rule was repealed.

The issues of communications between a predecessor auditor (auditor replaced) and the successor auditor (auditor accepting or invited to make a proposal on the engagement) is still covered in *SAS No. 7.*[18]

Before accepting an engagement, the prospective successor auditor should ask the prospective client to authorize the predecessor auditor to respond to his or her inquiries. Under Rule 301 this permission is required if the predecessor auditor is to respond. Failure of the prospective client to grant permission should raise serious questions as to whether the potential successor auditor should accept the engagement.

Once permission of the client is obtained, the prospective successor auditor should inquire into matters that may affect acceptance of the engagement. This includes questions relating to: (1) the integrity of management; (2) disagreements with management on accounting or auditing matters; and (3) the reason for the change in auditors. The predecessor should respond fully except when an unusual circumstance (such as pending litigation) limits the response. Either prior to or after acceptance of the engagement, the successor auditor should

[17] *Referendum: Background Information on Proposed Amendments to the Code of Ethics,* January 30, 1979, American Institute of Certified Public Accountants, 1979, p. 8.
[18] The remainder of this section is based on *Statement on Auditing Standards No. 7.* "Communications between Predecessor and Successor Auditors," American Institute of Certified Public Accountants. Copyright © 1975 by the American Institute of Certified Public Accountants, Inc.

review the predecessor's working papers (after obtaining permission of the client and agreement of the predecessor auditor) and make such other inquiries of the predecessor auditor as are needed to obtain evidence for expressing an auditor's report.

Discreditable Acts (Rule 501). The code contains a "catchall" clause which prohibits acts that are discreditable to the profession. This provision enables the Institute to bring action under its code of professional ethics against members who have committed undesirable acts that are not specifically covered in the other sections of the code.

Commissions (Rule 503). Commissions and fee splitting are not usually in the best interest of the clients. Fee splitting often raises the specter of conflict of interest. Also, such fees are often charged back to the client, either directly or indirectly. Consequently, the code prohibits a practitioner from paying a commission to obtain a client or accepting a fee for referring a client to another CPA.

WHO IS OBLIGATED

The AICPA code of ethics and the codes that have been adopted by the state societies and boards of accountancy are primarily directed toward the CPA in public practice. The AICPA member in public practice must observe all of the rules of professional conduct. The CPA who is not in public practice, however, is required to observe the rules relating to integrity and objectivity (Rule 102) and acts discreditable to the profession (Rule 501). Recently, there has been some interest in a code for CPAs not in public practice.

Under the AICPA code, CPAs are held responsible for the actions of all persons who are associated with them in their practice. Thus, CPAs are responsible for the professional conduct of any non-CPAs who work under their supervision.

ENFORCEMENT OF THE CODE

Formal Control Mechanisms

The AICPA, the state societies, and the various boards of accountancy each have the authority to enforce their individual codes of ethics. However, the nature of this authority varies somewhat. The AICPA can expel, suspend, censure, or warn a member. Both the AICPA and the state societies are voluntary, professional associations. Thus, the right of a CPA to practice is not affected by termination of membership in either of these organizations. If a CPA were suspended or expelled from both the AICPA and the state society of CPAs, he or she would still be able to practice. The real power to enforce the code of ethics, however, lies with the various boards of accountancy. These boards generally have the power to revoke or suspend the practitioner's CPA certificate or the right (license) to practice. Furthermore, the board can censure or warn the individual at its discretion.

Disciplinary Proceedings

The disciplinary proceedings of the professional accounting associations usually involve providing hearings for accused violators before a group of their peers. Accused violators have the right to be present and usually have the right to be represented by counsel. The determination made at such a hearing sometimes may be appealed to another board.

In a disciplinary proceeding brought by a board of accountancy, the accused is normally asked to appear in person before the board. The individual usually has the right to be represented by legal counsel. Often an accused violator has a right to appeal a decision to the courts.

Problems with Enforcement

The profession's mechanisms for enforcing the code have some problems. CPAs are often reluctant to report the violations of fellow practitioners. Additionally, CPAs who serve on the trial boards of the professional associations are called upon to spend a great deal of time in these activities without compensation. The costs to the associations can be high since they often must retain legal counsel.[19]

Members of the various boards of accountancy usually are busy practitioners. While they often receive some compensation for meetings, it is usually quite limited. Professional associations and boards of accountancy generally do not have staffs that are of sufficient size to handle a heavy work load.[20]

The punishments meted out by the different agencies may vary. Different bodies, professional associations or boards of accountancy, may disagree in a particular situation as to guilt or innocence or as to the sanction to be imposed if the individual is found guilty.[21]

The accounting profession is aware of the problems in its ethics enforcement procedures. Efforts are currently under way to overcome these problems, and hopefully they will be successful.

---

[19] John L. Carey, *The CPA Plans for the Future* (New York: American Institute of Certified Public Accountants, 1965), p. 334.

[20] Ibid., p. 338.

[21] Ibid., pp. 336–37.

Ethics Education

In recent years the professional accounting associations have begun to place a good deal of emphasis on education in the area of professional ethics. Also, professional development sessions have been devoted to ethics, and accounting newsletters and journals are allocating additional space to this important topic.

The boards of accountancy in many states are now requiring CPA candidates to take a special examination in professional ethics. Such an examination will help assure that younger members of the profession have an understanding of the code.

TAX PRACTICE[22]

Most CPAs engage in activities that are related to tax practice. Carey and Doherty suggest that in tax practice CPAs have several responsibilities: (1) to the client; (2) to the government; and (3) to the public. These authors note that the AICPA code of ethics definitely applies to tax practice. The AICPA has sanctioned members for improper actions relating to tax practice. Generally, these actions pertain to the provision prohibiting acts discreditable to the accounting profession.[23]

The AICPA has a program under way to provide guidance to members in their tax practices. More specifically, the Institute's Federal Taxation Division issues *Statements on Responsibilities in Tax Practice*. These are a "... series of statements ... intended to constitute a body of advisory opinion on what are good standards of tax practice, delineating the extent of a CPA's responsibility to his client, the public, the Government, and his profession."[24] Additionally, "the statements are not intended to establish a separate code of conduct in tax practice, apart from the general ethical precepts of the Institute's Code of Professional Ethics."[25]

Statements on Responsibility

To date the AICPA has issued ten *Statements on Responsibilities in Tax Practice*. These ten statements are discussed briefly in the following paragraphs.

[22] This section is based in part on Walter C. Frank, "The CPA and Ethics in Tax Practice," *The Tax Adviser*, December 1973, pp. 716–22. Copyright © 1973 by the American Institute of Certified Public Accountants, Inc.

[23] Carey and Doherty, *Ethical Standards of the Accounting Profession*, pp. 82–83.

[24] *Statements on Responsibilities in Tax Practice*, "Introduction," American Institute of Certified Public Accountants, Revised 1969, p. 1.

[25] Ibid., p. 3.

No. 1. Signature of Preparer. Statement No. 1 suggests that a CPA should sign any tax return that he or she prepares. The CPA should sign as a preparer regardless of whether the return was prepared for compensation.

No. 2. Signature as a Reviewer. Statement No. 2 suggests that a CPA who only reviews a return, may at his or her option, sign the return as a preparer if the CPA acquires the knowledge of the return that is substantially equivalent to the knowledge a preparer would have acquired.

No. 3. Questions on Returns. Tax returns often contain questions. If the client does not answer all of the questions, the CPA must be satisfied that a reasonable effort was made to answer all questions. Reasons should be stated when questions are left unanswered. Failure of the client to comply with these requirements should result in the CPA declining to sign the return.

No. 4. Recognition of an Administrative Proceeding from a Prior Year. This statement indicates that in preparing a tax return a CPA should consider the facts and the rules existing in the current year. The practitioner need not be governed this year by the disposition of an item in an administrative proceeding for a prior year.

No. 5. Using Estimates. Statement No. 5 suggests that it is permissible for a CPA to prepare a tax return that involves the use of estimates if *(a)* the use of estimates is generally acceptable or *(b)* if it is not practicable to obtain the actual data. Estimates should not be presented in a manner that implies greater accuracy than actually exists.

Nos. 6 and 7. Knowledge of Errors. Statement No. 6 suggests that, if a CPA learns of an error in a client's previously filed tax return or of a client's failure to file a tax return, the CPA should discuss the matter with the client. If the CPA is requested to prepare the current year's tax return and the client has not rectified an error in a prior return that resulted or might result in a material understatement of a tax liability, the CPA should consider whether or not to prepare the return. Furthermore, if the CPA does prepare the return, he or she should make sure the error is not repeated in the current year. The CPA is, however, under no obligation to report this situation to the Internal Revenue Service (IRS).

Statement No. 7 discusses the CPA's actions on finding an error in the course of representing a client in an administrative proceeding. The CPA should ask the client for permission to explain the error to the IRS. If the client does not agree, the CPA should consider withdrawing from the engagement.

No. 8. Advising Clients. In giving tax advice to clients, the CPA should provide the client with high quality service. The CPA may contact the client when subsequent developments relate to advice previously given. However, *Statement No. 8* notes that the CPA "... cannot be expected to have assumed responsibility for initiating such communications except while he is assisting a client in implementing procedures or plans associated with the advice provided. Of course, the CPA may undertake this obligation by specific agreement with his client."[26]

No. 9. Various Procedural Aspects of Return Preparation. In most instances in preparing a tax return a CPA is justified in relying on information supplied by the client. Where appropriate the client should provide supporting data. The CPA should consider the implications of all information available and make inquiries when it appears reasonable to do so. Finally, the CPA, when signing a federal tax return, should not alter the preparer's declaration.

No. 10. Positions Contrary to Treasury Department or IRS Interpretations. This statement indicates that the CPA is allowed while preparing a tax return to take a position that is contrary to Treasury Department or IRS interpretations of the Internal Revenue Code without disclosure. When doing so, however, there should be reasonable support for the position. Additionally, the CPA, where there is reasonable support, may take a position contrary to a particular section of the Internal Revenue Code.

Treasury Department Circular 230

Another source of guidance for the CPA in tax practice is Treasury Department Circular 230. This circular governs all individuals practicing before the IRS. Practice before the IRS includes representing a client before the IRS as well as corresponding with and communicating with the IRS. However, the preparation of tax returns would not be included here. Some of the areas covered by Treasury Department Circular 230 include: (1) submission of records and information; (2) knowledge of an error; (3) fees; (4) conflict of interest; and (5) suspension or disbarment of a practitioner from practice.

Technical Tax Standards

Tax practice falls under the areas covered in new Rules 201 and 204. As was noted earlier, it is anticipated that in the future the Council of the AICPA will instruct the Federal Taxation Executive Committee to establish standards in the tax area. It is possible that the committee will look to the *Statements on Responsibility in Tax Practice* in the process of establishing tax standards.

---

[26] "Advice to Clients," *Statement on Responsibilities in Tax Practice No. 8*, American Institute of Certified Public Accountants, 1970, p. 1.

MANAGEMENT SERVICES

During the past 25 years, CPAs have increased their management consulting activities substantially. CPA firms have performed many diverse services for clients including industrial engineering, systems analyses, and budgeting.

The performance of management services by CPAs raises several issues relating to accounting ethics. First, does the code apply to the practitioner who is performing management services? As outlined in the appendix to this chapter, under "Applicability of Rules," there is no doubt that the code does in fact apply to such work.

Another important question is: Can CPAs perform management services for a client and still be regarded as independent in performing an audit examination? Generally, it is felt that as long as CPAs merely give advice to the client and do not actually make the decisions, they do not lose their independence.

The AICPA established an independent commission called "The Commission on Auditors' Responsibilities" (or the "Cohen Commission" after its chairman) to develop ideas concerning the responsibilities of independent auditors. One area considered by the Cohen Commission was management consulting. The Commission noted:

> ... There is little question that the provision of some other services to audit clients poses an obvious *potential* threat to the auditor's independence. . . .
>
> Public accounting firms have indicated that they make substantial effort to avoid conflicts of interest. Such statements recognize the undeniable fact that a potential for such conflict exists. However, this recognition and the efforts to avoid conflicts appear to have been successful:
>
> * * * * *
>
> ... On balance, the Commission concludes that the relevant facts do not support a prohibition against any particular services that auditors are now permitted to offer.[27]

On the other hand, the original document establishing the SEC Practice Section of the AICPA Division of Firms approved by the AICPA's Council puts some restrictions on the type of management consulting that can be performed by a CPA firm for audit clients who have securities registered with the SEC (e.g., prohibiting public opinion polls, psychological testing, and executive recruiting). The document indicated that the SEC Practice Section would continue to study the question of management services.

---

[27] *The Commission on Auditors' Responsibilities: Report, Conclusions, and Recommendations,* 1978, p. 102.

At the request of the Executive Committee of the SEC Practice Section, its Public Oversight Board examined the question of management services and independence. In the Spring of 1979, this Board issued a report which among other things concluded that "mandatory limitations on scope of services should be predicted only on the determination that certain services, or the role of the firm performing certain services, will impair a member's independence in rendering an opinion on the fairness of a client's financial statements or present a strong likelihood of doing so."[28] The report went on to note that "at this time no rules should be imposed to prohibit specific services on the grounds that they are or may be incompatible with the profession of public accounting, might impair the image of the profession, or do not involve accounting or auditing related skills."[29]

A third important issue relates to competence. Rule 201(A) notes that "a member shall undertake only those engagements which he or his firm can reasonably expect to complete with professional competence." If a CPA firm does not have the competence or is unable to acquire the competence to perform an engagement, the firm should decline the job, referring the work to a practitioner who is competent in that particular area.

In 1975 the AICPA's Management Advisory Services Executive Committee issued a number of Management Advisory Services Practice Standards. These standards were intended to apply to formal consulting services and not to informal advice given to clients. The standards include the following areas: (1) personal characteristics of the practitioner (e.g., integrity, objectivity, independence); (2) competence of practitioners; (3) due care; (4) client benefit (notifying a client before starting an engagement of reservations concerning anticipated benefits); (5) understandings with the client; (6) planning, supervision, and control of engagements; (7) sufficient relevant data for the conclusions and recommendations; and (8) the communication to the client of significant matters relating to the results.

These standards are guides to CPAs practicing in the consulting area. The standards are not an integral part of the code. However, AICPA members may be asked to justify departures from these standards.

Management Advisory Services do, however, fall under the areas covered in new Rules 201 and 204. As mentioned earlier, in October 1978 the AICPA's Council approved a resolution authorizing the

---

[28]*Public Oversight Board Report: Scope of Services by CPA Firms*, Public Oversight Board, SEC Practice Section, American Institute of Certified Public Accountants, 1979, pp. 4–5.

[29]Ibid., p. 5.

Management Advisory Services Executive Committee to establish standards in that area. This resolution read in part as follows:

> Resolved: That the Management Advisory Services Executive Committee is hereby designated to promulgate technical standards under Rule 204 with respect to the offering of management advisory services provided, however, that such standards do not deal with the broad question of what, if any services should be proscribed, and provided further that any such statements are subject to review by affected senior technical committees of the Institute prior to issuance.[30]

The eight practice standards issued in 1975 do not come under the jurisdiction of Rule 204. However, in the future, technical standards issued by the Management Advisory Services Executive Committee will fall under Rule 204.

The area of ethical behavior is one that will continue to receive increasing attention within the accounting profession in the future.

APPENDIX

A REPRODUCTION OF THE AICPA RULES OF CONDUCT*

DEFINITIONS

The following definitions of terminology are applicable wherever such terminology is used in the rules and interpretations.

Client The person(s) or entity which retains a member or his firm, engaged in the practice of public accounting, for the performance of professional services.

Council The Council of the American Institute of Certified Public Accountants.

Enterprise Any person(s) or entity, whether organized for profit or not, for which a CPA provides services.

Firm A proprietorship, partnership or professional corporation or association engaged in the practice of public accounting, including individual partners or shareholders thereof.

---

[30] *AICPA Professional Standards*, vol. 2. American Institute of Certified Public Accountants, p. 5143.

*Source: *Restatement of the Code of Professional Ethics*, Copyright © 1972 by the American Institute of Certified Public Accountants, Inc. The 1978 amendments per AICPA Professional Standards, vol. 2. The 1979 amendments per *Referendum: Background Information on Proposed Amendments to the Code of Ethics*, January 30, 1979, American Institute of Certified Public Accountants, 1979.

Financial statements Statements and footnotes related thereto that purport to show financial position which relates to a point in time or changes in financial position which relate to a period of time, and statements which use a cash or other incomplete basis of accounting. Balance sheets, statements of income, statements of retained earnings, statements of changes in financial position and statements of changes in owners' equity are financial statements.

Incidental financial data included in management advisory services reports to support recommendations to a client, and tax returns and supporting schedules do not, for this purpose, constitute financial statements; and the statement, affidavit or signature of preparers required on tax returns neither constitutes an opinion on financial statements nor requires a disclaimer of such opinion.

Institute The American Institute of Certified Public Accountants.

Interpretations of rules of conduct Pronouncements issued by the Division of Professional Ethics to provide guidelines as to the scope and application of the Rules of Conduct.

Member A member, associate member or international associate of the American Institute of Certified Public Accountants.

Practice of public accounting Holding out to be a CPA or public accountant and at the same time performing for a client one or more types of services rendered by public accountants. The term shall not be limited by a more restrictive definition which might be found in the accountancy law under which a member practices.

Professional services One or more types of services performed in the practice of public accounting.

APPLICABILITY OF RULES

The Institute's Code of Professional Ethics derives its authority from the bylaws of the Institute which provide that the Trial Board may, after a hearing, admonish, suspend, or expel a member who is found guilty of infringing any of the bylaws or any provisions of the Rules of Conduct.

The Rules of Conduct which follow apply to all services performed in the practice of public accounting including tax and management advisory services, except (a) where the wording of the rule indicates otherwise and (b) that a member who is practicing outside the United States will not be subject to discipline for departing from any of the rules stated herein so long as his conduct is in accord with the rules of the organized accounting profession in the country in which he is practicing. However, where a member's name is associated with financial statements in such a manner as to imply that he is acting as an independent public accountant and under circumstances that would entitle the reader to assume that United States practices were followed, he must comply with the requirements of Rules 202 and 203.

A member may be held responsible for compliance with the Rules of Conduct by all persons associated with him in the practice of public accounting who are either under his supervision or are his partners or shareholders in the practice.

A member engaged in the practice of public accounting must observe all the Rules of Conduct. A member not engaged in the practice of public accounting must observe only Rules 102 and 501 since all other Rules of Conduct relate solely to the practice of public accounting.

A member shall not permit others to carry out on his behalf, either with or without compensation, acts which, if carried out by the member, would place him in violation of the Rules of Conduct.

INDEPENDENCE, INTEGRITY AND OBJECTIVITY

Rule 101-Independence. A member or a firm of which he is a partner or shareholder shall not express an opinion on financial statements of an enterprise unless he and his firm are independent with respect to such enterprise. Independence will be considered to be impaired if, for example:

A. During the period of his professional engagement, or at the time of expressing his opinion, he or his firm
    1. (a) Had or was committed to acquire any direct or material indirect financial interest in the enterprise; or
        (b) Was a trustee of any trust or executor or administrator of any estate if such trust or estate had or was committed to acquire any direct or material indirect financial interest in the enterprise; or
    2. Had any joint closely held business investment with the enterprise or any officer, director, or principal stockholder thereof which was material in relation to his or his firm's net worth; or
    3. Had any loan to or from the enterprise or any officer, director, or principal stockholder thereof. This latter proscription does not apply to the following loans from a financial institution when made under normal lending procedures, terms, and requirements:
        (a) Loans obtained by a member or his firm which are not material in relation to the net worth of such borrower.
        (b) Home mortgages.
        (c) Other secured loans, except loans guaranteed by a member's firm which are otherwise unsecured.

B. During the period covered by the financial statements, during the period of the professional engagement, or at the time of expressing an opinion, he or his firm

    1. Was connected with the enterprise as a promoter, underwriter or voting trustee, a director or officer or in any capacity equivalent to that of a member of management or of an employee; or

    2. Was a trustee for any pension or profit-sharing trust of the enterprise.

The above examples are not intended to be all-inclusive.

Rule 102–Integrity and Objectivity. A member shall not knowingly misrepresent facts, and when engaged in the practice of public accounting, including the rendering of tax and management advisory services, shall not subordinate his judgment to others. In tax practice, a member may resolve doubt in favor of his client as long as there is reasonable support for his position.

COMPETENCE AND TECHNICAL STANDARDS

Rule 201–General Standards. A member shall comply with the following general standards as interpreted by bodies designated by Council, and must justify any departures therefrom.

A. Professional competence. A member shall undertake only those engagements which he or his firm can reasonably expect to complete with professional competence.

B. Due professional care. A member shall exercise due professional care in the performance of an engagement.

C. Planning and supervision. A member shall adequately plan and supervise an engagement.

D. Sufficient relevant data. A member shall obtain sufficient relevant data to afford a reasonable basis for conclusions or recommendations in relation to an engagement.

E. Forecasts. A member shall not permit his name to be used in conjunction with any forecast of future transactions in a manner which may lead to the belief that the member vouches for the achievability of the forecast.

Rule 202–Auditing Standards. A member shall not pemit his name to be associated with financial statements in such a manner as to imply that he is acting as an independent public accountant unless he has complied with the applicable generally accepted auditing standards promulgated by the Institute. Statements on Auditing Standards issued by the Institute's Auditing Standards Executive Committee† are, for purposes of this rule, considered to be interpretations of the generally accepted auditing standards, and departures from such statements must be justified by those who do not follow them.

Rule 203–Accounting Principles. A member shall not express an opinion that financial statements are presented in conformity with generally accepted accounting principles if such statements contain any departure from an accounting principle promulgated by the body designated by Council to establish such principles which has a material effect on the statements taken as a whole, unless the member can demonstrate that due to unusual circumstances the financial statements would otherwise have been misleading. In such cases his report must describe the departure, the approximate effects thereof, if practicable, and the reasons why compliance with the principle would result in a misleading statement.

Rule 204–Other Technical Standards. A member shall comply with other technical standards promulgated by bodies designated by Council to establish such standards, and departures therefrom must be justified by those who do not follow them.

RESPONSIBILITIES TO CLIENTS

Rule 301–Confidential Client Information. A member shall not disclose any confidential information obtained in the course of a professional engagement except with the consent of the client.

This rule shall not be construed (a) to relieve a member of his obligation under Rules 202 and 203, (b) to affect in any way his compliance with a validly issued subpoena or summons enforceable by order of a court, (c) to prohibit review of a member's professional practices as a part of voluntary quality review under Institute authorization, or (d) to preclude a member from responding to any inquiry made by the ethics division or Trial Board of the Institute, by a duly constituted investigative or disciplinary body of a state CPA society, or under state statutes.

Members of the ethics division and Trial Board of the Institute and professional practice reviewers under Institute authorization shall not disclose any confidential client information which comes to their attention from members in disciplinary proceedings or otherwise in carrying out their official responsibilities. However, this prohibition

---

†*Authors' Note:* The Auditing Standards Executive Committee has been replaced by the Auditing Standards Board.

shall not restrict the exchange of information with an aforementioned duly constituted investigative or disciplinary body.

Rule 302 – Contingent Fees.   Professional services shall not be offered or rendered under an arrangement whereby no fee will be charged unless a specified finding or result is attained, or where the fee is otherwise contingent upon the findings or results of such services. However, a member's fees may vary depending, for example, on the complexity of the service rendered.

Fees are not regarded as being contingent if fixed by courts or other public authorities or, in tax matters, if determined based on the results of judicial proceedings or the findings of governmental agencies.

OTHER RESPONSIBILITIES AND PRACTICES

Rule 501 – Acts Discreditable.   A member shall not commit an act discreditable to the profession.

Rule 502 – Advertising and Other Forms of Solicitation.   A member shall not seek to obtain clients by advertising or other forms of solicitation in a manner that is false, misleading, or deceptive.

Rule 503 – Commissions.   A member shall not pay a commission to obtain a client, nor shall he accept a commission for a referral to a client of products or services of others. This rule shall not prohibit payments for the purchase of an accounting practice or retirement payments to individuals formerly engaged in the practice of public accounting or payments to their heirs or estates.

Rule 504 – Incompatible Occupations.   A member who is engaged in the practice of public accounting shall not concurrently engage in any business or occupation which would create a conflict of interest in rendering professional services.

Rule 505 – Form of Practice and Name.   A member may practice public accounting, whether as an owner or employee, only in the form of a proprietorship, a partnership or a professional corporation whose characteristics conform to the resolutions of Council.

A member shall not practice under a firm name which includes any fictitious name, indicates specialization or is misleading as to the type of organization (proprietorship, partnership, or corporation). However, names of one or more past partners or shareholders may be included in the firm name of a successor partnership or corporation. Also, a partner surviving the death or withdrawal of all other partners may continue to practice under the partnership name for up to two years after becoming a sole practitioner.

A firm may not designate itself as "Members of the American Institute of Certified Public Accountants" unless all of its partners or shareholders are members of the Institute.

GLOSSARY

Code of ethics A body of rules which define acceptable and unacceptable professional behavior. [see page 46]

Contingent fees When the fee an auditor is to receive for services is based on the findings of the engagement. Contingent fees are prohibited by the code of ethics.

Council The governing body of the AICPA. It is composed of AICPA members who are elected to Council or are members of Council due to their position (e.g., all past Chairmen of the Board of the Institute who are still AICPA members are members of Council). Note that between meetings of Council the AICPA is directed by the Board of Directors [AICPA Standards, Volume 2].

Discreditable acts Actions by a CPA that would bring discredit to the profession.

Incompatible occupation An occupation that would create a conflict of interest when a public accountant renders a service.

(Also see the definitions contained in the beginning of the appendix.)

QUESTIONS AND PROBLEMS

2-1. Is there a single code of ethics for the accounting profession? Explain.

2-2. To what groups does the CPA have ethical responsibilities?

2-3. R. Jones, CPA, placed an ad in a charity program saying "Compliments of R. Jones, CPA." Is this ethical? Explain.

2-4. CPA J is called into Federal District Court. The government subpoenas his working papers for a particular client. J refuses, claiming that he is a professional and therefore has "privileged communication" with that client. Is CPA J's position correct? Explain.

2-5. Steve Smith, CPA, is moving his office to a new building. He sends a notice to this effect to the local newspaper which published it. Is his action correct? Explain.

2-6. Rule 201 contains five general standards that are applicable to all areas of public accounting. List and discuss these standards.

2-7. In 1978 and 1979, the AICPA's membership voted to allow certain forms of advertising and other types of solicitation.
   a. Discuss the kinds of advertising and other types of solicitation in which CPAs are allowed to engage.
   b. What kinds of media may CPAs use to advertise?
   c. How often may a CPA advertise?
   d. What information may a CPA include in an advertisement?

2-8. List some kinds of advertising and other types of solicitation that if engaged in by CPAs would be considered false, misleading, or deceptive.

2-9. Does the AICPA Code of Ethics cover tax practice? Management services? Explain.

2 / The Code of Professional Conduct 69

2-10. Will suspension of a CPA from the AICPA prevent the individual from practicing as a CPA? Explain.

2-11. S. H. Smith, CPA, is building her own office building. She erects a sign on the building site which reads: "This is the future home of S. H. Smith, CPA." Comment on the CPA's action.

2-12. List the areas included in the Management Advisory Services Practice Standards.

2-13. Discuss the significance of *Treasury Department Circular 230.*

2-14. Select the *best* answer for each of the following items:

    a. A CPA accepts an engagement for a professional service *without* violating the AICPA Code of Professional Ethics if the service involves

        1. The preparation of cost projections for submission to a governmental agency as an application for a rate increase, and the fee will be paid if there is a rate increase.

        2. Tax preparation, and the fee will be based on whether the CPA signs the tax return prepared.

        3. A litigatory matter, and the fee is *not* known but is to be determined by a district court.

        4. Tax return preparation, and the fee is to be based on the amount of taxes saved, if any.

    b. Which of the following statements *best* describes why the profession of certified public accounting has deemed it essential to promulgate a code of ethics and to establish a mechanism for enforcing observance of the code?

        1. A distinguishing mark of a profession is its acceptance of responsibility to the public.

        2. A prerequisite to success is the establishment of an ethical code that stresses primarily the professional's responsibility to clients and colleagues.

        3. A requirement of most state laws calls for the profession to establish a code of ethics.

        4. An essential means of self-protection for the profession is the establishment of flexible ethical standards by the profession.

    c. The AICPA Code of Professional Ethics states, in part, that a CPA should maintain integrity and objectivity. Objectivity in the code refers to a CPA's ability

        1. To maintain an impartial attitude on all matters which come under the CPA's review.

        2. To independently distinguish between accounting practices that are acceptable and those that are *not*.

        3. To be unyielding in all matters dealing with auditing procedures.

        4. To independently choose between alternate accounting principles and auditing standards.

    d. A CPA who has given correct tax advice which is later affected by changes in the tax law is *required* to

1. Notify the client upon learning of any change.
2. Notify the client only when the CPA is actively assisting with implementing the advice or is obliged to so notify by specific agreement.
3. Notify the Internal Revenue Service.
4. Take no action if the client has already followed the advice unless the client asks the question again.

e. A CPA's retention of client records as a means of enforcing payment of an overdue audit fee is an action that is
1. Considered acceptable by the AICPA Code of Professional Ethics.
2. Ill-advised since it would impair the CPA's independence with respect to the client.
3. Considered discreditable to the profession.
4. A violation of generally accepted auditing standards.

f. Upon discovering irregularities in a client's tax return that the client would *not* correct, a CPA withdraws from the engagement. How should the CPA respond if asked by the successor CPA why the relationship was terminated?
1. "It was a misunderstanding."
2. "I suggest you get the client's permission for us to discuss all matters freely."
3. "I suggest you ask the client."
4. "I found irregularities in the tax return which the client would not correct."

g. A CPA, who is a member of the American Institute of Certified Public Accountants, wrote an article for publication in a professional journal. The AICPA Code of Professional Ethics would be violated if the CPA allowed the article to state that the CPA was
1. A member of the American Institute of Certified Public Accountants.
2. A professor at a school of professional accountancy.
3. A partner in a national CPA firm.
4. A practitioner specialized in providing tax services.

(AICPA, adapted)

2-15. CPA J is appointed by the governor of his state as the State Comptroller. As comptroller of the state CPA J will maintain control over accounts for all state funds, administer disbursements, allocate revenue among county and local governments, and serve as an ex officio member of several committees, boards, and commissions. At the time of his appointment, CPA J is in public practice. May CPA J remain in public practice while serving as state comptroller?

(AICPA, adapted)

2-16. H. T. Smith, CPA, is asked by a prospective client to perform a management services engagement. Smith, realizing the engagement is beyond her abilities, refers the prospective client to R. Jones, CPA, who performs the engagement. R. Jones sends H. T. Smith 10 percent of the fee in payment for the referral. Comment.

2-17. E. E. Johne is a CPA. She also is an attorney. Johne lives in a small town that has very few CPAs and very few lawyers. In order to supply the residents of the community with full professional services, Johne decides to practice both as a CPA and as an attorney. Comment on this situation.

2-18. Joe Tack, CPA, performed tax and bookkeeping services for I.M. Cheap, Inc., for the fiscal year ended December 31, 1981. Tack billed Cheap, Inc., $8,000 for his services. Cheap feels the fee is too high and refuses to pay anything. Since Tack is holding all of Cheap's journals and ledgers, he informs the president of Cheap, Inc., that he will retain Cheap's books until the fee is paid. Comment on this situation.

2-19. Sally Root, CPA, has a large practice that consists mostly of opinion audits. Being a sole practitioner, Root is concerned that her work papers and reports do not receive as much review as the work papers and reports receive in larger firms. As a consequence, she asks the AICPA to periodically send in CPAs from other firms to review her papers and reports in order to offer constructive criticisms. Is Root violating the rule on confidentiality?

2-20. Alan Room, CPA, a partner of Room & Room, CPAs, meets Alvin Staffman, a senior accountant with another CPA, at a state society meeting. Room is very impressed with Staffman and during their conversation offers Staffman a job at a very high salary. Comment.

2-21. J. C. Conman, president of Marginal Corp., is in need of audited financial statements. He asks Sandra Honest, CPA, to estimate her fees for such an engagement. After a careful evaluation Honest gives Conman an estimate range. Conman says that the estimate is too high but says he would be happy to pay Honest 4 percent of net income for that year. Comment on this situation.

2-22. J. C. Wise, CPA, has a very large client, Future Inc., that is in need of a large bank loan. The bank, as part of the loan application, asks Future for a forecast of its operations for the next three years. The president of Future is very anxious to obtain the loan. He asks Wise to attest to the forecast. Comment.

2-23. I. M. Old, CPA, has a large practice. He is 65 years old and would like to retire. J. C. Young, CPA, is interested in purchasing Old's practice. In order to determine a fair purchase price Old lets Young examine all of his records, working papers, and so on. Comment.

2-24. R. A. Sideline, CPA, decides to render an additional service for her clients by arranging for her clients to purchase office supplies from a particular company at a reduced price. The supplier gives Sideline 1 percent of all such sales. Comment.   (AICPA, adapted)

2-25. R. A. Bill, CPA, is asked by Small, Inc., a tax client, whether the corporation should file Form 8982 with its state income tax return.

Form 8982 requires Small, Inc., to disclose the amount of inventory on hand. The state department of taxation always passes copies of Form 8982 on to the county property tax assessor. Since the penalty for not filing a Form 8982 is a $10 fine, Bill advises Small, Inc., not to file a Form 8982. Comment on this advice.

2-26. An auditor's report was appended to the financial statements of Worthmore, Inc. The statements consisted of a balance sheet as of November 30, 1980 and statements of income, retained earnings, and changes in financial position for the year then ending. The first two paragraphs of the report contained the wording of the standard unqualified (short-form) report, and a third paragraph read as follows:

> The wives of two partners of our firm owned a material investment in the outstanding common stock of Worthmore, Inc. during the fiscal year ending November 30, 1980. The aforementioned individuals disposed of their holdings of Worthmore, Inc. on December 3, 1980 in a transaction that did not result in a profit or a loss. This information is included in our report in order to comply with certain disclosure requirements of the *Code of Professional Ethics* of the American Institute of Certified Public Accountants.
>
> Bell & Davis
> Certified Public Accountants

Required:

a. Was the CPA firm of Bell & Davis independent with respect to the fiscal 1980 examination of Worthmore, Inc.'s financial statement? Explain.

b. Do you find Bell & Davis' auditor's report satisfactory? Explain.

c. Assume that no members of Bell & Davis or any members of their families held any financial interests in Worthmore, Inc., during 1980. For each of the following cases, indicate if independence would be lacking on behalf of Bell & Davis, assuming that Worthmore, Inc. is a profit-seeking enterprise. In each case, explain why independence would or would not be lacking.

1. Two directors of Worthmore, Inc. became partners in the CPA firm of Bell & Davis on July 1, 1980, resigning their directorships on that date.

2. During 1980 the former controller of Worthmore, now a Bell & Davis partner, was frequently called on for assistance by Worthmore. He made decisions for Worthmore's management regarding fixed asset acquisitions and the company's product marketing mix. In addition, he conducted a computer feasibility study for Worthmore.

(AICPA, adapted)

2-27. Shortly before the due date Daniel Burr requested that you prepare the 1980 federal income tax return for Burr Corporation, a small closely held service corporation that he controlled. Burr placed a package on your desk and said, "Here is all the information you need.

I'll pay you $300 if you prepare the return in time for filing by the deadline with no extension—and if the tax liability is less than $2,000 I'll increase your fee to $500." The package contained the corporation's bank statements and paid checks, prior years' tax returns prepared on the accrual basis, and other financial and tax information. The books of account were not included because they were not posted up to date.

You found that deposits shown on the bank statements substantially exceeded Burr's sales figure and the expenses listed seemed rather large in relation to sales. Burr explained that he made several loans to the corporation during the year and expenses just seemed to "mount up."

Required:

1. What ethical issues should you consider before deciding whether or not you should prepare the federal income tax return for Burr Corporation?
2. If you prepare this return, must you sign it? Explain.
3. If you sign the return, what does your signature imply?

(AICPA, adapted)

2-28. *Part a.* During 1980, your client, Big Corporation, requested that you conduct a feasibility study to advise management of the best way the corporation can utilize electronic data processing equipment and which computer, if any, best meets the corporation's requirements. You are technically competent in this area and accept the engagement. Upon completion of your study the corporation accepts your suggestions and installs the computer and related equipment that you recommended.

Required:

1. Discuss the effect the acceptance of this management services engagement would have upon your independence in expressing an opinion on the financial statements of the Big Corporation.
2. Instead of accepting the engagement, assume that you recommended Ike Mackey, of the CPA firm of Brown and Mackey, who is qualified in specialized services. Upon completion of the engagement your client requests that Mackey's partner, John Brown, perform services in other areas. Should Brown accept the engagement? Discuss.
3. A local printer of data processing forms customarily offers a commission for recommending him as supplier. The client is aware of the commission offer and suggests that Mackey accept it. Would it be proper for Mackey to accept the commission with the client's approval? Discuss.

Part b. Alex Pratt, a retired partner of your CPA firm, has just been appointed to the board of directors of Palmer Corporation, your firm's client. Pratt is also a member of your firm's income tax committee which meets monthly to discuss income tax problems of the partnership's clients. The partnership pays Pratt $100 for each committee meeting he attends and a monthly retirement benefit of $1,000.

Required:

Discuss the effect of Pratt's appointment to the board of directors of Palmer Corporation on your partnership's independence in expressing an opinion on the Palmer Corporation's financial statements.

(AICPA, adapted)

2–29. The attribute of independence has been traditionally associated with the CPA's function of auditing and expressing opinions on financial statements.

Required:

a. What is meant by "independence" as applied to the CPA's function of auditing and expressing opinions on financial statements? Discuss.

b. The Rocky Hill Corporation was formed on October 1, 1980, and its fiscal year will end on September 30, 1981. You audited the corporation's opening balance sheet and rendered an unqualified opinion on it.

A month after rendering your report you are offered the position of secretary of the company because of the need for a complete set of officers and for convenience in signing various documents. You will have no financial interest in the company through stock ownership or otherwise, will receive no salary, will not keep the books, and will not have any influence on its financial matters other than occasional advice on income tax matters and similar advice normally given a client by a CPA.

Assume that you accept the offer but plan to resign the position prior to conducting your annual audit with the intention of again assuming the office after rendering an opinion on the statements. Can you render an independent opinion on the financial statements? Discuss.

(AICPA, adapted)

2–30. Tom Jencks, CPA, conducts a public accounting practice. In 1980 Mr. Jencks and Harold Swann, a non-CPA, organized Electro-Data Corporation to specialize in computerized bookkeeping services. Mr. Jencks and Mr. Swann each supplied 50 percent of Electro-Data's capital, and each holds 50 percent of the capital stock. Mr. Swann is the salaried general manager of Electro-Data. Mr. Jencks is affiliated with the corporation only as a stockholder; he receives no salary and does not participate in day-to-day management. However, he has transferred all of his bookkeeping accounts to the corporation and recommends its services whenever possible.

Required:

Organizing your presentation around Mr. Jencks' involvement with Electro-Data Corporation, discuss the propriety of:

a. A CPA's participation in an enterprise offering computerized bookkeeping services.
b. The use of advertising by an enterprise in which a CPA holds an interest.
c. A CPA's transfer of bookkeeping accounts to a service company.
d. A CPA's recommendation of a particular bookkeeping service company.

(AICPA, adapted)

2-31. Judd Hanlon, CPA, was engaged to prepare the federal income tax return for the Guild Corporation for the year ended December 31, 1980. This is Mr. Hanlon's first engagement of any kind for the Guild Corporation.

In preparing the 1980 return, Mr. Hanlon finds an error on the 1979 return. The 1979 depreciation deduction was overstated significantly—accumulated depreciation brought forward from 1978 to 1979 was understated, and thus the 1979 base for declining balance depreciation was overstated.

Mr. Hanlon reported the error to Guild's controller, the officer responsible for tax returns. The controller stated: "Let the revenue agent find the error." He further instructed Mr. Hanlon to carry forward the material overstatement of the depreciable base to the 1980 depreciation computation. The controller noted that this error also had been made in the financial records for 1979 and 1980 and offered to furnish Mr. Hanlon with a letter assuming full responsibility for this treatment.

Required:

a. Evaluate Mr. Hanlon's handling of this situation.
b. Discuss the additional action that Mr. Hanlon should now undertake.

(AICPA , adapted)

Learning Objectives

Study of this chapter is intended to accomplish several learning objectives. Included among these are to achieve:

1. An understanding of accountants' legal liability under common law to clients, subrogees, primary beneficiaries, and to third parties other than primary beneficiaries.
2. Some familiarity with some of the landmark court cases involving accountants' legal liability under the common law.
3. An appreciation for the importance of a well-written audit engagement contract or letter.
4. An appreciation for the care that must be taken in each engagement to avoid liability exposure under the common law.

3

Accountants' Legal Liability under Common Law*

Certified public accountants may be held liable for both civil and criminal actions which arise out of their acts, errors, or omissions. Civil actions may be initiated against CPAs because of breach of contract, tortious conduct (a civil wrong independent of a contract), or violation of a civil section of a statute; the first two categories are usually referred to as violations of common law (unwritten law as opposed to statute law). In general, civil actions are introduced by private parties in an attempt to obtain compensation through the courts for alleged losses caused by the direct or indirect actions of the certified public accountant. Damages in the form of money are awarded in civil actions. Any criminal action introduced against the accountant will be brought by the state or federal government or their agencies because of alleged violations of a statute. Imprisonment and/or fines are the penalty for the accountant who is found guilty of criminal charges.

GENERAL BASIS FOR ACTIONS

The auditing function is the main area of risk faced by the auditor, but it is not the only risk area. The auditor also may face specialized professional liability exposure arising from engagements in which other services are rendered, such as tax work or management services.

The accountant also may be held liable by clients for breaching the auditor-client confidential relationship that exists. For example, if an auditor divulges confidential information to a third party which results in a loss to the client, the client may recover damages from the auditor.

*This chapter was prepared by Professor Arthur J. Francia, The University of Houston.

If the divulging of information does not result in loss to the client, the client probably would not be able to recover damages.

Under the common law there is no *privileged communication* between accountants and their clients. This means that an accountant can be called as a witness and may be required to show the audit working papers in a court case involving a client. Some states have statutes which grant privileged communications to the accountant-client relationship. (As mentioned in Chapters 1 and 2, there is no such federal statute.) Some of these state statutes make no restriction as to the type of legal proceedings to which the privilege applies, but others do specify certain situations to which it does not apply (e.g., criminal cases). Where the accountant is required by law to reveal information about a client, the client cannot hold the accountant liable for breaching the auditor-client confidential relationship that normally exists.

During the course of an audit, the auditor may investigate the character and acts of the employees of the client. If the accountant makes derogatory oral statements (slander) or written statements (libel) concerning these persons to third parties, the auditor may be held liable for damages if these statements are found to be incorrect.

LIABILITY FOR THE ACTS OF OTHERS

The work of the CPA firm organized as a partnership is performed in the name of the partnership. This means that all partners are jointly liable for acts or omissions of any one of them.

The partners in a CPA firm are also required to rely on the work of subordinates in their firm, other CPAs not in the firm, third-party experts, and, in some cases, foreign accounting firms. Because of the law of agency, the partnership may be held liable for the faulty performance or conduct of these or any other persons engaged in the audit. If a firm is held liable for the negligent act of one of its agents, it will usually have a cause of action against (it will be able to sue) the agent.

The agency problem is especially prevalent in the CPA firm because of the hierarchy of employees who actually perform the audit work. Audit examinations are performed under the direction and control of partners. Employees work under the supervision of the partners and are acting within the law of agency. Thus, a master-servant relationship is established in which any liability may ultimately be traced directly to the partners in the firm.

If a firm engages another CPA firm to perform some aspect of an audit and if the conduct of the hired firm proves to be faulty, the law of agency may be applicable. (Chapter 14 covers this situation in greater detail, specifically dealing with the effect of whether and how the hired firm is mentioned in the audit report.) The hired firm may be under the control and supervision of the principal auditor, thus making the liability traceable to the principal auditor.

Auditors must rely on their professional judgment in expressing an opinion as to the fairness of presentation of the financial statements. Since they cannot reasonably be expected to be experts in all areas, they may have to rely on the opinions of other third-party experts for certain information from time to time. For example, if an auditor has a financing question, an underwriter or banker may be consulted for an opinion. This consultation could, of course, influence the auditor's judgment in a given situation. A lawyer may be engaged to render an opinion as to the potential impact of certain contingent liabilities or contracts on the client's financial position, operating results, or changes in financial position, and thus may influence the decisions made by the auditor. Under certain circumstances, it is possible for the auditor to be held liable under the common law for his or her actions even when the advice of third-party experts was relied upon in taking these actions.

THE AUDITOR'S LIABILITY UNDER COMMON LAW TO CLIENTS AND SUBROGEES

Clients and subrogees (those who acquire by substitution rights belonging to another) may be treated as one distinct group. Subrogees are normally surety companies that carry fidelity bonds on the employees of a company. If, for example, an employee of a business firm absconds (flees) with assets, usually money, the surety company reimburses the business firm for the amount of the loss. When a surety company pays a loss, it is legally entitled to stand in the business firm's place (subrogation) with regard to any legal alternatives that the business firm has available in order to recover the loss.

Breach of Contract Liability to Clients and Subrogees

This section is concerned mainly with breach of contract considerations. However, the section does include some discussion of tort liability, which is more thoroughly covered later in the chapter.

The auditor generally performs an audit under the specifications of a contract agreed upon between the client and the public accounting firm. In some instances, this contract may be very specific (as it should be), while in others it may be of a somewhat general nature. In any case, it is normally implied that the audit will be made in accordance with generally accepted auditing standards unless specific provisions are made to the contrary.

The public accounting firm is operating as an independent contractor and, as such, is not bound to follow the explicit instructions of the client, except possibly in the case of certain special-purpose examinations. Independence and objectivity should, of course, always prevail when the CPA performs an audit examination. If the obligor (the auditor in this instance) in a personal service contract is unable to complete the performance called for in the contract because of disability, the contract is discharged (invalidated). In this event, the obligor can only collect from the other party to the contract to the extent that he or she can prove that the services actually performed were of value to that party.

The rights of the parties under contract law are established by the terms of the contract. The contractual relationship between the parties is referred to as "privity." The rights of the parties involved in a tort action (a civil wrong independent of a contract) are established by law. However, it may be possible for an act, error, or omission to be both a breach of contract and tortious conduct (e.g., negligence). A CPA might be liable to the client on either basis. The theory of law which the plaintiff elects to use could have an effect on certain factors including the statute of limitations (a statute designating a certain time after which rights cannot be enforced by legal action), the available defenses (the methods and facts adopted to protect the defendant against the plaintiff's action), and the amount of damages.

The next two cases illustrate the liability which the auditor faces from subrogees (those who acquire by substitution the rights belonging to another). The second case (and two others) also points out the importance of a clearly written contract or engagement letter.

Three firms of public accountants were involved in the *National Surety Corporation* case. The client's cashier embezzled $329,300 and covered the defalcation by "kiting" bank deposits (a form of cash manipulation that is described in Chapter 9) at or near audit dates. The National Surety Corporation held a fidelity bond on the cashier and reimbursed the cashier's firm, Halle & Stieglitz, for the loss. The surety, under its right of subrogation to the client's claim, brought suit against the public accountants. The charge was based on four factors:

1. Failure to properly perform their audit as per contract.
2. Breach of warranty in their reports.
3. Negligence in their work.
4. Fraudulently misrepresenting material facts in their reports.[1]

---

[1] *National Surety Corporation* v. *Lybrand,* 256 App. Div. 226, 9 N.Y.S. 2d 554 (1st Dept. 1939).

The defendants claimed that Halle & Stieglitz were negligent because they should have discovered the "kiting" themselves at the time they prepared their bank reconciliations.

The court felt that an examination of cash was a basic audit procedure and that the accountants in question had failed to make an adequate verification of cash. In this case the embezzler was a mere cashier whose accounts would normally be tested by any reasonable auditor. This case is discussed more fully later in this chapter.

The Importance of a Well-Written Audit Contract or Engagement Letter. The auditor has a contractual relationship with the client. Consequently, it is recommended that the auditor should place in a letter to the client the various aspects and details of the agreement with the client. This letter is referred to as an engagement letter and evidences the auditor's agreement with the client. The letter containing the client's signature should be retained by the auditor. The engagement letter can serve as a contract between the two parties, or a separate contract may be drawn between the parties.

An example of an engagement letter is presented in Figure 3-1.

The importance of a well-written contract or engagement letter was illustrated in the case of *Maryland Casualty Co. v. Jonathon Cook.*[2] This case involved the embezzlement of $12,969.15 by the city treasurer of Flint, Michigan, during the period April 5, 1928, to October 24, 1935. Jonathon Cook & Company performed the audit of the city of Flint for the period of July 1, 1931, to June 30, 1932.

The city of Flint prepared audit specifications when they let the contract for bids. After Jonathon Cook accepted the engagement, an audit contract was drawn which included the audit specifications as a part of the contract. The city employees, who were the drawers of the specifications and the contract, did not use technical terms in preparing either document.

The Maryland Casualty Co. carried a surety bond on the treasurer of the city of Flint. The treasurer embezzled funds, and when this fact was exposed the surety company paid the city for its loss and became a subrogee. Under their right of subrogation they instituted litigation against the auditors, Jonathon Cook & Company.

Other CPAs testified as to the type of audit specified by the contract. The testimony of these accountants was summarized by the court as follows:

> Some of the accountants here testifying have said that this contract and specifications required a cash audit. Some have said it required a balance sheet audit. Some have said it required a combination of a cash and

---

[2] *Maryland Casualty Co. v. Jonathon Cook*, 35 F. Supp. 160 (E. D. Mich. 1940).

FIGURE 3-1

JONES & ROME, CPAs
Main Street
Baltimore, Md.

August 31, 1980

Mr. Sam Smith, President
XYZ Corporation
9 Arbor Lane
Gold Spring, Md.

Dear Mr. Smith:

This letter is to confirm our understanding of the arrangements to examine the financial statements of XYZ Corporation for the year ended December 31, 1980, for the purpose of expressing an opinion as to the fairness of the presentation of the financial statements.

We shall examine the financial statements of XYZ Corporation as of December 31, 1980, and provide such services that are needed. Our examination will be conducted in accordance with generally accepted auditing standards and will include such tests and procedures as we think are needed. The examination will be directed to commenting on the fairness of the presentation of the financial statements as a whole in conformity with generally accepted accounting principles.

An examination directed to the expression of an opinion on the financial statements is not primarily or specifically designed, and cannot be relied upon, to disclose defalcations or other similar irregularities should any exist, although their discovery may result.

Our charge for this work will be at our regular rates. A billing will be rendered at the completion of the engagement.

We are pleased that you have selected us as your independent auditor and look forward to a continuing pleasant relationship with you. Please indicate your agreement with the arrangements discussed in this letter by signing and returning the enclosed copy.

Sincerely,

J. R. Rome, CPA

Source: This letter is based on the suggested wording in Earl F. Davis and James W. Kelley, "The Engagement Letter and Current Legal Developments," *The Journal of Accountancy* (December 1972), pp. 56–57.

balance sheet audit, and some others have said that it required a detailed audit.[3]

The court interpreted the contract using the normal, everyday meaning of the terms in the documents. The court said:

> I think it is high time for accountants to know that if they want a particular contract which they enter into to be measured in the technical terms of a cash audit, or a balance sheet audit, or a detailed audit, they should insist that their contract and the specifications which they agree to comply with in their contract should plainly state the facts.[4]

Jonathon Cook initially had a discussion with the Director of Finance of the city of Flint concerning the work to be performed and had entered into the contract in reliance on this prior discussion. The court said, "That conversation with the Director of Finance does not mean a thing. The contract was with the city of Flint and not with the Director of Finance."[5]

The actual suit was brought on the grounds of the negligence of Jonathon Cook in performing the function as an auditor. With regard to the relationship of the scope of the contract and the finding of the defendant guilty of negligence, the court said:

> An auditor performing on the basis of *this contract* and these specifications and doing his work as a reasonably prudent, careful auditor would have done his work, would have, and should have, discovered some of these many, many irregularities; and, having discovered some of them, all of the others would have been found.[6] (Emphasis added.)

The court brought the relationship between the audit contract and the negligence action into its proper perspective in this case. The court said:

> For the failure to perform this audit engagement in accordance with the terms of this contract as a reasonably prudent and careful auditor would and because of such negligence, this defendant auditor, Jonathon Cook, must respond in damages.[7]

Jonathon Cook was required to reimburse the Maryland Casualty Company in the amount of $11,169.09—the loss that occurred subsequent to the audit.

The protection that a contract can provide was aptly illustrated in

---

[3] Ibid., p. 164.
[4] Ibid., pp. 164–65.
[5] Ibid., p. 165.
[6] Ibid., p. 166.
[7] Ibid., p. 166.

84

the case of *O'Neill* v. *Atlas Automobile Finance Corporation.*[8] The auditors sued their client for fees for professional services rendered during July and August 1936. The client introduced a counterclaim for damages suffered as a result of defalcations made by their bookkeeper during prior periods.[9] In reply to the countersuit, the auditors' contention was ". . . that their contract was for a limited examination, and a financial review of defendant's books, without verification."[10] The client claimed ". . . that the terms of plaintiffs' employment contemplated the making of a complete and detailed audit and the furnishing of certified reports which should have uncovered the shortage."[11] The auditors admitted that their original employment was under oral contract. In a July 1935 letter to the client that confirmed reengagement for the period July 1935 through May 1936, the auditors stated:

> Confirming our recent conversation we agree with respect to the Atlas Automobile Finance Corp. and the Universal Auto Loan Co., *to make a monthly examination of the transactions and submit monthly reports in substantially the same form as heretofore.* (Emphasis by court.)[12]

With the reports that were submitted in prior periods, O'Neill sent a letter of transmittal that read in part:

> We have prepared *from the records* of Atlas Automobile Finance Corporation and *information* submitted to us a balance sheet as of (designated month and year) and a comparative statement of profit and loss based on the month of (name of month). (Emphasis by court.)[13]

The client brought the countersuit under the law of negligence claiming that the auditors had failed to discover that certain tapes prepared by the bookkeeper were incorrect. In a detailed audit these incorrect tapes probably would have been discovered.

The judgment of the court was for the auditors in both suits. In the countersuit it was decided by the court that the prior periods' reports were not certified. The letter that was sent when the auditing firm was reengaged was satisfactory to the defendant company. In its decision, the court indicated that this letter established the scope of the audit and the duties and standard of care to be exercised by the auditors.

---

[8] *O'Neill* v. *Atlas Automobile Finance Corporation,* 139 Pa. Super. 346, 11A. 2d 782 (1940).

[9] 1933 to May 1936, except for January 1935, to May 1935. Another accounting firm was employed by the defendant during the latter period.

[10] *O'Neill* v. *Atlas Automobile Finance Corp.,* p. 784.

[11] Ibid.

[12] Ibid.

[13] Ibid.

The *1136 Tenants' Corporation* case[14] is a more recent case which deals with the failure of an auditor to have an engagement letter which was clear in every respect. In this important case a cooperative apartment corporation (1136 Tenants' Corporation) sued a CPA firm (Max Rothenberg & Co.) alleging that the CPAs had failed to uncover defalcations of 1136 Tenants' Corporation's funds by the former managing agent for the plaintiff. Max Rothenberg & Co. had been engaged in August 1963 by an officer of the managing agent to perform certain accounting services for the plaintiff under an oral agreement for a fee of $600 per year.[15]

The CPA firm continued to provide services to the plaintiff until March 1965, when the plaintiff found that the managing agent had not paid certain of the plaintiff's obligations that were supposed to have been paid.[16]

The defendant CPAs sent 1136 Tenants' Corporation financial statements for 1963 and for the first six months of 1964. These statements were accompanied with transmittal letters each of which in part said:

> Pursuant to our engagement, we have reviewed and summarized the statements of your managing agent and other data submitted to us by [the managing agent] . . . pertaining to 1136 Tenants' Corporation. . . . The following statements . . . were prepared from the books and records of the Corporation. No independent verifications were undertaken thereon. . . .[17]

The financial statements referred the reader to the letter of transmittal. However, the statements did not indicate that an officer of the managing agent had diverted funds for his own use. The plaintiff contended that the defendants should have performed an audit. The defendants argued that they had not agreed to perform an audit, although the term "audit expense" was used in a schedule prepared by the accountant. The lower state court held for the plaintiff as did the state appellate court.[18] The damages which the auditor had to pay amounted to almost $240,000.

The defendant had performed certain auditing procedures in addition to write-up work (write-up work is work done which leads to and

---

[14] For a synopsis of this case, see *The Journal of Accountancy* (November 1971), pp. 67–73.

[15] Emanuel Saxe, "Accountants' Responsibility for Unaudited Financial Statements," *The New York Certified Public Accountant* (June 1971), p. 420.

[16] Ibid.

[17] AICPA-NYSSCPA *Amicus Curiae* submitted to the Court of Appeals of the State of New York, *The Journal of Accountancy* (November 1971), pp. 68–69.

[18] Ibid., p. 69.

includes the preparation of financial statements for the client). The firm's work sheets "... indicate that defendant did examine plaintiff's bank statement, invoices and bills. ..."[19]

In this case the defendant had not obtained a signed engagement letter that set forth the scope of the engagement. Two authors noted:

> The engagement letter is a critical first line of defense in conducting any engagement, whether it is to be in accordance with generally accepted auditing standards or not. This is true because, when such a letter is properly drafted there can be no room for arguments as to what was contemplated by the parties and what degree of responsibility the accountant agreed to undertake.[20]

Tort Liability to Clients and Subrogees

As defined earlier, torts are any civil wrong other than breach of contract. (Technically, breach of either trust or some other equitable obligation is also considered a tort, but for purposes of this discussion the definition given will suffice.) The CPA has been held to be liable to clients and subrogees under the theory of law commonly considered tort law. The charges of ordinary negligence, gross negligence, or fraud usually arise from audits where the accountant has made an error, mistake, omission, or misrepresentation.

Probably the allegation of ordinary negligence is the most common. This is because of the contract-negligence relationship and the relative ease of proving ordinary negligence as opposed to establishing gross negligence or legal fraud. *Ordinary negligence* (also referred to simply as "negligence") is a lack of *reasonable* care in the exercise of a legal duty. *Gross negligence* is a lack of even *minimum* care in the exercise of a legal duty. *Fraud* is an actual *misrepresentation* of a material fact known by the auditor to be false (or made without regard for the truth) with the purpose of deceiving another party who is then injured. In order to bring suit on the basis of ordinary negligence there must have been a clear chain of events or actions:

1. There must have been a legal duty on the part of the CPA either to act or not to act. This duty may be created by contract, and the relationship between the parties to a contract is referred to as *privity*.
2. There must have been a breach of this duty.

---

[19] Decision of the Appellate Division of the Supreme Court of the State of New York, *The Journal of Accountancy* (November 1971), p. 67.

[20] Charles Chazen and Kenneth L. Solomon, "The Unaudited State of Affairs," *The Journal of Accountancy* (December 1972), p. 43.

3. Injuries must have been sustained. (Naturally, the injuries here would be monetary and not physical.)
4. The proximate (direct) cause of the injuries must be established as the breach of legal duty.

In addition, the plaintiff's interest must have fallen within the zone of risk; that is, it must have been reasonably foreseeable that the plaintiff could be injured financially if the defendant was negligent.

The questions that must be answered in all potential tort cases are: "What are the duties and standards of care the CPA must use?" and "What standards of care did the CPA use in carrying out these duties?" Once these two issues are resolved, the outcome of the case is reasonably predictable.

There have been various attempts to establish the accountant's duties and standards of care. For example, the American Institute of Certified Public Accountants has numerous publications including books, pamphlets, and cases that attempt to establish guidelines that define these duties and standards of care.[21] Generally, these attempts at establishing an accountant's duties and standards of care have not been very effective in serving as the basis for either legal charges or defenses of the accountant to date. Instead, often the decisions seem to reflect the judge's sense of propriety or fairness in each circumstance.

In the previously discussed cases of *Maryland Casualty Co.* v. *Jonathon Cook* and *National Surety Corp.* v. *Lybrand*, negligence was the basis for suit, and the negligence arose directly in conjunction with or from a breach of contract. The next two cases are presented to illustrate what the CPA must do to maintain the standard of care necessary to eliminate tortious conduct with regard to the client.

In one case[22] the court held that a breach of contract could give rise to a charge of negligence or fraud if professionals are careless in the execution of a contract. The court held that the major portion of the loss was the result of ". . . the failure of [the auditors] to use due care and vigilance, and to properly perform their contract to examine all cash transactions and supporting data."[23]

In another case[24] the court outlined the CPA's duty to the parties involved as follows:

---

[21] For example, *Auditing Standards and Procedures* (1933), *Audits by Certified Public Accountants* (1950), *Generally Accepted Auditing Standards* (1954), and various *Statements on Auditing Standards* (1973–present).

[22] *Dantzler Lumber & Export Company* v. *Columbia Casualty Co.*, 115 Fla. 541, 156 So. 116 (1934).

[23] Ibid., p. 543.

[24] *Fidelity & Deposit Co. of Maryland* v. *Atherton*, 47 N.M. 443, 144 P. 2d 157 (1943).

The appellees [CPAs] owed to the board of county commissioners [the clients] a legal duty to make their reports without fraud and a contractual duty to make them, under the terms of their contract, with the care and caution required of experts.[25]

If the CPA must use "... the care and caution required of experts" when dealing with a client, then the CPA can be held liable to the client for ordinary negligence. Thus, if there is a contractual relationship between the parties (privity), the CPA may be held liable for *ordinary negligence.*

There are many cases illustrating that the accountant may be held liable for ordinary negligence by either clients or subrogees when failing to check carefully any item that normally would arouse suspicion.[26] The next two cases illustrate two different situations concerned with charges of fraud and negligence against the CPA.

In the case of *Flagg* v. *Seng*[27] a trustee for a bankrupt land syndicate initiated a suit against the auditors of the land syndicate in order to recover $68,000 in dividends that were illegally declared and paid by the board of directors of the land syndicate.

The syndicate had a policy of recognizing income on transactions such as exchanges of land for land or the corporation's stock for land even though cash was not involved.[28] The trustee charged that the accountant knowingly submitted false reports that recognized the unearned income items and the board of directors, acting on the accountants' reports, declared illegal dividends. But the accountants involved were not fully cognizant of the revenue recognition practices used by the land syndicate. In the process of auditing the corporation they noted one of the questionable sales and sought legal advice. Legal counsel for the corporation advised the auditors that the sale was perfectly legal.

A lower court found the accountants not guilty and this judgment was upheld by the court of appeals. The basis for the judgment centered on the fact that the illegal revenue recognition policy was known to the board of directors and therefore *they were not deceived* by the auditor's report. The fact that the auditors sought legal counsel on the questionable transaction they did uncover was sufficient to make the court view their investigation of the revenue recognition technique as adequate.

In the *National Surety Corporation* v. *Lybrand* case, the client

[25] Ibid., p. 449.

[26] For example, *Dantzler Lumber & Export Co.* v. *Columbia Casualty Co.; National Surety Corp.* v. *Lybrand; Maryland Casualty Co.* v. *Jonathon Cook,* all cited above.

[27] *Flagg* v. *Seng,* 16 Cal. App. 2d 545, 60 P. 2d 1004 (1936).

[28] This procedure was in violation of acceptable accounting principles.

brought charges for breach of contract, breach of warranty, negligence, and fraud. A cashier was "kiting" and also "lapping" (techniques of misappropriating cash which are described in Chapter 9) and the auditors failed to discover the defalcations. There were late deposits, and bank transfers were made by the cashier to cover a shortage. The accountants never checked the deposit slips against the entries in the accounts, nor did they follow the standard cash audit procedure of checking the balances in all the banks as of the same day.

The trial court found the accountants innocent (the judge dismissed the case) because of contributory negligence, but the Appellate Division reversed the decision stating:

> It was for the jury to say whether the practice of "lapping" and "kiting" of checks should have put the defendants upon inquiry which would have led to discovery of the defalcations, and whether, if defendants had exercised ordinary care and used proper methods of accounting as established by the expert testimony, they would have observed checks drawn out of numerical order. . . . Their representations that there had been a verification of cash was a pretense of knowledge when they did not know the condition of the bank accounts and had no reasonable basis to assume that they did. This the jury could have found, amounted to at least constructive fraud.[29]

The issue of the accountants' negligence or fraud was not decided in the trial court because of the acceptance of the contributory negligence defense. The Appellate Division felt the issues should have gone to the jury, and the Appellate Court did not feel that contributory negligence was an acceptable defense in this case because "Negligence of the employer is a defense only when it has contributed to the accountant's failure to perform his contract and to report the truth."[30] This was not the situation in this case. The original verdict would probably have been reversed had the case gone to trial again.

THE AUDITOR'S LIABILITY TO PRIMARY BENEFICIARIES UNDER THE COMMON LAW

A *primary beneficiary is a third party for whose primary benefit the audit is being undertaken.* Any primary beneficiary will be *identified* by name to the auditor *prior* to the audit, and the CPA will have knowledge of the fact that the audit report will affect the primary beneficiary's decisions.

The following third parties are examples of primary beneficiaries,

[29] *National Surety Corporation* v. *Lybrand*, p. 562.
[30] Ibid., p. 563.

and examples of the types of information that they may wish the auditor to provide for them are given. Landlords of commercial tenants may have leases drawn so that the rental charge will consist of a fixed rental plus a percentage of sales. The landlord would be interested in a sales audit; the rental income depends in part on the sales of the lessee. Banks and other creditors with loans outstanding that include loan covenants requiring specific actions by the debtor will often require a special report from the auditors denoting the specific adherence to the loan or debenture covenant requirements. *In many cases this report will be addressed directly to the creditor. The actual audit contract will probably still be between the auditors and the client with the client paying the audit fee.*

The next two cases presented do not involve accountants. However, the relationships of the parties involved are similar to that of the auditor versus primary beneficiary situation so that the legal principles involved could be used as case precedents. These two cases suggest that an expert may be held liable by a primary beneficiary for ordinary negligence. If the auditor can be held liable for ordinary negligence by primary beneficiaries this indicates that the standard of care required when providing financial information for the benefit of primary beneficiaries is at least as high as that necessary when dealing with clients or subrogees.

In a New York case,[31] a seller of beans hired public weighers to weigh the beans and provide a weight certificate for the buyer. It was understood by all parties that the payment for the beans was to be made in accordance with the certified weight sheets. The Glanzer brothers (plaintiffs), purchasers of the beans, found the actual weight of the beans to be 11,854 pounds less than the weight as certified by the public weighers. They brought suit against the public weighers for ordinary negligence in performing their duty and recovered their overpayment plus costs.

The court stressed that the key factor of the intimate relationship between the third party and the defendant played a major role in arriving at the defendant's liability.

> The controlling circumstance is not the character of the consequence, but its proximity or remoteness in the thought and purposes of the actor.
>
> * * * * *
>
> The defendants, acting not casually nor as mere servants, but in the pursuit of an independent calling, weighed and certified at the order of one with the very end and aim of shaping the conduct of another. Diligence was owing, not only to him who ordered, but to him who also relied.[32]

---

[31] *Glanzer v. Shepard*, 233 N.Y. 236, 135 N.C. 275 (1922).
[32] Ibid., pp. 240, 242.

The ability of a primary beneficiary to bring tort actions against a defendant when a contract is improperly executed was also brought out in this case.

> In such circumstances, assumption of the task of weighing was the assumption of a duty to weigh carefully for the benefit of all whose conduct was to be governed. We do not need to state the duty in terms of contract or of privity. Growing out of a contract, it has nonetheless an origin not exclusively contractual. Given the contract and the relation, the duty is imposed by law.[33]

In another case[34] a trustee for a bond issue was required only to certify the right to issue bonds when collateral in the amount of 110 percent was received from the issuing company. This collateral was required to be in the form of cash, current funds, first lien mortgages or trade acceptances for motor vehicle purchases. Once the collateral was received by the trustee, the trustee would authenticate the debentures and return them to the company. The company would then issue the bonds. The issuing company placed worthless collateral in the hands of the trustee. In addition, the collateral was not of the type required by the debenture, that is, cash, current funds, first lien mortgages, or trade acceptances for motor vehicle purchases. Without the trustee's authorization the bonds were worthless. The trustee authenticated the bonds and held the worthless collateral. The issuing corporation went into bankruptcy and a bondholder sued the trustee. The courts felt the trustee was guilty of negligently making a misrepresentation of fact when certifying the bonds because the collateral failed to meet the specific terms of the covenant clause in the debenture.

THE AUDITOR'S LIABILITY UNDER COMMON LAW TO THIRD PARTIES WHO ARE NOT PRIMARY BENEFICIARIES

The CPA also can be held liable to third parties other than primary beneficiaries. Opinions rendered by CPAs, when exhibited to such parties, can serve as a basis for adverse legal action. These additional third-party groups are usually user groups such as creditors, investors, or potential investors who rely on the CPA's opinion as to the fairness of presentation of the financial statements but are not identified by name to the auditor prior to the audit. Since third parties are not considered to be parties to the audit contract (therefore lacking privity) nor the primary benefactors of an audit, they would have little or no basis for a breach of contract action against an auditor.

---

[33] Ibid., p. 239.

[34] *Doyle v. Chatham & Phenix National Bank*, 253 N.Y. 369, 171 N.E. 574 (1930).

In the earliest American case involving the accountant's liability to third parties, the *Landell* v. *Lybrand* case, it was found that a third-party investor who relied on audited financial statements when making investment decisions could not hold a CPA liable for investment losses even if the CPA was guilty of ordinary negligence in performing the audit in question.[35]

In the lower court the *Landell* v. *Lybrand* case was decided for the defendant CPAs because the complaint failed to state a cause of action. The judgment was affirmed upon appeal by the plaintiff. The Supreme Court of Pennsylvania heard the appeal and this court stated:

> There were no contractual relations [no privity] between the plaintiff and defendants, and, if there is any liability from them to him, it must arise out of some breach of duty, for there is no averment [an allegation] that they made the report with intent to deceive him. The averment in the statement of claim is that the defendants were careless and negligent in making their report; but the plaintiff was a stranger to them, and to it, and, as no duty rested upon them to him, they cannot be guilty of any negligence of which he can complain. (Definitions added.)[36]

The *Ultramares* case was significant in establishing the accountant's liability to unidentified third-party beneficiaries in tort actions.[37] In this case the defendant CPAs had audited the client firm and certified the financial statements. The accountants prepared 32 copies of the financial statements for the client firm, thus making it obvious that the client was going to seek credit that it needed.

The accounting firm's client had included fictitious balances in the various ledger accounts. The auditor did not uncover the manipulations because they failed to verify the underlying documents that would have exposed the proper balances of the ledger accounts. Actually, the client was near bankruptcy.

The plaintiff creditor made loans to the client; the client went bankrupt and the creditor charged the CPAs with negligent misrepresentations and fraudulent misrepresentations.

The court recognized that the audit *was made for the primary benefit of the client, not the third-party creditor.* Thus, the third party was not considered to be a primary beneficiary. In this case the judge, Justice Cardozo, established some dimensions for the CPA's liability to these third parties.

> The defendants owed to their employer a duty imposed by law to make their certificate without fraud, and a duty growing out of contract

[35] *Landell* v. *Lybrand*, 264 Pa. 406, 107 Atl. 783 (1919).

[36] Ibid., p. 408.

[37] *Ultramares Corp.* v. *Touche*, 255 N.Y. 170, 174 N.E. 441 (1931).

to make it with the care and caution proper to their calling. . . . To creditors and investors to whom the employer exhibited the certificate, the defendants owed a like duty to make it without fraud, since there was notice in the circumstances of its making that the employer did not keep it to himself. . . . If liability for negligence exists, a thoughtless slip or blunder, the failure to detect 'a theft or forgery beneath the cover of deceptive entries, may expose accountants to a liability in an indeterminate amount for an indeterminate time to an indeterminate class. The hazards of a business conducted on these terms are so extreme as to enkindle doubt whether a flaw may not exist in the implication of a duty that exposes to these consequences.[38]

This ruling definitely eliminated the charge of ordinary negligence as an acceptable basis for suit for third parties other than primary beneficiaries. In the same case, Justice Cardozo, recognizing that accountants only express an opinion on financial statements, explicitly established law defining the basis on which accountants could be held liable in third-party suits.

Even an opinion, especially an opinion by an expert, may be found to be fraudulent if the grounds supporting it are so flimsy as to lead to the conclusion that there was no genuine belief back of it. . . .

* * * * *

Our holding does not emancipate accountants from the consequences of fraud. . . .

* * * * *

. . . negligence or blindness, even when not equivalent to fraud, is none the less evidence to sustain an inference of fraud. At least this is so if the negligence is gross.[39]

This was considered a landmark case at least in part because of the great stature which Justice Cardozo held in the legal profession. The legal theory enunciated by Justice Cardozo made it very difficult for these third parties to win suits against public accountants. They could only do so if there was gross negligence or fraud. In such situations lack of privity is not a valid defense.

The legal principles set forth in the *Ultramares* case were upheld in the *State Street Trust Company* v. *Ernst* case. In the *State Street Trust Company* case the client firm was engaged in the factoring business. A large part of the client's available funds were obtained from 17 banks. The client firm was audited and the audited statements were sent to the creditor banks by the client. About 30 days later the

---

[38] Ibid., p. 444.
[39] Ibid., pp. 447, 448, and 449.

auditors sent a long-form report (described in Chapter 14) to the client. The cover letter, which was considered an integral part of the report, indicated that the reserve for doubtful accounts was grossly inadequate. The short-form report sent to the banks by the client failed to mention this fact. About 13 months later the client was petitioned into bankruptcy.[40]

The action against the auditors was initiated by a creditor bank that had advanced $300,000 to the client after receiving the short-form report 13 months earlier. There was no question that the creditor bank relied upon the audited financial statements in making the loan. It had been unwilling to advance any funds to the client until it had received the statements.

In this case, the original trial court jury found the defendants liable, but the trial judge set aside the verdict on the grounds that it was not supported by the evidence presented. The Appellate Division supported the trial judge and finally the Court of Appeals reversed the prior judgments and granted a new trial in 1938.

The Court of Appeals reiterated various findings and upheld the findings of the *Ultramares* case. The Court defined the fact situation that would probably call for a finding of fraud in the absence of active or deliberate intent.

> Accountants, however, may be liable to third parties, even where there is lacking deliberate or active fraud. A representation certified as true to the knowledge of the accountants when knowledge there is none, a reckless misstatement, or an opinion based upon grounds so flimsy as to lead to the conclusion that there was no genuine belief in its truth, are all sufficient upon which to base liability. A refusal to see the obvious, a failure to investigate the doubtful, if sufficiently gross, may furnish evidence leading to an inference of fraud so as to impose liability for losses suffered by those who rely on the balance sheet. In other words, heedlessness and reckless disregard of consequence may take the place of deliberate intention.[41]

In recent years the fact that third parties who are not primary beneficiaries could not hold the auditor liable for ordinary negligence may be undergoing a change. This is illustrated in the ruling in the *Rusch Factors, Inc.* v. *Levin* case[42] where Rusch Factors, Inc. had asked for certified financial statements of a corporation seeking a loan. The defendant accountant audited and certified the financial statements which showed the corporation to be solvent. Actually, the cor-

---

[40] *State Street Trust Co.* v. *Ernst*, 278 N.Y. 104, 15 N.E. 2d 415 (1938). See Saul Levy, *Accountants' Legal Responsibility* (New York: American Institute of Accountants, 1954), pp. 34–39 for more details of this case.

[41] Ibid., p. 112.

[42] *Rusch Factors, Inc.* v. *Levin*, 284 F. Supp. 85 (D.C.R.I. 1968).

poration was insolvent. The corporation later submitted the certified financial statements to Rusch Factors, Inc., and received the loan. The company subsequently went into receivership. Rusch Factors sued the auditor for damages resulting from its reliance on the fraudulent or negligent misrepresentations in the financial statements. The defendant moved for dismissal on the basis of privity of contract. Here the court said:

> . . . this court holds that an accountant should be liable in negligence for careless financial misrepresentations relied upon *by actually foreseen and limited classes of persons.* According to the plaintiff's complaint in the instant case, *the defendant knew that his certification was to be used for,* and had as its very aim and purpose, *the reliance of potential financiers* of the . . . corporation . . . (Emphasis added.)[43]

One source commenting on the court's ruling in the case stated that "in fact, the Court need not have gone even that far, for as the Rhode Island Court recognized, the circumstances were such as to come squarely within the primary benefit role as enunciated by Judge Cardozo in *Ultramares.*"[44]

This case would seem to indicate that some courts are changing the liability to third parties who are not primary beneficiaries from not being liable to these third parties for ordinary negligence to being liable for ordinary negligence *if* the accountant is *informed* of a specific use (the category of user and the type of decision to be made) that is to be made of the certified statements even though he or she does not know the exact identity by name (e.g., The 1st National Bank) of the one who is to rely on them.

In another recent case, the *Rhode Island Hospital Trust National Bank* v. *Swartz,*[45] the auditor was held liable to a third party for ordinary negligence (the court used the *Rusch Factors* precedent) even though the auditor issued a disclaimer of opinion (discussed in detail in Chapter 14) on the fairness of the presentation of the financial statements. The plaintiff in the case was a bank which had made a loan to the International Trading Corporation (the borrower) relying on the financial statements which had been certified by a firm of CPAs. The borrower had represented to the bank that it had made certain leasehold improvements when in fact it had made none. The financial statements capitalized certain labor expenses as part of the cost of leasehold improvements. No mention was made of any cost of mate-

---

[43] Ibid., pp. 92–93.

[44] David B. Isbell and D. R. Carmichael, "Disclaimers and Liability—The Rhode Island Trust Case," *The Journal of Accountancy* (April 1973), p. 41.

[45] *Rhode Island Hospital Trust National Bank* v. *Swartz,* 455 F. 2d 847 (4th Cir. 1972). (For the full details of this case see "Rhode Island Hospital Trust Decision," *The Journal of Accountancy* (April 1973), pp. 63–66.)

rials for the improvements. Net income and net worth were both over-stated by about $200,000 as a result of the capitalization of these labor costs which were actually utilized in operations.

In a cover letter accompanying the financial statements and ad-dressed to the client, the accountants said:

> *Additions* to fixed assets in 1963 *were found* to include principally warehouse improvements and installation of machinery and equipment in Providence, Rhode Island, Brunswick, Georgia, and Palm Beach, Florida. Practically *all of this work was done by company employees and materials and overhead were borne by the International Trading Corporation and its affiliates.* Unfortunately, fully complete detailed cost records were not kept of these capital improvements and no exact determination could be made as to the actual cost of said improvements. (Emphasis was added by the Court.)[46]

Later in the letter they stated:

> Because of the limitations upon our examination expressed in the preceding paragraphs and the material nature of the items not confirmed directly by us, we are unable to express an opinion as to the fairness of the accompanying statements.[47]

The Court said, "... While industry standards may not always be the maximum test of liability, certainly they should be deemed the minimum standard by which liability should be determined...."[48] It then went on to quote from Chapter 10, paragraph 1 of *Statement on Auditing Procedure No. 33* (1963) which requires that *"When an over-all opinion cannot be expressed, the reasons therefore shall be stated...."*[49] (Emphasis added by the Court.) Reference was also made to paragraph 16 of *SAP No. 33* which reads, " '[w]henever the independent auditor disclaims an opinion, he should give *all* substantive reasons for doing so,' ... (emphasis in original.)"[50] The Court did not believe this had been done.

This case is another illustration of the auditor being held liable for ordinary negligence to a third party who was not a primary bene-ficiary. This is another indication of what may be a trend toward in-creasing liability for the auditor to third parties under the common law.[51]

---

[46] Ibid., p. 849.

[47] Ibid., p. 850.

[48] Ibid., p. 852.

[49] Ibid.

[50] Ibid.

[51] For an excellent expanded coverage of the subject of legal liability of the auditor, see Denzil Y. Causey, Jr., *Duties and Liabilities of Public Accountants* (Homewood, Ill.: Dow Jones-Irwin, 1979), 268 pages © 1979 by Dow Jones-Irwin.

GLOSSARY

Breach of contract When a party to a contract does not perform the required obligation(s).

Civil actions Introduced by private parties in an attempt to obtain compensation through the courts for alleged losses caused by the direct or indirect actions of another party.

Common law Unwritten law as opposed to statute law.

Contributory negligence When the party that is injured contributed to the loss through his or her own negligence.

Criminal actions Brought by the state or federal government or their agencies because of alleged violations of a statute. Imprisonment and/or fines may be the penalty if found guilty.

Engagement letter A letter to the client by the auditor which presents the various aspects and details of the agreement with the client. This letter is evidence of the auditor's agreement with the client. For an example, see Figure 3-1.

Fraud An actual misrepresentation of a material fact known by the perpetrator to be false (or made without regard for the truth) with the purpose of deceiving another party who is then injured.

Gross negligence A lack of even minimum care in the exercise of a legal duty.

Kiting See "Glossary," Chapter 9.

Lapping See "Glossary," Chapter 9.

Libel A false derogatory written statement concerning a person which is made available to a third party.

Ordinary negligence A lack of reasonable care in the exercise of a legal duty.

Primary beneficiary A third party for whose primary benefit the audit (or other service) is being undertaken.

Privity The contractual relationship between the parties to a contract.

Slander A false derogatory oral statement concerning a person made to a third party.

Statute of limitations A statute designating a certain time after which rights cannot be enforced by legal action.

Subrogees Those who acquire by substitution rights belonging to another.

Tort A civil wrong other than breach of contract.

Write-up work Work done which leads to and includes preparation of financial statements for the client.

QUESTIONS AND PROBLEMS

3-1. Describe the auditor's liability to clients and subrogees. Define a subrogee.

3-2. Describe the auditor's liability to primary beneficiaries.

3-3. Describe the auditor's liability to unidentified third parties.

3-4. Distinguish between civil actions and criminal actions.

3-5. In which areas of activity does a CPA face legal liability?

3-6. Is the relationship between an auditor and the client a confidential relationship? Does the auditor have privileged communications; that is can the CPA refuse to divulge information concerning a client in a courtroom when directed to do so?

3-7. Is it true that a partner in a CPA firm can be held liable for acts of the other partners and of employees in the firm?

3-8. Is it true that an auditor may be held liable for his or her actions even though the advice of third-party experts was relied on in taking these actions?

3-9. Define what is meant by the term "privity." Of what significance is privity?

3-10. What was the relationship of the two parties involved in the *Maryland Casualty Co.* v. *Jonathon Cook* case? What was the allegation and the final outcome?

3-11. Is negligence of a client a valid defense for the independent auditor whenever it can be proved? Comment.

3-12. Describe the importance of having a clearly worded contract or engagement letter.

3-13. Distinguish between ordinary negligence, gross negligence, and fraud.

3-14. What chain of events is necessary to bring suit on the basis of ordinary negligence?

3-15. Is the auditor liable to clients, subrogees, and primary beneficiaries for gross negligence and fraud? Comment.

3-16. In the *Ultramares* case why was the plaintiff creditor not considered to be a primary beneficiary?

3-17. Is it true that the accountant's liability to third parties may be shifting (increasing)? Give your reasons.

3-18. Describe the purpose of an engagement letter.

3-19. Select the *best* answer for each of the following questions:

   a. The traditional common-law rules regarding accountants' liability to third parties for negligence
   1. Remain substantially unchanged since their inception.
   2. Were more stringent than the rules currently applicable.
   3. Are of relatively minor importance to the accountant.
   4. Have been substantially changed at both the federal and state levels.

   b. Gaspard & Devlin, a medium-sized CPA firm, employed Marshall as a staff accountant. Marshall was negligent in auditing several of the firm's clients. Under these circumstances which of the following statements is true?
   1. Gaspard & Devlin is *not* liable for Marshall's negligence because CPAs are generally considered to be independent contractors.
   2. Gaspard & Devlin would *not* be liable for Marshall's negli-

gence if Marshall disobeyed specific instructions in the performance of the audits.

3. Gaspard & Devlin can recover against its insurer on its malpractice policy even if one of the partners was also negligent in reviewing Marshall's work.

4. Marshall would have *no* personal liability for negligence.

c. For what minimum period should audit working papers be retained by the independent CPA?

1. For the period during which the entity remains a client of the independent CPA.

2. For the period during which an auditor-client relationship exists but not more than six years.

3. For the statutory period within which legal action may be brought against the independent CPA.

4. For as long as the CPA is in public practice.

d. *The 1136 Tenants* case was chiefly important because of its emphasis upon the legal liability of the CPA when associated with

1. A review of interim statements.

2. Unaudited financial statements.

3. An audit resulting in a disclaimer of opinion.

4. Letters for underwriters.

e. You are a CPA retained by the manager of a cooperative retirement village to do "write-up work." You are expected to prepare unaudited financial statements with each page marked "unaudited" and accompanied by a disclaimer of opinion stating no audit was made. In performing the work you discover that there are no invoices to support $25,000 of the manager's claimed disbursements. The manager informs you that all the disbursements are proper. What should you do?

1. Submit the expected statements but omit the $25,000 of unsupported disbursements.

2. Include the unsupported disbursements in the statements since you are not expected to make an audit.

3. Obtain from the manager a written statement that you informed him of the missing invoices and his assurance that the disbursements are proper.

4. Notify the owners that some of the claimed disbursements are unsupported and withdraw if the situation is not satisfactorily resolved.

f. Winslow Manufacturing, Inc., sought a $200,000 loan from National Lending Corporation. National Lending insisted that audited financial statements be submitted before it would extend credit. Winslow agreed to this and also agreed to pay the audit fee. An audit was performed by an independent CPA who submitted his report to Winslow to be used solely for the purpose of negotiating a loan from National. National, upon reviewing the audited financial statements, decided in good faith *not* to extend the credit desired. Certain ratios, which as a matter of policy were used by National in reaching its decision, were deemed too low. Winslow used copies of the audited financial statements to obtain credit elsewhere. It was subsequently learned that the CPA, despite the exercise of reasonable care, had failed to discover a sophisticated embezzlement scheme by Winslow's chief accountant. Under these circumstances, what liability does the CPA have?

   1. The CPA is liable to third parties who extended credit to Winslow based upon the audited financial statements.
   2. The CPA is liable to Winslow to repay the audit fee because credit was *not* extended by National.
   3. The CPA is liable to Winslow for any losses Winslow suffered as a result of failure to discover the embezzlement.
   4. The CPA is *not* liable to any of the parties.

  g. Martinson is a duly licensed CPA. One of his clients is suing him for negligence alleging that he failed to meet generally accepted auditing standards in the current year's audit thereby failing to discover large thefts of inventory. Under the circumstances

   1. Martinson is *not* bound by generally accepted auditing standards unless he is a member of the AICPA.
   2. Martinson's failure to meet generally accepted auditing standards would result in liability.
   3. Generally accepted auditing standards do *not* currently cover the procedures which must be used in verifying inventory for balance sheet purposes.
   4. If Martinson failed to meet generally accepted auditing standards, he would undoubtedly be found to have committed the tort of fraud.

(AICPA, adapted)

3-20. Jones, a CPA engaged in practice without any partners or associates, was retained by Abrams to audit his accounts and prepare a report including his professional opinion for submission to a prospective purchaser of Abrams's business. When the field work was about half completed Jones became seriously ill, and was unable to complete the engagement. The prospective buyer lost interest and the sale of the business fell through.

  a. Abrams sues Jones for breach of his contract. Does he have a valid right of action for damages? Explain the legal principles involved.
  b. Jones sues Abrams for his fee for the work he was able to complete. Does he have a valid right of action? Explain the legal principles involved.

(AICPA, adapted)

3-21. Abraham Jenkins, a CPA, performed an audit for Hiram Blanchard. Later, in a legal proceeding involving Blanchard as a party, Jenkins was subpoenaed as a witness. He was asked to testify concerning Blanchard's financial affairs based on information he acquired during his audit. He refused to testify on the ground that such information is confidential and is privileged as between accountant and client.

a. The proceeding is a civil action for breach of contract in a state court. There is no applicable state statute with respect to privileged communications between accountants and their clients, and the common law prevails. Would Blanchard's refusal to testify be upheld? Explain.

b. The proceeding is in a state where there is a statute relating to communications between accountants and clients. Describe generally how such state statutes vary as to the types of legal proceedings to which they apply.

(AICPA, adapted)

3-22. Meglow Corporation manufactured ladies' dresses and blouses. Because its cash position was deteriorating, Meglow sought a loan from Busch Factors. Busch had previously extended $25,000 credit to Meglow but refused to lend any additional money without obtaining copies of Meglow's audited financial statements.

Meglow contacted the CPA firm of Watkins, Winslow & Watkins to perform the audit. In arranging for the examination, Meglow clearly indicated that its purpose was to satisfy Busch Factors as to the Corporation's sound financial condition and thus to obtain an additional loan of $50,000. Watkins, Winslow & Watkins accepted the engagement, performed the examination in a negligent manner (ordinary negligence) and rendered an unqualified auditor's opinion. If an adequate examination had been performed, the financial statements would have been found to be misleading.

Meglow submitted the audited financial statements to Busch Factors and obtained an additional loan of $35,000. Busch refused to lend more than that amount. After several other factors also refused, Meglow finally was able to persuade Maxwell Department Stores, one of its customers, to lend the additional $15,000. Maxwell relied upon the financial statements examined by Watkins, Winslow & Watkins.

Meglow is now in bankruptcy and Busch seeks to collect from Watkins, Winslow & Watkins the $60,000 it loaned Meglow. Maxwell seeks to recover from Watkins, Winslow & Watkins the $15,000 it loaned Meglow.

Required:

a. Will Busch recover? Explain.
b. Will Maxwell recover? Explain.

(AICPA, adapted)

3-23. The CPA firm of Winston & Mall was engaged by the Fast Cargo Company, a retailer, to examine its financial statements for the year ended August 31, 1980. It followed generally accepted auditing standards and examined transactions on a test basis. A sample of 100 disbursements was used to test vouchers payable, cash disbursements, and receiving and purchasing procedures. An investigation of the sample disclosed several instances where purchases had been recorded and paid for without the required receiving report being included in the file of supporting documents. This was properly noted in the working papers by Martin, the junior who did the sampling. Mall, the partner in charge, called these facts to the attention of Harris, Fast Cargo's chief accountant, who told him not to worry about it, that he would make certain that these receiving reports were properly included in the voucher file. Mall accepted this and did nothing further to investigate or follow up on this situation.

Harris was engaged in a fraudulent scheme whereby he diverted the merchandise to a private warehouse where he leased space and sent the invoices to Fast Cargo for payment. The scheme was discovered later by a special investigation and a preliminary estimate indicates that the loss to Fast Cargo will be in excess of $20,000.

Required:

a. What is the liability, if any, of Winston & Mall in this situation? Discuss.

b. What additional steps, if any, should have been taken by Mall? Explain.

(AICPA, adapted)

3-24. Barton and Co. have been engaged to examine the financial statements for Mirror Manufacturing Corporation for the year ended September 30, 1980. Mirror Manufacturing needed additional cash to continue its operations. To raise funds it agreed to sell its common stock investment in a subsidiary. The buyers insisted upon having the proceeds placed in escrow because of the possibility of a major contingent tax liability. Carter, president of Mirror, explained this to Barton, the partner in charge of the Mirror audit. He indicated that he wished to show the proceeds from the sale of the subsidiary as an unrestricted current account receivable. He stated that in his opinion the government's claim was groundless and that he needed an "uncluttered" balance sheet and a "clean" auditor's opinion to obtain additional working capital. Barton acquiesced in this request. The government's claim proved to be valid and, pursuant to the agreement with the buyers, the purchase price of the subsidiary was reduced by $450,000. This, coupled with other adverse developments, caused Mirror to become insolvent with assets to cover only some of its liabilities. Barton and Co. is being sued by several of Mirror's creditors who loaned money in reliance upon the financial statements upon which it rendered an unqualified opinion.

Required:

What is the liability, if any, of Barton and Co. to the creditors of Mirror Manufacturing? Explain.

(AICPA, adapted)

3-25. In conducting the examination of the financial statements of the Farber Corporation for the year ended September 30, 1981, Harper, a CPA, discovered that Nance, the president who was also one of the principal stockholders, had borrowed substantial amounts of money from the Corporation. He indicated that he owned 51 percent of the Corporation, that the money would be promptly repaid, and that the financial statements were being prepared for internal use only. He requested that these loans not be accounted for separately in the financial statements, but be included in the other current accounts receivable. Harper acquiesced in this request. Nance was correct as to his stock ownership and the fact that the financial statements were for internal use only. However, he subsequently became insolvent and was unable to repay the loans.

Required:

What is Harper's liability? Explain.

(AICPA, adapted)

3-26. Risk Capital Limited, a Delaware corporation, was considering the purchase of a substantial amount of the treasury stock held by Florida Sunshine Corporation, a closely held corporation. Initial discussions with the Florida Sunshine Corporation began late in 1980.

Wilson and Wyatt, Florida Sunshine's accountants, regularly prepared quarterly and annual unaudited financial statements. The most recently prepared financial statements were for the year ended September 30, 1981.

On November 15, 1981, after protracted negotiations, Risk Capital agreed to purchase 100,000 shares of no par, Class A Capital Stock of Florida Sunshine at $12.50 per share. However, Risk Capital insisted upon audited statements for calendar year 1981. The contract specifically provided:

> Risk Capital shall have the right to rescind the purchase of said stock if the audited financial statements of Florida Sunshine for calendar year 1981 show a material adverse change in the financial condition of the Corporation.

Wilson and Wyatt were informed as to the specific use to be made of the audited financial statements but did not know the identity (name) of the user.

The audited financial statements furnished to Florida Sunshine by Wilson and Wyatt showed no such material adverse change. Risk Capital relied upon the audited statements and purchased the treasury stock of Florida Sunshine. It was subsequently discovered that, as of the balance sheet date, the audited statements were incorrect and that in fact there had been a material adverse change in the financial condition of the Corporation. Florida Sunshine is insolvent and Risk Capital will lose virtually its entire investment.

Risk Capital seeks recovery against Wilson and Wyatt.

Required:

Assuming that only ordinary negligence is proved, would Risk Capital prevail:

a. Under the Ultramares precedent?

b. Under the Rusch Factors precedent?

State "yes" or "no" and explain.

(AICPA, adapted)

3-27. Wells and White, the accountants for the Allie Corporation, provided various professional services for Allie over 15 years under annual retainer agreements. The services included tax return preparation, special cost analyses, and the preparation of the corporation's audited and unaudited financial statements.

The relationship had been quite harmonious until the retirement of Roberts, the president and founder of Allie Corporation. His successor, Strong, was a very aggressive, expansion-oriented individual who lacked the competence and personal attraction of his predecessor. Two years after Roberts' retirement the unbroken record of increases in annual earnings was in jeopardy.

Strong realized that a decrease in earnings would have an unfavorable impact on his image and on his plans to merge with a well-known conglomerate. He called Wells, the senior partner of Wells and White, and demanded that the method of computing and reporting the current year's earnings be changed in a way that would preserve the upward trend in earnings.

Although the proposed method would be within the realm of generally accepted accounting principles, Wells subsequently told Strong that, in the exercise of its professional judgment, the firm could not agree to such a change. Strong promptly dismissed the firm and refused to pay the final billing of $1,750 for services rendered to the date of dismissal under its agreement with Wells and White.

Wells and White have brought suit against Allie Corporation for the $1,750. Allie Corporation responded by denying liability on the ground that the firm's refusal to cooperate constituted a breach of contract which precluded recovery. Allie also counterclaimed by demanding the return of all audit working papers, correspondence, and duplicate tax returns and supporting explanations pertaining to Allie Corporation. The counterclaim was denied since the working papers and duplicate tax returns are the property of the CPA firm (Wells and White).

Strong was unable to find other accountants who approved of the proposed change in the method of computing and reporting earnings, so he abandoned this demand and then engaged new accountants, Bar & Cross. Income continued to decrease in the next two quarters and Strong became convinced that the cause of this must be defalcations by some dishonest employee. Therefore, he engaged Bar & Cross to make a special study to discover the guilty person. After several months of intensive work Bar & Cross were able to discover minor defalcations of $950. Of this amount, $600 was stolen during the last two years while Wells and White were Allie Corporation's accountants. Allie Corporation sues Wells and White for the loss.

Required:

a. Is the Wells and White account receivable valid and enforceable against the Allie Corporation? State "yes" or "no" and explain.

b. Will Allie Corporation recover the loss from Wells and White? State "yes" or "no" and explain.

(AICPA, adapted)

3-28. a. What is the legal relationship of the accountant to the client? Explain.

b. What is the legal duty of skill and care that the accountant-client relationship imposes upon the accountant? Explain.

c. Compare the accountant's common-law liability to clients and third parties for actual fraud committed by the accountant with his or her liability to them for ordinary negligence. Explain.

(AICPA, adapted)

3-29. Charles Worthington, the founding and senior partner of a successful and respected CPA firm, was a highly competent practitioner who always emphasized high professional standards. One of the policies of the firm was that all reports by members or staff be submitted to Worthington for review.

Recently, Arthur Craft, a junior partner in the firm, received a phone call from Herbert Flack, a close personal friend. Flack informed Craft that he, his family, and some friends were planning to create a corporation to engage in various land development ventures; that various members of the family are presently in a partnership (Flack Ventures) which holds some land and other assets; and that the partnership would contribute all of its assets to the new corporation, and the corporation would assume the liabilities of the partnership.

Flack asked Craft to prepare a balance sheet of the partnership that he could show to members of his family, who were in the partnership, and friends to determine whether they might have an interest in joining in the formation and financing of the new corporation. Flack said he had the partnership general ledger in front of him and proceeded to read to Craft the names of the accounts and their balances at the end of the latest month. Craft took the notes he made during the telephone conversation with Flack, classified and organized the data into a conventional balance sheet, and had his secretary type the balance sheet and an accompanying letter on firm stationery. He did not consult Worthington on this matter or submit his work to him for review.

The transmittal letter stated: "We have reviewed the books and records of Flack Ventures, a partnership, and have prepared the attached balance sheet at March 31, 1981. We did not perform an examination in conformity with generally accepted auditing standards, and therefore do not express an opinion on the accompanying balance sheet." The balance sheet was prominently marked "unaudited." Craft signed the letter and instructed his secretary to send it to Flack.

Required:

What legal problems are suggested by these facts? Explain.

(AICPA, adapted)

3-30. One of the major written understandings between a CPA and his client, in connection with an examination of financial statements, is the engagement (arrangements) letter.

Required:

a. What are the objectives of the engagement (arrangements) letter?
b. A CPA's responsibilities for providing accounting services sometimes involve his association with unaudited financial statements. Discuss the need in this circumstance for an engagement letter.

(AICPA, adapted)

3-31. Millard & Hans, CPAs, has been engaged for several years by Happy Toys, Inc., to perform the "usual" examination of its financial statements and provide other accounting services. The understanding was oral, and the fee was based on an annual retainer.

Millard & Hans regularly prepared unaudited quarterly financial statements and examined and reported on Happy Toys' annual financial statements. During the current year's examination, Happy Toys decided to go public and requested that Millard & Hans assists in preparing all the necessary financial statements and other financial information and supply the independent auditor's reports as necessary for inclusion in a registration statement to be filed with the Securities and Exchange Commission (SEC). Millard & Hans is independent in accordance with SEC rules and regulations. Millard & Hans complied with Happy Toys' request and subsequently submitted a bill to Happy Toys for $15,000 for the additional work performed in connection with the SEC filing. Happy Toys refused to pay, claiming the additional work was a part of the "usual" engagement and was covered by the annual retainer.

Required:

a. If Millard & Hans sues Happy Toys for its $15,000 fee, who is likely to prevail? Explain.
b. Discuss how Millard & Hans can avoid similar problems in the future with Happy Toys and other clients.

(AICPA, adapted)

3-32. Jackson was a junior staff member of an accounting firm. She began the audit of the Bosco Corporation which manufactured and sold expensive watches. In the middle of the audit she quit. The accounting firm hired another person to continue the audit of Bosco. Due to the changeover and the time pressure to finish the audit, the firm violated certain generally accepted auditing standards when they did not follow adequate procedures with respect to the physical inventory. Had the proper procedures been used during the examination they would have discovered that watches worth more than $20,000 were missing.

The employee who was stealing the watches was able to steal an additional $30,000 worth before the thefts were discovered six months after the completion of the audit.

Required:

Discuss the legal problems of the accounting firm as a result of the above facts.

(AICPA, adapted)

3-33.   A CPA firm was engaged to examine the financial statements of Martin Manufacturing Corporation for the year ending December 31, 1980. The facts revealed that Martin was in need of cash to continue its operations and agreed to sell its common stock investment in a subsidiary through a private placement. The buyers insisted that the proceeds be placed in escrow because of the possibility of a major contingent tax liability that might result from a pending government claim. The payment in escrow was completed in late November 1980. The president of Martin told the audit partner that the proceeds from the sale of the subsidiary's common stock, held in escrow, should be shown on the balance sheet as an unrestricted current account receivable. The president was of the opinion that the government's claim was groundless and that Martin needed an "uncluttered" balance sheet and a "clean" auditor's opinion to obtain additional working capital from lenders. The audit partner agreed with the president and issued an unqualified opinion on the Martin financial statements which did not refer to the contingent liability and did not properly describe the escrow arrangement.

The government's claim proved to be valid, and pursuant to the agreement with the buyers, the purchase price of the subsidiary was reduced by $450,000. This adverse development forced Martin into bankruptcy. The CPA firm is being sued for deceit (fraud) by several of Martin's unpaid creditors who extended credit in reliance upon the CPA firm's unqualified opinion on Martin's financial statements.

Required:

Based on these facts, can Martin's unpaid creditors recover from the CPA firm? Explain your answer.

(AICPA, adapted)

3-34.   The CPA firm of Martinson, Brinks & Sutherland, a partnership, was the auditor for Masco Corporation, a medium-sized wholesaler. Masco leased warehouse facilities and sought financing for leasehold improvements to these facilities. Masco assured its bank that the leasehold improvements would result in a more efficient and profitable operation. Based on these assurances, the bank granted Masco a line of credit.

The loan agreement required annual audited financial statements. Masco submitted its 1979 audited financial statements to the bank which showed an operating profit of $75,000, leasehold improvements of $250,000, and net worth of $350,000. In reliance thereon, the bank loaned Masco $200,000. The audit report which accompanied the financial statements disclaimed an opinion because the cost of the leasehold improvements could not be determined from the company's records. The part of the audit report dealing with leasehold improvements reads as follows:

Additions to fixed assets in 1979 were found to include principally warehouse improvements. Practically all of this work was done by company employees and the cost of materials and overhead were paid by Masco. Unfortunately, fully complete detailed cost records were not kept of these leasehold improvements and no exact determination could be made as to the actual cost of said improvements.

In late 1980 Masco went out of business, at which time it was learned that the claimed leasehold improvements were totally fictitious. The labor expenses charged as leasehold improvements proved to be operating expenses. No item of building material cost had been recorded. No independent investigation of the existence of the leasehold improvements was made by the auditors.

If the $250,000 had not been capitalized, the income statement would have reflected a substantial loss from operations and the net worth would have been correspondingly decreased.

The bank has sustained a loss on its loan to Masco of $200,000 and now seeks to recover damages from the CPA firm, alleging that the accountants negligently audited the financial statements.

Required:

Answer the following, setting forth reasons for any conclusions stated.

    a.   Will the disclaimer of opinion absolve the CPA firm from liability?

    b.   Are the individual partners of Martinson, Brinks & Sutherland, who did not take part in the audit, liable?

    c.   Briefly discuss the development of the common law regarding the liability of CPAs to third parties.

(AICPA, adapted)

3–35.   CPA J has been asked to audit the financial statements of a publicly held company for the first time. All preliminary verbal discussions and inquiries have been completed between the CPA, the company, the predecessor auditor, and all other necessary parties. CPA J is now preparing an engagement letter.

Required:

List the items that should be included in the typical engagement letter in these circumstances and describe the benefits derived from preparing an engagement letter.

(AICPA, adapted)

Learning Objectives

Study of the material in this chapter is designed to achieve the following learning objectives:

1. A basic understanding of the reporting requirements of the Securities and Exchange Commission (SEC).
2. A knowledge of the organization of the SEC.
3. An understanding of "materiality" and "independence" as they relate to SEC matters.
4. An understanding of the specific provisions of the 1933 and 1934 acts.
5. A knowledge of the steps in the typical registration process.
6. An understanding of accountants' legal liability under the 1933 and 1934 acts.
7. A familiarity with some of the cases which have occurred regarding accountants' legal liability under the SEC acts and their implications.

4

The SEC and Accountants' Liability under Statute Law*

INTRODUCTION[1]

There are both state and federal regulations that create a liability to third parties, other than creditors, who rely on financial statements when purchasing securities under certain specified conditions.

Most states have "Blue Sky Laws" for the purpose of regulating the issuance and trading of securities within their respective state. The general tone of the "Blue Sky Laws" in these states is to create a duty by statute that requires the auditor to make any audit of any financial statements related to securities registration without fraud or carelessness. Due care and caution must be exercised by the auditor. Each state can regulate the public accountants engaged in any activity related to securities registration within its jurisdiction, but this is now under challenge regarding tender offer legislation.

The federal legislation that has been enacted in order to protect purchasers and owners of securities (thus creating a potential basis of liability for the auditor) includes: the Securities Act of 1933, the Securities Exchange Act of 1934, the Public Utility Holding Company Act of 1935, the Trust Indenture Act of 1939, the Investment Company Act of 1940, and the Investment Advisors Act of 1940.

The two most significant federal statutes are the Securities Act of 1933 and the Securities Exchange Act of 1934. These acts have required that audited statements be filed with the Securities and Exchange Commission (SEC or Commission). The two acts and their

---

*Designated portions of this chapter were prepared by Professor Arthur J. Francia, the University of Houston.

[1]This section of the chapter was prepared by Professor Arthur J. Francia, the University of Houston.

111

legal liability implications are discussed in detail in this chapter. But first it is necessary to cover some background information on the SEC.

BACKGROUND

The auditor needs a basic understanding of the reporting requirements of the Securities and Exchange Commission in order to serve clients subject to the SEC's jurisdiction. The Commission's actions directly affect the following activities of many companies:

1. Selling their securities to the public (except for certain "exempt offerings").
2. Listing their securities on a national stock exchange and registering certain securities which are traded over-the-counter.
3. Furnishing proxy information to shareholders.
4. Furnishing periodic information, such as annual and interim reports, to the public.
5. Trading of their securities by insiders (i.e., directors, officers, and shareholders with more than 10 percent ownership in the company).

The first four of these activities require that certain financial information be filed with the Commission before being made available to the public. The auditor often examines these reports prepared for filing with the SEC. To do this the auditor needs a working knowledge of Regulation S-X which prescribes the form and content of financial statements to be submitted. The auditor should also be familiar with the rules and regulations for filing and the related instructions for the specific forms which the client is required to file. An understanding of the governing acts covered in this chapter is also necessary.

Companies have not always been required to provide information of the type required now. For example, late in the 19th century, in response to a request for information from the New York Stock Exchange (NYSE), a large listed railroad indicated that it did not make reports or publish financial statements.

The stock exchanges, together with the predecessor to the American Institute of Certified Public Accountants and other interested parties, sought to require that financial statements be sent to shareholders and also sought to improve their form, content, and dependability. These efforts met with limited success. By 1926, a company listed on the NYSE had to provide its shareholders with an annual report containing financial statements at least 15 days before its annual meeting. However, the quality and extent of disclosures contained in these reports were subject to question. Companies whose securities were not listed on the NYSE were not even subject to the requirement. The preparation of financial statements (and audits of these) had the primary purpose of being used to obtain loans or lines of credit.

In the 1930s efforts to obtain more fully informative reports were aided by federal regulation of security issues and trading. After the crash of 1929, Congress enacted the Securities Act of 1933 and the Securities Exchange Act of 1934. Under these acts, all companies having securities traded publicly (with some exceptions to be explained later) must register and file periodic reports with the SEC. Registration statements and annual reports filed with the SEC must contain financial statements audited by independent accountants, with certain exceptions. In many cases, a request to a shareholder for his or her vote (on a proxy form) must also be accompanied by financial statements. These acts are described in more detail later in this chapter.

Accounting Series Release No. 81 comments on the origin of the independent accountant's role in SEC practice:

> The passage of the Securites Act . . . [was] an important landmark in the development of the concept of the responsibility of the independent accountant to the investor and the public. The original draft of the Securities Act did not require certification by independent accountants. A representative of the accounting profession appeared at the hearings on the bill before the Committee on Banking and Currency of the U.S. Senate to suggest revisions of the bill. . . . He pointed out that the bill as drafted imposed "highly technical responsibilities upon the Commission as to accounting principles, their proper application and their clear expression in financial statements," and suggested the bill be revised to require that "the accounts pertaining to such balance sheet, statement of income and surplus shall have been examined by an independent accountant and his report shall present his certificate wherein he shall express his opinion. . . ."
>
> The committee considered at length the value to investors and to the public of an audit by accountants not connected with the company or management and whether the additional expense to industry of an audit by independent accountants was justified by the expected benefits to the public. The committee also considered the advisability and feasibility of requiring the audit to be made by accountants on the staff of the agency administering the Act.
>
> In the report on the bill the Senate committee stated that it was intended that those responsible for the administration and enforcement of the law should have full and adequate authority to procure whatever information might be necessary in carrying out the provisions of the bill, but it was deemed essential to refrain from placing upon any Federal agency the duty of passing judgment upon the soundness of any security. The proposal to require certification by independent public accountants was incorporated in the bill as passed.

Organization of the SEC

The Securities and Exchange Commission was created by Congress under the Securities Exchange Act of 1934. It is an independent, regulatory agency of the federal government. Its principal responsibility is to administer the following federal laws governing the sale and trading of securities:

Securities Act of 1933

Securities Exchange Act of 1934

Public Utility Holding Company Act of 1935

Trust Indenture Act of 1939

Investment Company Act of 1940

Investment Advisors Act of 1940

These laws, as they relate to registration of annual periodic reporting requirements, are intended to provide the investor with information about the issuer of a security so an informed decision can be made as to the merits of that security. The emphasis of these laws is on *disclosure.* (However, the SEC does not prohibit the sale or trading of highly speculative securities if they are characterized as such in the filing.) Of the above listed laws the coverage in this text will be concerned with describing the provisions and implications of the Securities Act of 1933 and the Securities Exchange Act of 1934.

The SEC is headquartered in Washington, D.C. It has regional offices in New York, Boston, Atlanta, Chicago, Fort Worth, Denver, Los Angeles, Seattle, and Washington, D.C. and also has numerous branches. The Commission has five members appointed to five-year terms by the President with the approval of the Senate. A maximum of three commissioners may be from the same political party. The Commission is assisted by a professional staff that is organized into divisions and offices. Figure 4–1 shows the organization of the SEC.

The independent accountant ordinarily works with the Division of Corporation Finance and the Office of Chief Accountant. The functions of these units of the SEC will now be described.

The Division of Corporation Finance establishes and enforces the SEC's requirements for the various information to be included in registration statements, applications, reports, and proxy statements filed with the SEC under the 1933 and 1934 acts. A director manages the division. The division has examining sections (called branches) each headed by a chief who reports to an assistant director of the division. Generally a section will handle everything relating to companies assigned to it. The division also has its own chief accountant and chief counsel. The division examines registration statements and applications, prospectuses, and various reports.

FIGURE 4-1
Securities and Exchange Commission

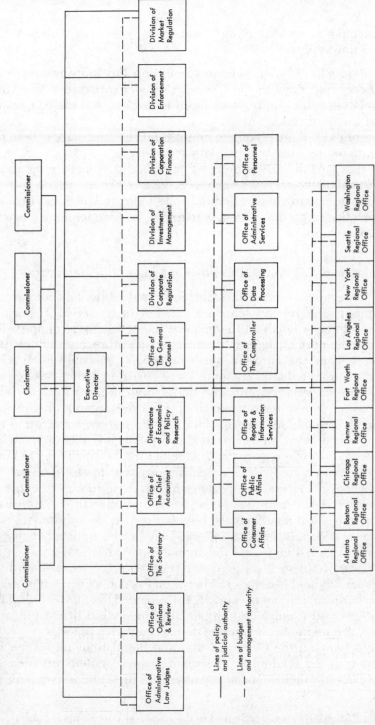

Lines of policy
and judicial authority

Lines of budget
and management authority

Office of Administrative Law Judges
Office of Opinions & Review
Office of The Secretary
Office of The Chief Accountant
Directorate of Economic and Policy Research
Commissioner
Commissioner
Chairman
Commissioner
Commissioner
Executive Director
Office of The General Counsel
Division of Corporate Regulation
Division of Investment Management
Division of Corporation Finance
Division of Enforcement
Division of Market Regulation
Office of Consumer Affairs
Office of Public Affairs
Office of Reports & Information Services
Office of The Comptroller
Office of Data Processing
Office of Administrative Services
Office of Personnel
Atlanta Regional Office
Boston Regional Office
Chicago Regional Office
Denver Regional Office
Fort Worth Regional Office
Los Angeles Regional Office
New York Regional Office
Seattle Regional Office
Washington Regional Office

Source: Adapted from material prepared by the Securities and Exchange Commission.

The chief accountant of the commission (who as of 1979 is A. Clarance Sampson):

1. Advises the Commission on accounting and auditing subjects,
2. Takes questions to the Commission and carries out its policies relating to accounting and auditing matters, and the composition of financial statements,
3. Replies to inquiries on accounting and auditing matters both from corporations and independent accountants,
4. Takes part in various proceedings relating to accounting and auditing subjects,
5. Considers situations relating to the independence and fitness to practice (e.g., the ethics or integrity) of independent practicing accountants.

Regulation S-X, Form and Content of Financial Statements

This regulation prescribes the form and content of all financial statements and related schedules filed with the SEC. There is no basic difference between the balance sheet, statement of operations, and statement of changes in financial position prepared under Regulation S-X and the same financial statements presented in an annual report to shareholders. In some instances, Regulation S-X requires disclosure of certain events and transactions other than those which the auditor would deem necessary for fair presentation in annual reports to shareholders. These additional disclosures are referred to as "compliance notes." The financial statements and schedules in SEC filings, as elsewhere, are management's representations. Financial statements in a published annual report (sent to stockholders on a regular basis) are essentially the same as those in a prospectus (the selling circular concerning securities being offered for sale) except that certain additional financial information may be required (as noted above) and certain information may have to be updated if the prospectus is issued long after the annual report is released.

In rare instances a subsequent event requiring recognition in the financial statements may occur between the date of the initial release of the financial statements and the filing date of the SEC report. These situations will require appropriate adjustment and disclosure in the financial statements and an updated accountant's report.

Rule 14a–3 of the General Rules and Regulations under the 1934 act controls the relationship between financial statements filed with the SEC and other financial statements of the same issuer. This rule says:

> Any differences, reflected in the financial statements included in the report to security holders, from the principles of consolidation or other

accounting principles or practices, or methods of applying accounting principles or practices, applicable to the financial statements of the issuer filed or proposed to be filed with the commission, which have a material effect on the financial position or results of operations of the issuer, shall be noted and the effect thereof reconciled or explained in such report. Financial statements included in the report may, however, omit such details or employ such condensation as may be deemed suitable by the management: *Provided,* That such statements, considered as a whole in the light of other information contained in the report shall not by such procedure omit any material information necessary to a fair presentation or to make the financial statements not misleading·under the circumstances.

Auditors involved in engagements which result in the filing of financial statements with the Securities and Exchange Commission should be thoroughly familiar with Regulation S-X, as well as Accounting Series Releases (ASRs) and Staff Accounting Bulletins (SABs). ASRs and SABs are two publications of the SEC which are important to accountants involved in filings with the Commission. ASRs cover accounting and financial matters and are used primarily by the SEC to issue (1) all official regulations and changes in regulations affecting the accounting and reporting policies of registrants and the responsibilities of their independent public accountants; (2) information deemed appropriate by the SEC regarding administrative and enforcement proceedings involving independent public accountants and others; and (3) official opinions and interpretations of the SEC on financial and accounting matters.

SABs describe some of the administrative accounting interpretations and practices followed by the SEC's Division of Corporate Finance and Office of the Chief Accountant. The SABs are not official rules of the Commission. However, because SABs represent staff policies, they should be viewed as authoritative references for SEC filings. The format of SABs is a series of questions and answers arranged under general topics with the surrounding facts, the question, and the staff's interpretation given for each item.

Unaudited Replacement Cost Information[2]

The SEC, in *Accounting Series Release No. 190,* amended Regulation S-X to require certain companies to include specified replacement cost information in a note or separate section of the audited statements filed with the SEC. These entities are required to explain

---

[2] This section is based on *Statement on Auditing Standards No. 18,* "Unaudited Replacement Cost Information," American Institute of Certified Public Accountants, 1977. Copyright © 1977 by the American Institute of Certified Public Accountants, Inc.

how they arrived at the amounts reported. *SAS No. 18* provides guidance to independent auditors concerning procedures to be applied to unaudited replacement cost information and any related information included in the audited statements filed with the SEC. Also, if a company includes replacement cost information with its audited statements, but is not required by Regulation S-X to do so, the auditor should follow the procedures mentioned in *SAS No. 18.*[3] (The requirements of *ASR No. 190* are to be phased out as companies begin reporting current costs as required by *FASB Statement No. 33.* See Chapter 13 for a discussion of *FASB Statement No. 33.*)

SAS No. 18 suggests that the auditor read the replacement cost information and apply limited procedures. The objective of these procedures (which involve selected inquiries)

> . . . is to provide the auditor with a reasonable basis for considering whether (a) the replacement cost information is prepared and presented in accordance with Regulation S-X of the Commission . . . and (b) management's disclosures with respect to the replacement cost information are consistent with management's responses to such inquiries. [*SAS No. 18*]

SAS No. 18 recommends that the auditor apply the following limited procedures to unaudited replacement cost information:

1. Discuss with management whether the replacement cost information is prepared in accordance to Regulation S-X.
2. Discuss with management ". . . the methods selected to calculate replacement cost information and the reasons for selecting them. . . ."
3. "Inquire of management as to procedures used to compile the data supporting the replacement cost information and to the relationship between data supporting the replacement cost information and data supporting the audited financial information. . . ."
4. "Inquire about the methods and bases used by management to calculate any supplemental replacement cost information. . . ."
5. "If management has changed the method of calculating replacement cost information, inquire as to the reasons for using a method different from that used in the previous fiscal period."

The auditor should see if management's answers to the above questions are consistent with the unaudited replacement cost information and other information gathered during the audit. However, the auditor is not obligated to use any procedures to corroborate management's responses.

---

[3] This is not necessary if the note or section of the financial statements containing the information are clearly marked "unaudited" and also indicates that the auditor has not applied any limited procedures.

Generally, the auditor, in a report on audited statements filed with the SEC, need not refer to the unaudited replacement cost information. If, however, the auditor feels there is ". . . a material inconsistency between the unaudited replacement cost information and the audited financial information, he should determine whether the audited financial statements, his report, or both require revision."[4] If they do not need revision and instead the unaudited replacement cost information needs revision, the client should be requested to make the appropriate change.

If the unaudited replacement cost information is not prepared or presented in accordance with Regulation S-X or if the auditor has been unable to apply limited procedures, then the auditor's report should be expanded to include an explanatory paragraph relating to the deficiency. Additionally, the auditor's report on the audited statements should include a disclaimer of opinion on the unaudited replacement cost information if that information (1) is not marked unaudited, or (2) contains ". . . an indication that the auditor performed any procedures regarding the information without also indicating that the auditor does not express an opinion. . . ."[5]

In *Accounting Series Release No. 203*, the SEC limited the liability of the auditor in reporting replacement cost information. The Commission stated:

> Current replacement cost information disclosed . . . shall be deemed not to be an untrue statement of a material fact; a statement false or misleading with respect to any material fact; an omission to state a material fact necessary to make a statement not misleading; or the employment of a manipulative, deceptive, or fraudulent device, contrivance, scheme, transaction, act, practice, course of business or an artifice to defraud; as those terms are used in the Securities Act of 1933, the Securities Exchange Act of 1934, or the Public Utility Holding Company Act of 1935, or rules and regulations thereunder, unless such information:
> 1. Was prepared without a reasonable basis; or
> 2. Was disclosed other than in good faith.

The reason the Commission gave for issuing this "safe harbor" rule was given in *ASR No. 203* as follows:

> The Commission is adopting the rule because of the imprecise nature of replacement cost information and its desire to encourage the development and disclosure of such information in good faith. The Commission recognizes that it is requiring companies to disclose data that is not subject to precise calculation. It is expected that there will be various approaches taken in the preparation and disclosure of replacement

---

[4]*SAS No. 18*, paragraph 7.
[5]Ibid., paragraph 9.

cost data. The Commission believes that persons required to disclose replacement cost data should be protected against the imposition of liability for such disclosures unless it can be clearly shown that the disclosures were prepared without a reasonable basis or disclosed in other than good faith.

The Concepts of "Materiality" and "Independence" in SEC Matters

The concept of *materiality* is as important in SEC matters as it is in other accounting matters. Rule 1–02 in Regulation S-X says, "the term 'material,' when used to qualify a requirement for the furnishing of information as to any subject, limits the information required to those matters as to which an average prudent investor ought reasonably to be informed before purchasing the security registered." Thus, the issue is whether a reasonable investor (not a particular investor) would attach importance to the matter. Judge McLean in the *BarChris* case (to be discussed in detail later in this chapter), had the following comment regarding materiality:

> What are "matters as to which an average prudent investor ought reasonably to be informed"? It seems obvious that they are matters which such an investor needs to know before he can make an intelligent, informed decision whether or not to buy the security.

> * * * * *

> The average prudent investor is not concerned with minor inaccuracies or with errors as to matters which are of no interest to him. The facts which tend to deter him from purchasing a security are facts which have an important bearing upon the nature or condition of the issuing corporation or its business.

> * * * * *

> Since no one knows what moves or does not move the mythical "average prudent investor," it comes down to a question of judgment, to be exercised by the trier of the fact as best he can in light of all the circumstances.[6]

In 1976, the Supreme Court adopted a narrow definition of materiality under a section of the 1934 act. In *TSC Industries, Inc.* v. *Northway, Inc.*,[7] the Supreme Court held that "an omission from a proxy solicitation is 'material' for the purposes of Section 14(a) only if 'there is a substantial likelihood that a reasonable shareholder *would* consider it important in deciding how to vote.' "[8]

---

[6] *Escott* v. *BarChris Construction Corporation*, 283 F. Supp. 653, pp. 681-82 (1968).

[7] *TSC Industries, Inc.* v. *Northway, Inc.*, 426 U.S. 438 (1976).

[8] *Harvard Law Review*, vol. 90 (November 1976), p. 255.

The criteria the Commission uses to judge the auditor's *independence* are stated in various Accounting Series Releases. Included among these ASRs are ASRs Nos. 47, 81, 112, 126, and 234. Some of the more significant comments from some of these are given below.

The following comments from *Accounting Series Release No. 47* dated July 25, 1944, concern the auditor's relations with clients:

> The requirement of the Securities and Exchange Commission that an accountant *be in fact independent* with respect to a company whose financial statements he certifies is grounded on the conviction that the existence of certain types of relationships between a company and its certifying accountant might bias the accountant's judgment on accounting and auditing matters. Certain relationships between an accountant and his client appear so apt to prevent the accountant from reviewing the financial statements and accounting procedures of a registrant with complete objectivity that the Commission has taken the position that existence of these relationships will preclude its finding that the accountant is, in fact, independent. (Emphasis added.)

Accordingly, Rule 2-01(b) of Regulation S-X provides that:

> The Commission will not recognize any certified public accountant or public accountant as independent who is *not in fact independent*. For example, an accountant will be considered not independent with respect to any person or any of its parents, its subsidiaries, or other affiliates (1) in which, during the period of his professional engagement to examine the financial statements being reported on or at the date of his report, *he or his firm or a member thereof had, or was committed to acquire, any direct financial interest or any material indirect financial interest, or* (2) *with which, during the period of his professional engagement to examine the financial statements being reported on, at the date of his report or during the period covered by the financial statements, he or his firm or a member thereof was connected as a promoter, underwriter, voting trustee, director, officer, or employee,* except that a firm will not be deemed not independent in regard to a particular person if a former officer or employee of such person is employed by the firm and such individual has completely disassociated himself from the person and its affiliates and does not participate in auditing financial statements of the person or its affiliates covering any period of his employment by the person. For the purposes of Rule 2-01 the term "member" means all partners in the firm and all professional employees participating in the audit or located in an office of the firm participating in a significant portion of the audit. (Emphasis added.)

The following comments are from *Accounting Series Release No. 126* dated July 5, 1972:

> *A part of the rationale which underlies any rule on independence is that managerial and decision-making functions are the responsibility of the client and not of the independent accountant.* It is felt that if the

independent accountant were to perform functions of this nature, he would develop, or appear to develop, a mutuality of interest with his client which would differ only in degree, but not in kind, from that of an employee. And where this relationship appears to exist, it may be logically inferred that the accountant's professional judgment toward the particular client might be prejudiced in that he would, in effect, be auditing the results of his own work, thereby destroying the objectivity sought by shareholders. *Consequently, the performance of such functions is fundamentally inconsistent with an impartial examination.* However, it is the role of the accountant to advise management and to offer professional advice on their problems. Therefore, the problem posed by this dilemma is to ascertain the point where advice ends and managerial responsibility begins.

In this context, *managerial responsibility begins when the accountant becomes, or appears to become, so identified with the client's management as to be indistinguishable from it.* In making a determination of whether this degree of identification has been reached, the basic consideration is *whether, to a third party, the client appears to be totally dependent upon the accountant's skill and judgment in its financial operations or to be reliant only to the extent of the customary type of consultation or advice. . . .*

. . . The Commission is aware of the fact that situations arise which require judgment in determining whether the Commission's standards of independence have been met and that a company or its accountants may wish assurance that no question as to independence will be raised if the company files financial statements with the Commission. *Where this is the case, the Commission urges the parties concerned to bring the problem to its attention so that a timely and informed decision on the matter may be made.* (Emphasis added.)

* * * * *

Business Relationships with Client

Direct and material indirect business relationships other than as a consumer in the normal course of business with a client or with persons associated with the client in a decision-making capacity, such as officers, directors or substantial stockholders, will adversely affect the accountant's independence with respect to that client. Such a mutuality or identity of interests with the client would cause the accountant to lose the appearance of objectivity and impartiality in the performance of his audit because the advancement of his interest would, to some extent, be dependent upon the client. In addition to the relationships specifically prohibited by Rule 2–01(b), joint business ventures, limited partnership agreements, investments in supplier or customer companies, leasing interests, except for immaterial landlord-tenant relationships, and sales by the accountant of items other than professional services are examples of other connections which are also included within this classification.

* * * * *

Occupations with Conflicting Interests

Certain concurrent occupations of certified public accountants engaged in the practice of public accounting involve relationships with clients which may jeopardize the certified public accountant's objectivity and, therefore, his independence. In general, this situation arises because the relationships and activities customarily associated with this occupation are not compatible with the auditor's appearance of complete objectivity or because the primary objective of such occupations are fundamentally different from those of a public accountant. Acting as counsel or as a broker-dealer, or actively engaging in direct competition in a commercial enterprise are examples of occupations so classified. . . .

The following comments are from *Accounting Series Release No. 234,* dated December 13, 1977 (some of these topics were mentioned also in earlier ASRs):

Family Relationships

The restrictions against holding interests in an audit client by an independent accountant set out in Rule 2–01(b)(1) and against holding official positions and associations with the client, as specified in Rule 2–01(b)(2), *are also applicable to relatives of the accountant in varying degrees depending on the closeness of the relationship. Family relationships in these situations require careful consideration in every case to determine whether independence in fact or the appearance of independence of the accountant may be impaired.* Many of these problems were discussed in ASR No. 126. In general, financial interests and business relationships of an accountant's immediate family or other dependent relatives with an audit client would be ascribed to the accountant and would accordingly impair his or his firm's independence with respect to that client. [Emphasis added.]

There would also be a presumption of impairment of independence *when other close relatives of the accountant have material financial interests or business relationships or hold important positions with a client.* . . . [Emphasis added.]

* * * * *

Retired Partners

Financial interests in or offical associations with a client or its affiliates by a retired partner of an accounting firm may affect the independence of the firm as if the partner were not retired, if any circumstances exist indicating that the retired partner in fact retains some influence or participation in the firm or that would give the appearance to an outside party that influence was retained. . . .

* * * * *

Accounting Services Rendered to a Client

It is the Commission's position that an accounting firm cannot be deemed independent with regard to auditing financial statements of a client if it has participated closely, either manually or through its computer services, in maintenance of the basic accounting records and preparation of the financial statements, or if the firm performs other accounting services through which it participates with management in operational decisions.

* * * * *

Unpaid Prior Professional Fees

In ASR No. 126 it was indicated that if fees for audit and other professional services are owed to an accountant for an extended period of time and become material in relation to the fee expected to be charged for a current audit there may be a question concerning the accountant's independence with regard to the current audit because the accountant may appear to have a direct interest in the results of operations of the client. It was also indicated that normally prior year audit fees should be paid before a current audit engagement is commenced in order for the accountant to be deemed independent with respect to the current audit. The prior year fees for all other professional services normally should be paid also for this determination to be made.

When this problem exists in connection with the required audits of financial statements to be included in annual reports filed with the Commission that position has been modified somewhat. In general a question would not be raised in such situations if, at the time the current audit engagement is commenced, a firm commitment is made by the client to pay the prior year fee before the audit report is issued, or an arrangement is agreed upon for periodic payments to settle the delinquent fee and there is reasonable assurance that the current audit fee can be paid on a timely basis. . . .

* * * * *

Litigation Involving Accountants and Their Clients

* * * * *

When an adversary position between a client and its accountant with respect to the audit services rendered or to be rendered is created as a result of litigation the accountant cannot be considered impartial or capable of exercising objective judgments in the performance of the audit work and could not be deemed to meet the Commission's requirements for independence. Other situations involving litigation or the possibility of litigation require careful consideration by the accountant to determine whether an adversary position is created which impairs his independence with respect to the audit work performed or to be performed.

In *Accounting Series Release No. 251*, dated July 6, 1978, the SEC set forth ". . . its interpretation that litigation between accountants and their clients which is not related to the audit work for that client is among the types of litigation which must be considered individually for its effects on independence." [*ASR No.* 251]

The *Accounting Series Releases* contain examples of situations brought to the attention of the SEC and the conclusions reached. Some of these are used in question 4–42 at the end of the chapter.

THE SECURITIES ACT OF 1933 (THE 1933 ACT)

Background

The 1933 act provides generally that public offerings of securities must be registered with the Commission before they may be sold. Issues of less than $1.5 million are dealt with under simplified provisions and may be exempt from registration under certain circumstances. Offerings restricted to the residents of the state in which the issuing company is organized and doing business are exempt, as are government securities and private sales. A sale is considered private if an entire issue is sold for investment to a limited number of knowledgeable investors and will not be distributed to the public.

The act's two objectives are: (1) to provide investors with information about securities offered for sale to the public; and (2) to prohibit misrepresentation or fraud in the sale of securities. Full and fair disclosure is to be made in a registration statement, which is a public document on file at the SEC offices.

Every registration statement includes a *prospectus* (selling circular), which is the principal source of information for an investor about the securities to be offered for sale. The prospectus must be furnished as a separate document to each person to whom the security is offered for sale. A prospectus for an S–1 filing (discussed below), for example, must contain the terms of the offering, information about management, description of the business and properties, audited financial statements, comparative financial data, and other information necessary for the prospective investor to make an informed investment decision. The only standard which must be met in the registration statement is an adequate and accurate disclosure of the material facts about the company and the securities it is planning to sell. Assuming proper disclosure, the Commission cannot deny registration or otherwise bar the securities from public sale. The investor must assess the riskiness of the securities.

The 1933 act provides for various registration statement forms, each for a particular class of issuer and security. Most common is *Form S–1*, a general form for registration of securities of all issuers for which no

other form is prescribed (see Code of Federal Regulations. Title 17—
Commodity and Securities Exchanges). Other forms in this series are
used for more specialized purposes. The forms and SEC reporting
services include instructions for preparing all registration forms. Each
registration form contains instructions describing the circumstances in
which that form may be used.

Registration Process

The registration process generally begins with negotiations between the company (and perhaps selling shareholders) and the "lead"
underwriter. The auditor's advice may be sought, and early participation of the auditor can be of great assistance.

The underwriting agreement between the lead underwriter and the
company selling the shares outlines their respective responsibilities
and duties. The auditor is not a party to the underwriting agreement.
The agreement does affect the auditor, however, because the client
usually agrees to obtain a letter from the auditor covering certain
representations made in the agreement. The letter from the auditor to
the underwriter states that the accountant has performed certain procedures and makes certain other general statements of fact. This letter
is generally referred to as a "comfort letter." *Statement on Auditing
Standards No. 1* describes the rules which the auditor should follow
in preparing such letters.

Preparing and filing a registration statement is a complex task. Registering securities is a major event for most companies, and the auditor's participation is an important service to the client. Although no
two filings are exactly alike, the main steps in most filings are similar.
They usually occur as follows:

1. The participating parties (client, legal counsel, independent
accountants, and underwriter) attend a preliminary planning meeting.
The parties establish a tentative timetable and assign tasks. Time is
usually an important element in the registration process, because the
underwriter wants the flexibility to market an issue at the most advantageous price for the registrant.

2. The auditor completes the examination of the financial statements and those schedules in the filing which are required to be
audited. Later, the auditor performs certain post-audit procedures relating to the audited financial statements as well as those procedures
agreed to in the underwriting agreements, reads basic documents, and
prepares the required accountant's reports. The post-audit procedures
are performed on interim period financial statements, subsequent
events, and on certain financial information as expressly requested by
one of the participating parties.

3. The client (through its attorneys) files the preliminary registration statement with the SEC.

4. The SEC (through its Division of Corporation Finance) normally reviews the registration statement and, if necessary, issues a letter of comments.

5. The parties respond to the commission's comments and an amended registration statement is filed if required.

6. The auditor obtains a letter of representation from the client.

7. The auditor prepares a letter for the underwriters if requested, "giving comfort" to them on specific accounting-related matters.

8. The auditor updates the post-audit procedures to the effective date of the registration statement and attends a meeting to ensure that all parties have performed their duties with "due diligence."

9. The SEC declares the registration statement effective.

10. The parties hold a closing meeting to exchange the securities and funds. The securities are then sold by the underwriters. (On a "best efforts" offering [where the underwriter uses its best efforts to sell securities, but does not guarantee the sale], securities are sold before the closing.)

ACCOUNTANTS' LIABILITY UNDER THE 1933 ACT[9]

As stated earlier, the Securities Act of 1933 requires certified financial statements to be included with the registration statement that must be filed with the Securities and Exchange Commission prior to the offering of certain securities for sale. Section 11 of the act, "Civil Liabilities on Account of False Registration Statement," is the most important noncriminal section for the accountant.

Saul Levy summarized the effect of this statute in 1954 as follows:

1. Any person acquiring securities described in the Registration Statement may sue the accountant, regardless of the fact that he is not the client of the accountant.

2. His claim may be based upon an alleged false statement or misleading omission in the financial statements, which constitutes his prima facie case. The plaintiff does not have the further burden of proving that the accountants were negligent or fraudulent in certifying to the financial statements involved.

3. The plaintiff does not have to prove that he relied upon the statement or that the loss which he suffered was the proximate result of the falsity or misleading character of the financial statement.

4. The accountant has thrust upon him the burden of establishing his freedom from negligence and fraud by proving that he had, after reasonable investigation, reasonable ground to believe and did be-

---

[9] This section of the chapter was prepared by Professor Arthur J. Francia, the University of Houston.

lieve that the financial statements which he certified, were true not only as of the date of the financial statements, but beyond that, *as of the time when the Registration Statement became effective.* (Emphasis by Levy.)

5. The accountant has the burden of establishing by way of defense or in reduction of alleged damages, that the loss of the plaintiff resulted in whole or in part from causes other than the false statements or the misleading omissions in the financial statements. Under the common law it would have been part of the plaintiff's affirmative case to prove that the damages which he claims he sustained were proximately caused by the negligence or fraud of the accountant.[10]

Any action that is brought against the auditor under the act must be filed within three years after the securities have been offered to the public and within one year after the discovery of the error or omission has been made.[11] Unless both of these conditions are met no action can be brought.

The BarChris Case

The auditor is also responsible for reporting any significant changes in the financial affairs of the firm offering the securities which occur between the audit date and the effective date of the registration statement. This review of events from the date of the certified audit until the effective date of the registration statement is called an S-1 review and is required by the act.

The courts had never defined what was required in an S-1 review until the case of *Escott v. BarChris Construction Corporation.*[12] One writer in commenting on the case stated:

The judge held that underwriters, lawyers, auditors and directors all were to blame for false financial information contained in a prospectus. It was believed to be the first time a judge had strictly defined standards for persons involved in procedures routine in the preparation of prospectuses.

The decision is likely to mean that everyone connected with a registration will be much more meticulous than in the past. It means that hardly anyone can safely take anyone else's word for anything. In theory, it means that nearly everyone involved must check every material fact himself by plodding through company records.[13]

---

[10] Saul Levy, *Accountants' Legal Responsibility* (New York: American Institute of Accountants, 1954), pp. 46–47. Copyright © 1954, by the American Institute of Certified Public Accountants, Inc.

[11] Securities Act of 1933, Public Law 22, 73d Cong. as amended, section 13.

[12] *Escott v. BarChris Construction Corporation*, 283 F. Supp. 643 (S.D.N.Y. 1968).

[13] "Getting at the Truth," *The Wall Street Journal*, May 14, 1968, p. 1. Reprinted with permission of *The Wall Street Journal*, © Dow-Jones & Company, Inc. (1968). All rights reserved.

Purchasers of the subordinated debentures of BarChris Construction Corporation initiated the action under Section 11 of the Securities Act of 1933 against any persons signing the registration statement, the underwriters, and the auditors. They charged that the registration statement directly relating to the bond issue contained material false statements and material omissions.

The impact of this case, from a liability standpoint, revolved around the S-1 review. The court recognized that the S-1 review should not be a complete audit. The auditors had prepared a written program for an S-1 review that the court found to be acceptable. This program included (1) a review of various minutes of meetings, latest interim financial statements, the more important financial records, and (2) an inquiry into changes in material contracts, significant bad debts, and newly discovered liabilities as well as other investigations. The court indicated that the senior auditor on the audit (who had not yet received his CPA certificate and was on his first assignment as a senior):

> ... asked questions, he got answers which he considered satisfactory, and he did nothing to verify them.

* * * * *

> There had been a material change for the worse in BarChris's financial position. That change was sufficiently serious so that the failure to disclose it made the 1960 figures misleading. [The senior] did not discover it. As far as results were concerned, his S-1 review was useless.[14]

The final paragraphs of the judge's decision concerning the auditor's liability in this case were probably the first outlining the standards of care the auditor must use in the S-1 review.

> Accountants should not be held to a standard higher than that recognized in their profession. I do not do so here. [The senior's] review did not come up to that standard. ... Most important of all, he was too easily satisfied with glib answers to his inquiries.
>
> This is not to say that he should have made a complete audit. But there were enough danger signals in the material which he did examine to require some further investigation on his part. Generally accepted accounting standards required such further investigation under these circumstances. It is not always sufficient to ask questions.[15]

The auditors were unable to prove that they acted with due diligence in this landmark case. They were found to be liable.

Criminal penalties under the 1933 act are contained in Section 24. Penalties are provided for *willfully* omitting a material fact or making an untrue statement in a registration statement.

---

[14] *Escott* v. *BarChris Construction Corporation*, p. 702.

[15] Ibid., p. 703.

SECURITIES EXCHANGE ACT OF 1934

Background

The specific purpose of the Securities Exchange Act of 1934 is:

To provide for the regulation of securities exchanges and of over-the-counter markets operating in interstate and foreign commerce and through the mails to prevent inequitable and unfair practices on such exchanges and markets. . . .[16]

The 1934 act as amended in 1964 extended the "disclosure" doctrine of investor protection to all securities listed and registered for trading on the national securities exchanges and to equity securities of many companies traded over-the-counter. Thus, the 1934 act pertains to securities *trading* instead of to the original *distribution* of securities. The 1934 act generally covers periodic reporting requirements for registered companies in reporting to the Securities and Exchange Commission.

Companies whose stock is listed on a national exchange are subject to the reporting requirements of the 1934 act. Also, every company (1) in interstate commerce, (2) with more than $1 million in total assets, (3) having 500 or more shareholders, *and* (4) having securities which are traded *over-the-counter* is subject to the 1934 act when it first meets these four requirements.

Forms

The 1934 act also prescribes the forms to be used.

Form 10 (not to be confused with Form 10-K) is a general form which requires information somewhat similar to that in Form S-1. It is filed by a company which attains more than 500 shareholders and assets of $1 million if the company is not filing annual SEC reports.

Once registered under the 1934 act, if the number of shareholders in a company whose stock is sold *over-the-counter* drops below 300, the company's registration will be terminated within 90 days after it officially notifies the SEC, and the company shall not be subject to SEC jurisdiction unless it otherwise falls within that jurisdiction.

All companies registered under the 1934 act are subject to SEC rules on: (1) annual and other periodic reporting, (2) proxies, (3) tender offer solicitations (as of a 1968 amendment), and (4) insiders' trading. Since 1964, companies registered under the 1933 act as well as companies registered before 1964 that have "undertaken" to do so,

---

[16] *Securities Exchange Act of 1934*, Public Law 291, 73d Cong. as amended to August 20, 1964, p. 1.

must file annual and other periodic reports. The auditor must know the client's SEC history as well as its present situation to determine exactly which SEC regulations and reporting requirements it must meet.

An annual report to the SEC (which usually includes by reference the financial statements from a company's annual report to shareholders and also includes other data about the company's activities during the year) is required to be filed by each company within 90 days after the end of its fiscal year. Domestic companies file this annual report on *Form 10-K*. Special industries and special situations may require other forms. Having to assist in preparing these periodic reports to the SEC often provides an accountant with his or her first SEC experience.

Registered companies are also required to file quarterly reports on *Form 10-Q* within 45 days after each of the first three fiscal quarters. A report need not be filed for the fourth quarter since Form 10-K is filed instead.

In 1975, the SEC issued *Accounting Series Release (ASR) No. 177* which significantly expanded Form 10-Q reporting for all registrants and mandated new requirements for the subsequent inclusion of certain quarterly data in the annual report of certain larger, actively traded companies. The following information is required in all Form 10-Q filings:

Financial statements (full or condensed):

1. Income statements for the quarter and year-to-date for the current and preceding year.
2. Balance sheets as of the end of the quarter for the current and preceding year.
3. Statements of changes in financial position for the year-to-date for the current and preceding year.

Management's narrative analysis of the results of operations.

In addition, disclosure in Form 10-Q is required upon the occurrence of the following events:

Business combinations (poolings and purchases).

Discontinued operations.

Accounting changes.

ASR No. 177 also requires the inclusion of comparative quarterly information in the registrant's annual report to shareholders. This has resulted in increased involvement of independent accountants in quarterly filings. Auditing and reporting on interim financial statements are discussed in Chapters 13 and 14.

Furthermore, registered companies must report events such as: (1) changes in control; (2) bankruptcy or receivership; (3) change in auditors; (4) acquisition or disposition of assets; and (5) other specified important events on *Form 8-K* soon after those events occur.

Proxy Solicitations

The 1934 act also requires every company registered under the act to furnish *proxy information* (if proxies are solicited from stockholders) to voting stockholders. A *proxy* authorizes another party (often management) to cast the shareholder's vote on various matters at the shareholders' meeting.

Although corporate reorganizations are often exempt from registration, shareholders receive substantially indentical types of information when they vote on a merger as they would in a prospectus. Proxy solicitations are required in most mergers and must let the stockholder vote "yes" or "no" on each matter. A proxy statement for a merger must accurately describe, among other things, the business and properties of each company, the plan of merger, and the rights of shareholders, including dissenters. The merger proxy statement differs from the registrants' prospectus in that it also must contain financial statements and other financial data relating to the other parties to the merger. A preliminary proxy statement must be furnished to the SEC at least ten days before the statement is mailed to the stockholders. The SEC reviews this material and furnishes the company with comments on deficiences, if any.

The National Student Marketing Case

In a case involving National Student Marketing Corporation two CPAs were accused and convicted (in December 1974) of making false and misleading statements in a 1969 proxy statement. One CPA (the audit partner) received a fine of $10,000 and was sentenced to a one-year jail term with all but 60 days suspended. The other (the audit supervisor) was fined $2,500 and was sentenced to a one-year jail term with all but 10 days suspended. The sentences were appealed. The federal appeals court affirmed the conviction of the audit partner, but it reversed the audit supervisor's conviction.[17]

---

[17] "Auditors Sentenced in National Student Marketing Case," *The Journal of Accountancy*, February 1975, p. 24. For other details of this case, see the March 12, 1970, March 23, 1970, February 4, 1972, January 18, 1974, July 29, 1975, December 6, 1976, January 19, 1977, and May 3, 1977 issues of *The Wall Street Journal*.

The auditing firm maintained that the two auditors were deliberately deceived by management and by employees of some of its customers and that the allegation of criminality against them was unjustified. This case illustrates that care must be taken to avoid legal liability when the auditor is associated with proxy statements.

Tender Offer Solicitations

The 1934 act, as amended, requires disclosure of relevant information by any person attempting to acquire over 5 percent of a company's securities by direct purchase or tender offer (an offer communicated to present shareholders offering to buy so many shares, usually at a price above the current market value). Any persons soliciting stockholders to accept or reject a tender offer also must disclose pertinent information.

Margin Requirements and Insider Trading

The 1934 act also establishes margin requirements (the limitation on the amount of credit which may be extended for the purpose of purchasing or carrying securities) which are regulated by the Board of Governors of the Federal Reserve System. For instance, if the margin requirement is 70 percent, a purchaser could only borrow 30 percent of the total required to purchase a security. The act also prescribes rules which govern security trading by "insiders." Insiders are stockholders who hold more than 10 percent of the outstanding shares (registered equity securities) of the corporation and all directors and officers of the company.

LEGAL LIABILITY UNDER THE 1934 ACT[18]

As stated earlier, the 1934 act requires companies whose securities are traded on the exchanges and certain companies whose shares are traded over-the-counter to file certified financial statements periodically with the Securities and Exchange Commission. The CPA can be held liable because of the audit and subsequent opinion given on the financial statements. Section 18(a) of the act points out the noncriminal liability of the accountant when it states that:

> Any person who shall make or cause to be made any statement in any application, report, or document filed pursuant to this title . . . which . . . was made false or misleading with respect to any material

---

[18] The first part of this section was prepared by Professor Arthur J. Francia, the University of Houston.

134

fact, shall be liable to any person (not knowing that such statement was false or misleading) who, in reliance upon such statement, shall have purchased or sold a security at a price which was affected by such statement, for damages caused by such reliance, unless the person sued shall prove that he acted in good faith and had no knowledge that such statement was false or misleading.[19]

Thus, the test for determining whether liability exists is whether the statements or reports misled the *average prudent investor* rather than whether they met professional standards. If the auditor can show that "due diligence" was used in performing the work this can also be used in the defense.

A somewhat similar one-year and three-year statute of limitations that is applicable to the 1933 act is found in the 1934 act (except for *Rule 10b-5*).

Section 10(b) of the 1934 act and the Securities and Exchange Commission's *Rule 10b-5*[20] have played a major role in current cases brought under the securities act. Section 10 states:

Sec. 10. It shall be unlawful for any person, directly or indirectly, by the use of any means or instrumentality of interstate commerce or of the mails, or of any facility of any national securities exchange—

(a) To effect a short sale, or to use or employ any stop-loss order in connection with the purchase or sale, of any security registered on a national securities exchange, in contravention of such rules and regulations as the Commission may prescribe as necessary or appropriate in the public interest or for the protection of investors.

(b) To use or employ, in connection with the purchase or sale of any security registered on a national securities exchange or any security not so registered, any manipulative or deceptive device or contrivance in contravention of such rules and regulations as the Commission may prescribe as necessary or appropriate in the public interest or for the protection of investors.[21]

Rule 10b-5, to some extent, reiterates Section 10(b) of the 1934 act but elaborates on or specifies what is illegal under Section 10(b) as follows:

SECTION 240.10b-5
EMPLOYMENT OF MANIPULATIVE
AND DECEPTIVE DEVICES

It shall be unlawful for any person directly or indirectly, by the use of any means or instrumentality of *interstate commerce*, or of the *mails* or

[19] Securities Exchange Act of 1934, Section 18(a).
[20] Code of Federal Regulations. Title 17—*Commodity and Securities Exchanges* (Revised as of January 1, 1968), Section 240.10b-5.
[21] Securities Exchange Act of 1934, Section 10.

of any facility of any *national securities exchange, (a)* To employ any device, scheme, or artifice to *defraud, (b)* To make *any untrue statement* of a material fact or *omit* to state a material fact necessary in order to make the statements made, in the light of the circumstances under which they were made, not misleading, or *(c)* To engage in any act, practice, or course of business which operates or would operate as a *fraud* or *deceit* upon any person in connection with the purchase or sale of any security. (Emphasis added.)[22]

From the standpoint of the accountants' liability, the questions raised under this section of the statute are concerned with the basic competence exhibited in protecting shareholders' interests and those of purchasers and sellers of securities.

Section 32 of the 1934 act describes criminal penalties for willfully and knowingly making a statement in any required report which was false or misleading with respect to any material fact. To illustrate, criminal fines were imposed on three CPAs in the *Continental Vending Machine Corporation* case (to be discussed later) under that section of the act and other statutes. For an auditor to defend against criminal liability it seems that it must be shown that he or she was not aware that the reports submitted would mislead the *average prudent investor.*

Enforcement Powers of the SEC

The following comments regarding the enforcement powers of the SEC are from *Accounting Series Release No. 81* dated December 11, 1958:

> . . . the Commission may disqualify, and deny, temporarily or permanently, the privilege of appearing or practicing before it to any accountant who is found by the Commission . . . not to possess the requisite qualifications to represent others; or to be lacking in character or integrity; or to have engaged in unethical or improper professional conduct. These proceedings are conducted privately and may or may not result in a published opinion. They have been rare. (Emphasis added.)

As a practical matter recently the SEC, rather than disqualifying and denying the privilege of CPAs to appear or practice before it, seems to be more inclined to have violating CPA firms submit to peer review to upgrade the quality of their procedures. A less stringent alternative is to censure a CPA firm. This latter alternative causes the firm some notoriety and embarrassment.

---

[22] *Code of Federal Regulations.* Title 17—*Commodity and Securities Exchanges* (Revised as of January 1, 1968), Section 240.10b-5.

In some recent cases[23] resulting from private investigations by the SEC of the conduct of CPA firms the settlements have included one or more of the following features:

a. Agreement by the CPA firm to (1) submit to a comprehensive "peer review" of the manner in which it conducts its practice with respect to audit clients whose financial statements are filed with the SEC; (2) to implement all reasonable recommendations of the peer review group; and (3) to submit to a subsequent review to determine whether implementation of the peer review group's recommendations have occurred.

b. Agreement that certain named individual partners of the CPA firm would not perform any audit work which would involve any filings with the SEC for a specified length of time.

c. Prohibition of the firm (or an office of the firm) from accepting any new publicly held clients for a specified period.

In commenting on the reasons for such an approach, former SEC Chief Accountant, John C. Burton, stated:

> ... the Commission has imposed a partial or complete limitation on new SEC business for a firm, either for a prescribed period or until such time as a peer review group is able to inspect a practice and report thereon to the Commission. In this way the Commission feels it has obtained outside evidence that the program has been effectively implemented before the firm is allowed to grow further. ... This seems particularly appropriate in cases where the problems have not been of a limited nature but have encompassed several areas of practice.[24]

OTHER RECENT CASES

Some of the other cases involving federal statute law that have received considerable publicity will now be discussed. Each of the cases selected seems to have had (or will have) a significant impact on the liability situation of accountants.

The Yale Express Case[25]

In this case the stockholders and creditors of Yale Express Systems, Inc., brought suit against a national CPA firm for issuing an unqualified opinion on its 1963 financial statements. The accountants' opinion was subsequently included in the 10-K report filed with the SEC.

---

[23] For example, see *Accounting Series Releases Nos. 153, 196, 210, 227, 238, and 241.*

[24] John C. Burton, "SEC Enforcement and Professional Standards: Philosophy, Objectives and Approach," 28 *Vanderbilt Law Review*, 19, 26 (1975).

[25] *Fischer* v. *Kletz*, 266 F. Supp. 180 (1967).

In 1964 the CPA firm performed management consulting services for Yale Express. While engaged in this management service work the CPA firm ". . . discovered that figures in the 1963 annual report were substantially false and misleading."[26] The CPA firm claimed that this discovery was made ". . . after the report was filed while plaintiffs contended discovery occurred before the SEC and others received the annual report."[27] The CPA firm did not report its discovery to the SEC or the public until March 1965.

When Yale Express later filed for bankruptcy, a number of shareholders and creditors filed suit against the CPA firm under Section 18(a) of the 1934 act and *Rule 10(b)-5*. The CPA firm moved to have certain aspects of the case dismissed. The court refused to dismiss the claim, and the CPA firm paid $650,000 in the settlement.

Later (1969) the AICPA issued *Statement on Auditing Procedure (SAP) No. 41* (which is now included in *SAS No. 1*, Section 561) on how and when to make appropriate disclosure of material facts obtained after the issuance of an audit report. *SAP No. 41* discussed the action that should be taken when an auditor becomes aware (after the date of the report on audited financial statements) of facts existing at the date of the report that could have affected the report had they been known. The auditor is required to investigate the facts immediately. If these facts are material, the auditor is required to prepare a revised report. The auditor should insist that the client notify anyone (including third parties, the SEC, stock exchanges, and other regulatory bodies) who is, or may be, relying on the auditor's report and the financial statements of the facts as they existed at the date of the original report. If the client does not do so, the auditors should do so.

The Continental Vending Case

In one of the more significant recent cases, two partners and a manager of a large CPA firm were found guilty of conspiring and adopting a scheme to violate federal criminal statutes as a result of issuing an opinion on financial statements. The CPAs were fined and the convictions were upheld under appeal. Eventually the accountants received a presidential pardon and the CPA firm settled the civil suit out of court. However, the fact that three professional accountants had received criminal sentences was (and is) of great concern to the accounting profession.

The CPAs were found guilty of certifying to the September 30,

---

[26] Henry B. Reiling and Russell A. Taussig, "Recent Liability Cases—Implications for Accountants," *The Journal of Accountancy* (September 1970), p. 50.
[27] Ibid.

138

1962, misleading financial statements of the Continental Vending Machine Corporation. The facts of the case are described below.

The president of Continental also operated Valley Commercial Corp. (an affiliate of Continental). Between 1958 and 1962 Continental's president borrowed money from Continental for his own personal use. Specifically, he caused Continental to lend the money to Valley which in turn lent the money to him (Continental's president).

On September 30, 1962, Valley owed Continental $3.5 million from these borrowings. Since Continental's president was unable to repay Valley he posted collateral, most of which was in the form of Continental stock. At the date of the opinion, the collateral had a value of $2.9 million. However, the auditors said the collateral was satisfactory since Continental also owed Valley about $1 million on the balance sheet date. Actually, Continental had issued about $1 million of notes to Valley, which had discounted the notes and turned the proceeds over to Continental.[28]

The footnote included in the financial statements which was related to this information read as follows:

> The amount receivable from Valley Commerical Corporation (an affiliated company of which [Continental's president] is an officer, director and stockholder) bears interest at 12 percent a year. Such amount, less the balance of the notes payable to that company, is secured by the assignment to the Company of Valley's equity in certain marketable securities. As of February 16, 1963, the amount of such equity at current market quotations exceeded the net amount receivable.[29]

The government, however, claimed the footnote should have stated:

> The amount receivable from Valley Commercial Corp. (an affiliated company of which [Continental's president] is an officer, director and stockholder), which bears interest at 12% a year, was uncollectible at September 30, 1962, since Valley had loaned approximately the same amount to [Continental's president] who was unable to pay. Since that date [Continental's president] and others have pledged as security for the repayment of his obligation to Valley and its obligation to Continental (now $3,900,000, against which Continental's liability to Valley cannot be offset) securities which, as of February 15, 1963, had a market value of $2,978,000. Approximately 80% of such securities are stock and convertible debentures of the company.[30]

The CPA firm involved in the case audited Continental, but did not audit Valley.

---

[28] Ibid., pp. 48–49.

[29] Ibid., p. 49.

[30] *United States* v. *Simon*, 425 F. 2d 796 (1969), p. 801.

The defendants called eight expert accounting witnesses who testified ". . . that neither generally accepted accounting principles nor generally accepted auditing standards required disclosure of the make-up of the collateral or of the increase of the receivable after the closing date of the balance sheet. . . ."[31] These expert witnesses also noted:

> . . . that disclosure of the . . . borrowings [of Continental's president] from Valley was not required, and seven of the eight were of the opinion that such disclosure would be inappropriate. The principal reason given for this last view was that the balance sheet was concerned solely with presenting the financial position of the company under audit; since the Valley receivable was adequately secured in the opinion of the auditors and was broken out and shown separately as a loan to an affiliate with the nature of the affiliation disclosed, this was all that the auditors were required to do.[32]

Circuit Judge Friendly noted that:

> Generally accepted accounting principles instruct an accountant what to do in the usual case where he has no reason to doubt that the affairs of the corporation are being honestly conducted. Once he has reason to believe that this basic assumption is false, an entirely different situation confronts him. Then, . . . he must "extend his procedures to determine whether or not such suspicions are justified." If as a result of such an extension or, as here, without it, he finds his suspicions to be confirmed, full disclosure must be the rule. . . .[33]

Evidently, the courts may hold CPAs to higher standards than those set by the profession.

The court noted that it could not find ". . . proof of motive in the form usual in fraud cases. . . . Ordinary commercial motivation [was] absent."[34] However, "the Government finds motive in defendants' desire to preserve [the CPA firm's] reputation and conceal the alleged dereliction of their predecessors and themselves in former years."[35]

The U.S. Financial, Inc. Case

The importance of this case is that it led to a large national accounting firm having to undergo mandatory review by persons outside

---

[31] Ibid., p. 805.
[32] Ibid.
[33] Ibid., pp. 806–807.
[34] Ibid., p. 808.
[35] Ibid.

the firm (mandatory peer review). As was noted earlier in this chapter, this is an alternative that the SEC appears to be selecting in an attempt to improve auditing practice.

The SEC found that financial statements and reports issued by U.S. Financial for the years ended 1970 and 1971 were false and misleading. *Accounting Series Release No. 153* which was issued as a result of this case stated:

> It appears that as part of a scheme to mislead the public by publishing false financial statements reflecting fictitious earnings, USF and certain of its officers, directors and associates *intentionally deceived* [the auditor] by making untrue representations and by furnishing false information in connection with its audits. The Commission has instituted legal proceedings against these parties.
>
> *Any such deception, however, did not relieve [the auditor] of its responsibilities to perform its audits in conformity with generally accepted auditing standards.* The information furnished to the Commission indicated that [the auditor's] conduct of the 1970 and 1971 audits in a number of respects *did not meet the professional standards required of public accountants who practice before the Commission.*
>
> Such information indicated that [the auditor] failed to obtain sufficient independent evidentiary material to support its professional opinion in regard to a number of highly material transactions which were constructed by management in such a way as to make it appear that income had been earned when in fact it had not been. In connection with these transactions it also appeared that [the auditor] failed to fully appraise the significance of information known to it and to extend sufficiently its auditing procedures under conditions which called for great professional skepticism. These transactions resulted in USF *improperly recognizing millions of dollars of revenues and profits in 1970 and 1971.* (Emphasis added.)

The auditor, without admitting or denying any violations or facts, consented to the entry of an order containing certain findings, conclusions, and remedial actions. The following remedial actions were prescribed by the SEC in *Accounting Series Release No. 153:*

> Accordingly, IT IS ORDERED that proceedings pursuant to Rule 2(e) of the Commission's Rules of Practice be, and they hereby are, instituted against [the auditor].
>
> IT IS FURTHER ORDERED that, subject to the terms and conditions provided in the offer of settlement [the auditor], be, and it hereby is:
>
> A. Censured by the Commission.
>
> B. Required to adopt, maintain and comply with procedures which shall be submitted to the Commission for its review and approval within thirty (30) days after the date hereof, to prevent future violations of the federal securities laws, which procedures shall provide, among other things, as a means of strengthening [the auditor's] procedures.

1.   That in all audit engagements specific review shall be made which is designed to determine the management's direct or indirect involvement in material transactions which are included in the financial statements;

2.   For the formulation and implementation of qualitative office review procedures requiring periodic review at least once every two years of all [the auditor's] offices under the control and supervision of [the auditor's] national staff to evaluate and ensure the quality of the audit engagements of such offices.

C.   In order to ascertain that [the auditor] is conducting its professional practice in compliance with paragraph B above, an investigation, which shall be conducted at the expense of [the auditor], *shall be conducted by the commission in accordance with methods and procedures adopted or approved by it by the use of members of the profession in public practice selected or approved by the Chief Accountant of the Commission or, at its option, by use of qualified professional accountants drawn from its own staff.* . . .

D.   For a period of twelve (12) months after the date of this order, [the auditor's] San Diego, California, branch office will not accept or undertake any new professional engagement which can be expected to result, within twelve (12) months from the date of such engagement, in filings, submissions or certifications with the Commission. . . .

E.   The auditor will not accept or undertake any new professional engagement of any client whose business, revenues and net profit (loss) is materially derived from real estate development or sales, including financing related thereto, as defined herein, which engagement can be expected to result, within twelve (12) months from the date of such engagement, in filings, submissions, or certifications with the Commission until the Chief Accountant of the Commission is satisfied that adequate audit guides and programs for application have been adopted, including appropriate testing thereof as applied to audits. . . .

F.   The Commission shall retain jurisdiction of this matter pending final receipt of a report of investigation referred to in paragraph C above and thereafter for either the taking, if necessary, of appropriate action to ensure compliance, including but not limited to the re-opening of these proceedings for the imposition of such other and further relief as may be required under the circumstances, or the approval of the report and termination, on notice, of this proceeding. (Emphasis added.)

Another development in this case which could have significant impact in the area of legal liability is that the national CPA firm has sued the client for supplying false and misleading information for audit. Specifically:

. . . [the auditor] filed a $50 million suit against USF [U.S. Financial, Inc.] and certain of its former officers, charging injury to the firm's professional reputation arising from the fraudulent actions with the specific intent to deceive. The firm stated that the charges are supported by the

SEC's findings that former officers of USF intentionally deceived the firm by making untrue representations and furnishing false information in connection with the audits for 1970 and 1971.[36]

As of 1979, the suit against the client had not been resolved.

An additional development was that in 1977 a jury awarded $30 million in damages to lending institutions that charged the CPA firm with negligence in auditing the financial statements.[37] As of 1979, this decision was being appealed.

The Equity Funding Case

A recent case which received substantial publicity is the *Equity Funding Life Insurance Co.* case. Of the $53 million settlement in this case, the CPA firms involved were required to pay $39 million.[38] Three of the auditors "after an arduous four-month trial . . . were found guilty on multiple criminal counts of securities fraud and filing falsified financial statements with the Securites and Exchange Commission."[39]

An article in *The Wall Street Journal* referred to a 239-page fraud report filed in federal court by the court-appointed trustee who was overseeing the company's reorganization under Chapter 10 bankruptcy proceedings. The article stated:

> . . . From 1964, when the company went public and the fraud was thought to begin, through 1972, Equity Funding put $143 million in income on its books that was completely bogus. Actually it had never made a profit and had been losing huge sums yearly.
>
> Apparently these losses were covered by the proceeds from loans and securities offerings.
>
> Investigations to date, however, have failed to turn up evidence that any of the fraud participants made large direct raids on the corporate treasury. They did well enough selling the inflated stock, some of it granted under a lavish stock bonus plan.[40]

---

[36] "SEC Imposes Sanctions on Accounting Firm," *The Journal of Accountancy*, April 1974, p. 12.

[37] See *The Wall Street Journal* (November 30, 1977), p. 31.

[38] "Equity Funding Suits are Settled for $53 Million," *The Wall Street Journal* (January 5, 1977), p. 4.

[39] "Three Former Equity Funding Auditors Convicted of Fraud, Filing False Data," *The Wall Street Journal* (May 21, 1975), p. 11. Reprinted with permission of *The Wall Street Journal*, © Dow-Jones & Company, Inc. (1975). All rights reserved.

[40] "Equity Funding Trustee Calls the Fraud an Inept, Slapdash, Pyramiding Scheme," *The Wall Street Journal* (November 4, 1974), p. 4. Reprinted with permission of *The Wall Street Journal*, © Dow-Jones & Company, Inc. (1974). All rights reserved. For more details on this case, see "Those Daring Young Con Men of Equity Funding," *Fortune* (August 1973), pp. 81-85, 120-32.

Earlier in the article it was stated that the:

> . . . fraud was neither brilliantly planned nor well executed, but a slap-dash, helter-skelter scheme in which one fraud had to be frantically covered by a greater and more blatant one. It would have finally collapsed of its own mushrooming weight and the fumblings of its perpetrators, who could no longer hide the enormity of their crime.[41]

The article related that the report dealt harshly with the performance of the auditors. It stated:

> The report makes another significant conclusion, sobering in its implications. It says, in effect, that the system of corporate checks and balances, including the presence of competent outside directors . . . , the reviews of regulatory agencies, the scrutiny of lenders and others, is worth little or nothing if the company's independent auditors haven't done their work properly. Like an inverted pyramid, the whole structure rests on reliable, tested financial figures.
>
> These, the trustee said, were conspicuously lacking in a fraud that lasted almost for a decade without detection, escalating year by year. The report is filled with samples of "red flag" transactions that should have prompted thorough checks by the auditors, but didn't.[42]

At the time, this case led some to believe that in the future accountants may be legally liable for not detecting material management fraud. It also caused some concern that the auditor's traditional reliance on internal control (where there is a division of responsibilities with checks and balances on the work of others within an organization) may need some reexamination. This important case proved that wide-spread collusion among employees is indeed possible.

The Hochfelder Case

In an article on this important case, J. Jay Hampson gave the facts as follows:

> First Securities Company of Chicago retained [the auditor] from 1946 to 1967 to do audit work and prepare the annual report for filing with the SEC. First Securities was a brokerage firm and member of the Midwest Stock Exchange. Leston B. Nay, president of the firm, owned 92 percent of its stock. Plaintiffs were customers of First Securities. Nay had persuaded them to invest funds in escrow accounts that he said would yield a high return. In 1968 Nay committed suicide, leaving a note that described First Securities as bankrupt and the escrow accounts as "spurious." In actuality there were no escrow accounts. Nay, after receiving the funds, diverted them to his own use. The transactions were not

---

[41] Ibid.
[42] Ibid.

recorded. The customers either wrote the checks to Nay or to a designated bank for his account. The customers never received records of the transactions or of the balances in the fictitious accounts.

The defrauded customers charged that Nay's scheme violated 10(b) and the SEC's Rule 10b-5, and that [the auditor] aided and abetted Nay's fraud by its failure to conduct proper audits of First Securities. More specifically, the customers charged that [the auditor] was negligent in failing to use appropriate auditing procedures, thereby not discovering the fraud. The customers alleged that Nay's "mail rule" was the principal means by which the fraud was perpetrated and that an effective audit would have revealed the scheme. Nay's "mail rule" provided that all mail addressed to him was to be opened only by him. In his absence, the mail was placed on his desk to be opened upon his return regardless of the duration of his absence. The customers expressly stated that they were not accusing [the auditor] of intentional fraud but, rather, with "inexcusable negligence."[43]

The question the court faced was whether the wording of *Rule 10b-5* limits the auditor's liability to intentional participation (fraud) or includes negligent conduct as well. The District Court found for the auditor. On appeal, a federal Court of Appeals reversed the decision and found for the plaintiffs. When the case was then appealed to the United States Supreme Court, the Court found that the auditor could not be held liable *because the auditor did not know of or intentionally participate in the fraud.*

The syllabus to the decision of the United States Supreme Court stated in part:

> ... A private cause of action for damages will not lie under § 10(b) and Rule 10b-5 in the absence of any allegation of "scienter," i.e., intent to deceive, manipulate, or defraud on the defendant's part. ...
>
> (a) The use of the words "manipulative," "device," and "contrivance" in § 10(b) clearly shows that it was intended to proscribe a type of conduct quite different from negligence, and more particularly the use of the word "manipulative," virtually a term of art used in connection with securities markets, connotes intentional or willful conduct designed to deceive or defraud investors by controlling or artificially affecting the price of securities. ...
>
> (b) The 1934 Act's legislative history also indicates that § 10(b) was addressed to practices involving some element of scienter and cannot be read to impose liability for negligent conduct alone. ...[44]

[43] J. Jay Hampson, "Accountants' Liability—The Significance of Hochfelder," *The Journal of Accountancy* (December 1976), p. 69.

[44] *Ernst & Ernst v. Hochfelder*, 425 U. S. 185 (1976).

This case seems to clarify the auditor's liability under Section 10(b). Only time will tell what the ultimate impact will be.

Other Cases

There are undoubtedly other cases which could have been mentioned in these last two chapters. Certain landmark cases (such as McKesson & Robbins, which resulted in the requirement to verify inventories and accounts receivable) were important in the development of auditing standards but they have little significance in describing the current legal environment. Some recent cases which received some publicity either have not yet been resolved, making it difficult to judge their impact at this time, or do not illustrate new points.

As the Hochfelder case illustrates, the auditors do not always lose these cases. Additionally, in early 1974, two auditors were acquitted in the *Four Seasons Nursing Home* case and a mistrial was declared for a third auditor.[45]

CONCLUDING COMMENTS

Chapters 3 and 4 have dealt with accountants' legal liability under the common law and under statute law. The increasing number of suits brought against accountants is a serious problem facing the profession. But it should not serve to discourage one from entering this challenging field of work.

A crucial issue is how a person entering the profession should react to the legal liability issue. Should that person develop an attitude of brooding suspicion and act like a super sleuth when performing an audit? We think not; rather, an attitude similar to the famous "I'm from Missouri, show me" seems to be called for. A feeling of healthy skepticism should be maintained, but it should not cause the auditor to treat everyone encountered with undue suspicion.

As long as an auditor does a top-flight job there is little to worry about. This includes not concentrating to such an extent on the detailed auditing steps or procedures (which are covered in the latter part of this text) that the overall purpose of those procedures is forgotten. As the auditor proceeds through the various stages of an audit, he or she must exercise considerable judgment and common sense (which unfortunately is not all that common). Questions such as the

---

[45] "Auditors Acquitted in *Four Seasons* Case," *The Journal of Accountancy* (April 1974), pp. 14–15.

146

following would be good to ask oneself (these are illustrative rather than all-inclusive):

1. Is each of the amounts presented in the financial statements fairly presented in accordance with generally accepted accounting principles?
2. Are there any ommissions of material items?
3. Are there any misstatements of material items?
4. Does this year's performance as reflected in the financial statements seem logical in view of previous years' performance?
5. Has "due care" been used in performing all phases of the audit?
6. Have all significant steps taken during the audit been recorded in the working papers? (These may be difficult to remember several years later.)
7. Have all necessary procedures in performing the audit been followed?
8. Have any procedures been rushed through just to stay within the time constraints of the audit?
9. Where knowledge and background were limited in a certain area were experts consulted?
10. Was everyone working on the audit supervised adequately and were all other generally accepted auditing standards complied with?
11. Were the quality control procedures adequate to ensure that performance of the audit was up to standard?
12. Near the conclusion of the audit and looking back did everything "seem" right or are there still some bothersome items that should be investigated further?
13. Was the *Code of Professional Ethics* complied with in all aspects of the engagement?

As you proceed through the remainder of the text you should keep these points in mind. Minor detailed steps are necessary in performing the audit just as it is necessary in driving an automobile to have your hands on the steering wheel, to use your right foot to operate the gas pedal and brake, and to look at the road, traffic, and signs. But you should concentrate on where you are going—your final destination. In an audit the final destination or goal is to express a professional opinion as to the fairness of the presentation of the financial statements. As will be described in following chapters, it is necessary to gather substantial audit evidence to be able to give this opinion with confidence so as to not expose yourself or the firm unduly to legal liability.

The firm can also take steps to minimize the chance of loss. Included among the steps it can take are the following:

1. When asked to take on a new client who has dismissed another auditor, discuss the situation with the other auditor (after receiving the client's permission) and review the working papers (after receiving the client's permission). Be very meticulous in looking into the background of these (and all) prospective clients. Many times firms have found that the risk of taking on certain new clients is not worth the reward.
2. Decrease the traditional emphasis on growth. Instead, concentrate on doing audits of firms in industries with which the firm is most familiar.
3. Use clearly worded engagement letters for all engagements and generally avoid associations with unaudited statements where possible.
4. Stay current with pronouncements of all authoritative bodies (AICPA, FASB, SEC, and so on) and provide continuing education on these matters to all employees.
5. Decrease time pressures to the extent possible in the performance of audit engagements. Long-run profitability may be increased.
6. Make sure that liability insurance coverage is adequate.

The legal environment for accountants will continue to change over the years. One must keep fully informed as to the current situation regarding this important topic.

GLOSSARY

Accounting Series Releases (ASR's)   The opinions and announcements issued by the SEC on accounting and auditing and related administrative matters.

"Best efforts" offering   Where an underwriter uses its best efforts to sell the securities. However, the underwriter does not guarantee the sale.

Blue Sky Laws   State laws which regulate the issuance and trading of securities within their respective state.

Comfort letter   A letter from the auditor to the underwriter stating that the accountant has performed certain procedures. The letter makes certain other general statements of fact.

Form 8-K   A form on which a company is to report to the SEC events such as: (1) changes in control; (2) bankruptcy or receivership; (3) change in auditors; (4) acquisition or disposition of assets; and (5) other specified important events.

Form 10   A form which is filed by a company which attains more than 500 shareholders and assets of $1 million if the company is not filing annual SEC reports.

Form 10-K   A form used by a domestic company to report annually to the SEC. It usually includes by reference the financial statements from a company's annual report to stockholders and also includes other data about the company's activities during the year. It must be filed within 90 days of the end of the company's fiscal year.

Form 10-Q   A form used by registered companies to file quarterly reports with the SEC (after each of the first three fiscal quarters).

Form S-1   A registration statement form, used under the 1933 act, for registration of securities of all issuers for which no other form is prescribed [Code of Federal Regulations].

Insiders   Directors, officers, and shareholders with more than 10 percent ownership in the company.

Margin requirement   The limitation on the amount of credit which may be extended for the purpose of purchasing or carrying securities.

Prospectus   A selling circular which must be furnished to each person to whom a security is offered for sale. It is the principal source of information for an investor about the securities to be offered for sale.

Proxy   Authorization given to another party (usually management) to cast the stockholder's vote on various matters at a stockholder's meeting.

Regulation S-X   Prescribes the form and content of all financial statements and related schedules filed with the SEC.

The Securities Act of 1933   The law that covers the public offerings of securities to be sold in interstate commerce, foreign commerce, or through the mails.

Securities and Exchange Commission   An independent, regulatory agency of the federal government charged with administering federal laws governing the sale and trading of securities.

Securities Exchange Act of 1934   The law that governs securities trading instead of the original distribution of securities. It regulates the securities exchanges and over-the-counter markets operating in interstate and foreign commerce and through the mails.

Staff Accounting Bulletins   Describes some of the administrative accounting interpretations and practices followed by the SEC's Division of Corporate Finance and Office of the Chief Accountant.

Tender Offer   An offer communicated to present shareholders offering to buy so many shares, usually at a price above the current market value.

Underwriting agreement   The agreement between the lead underwriter and the company selling shares. It outlines their respective responsibilities and duties.

QUESTIONS AND PROBLEMS

4-1.   Briefly describe the "Blue Sky Laws" and their impact on the auditor.

4-2.   List the various activities over which the SEC has jurisdiction.

4-3.   What are the provisions of Regulation S-X?

4-4.   One of your fellow students says to you, "The underlying purpose of the federal laws governing the sale and trading of securities is to make recommendations to potential purchasers of these securities as to which one to buy." Comment.

4-5. Refer to Figure 4-1. With which two units of the SEC do independent accountants ordinarily deal?

4-6. What are the principal duties of the Chief Accountant of the SEC?

4-7. Briefly describe the purpose and significance of:

   a.   The Securities Act of 1933.
   b.   The Securities Exchange Act of 1934.

4-8. The sales of certain securities are exempted from the requirements of the Securities Act of 1933. Describe the characteristics which make these securities exempt.

4-9. What types of information are required in a prospectus for an S-1 filing?

4-10. Describe the main steps in the "typical" registration filing.

4-11. Describe the accountant's noncriminal liability under the 1933 act.

4-12. What is the statute of limitations under the 1933 and 1934 acts?

4-13. What is an S-1 review?

4-14. In the *BarChris Construction Corporation* case did the court find that the written program for the S-1 review was inadequate? Explain.

4-15. Is it accurate to say that the 1933 act is concerned with the distribution of securities while the 1934 act is concerned with the trading of securities?

4-16. Which companies are subject to the reporting requirements of the 1934 act?

4-17. In recent years it has been fairly common for "over-the-counter" companies to "go private" to avoid being subject to the reporting requirements under the 1934 act. Once a company is registered under the 1934 act, what actions can it take to avoid being subject to the reporting requirements of the act in the future?

4-18. What is a 10-K report?

4-19. What is a 10-Q report?

4-20. What are some of the types of information that registered companies are required to report to the SEC on Form 8-K?

4-21. What information must be included in a proxy statement for a merger? How does such a proxy differ from the registrants' prospectus?

4-22. What basic issue did the *National Student Marketing Corporation* case involve? What was the nature of the penalties imposed?

4-23. Are tender offer solicitations covered by the 1934 act?

4-24. If the margin requirement is 60 percent and a purchaser of securities desires to buy $10,000 (market value) of stock, how much can be borrowed to complete the transaction?

4-25. Who qualifies as an "insider"?

4-26. What is the auditor's objective in applying limited procedures to replacement cost information?

4-27. Describe the accountant's noncriminal legal liability under the 1934 act. What effect did the *Hochfelder* case have in clarifying this?

150

4-28. What acts are considered to be illegal acts under the SEC's *Rule 10b-5?*

4-29. How does the SEC define the following?

    a. Materiality

    b. Independent accountants.

4-30. Discuss the significance of the *Yale Express* case.

4-31. Can both civil and criminal liability result from the same case? Did this happen in the *Continental Vending* case?

4-32. What actions did the SEC take against the auditors in the *U.S. Financial, Inc.,* case?

4-33. What are the likely implications of the *Equity Funding* case?

4-34. What is the likely effect of the *Hochfelder* case?

4-35. Select the best answer for each of the following items.

    a. An investor seeking to recover stock market losses from a CPA firm, based upon an unqualified opinion on financial statements which accompanied a registration statement, must establish that

        1. There was a false statement or omission of material fact contained in the audited financial statements.

        2. He relied upon the financial statements.

        3. The CPA firm did *not* act in good faith.

        4. The CPA firm would have discovered the false statement or omission if it had exercised due care in its examination.

    b. Josephs & Paul is a growing medium-sized partnership of CPAs. One of the firm's major clients is considering offering its stock to the public. This will be the firm's first client to go public. Which of the following is true with respect to this engagement?

        1. If the client is a service corporation, the Securities Act of 1933 will *not* apply.

        2. If the client is *not* going to be listed on an organized exchange, the Securities Exchange Act of 1934 will *not* apply.

        3. The Securities Act of 1933 imposes important additional potential liability on Josephs & Paul.

        4. As long as Josephs & Paul engages exclusively in intrastate business, the federal securities laws will *not* apply.

    c. A CPA is subject to *criminal* liability if the CPA

        1. Refuses to turn over the working papers to the client.

        2. Performs an audit in a negligent manner.

        3. Willfully omits a material fact required to be stated in a registration statement.

        4. Willfully breaches the contract with the client.

    d. The Securities Act of 1933, in general, exempts certain small stock offerings from full registration. What is the maximum dollar amount which would qualify for this exemption?

        1. $300,000.

        2. $1,500,000.

        3. $2,000,000.

        4. $4,000,000.

    e. The most significant aspect of the *Continental Vending* case was
that it

      1. Created a more general awareness of the auditor's exposure to
criminal prosecution.

      2. Extended the auditor's responsibility for financial statements
of subsidiaries.

      3. Extended the auditor's responsibility for events after the end
of the audit period.

      4. Defined the auditor's common-law responsibilities to third
parties.

    f. A third-party purchaser of securities has brought suit based upon
the Securities Act of 1933 against a CPA firm. The CPA firm will
prevail in the suit brought by the third party even though the CPA
firm issued an unqualified opinion on materially incorrect financial statements if

      1. The CPA firm was unaware of the defects.

      2. The third-party plaintiff had *no* direct dealings with the CPA
firm.

      3. The CPA firm can show that the third-party plaintiff did *not*
rely upon the audited financial statements.

      4. The CPA firm can establish that it was *not* guilty of actual
fraud.

(AICPA, adapted)

4-36. J. Kone, CPA, has been controller of Big Co. for five years. Before that
she was a staff accountant for Little & Small, CPAs. The Big Co. decides to hire Little & Small as auditors. Would the CPA firm meet the
SEC's independence requirements?

4-37. Sam Adams, CPA, owns ten shares of Tiny Co. Tiny Co. has just hired
Adams to be its independent auditor. Would the SEC consider Adams
to be independent?

4-38. CPA J is a partner in the CPA firm of JKL & M, CPAs. CPA J is a
member of the board of directors of Mill, Inc. CPA M (a partner of CPA
J) makes an agreement with Mill, Inc., to do the annual audit. Since J is
on the board, it is agreed that J will not participate in the audit. Would
the SEC consider this arrangement to be independent?

4-39. The Chriswell Corporation decided to raise additional long-term capital by issuing $3 million of 8 percent subordinated debentures to the
public. May, Clark & Co., CPAs, the company's auditors, were engaged to examine the June 30, 1981, financial statements which were
included in the bond registration statement.

    May, Clark & Co. completed its examination and submitted an un-
qualified auditor's report dated July 15, 1981. The registration statement was filed and became effective on September 1, 1981. Two
weeks prior to the effective date one of the partners of May, Clark &
Co. called on Chriswell Corporation and had lunch with the financial
vice president and the controller. He questioned both officials on the
company's operations since June 30 and inquired whether there had
been any material changes in the company's financial position since

that date. Both officers assured him that everything had proceeded normally and that the financial condition of the company had not changed materially.

Unfortunately the officers' representation was not true. On July 30, a substantial debtor of the company failed to pay $400,000 due on its account receivable and indicated to Chriswell that it would probably be forced into bankruptcy. This receivable was shown as a collateralized loan on the June 30 financial statements. It was secured by stock of the debtor corporation which had a value in excess of the loan at the time the financial statements were prepared but was virtually worthless at the effective date of the registration statement. This $400,000 account receivable was material to the financial condition of Chriswell Corporation, and the market price of the subordinated debentures decreased by nearly 50 percent after the foregoing facts were disclosed.

The debenture holders of Chriswell are seeking recovery of their loss against all parties connected with the debenture registration.

Required:

Is May, Clark & Co. liable to the Chriswell debenture holders? Explain.

(AICPA, adapted)

4-40. Each of the lettered statements of fact below is followed by numbered sentences that state legal conclusions relating to those facts. You are to determine whether each legal conclusion is true or false according to the general principles of accountants' legal responsibility and federal securities regulation.

A. James Sack, a partner in the firm of Walters, Jones, & Sack, CPAs, prepared tax returns for Ominus, a closely held family corporation. The corporation's books were kept by a family member. While preparing the tax returns, Sack realized that the books and records were poorly kept and contained several inaccuracies. However, he relied upon them and based his tax computations exclusively upon them. As a result, Sack erroneously included in taxable income some items which did not actually represent income. The errors subsequently were discovered, but, by that time, it was too late to file an amended return or claim for refund to recover the excess taxes paid.

 1. James Sack was negligent in preparing the tax return.
 2. The Internal Revenue Service would be unable to subpoena Walters, Jones, & Sack's working papers because they are privileged communications.
 3. Walters, Jones, & Sack will be liable for the excess amount of taxes paid by Ominus.
 4. Only Sack, and not the CPA firm, would be liable under the circumstances described.
 5. Sack's firm could defend successfully a suit brought by Ominus to recover the excess amount of tax by establishing the contributory negligence of Ominus.

      6.   The fact that Sack had not been informed of the inadequacy of the records totally exonerates him from liability.

      7.   Sack has committed a fraud.

      8.   If Sack had joined Ominus in willfully attempting to evade taxes, he would be guilty of a felony.

B. The partnership, Winslow, Wilson & Carr, CPAs, prepared the income tax returns for Charles Bosphor for several years. The staff accountant who prepared Bosphor's tax return for 1981 properly elected to report certain income as an installment sale.

    The next year a new staff man was assigned to the task of preparing Bosphor's return. He inadvertently failed to check the returns for prior years. Consequently, he failed to include the installment income for 1981. An audit of the return by the Internal Revenue Service revealed the error, and additional tax and interest were assessed.

      9.   Winslow, Wilson, & Carr were negligent in the preparation of the tax return in question.

   10.   Winslow, Wilson, & Carr will be liable for the tax assessed.

   11.   Winslow, Wilson, & Carr will be liable for the interest assessed.

   12.   It was Charles Bosphor's responsibility to check the returns and inform Winslow, Wilson & Carr of the error.

   13.   Good accounting practice would dictate that a new man on an engagement review his predecessor's work for the past several years.

C. Kenneth Chance, a senior accountant with the partnership of South, Wall, Evers, & Co., CPAs, resigned after several years with the firm. During his employment, he had examined the financial statements of Zelex Corporation and became a close friend of the controller and the financial vice president of Zelex.

    After establishing his own firm, Chance actively solicited the business of Zelex, even though the South firm had been engaged to perform the current year's audit. During the audit, Zelex dismissed the South firm alleging that Chance's replacement was personally obnoxious, performed his work in a slipshod manner, and was dating one of the company's female bookkeepers. Zelex demands the return of all of its books and records and the firm's working papers.

   14.   Zelex could dismiss the South firm without liability solely upon the personality conflict that arose with respect to Chance's replacement.

   15.   If Chance's replacement was negligent in performing his work, Zelex could terminate the relationship and recover damages.

   16.   Zelex has the right to the return of its books and records.

   17.   The South firm must turn over its working papers to Zelex.

   18.   If none of Zelex's allegations are true, Zelex will be liable for breach of contract.

D. Xavier, Frances, & Paul are a growing medium-sized partnership of CPAs located in the midwest. One of the firm's major clients is considering offering its stock to the public. This will be the firm's first client to go public.

19. The firm should thoroughly familiarize itself with the Securities Act of 1934, and Regulation S–X.
20. If the client is unincorporated, the Securities Act of 1933 will not apply.
21. If the client is going to be listed on an organized exchange, the Securities Exchange Act of 1934 will not apply.
22. The Securities Act of 1933 imposes an additional potential liability on firms such as Xavier, Francis, & Paul.

(AICPA, adapted)

4-41. Whitlow and Wyatt, CPAs, has been the independent auditors of Interstate Land Development Corporation for several years. During these years, Interstate prepared and filed its own annual income tax returns.

During 1980, Interstate requested Whitlow and Wyatt to examine all the necessary financial statements of the corporation to be submitted to the Securities and Exchange Commission (SEC) in connection with a multistate public offering of 1 million shares of Interstate common stock. This public offering came under the provisions of the Securities Act of 1933. The examination was performed carefully and the financial statements were fairly presented for the respective periods. These financial statements were included in the registration statement filed with the SEC.

While the registration statement was being processed by the SEC but prior to the effective date, the Internal Revenue Service (IRS) subpoenaed Whitlow and Wyatt to turn over all its working papers relating to Interstate for the years 1977–1979. Whitlow and Wyatt initially refused to comply for two reasons. First, Whitlow and Wyatt did not prepare Interstate's tax returns. Second, Whitlow and Wyatt claimed that the working papers were confidential matters subject to the privileged-communications rule. Subsequently, however, Whitlow and Wyatt did relinquish the subpoenaed working papers.

Upon receiving the subpoena, Wyatt called Dunkirk, the chairman of Interstate's board of directors and asked him about the IRS investigation. Dunkirk responded, "I'm sure the IRS people are on a fishing expedition and that they will not find any material deficiencies."

A few days later Dunkirk received written confirmation from the IRS that it was contending that Interstate had underpaid its taxes during the period under review. The confirmation revealed that Interstate was being assessed $800,000 including penalties and interest for the three years.

This $800,000 assessment was material relative to the financial statements as of December 31, 1980. The amount for each year individually exclusive of penalty and interest was not material relative to each respective year.

Required:

1. Discuss the additional liability assumed by Whitlow and Wyatt in connection with this SEC registration engagement.
2. Discuss the implications to Whitlow and Wyatt and its responsibilities with respect to the IRS assessment.
3. Could Whitlow and Wyatt have validly refused to surrender the subpoenaed materials? Explain.

(AICPA, adapted)

4-42. The following situations (taken from *ASR No. 234*) were ones that were presented to the SEC for their interpretation concerning any effect on the independence of the accountant. Decide in each instance what your ruling would have been had you been asked to make the decision.

a. A large accounting firm employed the son of the president of a very large client as a professional accountant in the local office which performed the continuing audits of financial statements of the client that are filed with the Commission. The son was not a dependent of his parents and did not reside with them.

b. An accounting firm inquired whether its independence would be impaired with respect to the audit of a client's financial statements to be filed with the Commission, if the firm gave summer employment as a professional accountant to the son of the president of the client. The son was a college student who was dependent on his parents and resided with them.

c. An accounting firm employed the son of a major stockholder of an audit client at the beginning level for professional accountants. The son is not dependent on the father, they do not live in the same community or have frequent contact, and the audit assignment would be performed by a branch office other than the branch to which the son is assigned.

d. A partner in an accounting firm who specialized in tax services was the brother-in-law of the treasurer and principal accounting officer of a client company planning to make an initial public offering of its securities. Although the tax partner had no audit responsibilities with regard to the client, he had given tax advice to the client and had reviewed its tax returns. The client and the accounting firm, as well as the residences of the brothers-in-law, were located in the same city.

e. A two-man partnership was merged into another accounting firm and immediately thereafter one of the two partners retired. Under the retirement agreement the retired partner would render without compensation ten hours of professional service per month for three years to the firm in connection with services that would be performed for the former clients of the merged partnership. He would receive percentages of the receipts from the services performed for the former clients and for new clients referred to the firm by him and of collections of the receivables of the merged partnership. The accounting firm inquired whether its independence would be adversely affected with respect to the audit of the financial statements of a new client with no prior connections with either the merged or present firms in which the retired partner had acquired a stock interest, if the firm waived the requirement for professional services by the retired partner.

f. A partner officially retired from his partnership in an accounting firm in 1969 and severed all active relationships with the firm in 1971. At the time of his retirement a fixed settlement for the repayment of his capital account and for retirement benefits was negotiated, the payments for which were completed in March 1974. The retired partner became director of a company in 1973 which proposed, near the end of 1974, to engage the firm to audit its financial statements for the years 1972, 1973, and 1974 to be filed with the Commission.

g. An accountant, who stated that he was a retired partner of a small firm which bears his name, inquired whether the firm could be considered independent with respect to the audit of financial statements to be included in a filing with the Commission by a client in which the accountant holds a financial interest. The accountant was receiving a small salary from the firm and a small participation in its professional fees, which were said to be in lieu of retirement payments.

h. An accounting firm inquired whether its independence would be adversely affected with respect to a client who has a retired partner on its board of directors and on the committee which selected this firm as the auditors. The retired partner utilizes office space and telephone service of the firm and continues to be listed as a partner in the office directory.

i. A computer firm is engaged exclusively in computer processing income tax return data for professional tax return preparers, including various local offices of many national accounting firms. When the computer company was contemplating making a public offering of its stock, an inquiry was made regarding whether an accounting firm which utilized this computer service could be deemed independent with respect to the audits of the financial statements of the computer firm required for the purpose of the public offering.

j. A partner in an accounting firm acquired, and assigned to his minor daughter, a 10 percent voting interest in a corporation which owned a retail store franchised from a proposed client that also operates similar stores directly.

k. Five partners of an accounting firm owned 10 percent of the voting interests in a small business investment company which planned to participate with another small business investment company in a loan to a client of the accounting firm. In conjunction with the loan the lending companies would receive warrants for 5 percent of the common stock of the audit client.

l. An accounting firm provided detailed guidance to personnel of a small client for the daily maintenance of the accounting records, reviewed and corrected such records periodically, and prepared the financial statements, which the client stated were the full responsibility of the accounting firm.

m. When an accounting firm was engaged to perform an audit of the financial statements of a client to be included in the annual report to the Commission, the fee for the prior year audit remained unsettled. As a condition for accepting the currect engagement the accounting firm specified that the prior fee must be paid in full prior to the issuance of the audit report.

n. When an accounting firm was engaged to perform an audit of financial statements to be included in a client's annual report to the Commission, a substantial portion of the prior year fees for audit and other professional services was unpaid. The client gave the firm promissory notes which provided for full payment of the unpaid balance of the fee within one year in equal monthly installments, and two principal stockholders of the client gave oral assurance of payment if the client failed to pay the debt.

o. When an accounting firm was engaged to perform an audit of financial statements to be included in a client's annual report to the Commission, the prior year fees for the annual audit and other audit services had not been paid. The client agreed to pay two thirds of the amount due before issuance of the current audit report and gave the firm a promissory note for the balance to be paid in ten equal weekly installments starting at the approximate date of the audit report.

4-43. A CPA firm has been named as a defendent in a class action by purchasers of the shares of stock of the Newly Corporation. The offering was a public offering of securities within the meaning of the Securities Act of 1933. The plaintiffs alleged that the firm was either negligent or fraudulent in connection with the preparation of the audited financial statements which accompanied the registration statement filed with the SEC. Specifically, they allege that the CPA firm either intentionally disregarded, or failed to exercise reasonable care to discover, material facts which occurred subsequent to January 31, 1980, the date of the auditor's report. The securities were sold to the public on March 16, 1980. The plaintiffs have subpoenaed copies of the CPA firm's working papers. The CPA firm is considering refusing to relinquish the papers, asserting that they contain privileged communication between the CPA firm and its client. The CPA firm will, of course, defend on the merits irrespective of the questions regarding the working papers.

Required:

Answer the following, setting forth reasons for any conclusions stated.

1. Can the CPA firm rightfully refuse to surrender its working papers?

2. Discuss the liability of the CPA firm in respect to events which occur in the period between the date of the auditor's report and the effective date of the public offering of the securities.

(AICPA, adapted)

part two

The Audit Process

Learning Objectives

Study of this chapter is designed to achieve several learning objectives. These include an understanding of:

1. The importance of internal control to the audit function.
2. The nature of internal control and its goals. This includes knowing the elements of an effective system of internal control.
3. The limitations of internal control procedures.
4. How the audit program is affected by the degree of internal control present.
5. How the auditor goes about reviewing, documenting, and evaluating the strength of an internal control system (including questionnaire and flowchart techniques).
6. The use of compliance tests.
7. The auditor's responsibility with regard to errors and irregularities.
8. The auditor's responsibilities if evidence is found of illegal acts by clients.

5

Internal Control

Basic to the audit process is an auditor's review, evaluation, and testing of the client's system of internal control. This analysis of internal control will affect the auditor's decisions regarding the audit program. This chapter discusses in detail internal control and the use of audit programs. Errors and irregularities which are related to internal control are also considered. Finally, there is a discussion of the auditor's actions and responsibilities if evidence is found of illegal acts by clients.

THE IMPORTANCE OF INTERNAL CONTROL

At the beginning of this century most businesses were small and owner-operated. These owner-managers were heavily involved with most of the decision making. As businesses grew in size and complexity professional managers replaced the owner-operators. Professional managers do not have the same firsthand knowledge of all aspects of the business as did the owner-operators. Consequently, they rely heavily on the information supplied to them by the accounting and other information systems. In order to assure management that the information it receives is both reliable and accurate, a system of internal control is developed. The system also helps ensure that assets are secure and that management policy is being followed.

Management is not the only group that looks to the system of internal control for assurance as to the reliability of information. Independent auditors also rely on the system of internal control in determining the timing, nature, and extent of their audit work.

As will be explained in later chapters, independent auditors usually do not verify every transaction that occurs during the year. To do so would be both unnecessary and uneconomical. Auditing standards require only that the auditor obtain "sufficient competent evidential matter" on which to base an opinion. Much of this evidence is obtained by "testing"—examining a representative sample. The extent of testing that is required in a particular circumstance depends on the auditor's evaluation of the effectiveness of the client's system of internal control. For example, usually the more effective the controls, the smaller the sample that will be required to test a year-end account balance.

The auditor frequently uses the phrases "study of internal control," "audit tests," and "audit program," and it is somewhat natural to assume that these are three separate and distinct functions. However they are actually closely interrelated parts, as will be evident in the remainder of this chapter.

The importance of the auditor's evaluation of internal control is recognized by its inclusion as one of the ten generally accepted auditing standards. The second standard of field work requires ". . . a proper study and evaluation of the existing internal control as a basis for reliance thereon and for the determination of the resultant extent of the tests to which auditing procedures are to be restricted."

The Nature of Internal Control

Statement on Auditing Procedure (SAP) No. 33 defined internal control as "the plan of organization and all of the co-ordinate methods and measures adopted within a business to safeguard its assets, check the accuracy and reliability of its accounting data, promote operational efficiency, and encourage adherence to prescribed managerial policies." This definition is extremely broad and recognizes that a system of internal control extends to functions which might not be directly related to either the accounting or financial departments. *SAS No. 1*, section 320.10 notes that the phrases "safeguarding of assets" and "reliability of financial records" were referred to as accounting controls. The phrases "promote operational efficiency" and "encourage adherence to prescribed managerial policies" suggest procedures of a nonaccounting nature (for example, quality control methods in the shop, performance reports for salespeople, statistical studies of plant efficiency, employee training programs, and labor turnover reports). These were usually referred to as administrative or managerial controls.

SAP No. 33 noted that "if the independent auditor believes . . . that certain administrative controls may have an important bearing on the reliability of financial records, he should consider the need for evaluating such controls." *SAS No. 1*, in section 320.12, suggests that this included under accounting controls any administrative control that the auditor believed affected the reliability of the financial statements.

SAS No. 1, in section 320.28, sharpened the definition of accounting control:

> Accounting control comprises the plan of organization and the procedures and records that are concerned with the safeguarding of assets and the reliability of financial records, and consequently are designed to provide reasonable assurance that:
>
> a. Transactions are executed in accordance with management's general or specific authorization.
> b. Transactions are recorded as necessary (1) to permit preparation of financial statements in conformity with generally accepted accounting principles or any other criteria applicable to such statements and (2) to maintain accountability for assets.
> c. Access to assets is permitted only in accordance with management's authorization.
> d. The recorded accountability for assets is compared with the existing assets at reasonable intervals and appropriate action is then taken with respect to any differences.

SAS No. 1, section 320.20, suggests that "transactions are the basic components of business operations." Section 320.21 states that ". . . [the] authorization of transactions refers to management's decision to exchange, transfer, or use assets for specified purposes under specified conditions."

Administrative control is also redefined in *SAS No. 1*, section 320.27, to include (but not be limited to)

> . . . the plan or organization and the procedures and records that are concerned with the decision processes leading to management's authorization of transactions. . . . Such authorization is a management function directly associated with the responsibility for achieving the objectives of the organization and is the starting point for establishing accounting control of transactions.

SAS No. 1, section 320.29, notes that these definitions of accounting and administrative controls ". . . are not necessarily mutually exclusive because some of the procedures and records comprehended in accounting control may also be involved in administrative control."

Management and Internal Control

The independent auditor evaluates internal control and (if engaged to do so) will *assist* management in the design, installation, and modification of the system. *SAS No. 1*, in section 320.31, notes that the *responsibility* for the establishment and the maintenance of internal control rests solely with management. Management must constantly review the system and initiate necessary changes and improvements.

Reasonable Assurance

SAS No. 1, section 320.32, recognizes that "the definition of accounting control comprehends reasonable, but not absolute, assurance that the objectives expressed in it will be accomplished by the system. The concept of reasonable assurance recognizes that the cost of internal control should not exceed the benefits expected to be derived." This cost-benefit relationship should, of course, be recognized by management and taken into consideration when designing a system of internal control.

Limitations of Internal Control

No system of internal control is perfect. There are always limitations that will be inherent in the system. *SAS No. 1*, section 320.34, suggests that such limitations may be due to such factors as: (1) misunderstanding of instructions; (2) errors in judgment; (3) carelessness; (4) distraction or fatigue; and (5) collusion.

FACTORS THAT CHARACTERIZE EFFECTIVE INTERNAL CONTROL

Various factors contribute to effective internal control. Included among these are: (1) personnel who are both competent and of high integrity; (2) a clear-cut and well-conceived organization structure; (3) a well-designed accounting system; (4) limited access to assets by unauthorized persons; and (5) existence of an effective internal auditing staff.

Employees

Particular attention should be given to the influence that client employees and executives may have on the effectiveness of internal control measures. A carefully designed procedure may be weakened or completely nullified by a careless, dishonest, or indifferent employee or executive, or by one who has not been properly trained. Consequently, in evaluating internal controls, the auditor should consider questions such as the following:

1. Have employees and executives been trained in their duties, and do they understand the reasons for performing them?

2. Are they competent to perform their assigned duties?
3. Are they adequately supervised from above and do they adequately supervise subordinates?
4. Are persons who handle funds or other negotiable assets bonded? (In addition to protecting the company against loss, a bonding investigation of employees may identify anyone with a history of being untrustworthy.)

Organization Structure

A clear-cut and well-conceived organizational structure should be designed around the basic functions of the business, and should provide for definite lines of responsibility. Certain items are of special importance in this regard. Each executive and employee of the client who has any effect on transactions of an accounting nature should have a clear understanding of his or her duties and should be competent to discharge them. No individual should handle all aspects of a transaction. Moreover, no individual employee should record a transaction and either have custody of the asset related to the transaction or be involved in the operating function related to the transaction. This segregation of duties helps assure that no one will misappropriate portions of assets and then be able to conceal this fact in the accounting records (see *SAS No. 1*, section 320.36).

Accounting System

One feature of a well-designed accounting system is that it includes a chart of accounts and a clear set of instructions for using the system, usually in the form of an accounting manual. Such a manual should describe in detail the procedures to be followed in processing, authorizing, and approving transactions of an accounting nature.

A well-defined and well-understood system for authorizing transactions also should be maintained. In general, the individual authorizing transactions should: (1) have no interest in the transaction other than to see that it conforms to company policy; (2) be at a level in the organization commensurate with the significance of the transaction (for example, purchase of a large amount of stock should have at least the authorization of a high executive); and (3) be sufficiently knowledgeable so that he or she understands the transactions and their consequences.

Limiting Access to Assets

Safeguarding assets means that only certain authorized personnel should have access to the assets. *SAS No. 1*, section 320.42, suggests

166

that ". . . access to assets includes both direct physical access and indirect access through the preparation or processing of documents that authorize the use or disposition of assets." The number and caliber of personnel to whom access is authorized should be influenced by the nature of the assets and the related susceptibility to loss through errors and irregularities. Limitation of direct access to assets requires appropriate physical segregation and protective equipment or devices.

One excellent means of controlling assets is to make a periodic comparison of book records with the physical assets themselves (see *SAS No. 1*, sections 320.43 to 320.48). Such comparisons, for example, may be made for cash, inventory, securities, and plant and equipment. The frequency of such counts or comparisons should vary with the materiality (or significance) of the assets, the susceptibility of the assets to loss, and the cost of making the comparison. The greater the materiality or susceptibility to loss, the more frequent should be the comparison (see *SAS No. 1*, section 320.46). Comparisons of book records with physical assets are also an important means of determining that transactions are being properly recorded.

Internal Auditing

Many companies have internal audit staffs. Depending on the company, these staffs vary in size and in their background and experience. The internal auditors often are involved in policing the effectiveness of internal control. To the extent they are successful, the internal auditors strengthen the effectiveness of the system of internal control. The effect of a client's internal audit group on the independent auditor's examination will be discussed at a later point in this chapter.

The factors discussed above are principles of internal control in terms of their most fundamental components. Some basic techniques commonly used in establishing internal control are double-entry bookkeeping (which in itself is an important form of internal control), control accounts, perpetual inventory records, periodic reconciliation of book amounts with physical counts (as noted above) or outside sources such as banks, and prenumbered documents together with a procedure for accounting for them. Another technique is the use of the "checks and balances" concept, in which the results of one type of action or the work of a person are checked or proved by independent means; e.g., the total of a "locked-in" register tape having to agree with the physical count of cash in that register, or the reconciliation of bank accounts by employees who are independent of the cash receipts, cash disbursements, accounts receivable, and accounts payable functions.

THE AUDITOR'S STUDY OF INTERNAL CONTROL

The auditor must be familiar with both the accounting controls and the administrative controls of the client's system.[1] However, the accounting controls normally will have the most direct bearing on the design of the audit program.

The auditor's review of internal control is made in order to determine the nature of the internal controls, whether such controls are capable of reasonably assuring that material errors and irregularities are avoided, and whether the prescribed controls have been maintained and are operating effectively. The findings developed during the course of this review determine to a large degree the audit procedures to be applied, the amount of detail testing, and certain other features of the audit program.

The actual steps in the review process are: (1) determining the procedures and controls which have been established by the client; (2) determining which ones the auditor wishes to rely on; (3) determining (by inquiry and by tests of recorded transactions) the extent to which the established procedures and controls upon which the auditor wishes to rely are functioning as intended; (4) evaluating the procedures and controls in order to determine the extent to which auditing procedures must be expanded or may be curtailed; and (5) determining recommendations that may be made to the client for improving the effectiveness of the procedures and controls. Chapter 15 contains a detailed discussion of reporting weaknesses in internal control to the client. This is especially significant since *SAS No. 20*[2] requires auditors to report to the client any material weaknesses in internal control that come to the auditor's attention during an audit.

It is not possible to set forth in specific detail all of the information an auditor seeks in the review of a client's internal controls. This is because no two companies are exactly the same, and even a single company may undergo significant changes in its operations and/or accounting system from one year to the next. There are many variables which must be considered; for instance, two companies with essentially identical plans of internal control may have a differing quality of personnel, materiality (or significance) of assets, and susceptibility of

---

[1] A clear-cut separation of administrative and accounting controls may not always exist in actual practice. For example, in some instances the auditor will not consider the shop production records of the client to be an accounting control, but in other cases these records may be considered as such because of their relationship to inventory records or payroll procedures.

[2] *Statement on Auditing Standards No. 20*, "Required Communication of Material Weaknesses in Internal Accounting Control," American Institute of Certified Public Accountants, 1977.

assets to loss. This would cause the adequacy of the controls of the two firms to be evaluated differently by the auditor.

As a minimum, the information obtained by the auditor would include the company's history, its products and processes, its organization plan (including the duties of employees and their functional relationships), a description of its accounting system, and a description of the internal audit function (if such a function exists).

DOCUMENTATION OF THE REVIEW OF INTERNAL CONTROL

The auditor's study of the client's system of internal control should be documented carefully. This record becomes an integral part of the working papers and is reviewed in subsequent engagements. Changes in internal accounting controls are evaluated by the auditor as to impact on the audit.

Three basic methods of documentation may be used alone or in combination. They are the narrative description, the questionnaire, and the flowchart methods. Each will now be described.

The narrative description of internal control is a description, in the auditor's own words, of the client's internal control system. Mention is made of any weaknesses noted in the review, and a description is made of the procedures and controls which are currently in effect.

As its name implies, the questionnaire method is a series of questions used by the auditor to evaluate the client's system of internal control. The answers are obtained by asking the appropriate person, observing the evidence, and/or conducting a test. An example of a partial internal control questionnaire is included in Appendix A to this chapter.

A third way to document and review a company's systems and procedures is by the use of flowcharts. Flowcharts are schematic drawings which show what happens and when, regarding systems and procedures in an organization. In many circumstances, flowcharts are easier for the auditor to prepare than a narrative description. An example and a further explanation of the flowchart method is presented as Appendix B.

COMPLIANCE TESTING

What client personnel tell the auditor regarding the system of internal control in use may not always be accurate. Formal policy sometimes may not be followed. Consequently, the auditor must always test the extent to which established procedures and controls are functioning *as intended*. These tests are one of two major categories of audit tests and are called *compliance tests*. The second category of audit tests—*substantive tests*—are performed to test or support the validity and propriety of accounting for specific transactions or account balances and thus provide the evidence required by the third standard of field work.[3] *SAS No. 1*, section 320.70 (as amended by SAS No. 23[4]), indicates that substantive tests consist of the following two general classes of auditing procedures: "... *(a)* tests of details of transactions and balances and *(b)* analytical review procedures applied to financial information."

Compliance testing is related to substantive tests. Certain auditing procedures may yield evidence for both compliance tests and substantive tests.

In this chapter we will discuss compliance testing in general terms. Chapters 9 through 13 will discuss compliance tests and substantive tests that can be used in evaluating financial statement accounts.

NATURE OF COMPLIANCE TESTING

The purpose of an audit examination is to determine whether the financial statements are fairly presented "... in conformity with generally accepted accounting principles applied on a basis consistent with that of the preceding period." Thus, auditors must be satisfied that the client's system of internal control will produce reasonably accurate accounting data from which financial statements may be prepared. Before they can formulate an opinion concerning the financial statements, auditors must examine transactions. Specifically, an auditor uses compliance testing to determine whether the internal control system generates reliable and accurate data and may therefore be relied upon. One major benefit of conducting these tests is that the auditor obtains an intimate knowledge of the details of the client's operations. This knowledge not only contributes to the quality of the audit examination, but also enables the auditor to make informed recommendations for improving the client's system of internal control.

It is usually both unnecessary and uneconomical for the auditor to examine all transactions. The theory of sampling or testing (as distinguished from the complete and detailed checking of every transaction included in the accounting records) rests on the assumption that the demonstrated quality of a properly selected sample is indicative of the probable quality of the universe from which the sample is selected. This assumption is valid only when the sample is truly representative of the whole, and extreme care must therefore be used to assure such representativeness. Since the process of sampling tests the whole by

---

[3]*SAS No. 1*, section 320.70.
[4]*Statement on Auditing Standards No. 23*, "Analytical Review Procedures," American Institute of Certified Public Accountants, 1978.

examining only a part, the auditor must be certain that all items in the sample are examined. A detailed audit of only a portion of the sample would yield inconclusive results.

The number of transactions selected, and the selection method, will vary according to each situation. *SAS No. 1*, section 320.61, states, "... tests of compliance ... ideally should be applied to transactions throughout the period under audit because of the general sampling concept that the items to be examined should be selected from the entire set of data to which the resulting conclusions are to be applied. Independent auditors often make such tests during interim work. When this has been done, application of such tests throughout the remaining period may not be necessary." Sampling, statistical or otherwise, is discussed in greater detail in Chapter 7.

Many CPA firms, in order to spread their work load more evenly throughout the year, no longer perform all of the audit work at the end of the fiscal year. Generally, a good deal of work is done during the year under audit. This is often referred to as interim work. Interim work often involves both compliance tests and substantive tests. As to the latter, the auditor often will test the accounts up to a specified interim date and then, during the year-end work, complete the analysis of the accounts.

When compliance tests have been performed during the interim work (at which time transactions for the entire year were not available for testing), the auditor should inquire of appropriate client personnel about any significant changes in internal control from the interim date to the end of the year under examination. The auditor also should determine from the response to that inquiry and from other evidential matter whether additional compliance tests may be necessary or desirable.

When compliance tests are conducted during the interim work, additional testing may or may not be done at year-end. In determining whether or not to test the remaining period, *SAS No. 1*, section 320.61, suggests that the factors to consider "... include *(a)* the results of the tests during the interim period, *(b)* responses to inquiries concerning the remaining period, *(c)* the length of the remaining period, *(d)* the nature and amount of the transactions or balances involved, *(e)* evidence of compliance within the remaining period that may be obtained from substantive tests performed by the independent auditor or from tests performed by internal auditors, and *(f)* other matters the auditor considers relevant in the circumstances."

Results of Interim Work

The less assurance of compliance provided by compliance tests for the first part of the year, the more likely is the auditor to decide that additional testing is desirable. Alternatively, satisfaction with compliance testing completed during interim work combined with continuation of essentially the same internal control procedures would usually call for no change in the audit program.

Inquiries about the Remaining Period

To the extent that any significant changes in internal control have occurred, the auditor's previous compliance tests may no longer be relevant to the remaining period. In these circumstances new tests should be applied. Changes in internal control should be viewed as being significant only if they could have significantly affected the validity of the amounts appearing in specific accounts to be tested in completing the audit. The auditor's inquiries and evaluation of responses should be addressed to specific parts of the internal control system such as those dealing with cash receipts, cash disbursements, sales and receivables, and issuance of credits and allowances rather than to the system as a whole. Strengths in one part of the system normally cannot compensate for weaknesses in another.

Length of the Remaining Period

Only if the auditor believes that the period covered by the interim tests is not representative of the full year will the length of the remaining period, in and of itself, make additional compliance tests necessary. If the auditor considers the period covered by the compliance tests to be representative, additional work is unnecessary unless other factors require it.

Nature and Amount of the Transactions or Balances Involved

In certain cases (e.g., cash balances, investments, and bad debt write-offs) the substantive test may be so thorough and detailed (using data generated outside the company) that very little reliance is placed on the system of internal control in forming the auditor's opinion. In other cases (e.g., cash transactions, sales, and inventories) the auditor may rely importantly on the effectiveness of the company's control procedures, and therefore should become satisfied about controls that were in effect throughout the year.

Evidence from Substantive Tests

The performance of certain substantive tests tells the auditor much about compliance. The examination of vendors' invoices in support of asset or expense account balances, for example, provides an opportu-

172

nity to review approvals on the invoices. To the extent that substantive audit work is performed so as to provide evidence of compliance for the period from the date of interim work to the end of the year, compliance testing that otherwise would be necessary can be reduced.

Other Matters

Such matters as the apparent competence and diligence of the employees who are concerned with internal control procedures, the nature of the industry, the type and quantity of transactions involved, the size of the company, an understaffed condition, the presence or absence of adequate training programs, a domineering personality in a sensitive position, and the auditor's experience with and knowledge of the company, may help determine the desirability of additional compliance tests after the interim work has been completed.

General Comment

In most cases, companies under audit will not have made significant changes in their internal control systems between completion of the interim work and the year-end. Thus, the auditor usually can be satisfied about internal control practices through compliance tests made during the interim work, but must determine that no significant changes in the system have occurred since that time.

Statistical Testing

Compliance tests may be performed using random sampling or subjective judgment sampling. *SAS No. 1*, section 320.62, notes that "tests of compliance may be applied on either a subjective or statistical basis. Statistical sampling may be a practical means of expressing in quantitative terms the auditor's judgment concerning reasonableness and for determining sample size and evaluating sample results on that basis."

APPROACHES TO COMPLIANCE TESTING

The auditor needs to test compliance with a particular internal control only if that control will be relied on in determining the nature, timing, or extent of substantive tests. Thus, to determine which compliance tests to perform, the auditor must determine which particular internal controls will be relied upon in the substantive testing. This point cannot be overemphasized and should be kept in mind in the later sections of this text where there is a discussion of the various tests that the auditor may use.

Compliance tests can be applied to individual transactions (e.g., cash receipts) that are selected randomly from throughout one particular month, a particular group of months, or even from the entire year. Additionally, the tests can be applied to a day's happenings (e.g., cash sales for a day, checks written during a day, daily mail receipts) that are also selected at random from a particular month, a particular group of months, or from the entire year. Finally, the tests may be applied to the happenings of an entire month (e.g., footing a purchases journal) selected randomly from months throughout the year.

Earlier we noted that ideally compliance tests should be applied to transactions throughout the period being audited. However, certain tests by their nature must be performed on a test period or test month coinciding with a client's normal accounting period. For example, in testing a book of original entry (such as the purchases journal) for arithmetic accuracy, the auditor will foot a particular month.

Although the mechanics involved in performing complicance tests vary, there are some general guides which are applicable to most situations. Before beginning a compliance test, the auditor must become familiar with the company's records and procedures. This is usually accomplished during the preliminary review of the system of internal control. If the auditor does not understand the client's procedures, any compliance test will be meaningless. Also, if the auditor does not understand the purpose of a test, time is likely to be wasted by using an approach which fails to meet the objectives of the test. Also the auditor should examine all items included in the sample.

There are two general approaches to compliance testing, each equally pertinent to the auditor's basic objective. These are sometimes designated as the *backward look* and the *forward look*.

With the backward look, auditors begin with a consideration of the whole or final result, the quality of which they wish to prove. Then they work back to the component transactions, selecting from such transactions a representative sample for purposes of detailed testing. The auditors are concerned with whether the transactions which have been recorded properly do, in fact, reflect bonafide transactions. An illustration of the use of this approach would be starting with the ending cash balance and then examining the evidence underlying recorded cash disbursements and cash receipts. Another example would be starting with the final balance in accounts receivable and then substantiating the authority (i.e., authorization) for noncash credits to accounts receivable.

With the forward approach, auditors select from the mass of transactions under examination a sample which is representative of the class as a whole. They begin with the inception of a transaction or at some intermediate point in the flow of a transaction and work forward to the ultimate recording of the transaction in the accounts. In this approach,

174

for each transaction, auditors are concerned with what should have been recorded and whether it is properly reflected both in the books and in the financial statements. A typical illustration of the use of this approach would be the investigation of scrap reports originating at the factory level in order to ascertain that the proceeds from disposal of the scrap have been properly accounted for.

COMPLIANCE TESTS: GENERAL JOURNAL AND GENERAL LEDGER

General journal entries may be used by the client to record transactions which are not included in special journals (e.g., the cash receipts book and other special journals) and to record the adjusting and closing entries. Auditors review the general journal entries for a test period and, in certain instances, for the entire period of the audit. In their examination they note whether the entries have been properly approved and are adequately supported, and they trace the postings to the general ledger.

Usually, auditors pay particular attention to unusual general journal entries because these entries may not be subjected to the controls which normally apply to other transactions of a more routine nature. Entries which reduce assets or increase liabilities often deserve the auditors' special attention. A credit to an asset account may conceal a misappropriation of cash. Fictitious liabilities may be recorded in the general ledger and, at a later date, paid without proper approval. The auditors should review the general ledger accounts and investigate all entries which appear to be unusual in nature or which do not represent postings from usual sources.

Improper footings of the general ledger accounts may be used to conceal the misappropriation of funds. The auditors will normally test the footings of general ledger accounts for the period selected for the compliance tests. If the controls are weak, the tests of the footings may become more extensive as the scope of the examination is increased.

Other compliance tests will be discussed in Chapters 9 through 13.

INTERNAL AUDITING AND THE SCOPE OF THE INDEPENDENT AUDITOR'S EXAMINATION[5]

Earlier in this chapter we noted that the existence of an effective internal auditing staff is a factor in the external auditor's evaluation of

[5] The material in this section is based on *Statement on Auditing Stundards No. 9,* "The Effect of an Internal Audit Function on the Scope of the Independent Auditor's Examination," American Institute of Certified Public Accountants, 1975. Copyright © 1975 by the American Institute of Certified Public Accountants, Inc.

internal control. *SAS No. 9* suggests that the independent auditor should, ". . . in determining the nature, timing, and extent of his own auditing procedures . . ." look at the work performed by the client's internal auditors. If the internal auditor's work may affect the external auditor's work, the latter ". . . should consider the competence and objectivity of internal auditors and evaluate their work."(*SAS No. 9*)

In evaluating competence the external auditor should consider the qualifications of the client's internal audit staff. Factors to be considered include hiring policies, training policies, and the quality of supervision.

In considering objectivity the external auditor should consider the level in the client's organization to which the internal auditor reports. Objectivity is more obtainable if the internal auditor does not report to someone who is responsible for an aspect of the entity audited by the internal auditor.

SAS No. 9 suggests a number of procedures that the independent auditor might employ in evaluating the work of the client's internal auditors. These include:

1. On a test basis examining documentary evidence of the internal auditor's work.
2. Consideration of the appropriateness of the scope of the internal auditor's work and the adequacy of the internal auditor's audit programs.
3. Consideration of the adequacy of the internal auditor's working papers.
4. Consideration of the appropriateness of the internal auditor's conclusions as well as the consistency of the internal auditor's reports with the findings of the work done.
5. Tests of the internal auditor's work by duplicating some tests and/or performing similar tests on a different sample.

SAS No. 9 indicates that the independent auditor may utilize the client's internal auditors to assist directly in performing the audit. This assistance may be in the performance of either substantive tests or compliance tests. In these instances, however, the independent auditor should both supervise and test the internal auditor's work.

THE AUDIT PROGRAM

An audit program is a set of audit procedures specifically designed for each audit. The audit program should include audit procedures that will enable the auditor to express an opinion on the statements taken as a whole. Thus, the audit procedures will include both substantive tests and compliance tests. The auditor follows the program in performing the audit engagement. When each procedure is performed

176

the auditor signs the program to indicate that the work has been accomplished. Appendix C contains a sample audit program for selected compliance tests.

The audit program provides a plan of the work to be done during the examination. However, the program also assists in assigning and distributing the work among the auditors working on the engagement, assists in controlling the work and establishing responsibility, provides a check against omission of necessary procedures, and aids in later reviewing the audit.

The design of the audit program, the study of internal control, and the compliance tests are interrelated elements in the audit, each supplying information which may modify consideration of the other two. None of these elements is fixed or static during the audit, but rather each is subject to continuing appraisal and adjustment as additional information is developed. As a result of the findings during the compliance tests, for example, the program of substantive tests may be altered.

On initial engagements the audit program typically will develop in three stages: (1) the broad phases of the program can be outlined at the time of engagement; (2) other details of the program can be sketched in after the review of internal control and accounting procedures has begun; and (3) procedures on specific phases of the audit can be further challenged and revised as the work progresses.

On recurring engagements, the program for the preceding audit should be studied before preparing the program for the current audit. The current audit program should reflect such modifications as are required by the experience gained in prior examinations and by changes in the business, internal control, or accounting methods of the client.

ERRORS AND IRREGULARITIES[6]

Every year American businesses lose a great deal of money through intentional misdeeds. Fraudulent activities are often concealed by falsifying records; and since part of auditors' work involves examining records and supporting documents, they sometimes uncover these irregularities in the course of the normal examination. On the other hand, the nature of fraud is oftentimes such that it cannot reasonably be expected to be uncovered during the course of a normal audit

[6] This section is based on *Statement on Auditing Standards No. 16,* "The Independent Auditor's Responsibility for the Detection of Errors or Irregularities," American Institute of Certified Public Accountants, 1977. Copyright © 1977 by the American Institute of Certified Public Accountants, Inc.

engagement. This might be the case if there is collusion on the part of key employees of the client.

SAS No. 16 differentiates *errors* from *irregularities*. Errors are defined in *SAS No. 16* as:

> ... unintentional mistakes in financial statements and include mathematical or clerical mistakes in the underlying records and accounting data from which the financial statements were prepared, mistakes in the application of accounting principles, and oversight or misinterpretation of facts that existed at the time the financial statements were prepared.

In contrast *SAS No. 16* defines irregularities as:

> ... intentional distortions of financial statements, such as deliberate misrepresentations by management, sometimes referred to as management fraud, or misappropriations of assets, sometimes referred to as defalcations. ...

Irregularities in financial statements may be due to many causes. *SAS No. 16* suggests they may be the result of:

> ... the misrepresentation or omission of the effects of events or transactions; manipulation, falsification, or alteration of records or documents; omission of significant information from records or documents; recording of transactions without substance; intentional misapplication of accounting principles; or misappropriation of assets for the benefit of management, employees, or third parties. Such acts may be accompanied by the use of false or misleading records or documents and may involve one or more individuals among management, employees, or third parties.

To what degree are independent auditors responsible for the detection of errors and irregularities? As noted in Chapter 1, it is the responsibility of the independent auditor to render an opinion as to the fair presentation of the finamcial statements of a client. *SAS No. 16* notes that:

> ... under generally accepted auditing standards the independent auditor has the responsibility, within the inherent limitations of the auditing process ..., to plan his examination ... to search for errors or irregularities that would have a material effect on the financial statements, and to exercise due skill and care in the conduct of that examination. The auditor's search for material errors or irregularities ordinarily is accomplished by the performance of those auditing procedures that in his judgment are appropriate in the circumstances to form an opinion on the financial statements; extended auditing procedures are required if the auditor's examination indicates that material errors or irregularities may exist. ...

Planning the Examination

SAS No. 16 indicates that "the independent auditor's plan for an examination in accordance with generally accepted auditing standards is influenced by the possibility of material errors or irregularities." In planning the examination, then, the auditor should consider the effectiveness of internal control in reducing the probability (while never eliminating the possibility) that significant errors or irregularities will occur. The auditor also should consider using substantive tests that will reveal existing material errors or irregularities.

In planning the examination the independent auditor should keep in mind the effect that the integrity of the client's management has on the audit. Management may be able to override controls that would normally prevent irregularities. *SAS No. 16* suggests that the following circumstances may make the auditor wary of the possibility of management making a material misstatement or the possibility of management overriding established internal control procedures:

1. The client does not correct material shortcomings in internal control that are practical to correct.
2. Constant turnover in important financial positions (e.g., controller).
3. Constant understaffed situation in the accounting and finance functions with the result being crisis conditions and loss of controls.

Inherent Limitations of an Audit

SAS No. 16 points out that independent audits are subject to certain inherent limitations. These include:

a. The fact that audits are a testing process. (See Chapter 7 for discussion of sampling.) There is always the possibility that material errors or irregularities may not be detected.
b. The risk that "... management's override of internal controls, collusion, forgery, or unrecorded transactions ..." *(SAS No. 16)* may result in material errors or irregularities being missed. *SAS No. 16* takes the position that "unless the auditor's examination reveals evidential matter to the contrary, his reliance on the truthfulness of certain representations [e.g., representations of management concerning the entity's records, confirmations and documents received from third parties] and on the genuineness of records and documents obtained during his examination is reasonable." The independent auditor is not obligated to extend

procedures to look for unrecorded transactions unless there is evidence that such transactions may exist.

The AICPA's position (as stated in *SAS No. 16*) is that "the auditor is not an insurer or guarantor; if his examination was made in accordance with generally accepted auditing standards, he has fulfilled his professional responsibility."

Suspicion of Errors or Irregularities

Material.   If independent auditors suspect errors or irregularities, they must decide whether it would be so material (or significant) as to affect their opinion on the financial statements. In the case of a possible material error or irregularity *SAS No. 16* suggests the following:

1. First discuss the matter with an appropriate member of the client's management who is at a minimum one level higher in the organization than the individuals who may be involved in the error or irregularity.
2. If after this discussion the auditors still feel the error or irregularities may exist, then the auditors should make sure that the board of directors or the audit committee of the board is aware of their suspicions.
3. Also the auditors should gather evidence as to the existence and effect of the suspected errors or irregularities. This might include discussion with the client's legal counsel.

SAS No. 16 suggests that in some cases the auditor may feel that irregularities or errors are present, but the auditor may find it ". . . impractical or impossible to obtain sufficient evidential matter to determine the existence, or related effect, of material errors or possible irregularities, or management may impose a limitation on the scope of the auditor's search for the evidential matter. . . ." In such instances when ". . . the auditor remains uncertain about whether these errors or possible irregularities may materially affect the financial statements, he should qualify his opinion or disclaim an opinion on the financial statements and, depending on the circumstances, consider withdrawing from the engagement, indicating his reasons and findings in writing to the board of directors." *(SAS No. 16)*

Immaterial.   If the independent auditors find errors or irregularities during their examination but conclude that the errors or irregularities are not material enough to affect the opinion, they should refer the matter to a level of the client's management that is at least one level higher than those involved.

ILLEGAL ACTS BY CLIENTS[7]

During the course of an audit, it is possible that the independent auditor may find evidence of possible illegal acts (e.g., bribes, illegal political contributions). *SAS No. 17* ("Illegal Acts by Clients") discusses the independent auditor's actions and responsibilities in such circumstances as well as how much attention, during an audit, an auditor should give to the possibility that illegal acts may have actually occurred.

SAS No. 17 indicates that an audit conducted in accordance with generally accepted auditing standards does not guarantee that all illegal acts will be uncovered. The independent auditor is not an expert in determining what is or is not illegal. However, it can happen in the course of an examination that an auditor may be able to identify an illegal act.

During the course of an audit, evidence is gathered concerning transactions (see Chapter 6 for a complete discussion of evidence). Transactions that appear to be unusual or questionable should raise a question to an auditor about the possibility of an illegal act. *SAS No. 17* mentions procedures and inquiries that may identify illegal acts. For example:

1. Consideration by an auditor of laws and regulations that may directly affect the financial statements (e.g., tax laws).
2. Inquiry of client's management or counsel concerning loss contingencies.
3. Inquiries about the client's compliance with laws and regulations and the client's policies for preventing illegal acts.
4. Examination of the client's internal communications.

Materiality

The independent auditor should consider the materiality of an illegal act. Such a consideration would include an evaluation of possible effects on the financial statements. Illegal acts can conceivably result in fines, penalties, and damages. Material effects should be adequately disclosed in the financial statements.

Once the independent auditor has ascertained that an illegal act has occurred, *SAS No. 17* suggests that

> ... the auditor should report the circumstances to personnel within the client's organization at a high enough level of authority so that appropriate action can be taken by the client with respect to—

---

[7] This section is based on *Statement on Auditing Standards No. 17*, "Illegal Acts by Clients," American Institute of Certified Public Accountants, 1977. Copyright © 1977 by the American Institute of Certified Public Accountants, Inc.

   a. consideration of remedial actions;
   b. adjustments or disclosures that may be necessary in the financial statements;
   c. disclosures that may be required in other documents (such as a proxy statement).

The Auditor's Report

The discovery of the occurrence of an illegal act may result in the independent auditor modifying the audit report. *SAS No. 17* notes that the auditor may be unable to ". . . determine the amounts associated with certain events, taken alone or with similar events, of which he becomes aware, or whether an act is, in fact, illegal, because of an inability to obtain sufficient competent evidential matter. . . . In those circumstances, the auditor should consider the need to qualify his opinion or disclaim an opinion because of the scope limitations. . . ." Alternatively, if the effect of an event is material and is not properly accounted for or disclosed, it may be necessary to give a qualified opinion or adverse opinion. Finally, if the effect of an illegal act on the financial statements cannot be estimated, then the auditor should modify the report in the manner used for disclosing uncertainties (see Chapter 14). If in the situations mentioned above the client is unwilling to accept the appropriate modified report, the auditor should consider withdrawing and reporting the situation to the client's board of directors.

Other Considerations

If an independent auditor finds an illegal act, regardless of the materiality of the act, the auditor must carefully consider management's response, once the matter is brought to their attention. Unless appropriate consideration is given to the reported illegal act, the auditor should consider withdrawing from the engagement or disassociating him or herself from this client.

It is up to the client's management to notify parties other than personnel within the client's organization of the existence of an illegal act. *SAS No. 17* indicates that "generally, the auditor is under no obligation to notify those parties. However, if the auditor considers the illegal act to be sufficiently serious to warrant withdrawing from the engagement, he should consult with his legal counsel as to what other action, if any, he should take."

In 1977, a federal law was passed which prohibits all U.S. companies and their officers, directors, agents, employees, and stockholders (who are acting on behalf of the company) from bribing foreign government or political officials. This law, the Foreign Corrupt Practices Act of 1977, is discussed in Appendix D to this chapter.

APPENDIX A

INTERNAL CONTROL QUESTIONNAIRE (PARTIAL)

INSTRUCTIONS FOR USE

1. This questionnaire has been designed to assist members of the staff in the determination of the adequacy or inadequacy of the client's system of internal control. It does not purport to be complete as regards all engagements and is not intended to preclude the insertion of additional questions which, in the opinion of the user, may be pertinent in considering the methods of internal control employed by a particular client.

2. The questionnaire is to be used subject to the modifications set forth in the succeeding paragraph. If the related examination covers the accounts of a group of companies, a questionnaire will usually be required for each company in the group. Similarly, if the client maintains branch plants and/or offices, a questionnaire should be developed for the head office, as well as for each branch plant or office, to the extent to which the decentralization of the accounting or other office routine renders such questionnaire applicable. For example, where a branch office has no general books of account but carries and records certain cash transactions and maintains a local payroll, only those sections of the questionnaire dealing with such matters should be used.

3. In the case of clients who employ a small number of persons, or who are engaged in certain special activities, such as brokerage firms, banks, etc., it may be found that the questionnaire is either entirely inappropriate or usable only in small part. In such instances it is expected that the matter of internal control will, nevertheless, have the full and adequate consideration of the accountant in charge, and separate supplemental pages should be used when the regular questionnaire is not appropriate.

4. The regular pages of the questionnaire have been prepared with spaces to indicate affirmative or negative answers to the majority of the questions. Each question should be answered by a check mark in the appropriate column, or a reason stated for there being no answer; e.g., "not applicable." This latter may be abbreviated as "N.A." and should be recorded in the "Yes" column.

5. The questions have been so devised that an affirmative answer would indicate a satisfactory degree of internal control. Negative answers should influence the examiner to consider whether, in order to make the questionnaire as informative as possible, such negative answers should be amplified or the related question

covered by a supplemental statement. For example, it may be that a negative answer should be coupled with a statement to the effect that some alternative procedure followed by the client has the same degree of adequate control in the circumstances.

6. The answering of the questions does not complete the investigation of the system of internal control; the accountant in charge must become satisfied, by observation and/or test check, that the procedures indicated by the answers are being carried out in practice.

7. Space is also provided at the end of each section of the questionnaire for notations as to the adequacy or inadequacy of the system as it relates to the particular section. (Use insert pages if necessary.)

8. Major shortcomings in the system as revealed by our survey, before being taken up with the client, should be discussed with the executive in charge, who will decide what action should be taken. Each section of the questionnaire should be signed by the accountant making the survey of that particular phase of the internal control; the questionnaire as a whole should be signed by the accountant in charge and, after a review by the executive in charge of the work, should be filed with the working papers in the permanent file.

9. During subsequent examinations, the questionnaire must be reviewed and brought up to date as follows:

   a. The auditor performing each section of the examination shall take the previously completed questionnaire and in conjunction with and as a part of the examination shall determine what changes, if any, have been made by the client in the system of internal control.

   b. The changes, if few in number for a particular section, will be made by crossing out the original answers and indicating the new answers, and the auditor's verifications in red.

   c. The changes, if numerous in a section, will be made by marking the original page superseded in the comment space provided for subsequent examinations, signing and dating the page and transferring it to the inactive file, and by filling out a revised section of the questionnaire as if it were a part of an original questionnaire and filing it in its proper place.

   d. The auditor, when the review of a section has been completed during each examination, shall sign and date each section, and shall note in the comment space the results of the review, i.e., "No change," "Control strengthened, see comments above," "Control weakened, see comments on supplemental page," and so on, as may be appropriate.

184

e. The in-charge senior and executive shall review the entire questionnaire at each examination date and indicate their review in the appropriate place on the title page.

Internal Control Questionnaire

CLIENT_____

ADDRESS_____

Accountant in charge		Executive	
Signed by:	Date:	Signed by:	Date:
_____	____	_____	____
_____	____	_____	____
_____	____	_____	____
_____	____	_____	____
_____	____	_____	____

I. GENERAL

	Answer Yes	No	Answer Based on Inquiry	Observation	Test

1. Does the client have a chart of organization?

2. Does the client have a chart of accounts?

3. Is the accounting routine set forth in accounting manuals?

4. Do we have copies of such charts and manuals in our permanent file for this client?

5. Does the client have:
   a. A controller?
   b. An internal auditor or audit staff?

6. If internal auditors are employed:
   a. Do they render written reports on the results of their examinations?

I. GENERAL *(continued)*	Answer Yes No	Answer Based on Inquiry Observation Test

I. GENERAL *(continued)*

    b. Are they directly responsible to, and do they report to, an executive officer other than the chief accounting officer? Designate:

    c. Have we reviewed their reports?

7. Is the general accounting department completely separated from:
    a. The purchasing department?
    b. The sales department?
    c. Manufacturing and/or cost departments?
    d. Cash receipts and disbursements?

8. Are all employees who handle cash, securities, and other valuables bonded?

9. Are all such employees required to take regular vacations, their regular duties then being assigned to other employees?

10. Does head office accounting control over branch offices appear to be adequate?

11. Are expenses and costs under budgetary control?

12. Is insurance coverage under the supervision of a responsible official or employee?

13. Are journal entries approved by:
    a. The controller?
    b. Other designated employee?

14. Does the client use standard journal entries for the regularly recurring monthly closing entries?

186

I. **GENERAL** *(continued)*

Answer: Yes / No — Answer Based on Inquiry, Observation, Test

15. Are journal entries adequately explained or supported by vouchers bearing adequate substantiating data?

16. Are periodic financial statements prepared for submission to management?

17. If so, are these sufficiently informative to bring to light abnormal fluctuations in costs, revenues, inventories, etc., and other discrepancies?

18. *a.* List names of officials and employees exercising the function noted:

Treasurer

Secretary

Controller

Internal auditor (chief)

Chief accountant

General ledger bookkeeper

Accounts receivable bookkeeper

Accounts payable bookkeeper

Cashier

Department heads:

Purchasing

Sales

Credit

Cost

Receiving

Shipping

I. GENERAL *(continued)*

	Answer		Answer Based on		
	Yes	No	Inquiry	Observation	Test

18. *a.* List names of officials and employees exercising the function noted *(continued)*

Payroll _____

Personnel _____

Tax _____

b. Is any one of the above, to the best of your information, a relative of any other? — — ___ _____ __

c. If so, who? _____

	Name	Date	Comment
Originally prepared by:	_____	_____	_____
Reviewed in subsequent examination by:	_____	_____	_____
	_____	_____	_____
	_____	_____	_____
	_____	_____	_____

II. CASH RECEIPTS

	Answer		Answer Based on		
	Yes	No	Inquiry	Observation	Test

A. Mail receipts:

1. Is the mail opened by someone other than the cashier or accounts receivable bookkeeper? — — ___ _____ __

2. Does the mail routine prohibit the delivery of unopened mail (other than personal mail) to employees having access to the accounting records? — — ___ _____ __

II. CASH RECEIPTS *(continued)*	Answer		Answer Based on		
	Yes	*No*	*Inquiry*	*Observation*	*Test*

3. *a.* Is a record of the money and checks received prepared by the person opening the mail? __ __ ____ _____ ___

   b. If so, is this record given to someone other than the cashier for independent verification of the amount recorded? __ __ ____ _____ ___

   c. Is this record compared with the cash receipts book regularly? __ __ ____ _____ ___

B. Other receipts:

1. Are the receipts of currency relatively insignificant? __ __ ____ _____ ___

2. Are receipts recorded by cash registers or other mechanical devices? __ __ ____ _____ ___

3. If so, are the machine totals checked independently by the accounting department? __ __ ____ _____ ___

4. Are sales books or receipts books used? __ __ ____ _____ ___

5. If so:

   a. Are the slips or receipts prenumbered? __ __ ____ _____ ___

   b. Are the daily totals and numerical sequence checked independently by the accounting department? __ __ ____ _____ ___

   c. Are unused books safeguarded? __ __ ____ _____ ___

6. If neither of the above methods is in use, is some other adequate system of control in force?
If so, explain. __ __ ____ _____ ___

7. Is there an adequate safeguard against misappropriation of cash through the recording of fictitious discounts or allowances by the cashier? __ __ ____ _____ ___

II. CASH RECEIPTS *(continued)*	*Answer*		*Answer Based on*		
	Yes	*No*	*Inquiry*	*Observation*	*Test*

8. Are miscellaneous receipts, such as from sale of scrap, salvage, etc. reported to the accounting department by the recipient as well as to the cashier?

9. Does the accounting department check such reports against the related cash book entries?

C. General:

1. Are each day's receipts deposited in the bank intact and without delay?

2. Does someone other than the cashier or accounts receivable bookkeeper take the deposits to the bank?

3. Is a duplicate deposit slip checked and held for the auditors by someone other than the employee making up the deposit?

4. Are bank debit advices (such as for N.S.F. checks) delivered directly to a responsible employee (other than the cashier) for investigation?

5. Are the duties of the cashier entirely separate from the recording of notes and accounts receivable?

6. Is the general ledger posted by an employee who is not from the cashier's department?

7. Is the office routine so arranged that the cashier is denied access to the accounts receivable ledgers and monthly statements?

8. Are all other cash funds (i.e., other than cash receipts) and securities handled by someone other than the cashier?

CASH RECEIPTS *(continued)*	*Answer*		*Answer Based on*		
	Yes	*No*	*Inquiry*	*Observation*	*Test*
9. If the cashier handles such funds: *a.* List the items hereunder:					
b. Are such items counted by us during our examination?	__	__	____	_____	__
10. Where branch offices make collections, are such collections deposited in a bank account subject to withdrawal only by the head office?	__	__	____	_____	__
11. Are rents, dividends, interest, and similar revenues adequately controlled in such manner that their nonreceipt would be noted and investigated?	__	__	____	_____	__
12. Is the cashier responsible for the cash receipts from the time they are received in his or her department until they are sent to the bank?	__	__	____	_____	__
13. Are proper physical safeguards and facilities employed to protect cash and cash transactions?	__	__	____	_____	__
14. Does any employee having custody of client funds also have custody of nonclient funds (e.g., credit union, employee benefit association, etc.)?	__	__	____	_____	__

Comment on adequacy of internal control:

	Name	*Date*	*Comment*
Originally prepared by:	_____	_____	_____
Reviewed in subsequent examination by:	_____	_____	_____
	_____	_____	_____
	_____	_____	_____

III. CASH DISBURSEMENTS	Answer		Answer Based on		
	Yes	No	Inquiry	Observation	Test
1. Are all disbursements, except from petty cash, made by check?	—	—	——	——	—
2. Are all checks prenumbered?	—	—	——	——	—
3. Are voided checks properly defaced or mutilated and held available for subsequent inspection?	—	—	——	——	—
4. Are checks required to be countersigned?	—	—	——	——	—
5. *a.* Is the signing of checks in advance prohibited?	—	—	——	——	—
b. Is the countersigning of checks in advance prohibited?	—	—	——	——	—
6. Are authorized signatures limited to officers or employees who have no access to accounting records or to cash?	—	—	——	——	—
7. Is the practice of drawing checks to "cash" or "bearer" prohibited?	—	—	——	——	—
8. If not, are checks so drawn limited to payrolls and/or petty cash reimbursement?	—	—	——	——	—
9. Are monthly bank statements and paid checks received directly by the accounting department?	—	—	——	——	—
10. Are the bank accounts independently reconciled by someone other than the employees who keep the cash records?	—	—	——	——	—
11. Is the sequence of check numbers accounted for when reconciling the bank accounts?	—	—	——	——	—
12. Is the practice of examining paid checks for date, name, cancellation, and endorsement followed by the employee reconciling the bank accounts?	—	—	——	——	—

III. CASH DISBURSEMENTS (continued)	Answer Yes No	Answer Based on Inquiry Observation Test

13. Are vouchers or other supporting documents presented together with the checks submitted for signature? — — —— —— —

14. Do the signers make adequate investigation before signing checks? — — —— —— —

15. If a check-signing machine is in use, are the machine and signature plates kept under effective control? — — —— —— —

16. Are checks mailed out without allowing them to return to the employee who drew the checks or to the accounts payable bookkeeper? — — —— —— —

17. Are the supporting documents impressed with a "paid" stamp or other mark so as to prevent their use for duplicate payment? — — —— —— —

18. Are payroll checks drawn against a separate payroll bank account? — — —— —— —

19. Is the payroll bank account on an imprest basis? — — —— —— —

20. Are dividend checks drawn against a separate dividend bank account? — — —— —— —

21. Are transfers from one bank to another under effective accounting control? — — —— —— —

IV. SECURITY INVESTMENTS

1. Are securities kept in a safe-deposit vault in the name of the client? — — —— —— —

IV. SECURITY INVESTMENTS *(continued)*	Answer Yes No	Answer Based on Inquiry Observation Test

2. If so:
   a. Does access thereto require the signature or presence of two or more designated persons? ___ __ ____ _____ ___
   b. Is a record maintained by the client of visits to the safe-deposit vault? ___ __ ____ _____ ___

3. If not:
   a. Are they kept in safekeeping by an independent person? ___ __ ____ _____ ___
   b. Are they kept in a safe place under control of an officer? ___ __ ____ _____ ___

4. Is a record kept by the accounting or the financial department of each security including certificate numbers? ___ __ ____ _____ ___

5. Are all securities, except "bearer" bonds, in the name of the client? ___ __ ____ _____ ___

6. Are securities periodically inspected and agreed with the record by internal auditors or other designated officers or employees? ___ __ ____ _____ ___

7. Are purchases and sales of securities authorized by:
   a. The board of directors? ___ __ ____ _____ ___
   b. An officer? ___ __ ____ _____ ___
   c. The financial department? ___ __ ____ _____ ___

8. Are securities held for others, or as collateral, recorded and safeguarded in a manner similar to those owned by the client? ___ __ ____ _____ ___

9. Are security investments which have been written off or fully reserved against followed up as to possible realization? ___ __ ____ _____ ___

194

IV. SECURITY INVESTMENTS *(continued)*	Answer Yes No	Answer Based on Inquiry Observation Test

10. Are satisfactory records kept to ensure the proper and prompt receipt of income on securities owned?

Comment on adequacy of internal control:

	Name	Date	Comment
Originally prepared by:	____	____	____
Reviewed in subsequent examination by:	____	____	____
	____	____	____
	____	____	____
	____	____	____

Only a few sections of an internal control questionnaire have been included in this appendix. Other sections of a complete internal control questionnaire might include: petty cash fund; notes and accounts receivable; inventories; properties and patents; notes and accounts payable and long-term debt; capital stocks; sales and shipping; purchases and expenses; and payrolls.

APPENDIX B
THE FLOWCHART METHOD OF DOCUMENTING THE INTERNAL CONTROL SYSTEM

Although flowcharts are common, they are sometimes difficult to understand because of a lack of standardization. The purpose of this appendix is to present a method of preparing flowcharts for inclusion in the audit working papers. The symbols described, except for the IBM symbols "transmittal tape" and "offpage connector," are those adopted by the American National Standards Institute (ANSI X3.5-1970) or those proposed by the International Organization of Standards (ISO). ANSI symbols are consistent with the more numerous ISO symbols.

Information for flowcharts can be obtained in three ways: (1) by interviewing the person responsible for the procedure; (2) by tracing documents through the steps in the procedure; and (3) by questioning each person about the documents he or she possesses, then compiling the procedures for each document. Interviewing the person responsible for the procedure is normally the most expedient course, because the person can usually describe major activities without unnecessary detail. Of course, the auditor must then ascertain that the procedures are, in fact, as described.

The flowcharting conventions to be used are described in Figure 5-1. The heading of a flowchart should normally include:

1. The name of the company.
2. The procedure being analyzed.
3. The person who originally prepared the flowchart.
4. The date of its original preparation.
5. The source of the information.
6. The person approving the chart.
7. The date of approval.

If the chart is subsequently revised, the persons making and approving the revision should also be noted on the chart together with applicable dates.

The flowchart is usually divided into columns separated by double lines. Each column represents an organizational unit, such as Accounting or Sales; or a function, such as Accounts Payable or Billing; or a person, such as Treasurer or Purchasing Agent.

Whether a column represents an organizational unit, a function, or a person depends on the procedure being charted, but each column should identify a distinct area of responsibility. A column at the left should be used for notes.

The flowchart usually is prepared starting at the upper left-hand portion of the page (next to the column for notes), and the movement of documents proceeds left to right and top to bottom unless the arrows direct the reader differently.

To conserve space a column may represent two organizational units, functions, or persons. This is accomplished by subdividing the column as shown in Figure 5-2. Information outside the subdivision—both above and below—is considered to be in the main column.

Crossing intermediate columns with flow lines is acceptable. However, to maintain clarity you may wish to avoid this by using a connector symbol in each column that would be connected by a flow line (Figure 5-3).

196

FIGURE 5–1
Flowchart symbols
Basic Symbols

Input/Output

Indicates the input or output of information. Can be used in place of the document symbol when a document first enters the system for processing (e.g., sales order from customer, customer remittance, invoice).

Process

Operation(s) causing the information to change in some manner without manual assistance (e.g., update of master payroll records or preparation of payroll checks in a computerized payroll system).

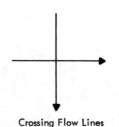

Crossing Flow Lines

If flow lines cross, they are not interrelated.

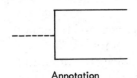

Annotation

For the addition of comments. May be connected to a symbol or a flow line.

Input/Output Symbols

The following specialized symbols may indicate an input/output function as well as the medium for recording or the means of handling information. When appropriate specialized symbols exist, they are used instead of the basic symbols.

Punched Card

Using any kind of punched card in an input/output function.

Card Deck

A deck of punched cards.

FIGURE 5-1 *(continued)*
Input/Output Symbols

Online Storage

Using some sort of on-line storage (e.g., payroll transaction tape loaded on a tape drive under the control of a central processing unit) in an input/output function.

Offline Storage

Storage of information or documents. The method of storage may be indicated inside the symbol (e.g., date, number).

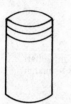

Magnetic Tape

Using magnetic tape in an input/output function.

Magnetic Disc

Using magnetic disc in an input/output function.

Punched Tape

Using punched paper tape in an input/output function.

Document

For example, sales invoice, purchase order, check, remittance advice.

Transmittal Tape

Adding machine tape proof, or similar batch control information.

Processing Symbols

Decision

An operation to determine which path to follow.

198

FIGURE 5-1 *(continued)*
Processing Symbols

The processing of data in a system by manual techniques.

Manual Operation

An operation done on equipment that is not controlled by a computer (e.g., card file sort by customer number).

Auxiliary Operation

Additional Symbols

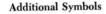

The entry or exit position in a system. Can be used to designate an organization, function, or person.

Terminal

Exit to, or entry from, another part of the flowchart on the same page. Use letters inside symbol to match entry and exit points.

Connector

Exit to, or entry from, another page of the same flowchart. Indicate page number and letter reference inside the symbol.

Offpage Connector

FIGURE 5-2
Column subdivision

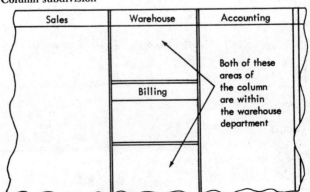

FIGURE 5-3
Connector

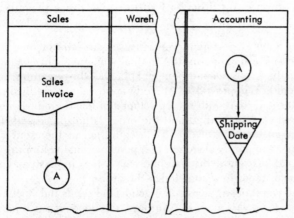

To help locate the connection, it is permissible to indicate
the column connected. This is done by indicating the column heading close to the connector symbol by the flow line.

Explanations should be written within the symbols if space allows.
If there is not sufficient space, use a circled capital letter to key to an
explanatory note. No writing should appear outside the symbols.

The origin and final disposition (e.g., discard, permanent file, or
transfer outside company or column) of each document must be shown
by the appropriate symbol.

Flow lines should not be drawn directly between two documents,
between two journals, or between a document and a journal. If, for
example, two documents are to be compared, they should be shown
flowing to an activity symbol. Flow lines should be horizontal or ver-
tical.

It should be remembered that the keys to a good flowchart are
neatness, proper spacing between the symbols, and a logical approach. A good approach may be outlined as follows:

Step 1. Define exactly what system or procedure is to be charted.
Step 2. Gather the necessary information through observations, interviews, and review of documents.
Step 3. Determine a tentative organization for the chart (i.e.,
whether columns should represent organizational units,
functions, or persons), and draw a rough sketch of the system
or procedures.
Step 4. Draw the flowchart.
Step 5. Trace a hypothetical transaction through the chart (with the
client's personnel, if possible) to see if any mistakes were
made in drawing the chart.

Illustrative Flowchart

The accompanying flowchart (Figure 5–4) was prepared from the following information:

> The Sales Department prepares a six-part sales invoice form from the customer's order and files the order alphabetically by customer. Part 2 is sent to the Credit Department for approval; the remaining parts are held until credit is approved. After credit approval, the credit slip is returned to Sales and filed with the customer's order. If credit is not approved, the customer is notified and the order is not processed. If approved, parts 1 (customer invoice) and 3 (accounting) are then sent to Billing and held in a temporary customer file; part 4 is sent to Shipping as a packing slip; part 5 is sent to the warehouse as a stock request; and part 6 is sent to the customer to acknowledge the order.
>
> The warehouse releases the goods and sends the stock request with the goods to Shipping. In Shipping, the goods are compared with the description on the stock request and units shipped are noted on this request and on the packing slip. Shipping then sends the packing slip with the goods to the customer. The stock request is sent to Billing. For back-ordered items, a back-order report is prepared in Billing after part 5 is returned from Shipping. The report is sent to the Sales Department for preparation of a new sales invoice.
>
> Billing enters the items shipped from the stock request on the customer invoice and accounting copy. Billing also makes extensions and checks them, compares prices to price list, and runs a tape of amounts on the accounting copies. The stock requests are filed numerically and numerical sequence is accounted for at this time. The customer invoice is sent to the customer.
>
> The accounting copy is sent to Accounting where it is posted to the customer ledger card and placed in the invoice file according to shipping date. A tape of invoices is also sent to Accounting where the total is posted to the general ledger sales and accounts receivable control accounts. The total daily posting to customer ledger cards is balanced to the general ledger sales entry. The tape of invoices is discarded after balancing.

APPENDIX C
EXAMPLE OF AUDIT PROGRAM FOR SELECTED COMPLIANCE TESTS

Voucher or Invoice Register

1. Compare vouchers and purchase invoices with register; check for proper classification of charges, approvals, evidence of receipt of goods, arithmetical accuracy, and authority for purchase. (The

FIGURE 3-4

General Corp.

Order, Shipping & Billing Procedure

Williams 11/7/80
Mitchell 11/21/80

NOTES		SALES	BILLING	WAREHOUSE	GENERAL ACCOUNTING

NOTES

The information for this chart was obtained from John Carr, the controller.

A. The sales invoice (SI) is prepared in 6 parts and indicates the customer name, part no. and description of the item. The parts of the sales invoice are as follows:
1. Customer invoice
2. Credit approval
3. Accounting
4. Packing slip
5. Stock request
6. Customer relations acknowledgment.

All parts, except 2, are held until the credit approval copy is returned and marked OK by the Credit Dept.

B. The goods are prepared with descriptions on stock request. Items shipped are marked on the stock request and packing slip included with the goods.

C. The quantities of items shipped are entered on the customer invoice and accounting copy from the stock request. These are checked, priced, and compared to price lists and are added by an adding machine. Copies run from the accounting copies represent the daily billing for the day. The summary is the beginning of invoices accounted for. All other the stock request copy is on file.

D. For back-ordered items, a back order report is prepared and sent to the sales Dept. kept for preparation of the new sales invoice.

SALES

CUSTOMER → SALES ORDER → Prepare Sales Inv. → SALES INVOICE
- 1 Customer Inv.
- 2 Credit Appr. → To Credit → A
- 3 To Shipping → C
- 4 To Warehouse → D
- 5 Stock Ship.
- 6 Cust. Ack. → CUSTOMER

I (from Billing) → Back Order Report → Cust. File (File by #)

SALES ORDER → Cust. File ← From Credit ← B

CREDIT

A → Perform Credit Check → Credit OK? → YES → B / NO → CUSTOMER

BILLING

F (from Shipping) → Cust. File → (merge) → ACCTG SI 3 → To Acctg. → G
- Customer Invoice SI 1 → CUSTOMER
- Stock Request SI 5 → File by # → ADD TAPE → To Acctg. → H
- Prepare Back Order Report → Back Order Report → To Sales → I

WAREHOUSE

D (from Sales) → Release Goods → To Shipping → E

SHIPPING

C (from Sales) → (merge) ← From Whse. E
From Sales Temp.
→ B → Packing Slip SI 4 → Cust. with Goods
→ Stock Request SI 5 → To Billing F

GENERAL ACCOUNTING

G (from Billing) → Post to Cust. Accts. → Balance Daily → ACCTG SI 3 → Ship Daily
H (from Billing) → Post to G/L Sales & A/R Cont. → Balance Daily → ADD TAPE → DISCARD

vouchers or invoices checked may be those selected for supporting cash disbursements or they may be selected as a separate sample.)
2. Check footings of register and trace postings to general ledger and subsidiary ledgers (e.g., expense ledger or inventory ledger).
3. Account for numerical sequence of vouchers.

Payrolls—Plant

1. Check recorded pay against original record of hours worked or units produced (i.e., clock cards, time sheets, etc.).
2. Compare rates paid with authorization forms, union-scale books, or other data.
3. Check computations of payroll, including footings.
4. Check deductions from pay of selected employees.
5. Check personnel records to ascertain whether persons being paid were employees during pay period being tested.
6. Examine paid payroll checks for employees included in test; for cash payments, examine receipts obtained from employees.
7. Be present to observe actual paying off of employees, or make a payoff on a surprise basis; observing or making a payoff is particularly advisable if employees are paid in cash.
8. Trace payroll tested to summaries; trace postings of summary totals to general ledger and subsidiary ledgers; check propriety of distribution.
9. Compare total of payroll tested with recorded disbursement from general bank account for such payroll.
10. Reconcile payroll bank account.
11. Investigate method of handling unclaimed pay.

Sales and Accounts Receivable

1. Account for numerical sequence of invoices and credit memoranda.
2. Prove footings of sales registers and credit-memorandum registers.
3. Trace postings of sales and credit-memorandum registers to general ledger accounts.
4. Trace postings of sales invoices and credit memoranda to customers' accounts.
5. Check sales invoices as to (a) arithmetical accuracy; (b) quantities invoiced, by comparison with shipping records; and (c) unit prices, by comparison with sales contracts or price lists (noting propriety of trade discounts granted).
6. Compare shipping records with sales records or invoices to see that all shipments have been billed.

7. Account for numerical sequence of shipping documents.
8. Review credit memoranda for approval.
9. Check credit memoranda covering returned goods as to *(a)* arithmetical accuracy; *(b)* quantities returned by reference to receiving records; and *(c)* unit prices by reference to original invoice or selling-price records.
10. Compare cash credit postings in customers' accounts with cash receipts records.
11. Inspect credit files in support of accounts charged off as uncollectible.

APPENDIX D

FOREIGN CORRUPT PRACTICES ACT OF 1977

The Foreign Corrupt Practices Act of 1977 prohibits all U.S. companies (as well as their officers, directors, agents, employees, and stockholders who are acting on behalf of the company) from bribing foreign governmental or political officials. Additionally, publicly held corporations are required to meet certain requirements concerning internal control and recordkeeping.

Foreign Corrupt Practices

The law prohibits any U.S. company (or any officer, director, employee, and so on) from using ". . . the mails or any means or instrumentality of interstate commerce corruptly in furtherance of an offer, payment, promise to pay, or authorization of the payment of any money, or offer, gift, promise to give, or authorization of the giving of anything of value to . . ." (1) a foreign official, (2) a foreign political party, (3) an official of a foreign political party, (4) a candidate for foreign political office, or (5) any person who will in turn give the money (etc.) to one of the aforesaid individuals or entities for purposes of influencing a decision or act in order to assist in obtaining or retaining business or directing business to a person. Penalties for conviction of such acts include fines and/or imprisonment.

Internal Control

The law also amends the Securities Exchange Act of 1934 by requiring public companies to

. . . devise and maintain a system of internal accounting control sufficient to provide reasonable assurance that—

204

(i) transactions are executed in accordance with management's general or specific authorization;

(ii) transactions are recorded as necessary (I) to permit preparation of financial statements in conformity with generally accepted accounting principles or any other criteria applicable to such statements, and (II) to maintain accountability for assets;

(iii) access to assets is permitted only in accordance with management's general or specific authorization; and

(iv) the recorded accountability for assets is compared with the existing assets at reasonable intervals and appropriate action is taken with respect to any differences.

These objectives were taken from *SAS No. 1*, section 320.28 and were incorporated in Section 13(b) of the 1934 Act. Consequently, the management and employees of a company may be civilly and criminally liable under the federal securities laws for the failure of a company to maintain a sufficient system of internal control.

Congress intended the internal control section of the law to strengthen the antibribery provisions. However, the internal control provision of the law is not limited to the detection or prevention of foreign bribery.

Recordkeeping

The law also requires public companies to "... make and keep books, records, and accounts, which, in reasonable detail, accurately and fairly reflect the transactions and dispositions of the assets of the issuer. . . ."

Responsibility under the Law

Management. Corporate management is responsible for seeing that corrupt practices do not occur in the conduct of their business. Businesses may want to establish codes of conduct for the guidance of officers and employees in their business activities. Companies (especially those involved in international activities) may want to monitor compliance with such codes of conduct. Internal or external auditors may be asked to review compliance with certain policies.

Management is also responsible for the establishment and maintenance of the system of internal control. This concept was discussed earlier in Chapter 5.

Independent Auditor. An audit of a company conducted by an independent public accountant does not guarantee that an illegal act will be detected. However, *SAS No. 16* notes that the "... auditor's plan for an examination . . . is influenced by the possibility of material errors or irregularities." And *SAS No. 17* says "the auditor should . . . inquire about the client's compliance with laws. . . ." Thus, the auditor may become aware of a violation of the Foreign Corrupt Practices Act and, if so, should follow the course of action outlined in Chapter 5 under "Illegal Acts by Clients."

An AICPA auditing interpretation clearly notes that ". . . there is nothing in the Act or the related legislative history that purports to alter the auditor's duty to his client or the purpose of his study and evaluation of internal accounting control. The Act creates express new duties only for companies subject to the Securities Exchange Act of 1934, not for auditors."[8]

As discussed in Chapter 15, *SAS No. 20* requires the auditor to inform the client of material weaknesses in internal accounting control disclosed during the audit. In communicating with management concerning material weaknesses the auditor should remember that ". . . the standards for determining a violation of the Act may differ from those applied by an auditor in determining material weaknesses. . . ."[9] Thus, ". . . the auditor may wish to include a statement to that effect in any communication concerning internal accounting control."[10] Furthermore, "the auditor should not issue a report that provides assurance on compliance with the internal accounting control provision of the Act."[11]

If an auditor finds a material weakness in internal accounting control, the matter should be discussed with the client's management and legal counsel to determine if the weakness violates the Act.[12] Consideration should be given to corrective action.[13] However, "if management has concluded that corrective action for a material weakness is not practicable, consideration should be given to the reasons underlying that conclusion, including management's evaluation of the costs of correction in relation to the expected benefit to be derived. . . . If it is determined that there has been a violation of the Act and appropriate consideration is not given to the violation, the auditor should consider withdrawing from the current engagement or dissociating himself from any future relationship with the client. . . ."[14]

---

[8] "Scope of Study and Evaluation of Accounting Control and the Foreign Corrupt Practices Act," *Auditing Interpretations—Internal Accounting Control and the Foreign Corrupt Practices Act, The Journal of Accountancy* (October 1978), p. 130.

[9] "Compliance with the Foreign Corrupt Practices Act of 1977," *Auditing Interpretations—Internal Accounting Control and the Foreign Corrupt Practices Act, The Journal of Accountancy* (October 1978), p. 130.

[10] Ibid.

[11] Ibid.

[12] "Material Weakness in Accounting Control and the Foreign Corrupt Practices Act," *Auditing Interpretations—Internal Accounting Control and the Foreign Corrupt Practices Act, The Journal of Accountancy* (October 1978), p. 131.

[13] Ibid.

[14] Ibid.

206

GLOSSARY

Accounting control ". . . comprises the plan of organization and the procedures and records that are concerned with the safeguarding of assets and the reliability of financial records. . . ."[*SAS No. 1*]

Administrative control ". . . the plan of organization and the procedures and records that are concerned with the decision processes leading to management's authorization of transactions. . . . Such authorization is a management function directly associated with the responsibility for achieving the objectives of the organization and is the starting point for establishing accounting control of transactions." [*SAS No. 1*]

Analytic review procedures ". . . substantive tests of financial information made by a study and comparison of relationships among data." [*SAS No. 23*].

Audit program A set of audit procedures specifically designed for each audit. These procedures enable the auditor to express an opinion on the financial statements taken as a whole.

Compliance tests Tests of the extent to which established procedures and controls are functioning as intended.

Errors ". . . unintentional mistakes in financial statements. . . ." [*SAS No. 16*]

Flowcharts (for documenting internal control) Schematic drawings which show what happens and when, regarding systems and procedures in an organization.

Illegal acts by clients Actions such as paying bribes, making illegal political contributions, and other actions which violate the law. [*SAS No. 17*]

Irregularities ". . . intentional distortions of financial statements. . . ." [*SAS No. 16*]

Narrative description (of internal control) A description, in the auditor's own words, of the client's internal control system.

Questionnaire method (of documenting internal control) A series of questions used by the auditor to evaluate the client's system of internal control.

Substantive tests ". . . (a) tests of details of transactions and balances and (b) analytical review procedures applied to financial information." [*SAS No. 1*, as amended by *SAS No. 23*]

QUESTIONS AND PROBLEMS

5–1. What is the independent auditor's responsibility for the client's system of internal control?

5–2. List and describe the various methods used by the auditor to document the internal control review.

5–3. In evaluating the competence of a client's internal auditing staff, the independent auditor will look at several factors. List some of these factors.

5–4. List and discuss four procedures that the independent auditor might employ in evaluating the work of the client's internal auditors.

5–5. What is accounting control?

5-6. What is administrative control?

5-7. What is the concept of "reasonable assurance" as it relates to internal control?

5-8. List some human limitations which can lessen the effectiveness of any system of internal control.

5-9. List some factors that contribute to effective internal control.

5-10. Should the independent auditor be familiar with both accounting controls and administrative controls? Why?

5-11. What are the two major categories of audit tests?

5-12. Name the two common approaches to compliance testing. Explain them.

5-13. Discuss the distinction that *SAS No. 16* makes between error and an irregularity.

5-14. List some possible causes of irregularities in financial statements.

5-15. What should an independent auditor do if he or she suspects the existence of a material error or irregularity? Would your answer change if the auditor suspected the existence of an error or irregularity that was not material?

5-16. List some specific procedures that may identify illegal acts.

5-17. The independent auditor's discovery of the occurrence of an illegal act may result in a modification of the audit report. Discuss these possible modifications.

5-18. Jane Smith, CPA, is a partner of the CPA firm of X, Y, Z, CPAs. During the course of her annual audit of the Small Co., Smith uncovers an illegal act committed by the head of purchasing. Smith reports the act to Small's president and board of directors. Since the effects of the acts are not material, the president and board decide to do nothing. What should Smith do?

5-19. The independent certified public accountant's report, opinion, or certificate as it is variously termed, normally includes the following: ". . . and, accordingly, included such tests of the accounting records . . . as we considered necessary in the circumstances."

Required:

Explain how the accountant determines what tests are necessary and the extent to which they are necessary.

(AICPA, adapted)

5-20. Adherence to generally accepted auditing standards requires, among other things, a proper study and evaluation of the existing internal control. The most common approaches to reviewing the system of internal control include the use of a questionnaire, preparation of a memorandum, preparation of a flowchart, and combinations of these methods.

208

Required:

a. What are the CPAs' objectives in reviewing internal control for an opinion audit?

b. Discuss the advantages to CPAs of reviewing internal control by using:

1. An internal control questionnaire.
2. The memorandum approach.
3. A flowchart.

(AICPA, adapted)

5-21. A company's system of internal control (which consists of accounting and administrative controls) is strengthened by including in the system procedures that have specific functions or purposes. For example, the system of internal control may include a voucher system that provides for all invoices to be checked for accuracy, approved for propriety, and recorded before being paid. The system reduces the likelihood that an invoice will be mislaid or the discount lost, and it provides assurance that improper or unauthorized disbursements are not likely to be made.

Required:

Give the purposes or functions of each of the following procedures or techniques that may be included in a system of internal control, and *explain* how each purpose or function is helpful in strengthening accounting and administrative internal control. (Use your background in this and other courses to answer.)

a. Fidelity bonding of employees.

b. Budgeting of capital expenditures.

c. Listing of mail remittances by the mail department when the mail is opened.

d. Maintaining a plant ledger for fixed assets.

(AICPA, adapted)

5-22. Jordan Finance Company opened four personal loan offices in neighboring cities on January 2, 1980. Small cash loans are made to borrowers who repay the principal with interest in monthly installments over a period not exceeding two years. Ralph Jordan, president of the company uses one of the offices as a central office and visits the other offices periodically for supervision and internal auditing purposes.

Mr. Jordan is concerned about the honesty of his employees. He came to your office in December 1980 and stated, "I want to engage you to install a system to prohibit employees from embezzling cash." He also stated, "Until I went into business for myself I worked for a nationwide loan company with 500 offices and I'm familiar with that company's system of accounting and internal control. I want to describe that system so you can install it for me because it will absolutely prevent fraud."

Required:

a. How would you advise Mr. Jordan on his request that you install the large company's system of accounting and internal control for his firm? Discuss.

b. How would you respond to the suggestion that the new system would prevent embezzlement? Discuss.

c. Assume that in addition to undertaking the systems engagement in 1981, you agreed to examine Jordan Finance Company's financial statements for the year ended December 31, 1980. No scope limitations were imposed.

1. How would you determine the scope necessary to satisfactorily complete your examination? Discuss.

2. Would you be responsible for the discovery of fraud in this examination? Discuss.

(AICPA, adapted)

5-23. The Kowal Manufacturing Company employs about 50 production workers and has the following payroll procedures.

The factory foreman interviews applicants and on the basis of the interview either hires or rejects the applicants. When applicants are hired they prepare a W-4 form (Employee's Withholding Exemption Certificate) and give it to the foreman. The foreman writes the hourly rate of pay for the new employee in the corner of the W-4 form and then gives the form to a payroll clerk as notice that the worker has been employed. The foreman verbally advises the payroll department of rate adjustments.

A supply of blank time cards is kept in a box near the entrance to the factory. Workers take a time card on Monday morning, fill in their name, and note in pencil on the time card their daily arrival and departure times. At the end of the week the workers drop the time cards in a box near the door to the factory.

The completed time cards are taken from the box on Monday morning by a payroll clerk. Two payroll clerks divide the cards alphabetically between them, one taking the A to L section of the payroll and the other taking the M to Z section. The clerks are fully responsible for their section of the payroll. They compute the gross pay, deductions, and net pay, post the details to the employee's earnings records, and prepare and number the payroll checks. Employees are automatically removed from the payroll when they fail to turn in a time card.

The payroll checks are manually signed by the chief accountant and given to the foreman. The foreman distributes the checks to the workers in the factory and arranges for the delivery of the checks to the workers who are absent. The payroll bank account is reconciled by the chief accountant who also prepares the various quarterly and annual payroll tax reports.

Required:

List your suggestions for improving the Kowal Manufacturing Com-

210

pany's system of internal control for the factory hiring practices and payroll procedures.

(AICPA, adapted)

5-24. You have been asked by the board of trustees of a local church to review its accounting procedures. As a part of this review you have prepared the following comments relating to the collections made at weekly services and recordkeeping for members' pledges and contributions.

The church's board of trustees has delegated responsibility for financial management and audit of the financial records to the finance committee. This group prepares the annual budget and approves major disbursements but is not involved in collections or recordkeeping. No audit has been considered necessary in recent years because the same trusted employee has kept church records and served as financial secretary for 15 years.

The collection at the weekly service is taken by a team of ushers. The head usher counts the collection in the church office following each service. He then places the collection and a notation of the amount counted in the church safe. The next morning the financial secretary opens the safe and recounts the collection. He withholds about $100 to meet cash expenditures during the coming week and deposits the remainder of the collection intact. In order to facilitate the deposit, members who contribute by check are asked to draw their checks to "cash."

At their request a few members are furnished prenumbered predated envelopes in which to insert their weekly contributions. The head usher removes the cash from the envelopes to be counted with the loose cash included in the collection and discards the envelopes. No record is maintained of issuance or return of the envelopes, and the use of the envelope system is not encouraged.

Each member is asked to prepare a contribution pledge card annually. The pledge is regarded as a moral commitment by the member to contribute a stated weekly amount. Based upon the amounts shown on the pledge cards, the financial secretary furnishes a letter to requesting members to support the tax deductibility of their contributions.

Required:

Describe the weaknesses and recommend improvements in procedures for:

a. Collections made at weekly services.
b. Recordkeeping for members' pledges and contributions.

(AICPA, adapted)

5-25. Eastern Meat Processing Company buys and processes livestock for sale to supermarkets. In connection with your examination of the company's financial statements, you have prepared the following notes based on your review of procedures:

a. Livestock buyers submit a daily report of their purchases to the plant superintendent. This report shows the dates of purchase and expected delivery, the vendor, and the number, weights, and type of livestock purchased. As shipments are received, any available plant employee counts the number of each type received and places a check mark beside this quantity on the buyer's report. When all shipments listed on the report have been received, the report is returned to the buyer.

b. Vendors' invoices, after a clerical check has been made, are sent to the buyer for approval and returned to the accounting department. A disbursement voucher and a check for the approved amount are prepared in the accounting department. Checks are forwarded to the treasurer for a signature. The treasurer's office sends signed checks directly to the buyer for delivery to the vendor.

c. Livestock carcasses are processed by lots. Each lot is assigned a number. At the end of each day a tally sheet reporting the lots processed, the number and type of animals in each lot, and the carcass weight is sent to the accounting department, where a perpetual inventory record of processed carcasses and their weights is maintained.

d. Processed carcasses are stored in a refrigerated cooler located in a small building adjacent to the employee parking lot. The cooler is locked when the plant is not open, and a company guard is on duty when the employees report for work and leave at the end of their shifts. Supermarket truck drivers wishing to pick up their orders have been instructed to contact someone in the plant if no one is in the cooler.

e. Substantial quantities of by-products are produced and stored, either in the cooler or elsewhere in the plant. By-products are initially accounted for as they are sold. At this time the sales manager prepares a two-part form; one copy serves as authorization to transfer the goods to the customer and the other becomes the basis for billing the customer.

Required:

For each of the lettered notes (a) to (e) above state:
1. What the specific internal control objective(s) should be at the stage of the operating cycle described by the note.
2. The control weaknesses in the present procedures, if any, and suggestions for improvement, if any.

(AICPA, adapted)

5-26. During your audit of the Pientak Corporation for 1980 you find that the corporation plans to install the following purchase order draft system for paying vendors:

a. The corporation will issue a draft in the form of a blank check attached to the purchase order for purchases. The purchase order draft (POD) form will combine a purchase order (upper half of form) with a blank check (lower half of form) and the two documents will be prenumbered with the same number and perforated so that the check can be easily detached.

b. The purchasing department will be responsible for the issuance and the PODs will be valid for a period of 90 days from the date of issuance. Each of eight buyers will maintain a supply of PODs. The supply will be replenished as needed.

c. The cashier's department will maintain a log of the numbers of the PODs given to each buyer. Unissued PODs will be kept in a safe in the cashier's office. The POD form will consist of five parts, which will be distributed as follows:

1. Copy no. 1 will be the purchase order and will be mailed to the vendor.
2. Copy no. 2 will be sent to the receiving department.
3. Copy no. 3 will be sent to the bookkeeping department.
4. Copy no. 4 will be filed numerically in the purchasing department.
5. Copy no. 5 will be kept by the buyer for follow-up purposes.

d. When the purchase order is issued, the buyer will enter the quantity, unit price, extended amount, and the total estimated amount of the order on the upper half of the POD form. The check will be made out in the vendor's name, dated and signed by the buyer. The original of the five-part form will then be mailed to the vendor.

e. Vendors will enter their invoice number, quantity, unit price, and total amount of goods to be shipped in the space provided on the check. When the goods are shipped the vendor will enter the total amount of the shipment on the face of the check and present the completed check to the bank for payment. No partially filled orders will be accepted. Vendors who deliver a quantity less than that ordered must receive a new purchase order for additional quantities to be delivered.

f. The bank will honor the check if it has not matured, stamp it "Paid," and charge the amount to the corporation's general cash account. The bank will send the paid checks to the cashier's department daily. After reviewing the paid checks the cashier's department will prepare an adding machine tape of the amounts and enter the total each day in the cash disbursements journal, debiting Accounts Payable. The paid checks will then be sent to the purchasing department.

g. When the goods are received, the receiving department will compare the quantity of items received to copy no. 2 of the POD, indicate the date the goods are received, initial copy no. 2 and route it to the purchasing department. The purchasing department will match the receiving department's copy no. 2 with the paid POD received from the cashier's department and enter the account distribution on the description section of the check. The extensions of unit prices multiplied by quantities entered by the vendor will be checked and the receiving department's copy no. 2

will be attached to the paid check and the documents sent to the bookkeeping department.

h.   The bookkeeping department will charge the appropriate asset or expense accounts at the time the paid checks are recorded in the accounts payable register. The checks, together with the related receiving reports, will then be filed by vendor.

Required:

1.   The treasurer of the corporation requests your aid in preparing a memorandum informing the bank of the new "POD" procedures. List the instructions that you would recommend be given to the bank regarding the POD bank account and the payment of "POD" checks.

2.   The internal control procedures within the corporation with regard to purchases in general are excellent. Suggest additional internal control measures needed for the use of purchase order drafts and verification of paid and unpaid PODs.

(AICPA, adapted)

5-27.   The customer billing and collection functions of the Robinson Company, a small paint manufacturer, are attended to by a receptionist, an accounts receivable clerk, and a cashier who also serves as a secretary. The company's paint products are sold to wholesalers and retail stores.

The following describes *all* of the procedures performed by the employees of the Robinson Company pertaining to customer billings and collections:

a.   The mail is opened by the receptionist who gives the customers' purchase orders to the accounts receivable clerk. Fifteen to twenty orders are received each day. Under instructions to expedite the shipment of orders, the accounts receivable clerk at once prepares a five-copy sales invoice form which is distributed as follows:

1.   Copy no. 1 is the customer billing copy and is held by the accounts receivable clerk until notice of shipment is received.
2.   Copy no. 2 is the accounts receivable department copy and is held for ultimate posting of the accounts receivable records.
3.   Copies no. 3 and no. 4 are sent to the shipping department.
4.   Copy no. 5 is sent to the storeroom as authority for release of the goods to the shipping department.

b.   After the paint ordered has been moved from the storeroom to the shipping department, the shipping department prepares the bills of lading and labels the cartons. Sales invoice copy no. 4 is inserted in a carton as a packing slip. After the trucker has picked up the shipment the customer's copy of the bill of lading and copy no. 3, on which are noted any undershipments, are returned to the accounts receivable clerk. The company does not "back order" in the event of undershipments; customers are expected to reorder the merchandise. The Robinson Company's copy of the bill of lading is filed by the shipping department.

c.   When copy no. 3 and the customer's copy of the bill of lading are received by the accounts receivable clerk, copies no. 1 and no. 2 are completed by numbering them and inserting quantities shipped, unit prices, extensions, discounts, and totals. The accounts receivable clerk then mails copy no.1 and the copy of the bill of lading to the customer. Copies no. 2 and no. 3 are stapled together.

d. The individual accounts receivable ledger cards are posted by the accounts receivable clerk by a bookkeeping machine procedure whereby the sales register is prepared as a carbon copy of the postings. Postings are made from copy no. 2 which is then filed, along with staple-attached copy no. 3, in numerical order. Monthly the general ledger clerk summarizes the sales register for posting to the general ledger accounts.

e. Since the Robinson Company is short of cash, the deposit of receipts is also expedited. The receptionist turns over all mail receipts and related correspondence to the accounts receivable clerk who examines the checks and determines that the accompanying vouchers or correspondence contains enough detail to permit posting of the accounts. The accounts receivable clerk then endorses the checks and gives them to the cashier who prepares the daily deposit. No currency is received in the mail and no paint is sold over the counter at the factory.

f. The accounts receivable clerk uses the vouchers or correspondence that accompanied the checks to post the accounts receivable ledger cards. The bookkeeping machine prepares a cash receipts register as a carbon copy of the postings. Monthly the general ledger clerk summarizes the cash receipts register for posting to the general ledger accounts. The accounts receivable clerk also corresponds with customers about unauthorized deductions for discounts, freight or advertising allowances, returns, etc., and prepares the appropriate credit memos. Disputed items of large amount are turned over to the sales manager for settlement. Each month the accounts receivable clerk prepares a trial balance of the open accounts receivable and compares the resultant total with the general ledger control account for accounts receivable.

Required:

Discuss the internal control weaknesses in the Robinson Company's procedures related to customer billings and remittances and the accounting for these transactions. In your discussion, in addition to identifying the weaknesses, explain what could happen as a result of each weakness.

(AICPA, adapted)

5-28. You have been engaged by the management of Alden, Inc., to review its internal control over the purchase, receipt, storage, and issue of raw materials. You have prepared the following comments which describe Alden's procedures.

Raw materials, which consist mainly of high-cost electronic components, are kept in a locked storeroom. Storeroom personnel include a supervisor and four clerks. All are well trained, competent, and adequately bonded. Raw materials are removed from the storeroom only upon written or oral authorization of one of the production foremen.

There are no perpetual inventory records; hence, the storeroom clerks do not keep records of goods received or issued. To compensate for the lack of perpetual records, a physical inventory count is taken monthly by the storeroom clerks who are well supervised. Appropriate procedures are followed in making the inventory count.

After the physical count, the storeroom supervisor matches quantities counted against a predetermined reorder level. If the count for a given part is below the reorder level, the supervisor enters the part number on a materials-requisition list and sends this list to the accounts payable clerk. The accounts payable clerk prepares a purchase order for a predetermined reorder quantity for each part and mails the purchase order to the vendor from whom the part was last purchased.

When ordered materials arrive at Alden, they are received by the storeroom clerks. The clerks count the merchandise and agree the counts to the shipper's bill of lading. All vendors' bills of lading are initialed, dated, and filed in the storeroom to serve as receiving reports.

Required:

Describe the weaknesses in internal control and recommend improvements of Alden's procedures for the purchase, receipt, storage, and issue of raw materials.

(AICPA, adapted)

5–29. Name each of the flowchart symbols shown below and describe what each represents.

Flowchart Symbols

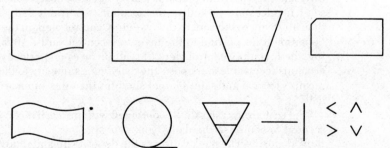

(AICPA, adapted)

5–30. Charting, Inc., a new audit client of yours, processes its sales and cash receipts in the following manner:

a. *Payment on account.* The mail is opened each morning by a mail clerk in the sales department. The mail clerk prepares a remittance advice (showing customer and amount paid) if one is not received. The checks and remittance advices are then forwarded to the sales department supervisor who reviews each check and forwards the checks and remittance advices to the accounting department supervisor.

The accounting department supervisor, who also functions as credit manager in approving new credit and all credit limits, reviews all checks for payments on past due accounts and then forwards all the checks and remittance advices to the accounts receivable clerk who arranges the advices in alphabetical order. The remittance advices are posted directly to the accounts receivable ledger cards. The checks are endorsed by stamp and totaled. The total is posted to the cash receipts journal. The remittance advices are filed chronologically.

After receiving the cash from the previous day's cash sales, the accounts receivable clerk prepares the daily deposit slip in triplicate. The third copy of the deposit slip is filed by date and the second copy and the original accompany the bank deposit.

b. *Sales.* Sales clerks prepare sales invoices in triplicate. The original and second copy are presented to the cashier. The third copy is retained by the sales clerk in the sales book. When the sale is for cash, the customer pays the sales clerk who presents the money to the cashier with the invoice copies.

A credit sale is approved by the cashier from an approved credit list after the sales clerk prepares the three-part invoice. After receiving the cash or approving the invoice, the cashier validates the original copy of the sales invoice and gives it to the customer. At the end of each day the cashier recaps the sales and cash received and forwards the cash and the second copy of all sales invoices to the accounts receivable clerk.

The accounts receivable clerk balances the cash received with cash sales invoices and prepares a daily sales summary. The credit sales invoices are posted to the accounts receivable ledger and then all invoices are sent to the inventory control clerk in the sales department for posting to the inventory control cards. After posting, the inventory control clerk files all invoices numerically. The accounts receivable clerk posts the daily sales summary to the cash receipts journal and sales journal and files the sales summaries by date.

The cash from cash sales is combined with the cash received on account to comprise the daily bank deposit.

c. *Bank deposits.* The bank validates the deposit slip and returns the second copy to the accounting department where it is filed by date by the accounts receivable clerk.

Monthly bank statements are reconciled promptly by the accounting department supervisor and filed by date.

Required:

Prepare a flowchart of the existing system of sales and cash receipts.

(AICPA, adapted)

5-31. The town of Commuter Park operates a private parking lot near the railroad station for the benefit of town residents. The guard on duty issues annual prenumbered parking stickers to residents who submit an application form and show evidence of residency. The sticker is affixed to the auto and allows the resident to park anywhere in the lot for twelve (12) hours if four quarters are placed in the parking meter. Applications are maintained in the guard office at the lot. The guard checks to see that only residents are using the lot and that no resident has parked without paying the required meter fee.

Once a week the guard on duty, who has a master key for all meters, takes the coins from the meters and places them in a locked steel box. The guard delivers the box to the town storage building where it is opened, and the coins are manually counted by a storage department clerk who records the total cash counted on a "Weekly Cash Report." This report is sent to the town accounting department. The storage department clerk puts the cash in a safe and on the following day the cash is picked up by the town's treasurer who manually recounts the cash, prepares the bank deposit slip, and delivers the deposit to the bank. The deposit slip, authenticated by the bank teller, is sent to the accounting department where it is filed with the "Weekly Cash Report."

Required:

Describe weaknesses in the existing system and recommend one or more improvements for each of the weaknesses to strengthen the internal control over the parking lot cash receipts.

(AICPA, adapted)

5-32. The first generally accepted auditing standard of field work requires, in part, that "the work is to be adequately planned." An effective tool that aids the auditor in adequately planning the work is an audit program.

Required:

What is an audit program, and what purposes does it serve?

(AICPA, adapted)

5-33. Select the *best* answer for each of the following items.

    a. When an independent auditor's examination of financial statements discloses special circumstances that make the auditor suspect that fraud may exist, the auditor's *initial* course of action should be to

       1. Recommend that the client pursue the suspected fraud to a conclusion that is agreeable to the auditor.

       2. Extend normal audit procedures in an attempt to detect the full extent of the suspected fraud.

    3. Reach an understanding with the proper client representative as to whether the auditor or the client is to make the investigation necessary to determine if a fraud has in fact occurred.

    4. Decide whether the fraud, if in fact it should exist, might be of such magnitude as to affect the auditor's report on the financial statements.

b. The independent auditor should acquire an understanding of a client's internal audit function to determine whether the work of internal auditors will be a factor in determining the nature, timing, and extent of the independent auditor's procedures. The work performed by internal auditors might be such a factor when the internal auditor's work includes

    1. Verification of the mathematical accuracy of invoices.

    2. Review of administrative practices to improve efficiency and achieve management objectives.

    3. Study and evaluation of internal accounting control.

    4. Preparation of internal financial reports for management purposes.

c. In connection with the examination of financial statements, an independent auditor could be responsible for failure to detect a material fraud if

    1. Statistical sampling techniques were *not* used on the audit engagement.

    2. The auditor planned the work in a hasty and inefficient manner.

    3. Accountants performing important parts of the work failed to discover a close relationship between the treasurer and the cashier.

    4. The fraud was perpetrated by one client employee, who circumvented the existing internal controls.

d. If an auditor was engaged to discover errors or irregularities and the auditor performed extensive detail work, which of the following could the auditor be expected to detect?

    1. Mispostings of recorded transactions.

    2. Unrecorded transactions.

    3. Counterfeit signatures on paid checks.

    4. Collusive fraud.

e. When preparing a record of a client's system of internal accounting control, the independent auditor sometimes uses a systems flowchart, which can *best* be described as a

    1. Pictorial presentation of the flow of instructions in a client's internal computer system.

    2. Diagram which clearly indicates an organization's internal reporting structure.

    3. Graphic illustration of the flow of operations which is used to replace the auditor's internal control questionnaire.

    4. Symbolic representation of a system or series of sequential processes.

f. Internal accounting control comprises the plan of organization and the procedures and records that are concerned with the safeguarding of assets and the
1. Decision processes of management.
2. Reliability of financial records.
3. Authorization of transactions.
4. Achievement of administrative objectives.

g. Effective internal control in a small company that has an insufficient number of employees to permit proper division of responsibilities can *best* be enhanced by
1. Employment of temporary personnel to aid in the separation of duties.
2. Direct participation by the owner of the business in the recordkeeping activities of the business.
3. Engaging a CPA to perform monthly "write-up" work.
4. Delegation of full, clear-cut responsibility to each employee for the functions assigned to each.

h. Which of the following is the *least* likely reason for the auditor's study and evaluation of internal control?
1. To determine the extent of audit testing.
2. To serve as a basis for reliance on the controls.
3. To determine the nature of transactions.
4. To serve as a basis for constructive service suggestions.

(AICPA, adapted)

Learning Objectives

Study of this chapter is designed to achieve several learning objectives. These include an understanding of:

1. The nature of evidence accumulated in an audit.
2. How to evaluate the quantity and quality of audit evidence.
3. The importance of working papers.
4. The nature and purposes of working papers.

6

Evidence and Working Papers

EVIDENCE

As was previously noted in Chapter 1, independent auditors give their opinion on the fair presentation of their client's financial statements. Before rendering such an opinion, auditors investigate the client's accounts to establish a basis for their opinion. In considering the investigative process, the American Accounting Association's Committee on Basic Auditing Concepts, 1969–71, noted that:

> The investigative process may be defined as an inquiry directed at establishing the degree of credibility of propositions. In auditing, the propositions always involve the degree of compliance of some accounting information with established criteria. The accounting information may be financial statements, accounting systems, or other accounting matters. The criteria comprise norms reflecting users' requirements, generally established by appropriate professional groups (e.g., accounting principles by the Accounting Principles Board).[1]

During the investigation, the auditor looks for evidence which will indicate the fair presentation of the client's financial accounts.

The AICPA strongly urges auditors to find sufficient, valid evidence to serve as a basis for their opinion. More specifically, the third standard of field work requires the auditor to obtain sufficient competent evidential matter before issuing an opinion as to the fair presentation of the client's statements. *SAS No. 1*, section 330.02, notes that the auditor both obtains and examines evidence. Furthermore, it is up to the auditor to evaluate the validity of the evidence by the exercise of professional judgment.

---

[1]Joseph A. Silvoso et al., "Report of the Committee on Basic Auditing Concepts," Supplement to vol. 47 of *The Accounting Review*, 1972, p. 35.

222

The Nature of Audit Evidence

Statement on Auditing Standards No. 1, section 330.03, states that "evidential matter supporting the financial statements consists of the underlying accounting data and all corroborating information available to the auditor." The data generated by the accounting system alone (e.g., journals, ledgers, manuals, work sheets) are not sufficient evidence on which to base an opinion. The accounting system might be producing inaccurate financial information. Consequently, the independent auditor must gather other information as well. The degree to which the auditor can rely on the evidence depends upon the source and form of the evidence. Since the auditor's *evaluation* of the fairness of the presentation of the financial statements is heavily dependent upon the *evidence* of their fairness, care must be taken to obtain as much evidence as is needed to make a proper evaluation.

The financial statements of an entity consist of many different accounts and their balances. In attempting to evaluate the fairness of the amounts in each account, the auditor must consider the basic nature of each account. For example, the nature of cash is very different from that of plant and equipment. Both are assets, but the risks of inaccuracies in each differ. Cash is generally much more susceptible to manipulation and theft. Thus, the auditor must, in each case, decide what is the best evidence under the circumstances to assure the fairness of each account.

Sufficient and Competent

Sufficiency of Evidence. Sufficiency is concerned with having enough evidence. It relates to the *quantity* of evidence that the auditor needs in a particular circumstance.

Competence of Evidence. Competence relates to the *qualitative* aspects of evidence. It relates to how qualified the evidence is to be used in the audit.

Statement on Auditing Standards No. 1, section 330.06, suggests that competent evidence is both valid and relevant. While validity may vary with the circumstances, section 330.08 mentions the following three presumptions concerning the validity of evidence:

    a. When evidential matter can be obtained from independent sources outside an enterprise, it provides greater assurance of reliability for the purposes of an independent audit than that secured solely within the enterprise.

    b. When accounting data and financial statements are developed under satisfactory conditions of internal control, there is more assurance as to their reliability than when they are developed under unsatisfactory conditions of internal control.

    c. Direct personal knowledge of the independent auditor obtained through physical examination, observation, computation, and inspection is more persuasive than information obtained indirectly.

Factors Affecting the Evidence to Be Gathered

Degree of Risk. *Statement on Auditing Standards No. 1,* section 330.09, suggests that the amount and kind of evidence required for the auditor to issue an opinion on a set of financial statements is up to the professional judgment of the auditor. Certainly the auditor should consider the degree of risk involved in the particular circumstance. According to section 330.09 of *SAS No. 1,* the degree of risk is a function of ". . . the adequacy of the internal control and susceptibility of the given item to conversion, manipulation, or misstatement. . . ."

Cost. Gathering large amounts of evidence is usually expensive. Consequently, in determining the quantity of evidence needed in a particular circumstance the auditor must consider the cost of gathering it. Section 330.13 of *SAS No. 1* states that "as a guiding rule, there should be a rational relationship between the cost of obtaining evidence and the usefulness of the information obtained. In determining the usefulness of evidence, relative risk may be properly given consideration. The matter of difficulty and expense involved in testing a particular item is not itself a valid basis for omitting the test."

Time. Generally, an audit cannot go on indefinitely. The client may desire that the audited statements be published within some reasonable time after the end of the year. But the auditor must not let a time constraint result in substandard work. Consequently, the auditor must take sufficient time to gather the amount and type of evidence to permit an informed opinion to be issued.

Materiality. The kind and amount of evidence gathered is also related to the materiality or significance of the account under consideration and the materiality of potential errors and irregularities (see *SAS No. 1,* section 330.09). An item is "material" if its omission or misstatement would affect a decision of a knowledgeable investor. What is a material item in a given circumstance is a matter of professional judgment. Items of little materiality require less consideration than do very material accounts. Furthermore, Mautz and Sharaf note that if ". . . some evidence is much more compelling or strong than other evidence, we are led to a conclusion that more compelling evidence is required for material assertions than for assertions that are not material. Note that the important point is not the quantity of evidence but rather the quality of evidence."[2]

---

[2]R. K. Mautz and Hussein A. Sharaf, *The Philosophy of Auditing* (American Accounting Association 1961), p. 104.

Types of Evidence

As noted earlier, there are various types of evidence. In this section they will be discussed in detail.

Data Generated. The data generated by the accounting system is one form of evidence. The extent to which the auditor can rely on this form of evidence is generally a function of the quality of the system of internal control which is present and operating in the entity being examined. If the system of internal control is strong, the auditor may rely to some extent on internally generated data. Thus with a strong system of internal control there is less need for large amounts of other kinds of evidence.

Physical Evidence. The actual physical inspection of many assets is the best evidence as to their existence. However, while inspection may prove existence, it does not tell the auditor very much about the ownership (who has title), quality, or value of the asset. These matters also must be investigated by the auditor.

Documents Created outside the Organization. There are two major types of documentary evidence created outside an organization—(1) evidence sent directly to the auditor and (2) evidence held by the client. Documents created by outside entities and sent directly to the auditor are perhaps the best type of documentary evidence. There is little possibility that client personnel have altered these documents with this sort of evidence. An example of such evidence is the auditor's confirmation of accounts and notes receivable.

Documents created externally but held by the client generally are not as good evidence as those created externally and sent directly to the auditor but often must be used. The degree of validity of such documents will depend on the ease with which client personnel could either alter or create such documents and on their motivation and inclination to do so under the circumstances. Insurance policies, deeds, brokers' advices, and bank debit memos are examples of such evidence.

Documents Internally Generated. Most documents created within a client's organization are generally considered to be a lower quality of evidence than those created outside the organization. The degree of reliance that an auditor can place on internally generated documents will depend in large measure on the quality of the system of internal control which is present and operating in the enterprise. If, for example, no one individual handles payroll transactions from start to finish, more reliance can be placed on payroll documents than in a system in which one individual performs all the payroll work. Generally, if a document is reviewed by one or more employees other than the preparer of the document, there is less chance that the preparer has falsified the document.

Internally generated documents such as canceled checks that circulate outside the client's organization, that are reviewed by outside agencies, and that are then returned to the client, have an added degree of reliability. A canceled check has been reviewed by the payee who endorsed the check as well as by various bank employees. These outside reviews give added reliability to canceled checks.

Examples of internally generated documents that generally do not circulate outside the client's organization include purchase requisitions and the corporate minutes.

Corporate minutes are a record of meetings and actions of the stockholders, board of directors, or any other group entrusted with the responsibility of administering corporate affairs. While the day-to-day, ordinary business activities of the corporation are seldom the subject of corporate resolutions, the minutes may contain authorizations to borrow money or references to contracts which obligate the company, or may mention claims or lawsuits, or authorize dividends, executive compensation, or major capital construction. Authorization for bank signatories and the opening or closing of bank accounts will also ordinarily appear in the minutes. Matters considered and actions taken by the stockholders or board of directors may be important, and the auditor should have knowledge of them. Such knowledge provides evidence of the validity of the accounts affected by board of directors or stockholder actions.

Whenever possible, the auditor should obtain from the client complete copies of minutes of meetings of stockholders, directors, and executive and other important committees. If the copies given to the auditor are not signed, the copies should be compared with the originals to make sure they are both accurate and complete. The minutes should be made a permanent part of the working papers.

If it is not possible to obtain copies of the minutes, the minutes books should be read and abstracted by the auditor. The excerpts recorded for the working papers should be those which have a bearing on the financial statements.

If the client is unwilling to make the minutes available at all, the auditor should explain to the client the importance of the minutes to the audit examination. The client should be told that without such access it might not be possible to issue an opinion on the financial statements.

Comparisons, Ratios, and Computations. Another form of evidence which an auditor may use is the comparison of account balances between and within periods. The auditor is looking for unusual changes that reveal something about the account in question. Likewise, comparison of budgeted to actual figures or industry data to actual figures may reveal useful information requiring further investigation (see *SAS No. 23*).

Identifying changes in financial ratios over time may reveal important financial changes worth investigating. Ratio analysis can have an important supplemental role in the auditor's examination, particularly in larger engagements where a relatively small portion of the direct evidence is reviewed. The use of ratio analysis gives the auditor a broad overview and aids in determining unusual areas where additional inquiry is necessary.[3] The comparisons and ratio analysis mentioned in the current and preceding paragraphs are examples of analytic review procedures.

The auditor will often perform independent calculations as a step in verifying an account balance. Such calculations may take the form of proving the footings on an invoice or independently calculating a payroll accrual.

Oral Evidence. A somewhat weak but useful type of evidence is information supplied by client personnel. An auditor frequently asks client personnel questions which are related to the various accounts under review. The responses to these questions can be very helpful, but as evidence they are not enough. When possible, oral evidence should always be confirmed by other types of evidence. Often the auditor can verify the client's statements by reference to various internally and/or externally created documents.

Written Representations.[4] Written representations are addressed to the auditor, signed by the client (although it is often prepared by the auditor), and contain representations made by the company officials to supplement information the auditor has obtained from the books and records of the company. They are often used to confirm information given to the auditor orally. The written representations are an integral part of the working papers. Among the areas covered are the representations listed in Figure 6-1. The written representations give the company's officials an opportunity to consider whether all important matters have been disclosed to the auditor, and also act as a reminder to the company of its primary responsibility for the fairness of presentation of the financial statements. However, the representations do not in any way relieve the auditor of the responsibility to follow generally accepted auditing standards in the examination.

Written representations may be limited to items that individually or in total are considered material to the financial statements. However materiality limitations would not apply to items 1, 2, and 3 in Figure 6-1. Furthermore, such limitations would not apply to item 6 in Fig-

---

[3]*Uniform CPA Examination*, May 1973, American Institute of Certified Public Accountants, p. 66.

[4]This section is based on *Statement on Auditing Standards No. 19*, "Client Representations", American Institute of Certified Public Accountants, 1977. Copyright © 1977 by the American Institute of Certified Public Accountants, Inc.

FIGURE 6-1
Possible areas for a client's written representations

1. Management acknowledgment of its responsibility for the fair presentation of the financial statements.
2. The availability of all financial records and any related data.
3. The completeness and availability of all minutes of meetings of stockholders, directors, and committees of directors.
4. The nonexistence of errors or unrecorded transactions in the financial statements.
5. Information concerning:
    a. Subsequent events.
    b. Noncompliance with contracts that may affect the financial statements.
    c. Losses from sales commitments.
    d. Obligations to repurchase assets that were previously sold.
    e. Related party transactions.
    f. The reduction of excess or obsolete inventories to net realizable value.
6. Irregularities involving the client's management or employees.
7. Communications that the client received from regulatory agencies relating to noncompliance with, or deficiencies in, financial reporting practices.
8. The client's plans or intentions that may affect the carrying value or classification of assets or liabilities.
9. The disclosure of compensating balances or other arrangements involving restrictions on cash balances, and disclosure of line-of-credit or similar arrangements.
10. The losses from purchase commitments for inventory quantities in excess of requirements or at prices in excess of market.
11. Violations or possible violations of laws or regulations whose effects should be considered for disclosure in the financial statements or as a basis for recording a loss contingency.
12. Other liabilities and gain or loss contingencies that are required to be accrued or disclosed by *FASB Statement No. 5*.
13. Unasserted claims or assessments that the client's lawyer has advised are probable of assertion and must be disclosed in accordance with *FASB Statement No. 5*.
14. Capital stock repurchase options or agreements or capital stock reserved for options, warrants, conversions, or other requirements.
15. Unaudited replacement cost information and interim financial information included in audited financial statements.
16. Other matters that the auditor may determine, based on the circumstances of the engagement, should be included in written representations from management.

Source: Adapted and/or quoted from *Statement on Auditing Standards No. 19*, "Client Representations," American Institute of Certified Public Accountants, 1977. Copyright © 1977 by the American Institute of Certified Public Accountants, Inc.

ure 6–1 in regard to management and to individuals significantly involved in the internal accounting control system.

The written representation should be signed by members of management who the auditor feels are responsible for the matters discussed. Generally this will be the client's chief financial officer and chief executive officer. However, depending on the circumstances, the auditor may want to obtain representations from others. For example, an auditor might want to obtain representations about the completeness of the minutes of board of directors meetings from the person responsible for keeping such records.

Failure of management to comply with an independent auditor's request for written representations on material matters may, due to scope limitations, necessitate the auditor rendering either an opinion that is qualified or a disclaimer of opinion (see Chapter 14 for a discussion of qualifications of opinion and disclaimers of opinions).

The representations should be addressed to the auditor and dated as of the date of the audit report. Such a date reflects the auditor's concern with events that might occur through the date of the report that may necessitate an adjustment or disclosure.

Using an Outside Specialist[5]

During an audit it may be necessary for the independent auditor to employ a person or firm with a particular skill or knowledge (outside of accounting and auditing), to aid in the conduct of an audit. Examples of such outside specialists include geologists, engineers, appraisers, actuaries, and attorneys. The employment of such individuals or firms raises a number of questions including: (1) when an outside specialist is needed; (2) how to select an outside specialist; (3) how to use the findings of an outside specialist; and (4) how the use of an outside specialist can affect the auditor's report.

When a Specialist Is Needed. A situation may arise during an audit in which an independent auditor requires the assistance of a specialist who is not a member of the CPA firm or the client's staff. The use of such a specialist is an audit procedure. For example specialists might be used to provide evidence concerning:

1. Valuation (e.g., jewelry).
2. Amounts derived by actuarial determinations.
3. Interpretations of agreements or regulations.

Selection of a Specialist. The independent auditor should ascer-

---

[5]This section is based on *Statement on Auditing Standards No. 11*, "Using the Work of a Specialist", American Institute of Certified Public Accountants, 1976. Copyright © 1976 by the American Institute of Certified Public Accountants, Inc.

tain the professional reputation and qualifications of the outside
specialist. Considerations should be given to factors such as (1) the
specialist's license or certification, (2) the reputation of the specialist
in his or her profession, and (3) the relationship of the specialist to the
independent auditor's client. It is best for the auditor to employ a
specialist who is independent of the client.

Using the Specialist's Findings.   The independent auditor may use
the work and findings of the outside specialist as evidential matter
supporting some aspect of the financial statements. Consequently, the
auditor should understand the methods and assumptions that the
specialist uses. The auditor should be satisfied that these methods and
assumptions are valid for purposes of providing evidence regarding
the items being tested. The auditor should consider testing any accounting data furnished to the specialist by the client (e.g., payroll
data furnished to an actuary for purposes of making pension plan calculations). Furthermore, the auditor should consider if the conclusions of the specialist substantiate the client's representations. If the
auditor is satisfied that the specialist's work is reasonable, then it is
appropriate to rely on that work. *SAS No. 11* notes that in cases in
which the specialist is related to a client ". . . the auditor should consider performing additional procedures with respect to some or all of
the related specialist's assumptions, methods, or findings to determine that the findings are not unreasonable or engage an outside
specialist for that purpose."

The Auditor's Report.   If the outside specialist's findings support
the client's representations, the independent auditor may conclude
(assuming no other information to the contrary) that sufficient competent evidence has been obtained. In such a situation, an unqualified
opinion should be given without any reference to an outside
specialist.

If there is a material difference between the client's representations and the specialist's findings (or if the auditor believes the
specialist's findings are not reasonable) the auditor should: (1) apply
additional procedures, and (2) if additional procedures are not satisfactory (i.e., do not resolve the matter), consider engaging another
specialist. If it appears that sufficient competent evidence cannot be
obtained, the auditor should ". . . qualify his opinion or disclaim an
opinion because the inability to obtain sufficient competent evidential matter as to an assertion of material significance in the financial
statements constitutes a scope limitation . . . " *(SAS No. 11)*. Alternatively, if the auditor concludes after additional procedures or obtaining a second specialist, that the client's representations are not in
accordance with generally accepted accounting principles, then a
qualified or adverse opinion should be given. Chapter 14 discusses

these various modifications of the auditor's report. If a modified auditor's report is given because of the report or findings of a specialist, the auditor may make reference to and identify the specialist in the audit report.

WORKING PAPERS

Statement on Auditing Standards No. 1, section 338.03 states that:

> Working papers are the records kept by the independent auditor of the procedures ... followed, the tests ... performed, the information ... obtained, and the conclusions ... reached pertinent to [the audit] examination. Working papers, accordingly, may include work programs, analyses, memoranda, letters of confirmation and representation, abstracts of company documents, and schedules or commentaries prepared or obtained by the auditor.

SAS No. 1, section 338.04 states:

> Working papers should fit the circumstances and the auditor's needs on the engagement to which they apply. The factors affecting the independent auditor's judgment as to the quantity, type, and content of the working papers desirable for a particular engagement include (a) the nature of the auditor's report, (b) the nature of the financial statements, schedules, or other information upon which the auditor is reporting, (c) the nature and condition of the client's records and internal controls, and (d) the needs in the particular circumstances for supervision and review of the work performed by any assistants.[6]

Importance of Working Papers

In Chapter 1, it was noted that the third standard of field work requires that the auditor accumulate sufficient competent evidential matter to use as a basis for issuing an opinion on the financial statements. Auditors accumulate on working papers evidence relating to the client's accounts. As a consequence, the working papers support the independent auditor's opinion.

Generally, a client's accounting records are maintained in chronological order, without any regard to the importance of the items. The auditor rearranges the data in the working papers so that the data become more meaningful and useful for the purpose of the audit. Consequently, working papers serve the auditor by being both a useful audit tool as well as a permanent record of the audit work performed.

A review of the audit work gives the CPA firm's partners assurance

---

that the audit work was both accurate and complete. The work of the staff accountant is reviewed by the senior accountant; the senior's work and often much of the staff accountant's work is subsequently reviewed by a manager; and so on. Working papers make these reviews possible. Reviewers need working papers to understand and correlate the work and findings of all of the members of the audit team. In this way, the CPA firm is assured that the opinion is supported by the findings of the audit team.

Filing of Working Papers

Working papers are generally filed in two principal categories: (1) working papers for each year audited (for example the 1980 audit) and (2) working papers in the permanent files. Permanent files normally contain information that will be used by the auditor on the engagement in future years. The information which may be included in the permanent file varies, but usually includes the following:

Notes for future audits.

Copies of letters of recommendation sent to clients.

Copy of articles of incorporation or excerpts therefrom.

Copy of bylaws or excerpts therefrom.

Sample of stock certificates or capital stock provisions.

Copy of indenture or loan agreements, with notations as to sections pertinent to the financial statements.

Computations of surplus restrictions under loan agreements.

Copies of bonus, pension, and profit sharing plans.

Copies of important royalty agreements, leases, management, and other contracts.

Analyses of capital stock and surplus accounts.

Trial balance of stock certificate books.

Depreciation schedules.

Data relating to stock options.

Data relating to income taxes.

Copies of union agreements.

Certain data relating to reports filed and correspondence with regulatory agencies.

Client's accounting manuals and charts of accounts.

Certain minutes of meetings of directors or stockholders.

Agreements with stock exchanges.

Registration statements, proxy statements, etc.

General Content of Working Papers

The audit working papers must contain a complete record of the audit procedures followed in the examination of the financial statements. They should be so clearly prepared that it will be possible at any time to determine from them the conditions present during the audit, the exact audit procedures employed, the evidence collected, and the conclusions reached.

These points are noted in *Statement on Auditing Standards No. 1*, section 338.05, as follows:

> Although the quantity, type, and content of working papers will vary with the circumstances, they generally would include or show:
>
> a. Data sufficient to demonstrate that the financial statements or other information upon which the auditor is reporting were in agreement with (or reconciled with) the client's records.
> b. That the engagement had been planned, such as by use of work programs, and that the work of any assistants had been supervised and reviewed, indicating observance of the first standard of field work.
> c. That the client's system of internal control had been reviewed and evaluated in determining the extent of the tests to which auditing procedures were restricted indicating observance of the second standard of field work.
> d. The auditing procedures followed and testing performed in obtaining evidential matter, indicating observance of the third standard of field work. The record in these respects may take various forms, including memoranda, check lists, work programs, and schedules and would generally permit reasonable identification of the work done by the auditor.
> e. How exceptions and unusual matters, if any, disclosed by the independent auditor's procedures were resolved or treated.
> f. Appropriate commentaries prepared by the auditor indicating his conclusions concerning significant aspects of the engagement.[7]

The working papers should include items that are pertinent to the audit examination. Data that is not relevant should be discarded. For example, if an auditor makes an analysis that proves to be incorrect, the analysis should not be included in the working papers. The inclusion of material that is not relevant tends to "clutter" the working papers and make them more difficult to review and interpret.

Kinds of Working Papers

Working papers generally are comprised of: (1) working trial balance; (2) assembly sheets; (3) adjusting entries; (4) audit schedules; (5)

---

[7]Copyright © 1973, by the American Institute of Certified Public Accountants, Inc.

audit memoranda; and (6) various other items. These items may appear in the current working paper file, in the permanent file, or in both.

Working Trial Balance.   The working trial balance consists of a trial balance of all of the client's accounts usually after the books have been closed for the period under audit. It is common for the client to prepare the working trial balance. The auditor then foots the trial balance and traces the account balances into the general ledger.

The working trial balance is central to the conduct of the audit. The auditor often keeps track of the progress of the audit through use of the trial balance. Adjusting entries suggested by the auditor and approved by the client and the resulting adjusted trial balance are summarized on the working trial balance.

Assembly Sheets.   Often special schedules will be used to show groupings of accounts entering into items appearing on the balance sheet or income statement. They are commonly called assembly sheets. For example, there might be two accounts payable accounts in the general ledger: Accounts Payable—Inventory Suppliers; and Accounts Payable—Other. The accounts payable assembly sheet summarizes the working papers for each of the accounts payable accounts. This facilitates the review of the working papers. A reviewer can easily tie the final balance figures into the working papers.

Adjusting Entries.   As the auditor analyzes the various accounts, items may be found which the auditor believes require adjustment. This may be due to a client error or simply to a difference of opinion regarding the accounting treatment to be accorded a particular item. In many instances the auditor and client may have different approaches to the recording of a transaction. If the difference is material the auditor will propose an adjustment to the client. If the client refuses to record a material adjustment, then the auditor may have to consider modifying the opinion.

If the client approves the adjustment, then the auditor will make an adjusting entry on the work paper related to the account under consideration. The entry will be made both on the working trial balance and also on a separate list of adjusting journal entries kept by the auditor.

Audit Schedules.   Audit schedules are the columnar work sheets which document and facilitate account analyses. These schedules generally make up much of the working paper volume. They consist of numerical data, captions, and explanations arranged to communicate information concerning certain transactions or balances. Since most numerical data in the schedules represent dollar amounts, dollar signs are usually omitted; however, the meaning of all other numbers (dates, percents, pieces, feet, and so on) should either be identified or be self-evident. Captions should be sufficiently descriptive and specific to enable the reader to understand the data.

Audit schedules may relate to: (1) a moment of time; (2) a period of time; or (3) a combination of *both*. A *moment of time analysis* analyzes an account balance as of a specific date (examples are an accounts receivable aging schedule, unexpired insurance analysis, and inventory price test). A *period of time analysis* summarizes transactions in an account or group of accounts for the period under examination (examples are income and expense analyses). It is possible for the auditor to use a *combination* of these analyses. This summarizes transactions during the year together with year-end detail.

Audit Memoranda. Audit memoranda supplement audit schedules by providing written comments on audit procedures or other useful information. Memoranda frequently explain audit procedures and findings.

Other Items. Other items may be included in the working papers. These include various questionnaires, flowcharts, the audit program, and documents created by others. Examples of the latter may include: letters of representation, letters from attorneys, other correspondence, copies of certain client documents, corporate minutes, a copy of bylaws, and a copy of the articles of incorporation.

Preparing Working Papers

Planning. Adequate planning before starting the preparation of a working paper can be helpful in improving its form and content. In recurring audit engagements, the prior year's working papers should be examined to determine whether they might be prepared in a manner that would be easier to prepare or would provide more informative data. The auditor also should be alert to changes in the client's procedures or organization or other circumstances that may require substantial changes in the working papers.

Client Preparation. Whenever possible the auditor should ask the client to prepare selected working papers. Obviously, client-prepared schedules should not be accepted as a part of the working papers until they have been subjected to the same auditing procedures that the auditor would have used if they had been prepared by him or her originally. Generally, verification of client-prepared schedules takes less time than if the auditor prepares the schedule. The time saved reduces the cost of the audit to the client. The fact that the client prepares the schedule always should be noted on the working paper so that a reviewer is aware of the identity of the preparer. Likewise, the auditor's verification procedures should be noted.

Independent auditors often arrange to have the client furnish assistance in locating and having available supporting data and files. This too will save time and reduce the cost of the audit. Similarly, the client's internal auditors may assist the independent auditors in observing the physical inventory. However, any assistance from the client should not be used as a substitute for normal audit procedures nor as a reduction of the requirements for the auditor's independent examination.

Form of Working Papers. Most firms have standards for the form and appearance of their working papers. However, generally each working paper should include the name of the person preparing the paper, the date of its preparation, and the name of the client. Usually working papers also contain the date of the balance sheet (when the audit covers a full year), a descriptive title of the data contained in the working paper, and the name of the individual(s) who reviewed the paper.

Outside Review of Working Papers

The work reflected in the working papers serves as the basis for the opinion rendered by the CPA firm on the financial statements of its clients. Working papers may be subject to review by third parties, sometimes years after the examination has been completed. The following are examples of situations in which such third-party review is possible:

1. Internal Revenue Service field agents may ask to examine the auditor's working papers when the agents are making a tax examination.
2. Parties to a legal action may subpoena and introduce the working papers as evidence.
3. The Securities and Exchange Commission may ask to review working papers in investigations where the SEC believes that inadequate audit procedures have been performed or disclosures are inadequate.
4. When a client merges with another company, the working papers may be reviewed by other independent auditors. Likewise, when an auditor is replaced, the new auditor may review (with the client's permission) the working papers of the old auditor.
5. Working papers may be reviewed by CPAs from one or more other CPA firms as part of a peer (quality) review program.

Arrangement of Working Papers

The completed working papers should be bound in folders. This helps to organize the papers and makes them easier to review. Folders should be marked clearly so that a reader will know whether they are current working paper folders or prior-year or permanent file folders.

The cover of each folder should have a list of the contents. Additionally, one folder should contain a listing of the contents of all of the folders prepared for the current audit.

The current working papers should be bound in some logical order. Consequently, some logical indexing system should be used. Many firms have standardized systems for indexing working papers.

The following is an example of the ordering that might be used in a set of working papers:

Working trial balance.

Adjustments.

Letters of representation.

Correspondence from attorneys.

Pertinent memoranda relating to the audit.

Data relating to commitments—purchase and sale.

Data relating to special matters.

Data relating to review of internal control.

Audit program for the year.

Assets and liabilities in balance sheet order.

Stockholders' equity and minutes.

Operations.

Compliance tests.

Note that the working trial balance is first, followed by the separate schedule of adjusting entries. The balance sheet accounts should be arranged in balance sheet order. Such arrangement gives order to the papers and helps to facilitate their review.

The index systems used by many CPA firms employ numbers, letters, or a combination of letters and numbers. For ease of reference, some firms "key in" the working paper analysis with the working trial balance by use of an indexing system. Thus, the identification number and/or letter given to each working paper is also placed on the corresponding account on the working trial balance. This facilitates cross-referencing between and among working papers.

"Tick" Marks

The auditor should include on each working paper an explanation of the auditing procedures employed. These explanations may be in the form of footnotes. More frequently, this is done by check marks or symbols (commonly called "tick" marks) that are keyed into the footnotes.

Ownership, Custody, and Filing of Working Papers

SAS No. 1, sections 338.06 through 338.08, discusses the ownership, custody, and filing of working papers. The *SAS* notes that the independent auditor owns the working papers. Many states, moreover, have laws that specifically state that the auditor owns the papers. However, the auditor must not use the papers in a manner that would violate the provisions of confidentiality in the code of ethics. Under a legal subpoena, the auditor may have to show the working papers to the proper authorities.

The auditor should retain custody of the working papers. *SAS No. 1*, section 338.08, notes that the auditor should carefully store the papers ". . . for a period of time sufficient to meet the needs of his practice and to satisfy any pertinent legal requirements of records retention."

Working Paper Review

Working papers are the primary evidence of the CPAs' audit work. They must contain sufficient competent evidence to support the claim to the adequacy of the examinations on which the auditors base their report. A planned series of reviews by auditors well qualified to determine the adequacy of the work helps to produce high-quality working papers and reports.

Performing a review of working papers aids in maintaining consistent work quality even though various staff members of the CPA firm have varying degrees of training and experience. The greatest difference between the senior accountant and assistants, and among the various assistants, is their level of on-the-job experience and training rather than their education. For example, an audit team may include an assistant on his or her first examination and others who have from a few weeks' to a few months' experience. Some staff members assigned to the audit team may have worked on previous engagements for the client, or for clients in related fields; while others may have had no previous contact with any similar business. Such differences require that staff persons be assigned only those duties they are competent to perform and that their working papers be thoroughly reviewed in order to determine that the work was properly performed.

GLOSSARY

Assembly sheets Special schedules used to show groupings of accounts entering into items appearing on the balance sheet or income statement.

Audit memoranda Supplement to audit schedules providing written comments on audit procedures or other useful information.

Audit schedules   Columnar work sheets which document and facilitate account analyses.

Competence of evidence   Relates to the qualitative aspects of evidence. It relates to how qualified the evidence is to be used in the audit.

Corporate minutes   A record of meetings and actions of the stockholders, board of directors, or any other group entrusted with the responsibility of administering corporate affairs.

Degree of risk   A function of ". . . the adequacy of the internal control and susceptibility of the given item to conversion, manipulation, or misstatement. . . ." [*SAS No. 1*]

Evidential matter supporting financial statements   ". . . the underlying accounting data and all corroborating information available to the auditor." [*SAS No. 1*]

Outside specialist   A person or firm (outside of accounting and auditing) with a particular skill or knowledge, such as a geologist or engineer [*SAS No. 11*].

Sufficiency of evidence   Concerned with having enough evidence. It relates to the quantity of evidence that the auditor needs in a particular circumstance.

"Tick" marks   Check marks or symbols that are keyed into the footnotes which explain the auditing procedures employed.

Working papers   ". . . the records kept by the independent auditor of the procedures . . . followed, the tests . . . performed, the information obtained, and the conclusions . . . reached pertinent to [the audit] examination." [*SAS No. 1*]

Written representations   Addressed to the auditor, signed by the client (although it is often prepared by the auditor), and contains representations made by the company officials to supplement the information the auditor has obtained from the books and records of the company.

QUESTIONS AND PROBLEMS

6-1.   Why is the independent auditor interested in evidence?

6-2.   List three factors that influence the evidence that the auditor gathers.

6-3.   Student B makes the following statement: "An independent auditor should spare no expense in obtaining evidence. Cost should never be a consideration." Comment on Student B's remark.

6-4.   Compare and contrast the competence of the following in terms of their use as evidence:
   a.   Purchase order.
   b.   Canceled check.
   c.   Confirmation sent directly to the auditor.

6-5.   CPA T is auditing The Large Co. During the audit T asks the president of Large if she (T) can see the minutes of the board of directors meetings for the year under audit. The president says: "No, the minutes are confidential." What should CPA T do?

6-6.   What is the significance of the auditor's working papers?

6-7. What are the two principal categories into which working papers are generally filed?

6-8. *a.* What should an independent auditor employ an outside specialist to aid in the conduct of an audit?

   b. Give some examples of circumstances in which an independent auditor would employ an outside specialist.

6-9. Discuss factors that an independent auditor should consider in ascertaining the professional reputation and qualifications of an outside specialist.

6-10. Is it proper for an independent auditor to question the methods and assumptions used by an outside specialist?

6-11. Discuss written representations. What are they?

6-12. Discuss the content of written representations.

6-13. Who should sign written representations?

6-14. What should an independent auditor do if the client declines to provide any written representations that the auditors feel are important?

6-15. Select the best answer for each of the following items:

   a. The following four statements were made in a discussion of audit evidence between two CPAs. Which statement is *not* valid concerning evidential matter?

      1. "I am seldom convinced beyond all doubt with respect to all aspects of the statements being examined."

      2. "I would not undertake that procedure because at best the results would only be persuasive and I'm looking for convincing evidence."

      3. "I evaluate the degree of risk involved in deciding the kind of evidence I will gather."

      4. "I evaluate the usefulness of the evidence I can obtain against the cost to obtain it."

   b. Evidential matter supporting the financial statements consists of the underlying accounting data and all corroborating information available to the auditor. Which of the following is an example of corroborating information?

      1. Minutes of meetings.

      2. General and subsidiary ledgers.

      3. Accounting manuals.

      4. Work sheets supporting cost allocations.

   c. From which of the following evidence-gathering audit procedures would an auditor obtain *most* assurance concerning the existence of inventories?

      1. Observation of physical inventory counts.

      2. Written inventory representations from management.

      3. Confirmation of inventories in a public warehouse.

      4. Auditor's recomputation of inventory extensions.

   d. The permanent section of the auditor's working papers generally should include:

240

1. Time and expense reports.
2. Names and addresses of all audit staff personnel on the engagement.
3. A copy of key customer confirmations.
4. A copy of the engagement letter.

e. During the course of an audit, an auditor required additional research and consultation with others. This additional research and consultation is considered to be:
1. An appropriate part of the professional conduct of the engagement.
2. A responsibility of the management, not the auditor.
3. A failure on the part of the CPA to comply with generally accepted auditing standards because of a lack of competence.
4. An unusual practice which indicates that the CPA should not have accepted the engagement.

(AICPA, adapted)

6-16. "Independent auditors should always prepare their own working papers. Client personnel should never be allowed to participate in the preparation of working papers." Comment on these statements.

6-17. What are assembly sheets?

6-18. Janice Smith, CPA, has performed the annual audit of Mean, Inc., for a number of years. In January of 1981 the board of directors of Mean, Inc., decided to change auditors. The president of Mean, Inc., asked Smith for all of her working papers for the Mean, Inc., audits. The president asserts that the working papers belong to Mean and he wants to give them to the new auditors.

Required:

a. Comment on the president's assertion that the working papers belong to Mean, Inc.
b. Comment on how the new auditor may gain access to the working papers.

6-19. What is the purpose of reviewing working papers?

6-20. CPA X is ordered by a federal court to submit to the court all of her working papers related to her client, The Small Co. CPA X declines to do so, claiming that the working papers are confidential. Comment.

6-21. I. M. Young is a new staff accountant with Big and Small, a public accounting firm. Young is assigned to his first task—auditing the cash account of a large client. After spending two hours on the task, Young shows the working papers to the senior in charge of the job. The senior finds that Young made some mistakes and consequently has to start over again. Young asks the senior what should be done with the working papers that reflect the incorrect work. The senior says: "They are of no value; however, you might as well include them in the working papers so that someone does not make the same mistake next year."

Required:

Comment on the senior's statement.

6-22. What are the general contents of working papers?

6-23. List the forms or types of working papers that you would expect to find in an ordinary annual audit.

(AICPA, adapted)

6-24. An auditor obtains data from several sources in the course of making an audit. These data and other details are incorporated in the working papers. List six general classifications of the content of working papers which are usually prepared in connection with an annual audit, and give an example of each classification. In classifying the content consider the source of evidence and the auditor's activities.

(AICPA, adapted)

6-25. Discuss the advantages to the CPA of the use of ratios as overall checks in an audit.

(AICPA, adapted)

6-26. An important part of every examination of financial statements is the preparation of audit working papers.

Required:

a. Discuss the relationship of audit working papers to each of the standards of field work.

b. You are instructing an inexperienced staffperson on her first auditing assignment. She is to examine an account. An analysis of the account has been prepared by the client for inclusion in the audit working papers. Prepare a list of the comments, commentaries, and notations that the staffperson should make or have made on the account analysis to provide an adequate working paper as evidence of her examination. (Do not include a description of auditing procedures applicable to the account.)

(AICPA, adapted)

6-27. The source of the accounting evidence is of primary importance in the CPA's evaluation of its quality. Accounting evidence may be classified according to source. List the classifications of accounting evidence according to source, briefly discussing the effect of the source on the reliability of the evidence.

(AICPA, adapted)

6-28. In evaluating the quality of the accounting evidence the CPA also considers factors other than the sources of evidence. List these other factors.

(AICPA, adapted)

6-29. The preparation of working papers is an integral part of the CPA's examination of financial statements. On a recurring engagement a CPA reviews the audit programs and working papers from the prior examination while planning the current examination to determine their usefulness for the current engagement.

Required:

a. 1. What are the purposes or functions of audit working papers?
   2. What records may be included in audit working papers?
b. What factors affect the CPA's judgment of the type and content of the working papers for a particular engagement?
c. To comply with generally accepted auditing standards a CPA includes certain evidence in the working papers—for example, "evidence that the engagement was planned and work of assistants was supervised and reviewed." What other evidence should a CPA include in audit working papers to comply with generally accepted auditing standards?
d. How can a CPA make the most effective use of the preceding year's audit programs in a recurring examination?

(AICPA, adapted)

6–30. You have been assigned by your firm to complete the examination of the 1981 financial statements of Carter Manufacturing Corporation because the senior accountant and his inexperienced assistant who began the engagement were hospitalized after an accident. The engagement is about half completed. Your auditor's report must be delivered in three weeks as agreed when your firm accepted the engagement. You estimate that by utilizing the client's staff to the greatest possible extent you can complete the engagement in five weeks. Your firm cannot assign an assistant to you.

The working papers show the status of work on the examination as follows:

a. *Completed*—Cash, fixed assets, depreciation, mortgage payable, and stockholders' equity.
b. *Completed except as noted later*—Inventories, accounts payable, tests of purchase transactions, and payrolls.
c. *Nothing done*—Trade accounts receivable, inventory receiving cutoff and price testing, accrued expenses payable, unrecorded liability test, tests of sales transactions, payroll deductions test and observation of payroll check distribution, other expenses, analytic review of operations, vouching of December purchase transactions, auditor's report, internal control investigation, internal control letter, minutes, preparation of tax returns, procedural recommendations for management, subsequent events, supervision and review.

Your review discloses that the assistant's working papers are incomplete and were not reviewed by the senior accountant. For example, the inventory working papers present incomplete notations, incomplete explanations, and no cross-referencing.

Required:

a. What field work standards have been violated by the senior accountant who preceded you on this assignment? Explain why you feel the work standards you list have been violated.

    b. In planning your work to complete this engagement you should scan work papers and schedule certain work as soon as possible and also identify work which may be postponed until after the report is rendered to the client.

       1. List the areas on which you should plan to work first, say in your first week of work, and for each item explain why it deserves early attention.
       2. State which work you believe could be postponed until after the report is rendered to the client and give reasons why the work may be postponed.

(AICPA, adapted)

6–31. In examining financial statements, an auditor must judge the validity of the audit evidence obtained.

Required:

Assume that you have evaluated internal control and found it satisfactory.

    a. In the course of the examination, the auditor asks many questions of client officers and employees.
       1. Describe the factors that the auditor should consider in evaluating oral evidence provided by client officers and employees.
       2. Discuss the validity and limitations of oral evidence.
    b. An auditor's examination may include computation of various balance sheet and operating ratios for comparison to prior years and industry averages. Discuss the validity and limitations of ratio analysis.
    c. In connection with the examination of the financial statements of a manufacturing company, an auditor is observing the physical inventory of finished goods, which consist of expensive, highly complex electronic equipment.

    Discuss the validity and limitations of the audit evidence provided by this procedure.

(AICPA, adapted)

6–32. The inspection of the minutes of meetings is an integral part of a CPA's examination of a corporation's financial statements.

Required:

    a. A CPA should determine if there is any disagreement between transactions recorded in the corporate records and actions approved by the corporation's board of directors. Why is this so and how is it accomplished?
    b. Discuss the effect each of the following situations would have on specific audit steps in a CPA's examination and on the auditor's opinion:
       1. The minute book does not show approval for the sale of an

244

important manufacturing division which was consummated during the year.

2. Some details of a contract negotiated during the year with the labor union are different from the outline of the contract included in the minutes of the board of directors.

3. The minutes of a meeting of directors held after the balance sheet date have not yet been written, but the corporation's secretary shows the CPA notes from which the minutes are to be prepared when the secretary has time.

c. What corporate actions should be approved by stockholders and recorded in the minutes of the stockholders' meetings?

(AICPA)

6-33. Auditors frequently refer to the terms "Standards" and "Procedures." Standards deal with measures of the quality of the auditor's performance. Standards specifically refer to the ten generally accepted auditing standards. Procedures relate to those acts that are performed by the auditor while trying to gather evidence. Procedures specifically refer to the methods or techniques used by the auditor in the conduct of the examination.

Required:

List at least eight different types of procedures that an auditor would use during an examination of financial statements. For example, a type of procedure that an auditor would frequently use is the observation of activities and conditions. *Do not discuss specific accounts.*

(AICPA, adapted)

Learning Objectives

Study of the material in this chapter is designed to achieve several learning objectives. These include an understanding of:

Part 1

1. The distinct objectives of testing in auditing—protection, estimation, discovery, correction, and prevention.
2. Statistical concepts including population, sample, mean, variability, normal distribution, precision, and reliability.
3. How to select a statistical sample.
4. How to determine sample size.

Part 2

5. Attribute estimation sampling.
6. Variables estimation sampling.
7. Discovery sampling.
8. How sampling is applied in practice.

7

Audit Sampling—Statistical and Otherwise*

PART 1

Auditing procedures consist principally of tests of the accounting records. The theory of testing accounting records, as distinguished from complete and detailed checking, rests on the assumption that the demonstrated quality or amount of a properly selected sample is indicative of the probable quality or amount of the whole (population) from which the sample is selected. The importance and complexity of deciding: (1) how many items to sample; (2) which items to sample; and (3) how to interpret the results in terms of audit objectives will be emphasized in this chapter.

TESTING OBJECTIVES AND SAMPLING

Several distinct objectives of testing in auditing can be identified. Among these are the following:

Protection Objective. The objective of protective testing is to guard against large dollar value items not being tested. Judgment often leads the auditor to select all items over a stated dollar amount as well as some smaller items.

Estimation Objective. The auditor's objective might be to project the total dollar value of a sample and to compare this estimate with a recorded book value. At other times, the auditor might wish to estimate an occurrence rate of a particular characteristic in a population. In making either kind of estimate, a properly designed statistical sam-

---

*This chapter has been divided into two reading parts for flexibility in assigning the chapter. The glossary and questions and problems have also been labeled as pertaining to Part 1 or Part 2.

248

ple allows the auditor to measure the probable difference between the estimated value and what would be obtained from a 100 percent sample. This difference, described as the *sampling error,* measures the extent to which the quality of a properly selected sample is indicative of the quality of the population.

Discovery Objective. The auditor's objective might be to ascertain whether a precisely defined occurrence does or does not exist with a specified minimum percentage of frequency. Consequently, the sample size must be large enough so that the auditor will have a specified probability of observing at least one example if the occurrences are so existent.

Correction Objective. If the primary purpose in examining individual items is to find the maximum number of errors which exist, this is known as corrective auditing. Corrective auditing usually will be used: (1) when the probable nature or location of errors in the population is known; (2) for special purpose examinations (including defalcation situations); or (3) as an extension of auditing procedures after analyzing errors found in a sample.

The correction objective often will be accomplished by a separate test of certain types of items rather than by an additional random sample selected from the entire population. Note, however, that items *added* judgmentally to a sample to accomplish correction objectives should *not* be combined with the random sample when making statistical evaluation. Otherwise, no valid statistical conclusions could then be drawn because of bias (nonrandomness) in the selection of these added items.

Prevention Objective. The prevention objective is to create in the client's employees uncertainty as to which items are likely to be selected for future testing. In addition to the selected sample, the auditor may wish to choose a few items each year, based on judgment, to ensure that certain types of transactions do not escape audit.

An Example Relating Sampling to Testing Objectives

The following example integrates these five distinct testing objectives into the audit tests. Where appropriate, statistical sampling has been used to help accomplish these objectives.

As a certain auditor begins his examination, he is given "a complete and accurate listing of raw material inventory." It is manually prepared, is 60 pages long, has 50 items to a page, and totals $540,000. The auditor has traced all test counts (counts of inventory made by the auditor while observing physical inventory) to the listing and found only isolated, very minor differences. Items which were test-counted were selected on a random basis from a daily stock status report, which proved to be an acceptable physical representation of the population. Other inventory audit procedures have produced satisfactory results, and the auditor now must determine that unit prices, extensions, and footings are accurate.

With a *protection objective,* the auditor decides to vouch unit prices and test extensions for all items with recorded extensions greater than $2,000 and also to test some smaller amounts. In sampling terminology, the auditor is stratifying the population by creating a 100 percent stratum of all items with recorded extensions of $2,000 or more.

To test unit prices and item extensions under $2,000, the auditor selects a statistical sample and uses dollar value estimation techniques to project an estimate of the population value based on the audited values of the sample items. This is the *estimation objective.*

To pursue the *discovery objective* the auditor would select a sufficiently large sample so that if defined errors (such as a decimal point in the wrong place or "per dozen" extended as "each") occurred with a specified frequency, there would be a certain selected probability (say 95 percent) of finding at least one occurrence in the sample. Finding an occurrence can provide the auditor with information that might help in estimating both the amount and nature of errors in the population.

If such an error were found (for example if 30 dozen of an item priced at $20 each were extended at $600 instead of $7,200) the auditor could "sight-test" extensions of all items with dozens in the quantity column or per dozen in the unit price column. Such sight-testing would serve a *correction objective.* In addition, the 60 page totals could be footed to the grand total and a number of randomly selected pages could be footed. If the list were known to be compiled and footed by several different employees, this might fulfill a *prevention objective* by including in the tests some portion of each person's work.

The preceding example shows that a specific audit problem might require a sampling plan which meets multiple objectives. An ideal sample would integrate all applicable testing objectives, but in practice the auditor must assign relative importance to the several objectives according to the circumstances. The auditor must (1) define the audit objectives of each test, (2) identify how to utilize sampling in testing, and (3) design an appropriate sampling plan.

Statement on Auditing Standards No. 1, section 320.62, states: "Tests of compliance may be applied on either a subjective or statistical basis. Statistical sampling may be a practical means for expressing in quantitative terms the auditor's judgment concerning reasonableness, and for determining sample size and evaluating sample results on that basis." Testing involves risk—the risk that the auditor might draw the wrong conclusions from the evidence gathered. The advantage of statistical sampling is that it enables the auditor to measure the risk of testing and to design sampling plans to control that risk.

In the remainder of this chapter the fundamental concepts of statistical sampling will be reviewed. It is assumed that the reader has taken a basic course in statistics. But to assist the reader in understanding the formulas and methods given, examples of calculations have been included throughout this chapter. If your coverage of statistics is fairly recent you may want to skip the examples which appear in boxes.

SOME STATISTICAL CONCEPTS

Population and Sample

A population is all items in a group being audited, for example, all documents, all accounting entries, or all inventory items in a given situation. *A sample is one or more items selected from that population.* By measuring and projecting certain characteristics of the items in a sample, the auditor obtains information about the population. Characteristics may be either quantitative or qualitative. A single sample can be used to estimate both types of characteristics. The auditor might wish to test the fairness of the total dollar value of accounts receivable as shown per books (quantity) using a *variables* estimation method and to estimate the percentage of entries posted to the wrong account (quality) using an *attribute* estimation method.

Mean

A measure of central tendency that occurs frequently in statistics is the *mean* or average. *The mean is obtained by totaling all the values and dividing by the number of items.* In a finite population of N items with values $X_1, X_2, X_3 \ldots, X_N$, the mean is represented by $\bar{X}$ and is computed as:

$$\bar{X} = \frac{\sum_{j=1}^{N} X_j}{N}$$

where Σ means "take the sum of the following quantities."

The expression $\sum_{j=1}^{N} X_j$ indicates that the values of the population $X_1 + X_2 + \ldots + X_N$ are to be summed; $j = 1$ indicates that the summa-

Example 1—Calculating the Mean

Given: A population of ten items with values of 14, 18, 15, 20, 24, 26, 22, 17, 25, 19.

Solution:

X
14
18
15
20
24
26
22
17
25
19

Formula:

$$\sum_{j=1}^{N} X_j = 200$$

$$\overline{X} = \frac{\sum_{j=1}^{N} X_j}{N}$$

$$\overline{X} = \frac{200}{10} = 20$$

tion should begin with the first item in the population and N indicates that summation should end with the last item in the population.

Variability

The extent to which the values of the items are spread about the mean is called the variability or dispersion of the population. While this variability can be measured in several ways, *the standard deviation is the most commonly used method in statistical sampling.* The population standard deviation is:

$$\sigma_{X_j} = \sqrt{\frac{\sum_{j=1}^{N} (X_j - \overline{X})^2}{N}}$$

where:

σ_{X_j} = Population standard deviation.
$\overline{X}$ = Mean of the population.
N = Number of items in the population.

The standard deviation of a sample is:

$$S_{X_j} = \sqrt{\frac{\sum_{j=1}^{n} (x_j - \overline{x})^2}{n - 1}}$$

Example 2—Calculating the Standard Deviation of the Population

Given: A population of ten items with values of 14, 18, 15, 20, 24, 26, 22, 17, 25, 19

Solution:

X	$\overline{X}$	$X - \overline{X}$	$(X - \overline{X})^2$
14	20*	−6	36
18	20	−2	4
15	20	−5	25
20	20	0	0
24	20	4	16
26	20	6	36
22	20	2	4
17	20	−3	9
25	20	5	25
19	20	−1	1

$$\sum_{j=1}^{N} (X_j - \overline{X})^2 = 156$$

Formula:

$$\sigma_{X_j} = \sqrt{\frac{\sum\limits_{j=1}^{N} (X_j - \overline{X})^2}{N}}$$

$$\sigma_{X_j} = \sqrt{\frac{156}{10}}$$

$$\sigma_{X_j} = 4 \ \text{(approximately)}$$

*This was calculated in Example 1.

where:

S_{X_j} = Sample standard deviation.
$\overline{x}$ = Mean of the sample.
$n - 1$ = Number of items in the sample minus one.

You will notice that the formula for the standard deviation of a sample includes the term $n - 1$ instead of N in the denominator of the fraction. This differs from the formula to compute the standard deviation of a population but the change in the denominator is mathematically necessary to prevent an underestimation of the population standard deviation. Using the standard deviation of the sample's audited values as an estimate of the population standard deviation of the audited values is an extremely important substitution but, unfortunately, the question of why the substitution is made is not always clearly understood. The population standard deviation of audited values would never be known unless all items in the entire population were audited. If this substitution were not made, there would be no way to relate the sample results to conclusions that may be drawn about the population. Because the sample standard deviation of au-

---

Example 3—Calculating the Standard Deviation of a Sample

Given: A sample of four items with values of 14, 15, 22, 25

Solution:

x	$\bar{x}$	$x - \bar{x}$	$(x - \bar{x})^2$
14	19*	−5	25
15	19	−4	16
22	19	3	9
25	19	6	36

$$\sum_{j=1}^{n} (x_j - \bar{x})^2 = 86$$

* The mean of the sample is:

$$\bar{x} = \frac{\sum_{j=1}^{n} x_j}{n}$$

$$\bar{x} = \frac{76}{4} = 19$$

Formula:

$$S_{X_j} = \sqrt{\frac{\sum_{j=1}^{n} (x_j - \bar{x})^2}{n - 1}}$$

$$S_{X_j} = \sqrt{\frac{86}{3}}$$

$$S_{X_j} = 5.3 \text{ (approximately)}$$

---

dited values is used as an estimate of the population standard deviation, the use of $n - 1$ in the denominator is imperative.

Another measure of variability is the range, or the difference between the largest and smallest values in a distribution. Although the range is easier to calculate than the standard deviation, it is not as meaningful a measure of variability. If there is one abnormally high or low value, the range is affected significantly while the standard deviation is not.

The range method often is applied to a small random presample to estimate the standard deviation when establishing the sample size.[1] In the range method, the sample items are distributed into equal groups of either 6 or 7 items each as they are randomly chosen. The range is computed for each group. The group ranges are averaged, then divided by a constant value known as the "d_2 factor" (which is obtained from a table) for group size 6 or 7, whichever is appropriate.

Consider the following population of 50 items (with the highest and lowest values underscored):

---

[1] See Herbert Arkin, *Handbook of Sampling for Auditing and Accounting* (New York: McGraw-Hill Book Company, Inc., 1963), pp. 106–10.

40	60	48	33	66	51	47	53	40	54	50	55	49	56	46
37	40	59	50	29	69	63	44	53	50	53	50	52	43	53
57	47	34	64	50	47	38	60	43	31	67	57	53	45	71
					36	63	50	47	47					

The sum of all these figures is 2,500. The mean is 50 (2,500 ÷ 50). The range is 42 (71-29). The standard deviation can be estimated using the range method as is illustrated in Example 4.

The actual standard deviation for the 50 items can be found by using the formula. In this case (Example 4), it is 9.77. This illustrates that the range method is at best a good approximation. The results of the range method can be manipulated easily by the distribution or concentration of extreme values among the groups. For this reason, it is important to list the items in the same order in which their corresponding random numbers were drawn. This method can be a useful timesaver when only a rough approximation is needed.

Normal Distribution

The distribution shown in Figure 7-1 is called a normal distribution. The important fact about this distribution is that the relative

---

Example 4—Calculating the Estimated Standard Deviation

Items

	1-7	8-14	15-21	22-24 26-29*	30-36	37-43	44-50
	40	53	46	63	53	38	45
	60	40	37	44	57	60	71
	48	54	40	53	47	43	36
	33	50	59	53	34	31	63
	66	55	50	50	64	67	50
	51	49	29	52	50	57	47
	47	56	69	43	47	53	47
Range	33	16	40	20	30	36	35

* The 25th item was ignored so the data could be divided into seven equal groups of seven items each.

$$\text{Average range} = \frac{33 + 16 + 40 + 20 + 30 + 36 + 35}{7} = 30$$

The d_2 factor for a group size of 7 is 2.704 (found in Arkin, p. 108—see footnote 1).

$$\text{Estimated standard deviation} = \frac{\text{Average range}}{d_2 \text{ factor}} = \frac{30}{2.704} = 11.09$$

FIGURE 7-1
Normal distribution with values of $\overline{X}$ = 50, σ = 10 (rounded)

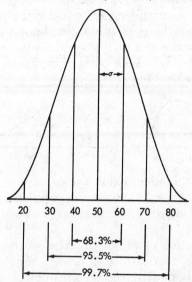

By examining Figure 7-1, you can see that if you randomly select one item from the population, you can predict the probability of its value falling within a certain interval. For example, if
you randomly select one item, you can tell that there is a 68.3 percent chance that its value
will be between 40 and 60 (the mean of 50± one standard deviation), there is a 95.5 percent
chance that it will fall between 30 and 70 (which is the mean of 50 plus or minus two standard
deviations), and a 99.7 percent chance that it will fall between 20 and 80 (the mean plus or
minus three standard deviations).

frequency of any interval of the normal curve (the percentage of observations in the interval) can be determined by knowing only the
mean ($\overline{X}$) and the standard deviation (σ). Normal distribution tables
are available that enable one to calculate the relative frequency of
items falling within any interval when the interval is expressed in
terms of the mean and multiples of the standard deviation. This is
done by measuring the interval from the mean to some point away
from the mean (see Figure 7-1).

Distribution of Sample Means

Suppose that several random samples, each containing the same
number of items, were drawn from the same population, and that the
mean was calculated for each sample. These means could be tabulated
and graphed as a *frequency distribution* (a chart or table that shows
the number of items in each class). One can refer to the population and
distribution of sample means in the same sense as one refers to the

population and distribution of sample items. With large sample sizes, the frequency distribution of sample means is approximately normal; with the mean of all the sample means equal to the population mean. This is true even when the population distribution is skewed which indicates that the frequency distribution does not represent a bell-shaped curve but instead the high point of the curve is to the right or left of the mean as shown below.

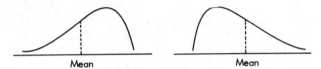

Most accounting populations exhibit some degree of skewness (are not symmetrical). Skewness in accounting populations usually means that the population contains a few very large items and many small items.

The standard deviation of the distribution of sample means (also known as "the standard error of the mean") equals the population standard deviation divided by the square root of the sample size. Symbolically:

$$\sigma_{\bar{x}} = \frac{\sigma_{x_j}}{\sqrt{n}}$$

In practice we do not know the population standard deviation because not all of the population items are audited. Hence we cannot compute the standard deviation of the distribution of sample means.

Example 5—Calculation of the Standard Error of the Mean (using the population standard deviation)

Given:

$$\sigma_{x_j} = 4 \text{ (See Example 2)}$$
$$n = 4 \text{ (See Example 3)}$$

Formula:

$$\sigma_{\bar{x}} = \frac{\sigma_{x_j}}{\sqrt{n}}$$

$$\sigma_{\bar{x}} = \frac{4}{\sqrt{4}} = 2$$

Example 6—Calculation of the Standard Error of the Mean
(using the sample standard deviation)

Given:

$$S_{x_j} = 5.3 \text{ (See Example 3)}$$
$$n = 4 \text{ (See Example 3)}$$

Formula:

$$\hat{\sigma}_{\bar{x}} = \frac{S_{x_j}}{\sqrt{n}}$$

$$\hat{\sigma}_{\bar{x}} = \frac{5.3}{\sqrt{4}} = 2.65$$

But we can use the standard deviation of the sample to estimate the population standard deviation. Consequently, we can estimate the standard error of the mean by dividing S_{x_j} (the sample standard deviation) by the square root of n. In symbols:

$$\hat{\sigma}_{\bar{x}} = \frac{S_{x_j}}{\sqrt{n}}$$

where:

$\hat{\sigma}_{\bar{x}} = Estimated$ standard error of the mean.

Precision and Reliability

The precision of an estimate is a measure of its accuracy—the closeness of the estimate to the true population value. The indicated reliability level R is the probability of achieving that degree of accuracy. If we are considering means, then the precision interval is that range surrounding the sample mean which has an $R\%$ probability of including the true population mean.

When considering means the following two statements can be made regarding precision and the precision interval:

1. The chance is $R\%$ that the absolute value (numerical value without regard to sign) of the difference between the sample mean and the population mean ($|\bar{x} - \bar{X}|$) is less than or equal to

$$U_R \cdot \frac{\sigma_{x_j}}{\sqrt{n}}$$

Example 7—Calculation of Precision (using the population standard deviation)

Given:

$\sigma_{x_j} = 4$ (See Example 2)
$n = 4$ (See Example 3)
$U_R = 2$ at a reliability of 95.5% (See Figure 7-1)

Formula:

$$\text{Precision} = U_R \cdot \frac{\sigma_{x_j}}{\sqrt{n}}$$

$$= 2 \cdot \frac{4}{\sqrt{4}} = 4$$

Thus, the chance is 95.5 percent that the absolute value of the difference between the sample mean and the population mean is less than or equal to 4.

Example 8—Calculation of the Precision Interval (using the population standard deviation)

Given:

$$U_R \cdot \frac{\sigma_{x_j}}{\sqrt{n}} = 4 \text{ (See Example 7)}$$

$$\bar{x} = 19 \text{ (See Example 3)}$$

Formula:

$$\text{Precision Interval} = \bar{x} - \left(U_R \cdot \frac{\sigma_{x_j}}{\sqrt{n}} \right) \text{ to } \bar{x} + \left(U_R \cdot \frac{\sigma_{x_j}}{\sqrt{n}} \right)$$

$$= 19 - 4 \text{ to } 19 + 4$$

$$= 15 \text{ to } 23$$

Thus, the chance is 95.5 percent that the interval 15 to 23 contains the population mean.

Example 9—Calculation of the Precision (using the sample standard deviation)

Given:

S_{x_j} = 5.3 (See Example 3. Even though the sample size should be at least 50 items the data from the earlier example will be used for illustrative purposes.)

n = 4 (See Example 3)

U_R = 2 at a reliability of 95.5% (See Figure 7-1)

Formula:

$$\text{Precision} = U_R \cdot \frac{S_{x_j}}{\sqrt{n}} = 2 \cdot \frac{5.3}{\sqrt{4}} = 5.3$$

Thus, the chance is 95.5 percent that the absolute value of the difference between the sample mean and the population mean is less than or equal to 5.3.

This calculation is referred to as the *precision*. The term U_R is the *reliability factor* (number of standard deviations) corresponding to a reliability of $R\%$ (a commonly used U_R value is 1.96 for a reliability of 95%). We can use the absolute value of the difference, $|\bar{x} - \bar{X}|$, because the normal distribution is symmetric.

2. The chance is $R\%$ that the interval:

$$\bar{x} - \left(U_R \cdot \frac{\sigma_{x_j}}{\sqrt{n}}\right) \text{ to } \bar{x} + \left(U_R \cdot \frac{\sigma_{x_j}}{\sqrt{n}}\right)$$

contains the population mean $\bar{X}$.

In practice, as stated earlier, we do not know the population standard deviation, but we can compute an estimate of this quantity by using the sample standard deviation (S_{x_j}). Replacing σ_{x_j} by S_{x_j} in (1) and (2) above is valid as long as the sample size is at least 50. Making this substitution, the formula becomes:

$$\text{The precision} = U_R \cdot \frac{S_{x_j}}{\sqrt{n}}$$

$$\text{The precision interval} = \bar{x} - \left(U_R \cdot \frac{S_{x_j}}{\sqrt{n}}\right) \text{ to } \bar{x} + \left(U_R \cdot \frac{S_{x_j}}{\sqrt{n}}\right)$$

That interval has an $R\%$ chance of including the population mean.

Example 10—Calculation of the Precision Interval (using the sample standard deviation)

Given:

$$U_R \cdot \frac{S_{x_j}}{\sqrt{n}} = 5.3 \text{ (See Example 9)}$$

$$\bar{x} = 19 \text{ (See Example 3)}$$

Formula:

$$\text{Precision interval} = \bar{x} - \left(U_R \cdot \frac{S_{x_j}}{\sqrt{n}}\right) \text{ to } \bar{x} + \left(U_R \cdot \frac{S_{x_j}}{\sqrt{n}}\right)$$

$$= 19 - 5.3 \text{ to } 19 + 5.3$$

$$= 13.7 \text{ to } 24.3$$

Thus, the chance is 95.5 percent that the precision interval 13.7 to 24.3 contains the population mean.

The formulas just given for precision are used for variables sampling. This is where the items to be sampled can be measured in terms of dollars or any other measure of quantity. In contrast, attribute sampling attempts to evaluate the frequency of occurrence of some event. Consequently, in attribute sampling, precision becomes:

$$\text{Precision} = U_R \cdot \sqrt{\frac{p(1-p)}{n}}$$

where: p = the occurrence rate of the event (e.g., an error) being measured in the population.

This formula is only an approximation. It is accurate only when the population rate of occurrence is 50 percent (in practice an auditor must estimate p). As the rate drops toward 0 percent, this formula becomes increasingly inaccurate. In auditing, the rate of occurrence is usually closer to 0 percent. Tables discussed later in this chapter are based on a method more applicable to auditing.

By examining the formulas for precision, one can see that precision and reliability are not independent terms. *Precision can only be defined for a specified reliability, and reliability can only be defined for a specified precision.* For example, if we decrease reliability from 95.5 percent to 68.3 percent, the U_R factor in the formula will correspondingly decrease from 2 to 1, causing the precision interval to become narrower (more precise).

Additionally, the sample size is related to precision. By examining

---

Example 11—Calculating Precision in Attribute Sampling

Given:

U_R = 2 at the 95.5% level of reliability (See Figure 7–1)
p = .6 (assumed rate of errors in a given population)
n = 50 (assumed)

Formula:

$$\text{Precision} = U_R \cdot \sqrt{\frac{p(1-p)}{n}}$$

$$= 2 \cdot \sqrt{\frac{.6(.4)}{50}}$$

$$= 0.139 \text{ (or 0.14 rounded)}$$

---

the formulas we see that if the sample size (n) is increased, the precision interval decreases *in size* (becomes more precise).[2]

SELECTING A STATISTICAL SAMPLE

Unrestricted Random Sampling

Unrestricted random sampling consists of drawing individual items at random from a population so that each item has an equal chance of being selected. If a sample item chosen is returned to the population so that it has a chance of being selected again, the method is called *with replacement.* If the item is not returned, it is called *without replacement.* Sampling without replacement gives greater sample efficiency (i.e., a smaller sample to achieve the same precision and reliability).

One method for drawing an unrestricted random sample would be to use a *random number table* (Figure 7–2 is an example of a random number table). Use of this method will help guard against *bias* in selection. It has the added advantage that a second, or reviewing, auditor can duplicate the exact sample using the same starting point and route through the table. The digits in most random number tables have been generated by a computer and subjected to statistical tests to ensure randomness. There is approximately an equal number of each of the digits 0 through 9 in these tables.

---

[2] Ibid., chapter 5 of Arkin.

262

FIGURE 7-2
Random number table excerpt

	Column				
Row	1	2	3	4	5
1	9588	3810	1161	5716	7048
2	6291	3964	9133	8362	7441
3	6766	8408	9939	1648	2143
4	2470	4741	5764	4033	7752
5	7647	4332	2897	8289	4810

The steps to follow when using a random number table to select an unrestricted random sample are:

1. Number the elements in the population to agree with the digits in the random number table.
2. Select and record a starting point in a random fashion (for example, pointing to a number on the page).
3. Select and record a route through the table (it may be sequential).
4. Record the stopping point.

It is a good auditing practice to record all random numbers selected and the method of corresponding these numbers with the items selected from the population.

**Example 12—Drawing an Unrestricted Random Sample
Using a Table of Random Number**

Assume there are approximately 10,000 items in a given population and that the items have been numbered 1–10,000. The items to be included in the sample could be selected by starting anywhere in the table. For instance, assume that it is decided to start with the first number in the table (Figure 7-2). The first number is 9,588, thus the 9,588th item in the population would be selected for inclusion in the sample. If a decision was made to proceed sequentially through the table, the next number in the table would then be used. The next number is 6,291, so the 6,291st item would also be included in the sample. The auditor would continue in this manner until enough items had been selected to meet the sample size requirements. Alternatively, a different route through the table could be selected as long as randomization is preserved (e.g., one would not be permitted to go through the table and select only those numbers starting with a 9 or some similar scheme).

> ### Example 13—Calculation of Skip Interval Assuming
> ### Multiple Random Starts
>
> Assume an auditor wishes to draw a sample of 300 from a population of 9,000. The auditor decides to use ten random starts. The skip interval will be 9,000/300 × 10 = 300. Consequently, after each of ten random starts, the auditor will select every 300th item.

Systematic Sampling

In systematic sampling, beginning sample item(s) are randomly chosen, a fixed number of items skipped, another item selected, and the same fixed number of items skipped. The process is continued throughout the frame (a frame is a listing of a population). The number of items skipped each time is called the *skip* interval.

A skip interval is obtained by dividing the sample size into the number of items in the population. To obtain comparable results from systematic sampling as from unrestricted random sampling, it is absolutely necessary that the frame be arranged in random order with respect to the population characteristic being measured. For example, if accounts receivable amounts are to be tested, systematic sampling might be used even though the accounts are filed alphabetically—provided the dollar amounts have no relation to the account names.

However, in many instances the frame may not be randomly arranged. But the auditor can guard against a nonrandom sample by using more than one random start. To reduce the possibility of bias, at least five to ten multiple starts should be used. In such instances the skip interval is found by dividing the sample size into the number of items in the population and then multiplying the result by the number of random starts (round downward, if necessary).

Systematic sampling often is easier to apply than unrestricted random sampling especially when the frame is a magnetic tape, computer tab listing, deck of keypunched cards, or file of ledger cards or vouchers. Only starting random numbers are required. The items in the frame need not be numbered consecutively to correspond with a random number table.

Stratified Random Sampling

When a population is highly variable (has a large standard deviation), the sample size required to achieve any given level of precision tends to be large. High variability of accounting populations usually is related to skewed distributions. One technique which may be used to reduce the required sample size is to divide the population into several strata.

An Auditor's Approach to Statistical Sampling, Volume 3, Stratified Random Sampling, indicates that there are three criteria that any stratification plan should meet[3]:

1. Every element [in a population] must belong to one and only one stratum.
2. There must be a tangible, specifiable difference that defines and distinguishes the strata. This must be known in advance.
3. The exact number of elements in each stratum must be known in advance.

The auditor can choose the stratum boundaries as he or she desires if they satisfy all three of these criteria. If logical divisions exist in the population, they can be used (e.g., by product line, type of item, location). By logical we mean based on the type of item being measured.[4] For example, a population of accounts receivable might be stratified by account value.

The stratification produces an estimate having a desired level of precision without using an extremely large sample. Such a sampling plan generally will be more efficient (require a smaller sample size to achieve the same precision) than unrestricted random sampling. Efficiency will be increased if each stratum has a relatively small standard deviation, and the weighted sum of the standard deviation is less than the standard deviation for the entire population.

To illustrate, assume that a population consists of seven items—five of which have a value of one and two of which have a value of three. The standard deviation of this population is greater than one, but by forming two strata with the five items of value one in the first stratum and the two items of value three in the second stratum, the standard deviation of each stratum is zero, and the weighted sum is also zero.

The procedures used to implement stratified random sampling are beyond the scope of this text. Before using stratified random sampling you should familiarize yourself with the subject.[5]

Judgment Sampling

If the auditor wishes to select a sample without using statistical selection techniques, then intuition, experienced judgment, and knowledge about the client may be used to select the sample. The

---

[3] *An Auditor's Approach to Statistical Sampling,* Vol. 3, *Stratified Random Sampling* (New York: American Institute of Certified Public Accountants, 1973), p. 8.

[4] See Arkin, *Handbook of Sampling for Auditing and Accounting,* p. 183.

[5] See for example, ibid., chapter 10.

resulting sample could be an effective sample for purposes of the audit. But judgmentally selected samples *cannot meet the criteria for statistical validity.* The auditor must recognize this fact when using judgment sampling.

Cluster Sampling

Cluster sampling may be a useful technique when the application of unrestricted random sampling to individual population items would be either too arduous or too expensive. It allows selection of more than one item at a time. In cluster sampling the population is divided into groups (clusters) of items, and a random sample of clusters is selected from all the clusters. Each cluster becomes a sampling unit.

After selecting the appropriate number of clusters, the auditor may either examine all items in a cluster (one-stage) or only a randomly chosen number of items in a cluster (two-stage).

For example, suppose an auditor has as a client a large hospital with 12,000 open accounts receivable due from discharged patients. The records are kept on ledger cards and filed alphabetically in ten trays, each 30 inches deep. The file has a large turnover of new records transferred in daily as patients are discharged and old records removed as accounts are paid.

To test the clerical accuracy of the control account balance and to select certain accounts for positive confirmation, the auditor has determined a sample size of 400 to be appropriate. The auditor concludes there is no convenient method to establish correspondence with a random number table.

Therefore, the auditor decides to use one-stage cluster sampling. Since there are about 40 cards per inch, the auditor could define a cluster as composed of one-half inch of cards. The frame then consists of 600 sampling units, from which the auditor will choose 20 at random using either an unrestricted or a systematic selection plan. For instance, if systematic selection were used with two random starts, two random numbers would be chosen between 1 and 60 and the skip interval of 60 sampling units ($600/20 \times 2 = 60$) would be used. The skip interval could also be expressed as 30 inches.

Generally, the "price" of relatively easy sample selection is "paid for" by the somewhat lesser statistical efficiency of cluster sampling. The procedures used to implement cluster sampling are beyond the scope of this book. Thus, before using cluster sampling, you should familiarize yourself with the subject.[6]

---

[6] See for example, ibid., chapter 11.

DETERMINING SAMPLE SIZE

The sample size formulas can be derived by rearranging the formulas for precision given earlier.

The formula given for attributes sampling was:

$$\text{Precision} = U_R \cdot \sqrt{\frac{p(1 - p)}{n}} \qquad \text{(See Example 11)}$$

Since "n" is the unknown, we wish to isolate it on the left-hand side of the equation.

First, both sides are squared yielding:

$$\text{Precision}^2 = U_R{}^2 \cdot \frac{p(1 - p)}{n}$$

So:

$$n = \frac{U_R{}^2 \cdot p(1 - p)}{\text{Precision}^2}$$

The formula given for variables sampling was:

$$\text{Precision} = \frac{U_R \cdot S_{X_j}}{\sqrt{n}} \qquad \text{(See Example 9)}$$

First, both sides are squared, yielding:

$$\text{Precision}^2 = \frac{(U_R \cdot S_{X_j})^2}{n}$$

So:

Example 14—Determining Sample Size for Attribute Sampling

Given:

$U_R = 2$ at the 95.5% level of reliability (See Figure 7-1)

$p = .6$ (Assumed rate of errors in the population. See Example 11)

Precision $= .139$ (See Example 11)

Formula:

$$n = \frac{U_R{}^2 \cdot p(1 - p)}{\text{Precision}^2}$$

$$n = \frac{2^2 \cdot .6(.4)}{(.139)^2} = \text{approximately 50 items}$$

Example 15—Determining Sample Size for Variables Sampling

Given:

$$U_R = 2 \text{ at a reliability of } 95.5\% \text{ (See Figure 7-1)}$$
$$S_{x_j} = 5.3 \text{ (See Example 9)}$$
$$\text{Desired Precision} = 5.3 \text{ (See Example 9)}$$

Formula:

$$n = \frac{(U_R \cdot S_{x_j})^2}{\text{Precision}^2}$$
$$= \frac{(2 \cdot 5.3)^2}{(5.3)^2} = 4$$

$$n = \frac{(U_R \cdot S_{x_j})^2}{\text{Precision}^2}$$

If the auditor is able to provide an estimate of p in the case of attribute sampling and S_{x_j} for variables sampling, then by specifying precision and reliability, the auditor would be able to establish the sample size. For attribute sampling, p may be established in a number of ways. Among the alternatives suggested by Arkin are (1) using the highest possible p that the auditor would expect; or (2) using a rate determined from a preliminary sample.[7]

It is not necessary to actually use the formula. Once the reliability, precision, and p have been established, tables can be used to find the sample size in sampling for attributes.[8]

Similar procedures apply to sampling for variables. The auditor again must establish the precision and reliability. Next, the auditor must estimate the standard deviation of the population. Arkin suggests that either of the following methods be used: (1) estimating the figure from the results found in a previous audit of the area involving the sample; or (2) estimating the figure from a preliminary sample.[9] Again, instead of using the formula, tables can be used to establish the sample size.[10]

---

[7] Ibid., pp. 96–103.
[8] Ibid., p. 97.
[9] Ibid., p. 107.
[10] Ibid., p. 109.

PART 2

ESTIMATION SAMPLING

Estimation sampling is a broad term which includes both sampling for attributes and sampling for variables. Acceptance sampling and discovery sampling are other methods (in addition to estimation sampling) which might be used. Acceptance sampling has not found much use in auditing and will not be discussed. Discovery sampling is discussed in a later section.

How should the auditor choose appropriate values for precision and reliability when determining sample size? These choices fall into the realm of audit judgment because no mathematical basis for definitive criteria is available and no authoritative pronouncement regarding their determination has been issued.

Whether sampling is on a statistical or nonstatistical basis, the auditor assumes risks of drawing wrong conclusions. Statistical sampling provides control and measurement of these risks; judgmental sampling does not. Consequently, the material in the remainder of this chapter focuses on conclusions which may be reached using samples selected according to sound statistical principles.

SAMPLING FOR ATTRIBUTES

When planning estimation sampling for attributes the auditor generally determines an estimated occurrence rate, together with a desired upper precision limit of a particular attribute in the population. It is, of course, possible to identify several attributes for a single sample item. It is necessary to define each attribute so that any sample item can be classified as either possessing or not possessing a particular attribute.

Because each item in the population either does or does not possess a particular attribute, the distribution of the population is specified completely by knowing how many, or what percentage of, items in the population possess the attribute. This percentage is called the *population rate of occurrence*. The mechanics of estimating this population rate of occurrence are: (1) count the number of occurrences in the sample and (2) divide by the sample size to produce the *sample rate of occurrence*. The sample rate of occurrence is the estimate of the population rate of occurrence.

To determine the precision of this estimate, the auditor can use tables instead of formulas. These tables are arranged so that the *upper precision limit* may be obtained directly. For most auditing purposes, knowing the achieved upper precision limit is sufficient. This evaluation allows the auditor to conclude (with a probability equal to the specified reliability) that the upper precision limit *will exceed* the population rate of occurrence.

Attribute sampling is useful in auditing mainly where the objective is to estimate the degree of compliance—such as a review of the effectiveness of accounting controls through compliance testing. If used for several years, it can also measure any improvement or deterioration in the effectiveness of the accounting controls from year to year.

After determining that attribute sampling will properly meet the audit objective(s), the auditor must define *precisely* the characteristic to be observed. For example:

In cash disbursements tests—discounts not taken, invoices not properly approved, invoices not checked for numerical accuracy, accounting distribution errors (both as to classification and posting).

In payroll tests—errors in hours, rates, extensions, deductions, lack of appropriate approval, excessive vacation time.

In cash receipts tests—erroneous discounts allowed, lack of credit memo documentation.

As integral parts of the sampling plan, the auditor must specify: (1) the desired reliability (confidence level) and (2) the desired upper precision limit. To determine the sample size, the auditor also must specify the *expected* rate of occurrence, which may be estimated from the experience of prior examinations or an initial presample of, say, 50 randomly selected items (which may be included in the final sample).

We previously noted that a table can be used to determine sample size in most situations where attribute sampling is used. (See Table 7–1.)

The steps for using such tables are:

1. Select the proper table. This will depend upon the reliability the auditor wishes to use.
2. Identify the column for the desired upper precision limit.
3. Identify the row corresponding to the expected rate of occurrence.
4. Read the sample size at the junction of the column and row.

When using attribute sampling, the auditor may use a single sample to test for several different attributes. The auditor not only must define each attribute, but also must specify exactly for each attribute what constitutes an occurrence. This is important so those who execute and review the work will each recognize the same items as occurrences. These precise definitions of attributes and occurrences should be retained as part of the working papers.

TABLE 7-1
Determination of sample size (reliability = 95%)

Expected Percent Rate of Occurrence	Upper Precision Limit: Percent Rate of Occurrence																				
	1	2	3	4	5	6	7	8	9	10	12	14	16	18	20	25	30	35	40	45	50
0.25	650	240	160	120	100	80	70	60	60	50	40	40	30	30	30	20	20	20	10	10	10
0.50	*	320	160	120	100	80	70	60	60	50	40	40	30	30	30	20	20	20	10	10	10
1.0		600	260	160	100	80	70	60	60	50	40	40	30	30	30	20	20	20	10	10	10
1.5		*	400	200	160	120	90	60	60	50	40	40	30	30	30	20	20	20	10	10	10
2.0			900	300	200	140	90	80	70	50	40	40	30	30	30	20	20	20	10	10	10
2.5			*	550	240	160	120	80	70	70	40	40	30	30	30	20	20	20	10	10	10
3.0				*	400	200	160	100	90	80	60	50	40	40	40	30	30	20	10	10	10
3.5					650	280	200	140	100	80	70	50	40	40	40	30	30	20	10	10	10
4.0					*	500	240	180	100	90	70	50	40	40	40	30	30	20	10	10	10
4.5					*	800	360	200	160	120	80	60	40	40	40	30	30	20	10	10	10
5.0						*	500	240	160	120	80	60	40	50	50	30	30	20	10	10	10
5.5						*	900	360	200	160	90	70	50	50	50	30	30	20	10	10	10
6.0							*	550	280	180	100	80	50	50	50	30	30	20	10	10	10
6.5							*	1,000	400	240	120	90	60	50	50	30	30	20	10	10	10
7.0								*	600	300	140	100	70	70	50	30	30	20	10	10	10
7.5								*	*	460	160	100	80	70	70	30	30	20	10	10	10
8.0									*	650	200	100	80	100	90	40	30	20	10	10	10
8.5									*	*	280	140	80	140	100	40	30	20	10	10	10
9.0										*	400	180	100	200	160	40	40	20	10	10	10
9.5										*	550	200	120	300	200	40	40	20	10	10	10
10.0											800	220	120	500	300	40	40	20	10	10	10
11.0											*	400	180	*	550	40	40	20	20	20	20
12.0												900	280	*	*	50	40	20	20	20	20
13.0												*	460		*	50	40	20	20	20	20
14.0													1,000			50	40	20	20	20	20
15.0													*			60	40	20	20	20	20
16.0																80	50	30	30	20	20
17.0																100	50	40	30	20	20
18.0																140	50	40	30	20	20
19.0																180	70	40	30	20	20
20.0																220	70	40	30	20	20
22.0																600	100	50	30	30	20
24.0																*	200	70	40	30	20
26.0																	400	100	50	30	30
28.0																	*	160	60	40	30
30.0																		280	80	40	30
33.0																		*	160	60	30
36.0																			460	100	50
39.0																			*	220	80
42.0																				800	140
46.0																					550

* = More than 1,000

In a plan to test cash disbursements, each disbursement would be considered a *sample item*. An example of an *attribute* might be a proper approval on the check request form. A lack of approval, or an improper approval, is an example of an occurrence. A particular sample item could be counted as an occurrence for several reasons: (1) it might have no approval, (2) the check request might be missing, (3) it might have a written approval by an unauthorized person, or (4) the dollar limit of the authorizing person might have been exceeded.

Note the term "occurrence" rather than "error" is used here because an auditor might be interested in an attribute which is not an error, but which affects an account and reflects the effectiveness of administrative internal controls, such as the percentage of accounts receivable having overdue amounts.[11]

AN EXAMPLE OF ATTRIBUTE SAMPLING

Let us assume an auditor wishes to appraise the effectiveness of the procedures for calculating factory payroll. Thus, the auditor will be interested in the existence of errors in the calculation of the payroll.

Assume there are 500 factory employees who are paid on a monthly basis. Since the payroll calculations are made monthly, there is a population of 6,000 calculations (500 × 12 months) during the year. The auditor specifies a reliability of 95 percent and an upper precision limit of 7 percent. The upper precision limit of 7 percent means that the auditor has determined judgmentally that a population occurrence rate of as high as 7 percent can be accepted without having to alter the scope of the other audit work. However, generally if the sample results in an upper precision limit in excess of 7 percent, the presumption is that the scope of the auditor's examination will be increased to account for the weaker internal control. The auditor feels that based on past experience with the client, the expected error rate is 3.5 percent.

We have noted that tables exist to aid the auditor in determining sample size for attributes. Table 7-1 is such an example. The table specifies sample sizes for various upper precision limits and various expected percentage rates of occurrence when the reliability is 95 percent. By examining this table the reader will note that the sample size should be 200.

Next, assume the auditor randomly samples 200 payroll calcula-

---

[11] There are two risks in attribute sampling that are analogous to the risks of variables estimation sampling plans as used in this chapter: (1) a risk similar to alpha risk, i.e., rejecting an accounting control as unreliable when it is effective, and (2) a risk similar to beta risk, i.e., of accepting as effective an accounting control that is unreliable. Further discussion of these risks is beyond the scope of this text.

TABLE 7-2
Evaluation of results (reliability = 95 percent). Numbers of observed occurrences

Upper Precision Limit: Percent Rate of Occurrence

Sample Size	1	2	3	4	5	6	7	8	9	10	12	14	16	18	20	25	30	35	40	45
10																	0		1	
20												0				1	2	3		4
30										0			1		2	3	4	5	7	8
40								0			1		2		3	5	6	8	10	12
50						0				1		2	3	4	5	7	9	11	13	16
60					0				1		2	3	4	5	6	9	11	14	17	20
70					0			1		2	3	4	5	7	8	11	14	17	20	24
80			0		1		2			3	4	5	7	8	9	13	16	20	24	28
90			0			1	2	3	4	5	6	8	9	11		15	19	23	27	32
100			0		1		2	3		4	6	8	9	11	13	17	22	26	31	36
120				0	1	2	3	4	5	6	8	10	12	14	16	21	27	33	38	44
140			0	1	2	3	4	5	6	7	10	12	14	17	19	26	32	39	46	52
160		0	1	2	3	4	5	6	8	9	12	14	17	20	23	30	38	45	53	61
180		0	1	2	3	5	6	8	9	11	14	17	20	23	26	35	43	52	60	69
200		0	1	3	4	6	7	9	11	12	16	19	23	26	30	39	48	58	68	77
220		0	2	3	5	7	8	10	12	14	18	22	25	29	33	44	54	64	75	86
240		1	2	4	6	8	10	12	14	16	20	24	28	33	37	48	59	71	83	94
260		1	3	4	7	9	11	13	15	17	22	26	31	36	41	53	65	77	90	103
280		1	3	5	7	10	12	14	17	19	24	29	34	39	44	57	71	84	98	111
300	0	1	3	6	8	11	13	16	18	21	26	31	37	42	48	62	76	91	105	120
320	0	2	4	6	9	11	14	17	20	22	28	34	40	45	51	66	82	97	113	128
340	0	2	4	7	10	12	15	18	21	24	30	36	42	49	55	71	87	104	120	137
360	0	2	5	8	10	13	17	20	23	26	32	39	45	52	59	76	93	110	128	146
380	0	2	5	8	11	14	18	21	24	28	34	41	48	55	62	80	98	117	135	154
400	0	3	6	9	12	15	19	22	26	29	37	44	51	59	66	85	104	123	143	163
420	0	3	6	9	13	16	20	24	27	31	39	46	54	62	70	90	110	130	151	171
460	0	4	7	11	15	18	22	26	31	35	43	51	60	68	77	99	121	143	166	188
500	1	4	8	12	16	21	25	29	34	38	47	56	66	75	84	108	132	157	181	197
550	1	5	9	14	18	23	28	33	38	43	53	63	73	83	94	120	146	173	200	227
600	1	6	10	15	20	26	31	36	42	47	58	69	80	92	103	132	161	190	219	249
650	2	6	12	17	23	28	34	40	46	52	64	76	88	100	112	143	175	207	239	271
700	2	7	13	19	25	31	37	43	50	56	69	82	95	108	122	155	189	223	258	292
800	3	9	15	22	29	36	43	51	58	65	80	95	110	125	141	179	218	257	296	336
900	4	10	18	26	34	42	50	58	66	74	91	108	125	142	159	203	247	291	335	379
1,000	4	12	20	29	38	47	56	65	74	84	102	121	140	159	178	227	275	324	374	423

Source: Ernst & Ernst Professional Development Series, *Audit Sampling Reference Manual*, 1974, p.

tions and finds errors in 6 calculations—a 3 percent sample occurrence rate. Once the auditor has found the rate of occurrence in the sample, other tables are available to give the achieved upper precision limit given the specified reliability.

Specifically, Table 7-2 can be used to evaluate the findings. To use this table the auditor should:[12]

1. Find the *row* corresponding to the sample size. Always be conservative. If the sample size selected falls between two rows, the row with the *smaller* size should be used.
2. Enter the row and find the *cell* corresponding to the *number* of occurrences in the sample. If the number of occurrences in the

---

[12] Tables 7-1 and 7-2 are exact for sampling with replacement and conservative approximation for sampling without replacement. These tables are intended for large populations where sample size will be less than 10 percent of the population.

sample falls between two cells, use the cell with the *higher* number of occurrences.

3. Read the upper precision limit percentage at the *top* of the *column* in which the cell appears. The findings of an attribute sample plan always should be stated in terms of: *(a)* the *estimated* actual occurrence rate in the population (which is the sample occurrence rate), and *(b)* the *estimated* upper precision limit at a specified reliability.

In the example the sample size is 200, the number of occurrences is 6, and thus the upper precision is 6 percent. Thus we can be 95 percent assured that the population error rate is less than 6 percent. This is less than the 7 percent originally deemed to be tolerable.

VARIABLES ESTIMATION SAMPLING

Risks of Using Variables Estimation Sampling

There are two risks to using variables estimation sampling in auditing. First is the risk of deciding a book balance is materially misstated when it really is fairly stated. This is called the *alpha* (α) risk. Additional testing might become necessary when it is decided that a book balance may be materially misstated. Such additional testing can be costly. Initially increasing the specified reliability level *decreases* the alpha risk and vice versa. This will be discussed further.

The second type of risk, which is much more serious in terms of ultimate liability in an audit situation, is the chance of not detecting a materially misstated book balance. This risk is called the *beta* (β) risk. Controlling this risk by adjusting precision and reliability also will be explained in this chapter.

Using the Estimation Objective in Testing

The audit objective in estimating the total audited value of a particular account is to decide whether its book value is fairly stated. The phrase "fairly stated" emphasizes concern with a particular aspect of the account balance—namely, whether the amount is reasonably correct insofar as the particular audit test or tests permit concluding. The statistical evidence supports "fair statement" when the estimated audited value is near the book value. Conversely, when the estimated audited value differs materially from the book value, the statistical evidence does not support "fair statement." For example, if the test involves selecting a sample of inventory items for price testing, and the statistical estimate of the inventory balance—based on audited prices—is near the book value, the auditor can conclude that the statistical evidence supports fair statement of inventory pricing. But if the estimated inventory balance is materially different from the book value, further testing might be necessary.

The previous material in this chapter discussed the precision of the estimated mean or average value. Now in discussing beta risk we are referring to the precision of the estimated total audited value. The precision of the estimated mean can be converted to the precision of the estimated total audited value by multiplying the precision of the estimated mean by N—the number of items in the population.

As stated earlier the precision of an estimate is a measure of its accuracy—the closeness of the estimate to the true population value. The indicated reliability level R is the probability of achieving that degree of accuracy. Stated another way, the reliability level indicates the chance that the precision interval around the estimate includes the true population value. For instance, there may be a 95 percent chance that the interval $300,000–$325,000 includes the true population value when the value of the estimate is $312,500. The true population value is defined as the value which would be obtained if 100 percent of the items in the population were tested.

Statistical evidence supports fair statement of a client's book value whenever the precision interval includes the book value *and* the precision is not too large in relation to an amount the auditor considers material.

More specifically, if the client's book value falls within the precision interval, the auditor can conclude that there is an $R\%$ chance that the difference between the true value and the book value does not exceed the length of the precision interval (see Examples 9 and 10). Remember that the length of the precision *interval* is twice the indicated precision. In order to arrive at meaningful conclusions, the indicated precision cannot be greater than an amount considered material.

Conversely, whenever a client's book value is outside the precision interval, statistical evidence fails to support fair statement. "Fails to support" does not mean that there is necessarily a material misstatement. Nevertheless, the failure of statistical evidence to support fair statement requires the auditor to obtain additional, competent evidential matter before the auditor can conclude that the book value is fairly stated.

As stated above, when statistical evidence is used to test the fairness of the book value, the auditor runs the risk of committing two types of error:

1. The statistical evidence might fail to support fair statement even though the difference between the book value and true value is fairly small. This is called *alpha* risk.

2. The statistical evidence might support fair statement when the book value is materially incorrect. This occurs when the precision interval includes the book value, even though the book value is materially misstated. This is called *beta* risk.

The auditor controls the first type of risk (alpha risk) by changing or setting the indicated reliability level, provided the procedures discussed in this chapter for controlling sampling risk are followed. In all cases, alpha risk is equal to 1.0 minus R (the complement of R). For example, if a reliability of 95 percent is selected, the auditor assumes a 5 percent alpha risk of deciding that a reasonably correct book value might be materially incorrect. This is because the precision interval surrounding 95 percent of all possible sample projections will include the true population value. Consequently, there is a 5 percent alpha risk (1.0—0.95) that the precision interval will fail to include the book value when the book value is equal to the true value.

This is shown in Figure 7–3, a distribution of the statistical estimates resulting from all possible samples of a given size that could have been taken. Statistical theory states that this distribution is centered at the true value. We *assume* that the true value is equal to the book value when measuring alpha risk. Let us further assume that book value equals $1 million and that a precision of $50,000 at the 95 percent reliability level would satisfy your audit objectives.

Because the curve represents the distribution of statistical estimates resulting from *all possible samples* that you could have taken, the single estimate which you obtain must come from some part of the

FIGURE 7–3
Illustration of 5 percent alpha risk. T(true value) is assumed equal
to B (book value) when measuring alpha risk

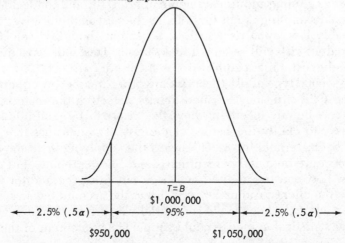

$T=B$
$1,000,000
$\longleftarrow$ 2.5% (.5α) $\longrightarrow$ | $\longleftarrow$ 95% $\longrightarrow$ | $\longleftarrow$ 2.5% (.5α) $\longrightarrow$
$950,000 $1,050,000

curve. If the precision interval of that estimate is to include the book value of $1 million, hence support fair statement of the book value, the estimate itself must have a value in the range of $950,000 to $1,050,000. In Figure 7–3 one can see that the chance of obtaining an estimate with a value in that range is 95 percent. Consequently, the chance of *not* obtaining an estimate with a value in that range (alpha risk) is 5 percent. That is, there is a 5 percent chance that the precision interval around an estimate will *not* include a correct book value.

The precision interval will include the book value of $1 million *only* when the value of the estimate itself is included within the interval from $950,000 to $1,050,000; therefore, we can state this decision rule: The statistical evidence supports fair statement whenever the estimate is included within the interval from book value minus precision to book value plus precision. This interval around the book value is called the *decision interval*.

Using a higher reliability level when calculating sample size increases the chance of obtaining an estimate within the decision interval, thereby decreasing alpha risk.

If the auditor selects a lower reliability level in the presence of excellent internal controls, the alpha risk increases of rejecting a book value which, with such excellent internal controls, has a very good chance of being reasonably stated. For instance, if a reliability level of 80 percent is selected, the alpha risk increases to 20 percent. Unnecessary audit time is the penalty for incurring alpha error (alpha error is where the statistical evidence fails to support fair statement of what later proves to be a reasonably stated book value) because the usual reaction of the auditor will be to examine evidence beyond the original sample. As a consequence, selection of an acceptable alpha risk should be based on the auditor's judgment of the cost and feasibility of examining additional sample items. If the auditor decides that additional sampling is not feasible, or the cost is prohibitive, then a reasonably low alpha risk, such as 5 percent should be selected. A higher alpha risk will reduce initial sample sizes and, consequently, total audit cost, unless alpha error is incurred.

The second type of risk (beta risk) involves greater consequences in that the CPA firm may be sued for not detecting the material misstatement. Before specifying how this risk can be controlled, it is necessary to clarify the nature of the risk. To state that the "book amount is materially incorrect" means that, applying the same auditing procedure on a 100 percent basis and finding the amount of difference between the audited and book amounts, the auditor would require the client to adjust or reconstruct the account balance.

Even when the book value is materially incorrect, there is a chance that the statistical evidence could support fair statement of the book value. The statistical evidence supports fair statement of a book value when the statistical estimate is included in the interval from book value minus precision to book value plus precision (the decision interval). However, the chance of this occurring when the book value is materially incorrect (beta risk) can be specified and controlled, thereby increasing the usefulness of a statistical test. *Beta risk is controlled by adjusting the ratio of the precision to the minimum amount that is considered material* by the auditor. The objective is, of course, to control this risk within acceptable levels. In other words, if the client's book value is incorrect by a material amount, the auditor wishes to be *reasonably sure* that the statistical evidence would *not* support fair statement of the book value.

More specifically, if the true value differs from the book value by at least *M* dollars (the minimum amount the auditor considers to be material in the circumstances), then the auditor does not want the estimate to fall within the decision interval (book value minus the precision to book value plus the precision). If the estimate does not fall within that interval, then the sample evidence does not support fair statement which, in this case, is the desired conclusion. There is no way to guarantee correct conclusions without a 100 percent examination; however, as stated above, beta risk can be controlled by adjusting the ratio of the specified precision to the amount considered to be material as will be shown later in this chapter.

Determination and Control of Beta Risk

Part of the auditor's examination is comprised of substantive tests which include both ". . . tests of details of transactions and balances and . . . analytic review procedures applied to financial information." (*SAS No. 1*, Section 320.70 as amended by *SAS No. 23*) In considering the possibility that the auditor's substantive tests would fail to detect a material error, tests of details conducted on a statistical basis can be distinguished from analytical review. In statistical tests, the beta risk is an *objective* measure of this possibility, while in analytical review, the evaluation of risk is *subjective*. Multiplying (1) the beta risk, by (2) the risk that other audit procedures *fail* to detect a material error quantifies subjectively the risk that all substantive tests of a particular account will fail to detect a material error.

If there were a 20 percent beta risk for a statistical sample conducted for a particular account coupled with a 30 percent risk that other supplemental audit procedures would fail to detect a material error in the same account, then the probability that both tests, taken together, would fail to detect a material error equals 6%— (20% × 30%).

Ultimate Risk. *SAS No. 1,* section 320A.14, states that "for the purpose of relating sampling reliability to the reasonableness of the basis for an opinion, it should be understood that the ultimate risk against which the auditor and those who rely on the opinion require reasonable protection is a combination of two separate risks. The first of these is that material errors will occur in the accounting process by which the financial statements are developed. The second is that any material errors that occur will not be detected in the auditor's examination."

Thus, ultimate risk is the chance that a material error will occur in the accounting process *and* the auditor's examination will not detect it. The effectiveness of internal control governs the chance of a material error occurring. Thus, multiplying (1) the risk that the internal control system allows a material error to occur, by (2) the beta risk, and (3) the risk that other audit procedures fail to detect the material error, quantifies the ultimate risk.

Let β = Beta risk.
C = Effectiveness of internal control.
SP = Effectiveness of supplemental audit procedures.

then

$$\text{Ultimate risk} = \beta(1 - C)(1 - SP)$$

Combined Reliability. The complement of ultimate risk is the combined reliability. If it is assumed that a 95 percent combined reliability level would be reasonable for a particular account balance, this would result from an ultimate risk of 5 percent (100% − 95% = 5%). This ultimate risk must be more than 0 percent because achiev-

---

Example 16—Calculating Ultimate Risk

Given:

$$\beta = 5\%$$
$$C = 80\%$$
$$SP = 20\%$$

Formula:

$$\text{Ultimate risk} = \beta(1 - C)(1 - SP)$$
$$= .05(1 - .8)(1 - .2) = .008$$

Thus, the ultimate risk is less than 1 percent that a material error will occur in the accounting process and the auditor's examination will not detect it.

ing a 0 percent risk level would require a 100 percent examination. Combined reliability (the complement of ultimate risk) can be stated as follows: $CR = 1 - [\beta(1 - C)(1 - SP)]$. Note that combined reliability (the complement of ultimate risk) is not synonymous with "reliability" (the complement of alpha risk).

Effectiveness of Internal Control.   The auditor should determine judgmentally the effectiveness (expressed as a percent) of the internal control system in preventing a material error from occurring. The second standard of field work regarding evaluation of internal control recognizes that the beta risk of substantive tests can vary directly with the evaluation of the system's effectiveness in preventing material misstatement.

The effectiveness of internal control should be determined separately for each population or account sampled. General or overall evaluations for an entire company are not appropriate because the degrees of control tend to vary from one account to another; also, strengths in one area may not offset or compensate for weaknesses in another. The quantification of internal control effectiveness necessarily falls into the realm of professional judgment. Although this may present certain practical problems, it is no different than the implicit evaluation of internal control when statistical sampling is not used.

Concluding that controls over a particular accounting population, such as accounts receivable, are 90 percent effective against the occurrence of material misstatement, means that there is a 10 percent chance that errors could occur on enough accounts or to such a degree that the *cumulative effect* would result in a material misstatement of the population value. This does *not* mean that 10 percent of the accounts are in error or that there is a 10 percent chance of any particular account being in error.

Effectiveness of Other Audit Procedures.   These other audit procedures may be trend analyses, gross margin reviews, comparisons of cost and selling prices of inventory items, review of variance accounts, and so on, and may be used to supplement the statistical test. Quantifying their effectiveness in detecting material errors is rather difficult, but very conservative estimates can be made quite easily which are still useful in practice.

Determination of Planned Beta Risk.   Earlier it was noted that combined reliability may be stated as:

$$CR = 1 - [\beta(1 - C)(1 - SP)]$$

In solving for β

$$[\beta(1 - C)(1 - SP)] = 1 - CR$$
$$\beta = \frac{(1 - CR)}{(1 - C)(1 - SP)}$$

Example 17—Calculating Planned Beta Risk

Given:

$CR =$ 99.2 percent (See Example 16—the ultimate risk was 0.8 percent so the combined reliability was 99.2 percent. In practice, the combined reliability generally is preset at 95 percent.)

$C =$ 80%

$SP =$ 20%

Formula:

$$\beta = \frac{(1 - CR)}{(1 - C)(1 - SP)}$$
$$= \frac{(1 - .992)}{(1 - .8)(1 - .2)} = .05$$

Thus, the planned beta risk is 5 percent given these facts.

This formula gives the amount of beta risk that the auditor can tolerate in a statistical test in the planning stage. In practice, the combined reliability level is generally preset at 95 percent. Then, after estimating the effectiveness of internal control and the effectiveness of supplemental audit procedures in detecting a material error, the auditor solves for the maximum planned beta risk as shown in Example 17.

Thus, the maximum planned amount of beta risk that should be present in statistical tests is governed by:

a. The desired combined reliability level.
b. The effectiveness of the internal control system in preventing a material misstatement from occurring.
c. The effectiveness of supplemental audit procedures in detecting a material misstatement.

Given the planned amount of beta risk, the auditor needs to (1) judgmentally determine the minimum amount considered material for the account being sampled, and (2) determine the amount of precision that will allow achievement of the planned level of beta risk.

Control of Beta Risk. As was mentioned previously, the beta risk is controlled by adjusting the ratio of the precision to the minimum amount that the auditor considers material in the circumstances. A low ratio results in a low beta risk.

After the auditor has determined judgmentally what amount shall be considered material, the desired ratio is achieved by increasing or decreasing the precision the auditor specifies when calculating sample size. In other words, once the auditor has calculated a beta risk consistent with his overall objectives, precision to be used to calculate sample size should be adjusted in relation to the amount considered material in order to attain that level of beta risk.

The precision to be used in determining sample size may be determined from the following formula:

$$A = \frac{M}{1 + \dfrac{Z_\beta}{Z_{\alpha/2}}}$$

where:

A = Precision to be used in determining sample size.
M = Minimum amount considered material.
Z_β = Normal table value of $.5 - \beta$.
$Z_{\alpha/2}$ = Normal table value of $.5 - \alpha/2$.

USING VARIABLES SAMPLING

Planning

The material in the prior sections relating to variables sampling described the risks in using variables sampling to decide fairness of an account balance. These risks are controlled by the auditor using judgment in the selection of two factors that affect the calculation of sample size: (1) reliability (complement of alpha risk), and (2) precision. These two choices affect alpha risk and beta risk. Beta risk, in turn, affects combined reliability and, consequently, ultimate risk. The discussion of these risks was confined principally to the planning stage of a sampling application.

At this point, we will summarize the steps an auditor would have performed in a sampling application. The auditor would have:

1. Evaluated the particular internal controls the auditor anticipated relying on, tested compliance with those controls, and judgmentally assigned a percentage effectiveness to their value in preventing a material error from occurring.
2. Selected a desired combined reliability level (probably at least 95 percent).
3. Assigned a percentage effectiveness of supplemental audit procedures representing the auditor's judgment of the probability that they would detect a material misstatement.
4. Calculated the maximum beta risk the auditor could tolerate in the statistical test. This calculation was based on the desired com-

---

Example 18—Calculation of Precision to Be Used in Determining Sample Size

Given:

Assume the auditor believes that an alpha risk (α) of 5 percent and a beta risk (β) of 5 percent are acceptable (see Example 17 to see how the auditor arrived at the 5 percent beta risk) and that the minimum material amount is $500,000.

Formula:

$$A = \frac{M}{1 + \dfrac{Z_\beta}{Z_{\alpha/2}}}$$

$$= \frac{\$500,000}{1 + \dfrac{Z.5 - .05}{Z.5 - .025}}$$

$$= \frac{\$500,000}{1 + \dfrac{Z.4500}{Z.4750}}$$

Next find the closest numbers in Table 7–3 to the Z values .4500 for beta and .4750 for alpha. If the .4500 does not appear in the table (as it does not) use the next higher number. The number .4505 appears in the 1.6 row and .05 column which means that the Z value for beta is 1.65. The number .4750 does appear in the table in the 1.9 row and .06 column. Thus, the Z value for alpha is 1.96. If it had not appeared the next *lower* number should be used.

Now substitute the Z values in the formula as follows and solve:

$$A = \frac{\$500,000}{1 + \dfrac{1.65}{1.96}} = \$271,468$$

Thus, in this example $271,468 is the precision to be used in determining the sample size.

---

    bined reliability and the effectiveness of both internal controls and supplemental audit procedures.

5. Judgmentally determined materiality for this particular account.
6. Selected an acceptable alpha risk based on the auditor's judgment of the cost and feasibility of additional sampling if the original sample fails to support fair statement of what later proves to be a reasonably stated book value.
7. Determined the amount of precision in order to achieve the auditor's planned beta risk and hence, the auditor's desired combined reliability.

TABLE 7-3
Normal curve area table

σ	.00	.01	.02	.03	.04	.05	.06	.07	.08	.09
0.0	.0000	.0040	.0080	.0120	.0160	.0199	.0239	.0279	.0319	.0359
0.1	.0398	.0438	.0478	.0517	.0557	.0596	.0636	.0675	.0714	.0753
0.2	.0793	.0832	.0871	.0910	.0948	.0987	.1026	.1064	.1103	.1141
0.3	.1179	.1217	.1255	.1293	.1331	.1368	.1406	.1443	.1480	.1517
0.4	.1554	.1591	.1628	.1664	.1700	.1736	.1772	.1808	.1844	.1879
0.5	.1915	.1950	.1985	.2019	.2054	.2088	.2123	.2157	.2190	.2224
0.6	.2257	.2291	.2324	.2357	.2389	.2422	.2454	.2486	.2518	.2549
0.7	.2580	.2612	.2642	.2673	.2704	.2734	.2764	.2794	.2823	.2852
0.8	.2881	.2910	.2939	.2967	.2995	.3023	.3051	.3078	.3106	.3133
0.9	.3159	.3186	.3212	.3238	.3264	.3289	.3315	.3340	.3365	.3389
1.0	.3413	.3438	.3461	.3485	.3508	.3531	.3554	.3577	.3599	.3621
1.1	.3643	.3665	.3686	.3708	.3729	.3749	.3770	.3790	.3810	.3830
1.2	.3849	.3869	.3888	.3907	.3925	.3944	.3962	.3980	.3997	.4015
1.3	.4032	.4049	.4066	.4082	.4099	.4115	.4131	.4147	.4162	.4177
1.4	.4192	.4207	.4222	.4236	.4251	.4265	.4279	.4292	.4306	.4319
1.5	.4332	.4345	.4357	.4370	.4382	.4394	.4406	.4418	.4429	.4441
1.6	.4452	.4463	.4474	.4484	.4495	.4505	.4515	.4525	.4535	.4545
1.7	.4554	.4564	.4573	.4582	.4591	.4599	.4608	.4616	.4625	.4633
1.8	.4641	.4649	.4656	.4664	.4671	.4678	.4686	.4693	.4699	.4706
1.9	.4713	.4719	.4726	.4732	.4738	.4744	.4750	.4756	.4761	.4767
2.0	.4772	.4778	.4783	.4788	.4793	.4798	.4803	.4808	.4812	.4817
2.1	.4821	.4826	.4830	.4834	.4838	.4842	.4846	.4850	.4854	.4857
2.2	.4861	.4864	.4868	.4871	.4875	.4878	.4881	.4884	.4887	.4890
2.3	.4893	.4896	.4898	.4901	.4904	.4906	.4909	.4911	.4913	.4916
2.4	.4918	.4920	.4922	.4925	.4927	.4929	.4931	.4932	.4934	.4936
2.5	.4938	.4940	.4941	.4943	.4945	.4946	.4948	.4949	.4951	.4952
2.6	.4953	.4955	.4956	.4957	.4959	.4960	.4961	.4962	.4963	.4964
2.7	.4965	.4966	.4967	.4968	.4969	.4970	.4971	.4972	.4973	.4974
2.8	.4974	.4975	.4976	.4977	.4977	.4978	.4979	.4979	.4980	.4981
2.9	.4981	.4982	.4982	.4983	.4984	.4984	.4985	.4985	.4986	.4986
3.0	.49865	.4987	.4987	.4988	.4988	.4989	.4989	.4989	.4990	.4990
3.1	.49903	.4991	.4991	.4991	.4992	.4992	.4992	.4992	.4993	.4993

Determining Sample Size

Next, using the selected reliability and precision, the auditor can determine sample size. Earlier in the chapter we noted that this can be done by using a formula or tables.

Drawing and Appraising Sample

The auditor will next draw the sample, perform the audit procedures and obtain a statistical estimate of the total audited value from the sample. Additionally, the auditor can determine from the sample the precision of the total audited value. This is the achieved precision. The achieved precision can be calculated by use of tables[13] or a formula.[14]

Further Quantitative Evaluation of Sample Results

At this point, the achieved precision frequently differs from the precision the auditor planned. This results from the sample standard deviation having a different value than the standard deviation used in calculating sample size. The achieved beta risk will differ from the planned beta risk whenever the achieved precision differs from the planned precision. Because the planned beta risk was based on (1) internal control, (2) other audit procedures, and (3) the desired combined reliability level, it follows that the beta risk the auditor calculated in the planning stage represents the maximum beta risk that should be present in the statistical test. Therefore, in the evaluation stage, the achieved beta risk should be less than or equal to the planned beta risk or the auditor will not attain the desired combined reliability level.

Whenever the achieved precision differs from the planned precision the auditor should use the following formula which will give a new precision (A'') resulting in a final beta risk equal to the planned beta risk:

$$A'' = A' + M(1 - A'/A)$$

where

A = Planned precision.
A' = Achieved precision.
M = Material amount.

---

[13] See Arkin, *Handbook of Sampling for Auditing and Accounting*, pp. 131–43 for a discussion of the use of such tables.

[14] The estimated audited value and achieved precision in some instances can be determined by difference estimation and ratio estimation. In difference estimation, for example, the auditor computes the mean value and standard deviation of the individual differences between each sample item's audited and book values. This mean is extended by the number of items in the population and this value is added to the total book value to obtain the estimated audited value. The standard deviation of the differences is used to compute the precision of the estimate. In ratio estimation, a composite ratio (the sum of audited values divided by the sum of book values) is calculated from the sample and projected to an estimated population total by multiplying this ratio by the total book value. Methods are available to enable the auditor to compute the precision of that estimate.

To use the ratio or difference methods, two conditions must be met: (1) the book or recorded value for each item in the population and total book value must be known *and* (2) differences between audited value and the book value must not be too rare. See Arkin, *Handbook of Sampling for Auditing and Accounting*, chapter 12, for a full discussion of both ratio and difference estimation.

As an example, assume:

Description	Amount
Book value	$20,751,533
Reliability (alpha risk—5%)	95%
Materiality	$ 1,000,000
Planned beta risk	30%
Planned precision	$ 787,000

Further assume that the estimated audited value was found to be $20,217,692 with an achieved precision of $279,235. Because the $279,235 achieved precision differs from the $787,000 planned precision, the auditor should compute a new precision (A''), which gives a final beta risk equal to the 30 percent the auditor had planned on:

$$A'' = A' + M(1 - A'/A)$$

Therefore,

$A'' = \$279,235 + \$1,000,000 \, (1 - \$279,235/\$787,000) = \$924,426$

A new decision interval is formed from $19,827,107 to $21,675,959 (book value of $20,751,533, plus and minus the new precision—$924,426). Because the estimated value ($20,217,692) falls within the new decision interval, the auditor can conclude that the statistical evidence supports fair statement of the book value. All of the original specifications for beta risk have been met. The specified reliability level (complement of the alpha risk) will change—either increase or decrease. However, this change in reliability level may be ignored because the estimated value falls within the final decision interval. (No alpha error was incurred.)

Reaching this conclusion as to fair statement would not have been obvious from the original sample results which were:

Book value	$20,751,533
Precision	$ 279,235
Decision interval	$20,472,298 to $21,030,768
Estimated audited value	$20,217,692

Notice that the estimated audited value did *not* fall within the decision interval. The initial reaction might have been that the statistical evidence failed to support fair statement. However, the beta risk achieved with the $279,235 precision would have been substantially less than the planned beta risk of 30 percent—actually it was less than 1 percent.

Therefore, the decision interval found with that precision was far too small. The formula to compute A'' gives a precision yielding a final beta risk equal to the planned beta risk and changes the reliability level. However, it is not necessary to know the amount of this new reliability level if the estimated value falls within the decision inter-

286

val formed by book value plus and minus A''. (If this happens, alpha error did not occur.)

However, the reliability of A'' can be found from the following formula:

$$U_{R'} = U_R \left[1 + \frac{M}{A} \left(\frac{A}{A'} - 1 \right) \right]$$

The reliability level can then be determined from a normal curve area table.

In the preceding illustration the statistical evidence supported fair statement of the book value. To illustrate another possibility let us use the same facts, except that the estimated audited value is $19,000,000 instead of $20,217,692. The formula computing A'' would still give a new precision of $924,426 yielding a 30 percent beta risk. However, the $19,000,000 estimate is not included in the final decision interval. In fact, it is $827,107 less than the lower decision interval limit.[15]

An Example of Sampling for Variables

Assume that statistical sampling is used in conjunction with the confirmation of notes receivable for a finance company. At the balance sheet date there are 5,100 loans outstanding totaling $10 million. One hundred of these loans have balances of $50,000 or more. These 100 loans total $7 million. It is decided to request confirmation of all the large accounts. Confirmations will be requested for a sample drawn from the remaining 5,000 loans based on a planned beta risk of 28 percent and a reliability of 90 percent. The purpose of the confirmation requests is to test the validity of the $10 million figure in notes receivable.

The 90 percent planned reliability is based on the auditor's willingness to accept a 10 percent alpha risk of erroneously concluding that the book balance might be materially misstated when, in fact, it later proves to be reasonably stated.

The planned beta risk of 28 percent is based on the auditor's desired combined reliability level of 95 percent, the evaluation of internal controls as being 80 percent effective in preventing material errors from occurring, and the estimate that other audit procedures would be

---

[15] Some of the alternatives available to the auditor when the statistical evidence does not support fair statement of the book value are:
1. Increase the sample size based on the achieved standard deviation to achieve lower risk levels acceptable for proposing an adjustment.
2. Request the client to revalue the account.
3. Judgmentally determine whether to accept book value based on the results of other additional audit procedures.

10 percent effective in detecting any material error in the account balance.
Therefore,

$$\beta = \frac{1 - CR}{(1 - C)(1 - SP)} = \frac{.05}{(.2)(.9)} \cong 28\%$$

Planned precision is calculated as follows assuming $40,000 is considered material.

$$A = \frac{M}{1 + \frac{Z_\beta}{Z_{\alpha/2}}} = \frac{\$40,000}{1 + \frac{.59}{1.64}} \cong \$30,000$$

The $30,000 planned precision will be used when calculating a sample size which should allow the auditor to achieve the desired combined reliability and alpha and beta risk levels.

In dollar terms the average precision is± $6 (that is, $30,000/5,000). The auditor draws a preliminary sample of 48 items in order to estimate the standard deviation of the population. By the use of the "range" method (discussed earlier on page 253) the standard deviation is estimated to be $100.

On page 266 we noted that a formula can be used to calculate sample size. If we label precision A, then:

$$n = \frac{(U_R \cdot S_{X_j})^2}{A^2} = \frac{(1.65 \times 100)^2}{(6)^2} = 756.25$$

The formula just used gives the sample size using sampling with replacement. Sample size for sampling without replacement can be found by using the following formula:

$$n = \frac{n'}{1 + \frac{n'}{N}}$$

where

n' = Sample size with replacement.
N = Population size.

When the fraction n/N is 0.05 or more this correction should be made. When the fraction is less than 0.05 the correction is optional since its effect is relatively immaterial.

In our example we will use sampling without replacement. Thus:

$$n = \frac{n'}{1 + \frac{n'}{N}} = \frac{756.25}{1 + \frac{756.25}{5,000}} \cong 657$$

Thus, the auditor must randomly sample at least another 609 accounts (657 less the 48 in the preliminary sample).

The auditor draws the sample, sends out the confirmation requests and (after a second request to nonreplies to the first request) receives back all 657. Let us assume that the 657 confirmations received totaled $390,915. (In most circumstances not all comfirmations sent out would be returned, and the auditor would use alternative procedures to test the balances of the nonreplies.) The average audited balance is $595 ($390,915 ÷ 657). If $595 is multiplied by the 5,000 loans $2,975,000 is obtained. This represents the probable audited value of the strata of notes receivable which have balances that are less than $50,000 each.

At this point, the achieved precision (A') for the $2,975,000 estimated audited value may be established. The standard deviation of the audited sample values is calculated and found to be $80.

Achieved average precision can be determined from the following formula:

$$A' = \frac{U_R S_{x_j}}{\sqrt{n}} = \frac{1.65 \times \$80}{\sqrt{657}} \cong \$5.15$$

Since n/N is more than 0.05, and we are using sampling without replacement a correction factor $\sqrt{1 - n/N}$ is multiplied by the achieved average precision. Thus, $5.15 is multiplied by $\sqrt{1 - n/N}$. In our example, the correction factor is $\sqrt{1 - 657/5000} \cong 0.932$. Then,

$$0.932 \times \$5.15 \cong \$4.80$$

The total achieved precision of the estimated audited value is found by multiplying $4.80 by N (in this example, 5,000).

$$5,000 \times \$4.80 = \$24,000 = A'$$

Since the achieved precision is less than planned precision we find a new precision A'' by the following formula

$$A'' = A' + M(1 - A'/A)$$
$$= \$24,000 + \$40,000 \left(1 - \frac{\$24,000}{\$30,000}\right)$$
$$= \$32,000$$

The decision interval becomes $3,000,000± $32,000 or $2,968,000 to $3,032,000. Since the audited value of $2,975,000 falls within the decision interval, we can conclude that the sample information supports fair statement of the book value. It is not necessary to know the new reliability level since the estimated value falls within the decision interval.

The audited value of the 100 largest accounts tested separately should be compared to their total book value of $7 million and a separate conclusion reached as to their fairness of presentation.

DISCOVERY SAMPLING

Thus far only estimation sampling has been discussed. Another type of sampling which is used by the auditor in special situations is discovery sampling. The objective of discovery sampling is to provide a specified assurance of locating at least one example of an attribute if its rate of occurrence in the population is at or above a specified rate. Discovery sampling is appropriate when the occurrence rate is quite low, yet the auditor wants to have a specified chance that the sample selected is large enough so that the observation of at least one occurrence may be expected.

The discovery sampling objective can be made a part of another test if the sample size is made large enough to satisfy all purposes simultaneously. On the other hand, there might be occasions when the sole objective of the sample is discovery. This is most likely to occur in special purpose examinations. For example, after dismissing an employee, a company might engage an auditor for a special purpose examination to determine whether errors (or defalcations) occurred in the employee's work. If the employee approved disbursements up to $2,000 from a special bank account, the auditor might select a sample large enough so that if 1 percent or more of the approved disbursements contained irregularities, the auditor would be 95 percent sure of finding at least one example. In such a case, seeing one example of fraudulent action would naturally lead to expanding the investigation.

While one function of discovery sampling is to locate an example, the auditor will always have the option of using a statistical sample for *estimation*. Thus, suppose that the sample fails to disclose any occurrences. In this case, the auditor is in the same position as with any sample with a sample occurrence rate of zero. The auditor can use the attribute tables to compute an upper precision limit. Likewise, if the sample produced at least one occurrence of the characteristic, in order to make an evaluation, the auditor should use the attribute tables to compute the upper precision limit of the population occurrence rate.

HARNESSING THE COMPUTER

Often, the best way to accomplish quantitative sampling plans is through the use of the computer. In addition to saving time, using a computer normally promotes greater accuracy. Computer programs exist which calculate the sample size, select the sample, and statistically evaluate the results.

SAMPLING IN PRACTICE[16]

The "art" of statistical sampling, discussed in this chapter, involves: (1) precisely defining the particular objective of each audit test and (2) translating these objectives into statistically meaningful audit procedures.

As an example, consider inventories. The objectives in auditing inventories are to determine that they physically exist, that they are the property of the client, that they are usable and salable, and that they are priced in accordance with the client's established policies and with generally accepted accounting principles. To accomplish these objectives, the audit program specifies a series of audit procedures. Suppose the auditor decides to use statistical sampling in the "price test." The purpose of the "price test" must be described so it can be translated into an appropriate sampling plan. The purpose might be one of the following:

1. To estimate the total dollar amount of pricing errors.
2. To estimate the percentage of items that have been priced incorrectly.
3. To discover some example(s) of pricing errors if they exist in a specified percentage of the items.

In many auditing situations the auditor will wish "to estimate the total dollar amount of pricing errors." Sampling for variables may be used here.

Because the second and third objectives mentioned above would yield information concerning the number of occurrences (attribute sampling in the second and discovery sampling in the third) rather than dollars, it usually will be more difficult to use such information to reach a conclusion about materiality. Two ways to translate attribute (occurrence) information into dollar estimates of *limited accuracy* follow.

1. If the sample error rate is 2 percent, and the upper precision limit is 6 percent at 95 percent reliability, the auditor can be 95 percent sure that the *maximum exposure* of overstatement of book value would be the total dollar amount of the largest 6 percent of the population's items. To the extent that any of the largest 6 percent of the

---

[16] Probability proportional to size or dollar-unit sampling has been advocated as an additional statistical sampling technique appropriate in auditing. Under this method the sampling unit in a population is an individual dollar rather than an individual item. It uses attribute sampling theory to draw dollar conclusions. The method eliminates the need to stratify the population since large dollar items have a greater chance of being selected. For a further discussion of this method, see R. Anderson and A. D. Teitlebaum, "Dollar-Unit Sampling," *Canadian Chartered Accountant* (April 1973), pp. 30–38.

population items were found acceptable in the sample, the next largest items below that point would be included.

2.   A reasonable estimate of the *probable exposure* might be computed by multiplying the sample mean by the sample error rate (2 percent in the example) by the number of items in the population. Unfortunately, in most attribute and discovery sampling situations, the sample mean and a listing of population items in descending amount will not be readily available.

These concepts do not apply to asset accounts in which the individual items can have credit balances or to liability accounts because the extent of potential differences is not limited by the amount of the recorded balance.

Also, these two concepts of exposure are, at best, approximations and are not necessarily close to the results of variables estimation methods. Therefore, attribute and discovery sampling may not be appropriate when the objective relates to a balance sheet account and the auditor expects to find some differences. However, such methods can be useful when combined with a variables estimation sampling plan.

Designing a Sampling Plan

Designing a sampling plan to accomplish audit objectives requires technical proficiency in statistics. It also requires a proficiency in the *art* of defining audit objectives and translating them into statistically meaningful audit procedures. If the auditor understands the principles in this chapter, appropriate sampling plans may be designed to cover many situations. When designing plans, two points should be considered.

1.   All plans should be reviewed to ensure (*a*) technical validity, and (*b*) appropriate application in the circumstances.

2.   A statistical specialist should be consulted concerning applications which require more advanced techniques than presented here. These would include: nonroutine problems, such as determining a Lifo index; testing a population of items in several physical locations when it is not possible to visit them all; and situations where sample sizes (determined by using the simple techniques described in this chapter) are too large for practical reasons.

Time and Cost Considerations

In certain situations, the use of statistical sampling will be beneficial because: (1) the audit evidence obtained will be objective and defensible, and (2) an estimate of the sampling error can be ascer-

292

tained readily. Sometimes, its use can save time and cost, but this should only rarely be the sole consideration.

Since there is nothing restrictive about an initial estimate of sample size, the auditor should always consider taking a few additional items whenever the sampling cost is small. An example would be accounts receivable confirmation requests where the cost of sending 25 additional requests (and performing alternative procedures on them, if necessary) might be nominal. This will be especially important if the auditor expects to find many differences, because otherwise there is a risk of not achieving the desired precision. It is almost always easier to select additional items initially rather than at a later date. For example, it would be difficult or impossible to go back to an open items account receivable file or work-in-process physical inventory weeks after the auditor initially selected a sample.

Statistical sampling, of course, is not appropriate in every auditing situation. For instance, sampling usually will be relatively inefficient for small populations. Also, if the auditor suspects that certain items in the population are more likely to contain errors, these items should be segregated before sampling the remainder. Finally, statistical sampling should generally not be used to obtain information about rare events. If errors are rare, sampling methods generally used may not provide much information about their occurrence rate or size.

Combining Results of Two or More Statistical Samples

In variables estimation, the results of two or more statistical samples can be combined if the precision around each estimate is expressed at the same reliability. The total population estimate is equal to the sum of the estimates being combined. The precision of the combined estimate is equal to the square root of the sum of the squares of each precision amount being combined. For example, if an auditor wished to combine these two results:

First: $1,000,000 ± $30,000 at 95% reliability.
Second: $2,500,000 ± $40,000 at 95% reliability.

The combined estimate is $3,500,000 and the precision around that estimate is ± $50,000 at 95 percent reliability. (The $50,000 is found by: $\sqrt{\$30,000^2 + \$40,000^2}$.)

Statistical Sampling and Confirmation Procedures

A frequently perplexing consideration when planning receivable confirmation procedures is the proper evaluation and handling of "nonresponse" to the requests. This consideration focuses attention on the underlying auditing decision of whether to use positive or negative requests. (See Chapter 10 for a discussion of positive and negative requests.) Statistical sampling makes the situation even more complex.

SAS No. 1, section 331.05, identifies three conditions that should be present if negative requests are to be used: "The negative form is useful particularly when internal control surrounding accounts receivable is considered to be effective, when a large number of small balances are involved, and when the auditor has no reason to believe the persons receiving the requests are unlikely to give them consideration."

Negative requests do not provide any measurement of nonresponse. In situations where it is judged that all three prerequisites are satisfied, *and* negative requests are used, conclusions drawn from the confirmation procedures will be *judgmental,* not statistically supportable. This is because variables estimation statistical projections for auditing purposes use the *audited* value of each sample item. If negative requests are used, the auditor would, in effect, be asserting that all nonresponding accounts were correct—that the audited value and book value are equal. Mathematically, every sample item, whether responding or not, has equal statistical importance; therefore, even one incorrect nonresponding account would destroy any possible *statistical* conclusion, even though *judgmentally* the auditor might have reason to believe that all errors on nonrespondent accounts would be immaterial in the aggregate.

Variables estimation sampling is a frequently used statistical approach. In such applications, where a statistical conclusion is desired, the auditor must use only positive confirmation requests and perform alternative procedures on every nonrespondent account in the sample.

The auditor may use negative requests with attribute or discovery sampling if there is a reasonable basis for estimating the extent of nonresponse. The complement of the response rate to first requests for positive-type confirmations used in the previous year for the same account may be a reasonable basis for making that determination. The sample size should be determined by dividing the indicated sample size from the table by the estimated *response* rate.

The evaluation would be based on the lower number; the sample size net of nonresponse. When using this approach, however, a sample conclusion might be, "To the extent that our assumption of the response rate is conservative, we are 95% confident that the upper precision limit is 6%."

CONCLUDING REMARKS

The use of statistical sampling techniques results in many advantages for the auditor. A major benefit is that it often saves considerable time. A statistical sampling plan might permit better advance planning of the audit since the accounts to be audited or the numbers of documents or transactions to be examined may be determinable in advance and work sheet formats prepared before regular field work begins. In addition, the extent of the auditor's work might be reduced because, without the use of statistical sampling techniques, a larger sample possibly might be chosen judgmentally. Furthermore, if during the course of the audit examination, the application of statistical sampling discloses the need for a substantial increase in the amount of audit testing, the auditor will promptly have grounds for estimating the additional audit costs involved and for related discussions with the client.

GLOSSARY—PART 1

Cluster sampling The population is divided into groups (clusters) of items, and a random sample of clusters is selected from all the clusters. Each cluster becomes a sampling unit.

Dispersion The extent to which the values of the items are spread about the mean.

Frequency distribution A chart or table that shows the number of items in each class.

Judgment sampling When the auditor selects a sample without using statistical selection techniques. Although intuition, experienced judgment, and knowledge about the client are used, judgmentally selected samples cannot meet the criteria for statistical validity.

Mean A measure of central tendency obtained by totaling all of the values and dividing by the number of items. See formula, page 250.

Normal distribution This term is illustrated by the normal bell-shaped curve (see Figure 7-1). The relative frequency of any interval of the curve can be determined by knowing the mean and the standard deviation.

Population All items in a group being audited.

Population rate of occurrence The percentage of items in a population which possess a particular attribute.

Precision (of an estimate) This is a measure of the closeness of a sample estimate to the true population value. See page 257.

Precision interval (of a mean) This interval is that range surrounding the sample mean which has an R% probability of including the true population mean. See formula, page 259.

Random number table A table of numbers running in no regular order which can be used to create probability samples. See Figure 7-2 for an illustration.

Range The difference between the largest and smallest values in a distribution.

Reliability (or confidence level) The probability of achieving a certain degree of precision. See page 257.

Sample One or more items selected from a population. The auditor may use the sample to obtain information about the population.

Sampling error The difference between the estimated value obtained from sampling and what would be obtained from examining all items in the population.

Skewness The measure of the asymmetry of a distribution.

Skip interval The number of items skipped each time when taking a systematic sample.

Standard deviation A unit of measure of the variability of a frequency distribution.

Standard error of the mean The standard deviation of the distribution of sample means. See formula, page 256.

Stratified random sampling Dividing the population into strata and then selecting random samples from the various strata.

Systematic sampling A method of drawing a sample in which the beginning sample item(s) are randomly chosen, a fixed number of items skipped, another item selected, and the same fixed number of items skipped.

Unrestricted random sampling Selecting a sample by drawing individual items at random from a population so that each item has an equal chance of being selected. If the sample item chosen is returned to the population so that it has a chance of being selected again, the method is called *with replacement*. If not, it is called *without replacement*.

Variability See dispersion.

GLOSSARY—PART 2

Alpha (α) risk The risk of deciding a book balance is materially misstated when it really is fairly stated.

Attribute sampling A procedure used to determine an estimated occurrence rate, together with an upper precision limit of a particular attribute in a population.

Beta (β) risk The risk of deciding a book balance is fairly stated when it really is materially misstated. See formula, page 279, for calculating planned beta risk.

Combined reliability The complement of ultimate risk. Thus, if ultimate risk is 5 percent, then combined reliability is 95 percent.

Discovery sampling Sampling for attributes so as to have a specified probability of locating an occurrence in a population.

Estimation sampling A broad term which includes both sampling for attributes and sampling for variables. It involves the projection of sample characteristics to a population. This can include quantitative or qualitative estimation.

Sample rate of occurrence The percentage of items in a sample which possess a particular attribute.

Ultimate risk The risk that a material error will occur in the accounting process and the auditor's examination will not detect it. See formula for calculating ultimate risk, page 278.

Variables sampling Projecting a quantitative characteristic (such as total dollar value) to the corresponding population quantity.

QUESTIONS AND PROBLEMS—PART 1

7-1. Define the following terms:
  - *a.* Precision.
  - *b.* Reliability.
  - *c.* Population.
  - *d.* Sample.
  - *e.* Mean.
  - *f.* Dispersion.
  - *g.* Range.
  - *h.* Unrestricted random sampling.
  - *i.* Systematic sampling.
  - *j.* Stratified random sampling.

7-2. What is the basic advantage systematic sampling has over unrestricted random sampling?

7-3. When should stratified random sampling be used?

7-4. A nonstratified sample of 80 accounts payable vouchers is to be selected from a population of 3,200. The vouchers are numbered consecutively from 1 to 3,200 and are listed, 40 to a page, in the voucher register. Describe at least four different techniques for selecting a random sample of vouchers for review.

(AICPA, adapted)

7-5. Tom Murrary, CPA, is conducting an audit of Jones Art Co. Mr. Murrary plans to select sufficient inventory items for test counts and pricing tests so that he can make a rough estimate of total inventory cost.
  - *a.* The standard deviation is a basic measure of variation. Define a standard deviation.
  - *b.* Will wide variability (as measured by the population standard deviation) in the cost of the items being sampled affect the sample size? Is so, in what manner?

(AICPA, adapted)

7-6. For each of the following questions select the *best* answer:
  - *a.* What is the primary objective of using stratification as a sampling method in auditing?
    1. To increase the confidence level at which a decision will be reached from the results of the sample selected.
    2. To determine the occurrence rate for a given characteristic in the population being studied.

3. To decrease the effect of variance in the total population.
4. To determine the precision range of the sample selected.
   b. How should an auditor determine the precision required in establishing a statistical sampling plan?
   1. By the materiality of an allowable margin of error the auditor is willing to accept.
   2. By the amount of reliance the auditor will place on the results of the sample.
   3. By reliance on a table of random numbers.
   4. By the amount of risk the auditor is willing to take that material errors will occur in the accounting process.
   c. Which of the following is an advantage of systematic sampling over random number sampling?
   1. It provides a stronger basis for statistical conclusions.
   2. It enables the auditor to use the more efficient "sampling with replacement" tables.
   3. There may be correlation between the location of items in the population, the feature of sampling interest, and the sampling interval.
   4. It does not require establishment of correspondence between random numbers and items in the population.
   d. Precision is a statistical measure of the maximum likely difference between the sample estimate and the true but unknown population total, and is directly related to
   1. Reliability of evidence.
   2. Relative risk.
   3. Materiality.
   4. Cost benefit analysis.

(AICPA, adapted)

7-7. Potter Company asks its auditor's assistance in estimating the average gross value of the 5,000 invoices during June 1981. The CPA estimates the population standard deviation to be $8. If the goal is to achieve a precision of ±$2 with a 95 percent level of confidence, what sample size should be drawn?

(AICPA, adapted)

7-8. One method used for drawing an unrestricted random sample is to use a random number table.
   a. List two advantages of using a random number table.
   b. List the steps to follow when using a random number table to select an unrestricted random sample.

7-9. During the course of an audit engagement, a CPA attempts to obtain satisfaction that there are no material misstatements in the accounts receivable of a client. *Statistical sampling* is a tool that the auditor often uses to obtain representative evidence to achieve the desired satisfaction. On a particular engagement an auditor determined that a material misstatement in a population of accounts would be $35,000. To obtain satisfaction the auditor had to be 95 percent confident that the population of accounts was not in error by $35,000. The auditor decided to use unrestricted random sampling with replacment and took a preliminary random sample of 100 items *(n)* from a population of 1,000 items *(N)*. The sample produced the following data:

Arithmetic mean of sample items $(\bar{x})$ $4,000
Standard deviation of sample items *(SD)* $ 200

The auditor also has available the following information:

Standard error of the mean (SE) = SD $\div \sqrt{n}$
Population precision (P) = N × R × SE

Partial List of Reliability Coefficients

If Reliability Coefficient (R) Is	Then Reliability Is
1.70	91.086%
1.75	91.988
1.80	92.814
1.85	93.568
1.90	94.256
1.95	94.882
1.96	95.000
2.00	95.450
2.05	95.964
2.10	96.428
2.15	96.844

Required:

a. Define the statistical terms "reliability" and "precision" as applied to auditing.
b. If all necessary audit work is performed on the preliminary sample items and no errors are detected,
   1. What can the auditor say about the total amount of accounts receivable at the 95 percent reliability level?
   2. At what confidence level can the auditor say that the population is not in error by $35,000?

(AICPA, adapted)

7-10. Balmes Company asks its auditor's assistance in estimating the proportion of its active 30-day charge account customers who also have an active installment credit account. The CPA takes an unrestricted random sample of 100 accounts from the 6,000 active 30-day charge accounts. Of the accounts selected, ten also have active installment credit accounts. If the CPA decides to estimate with 95 percent confidence, the estimate is that (select the best answer):

a. At most, 10 percent of the active 30-day charge account customers also have active installment credit accounts.
b. At least, 10 percent of the active 30-day charge account customers also have active installment credit accounts.
c. Between 7 percent and 13 percent of the active 30-day charge account customers also have active installment credit accounts.

    d. Between 4 percent and 16 percent of the active 30-day charge account customers also have active installment credit accounts.

(AICPA, adapted)

7-11. Statistical sampling techniques are being used in auditing. A sample is taken and analyzed to draw an inference or reach a conclusion about a population, but there is always a risk that the inference or conclusion may be incorrect. What is the value, then, in using statistical sampling techniques?

(AICPA, adapted)

7-12. You are now conducting your third annual audit of the financial statements of Elite Corporation for the year ended December 31, 1981. You decide to employ unrestricted random number statistical sampling techniques in testing the effectiveness of the company's internal control procedures relating to sales invoices, which are all serially numbered. In prior years, after selecting one representative two-week period during the year, you tested all invoices issued during that period and resolved all of the errors which were found to your satisfaction.

Required:

    a. Explain the statistical procedures you would use to determine the size of the sample of sales invoices to be examined.

    b. Once the sample size has been determined, how would you select the individual invoices to be included in the sample?

    c. Would the use of statistical sampling procedures improve the examination of sales invoices as compared with the selection procedure used in prior years?

    d. Assume that the company issued 50,000 sales invoices during the year and the auditor specified a confidence level of 95 percent with a precision range of ± 2%.

        1. Does this mean that the auditor would be willing to accept the reliability of the sales invoice data if errors are found on no more than 4 sales invoices out of every 95 invoices examined? Discuss.

        2. If the auditor specified a precision range of ± 1%, would the confidence level be higher or lower than 95 percent assuming that the size of the sample remains constant? Why?

(AICPA, adapted)

QUESTIONS AND PROBLEMS—PART 2

7-13. Describe "attribute sampling."

7-14. What is discovery sampling?

7-15. The use of statistical sampling techniques in an examination of financial statements does not eliminate judgmental decisions. Identify and explain at least four areas where judgment may be exercised by a CPA in planning a statistical sampling test.

(AICPA, adapted)

7–16. Assume that a CPA's sample shows an unacceptable error rate in a compliance test of internal control. Describe the various actions that the auditor may take based upon this finding.

(AICPA, adapted)

7–17. Refer back to Question 7–9. Assume that the preliminary sample was sufficient. Compute the auditor's estimate of the population total.

(AICPA, adapted)

7–18. For each of the following select the best answer:

    a. For a large population of cash disbursement transactions, Smith, CPA, is testing compliance with internal control by using attribute sampling techniques. Anticipating an occurrence rate of 3 percent Smith found from a table that the required sample size is 400 with a desired precision limit of 5 percent and reliability of 95 percent. If Smith anticipated an occurrence rate of only 2 percent but wanted to maintain the same desired upper precision limit and reliability the sample size would be closest to

        1. 200.
        2. 400.
        3. 533.
        4. 800.

    b. Which of the following *best* describes what the auditor means by the rate of occurrence in an attribute sampling plan?

        1. The number of errors that can reasonably be expected to be found in a population.
        2. The frequency with which a certain characteristic occurs within a population.
        3. The degree of confidence that the sample is representative of the population.
        4. The dollar range within which the true population total can be expected to fall.

    c. The purpose of tests for compliance is to provide reasonable assurance that the accounting control procedures are being applied as prescribed. The sampling method that is *most* useful when testing for compliance is

        1. Judgment sampling.
        2. Attribute sampling.
        3. Unrestricted random sampling with replacement.
        4. Stratified random sampling.

    d. When using statistical sampling for tests of compliance an auditor's evaluation of compliance would include a statistical conclusion concerning whether

        1. Procedural deviations in the population were within an acceptable range.
        2. Monetary precision is in excess of a certain predetermined amount.
        3. The population total is not in error by more than a fixed amount.

4. Population characteristics occur at least once in the population.

(AICPA, adapted)

7-19. An auditor believes that the error occurrence rate of expensing capital items is 2 percent which will have an immaterial effect upon the financial statements. The maximum acceptable occurrence rate is 3 percent. What type of sampling plan should the auditor select in the circumstances?

(AICPA, adapted)

7-20. Assume that an auditor is interested in appraising the effectiveness of the calculation of payroll taxes. Also, assume the auditor specifies a reliability of 95 percent and an upper precision of 6 percent. The auditor, based on past experience with this client, feels that the expected error rate is 3 percent.

Required:

Using Table 7-1 determine the size of the sample that the auditor should draw.

7-21. Referring to Question 7-20, the auditor finds ten errors in calculation. Using Table 7-2 find a more exact upper precision limit given the specified reliability.

7-22. List and discuss four advantages of applying statistical sampling techniques to audit testing.

(AICPA, adapted)

7-23. A CPA's client maintains perpetual inventory records. In the past, all inventory items have been counted on a cycle basis at least once during the year. Physical count and perpetual record differences have been minor. Now, the client wishes to minimize the cost of physically counting the inventory by changing to a sampling method in which many inventory items will not be counted during a given year. Under what circumstances will the auditor accept the sampling method?

(AICPA, adapted)

7-24. Assume an auditor, in auditing an account, determines that an α risk of 5 percent and a β risk of 25 percent are acceptable. The auditor considers that for this account the minimum material error is $400,000.

Required:

Determine the precision to be used in determining sample size so that the auditor can attain that level of beta risk.

7-25. The Cowslip Milk Company's principal activity is buying milk from dairy farmers, processing the milk and delivering the milk to retail customers. You are engaged in auditing the retail accounts receivable of the company and determine the following:

1. The company has 50 retail routes; each route consists of 100 to 200 accounts, the number that can be serviced by a driver in a day.

2. The driver enters cash collections from the day's deliveries to

each customer directly on a statement form in record books maintained for each route. Mail remittances are posted in the route record books by office personnel. At the end of the month the statements are priced, extended and footed. Photocopies of the statements are prepared and left in the customers' milk boxes with the next milk delivery.

    3.   The statements are reviewed by the office manager, who prepares a list for each route of accounts with 90-day balances or older. The list is used for intensive collection action.

    4.   The audit program used in prior audits for the selection of retail accounts receivable for confirmation stated: "Select two accounts from each route, one to be chosen by opening the route book at random and the other as the third item on each list of 90-day or older accounts."

Your review of the accounts receivable leads you to conclude that statistical sampling techniques may be applied to their examination.

Required:

a.   Since statistical sampling techniques do not relieve the auditor of responsibilities in the exercise of professional judgment, of what benefit are they to the auditor? Discuss.

b.   Give the reasons why the audit procedure previously used for selection of accounts receivable for confirmation (as given in [4] above) would not produce a valid statistical sample.

c.   What are the audit objectives or purposes in selecting 90-day accounts for confirmation? Can the application of statistical sampling techniques help in attaining these objectives or purposes? Discuss.

d.   Assume that the company has 10,000 accounts receivable and that your statistical sampling disclosed 6 errors in a sample of 200 accounts. Is it reasonable to assume that 300 accounts in the entire population are in error? Explain.

(AICPA, adapted)

7-26. Answer the following questions using Table 7-1 and Table 7-2.

a.   Assume that you are testing a client's cash disbursements. More specifically, you are testing the propriety of account distributions. Also assume that a sample occurrence rate of errors of 4 percent is expected, but the substantive tests of operations would have to be expanded only if the occurrence rate were above 8 percent. You want 95 percent reliability. What sample size should be used?

b.   Under the conditions in (a) above, assume you selected the sample and found five occurrences of errors. What is the achieved upper precision level?

7-27. You desire to evaluate the reasonableness of the book value of the inventory of your client, Jones, Inc. You satisfied yourself earlier as to inventory quantities. During the examination of the pricing and extension of the inventory, the following data were gathered using appropriate unrestricted random sampling with replacement procedures.

Total items in the inventory $(N) = 12,700$

Total items in the sample (n) = 400
Total audited value of items in the sample = \$38,400

$$\sum_{j=1}^{400} (x_j - \bar{x})^2 = 312,816$$

Formula for estimated population standard deviation

$$S_{x_j} = \sqrt{\frac{\sum_{j=1}^{j=n} (x_j - \bar{x})^2}{n - 1}}$$

Formula for estimated standard error of the mean

$$SE = \frac{S_{x_j}}{\sqrt{n}}$$

Confidence level coefficient of the standard error of the mean at a 95 percent confidence (reliability) level = $\pm$ 1.96.

Required:

a. Based on the sample results, what is the estimate of the total value of the inventory? Show computations in good form where appropriate.

b. What statistical conclusion can be reached regarding the estimated total inventory value calculated in (*a*) above at the confidence level of 95 percent?

(AICPA, adapted)

7-28. Assume the following data in the audit of accounts receivable of Smith Co.

Amount considered material	\$ 100,000
Desired reliability	95%
Population size	5,000
Desired combined reliability	95%
Internal control effectiveness	80%
Supplemental audit procedure effectiveness ...	20%
Estimated population standard deviation	\$ 100
Book value	\$5,080,000

Required:

a. Calculate the sample size.

b. Assume 150 positive confirmations are sent out and returned. Also, assume the 150 returned confirmations totaled \$150,000 with a standard deviation of \$50. Is the account fairly stated?

7-29. Levelland, Inc., a client of your firm for several years, uses a voucher system for processing all cash disbursements which number about 500 each month. After carefully reviewing the company's internal controls, your firm decided to statistically sample the vouchers for 11 specific characteristics to test operating compliance of the voucher system against the client's representations as to the system's operation. Nine of these characteristics are noncritical; two are critical. The characteristics to be evaluated are listed on the accompanying work sheet.

Pertinent client representations about the system follow:

1. Purchase orders are issued for all goods and services except for recurring services such as utilities, taxes, and so on. The controller issues a check request for the latter authorizing payment. Receiving reports are prepared for all goods received. Department heads prepare a services-rendered report for services covered by purchase orders. (Services-rendered reports are subsequently considered receiving reports.)

2. Copies of purchase orders, receiving reports, check requests, and original invoices are forwarded to accounting. Invoices are assigned a consecutive voucher number immediately upon receipt by accounting. Each voucher is rubber-stamped to provide spaces for accounting personnel to initial when (a) agreeing invoice with purchase order or check request, (b) agreeing invoice with receiving report, and (c) verifying mathematical accuracy of the invoice.

3. In processing each voucher for payment, accounting personnel match each invoice with the related purchase order and receiving report or check request. Invoice extensions and footings are verified. Debit distribution is recorded on the face of each invoice.

4. Each voucher is recorded in the voucher register in numerical sequence after which a check is prepared. The voucher packets and checks are forwarded to the treasurer for signing and mailing the checks and canceling each voucher packet.

5. Canceled packets are returned to accounting. Payment is recorded in the voucher register, and the voucher packets are filed numerically.

Following are characteristics of the voucher population already determined by preliminary statistical testing. Assume that each characteristic is randomly distributed throughout the voucher population.

1. Eighty percent of vouchers are for purchase orders; 20 percent are for check requests.

2. The average number of lines per invoice is four.

3. The average number of accounts debited per invoice is two.

Appropriate statistical sampling tables follow. For values not provided in the tables, use the next value in the table which will yield the most conservative result.

TABLE 1
Evaluation of results: number of occurrences
in sample. Reliability (confidence level):
95 percent

Sample Size	Precision (Upper Limit) Percentage					
	1	2	3	4	5	6
90				0		1
120			0	1		2
160		0	1	2	3	4
240		1	2	4	6	8
340	0	2	4	7	10	12
460	0	4	7	11	15	18
1,000	4	12	20	29	38	47

TABLE 2
Probability in percent of including at least one occurrence in
a sample (for populations between 5,000 and 10,000)

Sample Size	If the True Population Rate of Occurrence is:					
	.1%	.2%	.3%	.4%	.5%	.75%
	The Probability of Including at Least One Occurrence in the Sample Is:					
240	22	39	52	62	70	84
300	26	46	60	70	78	90
340	29	50	65	75	82	93
400	34	56	71	81	87	95
460	38	61	76	85	91	97
500	40	64	79	87	92	98
600	46	71	84	92	96	99
700	52	77	89	95	97	99+
800	57	81	92	96	98	99+
900	61	85	94	98	99	99+
1,000	65	88	96	99	99	99+

Note: 99+ indicates a probability of 99.5 percent or greater.

LEVELLAND, INC.
Voucher Test Work Sheet
Years Ended December 31

Characteristics	Year 1	Year 2						
	Column A	Column B	Column C	Column D	Column E	Column F	Column G	Column H
	Sample Size	Estimated Error Rate	Specified Upper Precision Limit	Reliability (confidence level)	Required Sample Size	Assumed Sample Size	Number of Errors Found	Upper Precision Limit
Noncritical								
1. Invoice in agreement with purchase order or check request.		1.1%	3	95%		460	4	
2. Invoice in agreement with receiving report.		.4	2	95		340	2	
3. Invoice mathematically accurate.								
Extensions		1.4	3	95		1,000	22	
Footings		1.0	3	95		460	10	
4. Account distributions correct.		.3	2	95		340	2	
5. Voucher correctly entered in voucher register.		.5	2	95		340	1	
6. Evidence of Accounting Department checks.								
a. Comparison of invoice with purchase order or check request.		2.0	4	95		240	2	
b. Comparison of invoice with receiving report.		1.3	4	95		160	2	
c. Proving mathematical accuracy of invoice.		1.5	3	95		340	10	
Critical								
7. Voucher and related documents canceled.		At or near 0	.75%	95%		600	5	
8. Vendor and amount on invoice in agreement with payee and amount on check.		At or near 0	.4%	95%		800	0	

TABLE 3
Determination of sample size: Percentage of occurrences in sample. Reliability (confidence level): 95 percent

Sample Size	Precision (upper limit) Percentage					
	1	2	3	4	5	6
90				0	0	
120			0	.8	.8	1.7
160		0	.6	1.2	1.9	2.5
240		.4	.8	1.7	2.5	3.3
340	0	.6	1.2	2.1	2.9	3.5
460	0	.9	1.5	2.4	3.3	3.9
1,000	.4	1.2	2.0	2.9	3.8	4.7

Required:

a. Year one:

An unrestricted random sample of 300 vouchers is to be drawn for year one. Enter in column A of the work sheet the sample size of each characteristic to be evaluated in the sample.

b. Year two:

1. Given the estimated error rates, specified upper precision limits, and required reliability (confidence level) in columns B, C, and D respectively, enter in column E the required sample size to evaluate each characteristic.

2. Disregarding your answers in column E and considering the assumed sample size and numbers of errors found in each sample as listed for each characteristic in columns F and G respectively, enter in column H the upper precision limit for each characteristic.

3. Identify each characteristic for which the sampling objective was not met and explain what steps an auditor might take to meet his or her sampling or auditing objectives.

(AICPA, adapted)

Learning Objectives

Study of the material in this chapter is designed to achieve several learning objectives. These include an understanding of:

1. How computerized accounting systems have affected the practice of auditing.
2. The various computer components and peripheral devices.
3. The nature and purpose of computer software.
4. The various types of computer installation —in-house, service bureau, time-sharing, and facilities management.
5. The flow of data within a computerized system.
6. Computer controls including general controls, hardware controls, and application controls.
7. How to evaluate computer controls.
8. Computer-assisted audit techniques including generalized audit software, test deck, and specialized programs.
9. Likely future developments.

8

Computer Controls and Audit Techniques*

The use of the computer in the accounting system has had a tremendous effect on how the auditor accomplishes the attest function. In computerized accounting systems, many procedures previously performed manually are performed by computer programs. Furthermore, the centralized processing of accounting information found in computerized systems reduces the segregation of duties normally found in manual systems. These changes in the processing of accounting information increase the opportunity for errors and irregularities unless computer controls are implemented. To properly study and evaluate internal control in computerized accounting systems, the auditor must not only understand computer controls, but also be able to utilize various techniques, such as generalized audit software, to test computerized procedures and accounting records. The significance of computerized accounting systems has been widely recognized in industry and the public accounting profession. In 1974, the AICPA issued *SAS No. 3*, which states that:

> When EDP is used in significant accounting applications, . . . the auditor should consider the EDP activity in his study and evaluation of accounting control. This is true whether the use of EDP in accounting applications is limited or extensive and whether the EDP facilities are operated under the direction of the auditor's client or a third party.[1]

Both internal auditors and CPA firms have developed approaches

---

*This chapter was written by Michael J. Jett, at the time a manager in the National Office of Ernst & Whinney.

[1]*Statement on Auditing Standards No. 3*, "The Effects of EDP on the Auditor's Study and Evaluation of Internal Control," American Institute of Certified Public Accountants, 1974, p. 2.

to evaluating computer controls and auditing through the computer to test programmed procedures and computerized accounting records. The evaluation of computer controls is performed as part of the overall evaluation of internal control and may be documented in questionnaires, flowcharts, or narratives. Personnel with specialized training may be required to make the evaluation.

THE COMPUTER ENVIRONMENT

Data processing is simply the collecting, processing, and distributing of information to achieve a desired result. The equipment and procedures through which the result is achieved constitute a data processing system. When a machine performs most of the procedures, the system is known as an automatic data processing system. More specifically, when the machine is an electronic digital computer, the system is described as an electronic data processing (EDP) system or computer system. Every computer system is designed to perform specific types of operations. The operations are *performed* by hardware—the physical components of the system, and are *controlled* by software—the computer programs.

Computer Hardware

The principal hardware component of a computer is the Central Processing Unit (CPU). The CPU consists of the main storage facility, the arithmetic and logic facility, and the control facility. Additionally, the CPU controls the input and output facilities.

Main Storage Facility. A computer's main storage facility (which also may be referred to as memory) consists of elements, such as ferrite core or semi-conductors, that take and hold a magnetic charge in one of two possible binary states, 0 and 1. Information that is stored in any element is referred to as a "bit." Since it is unlikely that one "bit" of storage will be useful, the bits are used in groups.

Main storage is used to temporarily store programs and data for processing. Furthermore, main storage is of a finite size. If greater storage capacity or a more permanent storage is needed, peripherial equipment which is not part of the CPU can be used as auxiliary storage. To process data that are in auxiliary storage, it is necessary to move the data from the peripherial equipment into the main storage facility.[2]

---

[2]See W. Thomas Porter and William E. Perry, *EDP Controls and Auditing*, 2d ed., Wadsworth Publishing Company, Inc., 1977, pp. 10–12.

Data may be retrieved from peripherial equipment in a sequential fashion—reading the data item-by-item from start to finish. Magnetic tape is an example of such equipment. Alternatively, data may be retrieved in a random manner by what is called a direct access device. Such a device allows one to read the 35th record, then the 48th, and then the 103rd, and so on. Magnetic disk packs (containing revolving plates) and magnetic drums (shaped like a barrel) are examples of direct access devices.

Arithmetic and Logic Facility. Arithmetic tasks (addition, subtraction, multiplication, and division), comparisons, and other types of data transformations are accomplished by the arithmetic and logic facility. The data and instructions needed for the operation are called from the computer's main storage. After the operation the results are returned to the main storage facility.

Input Facility. An input facility permits the computer to receive both data and instructions for processing. The data and instructions may be submitted through media such as punched cards, magnetic tape, magnetic drums or disks. While punched cards are perhaps the most popular media for inputting information, magnetic tapes or disks and direct entry remote terminals are becoming popular.

Output Facility. The output facility returns information from the computer to the user. The output may be put onto media such as punched cards, magnetic tape or disk pack, paper tape, paper (via a printer), or transmitted to remote terminals.

Control Facility. The control facility regulates the activities of the other facilities by retrieving machine language instructions from the main storage facility and then interpreting the instructions. Next, the control facility generates the signals and commands that cause the other facilities to perform their operations at the appropriate times.

Computer Software

Software is a series of programs or routines that provide instructions for operating the computer. There are two broad categories of computer software—application programs and systems software. Application programs (sometimes referred to as user or problem programs) are designed to accomplish specific objectives for users, such as processing payroll or pricing the inventory. In the early days of computers, they were written in machine language (also known as object language or object code). Today, however, programming in an English-like language, such as COBOL (Common Business Oriented Language) and RPG (Report Program Generator), is made possible by an element of software known as a compiler. Compilers are programs which translate the application programs written in COBOL, RPG, or other high-level languages (known as source code) into machine language, which can be placed into main storage and executed.

Programmers do not write all the instructions necessary to control a computer system. Computer manufacturers usually provide programs, known as systems software, which operate the computer system and perform routine tasks for users. Important elements of systems software are the operating system and utilities. An operating system is a highly complex set of programs designed to:

1. Serve as a means of communication between the computer hardware and the human operator.
2. Schedule, load, initiate, and supervise the execution of programs.
3. Initiate and control input and output operations.
4. Manage and control compilers and utility programs.

Operating systems are given various names by computer vendors, such as "control programs," "executives," or "supervisors." Utilities are a program or group of programs designed to perform commonly encountered data handling functions, such as sorting files, merging files, and copying data from one file to another. Most computer manufacturers provide comprehensive libraries of utility programs.

Computer Installations

Computer installations are the physical facilities where the computer hardware and personnel are located. Computer installations are generally organized into one of the following categories:

1. *In-House or Captive Computer.* The organization owns or leases the equipment and hires the necessary trained personnel to program, operate, and control the various applications processed with the equipment. This is the most common arrangement in use today. Large organizations can have one or several computer systems handling the needs of various divisions of the business.
2. *Service Bureau Computer.* The computer is owned by an independent outside agency which rents computer time and provides programming, keypunching, and other services. The user organization pays only for the computer time and other services it uses. Rates are generally based on some measurable quantity, such as the number of computer hours used to process the data.
3. *Time-sharing.* Under this system, the organization acquires a keyboard device capable of transmitting and receiving data and, by agreement, the right to use a central computer facility. This facility will furnish service to several users at the same time. The

user company does most of its own programming and treats the
computer as though the company were the only one using it.
When the company needs service it telephones the computer
facility, and, using an acoustical coupler between the telephone
and the terminal, submits its user number and password, calls for
its files, and then begins to process the necessary data.
4. *Facilities Management.* This is the latest type of computer service arrangement to be developed. It falls somewhere between
the captive computer and the service bureau computer categories.
Under facilities management, the organization needing computer
services may lease or purchase the necessary hardware and install
it on its own premises. Then, by negotiation, an outside contractor
with the necessary staff of programmers and operators agrees to
manage the facility. In some instances, the contractor may own or
lease the equipment. Facilities management is usually covered by
a long-term contract typically of three to six years. All of the
people necessary to manage the installation are employees of the
contractor. The agreement usually specifies that the user organization must use the contractor for all present and future computer services, although there are termination clauses in these
contracts.

COMPUTER CONTROLS

Section 320.33 of *SAS No. 1* states that:

> Since the definition and related basic concepts of accounting control
> are expressed in terms of objectives, they are independent of the
> method of data processing used; consequently, they apply equally to
> manual, mechanical, and electronic data processing systems. However,
> the organization and procedures required to accomplish those objec-
> tives may be influenced by the method of data processing used.

In other words, the use of the computer in an accounting system
does not change the objectives or essential characteristics of accounting control discussed in Chapter 5. Both manual and computerized
accounting systems are comprised of attributes and procedures designed to achieve the objectives. In manual systems, control objectives are achieved through manual procedures and segregation of
functions. In computerized systems, however, many procedures previously performed manually are performed within computer programs
and systems software. Furthermore, because accounting data and
transactions are processed centrally, various accounting functions become centralized. The elimination of manual procedures and centralization of functions increases the opportunity for errors and ir-

regularities, unless compensating controls are implemented. These compensating controls are known as computer controls. Some computer controls are programmed procedures within computer programs and systems software. Others are manual procedures, such as the use of batch control totals and review of output, often referred to as computer controls because they are related to the use of the computer in the accounting system.

SAS No. 3 recognizes the effect of the computer upon traditional accounting control concepts. It classifies accounting controls in computerized systems into the categories of general controls and application controls. General controls relate to all computer applications, and not to any specific application. *SAS No. 3* indicates that included among general controls are:

1. The plan of organization and operations of the computer department.
2. The procedures for documenting, testing, and approving computer systems and applications and changes thereto.
3. Hardware controls.
4. Controls over access to computer files and programs.

Application controls, on the other hand, relate to specific tasks that the computer performs for users. They are discussed later in the chapter.

General Controls

The Organization of the Computer Department. The use of a computer affects the basic organization of most businesses. In accounting systems where a computer is not used, the processing of data relating to a particular business function, such as sales, is normally centralized within one department under one department head who is responsible for the processing of the particular accounting information. In computerized accounting systems, the responsibility is shared with the computer department, which processes and usually maintains custody of the information on computer files. The computer department will usually share this responsibility with several different departments, known as user departments, which use its processing services. Thus, although most accounting information will be processed centrally, the responsibility for processing is decentralized, and both the computer department and user department must develop and maintain computer controls.

The consolidation of functions found in computerized accounting systems can combine incompatible functions, unless a proper organization within the computer department is maintained. The organizational plan of the computer department should, therefore, clearly define lines of authority, responsibility, and duties for each employee, and provide for the segregation of incompatible functions. Figure 8–1 shows the basic organizational plan for a computer department.

Ideally, the organization should be divided into an administrative function (including a steering committee and EDP manager), an applications and programming function, an operations function, and a data control function, which acts as an interface between the computer department and the users. It is important that the computer department not be under the direct control of any user department. Otherwise, the user may have the authority to require the computer department to circumvent established controls. Organizational independence of the data processing function from the user departments creates a framework within which user controls may be performed independently of data processing controls.

Steering Committee. The steering committee should be composed of a senior executive from each functional area of the organization which is affected by data processing. The EDP manager should be on the steering committee. If the organization has an internal audit department, it is advisable that a representative of that department be a member of the committee. The purpose of the steering committee is to:

FIGURE 8–1
Basic organizational structure of a computer department

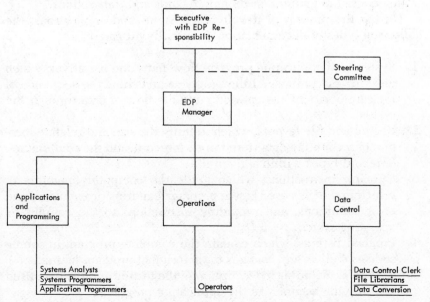

1. Review, evaluate, and approve planned computer systems and applications.
2. Evaluate and monitor progress in developing the computer systems and applications.
3. Evaluate and approve proposals concerning the acquisition of EDP equipment and facilities.

EDP Manager.   The manager of the computer department directs the overall operation of the department. He or she should report to a top executive of the company, such as the controller, financial vice president, or information systems vice president. The EDP manager is responsible for providing managerial guidance to the systems and programming, operations, and data control staffs; and developing standards, policies, priorities, and short- and long-range plans for the department.

Applications and Programming.   This function consists of systems analysts, systems programmers, and application programmers. Systems analysts are responsible for evaluating and designing new or improved computer systems. Systems programmers maintain the software which controls the hardware and the application programs. Application programmers prepare, test, and update the application programs required to accomplish user objectives. They prepare program flowcharts in accordance with the specifications provided by the systems analysts, and then code the required programs in source languages, such as COBOL. The programs are then tested using test data, which consist of genuine or dummy records and transactions.

During the process of developing systems and applications, the following types of documentation are usually prepared:

1. System and application program flowcharts and narratives, which describe the purpose of the programs and show the sequence of logical operations they perform and the flow of data through the system.
2. Record and file layouts, which identify the size and relative location of accounting data stored in each record, and the combination of record types within a given file.
3. Operator instructions, which guide the computer operators in selecting the files used by the program, handling program halt and error conditions, and providing instructions to the computer's operating system.
4. Program listings, which contain the complete program in source code as well as any changes to the original program listing.
5. Test data, including a description of the testing and the data used to verify the accuracy of the application programs.

6. Application approval and change sheets, which evidence approval
    of the application programs and changes to them.

Documentation is important because it is frequently the best source
of information on control features within computer programs. Therefore, the review of computer controls may depend, in part, on
adequate documentation. Furthermore, a lack of proper documentation can make the installation dependent upon the individuals who
prepared the programs, since they would be the only persons capable
of maintaining them.

Computer Operations.   Computer operators are responsible for
running the computer and executing jobs in accordance with operator
instructions and a job schedule. In most cases, the operations manager
or supervisor will prepare the job schedule, although this may be done
by the EDP manager in smaller installations. The operators execute
jobs via a computer console, which enables them to communicate with
the computer's operating system.

Data Control.   Data control is responsible for controlling the
timely receipt of data for computer processing and the distribution of
computer output to user departments. In addition, the function usually includes the conversion (keypunching) of data into machine-sen-
sible form, and the maintenance of a computer file library. The control
group logs input data and control totals when the data are received for
processing. It maintains contact with users regarding input errors and
follows up on corrections. When output is received, the control group
reconciles it to the input, reviews it for accuracy, and supervises its
distribution to users. A file library should be maintained to protect
computer tape or disk files and other records from loss, damage, and
unauthorized use. To ensure adequate control, there should be a librarian or library staff responsible for keeping track of the files and
their use. Provision should be made for off-premise storage of copies
of critical data files and programs.

Applications Development, Acquisition, and Changes.   Applications development includes the activities of the systems analysts and
programmers who develop computer systems and applications. Good
systems and applications development requires documentation, management and user review and approval procedures, technical review
and approval, and involvement of the internal and external auditors.
Without these, the resulting applications may result in inaccurate recordkeeping. In particular, user department and auditor involvement
are needed to determine that an adequate audit trail or link between
the original source documents and the summary figures in the financial statements has been established.

Applications acquisition is the purchase of systems and applications from outside vendors. The procedures used to control the acquisition of systems and applications are very similar to the applications development procedures.

Often, shortly after a system is implemented, it becomes necessary to make changes to the various programs. The process of requesting, approving, testing, and implementing the changes is known as program maintenance. Changes to application programs should be requested and approved in writing, and subjected to testing before final implementation. Documentation should be updated to reflect the changes.

Hardware Controls. Computer manufacturers build into their equipment features which will detect and sometimes correct machine-based errors. Most of these features operate on the principle of adding an extra element to a machine process or data code to detect any error which can occur. The following are the more common hardware controls.

1. *Parity Check.* The computer processes data in arrays of binary digits ("bits") of "1" and "0", which denote alphabetic and numeric characters. In addition to the bits necessary to denote the character, an extra or parity bit is added to bring the sum of the "1" bit to an even (even parity check) or odd (odd parity check) number, depending upon the make of the computer. The parity check is applied as data are transferred among the various components of the computer to ensure that bits are not lost during the transfer process.
2. *Valid Character Check.* Established patterns are used to identify and accept valid bit combinations for input and output devices. If nonconforming combinations are detected, an error condition is created.
3. *Dual Read and Read-after-Write.* Data read from punched cards are read by two separate reading stations, and the results of the two operations are compared to detect errors. Similarly, data written to magnetic tape or disk are read again to detect errors.
4. *Validity Check.* The central processing unit checks operation codes and memory addresses against those allowed prior to execution.
5. *Echo Check.* The central processing unit transmits a signal to the printer or card punch, which activates the print or punch mechanism for each character. Before printing or punching, a signal is sent back to the CPU verifying that the proper print or punch position has been activated.

Access to Computer Equipment, Data Files, and Programs. Computer data files and programs cannot be altered without the use of computer equipment. Therefore, controlling access to computer equipment is an extremely important control consideration. One of the basic objectives of accounting control—safeguarding—stresses that access to assets should be permitted in accordance with management's authorization. In EDP environments, assets take the form of the accounting information (data) on computer files, the computer programs, and the computer equipment itself.

In general, only operations personnel should be allowed in the computer room. There are several methods of restricting access. These may include the use of a locked door to which only authorized personnel have keys, or the use of sliding doors which have cipher locks or require magnetic cards. Proper segregation of duties helps to enforce access controls. Programmers, for example, should not be allowed to operate the computer, and operators should not be allowed to program or have access to program documentation.

Control over access to data files is important because it helps ensure that the correct file is used in an application, and that files are restricted to authorized users. A data file, which is simply a collection of related records, can be stored on punched card, perforated tape, and magnetic tape, drum, or disk. The file can be a master file or a transactions file. A master file contains relatively permanent information. In a payroll application, for example, it would contain the employee number, name and address, department, rate of pay, withholding information, and year-to-date gross and net pay. Transactions files contain temporary information, such as the payroll for a certain weekly or monthly period. Master files are particularly important because errors in master file data can cause errors in the processing of transactions against the master file. Most installations maintain three generations of master files to enable recreation of any tape files lost or destroyed. This is known as the grandfather-father-son principle of file retention. The current version is the son; the previous version the father; and the previous father is the grandfather.

In addition to maintaining a file library, external and internal labels should also be used. An external label, affixed to card and magnetic tape files, should be checked by the operator to see if it is the correct file. There are no specific requirements as to how much information should be on the label. Some installations include the file name, volume serial number, date created, version number, and other items. Other installations simply use a volume serial number. Internal labels, such as header labels containing information which identifies the file, can be checked by the operating system or application programs to help ensure that the correct file is used. Many installations also use another internal label, known as a trailer label, which is a record at the end of a file that contains control information, such as the number of records on the file and total dollar amounts.

Although programs can be physically stored on punched card, magnetic tape, or disk, they are most commonly stored on disk. When stored on disk, they are often grouped together into a file called a program library, which has a directory within it to identify each program stored. The programs are physically stored in one of two logical forms—source code or object code. In order to execute a program, a person must (1) know the program name and location, (2) have sufficient technical knowledge to run the program, and (3) have access to the computer. Controls over program access, therefore, focus on restricting one or more of these execution requirements. Restricting access to the computer room or terminals, for example, limits the number of persons who can access a program. Prohibiting operator access to program documentation prevents operators from knowing program names and storage locations.

Other control techniques which may be used are passwords, special software librarian packages, and job accounting. It is becoming increasingly popular to establish security systems over files so that the user of the file must not only know its name, but also a security code or password. In controlling access to program libraries, passwords are commonly used in conjunction with special software, which prevents unauthorized attempts to change programs. Job accounting, which provides an audit trail of machine activity in the form of reports of jobs run on the computer, can be used to identify unauthorized execution of programs or use of program libraries.

Application Controls

Computer Applications. The computer department performs specific tasks for users through computer applications, which are a group of related computer programs and data files designed to accomplish the accounting objectives of user departments, such as generating customer invoices. Any computer application, even the most complex, can be viewed in terms of the accounting information it processes. In fact, regardless of the type of data processed or the kind of equipment used, all data processing usually involves these four basic functions.

1. *Input Function.* The acceptance of information (source data) from other parts of the system.
2. *Processing Function.* The calculation or generation of new data.
3. *Output Function.* The return of information (data on output reports, documents, transaction files, or terminals) to other parts of the accounting system.
4. *Master Files Function.* The storage of relatively permanent in-

formation (data on magnetic tape or disk files) necessary to sustain the processing of accounting transactions.

Figure 8–2 is a flowchart of an invoicing application. It shows how the billing function, described in Figure 5–4, Chapter 5, might be accomplished in a computerized accounting system. The purpose of the application is to generate customer invoices and a daily sales journal. To accomplish this purpose, the application:

1. *Accepts* shipping information (customer number, customer name and address, part number, quantity shipped, date shipped, and so on) as input from the billing department through the use of a terminal which is "online" to the computer.
2. *Calculates or generates* an invoice amount (new accounting information) which did not previously exist in the accounting system. In performing the calculation, the application uses the sales price for the respective part number on the sales price master file and other billing information, such as discount and credit terms, from the customer master file.
3. *Returns* accounting information in the form of the daily sales journal and customer invoices to the billing department. In addition, a magnetic tape of daily sales transactions is created for input to the general ledger application.
4. *Stores* sales transactions (accounting information) on the customer master file as additions to outstanding customer balances.

Note that both the billing department and the computer department share in the responsibility for the billing function. The computer is used to perform many procedures, such as calculating the invoice amount, preparing the customer invoice, and posting the sale to the customer's account, which were previously performed manually in the billing department.

Application Control Objectives.   Application controls are the procedures of a specific computer application and are designed to control the processing of specific accounting transactions and data. As previously discussed, both the computer department and user departments share responsibility for the correct processing of accounting information of any particular function. For example, using the computer to process payroll transactions necessitates a "shared responsibility" between the payroll and computer departments for the correct processing of payroll transactions. The shared responsibility begins during the application development stage of the payroll application, and continues throughout its life cycle. User departments share their responsibility through procedures which are designed to provide reasonable assurance that their data and transactions are processed as

FIGURE 8-2

General Corporation
Invoicing Application

PREPARED Williams 11/7/80
APPROVED Michael 11/21/80

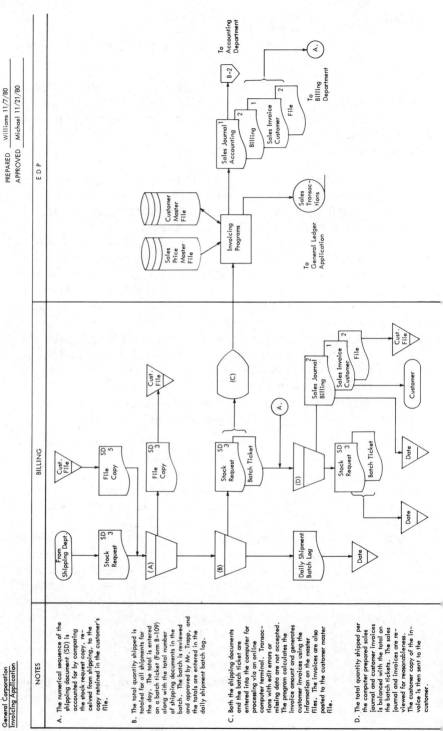

NOTES

A. The numerical sequence of the shipping document (SD) is accounted for by comparing the stock request copy, received from shipping, to the copy retained in the customer's file.

B. The total quantity shipped is totaled for all shipments for the day. The total is entered on a batch ticket (Form B-109) along with the total number of shipping documents in the batch. The batch is reviewed and approved by Mr. Trapp, and the totals are entered in the daily shipment batch log.

C. Both the shipping documents and the batch ticket are entered into the computer for processing via an online computer terminal. Transactions with edit errors or missing data are not accepted. The program calculates the invoice amount and generates customer invoices using the information on the master files. The invoices are also posted to the customer master file.

D. The total quantity shipped per the computer prepared sales journal and customer invoices is balanced with the total on the batch tickets. The sales journal and invoices are reviewed for reasonableness. The customer copy of the invoice is then sent to the customer.

authorized, and are accurately and completely recorded. The procedures employed by user departments are manual procedures. The computer department, on the other hand, shares its responsibility through procedures which may be manual or programmed. The programmed procedures are contained within computer application programs or systems software, and are also designed to ensure that accounting data and transactions are processed as authorized and are accurately and completely recorded. The programmed procedures may be a substitute for or supplement to the manual procedures of the user departments. In processing customer orders, for example, the credit department will usually compare the customer's balance to the dollar amount of the transaction to ensure that the customer's credit limit is not exceeded. This same procedure can be part of the sales application program. Figure 8–3 provides examples of manual and programmed procedures which may help achieve the authorization and recording objectives defined in *SAS No. 1*, section 320.28 (see Chapter 5, page 163).

In order to achieve the objectives, the procedures must be applied to the transactions at certain points (functions) within the application. Authorization procedures are applied to ensure that only authorized transactions are input to the application, and that data on application master files remain authorized. Procedures designed to ensure that transactions are accurately recorded are applied throughout the appli-

FIGURE 8–3
Computer application controls

| Accounting Control Objective | Examples of Procedures Which Help Achieve the Objective | |
	Manual	*Programmed*
Authorization	The use and checking of approvals on source, batch, and transmittal documents; approvals for error corrections; and controlling access to computer terminals located in user departments.	The use and checking of passwords, terminal authority levels, and terminal identification by computer programs and systems software.
Accuracy	The general or specific manual review of computer documents and reports.	Tests made by computer programs or systems software to edit input or created data for validity or reasonableness.
Completeness	The use and checking of batch, hash, or control totals for transactions processed and data on computer files.	The use of computer programs and systems software to reconcile transactions and balance computer files (e.g., trailer labels, run-to-run totals).

324

cation. They are needed in the input function to ensure that transactions accepted by the application are accurate; in the processing function to ensure that data calculated or generated by the application are accurate; and in the output function to ensure that transactions output from the application are accurate. In the master files function, they are needed to ensure that the data on master files remain accurate. Procedures which ensure that transactions are completely recorded are needed in the input function to keep track of the transactions until they are accepted by the application. In the output function, they are needed to keep track of transactions which have been accepted or created by the application and output to a report or transactions file. They are needed in the master files function to reconcile the data stored on the file to control totals.

Controls over Input. Input controls are designed to provide reasonable assurance that information accepted by the application from other parts of the accounting system is authorized, accurate, and complete. Controls over input begin in user departments where, traditionally, control has been established through the use of batch controls. A batch is a group of transactions to be processed in sequence as one lot. The batching technique generally consists of collecting input documents in the user department, manually counting the number of documents, and computing a control total on key numeric data fields (usually dollar or quantity amounts). Batch controls are usually extended another step to include a sequential batch number to ensure that all batches are accounted for by the user department and the computer department. Such batch data are usually noted on a batch control document, a copy of which is retained in the user department for later verification that the batch was properly processed. User department approval should be indicated on the batch control document, which is then forwarded with the batched transactions to data processing.

The effectiveness of batch control is greatly dependent upon the nature of batch checking performed in the computer department. As a minimal check, the data control department should verify the authorization of the batch and record the control totals and batch serial numbers in a batch log. Batch control effectiveness is increased with manual recounting of items or recomputation of control amounts. Program checking of batch controls is accomplished when the information on the batch control document is captured by the application program and compared with detail information accumulated by the program from detail batch documents. Differences in item counts or control totals should result in batch error messages being generated, and could result in rejection of the batch from further processing. Other examples of edit tests which may be performed in the application are:

1. Verifying that all required data are present.
2. Verifying proper data format.
3. Matching data to a set of allowable entries.
4. Matching data to a set of previously established values, such as a customer account number.
5. Checking the numerical sequence of the documents.
6. Recalculating check digits.
7. Performing reasonableness or limit tests.

Although batched input transactions are usually edited when they are entered into the application, they may also be edited later in the application.

Errors detected during the editing process may be handled in one of four different ways.

1. Edit errors in a batch result in the entire batch being rejected. Only batches containing no edit errors are processed beyond the edit routines.
2. Within a given batch, transactions with edit errors are rejected, but those without errors are accepted and processed further.
3. Within a given batch, all transactions are accepted and processed. Those with edit errors are posted to a suspense account or file until a subsequent correction is posted. Unlocated differences may also be posted to the file until corrected.
4. Within a given batch, all transactions are accepted and processed. Those with edit errors are posted to the appropriate master or transaction file with some indication (such as a code) that the transaction contained an error. The code is removed when the error is subsequently corrected.

Edit errors (except possible data conversion errors, such as keypunch errors) should be returned to user departments for correction and re-submission.

Controls over Processing. Processing controls are designed to provide reasonable assurance that accounting information calculated or generated by the application is accurate. Because the generation or calculation of new data is often done in a manner which is difficult for the user to verify, minimal manual controls are often found in this area. When manual controls are present, they generally consist of someone performing tests over a limited number of items which have been calculated or generated, such as a review for reasonableness, manual recalculation of detail items, and manual recalculation of totals.

In some cases, programmed checks may be performed over calculated items, but since they are usually subject to the same application

326

development criteria as the original calculation, they do not provide the independence found in manual tests performed by the user. Furthermore, they can be difficult to identify and compliance-test. In general, programmed checks are similar to edits performed over input data. Typical checks include:

1. Verifying the proper format (alpha, numeric, significant digits).
2. Verifying the range or sign of resulting values (positive, negative, zero-balance).
3. Matching data to a set of allowable entries.
4. Reasonableness and limit tests.
5. Recalculation using different methods.

Controls over Output. Output controls are designed to provide reasonable assurance that accounting information returned to other parts of the system is complete and accurate. Output can include printed reports, documents, special forms, and transaction (temporary) files. Obviously, the completeness and accuracy of output cannot be verified unless the physical output item is properly distributed to users. Data control should have responsibility for distributing the output to the appropriate users and should maintain a routing or distribution schedule.

Initial control over completeness and accuracy of output is dependent upon the quality of input information, the accuracy of data stored on master files used by the application, and the accuracy of processing performed by the application.

Control totals established by the user enable further verification that all transactions have been completely recorded. Manual procedures, such as recalculation of amounts, comparison of certain data items to detailed manual records, or a visual scan or review, can be used to help determine that the output data are accurate.

Controls over Master Files. As previously mentioned, there are two basic types of computer files: transactions files and master files. Transactions files contain information of a less permanent nature than master files, such as individual sales transactions, which are used to update master files. Master files contain information that is usually considered permanent, such as a customer number, name and address, credit limit and terms, and account balance; and that is periodically updated by accounting transactions. Once a master file is updated, another version or generation of that file exists.

The audit significance of master files is that many amounts later calculated or generated by the application depend upon the data contained in the master file. The accuracy of invoice amounts, for example, depends upon the accuracy of the unit sales price for each part number stored in the sales price (or inventory) master file. Therefore, master file controls are designed to prôvide reasonable assurance that the data stored in master files remain authorized, accurate, and complete.

Changes to master files can occur in one of two ways. First, normal transactions processed by application programs can cause changes to master files, such as the updating of an accounts receivable master file from sales invoice, customer payment, and debit or credit memo transactions. Second, additions, deletions, and adjustments to master files may be caused by changes initiated outside the normal transaction flow. Examples include the addition of a new customer to an accounts receivable master file, or the deletion of old inventory items from an inventory master file. Changes of this latter nature are often referred to as file maintenance transactions. Application controls dealing with input and processing apply to both types of master file changes.

To ensure that the data on master files remain authorized, accurate, and complete, user departments generally obtain periodic reports containing the contents of the master file. An aged trial balance of accounts receivable or a listing of current customers, for example, may be used to ensure that customer information on the customer master file is authorized, accurate, and complete; or user departments may obtain a listing of all changes to the master file. Another important control is balancing the number of records and dollar amounts contained on the file to other accounting records. Where separate generations or versions of the file are maintained, procedures should exist to verify that the correct version is used in processing transactions. Computer department verification consists of adequate library procedures, and internal and external file label checking. User verification of the correct file version consists of a detailed examination of application output and periodic review of master file contents.

Online, Real-Time Systems. Most computer installations with earlier generations of computers exclusively use batch processing where source documents are accumulated into batches over a period of time, arranged in sequence, and processed against the master file. However, the advent of telecommunications and direct access files made possible real-time processing where the computer system can accept input at any time, execute the program or programs required to process the input, access and update the required master files, and respond to the user with accurate information. This is done in no more than a few seconds and without the presequencing of data required in batch systems. The concept of real-time is commonly associated with systems whose response times are in microseconds, and this is viewed as an essential characteristic of real-time processing.

Real-time processing, by its very nature, requires the use of online devices. An online system is one in which computer equipment and devices are in direct contact with the computer's central processing unit and usually under its direct control. The online devices are most commonly computer terminals remotely located from a central facility. An online system need not also be a real-time system. An online system may use batch processing, where transactions are submitted through a remotely located terminal, transmitted to the central facility where they are stored on magnetic tape or disk, and processed as a batch at a later time. A real-time system, however, must be an online system. The most familiar example of online, real-time (OLRT) systems are those used by commercial airlines for processing reservations.

OLRT systems have several audit implications, the most important of which is the elimination of the time interval usually found in batch systems between the point where a transaction occurs and the point at which it is processed. In batch systems, this time period permits the examination of the transactions and the accumulation of balancing control totals. Another implication of OLRT systems is the potential loss of audit trail from reduction in the amount of hard-copy source documentation, which is an integral part of batch systems. Since the users of the terminals are essentially computer operators, they bypass the data control and operations function which help control transactions processed in batch systems. Therefore, controls over authority to submit information must be a combination of user and system procedures, and it is the responsibility of the user to ensure that input errors are corrected and that all data are submitted for processing.

Adequate online controls begin with procedures which limit access to the online terminals. User departments should have procedures which limit physical access to authorized users. The online systems software should require the use of a password or security code which identifies the user. Some online systems require thumbprints or plastic cards with magnetic strips to identify users. As a further control, the system may have several levels of passwords (terminal authority levels) which the user must submit as more processing authority is requested. Unauthorized access attempts should be recorded and investigated. In some online systems, repeated unauthorized access attempts will cause the terminal to "lock" and prevent its further use until it is reactivated. To provide an audit trail, there should be some procedure to log input transactions. The procedures commonly used include manual logging procedures at the terminal site, attaching a printer to the terminal, or the use of a transactions log at the central facility where transactions entered into the system are recorded on magnetic tape or disk to provide an after-the-fact batch control.

Data Base Systems.[3] In conventional data processing file systems, all data associated with a specific application are stored in one or more files belonging only to that application. For example, the data stored in the inventory master file are associated with the specific program or programs of the inventory application. Since each application has its own programs and files, there may be a great deal of data redundancy. The inventory part number stored in the inventory master file would also be stored in files associated with other applications, such as the purchase order file, vendor master file, and job costing detail file. Redundancy in stored data has several disadvantages, such as extra storage costs, the requirement for multiple updating operations whenever the data are changed, and the difficulty of keeping all copies of the data at the same update level.

Data base systems (sometimes referred to as integrated file systems) greatly reduce the amount of redundant data stored. This is achieved by storing the data in one central physical location on magnetic disk (the data base) and allowing each application to have a unique logical view of the data. The inventory part number would be physically stored once on magnetic disk, but logically associated with other data items, such as quantity on hand, vendor name, quantity on order, and unit cost. Each application program is allowed to use only those logical associations necessary to accomplish its processing function. These logical associations are known by a software package, the data base management system (DBMS), which controls the use of the data base and has the logical associations stored in the DBMS library. The logical association between the inventory part number and quantity on hand is used by the inventory application, but may not be necessary for the purchases application. However, the purchases application would certainly use the logical association between inventory part number and vendor name.

There are several control considerations for data base systems. In conventional file systems, an error in master file data affects only those transactions of the specific application associated with the master file. Errors in data stored in data bases, however, can cause errors in all applications sharing the data. Therefore, the validation of input data takes on greater importance. In addition to the general controls previously discussed, general controls in data base systems depend upon the data base administrator (DBA) and the DBMS library. The DBA has custody of the data stored in the data base and is responsible

---

[3]This section is based in part on J. Hal Reneau, "Auditing in a Data Base Environment," *The Journal of Accountancy,* (December, 1977), pp. 59–65. Copyright © 1977 by the American Institute of Certified Public Accountants, Inc.

for controlling its use and overall structure. The data base administrator may be one person or a group of persons. The DBA function should be separate from the operations, data control, and applications development and programming functions. If an application programmer wants to create a new data item or change a logical association, he or she must apply to the DBA for permission. The DBA will then make the appropriate changes to the DBMS library. Proper controls require that only the DBA have authority to make changes to the DBMS library, and that all changes be documented and approved. The DBA should not be allowed to operate the computer or initiate transactions without user department approval. Application programmers should not have knowledge of data items and logical associations which are not related to their own applications.

Minicomputers. Since their introduction in 1959, minicomputers have become increasingly popular. While there is no universally accepted definition of a minicomputer, they are typically low-cost, physically small, general-purpose computers. Like large computer systems, minicomputer systems consist of a central processing unit, input devices, and output devices. Minicomputers are primarily marketed for small- and medium-sized businesses that have been using manual, mechanical, and punched-card data processing systems for bookkeeping and accounting functions.

In reviewing computer controls in minicomputer environments, the auditor is likely to find general control weaknesses. The size of the organizations which employ minicomputers does not lend itself to many of the standard computer controls expected in larger computer installations. Most minicomputer installations have few employees and little, if any, segregation of duties. In many cases, the person having responsibility for the computer will also have responsibilities in user departments. Controls over access to the computer equipment, programs, and data files may also be weak. Some programs for minicomputers are written in interpretive languages rather than compiler languages. A compiler language (such as COBOL) must first be converted from source code to object code before it can be executed. The nature of object code makes it difficult to modify. Therefore, changes to compiler language programs normally involve changing the source code, recompiling the program, and creating a new object program. Interpretive languages, on the other hand, do not require a compiler. They are executed directly from the source code and no separate object program is created. Consequently, a person authorized to process a program written in an interpretive language has a greater opportunity to make unauthorized changes to the program.

Although weak general controls may exist in minicomputer environments, the auditor may still be able to place reliance on application controls. When general controls are weak, the auditor may find that user controls are more reliable than programmed controls as a basis for audit reliance. The auditor may, for example, identify strong manual procedures in user departments over the review and balancing of computer input and output.

Distributed Data Processing. Until the early 1970s, business organizations primarily used centralized data processing, where a single, centrally located computer processed accounting data from various geographical locations or management levels. In recent years, however, distributed data processing has become one of the fastest growing segments of the data processing industry. The essence of distributed data processing is the capture, processing, and use of accounting data at its source or point of origin and the communication of the data to larger computers only when it must be further processed, stored, or made available to other areas of the business organization. Distributed data processing evolved from the decentralized system philosophy of installing minicomputers at remote locations to work in a cooperative manner with a larger computer at a central site. A typical distributed data processing system consists of minicomputers, microcomputers, or intelligent terminals which can process data at its origin and communicate with other computers in the system. Such a system may not have a larger computer at a central location.

Distributed processing involves the distribution of application processing. Therefore, each remote location must develop and maintain adequate general controls and application controls. The degree to which the auditor will be concerned with the computer controls at any one location will depend upon the significance of the applications processed by the location and the extent of the processing. Since distributed data processing involves the use of minicomputers and online processing, the applicable control considerations should be considered by the auditor for each significant location.

EVALUATING COMPUTER CONTROLS[4]

The study and evaluation of computer controls should be performed as part of the overall study and evaluation of internal control. SAS No. 3 divides the review of computer controls into two phases—the preliminary phase and the completion phase. The preliminary phase is used by the auditor to understand the overall accounting system, including the computerized portion, and the com-

[4]Portions of this section were adapted from *The Auditor's Study and Evaluation of Internal Control in EDP Systems,* American Institute of Certified Public Accountants, 1977, pp. 9–20. Copyright © 1977 by the American Institute of Certified Public Accountants, Inc.

pletion phase is used to evaluate the computer controls upon which the auditor intends to place reliance. Both phases of the review include general controls and application controls. The review can be documented in questionnaires, system flowcharts, or narratives.

The purpose of the preliminary phase of the review is to enable the auditor to understand the flow of transactions through the overall accounting system, the extent of computer involvement in accounting applications, and the basic structure of accounting control. During the preliminary phase, the auditor focuses on identifying and understanding how the structure of computer controls relates to the overall structure of accounting control. The preliminary phase of the review covers both the manual and computerized portions of the accounting system. To understand the flow of transactions through the accounting system, the auditor will ordinarily relate significant computer applications to the overall accounting system. This may be achieved by identifying the significant inputs, outputs, master files, and processing of those applications which process accounting information that can materially affect the financial statements, and tracing the flow of a limited number of transactions through the application.

The extent of computer involvement in accounting applications may be assessed by considering the number, type, and dollar amount of transactions processed by the computer and the nature and extent of the processing. To understand the basic structure of accounting control, the auditor will usually consider the controls that are provided in the overall accounting system, the division of control responsibility between the manual and computerized portions of the system, and the relationship between the existing manual and computer controls.

Upon completion of the preliminary phase of the review, the auditor assesses both general and application controls to determine whether they appear to provide a basis for audit reliance. If the auditor plans to place reliance on computer controls, the review is completed for those specific controls on which audit reliance is planned. The completion phase consists of making further inquiries and observations for the relevant computer controls, performing tests of compliance, and making an overall evaluation. Most CPA firms and internal auditors have developed structured approaches to reviewing computer controls. The various approaches usually require the use of questionnaires, although flowcharts and narratives may also be used. Figure 8–4 illustrates a portion of a general controls review questionnaire used by an international CPA firm.

The procedures used to compliance-test computer controls depend upon the nature of the controls. General controls are usually tested by observing the performance of duties by installation personnel, and reviewing authorizations, application documentation, and approvals.

FIGURE 8–4
Portion of a general controls review questionnaire

Application Development, Programming And Documentation

Discussed with:_____

4.1 Are there written policies and procedures for application development or acquisition?

	Application Development		Application Software Acquisition	
	Yes	No	Yes	No

If YES, review the written policy and indicate below the operating practices it provides. If NO, determine the practices usually followed through discussion with client personnel, and indicate these practices below.

	Development		Acquisition	
	Yes	No	Yes	No
User participation	—	—	—	—
User approval at key development points	—	—	—	—
Procedures for user acceptance of completed applications or acquired software	—	—	—	—
DP management approval at key development points	—	—	—	—
DP management approval of completed applications or acquired software	—	—	—	—
Formal testing procedures	—	—	—	—
User participation in testing	—	—	—	—
Procedures for initial file creation	—	—	—	—
Procedures for formal conversion and implementation	—	—	—	—
Guidelines for training user department personnel	—	—	—	—
Guidelines for training DP personnel	—	—	—	—
User department review and appraisal of internal controls	—	—	—	—
Internal audit review and appraisal of internal controls	—	—	—	—
Other review and appraisal of internal controls (describe)	—	—	—	—

Source: Reprinted with special permission of Ernst & Whinney.

The procedures used to test application controls depend upon whether the controls represent manual or programmed procedures. Manual procedures can usually be tested as part of the customary compliance tests. Programmed procedures, on the other hand, will usually require the use of computer-assisted audit techniques, discussed in the following section. An AICPA audit and accounting guide, "The Auditor's Study and Evaluation of Internal Control in EDP

334

Systems," recognizes the effect of the computer on audit procedures, and provides examples of compliance tests for both general and application controls.

The overall evaluation of computer controls is made on the same basis as for other elements of accounting control. In making the evaluation, the auditor should (1) consider the types of errors and irregularities that could occur, (2) determine the computer controls that should prevent or detect such errors and irregularities, (3) determine whether the necessary computer controls are prescribed and are being followed satisfactorily, and (4) evaluate any weaknesses. The evaluation should consider not only the strengths and weaknesses of the general controls and application controls, but also the effect that general control weaknesses can have on application controls. As stated by SAS No. 3: "Weaknesses in general controls often have pervasive effects. When general controls are weak or absent, the auditor should consider the effect of such weaknesses in the evaluation of application controls." Because general controls relate to all applications and not to any specific application, general controls create the environment or framework within which application controls are exercised. For example, weak segregation of duties within the computer department can undermine otherwise strong application controls. Operators may be able to write computer programs or obtain access to program documentation. This would enable the operators to make unauthorized changes to application programs or to execute application programs other than those authorized, thus circumventing those controls programmed into the authorized application programs. On the other hand, strong general controls do not, in and of themselves, provide a basis for audit reliance. To achieve accounting control objectives, they must be coupled with adequate application controls.

The following table and discussion summarizes the relationship between general controls and application controls, and how that relationship may affect the auditor's overall evaluation of computer controls. (Discussion point (1) relates to column (1) in the table and so on.)

Type of Computer Control	Possible Outcome of Computer Controls Reviews			
	(1)	(2)	(3)	(4)
General controls	Strong	Strong	Weak	Weak
Application controls	Strong	Weak	Strong	Weak

(1) Computer controls appear to provide a basis for audit reliance. In this case, the auditor would most likely rely on the computer controls and restrict the extent of substantive tests.

(2) Although general controls provide an environment for controlled

computer applications, the application programs may not contain sufficient programmed controls to accomplish control objectives or manual application control procedures may be weak or absent. Accordingly, the auditor may attempt to identify compensating controls or devote audit effort to performing substantive tests.

(3) Application controls are designed to prevent or detect errors and irregularities, but personnel within the computer department may have incompatible functions or general controls may otherwise be weak or absent. Although application controls appear to provide a basis for audit reliance, the auditor may not be able to obtain reasonable assurance that application controls can be relied upon throughout the audit period, in which case subsequent audit effort would be directed toward testing compensating controls or performing substantive tests.

(4) Unless user department controls include extensive review of output (comparison to source documents, and so on) and adequate balancing procedures (dollar control totals, and so on), the auditor may have to perform significant substantive tests at the balance sheet date.

COMPUTER-ASSISTED AUDIT TECHNIQUES[5]

Computer-assisted audit techniques (CAAT) are the tools and techniques employed by auditors to "audit through (or with) the computer." As computerized accounting systems have become logically and technologically more complex, auditors have found it increasingly difficult to either ignore the existence of the computer altogether ("audit around the computer"), or not make use of the computer in formulating audit tests ("audit without the computer"). Computer-assisted audit techniques enable the auditor to audit through the computer to perform substantive testing and compliance testing. The following table summarizes some of the more common computer-assisted audit techniques and their uses.

Computer-Assisted Audit Techniques	Compliance Tests	Substantive Tests
Generalized audit software	X	X
Test deck	X	
Integrated test facility	X	
Specialized audit programs	X	X
Additional techniques	X	X

---

[5]A portion of this section was adapted from a draft of "Proposed Audit Guide: Computer Assisted Audit Techniques," American Institute of Certified Public Accountants, 1978. Adapted with permission.

Generalized Audit Software

A generalized audit software package is a computer program or group of programs which can perform certain data processing functions, such as reading computer files, performing calculations, printing reports, and selecting desired records. It is the most widely used computer-assisted audit technique for compliance and substantive testing. There are several advantages to using generalized audit software, such as:

1. The applications can be written using a coding technique that is easily learned.
2. The functions provided by the packages are specifically designed to accomplish audit tasks.
3. Audit documentation is a regular by-product of its use.
4. It enables independent processing of live client data.

Many large CPA firms and software vendors have developed generalized audit software packages. They require a minimal amount of programming and EDP technological knowledge, yet increase the auditor's independence from client EDP personnel. In most instances, personnel can be trained in one or two weeks to code an application and operate the package. In general terms, audit software applications can (1) test records for correctness, consistency, and completeness, (2) test calculations and make computations, (3) compare data on separate files, (4) select and print audit samples, and (5) summarize or resequence data. Audit software is particularly useful for calculating and selecting statistical samples because it enables the auditor to use the speed and accuracy of the computer.

One common application of generalized audit software is for parallel simulation, where the same data files used by the client's programs are used by the audit software package to simulate the processing performed by the client's programs. The simulated output is compared to the client's records and differences are followed up and reconciled. Parallel simulation can be used for compliance testing of programmed procedures and controls or substantive testing.

Test Deck and ITF

Use of the test deck is one of the earliest techniques developed to compliance test programmed procedures and controls. A test deck consists of test data, which is a set of transactions selected from previously processed transactions or created by the auditor. The test data are processed against the client's application programs and the actual results compared to the expected results. The expected results are independently determined on the assumption that the application contains effective programmed controls and will perform as specified in the program documentation. In using a test deck, the auditor is generally interested in determining that valid transactions are processed correctly, and that invalid transactions are detected by the programmed controls. Although very effective for testing programmed controls, the use of a test deck has some shortcomings. The most significant shortcoming is that it tests only preconceived situations and may include the same oversights as exist in the program documentation. The tests may lack objectivity because they are directed toward documented controls only.

Whereas test deck transactions are not processed with regular input, a modification of the test deck, known as integrated test facility (ITF), creates a dummy entity (a fictitious customer, employee, store) through which test transactions are processed with regular transactions through the client's records to the general ledger, at which point they are reversed by journal entry. The advantage of this approach is that it tests the whole system, the manual procedures as well as the programmed procedures.

Specialized Audit Programs and Additional Techniques

Other special audit programs may be written to perform specific audit tasks. They may be written by the auditor or by the client, or client programs may be modified. If not prepared by the auditor, he or she has an obligation to determine that the program will perform as it is purported to perform.

Other computer-assisted audit techniques include the review and comparison of program logic, the use of time-sharing, and utility programs. By reviewing and comparing program logic, the auditor can enhance his or her understanding of a particular program and identify any changes that have occurred during the audit period. Many major time-sharing vendors have libraries of programs that can be helpful to auditors, such as programs for statistical sampling and analytical review. Utility programs may be used by auditors to print all or part of a computer file or to support an audit software application by sorting records or creating a test file. In addition, internal auditors frequently use embedded audit modules, which are sections of program code that perform audit functions and are incorporated into regular application programs. This technique is most efficient when developed during the design of new applications.

FUTURE DEVELOPMENTS

Most authorities believe that it will become cheaper to store data on computer files than on paper. Several technological developments are contributing to this, including the decreasing costs of digital circuitry and computer storage. Tiny pocket computers with microscopic circuitry are now being mass produced. Some have as much processing power as the "second generation" IBM 1401 computer, but four times as much memory. The first trillion-bit online storage devices are now in use, and further increases in storage capacity are anticipated.

To utilize the large amount of stored data, the ability to access the data from remote locations (data transmission) and the ability to converse with the computer (person-computer dialogues) are needed. Advances in these areas are being made. Laser transmission with optical fibers is increasing the capacity of telecommunications and lowering its cost. The computer industry is placing increasing emphasis on developing effective communications between an individual and the computer. Systems design is now being made from the "end-user" perspective, where the terminal or console operator is no longer a secondary consideration, but the prime focus of the design process.

These developments have important implications for the auditor. The decreasing costs of computer hardware and telecommunications will mean increased usage of computers, both in small and large business enterprises. Batch systems will be replaced with online, real-time systems, file systems with data base systems, and centralized processing with distributed processing. In order to effectively audit in a computerized environment, the auditor will find it essential to understand computerized accounting systems, computer controls, and computer-assisted audit techniques.

GLOSSARY*

Application A group of related computer programs and data files designed to accomplish certain user accounting objectives.

Application controls Internal accounting controls relating to specific computer applications.

Arithmetic and logic facility The portion of the central processing unit that performs arithmetic tasks, comparisons, and data transformations.

Audit trail The trail of evidence linking individual accounting transactions to the summary totals in the books of account.

Batch total A sum of a set of items which is used to check the accuracy of operations on a particular batch of records.

Central processing unit (CPU) The principal hardware component of a computer. The CPU consists of the main storage facility, the arithmetic and logic facility, and the control facility. Additionally, the CPU controls the input and output facilities.

---

*Some of the terms in the glossary were taken or adapted from *IBM: Data Processing Glossary*, 5th ed., December 1972. Also, some were taken or adapted from Gordon B. Davis, *Auditing and EDP*, American Institute of Certified Public Accountants, 1968. Copyright 1968 by the American Institute of Certified Public Accountants, Inc.

Check digit   A digit associated with a word or group of words for the purpose of checking for the absence of certain classes of errors.

Common Business Oriented Language (COBOL)   A programming language for business applications.

Compiler   A computer program that converts (compiles) a program written in a source language, such as COBOL, into machine language.

Computer-assisted audit techniques (CAAT)   The tools and techniques, such as audit software and integrated test facility (ITF), used by auditors to audit through the computer.

Control facility   The portion of the central processing unit which controls the other facilities by retrieving machine language instructions from main storage and then interpreting the instructions. Next, the control facility generates the signals and commands that cause the other facilities to perform their operations at the appropriate times.

Data base administrator (DBA)   A person or group of persons responsible for the safekeeping and overall structure of the data stored in a data base.

Data base management system (DBMS)   The software package which controls a data base system.

Data base systems   The storing of data items in a central physical location, and in a manner which enables the data to be shared by several different applications.

Direct Access Storage Device (DASD)   A storage device, such as magnetic disk or drum, which enables data to be written or retrieved in a random manner.

Disk   A direct access storage device consisting of circular metal plates coated with magnetic oxide.

Echo check   The transmitting of data received by an output device back to the source unit for comparison with the original data.

Editing   Input controls such as verifying that all required data are present, verifying proper data format, performing reasonableness or limit tests, and so on.

Embedded audit modules   Audit routines contained within application programs.

External labels   A paper label attached to a magnetic tape or disk to identify its contents.

File   A collection of related records, such as a payroll file, arranged in sequence according to a key value contained within each record.

File system   The storing of data items in files so that each file is associated only with the program or programs of a specific application.

General controls   Internal accounting controls in computerized systems which relate to all computer applications.

Generalized audit software   A computer program or group of programs which can perform certain data processing functions, such as reading computer files, performing calculations, printing reports, and selecting desired records. It is the most widely used computer-assisted audit technique for compliance and substantive testing.

Hardware   The physical components of a computer system, such as CPU, tape and disk drives, card reader, terminals, and so on.

Hash total   A control total created by the addition of numbers that usually would not be added. For example, the addition of a list of part numbers.

Header label   A machine readable record at the beginning of a file which contains data identifying that file.

Integrated test facility (ITF)   A computer-assisted audit technique in which a dummy entity is created (a fictitious customer, employee, store) through which test transactions are processed with regular transactions through the client's records to the general ledger, at which point they are reversed by journal entry.

Intelligent terminal   An input/output device that can be programmed to perform certain functions, such as data editing.

Internal labels   A record magnetically recorded on tape, such as a header label or trailer label, to identify its contents.

Machine language   As opposed to source language, a language which a computer can execute without any translation. Synonymous with object code or object language.

Main storage   The portion of the central processing unit (CPU) in which various kinds of information is stored.

Master file   A file containing relatively permanent data and which is periodically updated.

Microcomputer   A computer system that is functionally and structurally similar to a minicomputer. However, the microcomputer is less expensive, smaller, and has less computing power than the minicomputer.

Minicomputer   A small, programmable, general-purpose computer which generally has less memory than larger computers.

Offline   Computer equipment or devices that are *not* in direct contact with the central processing unit (CPU).

Online   Computer equipment or devices which are in direct contact with the central processing unit (CPU) of a computer system and usually under its direct control.

Operating system   The organized collection of programmed procedures and routines used to operate a computer.

Parallel simulation   The use of generalized audit software to perform functions essentially equivalent to those of the client's programs.

Parity check   A check that tests whether the number of one bits in an array is even (even parity check) or odd (odd parity check).

Real-time   The processing of transactions as soon as they occur and in such a manner as to provide an immediate response to the user.

Run-to-run totals   Control totals that facilitate the identification of the addition of unauthorized data or the occurrence of loss of data between different steps of computer processing.

Software   The collection of programs and routines, such as compilers, operating systems, and utility programs, that facilitate the use of hardware.

Source code   A language, such as COBOL or RPG, that must be translated (for example, by a compiler) into machine language, which can be placed into main storage and executed.

Terminal   An online device through which data are entered using a typewriter keyboard or optical scanner.

Terminal authority levels   Several levels of passwords which the users of online systems must submit as more processing authority is requested.

Test deck   A technique to compliance-test programmed procedures and controls. The test deck consists of a set of transactions either selected from previously processed transactions or created by the auditor. These transactions are processed against the client's application programs and the actual results compared to expected results.

Trailer label   A record that follows a group of records on a file and contains summary information related to those records.

Transactions file   A file containing detail records of temporary data, which occurred during a specific period of time.

Utility program   A standard program that performs routine tasks, such as sorting or merging files.

QUESTIONS AND PROBLEMS

8-1.   What techniques can be used to document an evaluation of computer controls?

8-2.   Carefully distinguish between computer "hardware" and "software."

8-3.   The principal hardware component of a computer system is the Central Processing Unit (CPU). It either consists of or controls five functional facilities. List these facilities.

8-4.   What is a direct access device?

8-5.   List and briefly describe four categories of computer installations that a business entity may use.

8-6.   Accounting controls in a computerized system can be classified into (a) general controls and (b) application controls. What are general controls? What do they include? What are application controls?

8-7.   In computerized accounting systems who is usually responsible for the processing of accounting information?

8-8.   Describe the composition and purpose of a steering committee.

8-9.   Briefly discuss the responsibilities of an EDP manager.

8-10.   Distinguish between "applications development" and "applications acquisition."

8-11.   What are minicomputers? Where are they likely to be used?

8-12.   "In reviewing computer controls in minicomputer environments, the auditor is likely to find general control weaknesses." Discuss the reasons why such a weakness in general controls may exist.

8-13.   What is distributed data processing?

8-14.   Most electronic data processing equipment manufacturers have built-in checks to ensure that information is correctly read, processed, transferred within the system, and recorded. One of these built-in checks is the parity bit.

    a.   What is the parity bit?

    b.   When would the parity bit control be used?

(AICPA, adapted)

342

8-15. Regardless of the type of data processed or the kind of equipment used, all data processing usually involves four basic functions. Identify and describe these functions.

8-16. Distinguish between transaction files and master files.

8-17. List and briefly discuss several audit implications of online, real-time systems.

8-18. List several advantages of using generalized audit software.

8-19. In general terms, describe what generalized audit software packages can do.

8-20. Select the best answer for each of the following items:

  a. The primary purpose of a generalized computer audit program is to allow the auditor to
   1. Use the client's employees to perform routine audit checks of the electronic data processing records that otherwise would be done by the auditor's staff accountants.
   2. Test the logic of computer programs used in the client's electronic data processing systems.
   3. Select larger samples from the client's electronic data processing records than would otherwise be selected without the generalized program.
   4. Independently process client electronic data processing records.

  b. Where computers are used, the effectiveness of internal accounting control depends, in part, upon whether the organizational structure includes any incompatible combinations. Such a combination would exist when there is *no* separation of the duties between
   1. Documentation librarian and manager of programming.
   2. Programmer and console operator.
   3. Systems analyst and programmer.
   4. Processing control clerk and keypunch supervisor.

  c. An auditor can use a generalized computer audit program to verify the accuracy of
   1. Data processing controls.
   2. Accounting estimates.
   3. Totals and subtotals.
   4. Account classifications.

  d. Which of the following *best* describes a fundamental control weakness often associated with electronic data processing systems?
   1. Electronic data processing equipment is more subject to systems error than manual processing is subject to human error.
   2. Electronic data processing equipment processes and records similar transactions in a similar manner.
   3. Electronic data processing procedures for detection of invalid and unusual transactions are less effective than manual control procedures.
   4. Functions that would normally be separated in a manual system are combined in the electronic data processing system.

e. Which of the following employees normally would be assigned the operating responsibility for designing an electronic data processing installation, including flowcharts of data processing routines?
   1. Computer programmer.
   2. Data processing manager.
   3. Systems analyst.
   4. Internal auditor.

f. An auditor should be familiar with a client's electronic data processing hardware and software. An important element of the client's software is the program. Another element of software is the
   1. Cathode ray tube (CRT).
   2. Central processing unit (CPU).
   3. Magnetic tape drive.
   4. Compiler.

g. Which of the following would *lessen* internal control in an electronic data processing system?
   1. The computer librarian maintains custody of computer program instructions and detailed listings.
   2. Computer operators have access to operator instructions and detailed program listings.
   3. The control group is solely responsible for the distribution of all computer output.
   4. Computer programmers write and debug programs which perform routines designed by the systems analyst.

(AICPA, adapted)

8-21. The Large Corporation has numerous small customers. A customer file is kept on disk storage. For each customer the file contains customer name, address, credit limit, and account balance. The auditor wishes to test this file to determine whether credit limits are being exceeded. Assuming that computer time is available, what is the best procedure for the auditor to follow?

(AICPA, adapted)

8-22. Payroll operations for Burns Corporation are processed on a tape-oriented computer. Some of their procedures are:

a. The personnel department does the following:
   1. Places new employees on the payroll.
   2. Assigns each new employee a permanent employee number.
   3. Initiates appropriate action for employee terminations or transfers.

b. Timekeepers keep a daily record of the hours worked in each department.

c. The payroll department keeps the deduction authorizations for all employees.

d. Some employees have their check mailed to their home.

e. The EDP department prepares the entire payroll. It automatically pays each employee for a 40-hour week unless it is notified otherwise. The department also prepares the checks and the withholding stubs accompanying the checks.

Given these circumstances, discuss some of the controls that might be used to prevent: (a) overpayment; (b) payment of nonexistent employees.

8-23. In converting an hourly payroll from a manual to a computer system, the rate file was established from rates received from the payroll department. Each rate combined the employee's base rate with a cost-of-living hourly bonus factor of $0.25. The program was written to pick up the combined rate from the file and add $0.25 before extending rate times hours worked. As a result, each employee was paid $0.50 in cost-of-living instead of the approved $0.25. What procedures might have detected this programming error?

8-24. Your company plans to have all payrolls processed by a local bank. At the end of each pay period, the company will give the bank a list of employees and the hours they worked during the period. Using the master rate file, the bank will calculate the net pay and deposit the net pay directly to each employee's bank account. The bank will send the company a withholding stub for each employee. The bank will prepare the payroll register, the quarterly and annual tax reports, and the annual W-2 statements. Identify several questions that might be asked regarding the company-bank relationship.

8-25. The Lake Utility District is installing an electronic data processing system. The CPA who conducts the annual examination of the Utility District's financial statements has been asked to recommend controls for the new system.

Required:

Discuss recommended controls over:
a. Program documentation.
b. EDP hardware.
c. Tape files and software.

(AICPA, adapted)

8-26. George Beemster, CPA, is examining the financial statements of the Louisville Sales Corporation, which recently installed an offline electronic computer. The following comments have been extracted from Mr. Beemster's notes on computer operations and the processing and control of shipping notices and customer invoices:

a. To minimize inconvenience, Louisville converted without change its existing data processing system, which utilized tabulating equipment. The computer company supervised the conversion and has provided training to all computer department employees (except keypunch operators) in systems design, operations, and programming.

b. Each computer run is assigned to a specific employee, who is responsible for making program changes, running the program, and answering questions. This procedure has the advantage of eliminating the need for records of computer operations because each employee is responsible for his or her own computer runs.

c. At least one computer department employee remains in the computer room during office hours, and only computer department employees have keys to the computer room.

d. System documentation consists of those materials furnished by the computer company—a set of record formats and program listings. These and the tape library are kept in a corner of the computer department.

e. The company considered the desirability of programmed controls but decided to retain the manual controls from its existing system.

f. Company products are shipped directly from public warehouses which forward shipping notices to general accounting. There a billing clerk enters the price of the item and accounts for the numerical sequence of shipping notices from each warehouse. The billing clerk also prepares daily adding machine tapes ("control tapes") of the units shipped and the unit prices.

g. Shipping notices and control tapes are forwarded to the computer department for keypunching and processing. Extensions are made on the computer. Output consists of invoices (in six copies) and a daily sales register. The daily sales register shows the aggregate totals of units shipped and unit prices which the computer operator compares to the control tapes.

h. All copies of the invoice are returned to the billing clerk. The clerk mails three copies to the customer, forwards one copy to the warehouse, maintains one copy in a numerical file, and retains one copy in an open invoice file that serves as a detail accounts receivable record.

Required:

Describe weaknesses in internal control over information and data flows and the procedures for processing shipping notices and customer invoices. Recommend improvements in these controls and processing procedures.

(AICPA, adapted)

8-27. CPAs may audit "around" or "through" computers in the examination of the financial statements of clients who utilize computers to process accounting data.

Required:

a. Describe the auditing approach referred to as auditing "around" the computer.

b. Under what conditions does the CPA decide to audit "through" the computer instead of "around" the computer?

c. How can the CPA become satisfied that the computer program tapes presented are actually being used by the client to process its accounting data?

(AICPA, adapted)

8-28. Examine the flowchart that follows and answer these questions. Indicate the flowchart step that relates to each question.

a. Is input to the EDP department precontrolled?
b. Are cards verified?
c. Who receives the output from the EDP department?
d. Is input edited manually? By computer?
e. In the master file updating run, is the detail input on cards? On tape?
f. What is the disposition of the "Payment Transaction" tape?

Flowchart for accounts payable

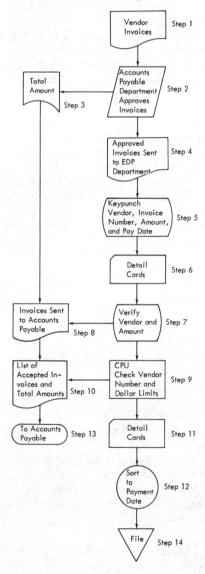

lowchart for accounts payable *(continued)*

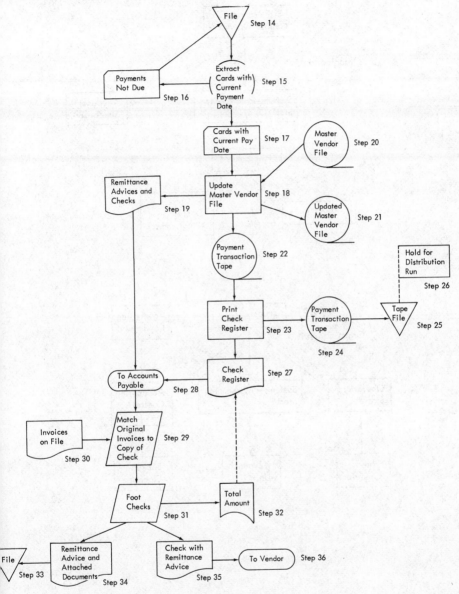

8–29. Discuss control weaknesses in the following four organizations:

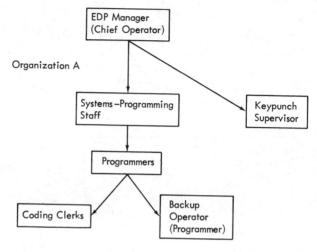

Organization A

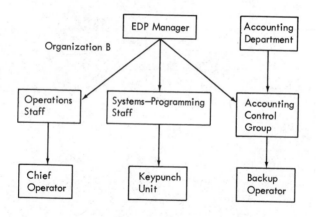

Organization B

8-29 *(continued)*

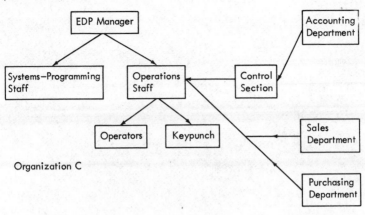

Organization C

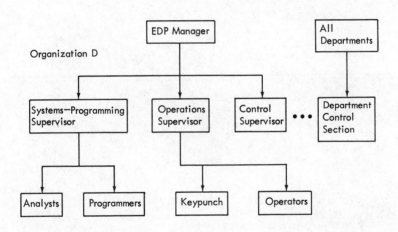

Organization D

part three

Audit Procedures

Learning Objectives

Study of the material in this chapter is designed to achieve several learning objectives. Among these are to acquire:

1. An understanding of the auditor's objective in the audit of cash.
2. A knowledge of the essential elements of internal control over cash.
3. A knowledge of testing cash transactions.
4. An understanding of the steps in the audit of cash during the year-end work, including auditing cash on hand and cash on deposit.
5. An understanding of the various schedules which may be used in the audit of cash.

9

Cash

The primary objectives of the auditor's examination of cash are to determine whether the cash balance is fairly stated in accordance with generally accepted accounting principles applied on a consistent basis and that cash is under the client's control.

Of all a company's assets, cash is the most liquid and, hence, potentially the most attractive to defalcators. Because of its high liquidity, the cash account should always receive the auditor's careful consideration. In almost every examination, cash transactions are so numerous and so common that the auditor may be tempted to regard cash work as somewhat routine or mechanical; such a frame of mind is to be avoided at all times.

INTERNAL CONTROL OVER CASH

Cash Receipts

Cash receipts may originate from numerous sources such as: receipts from customers on account; receipts from cash sales for the regular goods or services of the company; and receipts from miscellaneous sources such as interest and dividends on investments and the sale of scrap (to name but a few). In most companies, cash receipts consist largely of checks which are received by mail. All receipts of cash (including checks) should be recorded immediately upon receipt. They should be deposited promptly and intact in the bank. There should be a segregation of duties between the employees who have custody of cash receipts and those who account for them. This is to avoid the possibility that an employee could misappropriate cash and then conceal the defalcation by altering the accounting records.

353

354

This segregation allows the work of one employee to act as a check on that of another.

Accounting for Mail Receipts. Mail receipts, like all cash, should be accounted for promptly. The ease with which an individual may be able to cash checks even though they are made payable to a company makes even checks readily subject to misappropriation. The misappropriation of receipts is more likely to occur prior to the time they are recorded than after, since it would be easier to conceal. Accountability may be established by having one person who is independent of other processors of cash prepare a listing of the receipts before the receipts are given to a second person for processing. Later, another individual can compare this listing with the total recorded receipts and to the amount shown on the bank deposit slip (and later to the bank statement).

Accounting for Cash Sales. Cash registers and other mechanical devices, or even simple procedures such as the issuance of a receipt to customers, assist in establishing prompt accountability at the point of sale whether the transaction is for cash, check, or on a credit basis. Cash registers may be used to provide locked-in totals which an independent employee can compare with the total recorded receipts on the books as well as to the related bank deposit. Cash registers display the amount of a cash transaction. This amount acts as a control feature since the customer can see the amount which is recorded.

Accounting for Miscellaneous Receipts. Rents, dividends, interest, and similar revenues should be controlled in such a manner that the failure to receive them on a timely basis would be noted and investigated. This can usually be accomplished by the use of normal accrual accounting procedures.

Depositing Receipts Promptly and Intact. As previously indicated, all cash receipts should be deposited promptly and intact in the company's bank account. This procedure makes it easier for the company to maintain effective control over its receipts. If all receipts are deposited intact in the bank and all disbursements are made by check, all of the company's cash transactions will be recorded twice, once on the books of the company and once by the bank. The risk of loss usually increases with the amount of time the receipts remain on the company's premises. Another advantage of depositing receipts promptly is that it permits the company to make use of the receipts sooner.

Segregation of Duties. The accounting for cash receipts should be handled by employees other than those having custody of cash receipts. For example, to achieve effective control over its cash transactions, a company may segregate its cash receipts duties among the mail room clerk (opening the mail), the cashier, the accounts receivable bookkeeper, and the general ledger bookkeeper. This division of responsibilities among several individuals helps to minimize the chances of error and/or misappropriation of funds since the work of one person serves as a "check" on the work of others.

Within the limits imposed by the importance of segregating functions, the handling of cash should be restricted to the fewest number of persons which is practical in the circumstances. Preferably one cashier should supervise and control these activities at each location. Persons handling cash receipts should not have access to, or authority over, accounts receivable records, nor should they be permitted to prepare bank reconciliations or post transactions to the general ledger.

Cash Disbursements

All disbursements, other than small payments made from petty cash funds, should be made by check. Disbursements should be made only for goods and services which are known to have been received and for other purposes which have been properly authorized. They should be made only after the appropriate documents have been properly approved and presented for payment.

Usually the primary document supporting a disbursement is the related vendor's invoice. Before an invoice is approved for payment, an employee should test its arithmetical accuracy; the quantities shown on the invoice should be compared with the quantities shown as having been received on the receiving report. If any differences are noted, they should be investigated and proper approval obtained before the invoice is paid. The fact that all the company's procedures for processing an invoice for payment have been performed also should be noted on the invoice. This may be accomplished by imprinting a checklist of the various procedures to be performed on the invoice when it is received and requiring employees to sign or initial their names after they have completed each of the procedures. If a voucher register is in use, these approvals will appear on the voucher jacket.

Invoices, purchase orders, and receiving reports are seldom available for disbursements such as contributions, legal retainers, and expense advances. In these circumstances, a memorandum of approval or a check request should be obtained from an authorized executive and retained in the files.

In order to increase the internal control over cash disbursements, the disbursing function may be subdivided into such functions as preparing, signing, and distributing each check.

Preparing the Check. Ordinarily checks should be prepared only after the related invoices or other appropriate documents have been approved for payment according to company procedures. The name of the payee should always be indicated on the check; checks should not be made payable to cash or to bearer since they could be cashed by anyone. Checks should be printed with serial numbers and accounted for by the client. The use of a check protector, a device which imprints the dollar amount on the check face mechanically, helps to prevent alteration of the amount on the check.

Signing the Check. Checks should be signed only by designated officers or employees of the client. Ordinarily, the person signing the check should not be directly involved in other cash handling functions. Blank checks should never be signed. Before signing a check, the signer should review the related invoice or other appropriate supporting documents. After the check is signed, the invoice and supporting documents should be marked "paid" or otherwise canceled to prevent their resubmission for payment.

Many companies require two signatures on a check in order to provide additional control over disbursements. In some companies checks written in excess of a specified dollar amount are signed manually, while smaller checks may be signed mechanically. Mechanical check signing devices should be maintained under the control of a designated employee or officer. Equipment is available which "protects" the check amount, signs the check, and produces a tape showing the amount of each check.

Distributing the Check. Once a check has been signed, it should be mailed or given directly to the payee by the signer or an employee operating under the direct control of the signer. It should never be returned to any employee who has participated in the check processing routine. This prevents someone from retrieving a check representing a fictitious payment.

COMPLIANCE TESTING: CASH

Since such a major proportion of a company's transactions involve the receipt or payment of cash, the examination of cash transactions provides the auditor with insight into the operation of the client's accounting system. In addition, the auditor is more likely to discover defalcations in analyzing cash transactions than in examining other types of transactions.

By discussing bank balances, cash receipts, and cash disbursements, the audit steps of reconciling the recorded amounts with bank amounts will be reviewed. A schedule showing a proof of cash is presented in Figure 9-1. This schedule may be prepared in conjunction with cash compliance testing.

Cash Funds and Bank Balances

Even though cash funds and bank balances are assets and not "transactions," they are discussed at this point because the tests relating to them (1) are closely interrelated with the tests of cash transactions and (2) usually include review and test of the client's cash reconciliation procedures which constitute a significant control feature of a company's cash accounting system.

Three audit steps that may be used in testing cash funds and bank balances during compliance testing include:

1. Count petty cash and cash for deposit on a surprise basis. Account for noncash items in funds. Determine that cash awaiting deposit has been recorded as cash received and is subsequently deposited.
2. Review the client's reconciliations of bank balances at both the beginning and end of the test period.
3. Test reconciling items appearing on reconciliations, such as undeposited receipts and unentered bank charges.

The audit procedures applied to petty cash fund balances may be performed at either year-end or at an interim date. There are two reasons why these procedures are performed at an interim date. First, normally the petty cash fund balance is not material, and therefore, the auditor is usually not concerned with substantiating the balance of the fund at the balance sheet date. The auditor's primary concern is determining whether the cash fund is adequately controlled by the client. Second, the element of surprise is important to petty cash audit procedures. A surprise count of cash funds is usually more effective if made at an interim date. A detailed discussion of cash count procedures will be discussed later in this chapter.

The client's cash reconciliation procedures usually constitute an important control feature over cash transactions (receipts and disbursements). For this reason, cash reconciliations are generally tested during compliance testing. These tests are usually made in the form of a proof of cash prepared for a test month (or a test period if the client's accounting records are maintained on other than a monthly basis) selected from the period under audit. An example of a proof of cash is shown in Figure 9–1. By preparing a proof of cash, an auditor satisfies two objectives of compliance testing: (1) to test the company's cash reconciliation procedures which usually constitute a significant feature of internal control; and (2) to ascertain that cash receipts and cash disbursements as recorded in the company's accounting records (from which individual transactions are to be selected to test the cash receipts and cash disbursements accounting systems) accurately reflect the cash receipts and cash disbursements that are being processed by the bank.

When examining a proof of cash, the auditor should perform the following tests:

1. Trace the bank balance from the bank statement to the reconciliation and the book balances from the reconciliation to the general ledger.
2. Prove the arithmetical accuracy of the footing of the outstanding checklist.
3. Prove the outstanding checklist by examining the preparation dates and the bank clearing dates of the checks which clear during the month after the reconciliation date. Be certain that all checks were properly included in or excluded from the list. Checks listed as outstanding which have not cleared at the time of the interim examination should be followed up at year-end.
4. Test deposits in transit by reference to cash receipts records and subsequent bank statements.
5. Investigate other reconciling items, such as undeposited receipts and unentered bank charges, by examining the underlying supporting documents.
6. Prove the arithmetical accuracy of the reconciliation.
7. Trace reconciled cash receipts and cash disbursements book balances to the books of original entry and to the gerneral ledger postings.

The extent of the auditor's review of the company's bank reconciliations will vary in each engagement. For example, footings may be sight-tested rather than machine-checked, outstanding checks may be accounted for on a selective basis, and reconciling items may be supported by examining underlying documents on a test basis.

Cash Receipts

In testing cash receipts (usually during the interim work), the auditor is attempting to determine if the client's controls and procedures are such that all payments intended for the company: (1) are received; (2) are properly and promptly recorded; and (3) are promptly and properly deposited in the bank. It usually is not difficult for the auditor to check the accuracy of recorded receipts, but it can be quite a different matter to determine whether all receipts have actually been recorded.

Companies use a variety of methods to ensure that all cash received is properly recorded and deposited. Where there are many cash transactions, as in a retail store, receipts are usually accumulated in a cash register which has a locked counter to record individual transactions and to accumulate totals. These readings may then be summarized and posted to a daily cash report, ideally by an employee other than those making cash sales. Other types of companies arrange to have their customers send payments directly to the company's bank under a "lockbox" arrangement. Under this arrangement, each day the bank credits all receipts to the company's account and sends the company a listing of them. This procedure provides the company with the immediate use of customers' payments, relieves it of considerable routine accounting work, and lessens the chances of manipulation of receipts by employees.

The following procedures may be used by the auditor in testing cash receipts transactions for the period under consideration.

1. Prove the arithmetical accuracy of the footings of the cash receipts record.
2. Test postings to the general ledger, to the customers' ledger, and to other subsidiary ledgers.
3. Compare the recorded receipts with individual deposits as shown by bank statements.
4. Compare remittance advices or other details of cash receipts with the entries in the receipts book.
5. Compare the composition of authenticated duplicate deposit slips with the recorded receipts.
6. Compare the recorded receipts with an independent record which is prepared before receipts are transmitted to the cashier.
7. Test cash discounts and noncash allowances or credits granted to customers.
8. Review the cash receipts records for unusual items and investigate any that are noted.

The following comments regarding each of the tests listed above will help to clarify the auditor's objectives in each test.

Footing Cash Receipts Records. This is a basic procedure performed in all phases of the audit. Before performing other tests of a client's records, the auditor must establish that the records are arithmetically accurate.

The auditor is concerned with the arithmetical accuracy of the cash receipts records and must also be constantly alert for the possibility that incorrect footings or postings may conceal a defalcation. If the client's accounting records are prepared manually, the extent of testing for clerical accuracy will usually be more extensive than if the client uses EDP equipment to process accounting data. This is because manual records are more susceptible to human error. Generally, once the reliability of the client's computer programs has been established through specific compliance tests, the auditor's tests of clerical accuracy can be limited.

Testing of Postings to Ledgers. The auditor must be satisfied that postings from the books of original entry to the general and subsidiary ledgers are properly made. Improper postings of credits to subsidiary ledgers, such as the customers' ledger or the investment ledger, may indicate possible defalcations. Postings in the detail ledgers which are not included in the control accounts or in the books of original entry may indicate a misappropriation of receipts.

Comparing the Recorded Receipts with Bank Statements. The auditor should compare the recorded receipts with the amounts shown on the bank statement, making sure that all receipts are deposited intact, and noting any unusual delays in deposits. In most instances, differences between the company records and bank statement, and unusual delays in deposits, are due to errors on the part of either the company or the bank, and these errors should be promptly corrected. The auditor, however, must be constantly alert for the possibility that an employee is withholding cash receipts. In addition, the auditor should reconcile the total of the recorded receipts with total receipts as shown on the bank statement. This may be accomplished during the preparation of a proof of cash (see Figure 9–1).

Comparing the Details of the Receipts with Recorded Entries. The auditor should ascertain whether the name, amount, and dates as shown on the remittance advices are in agreement with the cash receipt records. This procedure is designed to detect the possible lapping of individual receipts.

Lapping is a method of concealing a cash shortage. It involves abstracting receipts from customers and covering the shortage with receipts from subsequent collections received from other customers. Later, this shortage is made up with receipts from still other customers; thus, the shortage is still there but never in the same accounts. Lapping is generally characterized by unreasonable delays in recording and depositing receipts.

This manipulation might be detected in other ways; for example, by comparing the list of individual receipts prepared in the mail room from customers' remittance advices with the detail of the recorded receipts (this assumes that mail room personnel are not part of the manipulation).

Comparing Deposit Slips with the Recorded Receipts. This procedure is also designed to detect lapping. The auditor must ascertain whether the details of the cash receipts record and its supporting documents agree with the amounts on the deposit slips.

Comparing the Recorded Receipts with an Independent Record. The independent record used by the auditor might be a listing of receipts prepared in the mail room or might be cash register tapes or collection reports. The use of this procedure assists the auditor in determining whether amounts recorded accurately reflect amounts received and to determine whether the company's system of controlling and recording all cash received is operating as intended. A common method which may be used for establishing control over receipts is the preparation of an independent record before the receipts are forwarded to the accounting department or to the cashier. Then, to ensure that no receipts have been withheld by the cashier or by an employee of the accounting department, an independent party compares the amount of this record with the total recorded receipts and with the daily bank deposit.

Testing of Cash Discounts and Other Allowances or Credits. This procedure enables the auditor to ascertain whether only proper credits (in terms of authorization, amounts, and compliance with invoice terms) have been made to the customers' accounts. The auditor will investigate unusual items to determine their nature and to become satisfied as to their propriety. An employee withholding cash receipts could conceal the defalcation by recording improper and fictitious discounts and allowances to customers' accounts, and the auditor must be alert for this possibility.

Reviewing Cash Receipts Records. To perform this test, the auditor must, of course, develop a keen understanding of what constitutes an unusual item in the particular circumstances faced by the client. What is considered unusual in one company may be commonplace in another. Examples of items which are normally considered to be unusual are checks included in cash receipts which were drawn by the company being audited and receipts from officers and employees. All items which seem to be unusual should always be investigated thoroughly by the auditor.

Cash Disbursements

In testing cash disbursements the auditor must determine whether all disbursements have been made according to the prescribed procedures of the company. In particular, it must be determined that they were properly authorized and were made only for goods and services that were actually received. Typical procedures employed by the auditor in testing disbursements for the period under consideration include:

1. Prove the arithmetical accuracy of the cash disbursements record and trace the postings to the general ledger.

2. Examine paid bank checks and compare them with the cash disbursements records.
3. Account for the numerical sequence of checks, and inspect any checks that were spoiled or voided.
4. Reconcile the total recorded disbursements with total disbursements as shown on the bank statement.
5. Test the recorded disbursements by inspecting supporting documents.
6. Scrutinize the cash disbursements records for unusual items and investigate any that are noted.

The following comments describe the auditor's objectives in performing each of the tests listed above.

Proving the Footings of Cash Disbursement Records and Tracing Totals to the General Ledger. The auditor is concerned with the footings of the cash records both as a test of the client's accounting system and because improper footings may indicate a defalcation. In tracing amounts to the general ledger, the auditor is concerned with the manner in which information flows into that ledger. The auditor should be particularly alert for the possibility of defalcations.

Comparing Bank Checks with the Cash Disbursements Records. The auditor should examine canceled checks and compare the date of the check, the check number, payee, and amount with the cash disbursements record. Any differences should be listed for further investigation. It should be ascertained whether each of the check signers is properly authorized; whether checks bear the endorsement of the payee as evidence that the payment was received by the proper person; and whether the date of the check and the bank cancellation date indicate the checks do, in fact, belong in the period under review.

Accounting for All Checks. A common means of guarding against unauthorized disbursements or misappropriation of assets is the use of prenumbered checks. The numerical sequence of these checks should be accounted for by the auditor.

Reconciling Recorded Disbursements with the Bank Statement. The amount of the recorded disbursements should be equal to the disbursements as shown on the bank statement, plus the checks outstanding at the end of the period, less the checks outstanding at the beginning of the period, and adjusted for any other reconciling items. The purpose of this type of reconciliation procedure is to reveal any differences between the disbursements per books and the disbursements per bank. The auditor normally accomplishes this objective by the preparation of a proof of cash. (See Figure 9-1.) A satisfactory explanation of any differences noted in the proof of cash should always be obtained by the auditor and included in the working papers.

FIGURE 9-1
Proof of cash

			Beginning Bank Reconciliation 9-30-80	Receipts	Disbursements	Ending Bank Reconciliation 10-31-80	
		Per bank statement	651176 00	14211 17 68	156557 0 54	50672314	CF
		Deposits in transit:					
		Beginning—deposited 10-1-80	2371404	(2371404)			
		Ending	–0–			–0–	
		Outstanding checks:					
		Beginning	(2115 84 83) #		(2115 84 83)		
		Ending			21020778	(21020778) #	
		Other reconciling items:					
		NSF check redeposited 11-2-80			(207361)	207361	
		Per books	463305 21	13974036 4	15621 19 88	298588 97	CF
				FD	FV		

OCTOBER PROOF OF CASH—FIRST NAT'L BANK
REGULAR ACCT.
RST INC.
12-31-80

	NAME	DATE
PREPARED	client Allen	1-14-81
APPROVED	Williams	1-18-81

Procedures Performed by Allen:
Ⓞ — Traced to bank statement.
✓ — Traced to 10/31/80 bank statement.
✗ — Traced to general ledger.
— Per adding machine tape attached.
F — Footed cash receipts journal and cash disbursements journal for October 1980.
V — Accounted for all checks and vouched all disbursements for October 1980.
D — Compared authenticated duplicate deposit slips with cash receipts record for October 1980.
✓ — Footed.
CF — Crossfooted.

As part of this test, the auditor should test the arithmetical accuracy of the bank statement and carefully review it for any evidence of erasures or alterations.

Examining Supporting Documents. As a further test of disbursements, the auditor will examine the underlying support for selected payments. The date, payee, and amount of the disbursements are compared with the information included on the supporting invoices. If more than one invoice is included in a check total, the auditor foots the invoices and compares their total with the total of the vouchers. Usually, the auditor would then proceed to a number of additional tests depending on the nature of the expenditure. The receiving records should be examined to determine that the goods were actually received. The prices, terms, and quantities on the invoice should be compared with those indicated on the purchase order. The arithmetical accuracy should be tested, and it should be ascertained whether invoices were effectively canceled to prevent their reuse, whether all available discounts were taken, and whether payments were properly authorized.

Reviewing Cash Disbursements Records for Unusual Items. Examples of items which may require investigation by the auditor include: payments to officers, directors, and employees (other than for compensation); checks payable to banks and lending institutions; payments to attorneys; and payments for unusually large amounts. The auditor's objective is, of course, to determine that the outlays were properly authorized and correctly recorded in the accounts.

SUBSTANTIVE TESTS: CASH

Much of the audit of cash, especially that related to cash receipts and disbursements, is performed during the auditor's interim examination. This portion of the cash examination has already been described. The cash work that is usually done by the auditor during the year-end examination is described in the paragraphs which follow.

Cash on Hand

Cash on hand includes petty cash funds, change funds, and undeposited receipts. The discussion of cash on hand is divided into five general parts—planning, cash count procedures, undeposited receipts, funds not counted, and general.

Planning. The careful planning of all cash counts to be made by the auditor is necessary for at least two reasons. The first, and most obvious, is to avoid unnecessary work. The second reason is to establish control over all cash funds and other negotiable assets, so that the items already counted cannot be subsequently substituted for those yet to be counted in an attempt to conceal a shortage. Control of these funds may be accomplished in a number of ways: by assembling them at a central location for simultaneous count; by using several auditors to count the funds at all locations at the same time; or by sealing each fund as it is counted and making certain that the seal is unbroken until the entire count is completed and all funds have been properly accounted for. All three of these methods may be used by the auditor in various combinations, depending, of course, on the size, nature, and location of the funds.

Securities are usually readily convertible into cash and vice versa; therefore, when the company has significant amounts of cash and securities, the auditor will want to control and count both the securities and the cash simultaneously. When securities are kept in a safe-deposit box under the control of two or more responsible employees of the client and access by one alone is never permitted, a simultaneous count may not be required if these controls are deemed to be effective by the auditor.

The relative materiality of the funds held by the client will also affect audit planning. A small fund, especially if maintained at a distant location, simply may not justify the time that might be required to count it. A more reasonable alternative might be to obtain a confirmation of the amount directly from its custodian, or, if the control is judged to be effective by the auditor, to do nothing more than summarize the small funds in the working papers and trace the totals to the accounting records. Surprise counts of cash on hand (and securities as well) are sometimes made. This is advisable when there is suspicion of lapping, a combination of the cash handling and recording functions, delays in providing fund information, general carelessness in the handling of funds, or a belief that internal controls are weak. In the examination of certain specialized businesses, such as brokerage houses, a surprise count may be a standard audit procedure. Surprise counts of branch office funds are sometimes made by the auditor at the request of management.

It should be emphasized that the auditor must always be careful to avoid making cash counts in a manner that may result in being accused or suspected of causing a shortage. Cash counts should always be made in the presence of the employee responsible for the funds. If this employee is called away before the count is completed, the auditor should terminate the count and return the cash to the custodian. If the auditor wishes to resume the same count at a later time, the fund should be sealed before returning it to the custodian. The auditor should be certain that the seal is unbroken when the count is resumed.

Cash Count Procedures. Figure 9–2 is an example of a convenient form which may be used by the auditor in making a cash count.

Most imprest and change funds are small and will require only a few minutes to count. In certain businesses, however, such as department stores or banks, these funds often amount to many thousands of dollars. In these circumstances, it is sometimes sufficient to account for all the bundles of currency and wrapped coin and test count the contents of only a representative number of bundles.

A listing of any noncash items in the fund should be included on the count sheet (along with the appropriate detail) and tested for propriety by the auditor at a later date. The nature of these items (as disclosed by the tests) should be fully described on the count sheet. The noncash items found by the auditor will vary according to the circumstances.

The auditor should obtain a signed receipt (in ink) from the custodian of the fund after the count has been completed. This receipt is an acknowledgment of the accuracy of the count and the return of the fund intact to the custodian.

If the cash fund includes checks held for deposit, the auditor may ask the client to cash or deposit these checks at the bank in the auditor's presence. Also, the client may ask the bank to notify the auditor directly of any checks which do not clear. This is done to ensure that the checks are valid.

When differences between the actual count and the recorded amount are noted, the auditor's working papers should include a full explanation of these differences. These differences should be discussed with an appropriate official of the company, for example, the fund custodian's supervisor. Any unusual items included in the fund such as the custodian's checks, old personal checks, or officers' checks should also be discussed with the appropriate company official. A memorandum of these discussions should be included in the auditor's working papers.

Undeposited Receipts. Undeposited cash receipts often consist of both checks and currency. These receipts normally will be counted only if the client's system of internal control is judged to be weak or if the amount of cash on hand at year-end is deemed to be material. Cash on hand is usually a material amount in businesses such as banks and department stores. The auditor should trace the undeposited receipts to both the cash receipts book and to the bank statement for the following period. If the receipts will be deposited by an employee who is involved in any phase of the recording process, the auditor may wish to control the receipts until they are deposited, mailed, or collected by an armored delivery service. The use of these procedures may prevent a manipulation of undeposited receipts.

FIGURE 9–2
Cash count

	Name	Date
Approved	*Williams*	10-29-80

CASH COUNT __PETTY CASH__
(Name of Fund)

CLIENT __RST, INC.__   AUDIT DATE __12-31-80__

COUNTED BY __Greg Allen__   DATE __10-15-80__   TIME __8:30 A.M.__

	QUANTITY	AMOUNT	TOTAL
CURRENCY			
Fifties			
Twenties	20	400 00	
Tens	20	200 00	
Fives	27	135 00	
Twos			
Ones	115	115 00	850 00
COIN			
Dollars			
Halves	12	6 00	
Quarters	44	11 00	
Dimes	22	2 20	
Nickels	51	2 55	
Pennies	75	75	22 50
WRAPPED COIN			
$10.00			

Checks for Deposit	list attached K.C. Carr 10-13-80 (payable to RST Inc.)		125 00
Cash Items	" "		
Advances	" "		
Undistributed Disbursements	" "		
Bad Checks	" "		
Other	" " *Stamps*		1 40
		TOTAL	998 90

Above listed cash and cash items in the amount of *Nine hundred ninety-eight and 90/100* Dollars

($ 998.90) were returned to me after count by a representative of Ernst & Whinney. All cash and cash items for which

I am accountable to __RST INC.__

have been presented for inspection and count.

__10-15-80__
Date

G. F. Drew
Signature of Custodian

(THIS RECEIPT MUST BE PREPARED IN INK)

BAL. PER FUND	$ 1,000.00
✓ PER COUNT	998.90
	1.10 NOT ADJUSTED

A-5   PRINTED IN U.S.A.

368

Certain situations require that the auditor obtain details of the receipts so that they may be subsequently traced to the accounts of individual customers. This would be the case, for example, in a situation where lapping is suspected by the auditor.

Funds Not Counted. As previously indicated, if funds are at a location which is not visited by the auditor, they may be confirmed directly with the custodian.

General. The auditor should prepare a summary of all funds held by the client and trace these totals to the general ledger. If a fund is not counted at year-end and the fund or its transactions are significant in amount, it may be desirable to test the interim transactions. Consideration should also be given to adjusting the accounts for any undistributed disbursements, payroll advances, and similar items.

Cash on Deposit

Cash on deposit includes demand deposits and time deposits. Time deposits normally represent investments of idle cash and usually will be stated separately in the balance sheet, either as a current or noncurrent asset depending on the nature and term of the investment. The audit procedures designed to test time deposits will normally include confirmation of the balance through direct correspondence with the bank.

Demand deposits (checking accounts) usually comprise the major portion of a company's cash balance. Most of the audit procedures employed during the examination of cash are designed to test demand deposit account balances. The discussion of demand deposits is divided into three major sections: confirmation of bank balances; tests of bank reconciliations; and cutoff bank statements.

Confirmation of Bank Balances. A Standard Bank Confirmation Inquiry (see Figure 9–3) should be mailed to each bank in which the company had a deposit or from which it borrowed funds or had other business during the current year. Whenever practicable, these confirmation requests should be mailed to the banks a few days before the balance sheet date. Ordinarily, confirmations are prepared in duplicate and signed by company personnel and then returned to the auditor for mailing.

In Figure 9–3, the information that is required to be included on the request prior to mailing is circled: the date signed by authorized signer (upper right-hand section of the form); the account name per bank records; the authorized signature of the client officer making the request (usually an authorized check signer); the bank name and address; whether the auditor is only interested in confirmation of bank

FIGURE 9–3

Standard bank confirmation inquiry

STANDARD BANK CONFIRMATION INQUIRY
Approved 1966 by
AMERICAN INSTITUTE OF CERTIFIED PUBLIC ACCOUNTANTS
NABAC, THE ASSOCIATION FOR BANK AUDIT, CONTROL
AND OPERATION

DUPLICATE
To be mailed to accountant

December 15 19 80

Dear Sirs:
Your completion of the following report will be sincerely appreciated. IF THE ANSWER TO ANY ITEM IS "NONE", PLEASE SO STATE. Kindly mail it in the enclosed stamped, addressed envelope direct to the accountant named below.

Report from   Yours truly,

(Bank) First National Bank   RST Inc.
                                               (ACCOUNT NAME PER BANK RECORDS)
First National Bank Building   By K. L. Good
                                                   Authorized Signature
Cleveland, Ohio 44115

Bank customer should check here if confirmation of bank balances only (item 1) is desired. ☐

ERNST & WHINNEY
1300 Union Commerce Building
Cleveland, Ohio 44115

NOTE — If the space provided is inadequate, please enter totals hereon and attach a statement giving full details as called for by the columnar headings below.

Dear Sirs:

1. At the close of business on December 31 1980, our records showed the following balance(s) to the credit of the above named customer. In the event that we could readily ascertain whether there were any balances to the credit of the customer not designated in this request, the appropriate information is given below.

AMOUNT	ACCOUNT NAME	ACCOUNT NUMBER	SUBJECT TO WITH-DRAWAL BY CHECK?	INTEREST BEARING? GIVE RATE
$ 669,935.	Regular	698-1362	yes	no
17,319.	Payroll	698-3491	yes	no

2. The customer was directly liable to us in respect of loans, acceptances, etc., at the close of business on that date in the total amount of $ 350,000.00 , as follows:

AMOUNT	DATE OF LOAN OR DISCOUNT	DUE DATE	RATE	PAID TO	DESCRIPTION OF LIABILITY, COLLATERAL, SECURITY INTERESTS, LIENS, ENDORSERS, ETC.
$ 350,000.00	3-1-71	10,000 quarterly	6%	12-1-80	Mortgage on building

3. The customer was contingently liable as endorser of notes discounted and/or as guarantor at the close of business on that date in the total amount of $ none , as below:

AMOUNT	NAME OF MAKER	DATE OF NOTE	DUE DATE	REMARKS
$				

1. discounted notes
2. Guarantor of notes of subsidiaries, officers, employees, etc.

4. Other direct or contingent liabilities, open letters of credit, and relative collateral, were
none

5. Security agreements under the Uniform Commercial Code or any other agreements providing for restrictions, not noted above, were as follows (if officially recorded, indicate date and office in which filed):
none

Yours truly, (Bank) First National Bank
By F. R. White
Authorized Signature

Date January 5 1981
A-4

balances (item 1) or desires additional information as well; the date as of which information is requested; and the bank account name and number.

Bank confirmation requests must be mailed by the auditor and not by company personnel in order to ensure that they are not altered

370

prior to mailing. The requests, along with the auditor's business reply envelope, should be mailed in an envelope bearing the auditor's return address. A record of all confirmations mailed should be maintained by the auditor. After a reasonable period of time, second requests should be sent to any banks which have not replied.

The information reported on the standard bank confirmation should be traced to the working papers as follows: bank account balances to bank reconciliations; direct and contingent liabilities to the appropriate sections of the auditor's working papers; and other information reported by the bank to the appropriate working papers. Banks are by no means infallible. Occasions may arise when the amount reported by the bank is not in agreement with the amount shown on the bank statement. In the event that the bank is in error, the auditor should obtain a corrected written confirmation from the bank.

Bank Reconciliations. In testing the company's reconciliations (see Figure 9–4), the auditor should:

1. Test the clerical accuracy of the reconciliations.
2. Test the footings of the listings of outstanding checks. (See Figure 9–5.)
3. Record on the listings of outstanding checks the date and payee of the following: checks for large amounts; checks drawn payable to cash, officers, employees, and affiliates; and all checks which may be considered unusual. The auditor should examine supporting data for these checks.
4. Trace checks for bank transfers to a schedule of such transfers in order to make sure all transfers are accounted for. (See Figure 9–6.)
5. Trace deposits in transit to the cutoff bank statements and indicate on the bank reconciliation the date of deposit. (See the next section for a discussion of cutoff bank statements.) The auditor should consider the advisability of comparing the individual items included in such deposits with the cash receipts record and with the detailed accounts receivable records on a test basis. If cutoff statements are not received directly from the bank, the auditor should also confirm the deposits in transit.
6. Determine that there are no omissions in the listings of outstanding checks. (The procedures for this step will be discussed in conjunction with cutoff bank statements.)
7. Investigate large checks outstanding at the balance sheet date that remain outstanding at the cutoff date.
8. Review supporting data for reconciling items other than deposits in transit and outstanding checks.
9. Trace book amounts to general ledger balances.

FIGURE 9-4
Bank reconciliation

	NAME	DATE
PREPARED	Client *Allen*	1-18-81
APPROVED	*Williams*	2-11-81

YEAR-END BANK RECONCILIATIONS
RST INC.
12-31-80

	First National		Second National
	Regular	Payroll	
12-31-80 Balance per bank statement	669935 12 ᶜ	17319 29 ᶜ	269450 60 ᶜ
Add deposit in transit			35000 00 ✗ *deposited 1-3-81*
	669935 12	17319 29	304450 60
Less outstanding checks— see list attached	107886 47	7319 29	47802 25
	562048 65	10000 00	256648 35
Add check of "RS Company" dated 12-23-80 charged to our account in error. Corrected by bank on 1-3-80	1427 16 ꓐ		
12-31-80 Balance per books	563475 81 ꜰ	10000 00 ꜰ	256648 35 ꜰ
	T/B	T/B	T/B

Procedures Performed by Allen:
C – Confirmed by bank – confirmation attached.
F – Footed.
✓ – Traced to 1-12-81 cut off bank statement received directly from the bank by Ernst & Whinney
ꓐ – Traced charge to December bank statement. Also examined correcting credit memo from bank received with cut off bank statement.
✗ – Traced to bank transfer schedule.
T/B – Traced to trial balance.

372

FIGURE 9-5
Outstanding check lists

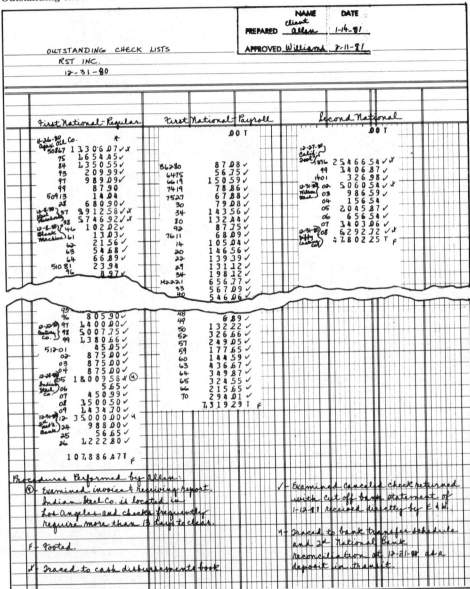

FIGURE 9-6
Schedule of bank transfers

		NAME	DATE
	PREPARED	*Client* Allen	2-2-81
YEAR-END BANK TRANSFERS	APPROVED	Williams	2-1-81
RST INC.			
12-31-80			

Checks drawn on First National Bank regular account

Check no.	Amount	Date per Books		Date Check Paid by Bank	Bank Deposit Date	
		Check	Deposit		1st Nat'l Payroll	2d Nat'l Regular
51085	46,096.54	12/21	12/21	12/22	12/21	
86	90,000.00	12/21	12/21	12/22		12/21
51210	47,243.24	12/28	12/28	12/29	12/28	
12	35,000.00	12/31	12/31	1/4 4		1/3
52690	49,204.11	1/4	1/4	1/5	1/4	
783	75,000.00	1/5	1/5	1/8		1/5
910	47,303.10	1/11	1/11	1/12	1/11	

This schedule was prepared by
examining cash disbursement
records for the period of 12/18/80
to 1/15/81.

4 - Traced to 12/31/80 outstanding
check list.

Cutoff Bank Statements. A cutoff bank statement is a statement with paid checks and other customary enclosures obtained from the bank by the auditor which shows transactions for a specified number of days following the bank reconciliation date. The auditor uses this statement in the examination of cash balances. Cutoff statements for significant bank accounts should normally cover at least ten business days following the balance sheet date. This is a general guideline which should be modified, if indicated, by the particular circumstances encountered by the auditor. If a cutoff statement covers too short a period, it will not allow a sufficient number of checks written in the period under review to clear. On the other hand, a statement obtained for too long a period will often include many checks written in the subsequent period, and therefore will require much more clerical effort than would otherwise be required on the part of the auditor.

A cutoff bank statement should be obtained directly from the bank so as to preclude any possible alteration by the client. (See Figure 9–7.)

When the auditor has not obtained the cutoff statement directly from the bank, certain additional procedures should be performed to assure the validity of the statement. The auditor should: (1) compare the beginning balance on the cutoff bank statement to the amount as shown on the bank confirmation; (2) examine the cancellation dates of all checks to determine if the checks have been canceled in the period covered by the cutoff statement and that the dates on the checks agree with the dates of the disbursements in the cash disbursements records; and (3) foot the checks and reconcile the total with the total charges on the bank statement. (The auditor may also decide to compare individual checks with the entries on the bank statement and the cash book.)

In certain instances, such as where there may be doubt concerning the validity and completeness of the reconciling items included on the year-end reconciliation, it may be desirable to prepare a second reconciliation as of the bank cutoff date.

All checks which clear with the cutoff statement and are dated prior to the balance sheet date should be examined and traced to the listing of outstanding checks by the auditor. Concealment of defalcations by manipulating the listing of outstanding checks can be accomplished, for example, by understating the total amount. This could be accomplished by either underfooting the list or by omitting checks from it. For this reason, the emphasis of this audit procedure should be on tracing *from* the checks received with the cutoff statement *to* the list of outstanding checks (rather than from the listing to the cutoff checks).

Checks dated subsequent to year-end for large amounts and for

FIGURE 9-7
Request for cutoff bank statements

R S T Inc.
17596 Superior Avenue
Cleveland, Ohio, 44115

January 3, 1981

First National Bank
First National Bank Building
Cleveland, Ohio   44115

Gentlemen:

Our auditors, Ernst & Whinney, 1300 Union Commerce Building,
Cleveland, Ohio, 44115, are making an examination of our financial
statements for the year ended December 31, 1980. In this connection,
please deliver or mail directly to them the bank statements, canceled
checks, and other customary enclosures for our accounts for the period
from January 1, 1981, to the close of business on January 12, 1981. Our
accounts are designated "Regular—number 698-1362" and "Payroll—
number 698-3491."

Very truly yours,

Oswald T. Good

Oswald T. Good
Treasurer

---

unusual items should be examined by the auditor to determine: (1)
whether the items should have been included in the financial statements for the year under examination; (2) the possible existence of
unrecorded liabilities; and (3) the possible existence of post-balance
sheet events which may require disclosures in the financial statements. Examples of unusual items would include payments to or from
officers, transfers between commercial accounts, or payments made to
vendors other than recognized suppliers.

FIGURE 9-8
Kiting

Date	Description	New York Bank		St. Louis Bank	
		Book	Bank	Book	Bank
1980					
12/30	Bank transfer not recorded on the books		6,000		
1981					
1/3	Record bank transfer on the books	6,000		⟨6,000⟩	
1/4	Bank transfer clears bank drawn on				⟨6,000⟩

Kiting

Kiting is made possible because time is required for a check to clear the bank on which it is drawn. It is used to conceal a cash shortage or keep a bank from detecting an overdraft.

Figure 9-8 shows how kiting may be accomplished. Assume that a company has its home office in New York City and a branch office in St. Louis. Further, assume that the company has bank accounts with a New York City bank and a St. Louis bank. Next, assume there is a shortage of $6,000 in the New York bank. A company official attempts to cover this shortage by drawing a check on December 30, 1980, on the St. Louis bank which is deposited to the account in the New York bank on the same day. The check is not recorded as a disbursement in the current period. The transaction is recorded on the books on January 3, 1981, and the check clears the St. Louis bank on January 4, 1981. Unless detected, the New York bank and book balances will be reconcilable on December 31, 1980, but not reconcilable on January 3, 1981.

This manipulation might be detected by reviewing all bank transfers before and after year-end, in order to determine that the book entry is recorded in the same year that the check is dated and the deposit in the New York bank is made. Such a review is generally done in the form of a schedule of interbank transfers (see Figure 9-6). This schedule should include all transfers of funds between bank accounts for a few business days both before and after the balance-sheet date. The schedule lists the date of withdrawal per the books and per the bank as well as the date of deposit per the books and the bank. Transfer checks in transit at year-end should be traced to the outstanding check list and to deposits in transit in the appropriate bank reconciliations. The deposit date of all transfers should be verified by tracing the deposit to the cutoff bank statement for the receiving bank.

Fictitious Reconciling Items

Deposits in transit, outstanding checks, special bank charges, and other reconciling items can be used to conceal a cash shortage. Figure 9-9 shows how a fictitious deposit in transit can be used to bring the books and bank account into agreement.

Assume that a company receives $131,000 on December 26, 1980. The bookkeeper who opens the mail and handles all cash work and all of the records makes two deposits that day ($119,000 and $8,000) totaling $127,000. The bookkeeper keeps $4,000.

At year-end, the bookkeeper prepares the bank reconciliation and lists the $4,000 as a deposit in transit. In first day's deposit after year-end (January 2, 1981) the bookkeeper splits the $116,000 receipts for the day into two deposits (of $112,000 and $4,000). The $4,000 on the January 2, 1981 deposit lends support to the fictitious reconciling item.

This manipulation might be detected by an audit procedure of comparing the recorded book amounts with the related bank amounts (per deposit slips and/or bank statements) using the January 1981 cutoff bank statement.

General Considerations

The auditor should review the cash transactions for several days prior to the balance-sheet date and until the completion of the field work, noting any unusual items of a material amount. Payments to or from officers, a temporary reduction in notes payable, new financing, delays in deposits of cash in transit, large receipts from a source other than regular customers, payments to vendors other than recognized suppliers, and so on, are examples of items which would ordinarily be investigated by the auditor. These items could indicate cash manipulations, unrecorded disbursements, or post-balance sheet events which should be disclosed in the financial statements.

The bank statements for all inactive bank accounts should also be reviewed by the auditor for the entire period under examination. Any transactions which are noted in these accounts should be investigated, since balances in inactive accounts may be compensating balances for loans which may require disclosure or, in some cases, even convenient sources of theft or of unauthorized borrowing by employees who may have access to these accounts.

FIGURE 9–9
Fictitious bank reconciliation

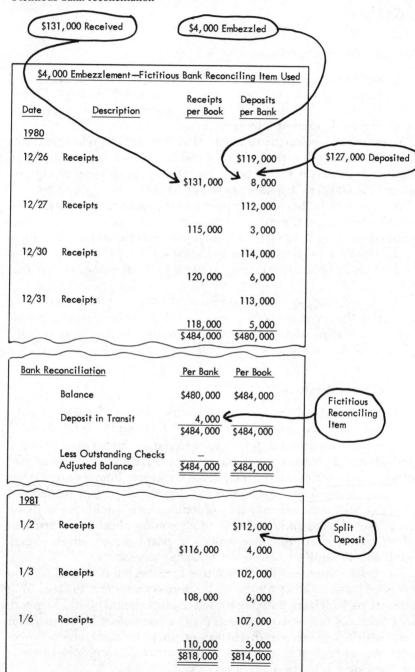

The auditor should review any bank overdrafts and note the existence of any funds that may be subject to withdrawal restrictions in order to determine the effect(s) (if any) on financial statement presentation. Information concerning withdrawal restrictions or other limitations on the use of funds may be disclosed by bank confirmations, minutes of board of directors meetings, loan agreements, bond indentures, published regulations concerning regulated businesses and industries, and escrow agreements.

AUDIT MEMORANDUM

The auditor should prepare a memorandum for the work papers which describe the work performed. This memorandum should clearly state the audit objectives, the work performed, the findings of the work performed, and the auditor's opinion as to whether the cash balance is fairly stated.

CONCLUDING REMARKS

Almost every transaction of any company will eventually result in either the receipt or disbursement of cash. The accounting procedures which enable a business to establish effective control over its cash transactions are among the most important, if not *the* most important, "controls" necessary for the successful operation of a business. Cash is more susceptible to misappropriation or theft than any other asset because it can easily be concealed and because it is not readily identifiable. This makes the auditor's cash work one of the most important segments of the examination.

GLOSSARY

Check protector A device which imprints the dollar amount on the check face mechanically.

Cutoff bank statement A statement with paid checks and other customary enclosures obtained from the bank by the auditor which shows transactions for a specified number of days following the bank reconciliation date.

Kiting A method used to cover a cash shortage. It involves writing a check on one bank account and depositing it in another just before the end of the accounting period. Since it takes several days for the check to clear, the amount of the check is included in the balance per bank of both banks involved. No entry is made in the company's records to record the transfer of funds until the next accounting period.

Lapping The act of abstracting receipts from customers and covering the shortage with receipts from subsequent collections received from other customers.

380

Lockbox An arrangement under which customers of a company send payments directly to the company's bank where they are credited to the company immediately.

Standard Bank Confirmation Inquiry A form mailed by the auditor to each bank in which a client had a deposit or from which it had borrowed funds or had other business during the current year. The form seeks verification of bank balances reported in the company's records. (See Figure 9–3 for an illustration.)

QUESTIONS AND PROBLEMS

9–1. What are the auditor's objectives in examining cash?

9–2. Briefly describe the proper accounting controls for the following:
 a. Mail receipts.
 b. Cash sales.
 c. Miscellaneous receipts.
 d. Cash disbursements.

9–3. What tests should be made of an invoice before it is approved for payment?

9–4. List and briefly describe three subdivisions of the cash disbursement function (for disbursements made by check).

9–5. What is included in Cash on Hand?

9–6. Why is careful planning of all cash counts necessary?

9–7. How can control of all cash funds be accomplished?

9–8. What is generally included in a bank confirmation?

9–9. What should the auditor generally do in testing the company's bank reconciliations?

9–10. What is a cutoff bank statement?

9–11. What procedures should the auditor perform when a cutoff statement has not been obtained directly from the bank?

9–12. What is the auditor's purpose in examining large or unusual checks dated subsequent to year-end?

9–13. What is kiting? Lapping? How can they be detected?

9–14. What is the auditor's objective in testing cash receipts?

9–15. List the procedures which should be applied when testing cash receipts.

9–16. What is the auditor's objective in testing cash disbursements?

9–17. List the procedures typically applied by the auditor when testing cash disbursements.

9–18. Prepare a simple illustration of "lapping" of cash receipts, showing actual transactions and the cash book entries.

(AICPA)

9–19. A new junior on the staff asks you why it is necessary to make any audit of petty cash when both the size of the fund and the total petty cash expenditures for the audit period appear to be immaterial. How would you answer the junior's question? Give the reasons for your answer.

(AICPA)

9-20. Select the best answer for each of the following items:

a. Internal control over cash receipts is weakened when an employee who receives customer mail receipts also
   1. Prepares initial cash receipts records.
   2. Records credits to individual accounts receivable.
   3. Prepares bank deposit slips for all mail receipts.
   4. Maintains a petty cash fund.

b. On the last day of the fiscal year, the cash disbursements clerk drew a company check on bank A and deposited the check in the company account bank B to cover a previous theft of cash. The disbursement has *not* been recorded. The auditor will *best* detect this form of kiting by
   1. Comparing the detail of cash receipts as shown by the cash receipts records with the detail on the confirmed duplicate deposit tickets for three days prior to and subsequent to year-end.
   2. Preparing from the cash disbursements book a summary of bank transfers for one week prior to and subsequent to year-end.
   3. Examining the composition of deposits in both bank A and B subsequent to year-end.
   4. Examining paid checks returned with the bank statement of the next accounting period after year-end.

c. An effective internal accounting control measure that protects against the preparation of improper or inaccurate disbursements would be to require that all checks be
   1. Signed by an officer after necessary supporting evidence has been examined.
   2. Reviewed by the treasurer before mailing.
   3. Sequentially numbered and accounted for by internal auditors.
   4. Perforated or otherwise effectively canceled when they are returned with the bank statement.

d. The cashier of Safir Company covered a shortage in the cash working fund with cash obtained on December 31 from a local bank by cashing but not recording a check drawn on the company's out-of-town bank. How would the auditor discover this manipulation?
   1. Confirming all December 31 bank balances.
   2. Counting the cash working fund at the close of business on December 31.
   3. Preparing independent bank reconciliations as of December 31.
   4. Investigating items returned with the bank cutoff statements.

(AICPA, adapted)

382

9-21. XYZ operates sales divisions in several cities throughout the country. In addition to other activities the sales divisions are charged with the collection of local receivables; each division maintains a bank account in which all collections are deposited intact. Twice a week these collections are transferred to the home office by check; no other checks are drawn on this bank account. Except for cash receipts and cash disbursements books, no accounting books are kept at the sales offices, but all cash records are retained by them in their files.

As part of your year-end audit you wish to include an audit of cash transfers between the sales divisions and the main office. It is intended that your representative will visit all locations.

Required:

a. What are the purposes of the audit of cash transfers?

b. Assuming that your representative has a full knowledge of audit procedures for regular cash collection to which he will attend at each location, design *only such additional specific* audit steps as he will be required to perform to audit the cash transfers from each sales division to home office.

(AICPA)

9-22. When you arrive at your client's office on January 11, 1981, to begin the December 31, 1980, audit, you discover the client had been drawing checks as creditors' invoices became due but not necessarily mailing them. Because of a working capital shortage, some checks may have been held for two or three weeks.

The client informs you that unmailed checks totaling $27,600 were on hand at December 31, 1980. He states these December-dated checks had been entered in the cash disbursements book and charged to the respective creditors' accounts in December because the checks were prenumbered. Heavy collections permitted him to mail the checks before your arrival.

The client wants to adjust the cash balance and accounts payable at December 31 by $27,600 because the cash account had a credit balance. He objects to submitting to his bank your audit report showing an overdraft of cash.

Required:

a. Submit a detailed audit program indicating the procedures you would use to satisfy yourself of the accuracy of the cash balance on the client's statements.

b. Discuss the propriety of reversing the indicated amount of outstanding checks.

(AICPA, adapted)

9-23. Your client is a small college in a small town. The college has recently elected as treasurer the president of the local bank in which the college keeps its cash funds. The bank is also the custodian of the college's endowment fund securities. Furthermore, certain short-term securities are held at the bank in a safe-deposit box to which the president has access.

Confirmation requests to the bank in the past have been signed by the former college treasurer and the bank's replies have been signed by the bank president.

Required:

a. What should you do about direct confirmations for the current fiscal year?
b. What effect would these circumstances have on your opinion?

(AICPA, adapted)

9-24. The Patrick Company had poor internal control over its cash transactions. Facts concerning its cash position at November 30, 1981 were as follows:

The cash books showed a balance of $18,901.62, which included undeposited receipts. A credit of $100 on the bank's records did not appear on the books of the company. The balance per bank statement was $15,550. Outstanding checks were: No. 62 for $116.25, No. 183 for $150.00, No. 284 for $253.25, No. 8621 for $190.71, No. 8623 for $206.80, and No. 8632 for $145.28.

The cashier abstracted all undeposited receipts in excess of $3,794.41 and prepared the following reconciliation:

Balance, per books, November 30, 1981		$18,901.62
Add: Outstanding checks:		
8621	$190.71	
8623	206.80	
8632	145.28	442.79
		19,344.41
Less: Undeposited receipts		3,794.41
Balance per bank, November 30, 1981		15,550.00
Deduct: Unrecorded credit		100.00
True cash, November 30, 1981		$15,450.00

Required:

a. Prepare a supporting schedule showing how much the cashier abstracted.
b. How did he attempt to conceal his theft?
c. Taking only the information given, name two specific features of internal control which were apparently missing.
d. If the cashier's October 31 reconciliation is known to be in order and you start your audit on December 5, 1981, what specific auditing procedures would uncover the theft?

(AICPA, adapted)

9-25. Your client, who sells on credit, has several bank accounts. A reconciliation of one of these accounts as of the balance sheet date appears as follows:

Balance per bank, December 31, 1981	$5,000
Add: Deposit in transit	1,000
Total	$6,000
Less: Outstanding checks	50
Balance per books, December 31, 1981	$5,950

The book balance of $5,950 is shown as cash on the balance sheet. As to the $1,000 shown as a deposit in transit, you are to:

a. Briefly describe the major possibilities of fraud or error in these circumstances.

b. List the audit procedures that might be followed in a regular annual audit which would help to verify the deposit in transit. Explain fully how these procedures would help to verify the deposit in transit and detect possible fraud or error.

(AICPA, adapted)

9-26. In connection with your audit of the ABC Co. at December 31, 1980, you were given a bank reconciliation by a company employee which shows:

Balance per bank	$15,267
Deposits in transit	18,928
	$34,195
Checks outstanding	21,378
Balance per books	$12,817

As part of your verification you obtain the bank statement and canceled checks from the bank on January 15, 1981. Checks issued from January 1 to January 15, 1981, per the books were $11,241. Checks returned by the bank on January 15th amounted to $29,219. Of the checks outstanding December 31st, $4,800 were not returned by the bank with the January 15th statement, and of those issued per the books in January 1981, $3,600 were not returned.

a. Prepare a schedule showing the above data in proper form.

b. Suggest four possible explanations for the condition existing here and state what your action would be in each case, including any necessary journal entry.

(AICPA, adapted)

9-27. Mr. William Green recently acquired the controlling financial interest of Importers and Wholesalers, Inc., importers and distributors of cutlery. In his review of the duties of employees Mr. Green became aware of loose practices in the signing of checks and the operation of the petty cash fund.

You have been engaged as the company's CPA and Mr. Green's first request is that you suggest a system of sound practices for the signing of checks and the operation of the petty cash fund. Mr. Green prefers not to acquire a check-signing machine.

In addition to Mr. Green, who is the company president, the company has 20 employees including four corporate officers. About 200 checks are drawn each month. The petty cash fund has a working balance of about $200 and about $500 is expended from the fund each month.

Required:

Prepare a letter to Mr. Green containing your recommendations for good internal control procedures for:

a. Signing checks. (Mr. Green is unwilling to be drawn into routine check signing duties. Assume that you decided to recommend two signatures on each check.)

b. Operation of the petty cash fund. (Where the effect of the control procedure is not evident, give the reason for the procedure.)

(AICPA, adapted)

9–28. Jerome Paper Company engaged you to review its internal control system. Jerome does not prelist cash receipts before they are recorded and has other weaknesses in processing collections of trade receivables, the company's largest asset. In discussing the matter with the controller, you find he is chiefly interested in economy when he assigns duties to the 15 office personnel. He feels the main considerations are that the work should be done by people who are most familiar with it, capable of doing it, and available when it has to be done.

The controller says he has excellent control over trade receivables because receivables are pledged as security for a continually renewable bank loan and the bank sends out positive confirmation requests occasionally, based on a list of pledged receivables furnished by the company each week (letters asking customers to confirm the amounts listed on the books as owed to the company). You learn that the bank's internal auditor is satisfied if he gets an acceptable response on 70 percent of his requests.

Required:

a. Explain how prelisting of cash receipts strengthens internal control over cash.

b. Assume that an employee handles cash receipts from trade customers before they are recorded. List the duties which that employee should not perform in order to withhold from him the opportunity to conceal embezzlement of cash receipts.

(AICPA, adapted)

9–29. A surprise count of the Y Company's imprest petty cash fund, carried on the books at $5,000, was made on November 10, 1981.

The company acts as agent for an express company in the issuance and sale of money orders. Blank money orders are held by the cashier for issuance upon payments of the designated amounts by employees. Settlement with the express company is made weekly with its representative who calls at the Y Company office. At that time he collects for orders issued, accounts for unissued orders, and leaves additional blank money orders serially numbered.

The count of the items presented by the cashier as composing the fund was as follows:

Currency (bills and coin)		$2,200
Cashed checks		500
Vouchers (made out in pencil and signed by recipient)		740
N.S.F. checks (dated June 10 and 15, 1981)		260
Copy of petty cash receipt vouchers:		
Return of expense advance	$200	
Sale of money orders (#C1015–1021)	100	300
Blank money orders—claimed to have been purchased for $100 each from the Express Company (#C1022 to 1027)		600

At the time of the count there was also on hand the following:

> Unissued money orders #C1028–1037.
> Unclaimed wage envelopes (sealed and amounts not shown).

The following day the custodian of the fund produced vouchers aggregating $400 and explained that these vouchers had been temporarily misplaced the previous day. They were for wage advances to employees.

a. Show the proper composition of the fund at November 10, 1981.
b. State the audit procedures necessary for the verification of the items in the fund.

(AICPA, adapted)

9–30. In connection with an audit you are given the following work sheet:

Bank Reconciliation
December 31, 1981

Balance per ledger 12/31/81	$17,174.86
Add:	
Collections received on the last day of December and charged to "cash in bank" on books but not deposited	2,662.25
Debit memo for customer's check returned unpaid (check is on hand but no entry has been made on the books)	200.00
Debit memo for bank service charge for December	5.50
	$20,142.61

Deduct:
Checks drawn but not paid by bank (see detailed list
 below) $2,267.75
Credit memo for proceeds of a note receivable
 which had been left at the bank for collection but
 which has not been recorded as collected 400.00
Check for an account payable entered on books as
 $240.90 but drawn and paid by bank as $419.00   178.10   2,945.85
Computed balance $17,196.76
Unlocated difference 200.00
Balance per bank (checked to confirmation) $16,996.76

Checks Drawn But Not Paid By Bank

No.	Amount
573	$ 67.27
724	9.90
903	456.67
907	305.50
911	482.75
913	550.00
914	366.76
916	10.00
917	218.90
	$2,267.75

Required:
a. Prepare a corrected reconciliation.
b. Prepare journal entries for items which should be adjusted prior to
    closing the books.

(AICPA, adapted)

9-31. One audit procedure which can be used to detect "kiting" at year-end
       is the reconciliation of all bank activity with the books (for all bank
       accounts) for the period just before and just after the year-end. Certain
       detailed comparisons can be avoided if this reconciliation is accom-
       plished in summary form.

   a. Using the data which follows, devise a good work-paper form to
       achieve the above-stated objective and reconcile thereon the bank
       balances at the three dates shown and the bank activity for the
       period December 1, 1980, to January 12, 1981. (Your work papers
       must include a "proof of cash transactions" but need not show the
       corrected balances or totals.)
   b. For each item on the work papers, you are to show by appropriate
       symbols all audit procedures you would take in completing your
       audit.
   c. Prepare journal entries needed as a result of your work.

ACB Corporation	11/30/80	12/31/80	1/12/81
Balance per bank statement	$27,324.08	$20,383.89	$29,514.84
Balance per cash book and general ledger	21,214.95	16,689.86	
Outstanding checks	7,324.13	8,231.12	3,172.50
Deposits in transit	2,200.00	3,750.00	1,625.00

	Period 12/1/80-12/31/80	Period 1/2/81-1/12/81
Receipts per cash book	$88,546.50	$21,473.26
Credits per bank statement	86,324.00	24,372.10
Disbursements per cash book	93,071.59	9,980.03
Charges per bank statement	93,264.19	15,241.15

The client obtained bank statements for November 30 and December 31, 1980, and reconciled the balances. You obtained the statements of 1/12/81 directly and obtained the necessary confirmations. *You have found that there are no errors in addition or subtraction in the books.* The following information was obtained:

1. Bank service charges of $11.50 were charged on the 11/30/80 statement and recorded in the cash disbursements on 12/5/80. Charges of $13.25 were charged on the 12/31/80 statement and recorded in the cash disbursements on 1/6/81.
2. A check (#28890) for $22.48 cleared the bank in December at $122.48. This was found in proving the bank statement. The bank made the correction on January 8.
3. A note of $1,000 sent to the bank for collection on 11/15/80 was collected and credited to the account on 11/28/80 net of a collection fee, $3.50. The note was recorded in the cash receipts on 12/10/80. The collection fee was then entered as a disbursement.
4. The client records returned checks in red in the cash receipts book. The following checks were returned by the bank.

Customer	Amount	Date Returned	Date Recorded	Date Redeposited
A. Black	$327.50	12/ 6/80	(Note)	12/ 8/80
C. Denny	673.84	12/27/80	1/3/81	1/15/81

Note: No entries made in either receipts or disbursement books for this item.

5. Two payroll checks for employees' vacations totaling $215.75 were drawn on January 3rd and cleared the bank January 8th. These were not entered on the books since semi-monthly payroll summaries (from payroll disbursement records) are entered in the disbursements on the 15th and 31st only.

(AICPA, adapted)

9–32. Glattelt Rural Electric Power Cooperative issues books of sight drafts to the foremen of its ten field crews. The foremen use the drafts to pay the expenses of the field crews when they are on line duty requiring overnight stays.

The drafts are prenumbered and, as is clearly printed on the drafts, are limited to expenditures of $300 or less. The foremen prepare the drafts in duplicate and send the duplicates, accompanied by expense reports substantiating the drafts, to the general office.

The draft duplicates are accumulated at the general office and a voucher is prepared when there are two or three draft duplicates on hand. The voucher is the authority for issuing a company check for deposit in an imprest fund of $5,000 maintained at a local bank to meet the drafts as they are presented for payment. The cooperative maintains a separate general ledger account for the imprest fund.

The audit of the voucher register and cash disbursements disclosed the following information pertaining to sight drafts and the reimbursement of the imprest fund:

1. Voucher no. 10524 dated 12/31/80, paid by check no. 10524 dated 12/31/80, for the following drafts:

Draft No.	Date	Crew No.	Explanation	Amount
6001	12/24/80	3	Expenses, 12/22-24	$160
2372	12/28/80	6	Expenses, 12/26–28	310
5304	12/30/80	7	Cash advance to foreman	260
			Voucher total	$730

2. Voucher no. 10531 dated 12/31/80, paid by check no. 10531 dated 1/3/80, for the following drafts:

Draft No.	Date	Crew No.	Explanation	Amount
4060	12/29/80	1	Expenses, 12/27–29	$150
1816	1/ 3/81	4	Expenses, 1/1–3	560
			Voucher total	$710

3. Voucher no. 23 dated 1/8/81, paid by check no. 23 dated 1/8/81, for the following drafts:

Draft No.	Date	Crew No.	Explanation	Amount
1000	12/31/80	9	Expenses, 12/28–31	$270
2918	1/ 3/81	10	Expenses, 12/28–31	190
4061	1/ 7/81	1	Expenses, 1/4–6	210
			Voucher total	$670

4. All of the above vouchers were charged to Travel Expense.
5. Examination of the imprest fund's bank statement for December,

the January cutoff bank statement, and accompanying drafts presented for payment disclosed the following information:

a. Reimbursement check no. 10524 was not credited on the December bank statement.

b. The bank honored draft no. 2372 at the established maximum authorized amount.

c. Original 1980 drafts drawn by foremen but not presented to the client's bank for payment by 12/31/80 totaled $1,600. This total included all 1980 drafts itemized above except no. 4060 and no. 2372, which were deducted by the bank in December.

d. December bank service charges listed on the December bank statement but not recorded by the client amounted to $80.

e. The balance per the bank statement at December 31, 1980, was $5,650.

Required:

a. Prepare the auditor's adjusting journal entry to correct the books at December 31, 1980. (The books have not been closed.) A supporting working paper analyzing the required adjustments should be prepared in good form.

b. Prepare a reconciliation of the balance per bank statement and the financial statement figure for the imprest cash account. The first figure in your reconciliation should be the balance per bank statement.

(AICPA, adapted)

9-33. Toyco, a retail toy chain, honors two bank credit cards and makes daily deposits of credit card sales in two credit card bank accounts (Bank A and Bank B). Each day Toyco batches its credit card sales slips, bank deposit slips, and authorized sales return documents, and keypunches cards for processing by its electronic data processing department. Each week detailed computer printouts of the general ledger credit card cash accounts are prepared. Credit card banks have been instructed to make an automatic weekly transfer of cash to Toyco's general bank account. The credit card banks charge back deposits that include sales to holders of stolen or expired cards.

The auditor conducting the examination of the 1980 Toyco financial statements has obtained the following copies of the detailed general ledger cash account printouts, a summary of the bank statements and the manually prepared bank reconciliations, all for the week ended December 31, 1980.

TOYCO
Detailed General Ledger Credit Card
Cash Account Printouts
For the Week Ended December 31, 1980

	Bank A	Bank B
	Dr. or (Cr.)	Dr. or (Cr.)
Beginning Balance		
December 24, 1980	$12,100	$ 4,200
Deposits		
December 27, 1980	2,500	5,000
December 28, 1980	3,000	7,000
December 29, 1980	0	5,400
December 30, 1980	1,900	4,000
December 31, 1980	2,200	6,000
Cash transfer		
December 27, 1980	(10,700)	0
Charge-backs		
Expired cards	(300)	(1,600)
Invalid deposits (physically		
deposited in wrong account)	(1,400)	(1,000)
Redeposit of invalid		
deposits	1,000	1,400
Sales returns for week ending		
December 31, 1980	(600)	(1,200)
Ending Balance		
December 31, 1980	$ 9,700	$29,200

TOYCO
Summary of the Bank Statements
For the Week Ended December 31, 1980

	Bank A	Bank B
	(Charges) or Credits	
Beginning Balance		
December 24, 1980	$10,000	$ 0
Deposits dated		
December 24, 1980	2,100	4,200
December 27, 1980	2,500	5,000
December 28, 1980	3,000	7,000
December 29, 1980	2,000	5,500
December 30, 1980	1,900	4,000
Cash transfers to general bank account		
December 27, 1980	(10,700)	0
December 31, 1980	0	(22,600)
Charge-backs		
Stolen cards	(100)	0
Expired cards	(300)	(1,600)
Invalid deposits	(1,400)	(1,000)
Bank service charges	0	(500)
Bank charge (unexplained)	(400)	0
Ending Balance—		
December 31, 1980	$ 8,600	$ 0

TOYCO
Bank Reconciliations
For the Week Ended December 31, 1980

Code No.		Bank A Add	or	Bank B (Deduct)
1.	Balance per bank statement—December 31, 1980	$8,600		$ 0
2.	Deposits in transit—December 31, 1980	2,200		6,000
3.	Redeposit of invalid deposits (physically deposited in wrong account)	1,000		1,400
4.	Difference in deposits of December 29, 1980	(2,000)		(100)
5.	Unexplained bank charge	400		0
6.	Bank cash transfer not yet recorded	0		22,600
7.	Bank service charges	0		500
8.	Charge-backs not recorded—Stolen cards	100		0
9.	Sales returns recorded but not reported to the bank	(600)		(1,200)
10.	Balance per general ledger—December 31, 1980	$9,700		$29,200

Required:

Based on a review of the December 31, 1980, bank reconciliations and the related information available in the printouts and the summary of bank statements, describe what action(s) the auditor should take to obtain audit satisfaction *for each item* on the bank reconciliations.

Assume that all amounts are material and all computations are accurate.

Organize your answer sheet as follows using the appropriate code number *for each item* on the bank reconciliations:

Code No.	Action(s) to Be Taken by the Auditor to Obtain Audit Satisfaction
1.	

(AICPA, adapted)

Learning Objectives

The study of the material in this chapter is designed to achieve several learning objectives. These include an understanding of the:

1. Objective of the auditor's examination of receivables.
2. Essential elements of internal control over receivables.
3. Specific audit procedures regarding accounts receivable, including the confirmation of accounts receivable.
4. Evaluation procedures for receivables, including the aging of receivables.
5. Other tests made by the auditor to determine that the sales cutoff was proper and that accounts sold or assigned are not included in the receivables balance.
6. Audit procedures involving notes receivable.

10

Receivables

In the examination of receivables the auditor evaluates receivable balances to determine whether they are fairly stated in accordance with generally accepted accounting principles applied on a consistent basis. Thus, the auditor attempts to establish: (1) the substantial accuracy of amounts recorded; (2) their validity as claims against recorded debtors; and (3) their collectibility. In addition, during the examination of receivables, the auditor should seek to obtain important evidence regarding related accounts, such as revenue from the sale of products or performance of services.

As audit procedures are applied to receivables, certain types of management problems may come to the attention of the auditor. Obviously, the collectibility of outstanding receivable balances is important both from the viewpoint of the auditor and from the viewpoint of management. The information the auditor develops during the review of the collectibility of receivables often provides information as to the status of the client's relations with customers. Past-due accounts may indicate dissatisfaction with the client's product, service or prices. Unprocessed credit memos for returned merchandise, pricing disputes, or claims concerning product quality could be indicative of other problems as well. For example, assume that the comments made on a number of replies to confirmation requests indicated frequent complaints with a particular product. This might suggest that the inventory of this product and its components should be reviewed for salability. Thus, by studying the management considerations which are noted during the examination of accounts receivable, the auditor may discover matters which will not only be of assistance to management in many areas, but will assist in the audit of receivables as well as other areas.

INTERNAL CONTROL OVER RECEIVABLES

The client must, of course, establish a number of controls over the accounts receivable from its customers. A formal procedure should exist for granting credit to customers. This task should be the responsibility of a particular employee (who preferably does not have other sales or receivable responsibilities). The accounts receivable department should receive duplicate sales invoices, customer remittance advices, and other source data for its use in recording and controlling receivables transactions. If possible, numerical control should be established over these documents. Control totals of the source documents should be included with the source data. The control totals should be reconciled periodically with the totals posted to the customer accounts, and any differences should be promptly investigated. Trial balances of customer accounts should be reconciled to the general ledger control account on a regular basis by an individual who does not have other receivable or general ledger responsibilities.

The employees who are involved in the processing of accounts receivable should not deal with the receipt of customer payments, the billing and credit processes, or any other related activities. One particular employee who is independent of other cash and receivable duties should be assigned the task of authorizing credits to receivable accounts from such sources as discounts and returns and allowances.

The postings to accounts receivable should be made on a timely basis. Current data regarding the status of accounts receivable are frequently required for credit and other management purposes.

Many companies mail monthly statements to their customers. This procedure is often not only helpful in collecting open accounts but also serves as a test of the accuracy of the accounts receivable records. Any differences reported by customers should be investigated promptly and resolved by an individual who, preferably, does not have other receivable responsibilities. An employee who, preferably, does not have other receivable responsibilities should be assigned the task of periodically aging all receivable accounts. Overdue accounts should be reviewed carefully to determine the steps that need to be taken to collect the amounts and whether any of them should be written off.

The write-off of uncollectible accounts should be approved by a knowledgeable officer or employee who has no other duties related to either accounts receivable or cash receipts. Before approving write-offs, this individual should examine evidence indicating that a reasonable effort has been made to collect the accounts. Even after accounts have been written off, the company should continue to maintain control over them by keeping an independent record of accounts written off to preclude misappropriation of any subsequent collections.

Notes receivable may be negotiable. Thus, they should be kept in a safe place with limited access, such as in a safe-deposit box. A subsidiary ledger of notes receivable should be kept. Periodic reconciliation of the notes to a notes subsidiary ledger and/or to the general ledger is an effective means of control. A designated official should be assigned the task of authorizing the acceptance of new notes or the renewal of old notes.

COMPLIANCE TESTING: RECEIVABLES

The procedures used by the auditor in the examination of receivables arising from trade sales include compliance testing and substantive testing.

The Compliance Tests

Trade receivables are naturally related to sales. Consequently, in compliance tests relating to receivables, sales will usually be involved. Thus, compliance testing of both of these areas will be discussed together. The audit of sales is discussed at greater length in Chapter 13.

The objective of compliance testing in these areas is to enable the auditor to ascertain whether the company's procedures are being followed. These procedures should be designed to ensure that: items sold by the company are to bona fide customers with reasonable credit standing; items sold are shipped; invoices for these items are promptly and properly prepared and recorded as a trade receivable; and billings to customers correspond to shipments.

Representative tests of sales and related trade receivables used by the auditor include the following:

1. Account for the numerical sequence of all invoices and credit memoranda.
2. Prove the footings of sales and credit memorandum registers.
3. Trace the postings of sales and credit memorandum registers to the general ledger.
4. Check sales invoices for arithmetical accuracy, quantities invoiced (by comparison with shipping records), and unit prices (by comparison with sales contracts or price lists, noting the propriety of any trade discounts granted).
5. Compare shipping records with sales records or invoices in order to ascertain that all shipments have been billed, and account for the numerical sequence of shipping documents.
6. Review credit memoranda for proper approval.
7. Check the credit memoranda covering returned goods for

arithmetical accuracy, quantities returned (by reference to receiving records), and unit prices (by reference to the original invoice or record of the selling price).

8. Compare cash credit postings in customers' accounts with the cash receipts records.

9. Inspect credit files in support of accounts written off as uncollectible.

The objectives of each of these tests will now be discussed in detail.

Accounting for Sales Invoices and Credit Memoranda. The failure of a company to process and properly record invoices and credit memos may seriously affect not only its profitability but its customer relations, operating efficiency, and the accuracy of its financial information as well. A good way to help prevent these problems from occurring is by the use of prenumbered documents. As a part of its system of internal control, the company should account for the numerical sequence of such documents, and the sequence should be checked by the auditor. If this is not done, errors which might cause sales to be either understated or overstated could go undetected.

One means of concealing an improper shipment or avoiding normal invoicing and collecting procedures is to suppress billing information. If this practice is undetected, employees having access to the applicable documents could direct shipments to themselves or an accomplice and suppress the billing or could arrange to divert collections from customers for bona fide sales. If procedures are in effect to ensure that all invoices are properly accounted for and recorded, such defalcations should be uncovered by the client's normal procedures of mailing statements to customers and following up on delinquent accounts. Customers will take issue with charges representing merchandise they never received or with those which they have already paid.

Proving the Footings of Sales and Credit Memorandum Registers. Accounting for the numerical sequence of all invoices and credit memos does not, in itself, ensure that the total sales and allowances for the period are necessarily correct. The additional step of testing the applicable journal or register totals for accuracy also must be taken by the auditor. The totals obtained from these books of original entry are important because of their effect on the receivable control accounts. The improper footing of these records could, for example, be used to conceal improperly recorded sales with the possible accompanying misappropriation of customer payments.

Tracing the Postings of Sales and Credit Memorandum Registers to the General Ledger. These tests are used by the auditor to determine whether accounting information is flowing properly and may help to detect errors or irregularities in processing invoices and credit memos.

Checking Sales Invoices for (a) Arithmetical Accuracy; (b) Quantities Invoiced (by comparison with shipping records); (c) Unit Prices; and (d) Approval by the Client.   This test enables the auditor to determine whether procedures designed to prevent clerical errors in billing are effective and to detect deviations from the company's pricing policies.

In testing prices, the auditor is primarily concerned with determining whether unit prices are in agreement with price lists, contracts, or other pricing authorizations. Frequently, the price of a product is determined by the sum of the various cost factors that were included in its fabrication—including materials, labor, and overhead. The computation and accumulation of these unit prices should be tested by the auditor.

Billings that are not in agreement with sales contracts or price lists may be due to clerical errors, to deliberate circumvention of company policy, or to the misappropriation of funds by withholding a portion of a customer's remittance and altering the selling price accordingly. The latter practice would normally be possible in those circumstances where sales representatives are allowed to accept payments from customers.

Comparing Shipping Records with Sales Records or Invoices and Accounting for the Numerical Sequence of Shipping Documents.   A company's procedures should be designed to assure that all shipments are billed to customers. The auditor should compare shipping records with sales records or invoices. The numerical sequence of shipping documents should also be accounted for and traced to the sales register or billing information. The auditor should also note whether billings are being prepared promptly after the goods are shipped. Delay in preparing billings and recording shipments as sales could impact the extent of the cutoff testing (which is discussed later) required at the balance sheet date.

Reviewing Credit Memoranda for Approval.   In commercial enterprises, credit is normally issued to customers for goods returned, to correct errors in either shipping or billing, or to maintain customer goodwill. Credits of this nature are normal. However, the auditor must be aware that credit memos also can be used to conceal errors or irregularities, for example, by issuing an improper credit memo to conceal the fact that a remittance from a customer may have been abstracted by a client employee.

Various forms and documents provide the underlying support for credit memos. In some companies the support will be a form designed specifically for this purpose. In others the supporting document may simply be a scrap of paper containing the relevant information. It may also take the form of interdepartmental correspondence, letters from customers, policy memos, or receiving reports. The methods of filing the support will also vary. For example, it may be attached to the credit memo or it may be filed numerically. The nature of the support and method of filing may vary according to the circumstances, but this does not alter the basic concept that credit memos must always be properly authorized, approved, and supported.

Approval is usually indicated by the initials of the responsible employee. The auditor should examine credit memos to determine whether they have, in fact, been properly approved. Further, the underlying support should be reviewed to ensure that it represents adequate authority for the credit.

Checking Credit Memoranda Covering Returned Goods for: (a) Arithmetical Accuracy; (b) Quantities Returned (by reference to receiving records); and (c) Unit Prices (by reference to the original invoice or record of the selling price). Tests of credit memoranda for returned goods are made in order to ensure that the credit has been issued in accordance with company policy. Frequently, the amount of the credit may be adjusted for a handling or usage charge. The tests of arithmetical accuracy, comparison of receiving records (customer name, date, description of merchandise, and quantities), review of approvals, and verification of prices are all tests used by the auditor which are necessary to ascertain whether credit for returned goods is being handled properly.

Comparing Cash Credit Postings in Customers' Accounts with the Cash Receipts Records. This procedure is a corollary to the tracing of amounts from the cash receipts journal to the customers' accounts. The purpose of this test is to determine whether credits in the subsidiary ledger accounts are based on valid entries in the books of original entry. This type of test is an example of the recommended practice of tracing transactions from, as well as to, the ledgers. In this manner, tests are made to ascertain whether the transactions which appear in the books of original entry are recorded in the ledgers and whether the ledgers are based on valid entries in the books of original entry. In applying this test to the accounts receivable, the auditor selects accounts for testing and traces the dates and amounts from the detail ledgers to the cash receipts records. Where the client's controls are weak, it may also be desirable to compare entries with the information included in remittance advices.

Inspecting Credit Files in Support of Accounts Written off as Uncollectible. Most write-offs of trade receivables are entirely proper. On the other hand, perfectly good accounts may have been inadvertently written off either because of a clerk's error or because a company employee has deliberately written off an account as uncollectible and kept the customer's payment.

In determining the propriety of write-offs, the auditor should examine the support maintained in the client's credit files. Correspondence with the debtor should be reviewed to establish whether an effort has been made to collect the amount due from the customer. Sometimes credit files contain correspondence with attorneys supporting the charge-offs. Supporting material may also be obtained from Dun & Bradstreet and other credit reports.

SUBSTANTIVE TESTS: ACCOUNTS RECEIVABLE

The auditor should first obtain an aged trial balance from the client. This trial balance may be as of the balance-sheet date or as of the confirmation date. Next, the auditor should foot and crossfoot the trial balance (generally on a test basis) and then reconcile the total with the general ledger control account. The accuracy of both the amounts and aging should be tested by reference to the individual accounts (aging will be discussed more fully later in this chapter). In checking the individual accounts, the auditor should be alert for debits, credits, or balances which are deemed to be of an unusual nature.

Confirming Receivables

SAS No. 1, section 331.01, states that the "confirmation of receivables and observation of inventories are generally accepted auditing procedures." In practice there are few instances where the correspondence with debtors is not practicable and reasonable. When it is not practicable and reasonable to confirm the receivable balances or when no replies are received, the auditor must become satisfied as to the reasonableness of the receivables by the use of "alternative procedures." Examples of alternative procedures that may be employed by the auditor include the examination of purchase orders, shipping records, contracts, correspondence, evidence of subsequent collection, and other documentary support. Alternative procedures are described in greater detail later in this chapter.

SAS No. 2 notes that circumstances may make it impracticable or impossible for the auditor to confirm receivables. If the auditor is, however, ". . . able to satisfy himself as to . . . accounts receivable by applying alternative procedures, there is no significant limitation on the scope of his work, and his report need not include reference to the omission of the procedures or to the use of alternative procedures." If the auditor is not satisfied with the results of the alternative procedures, this limitation on the work should be referred to in the scope paragraph, described in an explanatory paragraph, and be referred to in the qualified opinion or disclaimer of opinion (whichever the auditor issues). If the sending of confirmations is both practicable and

402

reasonable, but is not done because of a client's wishes, generally this should be mentioned in the scope paragraph, described in an explanatory paragraph, and referred to in a disclaimer of opinion (if receivables are material in amount).

SAS No. 1, section 331.03, also indicates that the method and timing of requesting such confirmations and the number of confirmations to be requested are determined by the auditor. It goes on to state, "such matters as the effectiveness of internal control, the apparent possibility of disputes, inaccuracies, or irregularities in the accounts, the probability that requests will receive consideration or that the debtor will be able to confirm the information requested and the materiality of the amounts involved are factors to be considered by the auditor in selecting the information to be requested and the form of confirmation, as well as the extent and timing of his confirmation procedures."

Method of Confirmation

Accounts receivable may be confirmed by either the positive request method, the negative request method, or by a combination of the two methods. With the positive request method, the debtor is asked to reply directly to the auditor stating whether the balance as indicated on the request is correct or, if it is incorrect, to indicate the correct balance and any possible explanation of the difference. A positive request is usually used (1) for individual account balances that are material in amount, (2) when there is reason to believe that the possibility of disputes, inaccuracies, or irregularities in the accounts is greater than usual, (3) when variables estimation sampling techniques are used, or (4) where there is reason to believe that a negative request will not receive adequate consideration. Positive-type confirmations are requested by sending either a standard printed form, a special form, or a letter using the client's letterhead. Figure 10-1 is an example of a positive request form.

With the negative request method, the debtor is asked to reply only if the balance as stated on the request is not in agreement with the debtor's records. *SAS No. 1* notes that this type of request is useful where internal control relating to receivables is effective, where there are many small balances, and where there are indications that the request will receive proper consideration. Examples of situations where the negative request would *not* be acceptable are (1) in the case of receivables from a debtor that is known for not responding to confirmation requests, (2) when internal controls are not adequate, and (3) where variables estimation sampling techniques are being used. Where the negative method is used, the request may be either rubber-stamped or attached in the form of a sticker on the company's

FIGURE 10-1
Positive confirmation request form prepared for mailing

CONFIRMATION REQUEST

Roberts Co.
2503 Woodward Avenue
Detroit, Michigan 66001

Gentlemen:
    Our auditors are making an examination of our financial statements
and wish to obtain direct confirmation of the correctness of the amount
owed us as of the date indicated. Please compare the balance shown
below with your records, noting details of any exceptions on the reverse
side. Then sign this letter in the space provided and return it directly to
our auditors, Ernst & Whinney. A reply envelope which requires no
postage is enclosed for your convenience.

    This is not a request for payment and remittances should not be made
to our auditors.

Audit date <u>10/31/80</u>   Very truly yours,

Account   Acme Manufacturing Company
    balance <u>$84,921.61</u>   *E. Z. Green*
                                     E. Z. Green
                                     Credit Manager

Ernst & Whinney:
    The balance shown above was correct on the date named. (If not
correct, check here ☐ and indicate difference on reverse.)

                                     _____
                                                        Company

                                     _____
                                                      Signed by

No. <u>2</u>

Return this confirmation to the <u>Atlanta, Georgia</u> *Office of Ernst &*
Whinney

regular statement to the customer, or it may be a special form or business reply card enclosed with the statement. Figure 10–2 is an example of a negative request.

Frequently both positive and negative requests are used in combination by the auditor during the course of the examination.

In some instances the usual form of confirmation requests will not be acknowledged, for example, by organizations such as the U.S. government and certain retail stores because it is not convenient for them to verify the balance shown. In these instances a confirmation request may be tailored in such a way as to bring a reply. For example, the auditor may find that a particular debtor will respond to a request which includes a listing of the details of purchases and payments received so they may be easily traced to the debtor's own records.

Timing of Confirmation

Accounts may be confirmed either at year-end or at an interim date near year-end. The advantages of selecting a date prior to year-end are: (1) there is more time to obtain replies from customers; (2) since more customers may reply, alternative procedures will be required on fewer accounts; and (3) reported differences can be investigated and disposed of by the auditor without delaying the issuance of the audit report. However, if the company's accounting records and controls are deemed to be weak, it may be necessary to circularize receivables at

FIGURE 10–2
Negative confirmation request form

PLEASE EXAMINE THIS STATEMENT CAREFULLY

If it does not agree with your records, report any differences in writing to our auditors

Ernst & Whinney
P.O. Box 6940
Cleveland, Ohio 44101

who are making an examination of our financial statements. If no differences are reported to them, this statement will be considered correct. This is not a request for payment and remittances should not be made to our auditors. A reply envelope, which requires no postage, is enclosed for your convenience.

year-end for the auditor to become satisfied as to the fairness of the receivable balances.

Extent of Confirmation

The extent to which the confirmation procedures will be used by the auditor is largely a matter of judgment, which is influenced by such factors as the evaluation of the system of internal control, the auditor's knowledge of the type of customer, and the dollar amount and number of accounts. For example, if a substantial portion of the client's sales is made to a very few customers, requests for confirmation (positive type) might be directed to all such debtors. In cases where the auditor tests only selected accounts, the accounts selected should be a representative sample selected by the use of statistical sampling techniques (see Chapter 7) or by the auditor's judgment. In such cases, it may also be desirable to request the confirmation of certain accounts such as those with large balances, past-due accounts, very active or inactive accounts, accounts with credit balances, accounts which have been written-off and/or turned over to an agency for collection, and any other accounts of an unusual nature which do not fall within the sample originally selected.

In selecting the sample the auditor must be certain that the population of accounts from which the sample is chosen is complete; i.e., that there is free access to all of the accounts which might be selected. As was noted earlier, the auditor should begin the audit of accounts receivable by obtaining a complete listing of all of the customer account balances. Hopefully, this will be in the form of an aged trial balance. In some instances a manual listing of balances, an adding machine tape, or a computer printout of the accounts will be used. In situations where the client has numerous accounts receivable and the computer is used, standard computer packages developed by certified public accounting firms may be used in testing the receivables and selecting individual accounts for confirmation. In any event, the arithmetical accuracy of the listing must be tested and the total reconciled to the general ledger control account.

When statistical sampling methods are used, the number of accounts to be circularized is determined using statistical formulas. Selection of accounts is performed randomly, e.g., through use of a random number table or other acceptable statistical method. As noted in Chapter 7, variables estimation sampling is a frequently used statistical approach. In such applications, where a statistical conclusion is desired, the auditor should use only positive confirmation requests and perform alternative procedures on every nonresponding account in the sample.

The auditor will select accounts for circularization according to the extent of the confirmation procedures outlined during the preliminary planning of the audit, modified for any significant changes noted in the composition of receivables which were not anticipated in the preliminary plan.

Recording Accounts Circularized

A record of the accounts selected for confirmation should be included in the auditor's working papers. If negative requests are used, a notation on the auditor's copy of the aged trial balance or on an adding machine tape of the customer balances will serve this purpose. For positive requests, this record may be a copy of the request itself, notations on the auditor's copy of the trial balance, or a work sheet indicating the customer's name, address, and account balance.

Controlling Customer Statements and Confirmation Requests

Requests or statements must be compared with the appropriate ledger accounts by the auditor to make certain the amounts are in agreement. To ascertain that all statements or requests will either reach their proper destination or be returned to the auditor by the post office, the auditor must mail out the confirmation requests in envelopes which bear the auditor's (and not the client's) return address. The auditor must maintain control over the statements or requests from the time they are compared with the ledger accounts until they are deposited in the mail. If the auditor fails to maintain this control, an employee could hide irregularities by removing statements with incorrect balances, altering balances to cover the manipulation of accounts, or mailing statements to fictitious addresses or to an accomplice.

When the negative method of confirmation is used, the request is frequently included with the client's monthly accounts receivable statement. (If the company does not prepare a regular monthly statement, the request may be in the form of a special letter or card on the company letterhead.) The auditor must determine that the name, address, and balance appearing on the statement correspond to the information included in the company's accounts receivable records. As previously indicated, the request may be rubber-stamped on the statement, attached in the form of a sticker, or printed on a special form enclosed with the statement.

Whenever possible the company's employees should be asked to assist the auditor in the confirmation process by stamping statements, stuffing envelopes, and so on (under the auditor's supervision), both to save time and reduce the auditor's fee. This imposes a need for careful planning to assure that the statements and requests remain under the auditor's control. The auditor must ascertain by means of personal supervision, observation, and testing that all statements are properly prepared and that none of the statements have been withdrawn or altered before mailing.

When positive confirmations are used, the company's employees will normally be asked to prepare the requests. The auditor must still control the confirmations, however. The procedures for preparing and mailing positive requests are the same as those for negative confirmations except that a self-addressed, stamped envelope is generally enclosed with positive requests (business reply envelopes are sometimes used for negative requests). As previously mentioned, all confirmations should be mailed in an envelope which bears the auditor's return address. If this procedure is followed and any requests are undeliverable, the auditor will have knowledge of this fact. Fictitious receivables, for example, might be disclosed by the use of this procedure.

With the positive confirmation request, every effort should be made by the auditor to obtain a reply from the debtor. Second requests should be mailed to customers who do not reply after a reasonable time, and in some cases telephone or telegraph follow-up may also be appropriate. For those customers who fail to reply at all, alternative procedures, described later in this chapter, should be followed.

Occasionally, during the preparation of the requests, the client may request a particular statement for various reasons; for example, because a "past-due" notice must be attached, an item must be checked, and so on. Such requests are generally valid; however, in each case the auditor should make a record of the statement withdrawn (name, address, and amount) and be certain that it is returned, unaltered, for mailing.

At times, the client may also request that the accounts of certain customers not be confirmed. Accounts may be in dispute, or some other reason may be given. The auditor should note the reason in the working papers and use alternative procedures to become satisfied as to the fairness of the account balance.

Investigating Exceptions to Confirmation Requests

Exceptions to receivables balances will be reported by some customers. Many differences result because of normal business reasons, such as shipments or customer payments in transit, unrecorded credits or allowances, disputes between buyer and seller, or clerical errors. But other differences could also indicate acccounts which have been

408

manipulated or are fictitious. All reported exceptions must be investigated by the auditor. If the exceptions are immaterial in amount or do not indicate serious weaknesses, the auditor may request that a responsible employee of the company investigate them. However, the auditor must control the replies and must become satisfied as to the reasons given for the exceptions. Any differences indicating that credit has not been given for a payment made or for merchandise returned prior to the statement date should be investigated by the auditor. The information and conclusions of the investigation should be included in the working papers.

Performing Alternative Procedures

Alternative procedures must be performed by the auditor to substantiate the balances of any customers who fail to respond to positive confirmation requests. Such procedures may include examining collections made subsequent to the confirmation date by inspection of incoming checks or remittance advices to see if the remittances apply to items open at the confirmation date; tracing invoice numbers and amounts collected to the individual customer's account, and tracing amounts collected to the record of cash receipts and to the bank deposit; examining the customer's purchase order, the client's shipping records, and the sales invoice; and taking such steps as are reasonable in the circumstances to establish the existence of the recorded debtor if there is any question as to the fact.

Interim Transactions from Confirmation Date to Balance-Sheet Date

If confirmation procedures are carried out prior to the year-end work, it is necessary for the auditor to review the intervening transactions in the receivables control accounts between the date of confirmation and the balance-sheet date and to consider confirming any accounts with large balances or any accounts that the auditor considers to be unusual which remain open at year-end. A review of interim transactions will normally include obtaining analyses prepared by the client of the entries in the general ledger control account for the intervening months; tracing the entries from the analyses to the books of original entry (which were tested as part of compliance testing); and reviewing the entries in the general ledger control account as to reasonableness and clerical accuracy.

The Evaluation Procedures

To conform with generally accepted accounting principles, accounts receivable should be included in the financial statements at their estimated realizable amount. Thus the auditor must not only become satisfied that the gross amount of the receivables is fairly stated, but that uncollectible accounts have been properly written off and that adequate provision has been made for potentially uncollectible amounts, credits, discounts, and so on. In reviewing the collectibility of accounts receivable and evaluating the adequacy of the allowance for doubtful accounts, the auditor will refer to various records of the client and to other information as well. This discussion of the evaluation procedures is divided into the following topics: aging of accounts, review of individual account balances, review of subsequent credits, prior experience of the company and changes in character of business, comparison of current year's statistics with prior experience, and changes in the business climate or environment.

Aging of Accounts.   Customer accounts are aged in order to determine the length of time that amounts have been outstanding. The longer an account is past due, the more likely it is to be uncollectible, other factors being equal. Therefore, the aging of receivables is of interest to the auditor in the evaluation of the adequacy of the allowance for uncollectible accounts. A comparison of the percentage of past due accounts with those of prior years is often useful to the auditor in evaluating the allowance.

As was noted earlier, the actual aging is often done by employees of the client. It may be done as of the confirmation date, the balance-sheet date, or both. If the receivables include a large number of small accounts, a listing of only those amounts which are past due may be acceptable. These would be tested by the auditor. Again, if the aging is prepared by the client, the auditor should test the accuracy of the amounts and of the aging by reference to the individual accounts, and the auditor should also test the arithmetical accuracy of the aging and reconcile the total amount to the general ledger control accounts. The aged trial balance should be included as a part of the auditor's working papers, and information obtained concerning the collectibility of accounts should be noted on this trial balance. Notations also may be made concerning payments of past due amounts, information obtained from the credit manager, and so on. Figure 10–3 is an example of an aged trial balance of accounts receivable.

Review of Individual Account Balances.   After the aged trial balance is initially reviewed by the auditor, certain accounts may be selected for further investigation. The collectibility of certain amounts may be discussed with the credit manager or other responsible company official(s). The results of these discussions should be summarized by the auditor for inclusion in the working papers. The auditor should check collections of past due amounts which have been made since the balance-sheet date, and should examine correspondence with customers, collection agency reports, and other rele-

FIGURE 10-3
Aged trial balance of accounts receivable

ACCOUNTS RECEIVABLE AGING SCHEDULE
ACME MANUFACTURING COMPANY
12-31-90

PREPARED: Client/Miller 2-21-91
APPROVED: Williams 2-25-91
4 of 4

Name	Balance Dr.	Balance Cr.	Dec.	Nov.	Oct.	Prior	
Roberts & Co.	7999675		40076657	35526.80	4593510		Pd. Inv. & Oct. charges (4379199.20) on 1-3-91
Jampson Steel	4598489		4536489				
Stabler Electric Co.		1343					
P. Julley	65269376		6526937				
Sallmon & Sons, Inc.	552619					552619	Pd. Inv. $3,000 (exam.) remit. 1-14-91 Pd. sales inv. on 12-31-91
Prebert Supplies Co.	114987					114987	Bankrupt-examined correspondence (see notes)
Undewater Corp.	548327			9217377	32659.00		Bona fide govt. perch. mgt.; verified by examination of customer records. Pd. $7,200 on 1-25-91.
Valley Distributors	5234					5234	
Walnut Mfg. Co.	323715		1716.15	1521.00			
Workman Bros., Inc.	26783467		14782467	10550000	1500.00		Pd. Nov. & Oct. charges on 1-26-91
Total page 4	1743990.34	1343	108746.77	50645.17	83592.00	6998.40	
1	210625.40	620.00	170298.60	30932.81	631.44	30899.54	
2	1927.22.62	2010	15400640	32467873	321.592	1821.60	
3	29284.283	1201.65	23464898	47221010	768875	3245.00	
	87105.81.19	177351	8467471.75	16237681	25578.00	151545.4	
	773.58	(77358)					
	8698076.61						

AJE #4 - to record c/h issued to salesman	(3000 00)							(3000 00)
AJE #5 - to write off bad account	(141 9 87)							(141 9 87)
AJE #- reclassify rec. from company officer	(6526 93) (B)		(6526 93)					
	858860 81		460171 24		16237681	255780?		1073467
	F		F		F	F		F
Percent of 1980 total	100 %		7.4 %		18.9 %	3.0 %		1.2 %
1979 percentage	72.0 %		72.0 %		20.0 %	4.3 %		3.2 %

Procedures Performed by W. Johnson:

√ - traced to detail ledger and aging report.

(A) - Automobiles purchased through company by Dudley president.

(B) - Credit balances not reclassified - amount insignificant.

F - footed and crossfooted total.

vant data included in the credit files of the client. It may also be advisable to obtain Dun & Bradstreet reports or independent information from other sources relating to customers whose accounts are material in amount.

Review of Subsequent Credits. The auditor should examine credit memos issued and recorded subsequent to year-end to ascertain whether these credit memos might affect the period under audit and therefore require an adjustment to be made. The auditor should also be alert for any indications of additional credits which may be required for the period under audit and, in the event any are noted, adjustments should be made to record them.

Prior Experience of the Company and Changes in Character of Business. The prior collection experience of the client, adjusted for any changes in the nature of the client's business or type of customer, may indicate what may be expected in the future. For example, if a company that was selling its product solely to jobbers in the past decides to sell directly to retail outlets, its previous collection experience would probably be of little or no use in predicting its experience in the future.

Comparison of Current Year's Statistics with Prior Experience. Comparison of significant statistics with those of the prior year can highlight potential weaknesses in the company's collection efforts which may have an impact on the overall collectibility of accounts receivable. These statistics include the percentage relationship of overdue accounts to the total receivable balance, number of average day's sales in accounts receivable, average annual accounts receivable turnover, and the percentage of bad debt write-offs to total sales.

Change in Business Climate. The increased likelihood of business failures during a business slowdown should be considered by the auditor in passing judgment as to the adequacy of the allowance for doubtful accounts.

Sales Cutoff

As part of the examination of accounts receivable, tests are made by the auditor to ascertain whether sales are recorded in the accounting period in which the title to the goods or services passes to the customer. This is normally a year-end audit procedure. The auditor usually tests the sales cutoff by examining invoices and shipping documents for several days both prior to and subsequent to year-end and by tracing such documents to the sales and accounts receivable records for the appropriate period. A test of the sales cutoff may occasionally be made at an interim date, to check the adequacy of the company's procedures. The sales cutoff is discussed in greater detail in Chapter 11, "Inventories."

Accounts Sold or Assigned

The selling or assigning of accounts receivable is not a widespread practice, but it is a method of financing used by some firms in certain industries. The minutes of directors' meetings and the bank confirmations may reveal this situation. If the auditor finds that accounts have been sold or assigned, the terms of these transactions should be investigated since disclosure of these transactions may be required in the financial statements if the amounts are material.

SUBSTANTIVE TESTS: NOTES RECEIVABLE

The auditor should obtain from the client a list of notes, acceptances, and other instruments evidencing indebtedness to the client. Next, the auditor should prove the arithmetic accuracy of the list and trace the totals to the general ledger. On a test basis, the details on the schedule should be traced to detailed records. The listing should indicate (and the auditor should verify) which notes are from trade debtors and which are from other sources such as stockholders, officers, directors, employees, and affiliated companies since these may require separate classification in the financial statements.

Generally, the auditor should inspect all of the actual notes and any collateral for the notes; preferably this inspection should take place during the counting of cash and examination of securities. If a client has a great number of notes receivable, the auditor might consider the possibility of examining a sample of the notes. Additionally, an auditor may wish to examine a note receivable owed to the client that is held by some other party. If it is not possible for the auditor to examine the note, the auditor should send a confirmation relating to the note to the holder of the note.

The auditor should confirm the notes and collateral (when notes are secured by collateral) with the makers. This includes notes discounted, assigned with recourse, or otherwise pledged. If positive confirmation methods are used, alternative procedures must be applied to those notes whose makers do not reply.

Additionally, the auditor should test the collectibility of the notes receivable balances. The auditor may age the receivables, discuss their origin and collectibility with the client, ascertain if there were any collections (including interest) since the balance-sheet date on questionable items, evaluate the adequacy of the collateral (if any), and determine if there is a reasonable allowance for uncollectible accounts. If the notes require regular payments, the auditor should determine if the payments have been made on a timely basis during the year and are not past due at the balance-sheet date. When relevant, a sales cutoff test should be performed.

The auditor should test the interest income from notes. This includes testing the calculations of accrued interest or of unearned interest if it is included in the face amount of the notes.

ITEMS FOR LETTER OF REPRESENTATION

The auditor should consider asking the client to include in a letter of representation matters concerning accounts receivable and notes receivable (see Chapter 6 for a general discussion of written representations). The letter might mention:

1. The dollar amount of accounts and notes receivable.
2. That the receivable balances on the balance-sheet date are valid receivables and do not include charges for goods shipped on consignment, on approval, or under repurchase agreements.
3. That receivables that are known to be uncollectible have been charged off, and adequate provision has been made for adjustments and losses in collection of receivables.

AUDIT MEMORANDUM

A memorandum describing the work performed on receivables should be prepared by the auditor and included in the working papers. This memorandum should clearly state the audit objectives, the work performed, the findings of the work performed, and the auditor's opinion as to whether the receivable balances are fairly stated. Specific comments relating to the auditor's evaluation of the allowances for doubtful accounts are also an important part of the memorandum.

GLOSSARY

Aging of accounts receivable A schedule showing the length of time that amounts have been outstanding.
Negative confirmation request Where the debtor is asked to reply only if the balance as stated on the request is not in agreement with the debtor's records. (See Figure 10-2 for an illustration.)
Positive confirmation request Where the debtor is asked to reply directly to the auditor stating whether the balance as indicated on the confirmation request is correct or, if it is incorrect, to indicate the correct balance and any possible explanation of the difference. (See Figure 10-1 for an illustration.)

QUESTIONS AND PROBLEMS

10-1. What is the overall objective of the auditor in examining receivables?

10-2. What is generally included in a good internal control system over receivables?

10-3. What audit procedures are used by the auditor in the examination of receivables?

10-4. How should the auditor begin the substantive tests of trade accounts receivable?

10-5. List some examples of "other procedures" available to the auditor when accounts receivable are not confirmed.

10-6. Describe the positive and negative confirmation procedures. When should each be used?

10-7. When during an audit should accounts receivable be confirmed?

10-8. What could cause exceptions to confirmation requests?

10-9. What alternative procedures need to be performed by the auditor in the cases where positive confirmations are unanswered?

10-10. What procedures should the auditor perform at year-end if receivables are circularized at an interim date?

10-11. What is a sales cutoff test? How is it performed?

10-12. List the procedures typically used in testing sales and related trade receivables.

10-13. You are making a regular annual audit of a retail furniture store that sells on an installment basis. Prepare an audit program for installment notes receivable.

(AICPA)

10-14. Select the best answer for each of the following:

a. Which of the following would be the *best* protection for a company that wishes to prevent the "lapping" of trade accounts receivable?
1. Segregate duties so that the bookkeeper in charge of the general ledger has *no* access to incoming mail.
2. Segregate duties so that *no* employee has access to both checks from customers and currency from daily cash receipts.
3. Have customers send payments directly to the company's depository bank.
4. Request that customers' payment checks be made payable to the company and addressed to the treasurer.

b. The use of the positive (as opposed to the negative) form of receivables confirmation is indicated when
1. Internal control surrounding accounts receivable is considered to be effective.
2. There is reason to believe that a substantial number of accounts may be in dispute.

3. A large number of small balances are involved.

4. There is reason to believe a significant portion of the requests will be answered.

c. It is sometimes impracticable or impossible for an auditor to use normal accounts receivable confirmation procedures. In such situations the *best* alternative procedure the auditor might resort to would be

1. Examining subsequent receipts of year-end accounts receivable.

2. Reviewing accounts receivable aging schedules prepared at the balance-sheet date and at a subsequent date.

3. Requesting that management increase the allowance for uncollectible accounts by an amount equal to some percentage of the balance in those accounts that *cannot* be confirmed.

4. Performing an overall analytic review of accounts receivable and sales on a year-to-year basis.

(AICPA, adapted)

10-15. A CPA accumulates various kinds of evidence upon which to base the auditor's opinion on the fairness of the presentation of the financial statements. Among this evidence are confirmations from third parties and written representations from the client.

Required:

a. 1. What is an audit confirmation?

2. What characteristics should an audit confirmation possess if a CPA is to consider it as valid evidence?

b. 1. What is a written representation?

2. What information should a written representation contain?

3. What effect does a written representation have on a CPA's examination of a client's financial statements?

c. 1. Distinguish between a positive confirmation and a negative confirmation in the auditor's examination of accounts receivable.

2. In confirming an audit client's accounts receivable, what characteristics should be present in the accounts if the CPA is to use negative confirmations?

(AICPA, adapted)

10-16. You are considering using the services of a reputable outside mailing service for the confirmation of accounts receivable balances. The service would prepare and mail the confirmation requests and remove the returned confirmations from the envelopes and give them directly to you.

What reliance, if any, could you place on the services of the outside mailing service? Discuss and state the reasons in support of your answer.

(AICPA, adapted)

10-17. In your examination of the financial statements of the Kay Savings and Loan Association for year ended December 31, 1981, you find a new account in the general ledger, Home Improvement Loans. You determine that these are unsecured loans not insured by any government agency, made on a discount basis to homeowners who are required to secure life insurance coverage provided by the association under a group life insurance policy for the outstanding amount and duration of the loan. Borrowers are issued coupon books which require monthly installment payments; however, borrowers may prepay the outstanding balance of the loan at any time in accordance with the terms of their loan contract. This account constitutes a material amount of the total assets of the association at December 31, 1981.

Required:

Prepare an audit program for the examination of the new account, Home Improvement Loans.

(AICPA, adapted)

10-18. Dodge, CPA, is examining the financial statements of a manufacturing company with a significant amount of trade accounts receivable. Dodge is satisfied that the accounts are properly summarized and classified and that allocations, reclassifications, and valuations are made in accordance with generally accepted accounting principles. Dodge is planning to use accounts receivable confirmation requests to satisfy the third standard of field work as to trade accounts receivable.

Required:

a. Identify and describe the two forms of accounts receivable confirmation requests and indicate what factors Dodge will consider in determining when to use each.

b. Assume Dodge has received a satisfactory response to the confirmation requests. Describe how Dodge could evaluate collectibility of the trade accounts receivable.

(AICPA)

10-19. Your examination of the financial statements of General Department Store, Inc. disclosed the following:

1. The store has 30,000 retail accounts which are billed monthly on a cycle basis. There are 20 billing cycle divisions of the subsidiary accounts receivable ledger, and accounts are apportioned alphabetically to the divisions.

2. All charge sales tickets, which are prenumbered, are microfilmed in batches for each day's sales. These sales tickets are then sorted into their respective cycle divisions, and adding machine tapes are prepared to arrive at the total daily sales for each division. The daily totals for the divisions are then combined for comparison with the grand daily total charge sales determined from cash

register readings. After the totals are balanced, the daily sales tickets are filed behind the related customer account cards in the respective cycle divisions.

3. Cycle control accounts for each division are maintained by postings of the tapes of daily sales.

4. At the cycle billing date the customers' transactions (sales, remittances, returns and other adjustments) are posted to the accounts in the individual cycle. The billing machine used automatically accumulates six separate totals: previous balances, purchases, payments, returns, new balances, and overdue balances. After posting, the documents and the customers' statements are microfilmed and then mailed to the customer.

5. Within each division a trial balance of the accounts in the cycle, obtained as a by-product of the posting operation, is compared with the cycle control account.

6. Credit terms for regular accounts require payment within ten days of receipt of the statement. A credit limit of $300 is set for all accounts.

7. Before the statements are mailed they are reviewed to determine which are past due. Accounts are considered past due if the full balance of the prior month has not been paid. Past due accounts are noted for subsequent collection effort by the credit department.

8. Receipts on account and customer account adjustments are accumulated and posted in a similar manner.

Required:

a. List the audit procedures that you would apply in the audit of the accounts comprising one billing cycle division. Confine your audit procedures to the sales tickets and charges to the accounts and to the verification of account balances. Do not discuss the audit of cash receipts or customer account adjustments.

b. Assume that the group of accounts selected for audit in part (a) was in the cycle division billed on January 19. List the additional overall audit procedures that you would apply to satisfy yourself as to the reasonableness of the total balance of accounts receivable at January 31, 1981, the fiscal year-end.

(AICPA, adapted)

10–20. You are in charge of your second yearly examination of the financial statements of Hillsboro Equipment Corporation, a distributor of construction equipment. Hillsboro's equipment sales are either outright cash sales or a combination of a substantial cash payment and one or two 60- or 90-day nonrenewable interest-bearing notes for the balance. Title to the equipment passes to the customer when the initial cash payment is made. The notes, some of which are secured by the customer, are dated when the cash payment is made (the day the equipment is delivered). If the customer prefers to purchase the equipment under an installment payment plan, Hillsboro arranges for the customer to obtain such financing from a local bank.

You begin your field work to examine the December 31 financial statements on January 5 knowing that you must leave temporarily for another engagement on January 7 after outlining the audit program for your assistant. Before leaving, you inquire about the assistant's progress in his examination of notes receivable. Among other things, he shows you a working paper listing the makers' names, the due dates, the interest rates, and amounts of 17 outstanding notes receivable totaling $100,000. The working paper contains the following notations:

1. Reviewed system of internal control and found it to be satisfactory.
2. Total of $100,000 agrees with general ledger control account.
3. Traced listing of notes to sales journal.

The assistant also informs you that he is preparing to request positive confirmation of the amounts of all outstanding notes receivable and that no other audit work has been performed in the examination of notes receivable and interest arising from equipment sales. There were no outstanding accounts receivable for equipment sales at the end of the year.

Required:

a. List the additional audit procedures that the assistant should apply in his audit of the account for notes receivable arising from equipment sales (Hillsboro has no other notes). No subsidiary ledger is maintained.

b. You ask your assistant to examine all notes receivable on hand before you leave. He returns in 30 minutes from the office safe where the notes are kept and reports that 1981 notes on hand total only $75,000.

List the possible explanations that you would expect from the client for the $25,000 difference. (Eliminate fraud or misappropriation from your consideration.) Indicate beside each explanation the audit procedures you would apply to determine if each explanation is correct.

(AICPA, adapted)

10-21. The Meyers Pharmaceutical Company, a drug manufacturer, has the following system for billing and recording accounts receivable:

1. An incoming customer's purchase order is received in the order department by a clerk who prepares a prenumbered company sales order form in which is inserted the pertinent information, such as the customer's name and address, customer's account number, quantity, and items ordered. After the sales order form has been prepared, the customer's purchase order is stapled to it.

2. The sales order form is then passed to the credit department for

420

credit approval. Rough approximations of the billing values of the orders are made in the credit department for those accounts on which credit limitations are imposed. After investigation, approval of credit is noted on the form.

3. Next the sales order form is passed to the billing department where a clerk types the customer's invoice on a billing machine that cross-multiplies the number of items and the unit price, then adds the automatically extended amounts for the total amount of the invoice. The billing clerk determines the unit prices for the items from a list of billing prices.

   The billing machine has registers that automatically accumulate daily totals of customer account numbers and invoice amounts to provide "hash" totals and control amounts. These totals, which are inserted in a daily record book, serve as predetermined batch totals for verification of computer inputs.

   The billing is done on prenumbered, continuous, carbon-interleaved forms having the following designations:

   a. "Customer's copy."
   b. "Sales department copy," for information purposes.
   c. "File copy."
   d. "Shipping department copy," which serves as a shipping order. Bills of lading are also prepared as carbon copy by-products of the invoicing procedure.

4. The shipping department copy of the invoice and the bills of lading are then sent to the shipping department. After the order has been shipped, copies of the bill of lading are returned to the billing department. The shipping department copy of the invoice is filed in the shipping department.

5. In the billing department one copy of the bill of lading is attached to the customer's copy of the invoice and both are mailed to the customer. The other copy of the bill of lading, together with the sales order form, is then stapled to the invoice file copy and filed in invoice numerical order.

6. A keypunch machine is connected to the billing machine so that punched cards are created during the preparation of the invoices. The punched cards then become the means by which the sales data are transmitted to a computer.

   The punched cards are fed to the computer in batches. One day's accumulation of cards comprises a batch. After the punched cards have been processed by the computer, they are placed in files and held for about two years.

Required:

List the procedures that a CPA would employ in the examination of the selected audit samples of the company's:

a. Typed invoices, including the source documents.

     b.   Punched cards.

    (The listed procedures should be limited to the verification of the sales data being fed into the computer. Do not carry the procedures beyond the point at which the cards are ready to be fed to the computer.)

(AICPA, adapted)

10-22. You have examined the financial statements of the Heft Company for several years. The system of internal control for accounts receivable is very satisfactory. The Heft Company is on a calendar year basis. An interim audit, which included confirmation of the accounts receivable, was performed at August 31 and indicated that the accounting for receivables was very reliable.

    The company's sales are principally to manufacturing concerns. There are about 1,500 active trade accounts receivable of which about 35 percent in number represent 65 percent of the total dollar amount. The accounts receivable are maintained alphabetically in five subledgers which are controlled by one general ledger account.

    Sales are machine-posted in the subledgers by an operation that produces simultaneously the customer's ledger card, his monthly statement, and the sales journal. All cash receipts are in the form of customer's checks and are machine-posted simultaneously on the customer's ledger card, his monthly statement, and the cash receipts journal. Information for posting cash receipts is obtained from the remittance advice portions of the customer's checks. The bookkeeping machine operator compares the remittance advices with the list of checks that was prepared by another person when the mail was received.

    Summary totals are produced monthly by the bookkeeping machine operations for posting to the appropriate general ledger accounts such as cash, sales, accounts receivable, etc. Aged trial balances by subledgers are prepared monthly.

    Sales returns and allowances and bad debt write-offs are summarized periodically and recorded by standard journal entries. Supporting documents for these journal entries are available. The usual documents arising from billing, shipping, and receiving are also available.

Required:

    Prepare in detail the audit program for the Heft Company for the year-end examination of the trade accounts receivable. Do not give the program for the interim audit.

(AICPA)

10-23. In your audit of the Longmont Company you prepared a schedule of notes receivable. This company, a manufacturer, does not have many notes receivable and therefore does not keep a note register. All notes have resulted from sales to customers. The following schedule was prepared:

Column Number		Column Heading
1.	....	Name of maker
2.	....	Names of endorsers
3.	....	Date of note
4.	....	Due date
5.	....	Principal
6.	....	Interest rate
		Discounted (To the bank)
7.	....	Date
8.	....	Rate
9.	....	Amount of discount
		Interest
10.	....	Collected
11.	....	Accrued
12.	....	Prepaid
13.	....	Payment on principal
14.	....	Balance due
15.	....	Collateral held

Required:

Draw a line down the middle of a lined sheet(s) of paper.

a. On the left of the line state the specific source(s) of information to be entered in each column and, where required, how data of previous columns are combined.

b. On the right of the line state the principal way(s) that such information would be verified.

(AICPA)

10–24. You are making an examination of the accounts of the Hardy Corporation. Accounts receivable represent a significant proportion of the total assets of the company. At the beginning of the audit you mailed out positive confirmations on a test basis. Included in your test were confirmations requested from several U.S. government departments; the confirmation requests for these accounts were returned along with the following notation:

> Your confirmation letter is returned herewith without action inasmuch as the type of information requested therein cannot be compiled by this office with sufficient accuracy to be of any value.

Your test also included customers whose accounts payable systems were either decentralized or who used a voucher system which made it impossible or impractical to give the requested information. These customers either informed you of their inability to comply with the request or did not reply.

Required:

Assuming the number and amount of responses to confirmation requests are unsatisfactory, what additional auditing procedures would you apply?

(AICPA, adapted)

10-25. As part of his examination of the financial statements of the Marlborough Corporation for the year ended March 31, 1981, Mario Romito, CPA, is reviewing the balance sheet presentation of a $1,200,000 advance to Franklin Olds, Marlborough's president. The advance, which represents 50 percent of current assets and 10 percent of total assets, was made during the year ended March 31, 1981. It has been described in the balance sheet as "miscellaneous accounts receivable" and classified as a current asset.

Mr. Olds informs the CPA that he has used the proceeds of the advance to purchase 35,000 shares of Marlborough's common stock, in order to forestall a take-over raid on the company. He is reluctant to have his association with the advance described in the financial statements because he does not have voting control and fears that this will "just give the raiders ammunition."

Mr. Olds offers the following four-point program as an alternative to further disclosure:

1. Have the advance approved by the board of directors. (This can be done expeditiously because a majority of the board members are officers of the company.)
2. Prepare a demand note payable to the company with interest of 7½ percent (the average bank rate paid by the company.)
3. Furnish an endorsement of the stock to the company as collateral for the loan. (During the year under audit, despite the fact that earnings did not increase, the market price of Marlborough common rose from $20 to $40 per share. The stock has maintained its $40 per share market price subsequent to year-end.)
4. Obtain a written opinion from the company attorney supporting the legality of the company's advance and the use of the proceeds.

Required:

a. Discuss the proper balance-sheet classification of the advance to Mr. Olds and other appropriate disclosures in the financial statements and footnotes. (Ignore SEC regulations and requirements, tax effects, creditor's restrictions on stock repurchase, the presentation of common stock repurchase, and the presentation of common stock dividends and interest income.)
b. Discuss each point of Mr. Olds' four-point program as to whether or not it is desirable and as to whether or not it is an alternative to further disclosure.
c. If Mr. Olds refuses to permit further disclosure, what action(s) should the CPA take? Discuss.
d. In his discussion with the CPA, Mr. Olds warns that the raiders, if successful, probably will appoint new auditors. What consideration should the CPA give to this factor? Explain.

(AICPA, adapted)

10-26. You are engaged in an audit as of December 31 of a medium-sized manufacturing company which has between 300 and 400 open trade receivable accounts. As a part of the interim work, you decide on October 10 to select approximately 100 customers' accounts for positive confirmations as of September 30. You obtain an aged trial balance of the accounts receivable as of September 30 and trace the balances of the open accounts to the trial balance from the subsidiary ledgers. In addition, you test the aging, foot the trial balance, and agree the total with the accounts receivable control account in the general ledger. Also, detailed tests of the sales and credit journals are made for the month of September.

Required:

a. Enumerate the types of accounts you would want to include in your selection of accounts to be circularized.
b. Outline the additional audit steps that should be undertaken at December 31 in support of the amounts shown as accounts receivable; the client is preparing for your use an aged trial balance of accounts receivable as of that date.

(AICPA)

10-27. The ABC Appliance Company, a manufacturer of minor electrical appliances, deals exclusively with 20 distributors situated at focal points throughout the country. At December 31, the balance sheet date, receivables from these distributors aggregated $875,000. Total current assets were $1,300,000.

With respect to receivables, the auditor followed the procedures outlined below in the course of the annual examination of the financial statements.

a. Reviewed system of internal control. It was found to be exceptionally good.
b. Tied detail with control account at year end.
c. Aged accounts. None were overdue.
d. Examined detail sales and collection transactions for the months of February, July, and November.
e. Received positive confirmations of year-end balances.

You are to criticize the completeness or incompleteness of the above program, giving reasons for your recommendations concerning the addition or omission of any procedures.

(AICPA)

Learning Objectives

The study of the material in this chapter is designed to achieve certain learning objectives. They include an understanding of the:

1. Essential elements of internal control over inventories.
2. Need for and methods of performing observations and tests of physical inventories.
3. Procedures used to determine that receiving and shipping cutoffs were proper.
4. Means of determining whether the basis of pricing inventory used by the client conforms to generally accepted accounting principles applied on a consistent basis.

11

Inventories

Inventories may be defined as those items of tangible personal property held by a company which are: (1) held for sale in the ordinary course of business; (2) in the process of production for sale in a business; or (3) to be consumed in the production of goods for sale in a business.[1]

The objective of the examination of inventories is for the auditor to determine whether inventories are presented fairly in the financial statements in conformity with generally accepted accounting principles applied on a consistent basis. Thus, the auditor must determine that the inventories physically exist; are the property of the company; are usable and salable; and are priced correctly. This involves investigating the care and accuracy with which the company has counted the inventories, the method and basis that have been followed in pricing them, and the arithmetical accuracy of the computations made. The auditor must also determine whether adequate provision has been made for obsolete and slow-moving inventory. Inventories are among the most difficult of the assets of the business for the auditor to evaluate because there are numerous types of inventories and many methods of costing and evaluating them.

METHODS OF DETERMINING COST

The primary basis of accounting for inventories is cost. The cost of inventories is the sum of all the expenditures and charges incurred, directly or indirectly, in bringing inventory items to their present condition and location. As the Committee on Accounting Procedure (of the AICPA) indicated in *Accounting Research Bulletin No. 43:* "Cost for inventory purposes may be determined under any one of several assumptions as to the flow of cost factors (such as first-in first-

---

[1]Committee on Accounting Procedure, American Institute of Certified Public Accountants, "Restatement and Revision of Accounting Research Bulletins," *Accounting Research Bulletin No. 43* (New York, 1953), p. 27.

out, average, and last-in first-out); the major objective in selecting a method should be to choose the one which, under the circumstances, most clearly reflects periodic income." It further stated that ". . . standard costs are acceptable if adjusted at reasonable intervals to reflect current conditions so that at the balance-sheet date standard costs reasonably approximate costs computed under one of the recognized bases," and that " in some situations a reversed mark-up procedure of inventory pricing, such as the retail inventory method, may be both practical and appropriate."

A departure from the cost basis of pricing inventory is required when the utility of the goods is no longer as great as their original cost. As the Committee on Accounting Procedure states (in *ARB No. 43*), "Where there is evidence that the utility of goods, in their disposal in the ordinary course of business, will be less than cost, whether due to physical deterioration, obsolescence, changes in price levels, or other causes, the difference should be recognized as a loss in the current period. This is generally accomplished by stating such goods at a lower level commonly designated as market."[2]

INTERNAL CONTROL OVER INVENTORY

Internal control over inventory affects many aspects of a business. It includes both safeguarding the inventory as well as accurately accounting for it.

Safeguarding Inventory

Safeguarding inventory involves control of the various aspects of inventory from the time that raw materials are received until the finished product is shipped. This includes control over the receiving of inventory, storage of inventory, movement of inventory within the business, processing and/or production of inventory, and ultimately shipping of inventory. From its receipt until its ultimate disposition, inventory must be carefully safeguarded. This safeguarding involves the use of a system of documents (preferably prenumbered) that acknowledges receipt of the goods and then authorizes the movement of goods through the production and shipping processes. These documents include receiving reports, material requisitions, and shipping authorizations.

Safeguarding inventory also involves assigning selected employees with the responsibility for the inventory at various clearly defined

---

[2]The AICPA lower-of-cost-or-market method defines "market" as replacement cost but sets an upper limit of selling price less costs to complete and sell and a lower limit of selling price less both costs to complete and sell and normal profit.

points in the production and shipping process. For example, inventory housed in a storeroom should be the sole responsibility of a designated employee in that storeroom. Additionally, at each point in the production and shipping process, detailed inventory records should be maintained on a current basis.

Accurate Accounting

An effective system of documentation and of detailed recordkeeping will help produce accurate inventory reporting. The maintenance of reliable, detailed records is enhanced when a business utilizes a strong perpetual inventory system. Also, accurate accounting regarding the various costs that are included in inventory is made possible by a well-conceived and properly functioning cost accounting system.

The detailed records of any perpetual inventory system should agree with the inventory control accounts. Additionally, businesses with perpetual inventory systems should periodically reconcile the perpetual inventory records with the actual inventory on hand by taking a physical count.

COMPLIANCE TESTING: INVENTORY

A company's accounting system should be designed so that it provides the information necessary to assign the proper cost to inventory and determine the proper amount of the cost of goods sold. The objective of compliance testing in this area is for the auditor to ascertain whether the company's procedures are being followed. Two general procedures for compliance tests of inventory are:

1. Test postings to detail inventory records for purchases, material requisitions, production, and shipments.
2. Review ledger accounts for periods not tested for unusual entries and investigate any found.

In addition, inventory is tested by the auditor as a part of the procedures for testing cash, vouchers, payrolls, and sales.

SUBSTANTIVE TESTING: INVENTORY

Observations and Tests of Physical Inventories

Statement on Auditing Standards (SAS) No. 1, section 331.01, indicates that the observation of inventories is a "generally accepted auditing procedure." In actual practice, the client's physical count of the inventories is almost always observed and tested by the auditor. However, if it is impracticable or impossible to observe the physical inventory, the auditor must become satisfied as to the fairness of the inventory balances by the use of alternative procedures. *SAS No. 1*, section 331.09, further states:

> When inventory quantities are determined solely by means of a physical count, and all counts are made as of the balance-sheet date or as of a single date within a reasonable time before or after the balance-sheet date, it is ordinarily necessary for the independent auditor to be present at the time of the count, and, by suitable observation, tests and inquiries, satisfy himself respecting the effectiveness of the methods of inventory-taking and the measure of reliance which may be placed upon the client's representations about the quantities and physical condition of the inventories.

SAS No. 1 sections 331.10–.11, note that when the client has reliable perpetual records that are compared periodically with physical counts, the auditor's observation procedures usually can be performed at any time, not necessarily at year-end. If a client uses statistical sampling to determine inventory quantity, the auditor must be satisfied with the sampling plan, counting procedures, and the counts (by observation).

SAS No. 2 notes that circumstances may make it impracticable or impossible to observe physical inventory. If the auditor is, however, ". . . able to satisfy himself as to inventories . . . by applying alternative procedures, there is no significant limitation on the scope of his work, and his report need not include reference to the omission of the procedures or to the use of alternative procedures."

In using alternative procedures, *SAS No. 1*, section 331.12, notes that such procedures should include the auditor making or observing physical counts of inventory, testing intervening transactions, and reviewing the client's counts and procedures relating to the physical inventory of the balance-sheet inventory figure. *SAS No. 2* suggests that if the auditor is not satisfied with the results of the alternative procedures, this limitation on his or her work should be referred to in the scope paragraph, described in an explanatory paragraph, and referred to in the qualified opinion or disclaimer of opinion (whichever the auditor issues). If observation of inventory is both practicable and reasonable and it is not done because of the client's wishes, generally this should be mentioned in the scope paragraph, described in an explanatory paragraph, and referred to in a disclaimer of opinion (if the inventories are material in amount).

Review of Company's Inventory Plans

It is extremely important that the auditor determine whether the client has planned properly for the taking of the physical inventory. In the typical manufacturing company, the inventory may consist of many hundreds or thousands of individual items. These items may be in various stages of completion, and may be located in various areas. The count and identification of these items must be completed accurately.

As a part of the procedures used to examine inventories, the auditor should review a copy of the company's inventory instructions. Complete instructions would normally include:

1. Names of the persons drafting and approving the instructions. Usually the controller or some other responsible client executive will approve the instructions.
2. Dates and times of the inventory taking. Many companies take a complete physical inventory at the end of their fiscal year. If a company's inventory controls are judged to be reliable, it is acceptable to take the physical inventory prior to year-end. This practice is usually desirable because it allows the company to complete a major part of its work in closing its books before the end of its fiscal year.
3. Names of the employees responsible for supervising the taking of the inventory.
4. Plans for rearranging and segregating stock, including the precaution of clearing work in process to natural cutoff points. Stock should be arranged in an orderly manner so as to make the counts by the inventory teams easier. When different items are intermingled or are at difficult-to-reach locations, the company risks counting the same item twice or overlooking items.
5. Provisions for control of receiving and shipping during the inventory count period and, if the plant is not shut down, provision for handling stock movement. Although not always practical, it is helpful if the receiving and shipping departments are cleared of all stock. If items must be transferred between departments, there should be procedures to ensure that each item is counted only once.
6. Instructions as to the use of inventory tags or sheets and their distribution, collection, and control. Generally, prenumbered tags are used, and they should be accounted for after the inventory count is completed.
7. Detailed instructions for accurate description of items and for determination of quantities by count, weight, or other measurement. Normally, all information recorded on the inventory tag should be checked or reviewed by an employee who did not participate in the original count. In order to attain assurance that all information is recorded properly, some companies require a "blind" second count. After the first employee lists a count, a second employee, without knowing what the first employee has recorded (because the count portion of the tag would have been removed), lists a count. Then, a

third employee compares the two counts and investigates any differences.

8. Instructions for identifying and segregating obsolete and slow-moving items of inventory.

9. Plans for determining quantities at outside locations.

10. Methods of transcribing original counts to final inventory sheets or summaries.

11. Methods followed in pricing inventory quantities, including the extent of recheck of prices.

12. Instructions for making extensions and footings and for the extent of recheck.

13. Instructions for review and approval of inventory by department heads or other supervisory personnel.

Observation of the Taking of the Physical Inventory

When the auditor plans an inventory observation, this assignment must be prepared for carefully. The company's inventory instructions should be reviewed, with particular attention given to those sections which describe the company's procedures for the counting of inventory and the control of inventory tags. The auditor should also review the timing and general plans for observing and testing the inventory counts. The auditor must be familiar with the client's inventory, the approximate volume, the proper units of measure, where the valuable items are located, and so on. The auditor should know when to arrive at the inventory location, who to ask for upon arrival, the areas of the plant for which he or she is responsible (plant layout sketches are helpful), and the extent of the specific audit procedures to be performed. Most points should be cleared in advance, including a tour of the storage area and a discussion of suitable clothing to wear.

When arriving at the client's plant, the auditor should meet with a supervisory employee of the client, and last-minute instructions should be discussed at that time. Also, it is good practice for the auditor to meet all the company's inventory supervisors and know where they can be contacted if the need arises. It is important to note that the auditor does not "take," "determine," or "supervise" a physical inventory, but rather "observes" and "tests" the inventory-taking procedures. The nature of his or her responsibility to "observe" and "test" must be clearly understood. It is important to note that the auditor does not give instructions to client personnel but reports any problems noted to the appropriate supervisor.

The auditor's responsibility to "observe" the taking of the inventory involves a number of important areas. These include observing:

1. Whether the company prepared adequately for taking the inventory. Stock should be arranged in an orderly manner. Shipping and receiving cutoffs (these are discussed later in this chapter) should be established. Movement of stock should be kept to a minimum.

2. Whether employees taking inventory appear to be conscientious and familiar with the stock and their duties, and whether they are adequately supervised.

3. Whether the inventory-counting teams are following the company's inventory instructions. Any deviations should be noted in the working papers and reported to the proper supervisor. Company procedures may require two independent counts of each inventory item; the results of these independent counts should be reviewed immediately.

4. The procedures of all counting teams in the departments for which the auditor is responsible.

The auditor should be alert for any possible double counting of inventory items. Inventories are sometimes counted twice when inventory teams skip around instead of counting items in location sequence. The use of inventory tags will assist in avoiding double counting. However, items may still be counted twice when the contents of several bins or boxes are recorded on a single inventory tag or listing.

The auditor also should be alert for any items not counted. Sometimes entire sections of a department may be missed inadvertently. To prevent this, inventory crews should place inventory tags on each item or inventory sheets in each location.

The auditor must be alert for "hollow squares" (empty spaces between stacks of boxes) and empty containers. A request may be made that containers be opened or piles of inventory be moved, although such requests are normally made on a limited basis.

Also, the auditor should watch for apparently unsalable, damaged, slow-moving, and obsolete items, and discuss these with the client personnel who are responsible for the inventory. In some circumstances it may be difficult to recognize these items, but any that appear to be questionable should be noted in the working papers for further investigation.

While observing the inventory, the auditor will also be testing the effectiveness of the procedures used by the client in taking the inventory. For example, the accuracy of the counts made by the company's employees will be tested. Special attention should be given to items of high value, but tests of the counts made by each inventory team and of all types of inventory in all departments will normally be included in the inventory work. It is difficult to suggest specific guidelines for the number of items to be counted in every instance. The nature of the inventory, the general arrangement of the stock, the type and extent of errors made by the inventory crews, and similar factors will all determine the extent of the tests made by the auditor.

For counting items which cannot be accumulated as individual units, special techniques or equipment may be used; e.g., scales, comparison with like items already counted, estimating tonnage of bulk storage items, aerial surveys of timber tracts and log storage ponds, and photographs of construction projects. The auditor must, of course, be familiar with and become satisfied as to the procedures used.

Ordinarily, the auditor is not expected to lift, sort, or stack inventory. In situations that require heavy lifting, the client's personnel should be asked for assistance.

When test counts disclose isolated or minor errors made by an inventory crew, they should be brought to the attention of an employee who is able to correct the error on the spot. It usually is not necessary to report minor errors to company supervisory personnel. However, if the auditor encounters a situation which might have a significant effect on the accuracy of the inventory, company supervisory personnel should be notified immediately so that corrective action can be taken. Examples of such situations include the disregarding of inventory instructions, general carelessness, or the existence of excessive errors.

The auditor should record some of the test counts in the working papers (see Figure 11-1). The information relating the numerical sequence of tags used and details relating to unused or voided tags in that sequence should be listed. Certain other information also will be listed, such as the details of any obsolete or slow-moving items and large quantity items. The auditor should indicate clearly those items which were counted and those about which information was merely listed. At a later date the auditor will trace this information to the final inventory listing prepared by the client. This will help determine the reliability of the procedures used by the company in compiling the final inventory. Generally, the following information should be included in the work sheet: (1) name of the auditor performing the tests; (2) name of the client; (3) page number; (4) location of items (plant, building, floor, and so on); (5) date of the count; (6) time of inventory observation; (7) tag number (if applicable); (8) quantity and unit of count; and (9) description of item. Regarding the description of inventory items, the auditor should use the same description that the company uses. Where applicable, part numbers, last completed operation, and other pertinent information should also be listed. To make the subsequent audit tests easier, the information listed should be both complete and accurate.

FIGURE 11–1
Inventory test count worksheet

APPROVED BY	NAME	DATE
	Williams	2-23-81

INVENTORY TEST COUNTS

E & W REPRESENTATIVE		NAME OF CLIENT					PAGE
J. Sanders		*Moore Machine Company*					4 OF 4

PLANT OR WAREHOUSE		BUILDING	FLOOR	SECTION	DEPARTMENT	
Denver		*Main St.*	*1*		*Machine Assembly*	

DATE	TIME	STAGE OF COMPLETION, DESCRIPTION, CONDITION, ETC.
12-30-80	FROM *2:30 P.M.* TO *4:00 P.M.*	

TAG NUMBER	PART NUMBER	UNIT	QUANTITY		STAGE OF COMPLETION, DESCRIPTION, CONDITION, ETC.
			(all counted)	1	
1100	*6072-51*	*ea.*	√ *1*	2	*4"-6" Modified press - w/o mounts*
				3	
1112	*301-10*	*pcs.*	√ *310*	4	*1/4" x 18" x 120" Stainless*
				5	
1157	*304-13*	*pcs*	√ *36*	6	*1/2" round - 6 ft. lengths - Stainless*
				7	
1210	*410-21*	*boxes*	Ⓐ *121*	8	*6" Mounting bolts - Heat treated*
				9	
1260	*4896-00*	*boxes*	√ *7*	10	*Pulley shaft - 1½" - 4 to a box*
				11	
1262	*7882-95*	*ea.*	√ *13*	12	*5" Rollers for Model 7820-10 mill*
				13	
				19	
1862	*3620-10*	*doz.*	√ *5*	20	*2 Ton fastening mounts*
				21	
1921	*1420-08*	*ea.*	√ *10*	22	*8" Mill housing - Last operation #972*
				23	
				24	
				25	

√ - *Traced to final inventory listing - Allen.*

Ⓐ - *Represents a portion of this item. Footed tags 1201, 1210, 1460, and 1692, and traced the total to the final inventory listing. - Allen*

A-9   PRINTED IN U.S.A.

During the taking of the physical inventory, the auditor should list receiving and shipping cutoff information. At a later date, this information should be traced to the company's accounting records. The objective is to ascertain (1) whether all items received up to the cutoff date were included in the physical inventory and charged to the purchases or inventory accounts (receiving cutoff), and (2) whether all items shipped up to the cutoff date were excluded from the physical inventory and have been credited to the inventory account (shipping cutoff) and included in sales and cost of goods sold.

The auditor should observe the following cutoff procedures:

1. Visit the receiving and shipping areas to observe whether cutoff procedures are being followed so as to achieve a clear separation between items to be included in the physical inventory and those to be excluded. This is particularly important in regard to items received during the inventory period and those awaiting shipment to customers.

2. When prenumbered receiving or shipping tickets are used, note the last number used preceding the cutoff. Any unused numbers should be noted. When prenumbered tickets are not used, obtain information about several shipments and receipts immediately prior to the inventory date. If the company receives or ships materials in freight cars, a listing of full and empty cars on the tracks plus notations on their inventory status should be made. (This matter requires special attention in most cases because of the substantial amounts involved.)

At the conclusion of the observation and tests, the auditor should prepare a memorandum which briefly and accurately describes the work done and the conclusions reached. A typical memorandum would include information concerning:

1. Location, time of visit, and department covered.
2. Whether the company's employees followed the inventory instructions. Any deviations should be noted, as well as the corrective actions which were taken.
3. Comments concerning the company's "housekeeping." (Were the inventory items neatly arranged, and so on?)
4. Procedures followed in observing and test counting. Degree of accuracy indicated by test counts. Notations of any unusual items or conditions observed, such as obsolete or slow-moving stock, damaged merchandise, consigned stock, and production and stock movement which occurred during the taking of the physical inventory.

5. Description of the procedures used by the company to obtain accurate shipping and receiving cutoffs and information obtained for future testing of the information.
6. An opinion, based on the results of tests and observations, as to whether the recorded quantities reasonably represent the quantities actually on hand at that time.

Figure 11-2 is an example of such a memorandum covering an inventory observation.

Tracing Test Counts, Checking Cutoffs, and Testing Clerical Accuracy

When the count has been completed, the client will price the inventory, extend (multiply) quantities by unit prices, and accumulate the extensions in order to arrive at a total amount for the inventory. Then the auditor must determine whether the final inventory has been compiled with care and accuracy by tracing test counts, checking cutoffs, and testing clerical accuracy.

Tracing Test Counts into Final Inventory Listing. During the observation of physical inventory, test counts which were made and listed in the auditor's counts should be traced to the company's final inventory listing. This test is made as a check of the final inventory tabulations of quantities. Often the final inventory is simply a listing of quantities noted on each inventory tag. Intermediate work sheets, adding machine tapes, or the computer may be used to group items by part number (or some other logical arrangement).

Sometimes only totals appear on the final inventory listing, and this may complicate the auditor's task. In this situation the auditor may trace the test counts to the applicable inventory tags (accounting for all tags), total the quantities on all the tags for a particular item, and compare this total to the quantity shown on the inventory listing.

Checking Receiving and Shipping Cutoff Procedures. The inventory account included in the general ledger must, of course, include all transactions which affect the status of the physical inventory at the time of the count; otherwise, the financial statements will be distorted. Therefore, it is important to ascertain that proper cutoffs were made. The test of the company's receiving and shipping cutoff procedures determines whether: (1) all materials received have been included in inventories; (2) liabilities have been recorded for all materials purchased on account and included in the inventories; (3) liabilities have not been recorded for any items excluded from the inventory; (4) receivables have been charged for all products sold on

438

FIGURE 11-2
Inventory observation memorandum

<table>
<tr><td></td><td></td><td>NAME</td><td>DATE</td></tr>
<tr><td rowspan="3">Observation of Inventory
Moore Machine Company
12-31-80</td><td>PREPARED</td><td>Smith</td><td>12-30-80</td></tr>
<tr><td>APPROVED</td><td>Williams</td><td>2-23-81</td></tr>
</table>

I was present at the Denver Plant of Moore Machine Company on 12-30-80, to observe the physical inventory procedures used.

I had previously read the attached "Moore-Inventory Instructions" and reviewed the portion of our audit program relating to inventories. Upon arrival, I met Mr. Frank Miller, the production control engineer. He was in charge of the physical inventory at this location. We toured all plant areas. I observed that items to be counted were neatly arranged which facilitated the inventory taking.

I observed the procedures being used by the inventory teams and made numerous tests of the counts recorded by each team. I listed representative test counts for subsequent tests. The personnel appeared familiar with the products and my tests indicated accurate recording of information. I noted that Team No. 4 failed to follow the section of the instructions which required the listing of the last operation completed as part of the description. I brought this matter to the attention of Mr. Miller, who had the tags corrected.

My comments about items which may be obsolete and data for testing Moore's cutoff procedures are attached.

Based on my observation, I believe the attached "Inventory Instructions" were adequate and were followed and that quantities and descriptions of items on hand at 12-30-80 were properly recorded on the inventory tags.

account; (5) all products sold have been excluded from inventory; and (6) receivables have not been recorded for products included in the inventory.

Particular attention should be given to inventory in transit, either from vendors or from branches, divisions, or subdivisions of the client. The auditor must determine whether these items have been recorded properly in the accounts. As part of this test, the auditor will note receiving and shipping cutoff data obtained during the taking of the physical inventory. The purchasing and receiving records and the sales and shipping records of the company will also be tested.

Testing Clerical Accuracy. Extensions and footings of inventories should always be tested by the auditor. Even though the calculations may have been performed on a computer, rechecked by client personnel, or made by an outside service agency under the control of the company, the auditor must check clerical accuracy. The extent of the auditor's tests will depend upon such factors as the procedures used by the client in compiling the final inventory listing, the care used by the client in making and checking the calculations, and the number and dollar amounts of the inventory items.

Some of the more common clerical errors which are made by the client in summarizing inventories include the following: transposition errors, misplaced decimal points, incorrect conversions and/or units of measure, errors in extensions (quantity times unit price), failure to carry page totals into the summary sheets, errors in footings, and errors in pricing.

When the auditor must undertake a substantial amount of checking of clerical accuracy, an outside service agency may be engaged or the computer may be used. If an outside service agency is employed, the auditor should not only pay for their services, but should also direct and supervise their work. In using the computer, the auditor may call upon EDP specialists for assistance and may use computer programs specifically developed for this purpose.

When the auditor performs tests of clerical accuracy, the work should be done carefully and yet as efficiently as possible. Since the auditor is primarily concerned with substantial errors, the tests are normally done on an approximate basis—that is, it is seldom necessary to prove extensions or footings to the exact dollar. For transpositions, misplaced decimals, and footings, the time-saving technique of sight testing (i.e., visually noting the reasonableness of the total) is often used. Large dollar or quantity items are usually checked for clerical accuracy. Where there are conversions, such as from feet to pounds, the auditor should test the source of information used for the conversion as well as the conversion itself. Although not all pages of the inventory detail are usually footed, ordinarily all page totals are traced to the summary, and the summary is footed. The working papers should include a description of the tests of clerical accuracy made by the auditor and a summary of the findings and conclusions.

If physical inventories are taken, priced, and compiled prior to the balance-sheet date, it is necessary for the auditor to ascertain that the proper adjustments have been recorded as of the inventory date. Also, tests must be made of the inventory transactions which occurred during the period from the time the physical inventory was taken to the balance-sheet date. The test of interim transactions normally includes:

1. A test of entries included in the inventory control accounts by reference to purchase journals, labor distributions, overhead allocations, or other records. It is important to make sure that all products billed have been removed from the inventory at the proper inventory cost amount.

2. A comparison of the gross profit margins of the current period with those of prior periods. All unusual variations must be investigated by the auditor and explained in the working papers.

Inventory Valuation

The auditor must determine whether the basis of pricing used by the client conforms to generally accepted accounting principles and whether it has been applied consistently. The procedures involved in meeting these objectives include: (1) examining inventory pricing and cost systems; (2) selecting items for price test; (3) pricing of purchased parts and materials; and (4) pricing of work-in-process and finished goods.

Inventory Pricing and Cost Systems. To test adequately inventory valuation, the auditor must understand the basic concepts of pricing and the more common cost systems. Common types of cost systems in use are job order and process cost. Either also may be used in combination with a standard cost system. In a job order cost system, job costs are tested by reviewing the pricing and accumulation of materials and labor used in producing the job lot and by testing the allocation of overhead. Process costs are tested by reviewing the pricing and accumulation of materials and labor used for each department or process over the accounting period and by testing the assignment of overhead to the units produced. This necessitates testing the computations of equivalent units of production for materials, labor, and overhead.

When standard costs are used, the auditor is interested in reviewing the standard costs to determine whether they result in an acceptable valuation of the inventory. The use of out-of-date standards may result in a significant misstatement of the inventory.

Selecting Items for Price Test. In a price test, the auditor tests a representative number of the prices of the items included in the inventory. The prices should conform with a generally accepted pricing method (for example, lower of FIFO cost or market). In selecting items for the price test, the auditor must exercise professional judgment. The use of statistical sampling techniques, a general knowledge of the business and the product, discussions with the company executives, and a review of inventory summary sheets and the prior year's price test are all helpful to the auditor in determining the specific items to be tested. Ordinarily, testing items of high dollar amount will give the auditor maximum assurance, with a minimum of time and effort, that the inventory is not substantially misstated. However, it is usually desirable to include a representative group of items of lesser dollar amount. It might also be appropriate to test items from principal product lines or from various departments. Purchased items or commodities of high value which are subject to wide or rapid price fluctuations—such as rubber, chemicals, wheat, textiles, or tin—should be included in the test if possible. The price test is usually evidenced in the auditor's working papers by means of a work sheet. (See Figure 11–3.)

Pricing of Purchased Parts and Materials. In order to test the prices of purchased parts and materials, the auditor will normally begin by preparing a list of items for testing. The listing will include a description of the inventory items selected, the stock number, the sheet number or tag number, and the inventory quantity, unit price, and extended amount. Price test work sheets should provide sufficient space to list several invoices making up the total of the inventory quantity. Once the items have been selected for testing, company personnel could be asked to locate supporting purchase invoices. When examining these items the auditor should consider the following matters:

1. Name of vendor. The vendor should be the usual and regular source of supply. This can be checked with the purchasing department.

2. Quantity. Invoices examined should cover the approximate quantity in inventory.

3. Unit price. The indirect cost of purchases (e.g., freight charges, discounts, insurance) may be accounted for in various ways. Generally, freight charges and insurance are included in the cost, while rebates and discounts, other than cash discounts, are excluded. Standard conversion tables are usually available from the client to aid the auditor when invoice prices are based on units which differ from those in the inventory, for example, steel bought by the pound but

FIGURE 11-3
Purchased items price test

PURCHASED ITEMS PRICE TEST
MOORE MACHINE COMPANY
12-31-80

PREPARED Malone 2-20-81
APPROVED Williams 2-23-81
NAME   DATE

INVT. PAGE NO.	DESCRIPTION	PER INVENTORY			INVENTORY OVER/(UNDER)	PER VENDOR'S INVOICE			VENDOR
		AMOUNT	QUANTITY	UNIT PRICE		UNIT PRICE	QUANTITY	DATE	
40	#462 - 2¼" x 36' x 320"	19,768.34	34,710 lb	.5385/lb		.5385/lb	32,600 lb	12-21-80	U.S. Steel
						.572/lb	6,210 lb(?)	12-2-80	Bethlehem Steel
							38,810 lb		
62	#628 - 2⅛" x 36' x 120"	16,146.81	28,880 lb	.5891/lb		.559/lb	21,000 lb	12-29-80	Republic Steel
						.559/lb	10,000 lb	12-19-80	-do-
							31,000 lb		
184	#667-92 - 3' stainless steel bolts	539.26	914 boxes	.590/box		.590/box	1,000 box	11-27-80	Allegheny Ludlum
188	#722-2 Wing supports	5,711.77	987 pcs	5.787 ea.		5.787 ea.	1,600 pcs	12-22-80	Alcoa
260	#1086-28 Windows	744.00	620 pcs	1.20 ea.		1.20 ea.	650 pcs	12-22-80	Corning Glass Works
120	#3626-10 Hydraulic pump	731.00	20 pcs	365.50 ea.		365.50 ea.	20 pcs	12-22-80	Curtis-Wright Corp

840	#721 Door bolts and nuts	32500	500 pcs	.65 ll	5000	.50 ea / .65 ea / .70 ea	350 pcs / 100 pcs / 50 pcs / 500 pcs	12-21-80 / 11-20-80 / 10-2-80	National Steel / -do- / -do-
920	#480 Rivets	100000	2000 lbs	.50/lb	13500	.50/lb / .50/lb	1000 lbs / 1000 lbs / 2000 lbs	12-21-80 / 12-1-80	Smith & Laughlin / -do-
1200	#820 Seats	600000	10 pcs	600.00 ea	600.00	575.00 ea / 600.00 ea / 600.00 ea	5 pcs / 2 pcs / 3 pcs / 10 pcs	12-2-80 / 11-27-80 / 11-2-80	Bendix Corporation / -do- / -do-
1261	#910-4 4" bolts - heat treated	72000	120 pcs	6.00 ea	66000 ⓑ	6.00 doz	120 pcs	12-11-80	Bendix Corporation
1300	#1200-1A compartment lights	30000	100 pcs	3.00 ea	83500	3.00 ea	100 pcs	12-2-80	General Electric
	Amount of purchased items inventory tested	585651 8		4 OK	835 00				

difference considered
minor - not adjusted

Ⓐ Represents emergency purchase from warehouse. Price that considered as new company normally buys from mill.
√ Examined vendor's invoice.
Ⓑ Item extended at $6.00 ea. instead of $6.00 per doz.

444

priced in lineal feet. If there have been no purchases of an item during the current period, the cost used is generally the same as in the prior year, subject to possible adjustment for the reduction in the utility of the goods.

4. Date of invoice. The invoices immediately preceding the inventory date should be used for a price test of FIFO values. If there are no current invoices, there is a possibility that the item is obsolete, slow-moving, or unsalable.

The lower-of-cost-or-market method generally is used for valuing inventory in the financial statements. A method of testing the market value of purchased items which is often satisfactory is to review the price paid for recent purchases. However, this procedure is not always adequate. For instance, if a commodity is subject to declining prices or rapid market fluctuations, supplementary tests and inquiries also should be made by the auditor. One source of this type of information is published quotations included in financial and trade publications; another is suppliers' price lists. The purchasing agent of the company may also be able to provide helpful information for the auditor's use in this regard.

Companies should have adequate procedures to control, remove from inventory, and determine the estimated realizable value of obsolete or slow-moving items. Such items should be reduced to their net realizable value. If a company does not employ such procedures, the auditor frequently will be required to extend the tests. The auditor's tests of inventory for slow-moving stock, obsolete stock, and similar items normally include the following procedures:

1. Discuss with responsible company personnel the procedures used to determine the quantities of such inventory and the related adjustments from cost, and test the reasonableness of the company's determinations.
2. Search for such items during the physical inventory observation, and check at a later date to see whether such items were considered by the company in its determination.
3. Review price-test work sheets for evidence of such items. The lack of recent purchases or the use of old standard costs are indications.
4. Check to determine that the current year's inventory does not include items excluded from the prior year's inventory.
5. Review inventory records on a test basis for items which appear to be inactive.
6. Evaluate inventory quantities in light of expected usage to determine that quantities on hand are not excessive. Turnover ratios,

sales forecasts, current sales, and unfilled orders are sometimes used as a basis for estimating usage.

Pricing of Work-in-Process and Finished Goods. The auditor will determine whether the costs included in the final inventory listing are in agreement with those in the supporting cost records, whether detailed cost records have been compiled in conformity with the company's cost system, and whether any significant clerical errors have been made in accumulating the cost.

As with purchased parts, the auditor normally will prepare a schedule of the individual inventory items to be tested. After the items have been selected, client personnel should be asked to locate the proper cost cards and all the supporting data and documents that the auditor will wish to examine. The test of the cost records will normally include tests of material, labor, and overhead costs. The auditor should test prices of materials by examining supporting invoices or by referring to the purchased parts and materials price test. The accuracy with which purchased units have been converted to production units shown in the cost records (for example, converting steel from dollars per ton purchase price to dollars per hundred pieces of manufactured parts) should be tested.

Labor costs on individual jobs or for processes or departments should be tested by tracing charges to both payroll records and time tickets. Both labor rates and hours worked should be tested. The compilation of the total cost should be checked for reasonableness.

To test overhead costs, the auditor must determine the procedures which are followed by the company in establishing rates and test the computation of these rates. Overhead usually is applied on the basis of direct labor hours or direct labor costs, although other bases such as machine hours are sometimes used. All manufacturing costs other than direct materials and direct labor are included as a part of manufacturing overhead. The auditor should test to determine whether a proper disposition was made of any over- or under-applied manufacturing overhead for the period.

The auditor must test the market price for items in work-in-process or for finished products. The price may be the cost of replacement, or it may be the selling price less the cost to complete and sell the item and, in some instances, a normal profit.[3] The selling prices may be obtained from the company's price list, from contracts, from catalogs, or from recent sales invoices. The auditor must be alert for trade discounts which reduce the listed selling price. As previously indicated, inquiries should be made concerning the existence of damaged,

[3]See footnote 2 for a further explanation.

slow-moving, overstocked, and obsolete inventories. It must be determined that adequate provision has been made for losses in disposing of these inventories, whether they are on hand or are committed to be acquired.

Physical Inventory Adjustments

When the amount of adjustment from book to physical inventory is considered abnormal, the company should find the reasons for the adjustment and prepare a summary of the reconciling items. The auditor should review the reconcilement and be satisfied as to the reasonableness of the items. A review of monthly gross profit margins, standard cost variances, methods of costing sales, provisions for inventory shrinkage, and methods of accounting for freight and discounts may help explain the adjustment.

Consignments, Purchase and Sales Commitments

The auditor should determine whether the company has established adequate control over merchandise which has been either received or shipped on consignment. Confirmation of quantities on hand may be requested by corresponding with outside consignors or consignees. In certain instances, the auditor may also personally observe this inventory. The auditor should ascertain that the consigned stock has been properly included in the inventory if it is a consignment out or excluded if it is a consignment from another firm.

The auditor should discuss with appropriate company officials the existence of any possible purchase commitments for quantities in excess of normal requirements or at prices in excess of current market. Purchase contracts may be examined on a test basis. A determination should be made as to whether any provision for losses from commitments is required in the circumstances.

The auditor also should review with company officials the possible existence of any commitments to sell products at prices below the cost of production and disposal. Sales contracts may be examined on a test basis and it should be determined whether a provision for losses from such commitments is required.

Items for Letter of Representation

The auditor should consider asking the client to include in a letter of representation matters relating to inventories. The letter may contain the balances in each classification of inventory at the balance-sheet date and a statement that the balances represent physical quantities determined by count, weight, or other measurement that have been priced at (here the appropriate description of the generally accepted basis such as LIFO or FIFO, or bases if the same basis was not used for all classes of inventories, should be inserted).

Also, the letter may contain an indication that:

a. In establishing the inventory amounts, appropriate allowance was made, in the pricing or otherwise, for slow-moving obsolete, damaged, or unsalable items.

b. Care was exercised in adjusting the book inventories to physical count to assure that: (1) all goods shipped to the company prior to the date of inventory determination were included in the inventory; (2) all items included in the inventory had been paid for or the liability had been recognized in the accounts at the date of determination; and (3) all items billed to customers on or before the date of inventory determination and all items held by the company that were the property of others were excluded from inventory.

AUDIT MEMORANDUM

A memorandum describing the work performed on inventories should be prepared by the auditor and included in the working papers. This memorandum should clearly state the audit objectives, the work performed, the findings of the work performed, and the auditor's opinion as to whether the inventory balance is fairly stated. Specific comments relating to the auditor's evaluation of any reserves for obsolete inventory, pricing policies, and consistency of pricing policies are an important part of this memorandum.

GLOSSARY

Cutoff procedures   Those procedures followed by the auditor to ensure that (1) all items received up to the cutoff date were included in the physical inventory and charged to the purchases or inventory accounts, and (2) whether all items shipped up to the cutoff date were excluded from the physical inventory and have been credited to the inventory account (under the perpetual system) and included in sales and cost of goods sold.

Inventories   Those items of tangible personal property held by a business which are: (1) held for sale in the ordinary course of business; (2) in the process of production for sale in a business; or (3) to be consumed in the production of goods for sale in a business. [*ARB 43*, p. 27.]

QUESTIONS AND PROBLEMS

11-1. Define inventories.

11-2. What are the objectives of the audit of inventories?

11-3. What is the "cost" of inventories?

11-4. What should be the objective in selecting among assumptions as to the flow of cost factors in determining inventory cost?

11-5. The lower-of-cost-or-market method generally is used for valuing inventory. How can the auditor check the market value of inventory consisting of purchased items?

11-6. List the auditing procedures an auditor can employ to determine whether slow-moving or obsolete items are included in the inventory.

(AICPA, adapted)

11-7. What should be done with the auditor's test counts that were made during the physical inventory and were listed in the auditor's working papers?

11-8. When is a departure from the cost basis of pricing inventory acceptable?

11-9. List some features of an inventory system that will help produce an accurate accounting for inventories.

11-10. What should be observed by the auditor during the taking of an inventory?

11-11. What is the purpose of testing the company's receiving and shipping cutoff procedures?

11-12. If physical inventories are taken, priced, and compiled prior to the balance-sheet date, tests must be made of the inventory transactions which occurred from the time the physical inventory was taken to the balance-sheet date. What does the test of interim inventory transactions normally include?

11-13. List some features of a system that provides for the safeguarding of inventory.

11-14. The client's cost system is often the focal point in the CPA's examination of the financial statements of a manufacturing company. For what purpose does the CPA review the cost system?

(AICPA, adapted)

11-15. The Summer Manufacturing Co. employs standard costs in its cost accounting system. List the audit procedures that you would apply to satisfy yourself that Summer's cost standards and related variance amounts are acceptable and have not distorted the financial statements. (Confine your audit procedures to those applicable to materials.)

(AICPA, adapted)

11-16. When a CPA has accepted an engagement from a new client who is a manufacturer, it is customary for the CPA to tour the client's plant facilities. Discuss the ways in which the CPA's observations made during the course of the plant tour would be of help in planning and conducting the audit.

(AICPA, adapted)

11-17. What is the auditor's objective in compliance tests concerning inventory?

11-18. Select the *best* answer for each of the following items:

a. Which of the following is the *best* audit procedure for the discovery of damaged merchandise in a client's ending inventory?
    1. Compare the physical quantities of slow-moving items with corresponding quantities of the prior year.
    2. Observe merchandise and raw materials during the client's physical inventory taking.
    3. Review the management's inventory representation letter for accuracy.
    4. Test overall fairness of inventory values by comparing the company's turnover ratio with the industry average.

b. When verifying debits to the perpetual inventory records of a non-manufacturing company, an auditor would be most interested in examining a sample of purchase
    1. Approvals.
    2. Requisitions.
    3. Invoices.
    4. Orders.

c. To *best* ascertain that a company has properly included merchandise that it owns in its ending inventory, the auditor should review and test the
    1. Terms of the open purchase orders.
    2. Purchase cutoff procedures.
    3. Contractual commitments made by the purchasing department.
    4. Purchase invoices received on or around year-end.

d. The primary objective of a CPA's observation of a client's physical inventory count is to
    1. Discover whether a client has counted a particular inventory item or group of items.
    2. Obtain direct knowledge that the inventory exists and has been properly counted.
    3. Provide an appraisal of the quality of the merchandise on hand on the day of the physical count.
    4. Allow the auditor to supervise the conduct of the count so as to obtain assurance that inventory quantities are reasonably accurate.

(AICPA, adapted)

11-19. Your audit client, Household Appliances, Inc. operates a retail store in the center of town. Because of lack of storage space Household keeps inventory that is not on display in a public warehouse outside of town. The warehouseman receives inventory from suppliers and,

450

on request from your client by a shipping advice or telephone call, delivers merchandise to customers or to the retail outlet.

The accounts are maintained at the retail store by a bookkeeper. Each month the warehouseman sends to the bookkeeper a quantity report indicating opening balance, receipts, deliveries, and ending balance. The bookkeeper compares book quantities on hand at month end with the warehouseman's report and adjusts his books to agree with the report. No physical counts of the merchandise at the warehouse were made by your client during the year.

You are now preparing for your examination of the current year's financial statements in this recurring engagement. Last year you rendered an unqualified opinion.

Required:

a. Prepare an audit program for the observation of the physical inventory of Household Appliances, Inc. (1) at the retail outlet and (2) at the warehouse.

b. As part of your examination would you verify inventory quantities at the warehouse by means of:

1. A warehouse confirmation? Why?
2. Test counts of inventory at the warehouse? Why?

c. Since the bookkeeper adjusts books to quantities shown on the warehouseman's report each month, what significance would you attach to the year-end adjustments if they were substantial? Discuss.

d. Assume you are unable to satisfy yourself as to the inventory at the audit date of Household Appliances, Inc. Could you render an unqualified opinion? Why?

(AICPA)

11-20. On January 10, 1981 you were engaged to make an examination of the financial statements of Kahl Equipment Corporation for the year ended December 31, 1980. Kahl has sold trucks and truck parts and accessories for many years, but has never had an audit. Kahl maintains good perpetual records for all inventories and takes a complete physical inventory each December 31.

The Parts Inventory account includes the $2,500 cost of obsolete parts. Kahl's executives acknowledge these parts have been worthless for several years but they have continued to carry the cost as an asset. The amount of $2,500 is material in relation to 1980 net income and year-end inventories but not material in relation to total assets or capital at December 31, 1980.

Required:

a. List the procedures you would add to your inventory audit program for new trucks because you did not observe the physical inventory taken by the corporation as of December 31, 1980.

    b.   Should the $2,500 of obsolete parts be carried in inventory as an asset? Discuss.

(AICPA, adapted)

11-21.   Ace Corporation does not conduct a complete annual physical count of purchased parts and supplies in its principal warehouse but uses statistical sampling instead to estimate the year-end inventory. Ace maintains a perpetual inventory record of parts and supplies and believes that statistical sampling is highly effective in determining inventory values and is sufficiently reliable to make a physical count of each item of inventory unnecessary.

Required:

    a.   Identify the audit procedures that should be used by the independent auditor that change or are in addition to normal required audit procedures when a client utilizes statistical sampling to determine inventory value and does not conduct a 100 percent annual physical count of inventory items.

    b.   List at least ten normal audit procedures that should be performed **to verify physical quantities** whenever a client conducts a periodic physical count of all or part of its inventory.

(AICPA)

11-22.   One of your clients, Bonded Warehousing Company, recently incorporated a subsidiary company to field warehouse petroleum products at a nearby industrial area. The parent company has engaged in terminal warehousing of lubricating oils and greases for a nearby petroleum refinery for some time. The refinery attempted to borrow against its light oil inventory but could do so only through a field warehousing arrangement. Bonded Warehousing was asked to field warehouse gasoline and diesel fuel for the refinery. The subsidiary leased the refinery's tank farm and undertook the field warehousing activity. The tank farm, which has adequate capacity for the refinery's output, has fifty tanks containing meters, alternate gauging openings, and protection devices such as valve locks. There are also burglar and fire alarms, and fire fighting equipment. Only nonnegotiable warehouse receipts are issued.

    The subsidiary employs only a stock record clerk, who keeps perpetual inventory records and issues warehouse receipts, and four yardmen, who do all loading and unloading of the tanks and take inventories. The parent company's home office receives all cash, writes all checks, and maintains all the records for the subsidiary company for a small monthly fee, and the home office internal control for these is excellent.

Required:

    List the features which you believe would be desirable in a system of internal control over inventories for the subsidiary. Classify these controls in the following categories:

a. Controls at the field warehouse over receipts and releases of goods.
b. Other inventory controls at the field warehouse.
c. Specific controls which should be exercised by the home office after subsidiary operations are commenced.
d. Other related organizational or administrative matters which should be considered by the home office on or before the date subsidiary operations are commenced.

(AICPA)

11-23. Late in December 1982 your CPA firm accepted an audit engagement at Rich Jewelers, Inc., a corporation which deals largely in diamonds. The corporation has retail jewelry stores in several Eastern cities and a diamond wholesale store in New York City. The wholesale store also sets the diamonds in rings and in other quality jewelry.

The retail stores place orders for diamond jewelry with the wholesale store in New York City. A buyer employed by the wholesale store purchases diamonds in the New York diamond market, and the wholesale store then fills orders from the retail stores and from independent customers and maintains a substantial inventory of diamonds. The corporation values its inventory by the specific identification cost method.

Required:

Assume that at the inventory date you are satisfied that Rich Jewelers, Inc., has no items left by customers for repair or sale on consignment and that no inventory owned by the corporation is in the possession of outsiders.

a. Discuss the problems the auditors should anticipate in planning for the observation of the physical inventory on this engagement because of the:
   1. Difficult locations of inventories.
   2. Nature of the inventory.
b. 1. Explain how your audit program for this inventory would be different from that used for most other inventories.
   2. Prepare an audit program for the verification of the corporation's diamond and diamond jewelry inventories, identifying any steps which you would apply only to the retail stores or to the wholesale store.
c. Assume that a shipment of diamong rings was in transit by corporate messenger from the wholesale store to a retail store on the inventory date. What additional audit steps would you take to satisfy yourself as to the gems which were in transit from the wholesale store on the inventory date?

(AICPA, adapted)

11-24. Often an important aspect of a CPA's examination of financial statements is the observation of the taking of the physical inventory.

Required:

a. What are the general objectives or purposes of the CPA's observation of the taking of the physical inventory? (Do not discuss the procedures or techniques involved in making the observation.)

b. For what purposes does the CPA make and record test counts of inventory quantities during the observation of the taking of the physical inventory? Discuss.

c. A number of companies employ outside service companies which specialize in counting, pricing, extending and footing inventories. These service companies usually furnish a certificate attesting to the value of the inventory.

Assuming that the service company took the inventory on the balance-sheet date:

1. How much reliance, if any, can the CPA place on the inventory certificate of outside specialists? Discuss.

2. What effect, if any, would the inventory certificate of outside specialists have upon the type of report the CPA would render? Discuss.

3. What reference, if any, would the CPA make to the certificate of outside specialists in the short-form report?

(AICPA, adapted)

11-25. The processing operations of Smith Co., your client, require a basic raw material, colgum, which is imported and refined by several domestic suppliers. Colgum is combined with other raw materials of the same general category to produce the finished product. Smith Co. has been disturbed by the unreliability of the supply because of the international situation and labor troubles of the suppliers and has stockpiled a large supply of colgum to assure continued operations. This supply of colgum is a substantial portion of Smith's inventory and you determine that it is a three-year supply. Colgum is a staple commodity widely used in manufacturing operations. Smith has consistently applied the "lower of cost or market" rule to the valuation of its total inventory. The year-end market price of colgum is less than Smith's cost.

Required:

a. What effect, if any, would this excess supply have upon the financial statements and your report? Discuss briefly.

b. What effect, if any, would this excess supply have upon the application of the rule of "cost or market, whichever is lower" to the valuation of individual items as against category totals in the total inventory? Discuss briefly.

(AICPA, adapted)

11-26. Coil steel comprises one half of the inventory of the Metal Fabricating Company. At the beginning of the year the company installed a system to control coil steel inventory.

The coil steel is stored within the plant in a special storage area.

When coils are received a two-part tag is prepared. The tag is pre-numbered and each part provides for entry of supplier's name, receiving report number, date received, coil weight, and description. Both parts of the tag are prepared at the time the material is received and weighed and the receiving report prepared. The "A" part of the tag is attached to the coil and the "B" part of the tag is sent to the stock records department with the receiving report. The stock records department files the tags numerically by coil width and gauge. The stock records department also maintains perpetual stock cards on each width and gauge by total weight; in a sense, the cards are a control record for the tags. No material requisitions are used by the plant, but as coils are placed into production, the "A" part of the tag is removed from the coil and sent to stock records as support of the production report which is the basis of entries on the perpetual inventory cards.

When the "A" part of the tag is received by the stock records department, it is matched with the "B" part of the tag and the "A" part is destroyed. The "B" part is stamped with the date of use, processed, and retained in a consumed file by width and gauge. The coils are neatly stacked and arranged and all tags are visible.

The balance of the inventory is examined by standard procedures and you are satisfied that it is fairly stated.

Physical inventories are taken on a cycle basis throughout the year. About one twelfth of the coil steel inventories are taken each month. The coil steel control account and the perpetual stock cards are adjusted as counts are made. Internal control of inventories is good in all respects.

In previous years the client had taken a complete physical inventory of coil steel at the end of the year (the client's fiscal year ends December 31) but none is to be taken this year. You are engaged for the current audit in September. You audited the financial statements last year.

Required:

Assuming that you decide to undertake some preliminary audit work before December 31, prepare programs for:

1. The verification of coil steel quantities previously inventoried during the current year.
2. Observation of physical inventories to be taken in subsequent months.

(AICPA, adapted)

11-27. In connection with his examination of the financial statement of Knutson Products Co., an assembler of home appliances, for the year ended May 31, 1982, Ray Abel, CPA, is reviewing with Knutson's controller the plans for a physical inventory at the company warehouse on May 31, 1982. Note: In answering the two parts of this question do not discuss procedure for the physical inventory of work in process, inventory pricing, or other audit steps not directly related to the physical inventory taking.

a. Finished appliances, unassembled parts and supplies are stored in the warehouse, which is attached to Knutson's assembly plant. The plant will operate during the count. On May 30 the warehouse will deliver to the plant the estimated quantities of unassembled parts and supplies required for May 31 production, but there may be emergency requisitions on May 31. During the count the warehouse will continue to receive parts and supplies and to ship finished appliances. However, appliances completed on May 31 will be held in the plant until after the physical inventory.

Required:

What procedures should the company establish to ensure that the inventory count includes all items that should be included and that nothing is counted twice?

b. Warehouse employees will join with accounting department employees in counting the inventory. The inventory takers will use a tag system.

Required:

What instructions should the company give to the inventory takers?

(AICPA, adapted)

11-28. Line-Rite Manufacturing Company, Inc. is a moderate-sized company manufacturing equipment for use in laying pipelines. The company has prospered in the past, gradually expanding to its present size. Recognizing a need to develop new products, if its growth is to continue, the company created an engineering research and development section. During 1983 at a cost of $70,000, this section designed, patented and successfully tested a new machine which greatly accelerates the laying of small-sized lines.

In order to adequately finance the manufacture, promotion and sale of this new product it has become necessary to expand the company's plant and to enlarge inventories. Required financing to accomplish this has resulted in the company engaging you in April 1983 to examine its financial statements as of September 30, 1983, the end of the current fiscal year. This is the company's initial audit.

In the course of your preliminary audit work you obtain the following information:

1. The nature of the inventory and related manufacturing processes do not lend themselves well to taking a complete physical inventory at year-end or at any other given date. The company has an inventory team which counts all inventory items on a cycle basis throughout the year. Perpetual inventory records, main-

tained by the accounting department, are adjusted to reflect the quantities on hand as determined by these counts. At year-end an inventory summary is prepared from the perpetual inventory records. The quantities in this summary are subsequently valued in developing the final inventory balances.

2. The company carries a substantial parts inventory which is used to service equipment sold to customers. Certain parts are also used in current production. The company considers any part to be obsolete only if it shows no usage or sales activity for two consecutive years. Parts falling into this category are reserved for fully. A reserve of $10,000 exists at present.

Your tests indicate that obsolescence in inventories might approximate $50,000.

As part of your audit you must deal with each of the foregoing matters.

Required:

a. With respect to inventories define the overall problem involved in this first audit.

b. Outline a program for testing inventory quantities.

c. Enumerate and discuss the principal problems involved in inventory obsolescence for the company assuming the amount involved was significant with respect to the company's financial position.

(AICPA, adapted)

11-29. A processor of frozen foods carries an inventory of finished products consisting of 50 different types of items valued at approximately $2,000,000. About $750,000 of this value represents stock produced by the company and billed to customers prior to the audit date. This stock is being held for the customers at a monthly rental charge until they request shipment and is not separated from the company's inventory.

The company maintains separate perpetual ledgers at the plant office for both stock owned and stock being held for customers. The cost department also maintains a perpetual record of stock owned. The above perpetual records reflect quantities only.

The company does not take a complete physical inventory at any time during the year since the temperature in the cold storage facilities is too low to allow one to spend more than 15 minutes inside at a time. It is not considered practical to move items outside or to de-freeze the cold storage facilities for the purpose of taking a physical inventory. Due to these circumstances, it is impractical to test count quantities to the extent of completely verifying specific items. The company considers as its inventory valuation at year-end the aggregate of the quantities reflected by the perpetual record of stock owned, maintained at the plant office, priced at the lower of cost or market.

Required:

a. What are the two principal problems facing the auditor in the audit of the inventory? Discuss briefly.

b. Outline the audit steps that you would take to enable you to render an unqualified opinion with respect to the inventory. (Your may omit consideration of a verification of unit prices and clerical accuracy.)

(AICPA)

11–30. The accounting and internal control procedures relating to purchases of materials by the Branden Company, a medium-sized concern manufacturing special machinery to order, have been described by your junior accountant in the following terms:

After approval by manufacturing department foremen, material purchase requisitions are forwarded to the purchasing department supervisor who distributes such requisitions to the several employees under his control. The latter employees prepare prenumbered purchase orders in triplicate, account for all numbers, and send the original purchase order to the vendor. One copy of the purchase order is sent to the receiving department where it is used as a receiving report. The other copy is filed in the purchasing department.

When the materials are received, they are moved directly to the storeroom and issued to the foremen on informal requests. The receiving department sends a receiving report (with its copy of the purchase order attached) to the purchasing department and sends copies of the receiving report to the storeroom and to the accounting department.

Vendors' invoices for material purchases, received in duplicate in the mail room, are sent to the purchasing department and directed to the employee who placed the related order. The employee then compares the invoice with the copy of the purchase-order on file in the purchasing department for price and terms and compares the invoice quantity with the quantity received as reported by the shipping and receiving department on its copy of the purchase order. The purchasing department employee also checks discounts, footings, and extensions, and initials the invoice to indicate approval for payment. The invoice is then sent to the voucher section of the accounting department where it is coded for account distribution, assigned a voucher number, entered in the voucher register, and filed according to payment due date.

On payment dates prenumbered checks are requisitioned by the voucher section from the cashier and prepared except for signature. After the checks are prepared they are returned to the cashier, who puts them through a check signing machine, accounts for the sequence of numbers, and passes them to the cash disbursement bookkeeper for entry in the cash disbursements books. The cash disbursements bookkeeper then returns the checks to the voucher section which then notes payment dates in the voucher register, places the checks in envelopes, and sends them to the mail room. The vouchers are then filed in numerical sequence. At the end of each month one of the voucher clerks prepares an adding machine tape of unpaid items in the voucher register and compares the total thereof with the general ledger balance and investigates any difference disclosed by such comparison.

Required:

Discuss the weaknesses, if any, in the internal control of Branden's purchasing and subsequent procedures, and suggest supplementary or revised procedures for remedying each weakness with regard to:

a. Requisition of materials.
b. Receipt and storage of materials.
c. Functions of the purchasing department.
d. Functions of the accounting department.

(AICPA)

Learning Objectives

Study of the material in this chapter is designed to achieve several learning objectives. Among these are:

1. An understanding of the auditor's objectives with regard to the examination of securities; property, plant, and equipment; prepaid expenses and deferred charges; intangible assets; and miscellaneous assets.
2. A knowledge of the essential elements of internal control over these assets.
3. An understanding of the audit procedures used in testing these various assets.

12

Other Types of Assets

This chapter discusses the auditor's examination of the remaining assets which are often included on the balance sheets of most clients. These assets include: securities, property, plant, and equipment; prepaid expenses and deferred charges; intangible assets; and miscellaneous assets.

SECURITIES

Securities include both temporary investments and long-term investments. *Temporary investments* include all securities that are listed on a recognized exchange and other securities that have a ready market and that management intends to convert to cash within a short period of time. They are held as a temporary investment of excess funds and are generally classified as a current asset. *Long-term Investments* are held for either long-term capital appreciation or to influence or control another company and are classified as a noncurrent asset.

Marketable equity securities are to be given separate consideration from other securities. The FASB in *Statement No. 12*,[1] requires that "marketable equity securities owned by an entity . . . be grouped into separate portfolios according to the current or noncurrent classifica-

---

[1]*Statement of Financial Accounting Standards No. 12*, "Accounting for Certain Marketable Securities," Financial Accounting Standards Board, 1975. Copyright © by Financial Accounting Standards Board, High Ridge Park, Stamford, Connecticut 06905, U.S.A. Reprinted with permission. Copies of the complete document are available from the FASB.

For purposes of FASB *Statement No. 12*, the term *marketable* ". . . means an equity security as to which sales prices or bid and ask prices are readily available on a national exchange (i.e., those registered with the Securities and Exchange Commission) or in the over-the counter market. . . ." [par. 7] An *equity security* ". . . encompasses any instrument representing ownership shares (e.g., common, preferred, and other capital stock), or the right to acquire (e.g., warrants, rights, and call options) or dispose of (e.g., put options) ownership shares in an enterprise at fixed or determinable prices." [par. 7] It does not include redeemable preferred stock, treasury stock, or convertible bonds.

462

tion of the securities for the purpose of comparing aggregate cost and market value to determine carrying amount. . . ." [par. 9] Each of the two categories (current and noncurrent) is to be carried at " . . . the lower of its aggregate cost or market value, determined at the balance sheet date." [par. 8] FASB *Statement No. 12* does not deal with certain investments (such as bonds). Therefore, *ARB 43*[2] still dictates the carrying value for these investments. Basically, it states that they should be carried at cost unless there is a permanent decline in market value.

The discussion regarding noncurrent market equity securities pertains to situations where the audited company owns less than 20 percent of the outstanding stock and therefore does not exert significant influence over that company. For situations where the audited company holds from 20 to 50 percent of the outstanding stock the auditor needs to make sure the provisions of APB *Opinion No. 18* have been applied.[3] In situations where the client owns a controlling interest (more than 50 percent) of a company, the auditor needs to be satisfied that *APB Opinions 16*[4] and *17*[5] have been applied. Further discussion of these latter two situations is beyond the scope of this text.

The auditor's objective in examining securities owned by the company is to be satisfied that they are fairly presented on the balance sheet and that any related income is also fairly stated. Specifically, that they are in the company's possession or held by others for the account of the company, that they are owned by the company, and that the basis at which the securities are carried and income is recognized conforms with generally accepted accounting principles applied on a consistent basis.

Internal Control over Securities

The responsibility for the purchase, sale, and custody of securities should be defined clearly and placed with a responsible officer of the business. However, the actual authorization of purchases and sales of securities is usually the responsibility of the board of directors of a corporation.

---

[2]*Accounting Research Bulletin No. 43*, "Restatement and Revision of Accounting Research Bulletins," American Institute of Certified Public Accountants, 1953.

[3]*Opinions of the Accounting Principles Board No. 18*, "The Equity Method of Accounting for Investments in Common Stock," American Institute of Certified Public Accountants, 1971.

[4]*Opinions of the Accounting Principles Board No. 16*, "Business Combinations," American Institute of Certified Public Accountants, 1970.

[5]*Opinions of the Accounting Principles Board Opinion No. 17*, "Intangible Assets," American Institute of Certified Public Accountants, 1970.

The accounting department should maintain detailed records of securities. The individual who keeps these records should not have access to the securities. Additionally, someone in the accounting department should keep detailed records on income derivable and derived from the securities.

Since securities offer a temptation for defalcation similar to cash, effective physical control is necessary. Stock certificates and registerable bonds should be made out in the company's name. Additionally, securities should be kept in a safe place, such as a safe-deposit box, or held by an independent custodian or broker. Access to the safe-deposit box ordinarily should require the presence of two officers or other responsible employees.

Periodically, the company should take an inventory of all the securities that it owns. This inventory should be compared with the accounting records. The inventory should be taken by an employee who has no other duties that relate to securities.

Audit Procedures

The auditor should obtain or prepare, in advance if possible, a listing of securities which includes information regarding: name of issuer and description of security; serial numbers; name of the owner and any endorsements; number of shares or principal amount; cost— and carrying amount, if other than cost; market price per unit; total market price; location of securities; if they are hypothecated (pledged without delivery of title or possession), with whom and for what purpose; and a summarization of equity securities and debt securities. If obtained from the client, the schedule should be footed and reconciled with the accounting records. Figure 12–1 is an example of a temporary investments listing prepared by the client for use during the audit.

The auditor should account for the securities owned by the company by inspecting the securities on hand and confirming any which are held by an outside custodian. The auditor should inspect the securities on hand in the presence of the company's representative and obtain a signed receipt for their return to the custodian. The receipt should be prepared in ink. If securities are held in more than one location, arrangements should be made to count securities at all locations at the same time to avoid the possibility of client personnel transferring securities from one location to another in an attempt to cover up theft or unauthorized use.

If securities are held by others for the account of the client, then the auditor should request confirmation of the securities as of the balance-sheet date. The holder of the securities should be requested to

FIGURE 12-1

	NAME	DATE
PREPARED	Client	
APPROVED		

Temporary Investments
Liquidity Enterprises, Inc.
7/31/80

Issuer and Description of Security	Certificate Number	No. of Shares or Principal Amount	Cost	(A) Market Value/Unit	Total Market Value
Equity Securities:					
ABC Corp. -- Common Stock	IA1234	1000	12000-	14.50	14500-
LNT, Inc. -- Common Stock	AB5678	500	4000-	6.50	3250-
XYZ Ltd. -- 6% Cumulative Preferred	OP9101	200	20000-	98.00	19600-
Total Equity Securities			36000-		37350-
Debt Securities:					
MG Corp. -- 9½% Subordinate Debentures due 7/1/97	ALK123	25000-	24500-	101	27500-
BTQ Enterprises -- 6½% Conv. Debentures -- due 9/1/80	RS4791	56000-	54500-	100	56000-
Total Debt Securities			79000-		83500-
TOTAL TEMPORARY INVESTMENTS			115000-		

All securities are located in the company's safety deposit box at the First Union Trust Bank.

(A) Market prices represent the final market quotes as of Friday - 7/30/80 -- listed in the 8/2/80 Wall Street Journal.

supply the auditor with information that (1) identifies the issuer, (2) describes the security, (3) indicates bond or stock certificate number, and (4) indicates the number of shares of stock or the face amount in the case of bonds. The request for confirmation should be mailed by the auditor and should include instructions to mail the reply directly to the auditor.

The auditor, when making a physical examination of securities, should note:

1. That the client's name appears on stock certificates and registered bonds.

2.   That past due coupons are not attached to coupon bonds. Also that coupons have not been clipped in advance of maturity dates. Any exceptions should be investigated.
3.   That the other information (e.g., number of shares, face amount of bonds, interest rates, and so on) obtained from the client is correct.

The information obtained during the physical examination of securities or by confirmation should be compared by the auditor to the information on the listing of securities obtained from the client. Any differences noted should be investigated. In making this comparison, the auditor should take special care to ascertain that the certificate numbers on the listing agree with those noted during the physical examination or listed on the confirmation. Differences in the certificate numbers may mean that there have been unauthorized or unrecorded securities—transactions during that year in which common stock or bonds were sold and later replaced with certificates of the same issuer.

If securities are inspected at a time other than the balance-sheet date, the auditor should account for any transactions which occurred in the intervening period. If, however, the securities are in a safe-deposit box, a letter from the safe-deposit company attesting to nonentry to the box during the interim period may eliminate the need to account for intervening transactions.

Once it has been ascertained that the securities listed on the schedule prepared by the client are under the control of the client, the auditor should test the carrying amount of the securities at the balance-sheet date and the realized gain or loss on sales made during the year. (For marketable equity securities, the auditor also should determine the appropriate carrying value in accordance with FASB *Statement No. 12.*) In doing this the auditor should perform the following procedures:

1.   The auditor should obtain from the client a schedule of all securities transactions (purchases and sales) that occurred during the year under audit. This schedule should describe fully the securities, cost, sales prices, and any gain or loss realized from a sale.
2.   All securities present at the beginning of the period should be accounted for (i.e., are either present at year end or have been disposed of). The serial numbers should be agreed to the prior year's work papers. The carrying value of securities acquired in prior years also can be verified by reference to the prior year's work papers.
3.   For purchases or sales during the year, the auditor should examine brokers' advices. Also, the auditor should check the approval of securities transactions by the board of directors, an investment committee, or an official designated by the board or committee.

When examining brokers' advices, the auditor should note the description of the security, name of the issuer, certificate number, number of shares or face amount of bonds, and the cost.

4. Any gains or losses on the disposal of securities during the year should be tested by the auditor. The total should be traced to the general ledger trial balance. Proceeds from the disposition of the securities may be checked by referring to brokers' advices and to the cash receipts record. The cost of the securities sold may be determined by FIFO (first-in, first-out), specific identification, or the average-cost method, and the method used should be applied consistently. The average-cost method may not be used for federal income tax purposes, however.

5. For current marketable equity securities taken as a group, the auditor should determine the aggregate lower of cost or market. If aggregate market is lower than aggregate cost, the auditor should determine that the securities have been written down to market. The unrealized loss is to be shown on the income statement. Later recoveries up to original cost are to be shown as unrealized gains on the income statement.

6. For noncurrent marketable equity securities the auditor should determine that any necessary write-down to market has been recorded. But the unrealized loss resulting from "temporary" declines is not to be shown on the income statement. Instead, it is included separately in the equity section on the balance sheet. Later recoveries up to original cost reduce the amount of the item appearing in the equity section. Declines in market value thought to be "permanent" are to be recorded as realized losses and shown on the income statement. Any later recoveries in market in this latter instance would be ignored until the securities are sold.

The auditor should test the dividends, interest income, and accrued interest receivable accounts. Dividends can be verified by reference to sources such as *Moody's* and *Standard & Poor's* and by the use of calculations. The auditor should also examine the client's cash receipts records. Interest income can be verified by calculation and reference to cash receipt records. Accrued interest receivable can also be verified by calculation. Discrepancies found in tests of securities income should be investigated.

When performing an audit of securities, the auditor needs to make sure that all information needed for financial statement disclosure is included in the work papers. This information includes a summary of marketable equity securities (cost and market) by current and noncurrent asset classification, and a summary of realized and unrealized gains and losses by current and noncurrent classification.

Market value at the balance-sheet date and as of the date of the accountants' report should be tested by reference to market quotations in published sources (e.g., *The Wall Street Journal, The New York Times, Commercial and Financial Chronicle,* or *Bank and Quotation Record*). When the securities held by the client are not actively traded, it may be necessary to obtain market quotations from brokers. Bonds frequently are quoted on the basis of yield to maturity, and it is necessary to examine the published yield figures to determine market value. For some bonds issued by the government, market value fluctuates in accordance with published tables.

PROPERTY, PLANT, AND EQUIPMENT

In the examination of property, plant and equipment, the auditor has three broad objectives. One is to determine whether the physical assets carried on the company's books do, in fact, exist, whether all existing assets are recorded, and whether all assets are being used in the manner the company claims they are being used. Another of the auditor's objectives is to determine the company's ownership of these assets and the presence of any related liens or other encumbrances. The third objective is to ascertain whether the company's methods of property accounting and valuation conform with generally accepted accounting principles and whether these principles have been consistently applied.

Internal Control over Property, Plant, and Equipment

The acquisition of items of property, plant, and equipment usually involves a major expenditure of funds by the client. It is essential, therefore, that accounting policies in this area be well defined and the responsibility for their administration and implementation clearly fixed. Proper control of property, plant, and equipment involves the use of budgets for plant and equipment, explicit accounting policies (regarding repairs, capitalization, and depreciation), and methods to ensure proper safeguarding of these assets.

All major expenditures for property, plant, and equipment should be made under budgetary control; and ordinarily, the capital budget should be approved by the client company's board of directors. Each expenditure made for a project included in the capital expenditure budget should be approved by a responsible executive. Authorization documents for asset acquisitions should be used. A description of the procedures to be employed for recording additions to and dispositions of property, plant, and equipment should be stated in writing. There should also be a written policy as to the type and minimum dollar amount of an expenditure to be capitalized.

Proper authority should always be obtained before assets are sold or abandoned. Documents should be used to authorize the disposition of assets. All retirements should be recorded on a current basis. In many instances, companies will take physical inventories of the fixed assets and compare these inventories with the accounting records.

The procedures used to exercise control over the costs of the individual assets acquired will, of course, depend to a large extent on whether the items are purchased or constructed. In either case, detailed property records should be maintained. In the case of a purchase, procedures which are similar to those employed for other types of acquisitions by purchase should be followed. When the asset is constructed by the company, actual costs should be compared to estimated costs. Significant differences should be investigated promptly. Where the asset is being constructed by an outside contractor on other than a fixed-price basis, the company should review the costing procedures of the contractor and make tests of these costs.

Auditing Property, Plant, and Equipment Accounts

Ordinarily the examination of property accounts is concentrated on a review and testing of changes in the account balances which occurred during the period under audit. During the initial audit of a company, the auditor should have established that the property accounts were fairly stated. Testing procedures for increases in these accounts are discussed in a following section. In testing the decreases in the account balances, the auditor refers to the amounts recorded in the accounts (some of which have already been tested in prior examinations) to determine whether asset retirements by sale or abandonment are properly recorded. The auditor must also ascertain (1) whether all fully depreciated assets have been eliminated from the accounts (if it is the company's policy to do so), and (2) whether assets which have become obsolete because of changes in the nature of the company's operations have been removed from the account in which they were recorded and set up in a separate account such as "Obsolete Machinery" at their salvage values. Procedures regarding disposals are also described in more detail later in this chapter.

As in any other phase of the audit, the auditor will begin the examination of property by reviewing internal control. Of particular importance in this review is the system of authorizations for asset acquisitions (including capitalization versus expense policies) and retirements and the depreciation policies of the client.

The auditor need not physically examine individual items of property, plant, and equipment in every case. These assets normally are not vulnerable to theft or fraud, and most companies have comparatively effective procedures for controlling additions, disposals, retirements, or abandonments of property. In some instances, however, the auditor may wish to inspect certain properties, both to obtain a better understanding of the company's operations and to become satisfied that these assets do, in fact, exist.

The examination of property, plant, and equipment normally requires three major audit procedures: analyzing and testing the changes in the asset balances; analyzing and testing the changes in the allowances for depreciation; and summarizing the transactions for the year.

Changes in Asset Balances. Balances in the property, plant, and equipment accounts may change because of additions, disposals, or transfers of assets, or because of a combination of these factors.

The examination of additions is ordinarily performed on a test basis, with particular attention given to the larger acquisitions. Smaller items are also investigated on a test basis in order to test the practices and procedures used by the company.

The cost of an asset includes its purchase price plus all expenditures which are necessary to place it in a position and condition for its intended use. Included are such items as invoice price, freight, handling charges, reconditioning costs, and installation costs. To support an addition to property, plant, and equipment, the auditor normally performs the following tests, either during compliance testing or during the property examination:

1. Examines the vendor's invoice noting the date of purchase, the price, the description of the asset, and the name of the purchaser.
2. Determines whether the purchase was properly authorized in accordance with the stated policies of the company.
3. Examines data evidencing the receipt of the asset.
4. For major additions to the land or building accounts, examines the deed, title policy, the closing statement, and similar documents in order to establish ownership.
5. For major acquisitions (and, on a test basis, for other selected purchases), inspects the asset.
6. Determines whether the asset life and salvage value as established by the company are reasonable.
7. Determines if the addition is eligible for the investment tax credit.
8. Verifies other costs charged to the assets such as freight, handling charges, reconditioning costs, and installation costs.

A company sometimes constructs its own additions to plant and equipment. The cost of this construction is normally accumulated in a work order and should include all direct material, direct labor, and the applicable overhead. The audit objectives of testing assets constructed by the company are similar to those for testing purchased assets. In examining constructed assets the auditor normally performs the following tests:

1. Determines whether the project was properly authorized in accordance with the company's stated policies.
2. Examines invoices for the purchased items.
3. Examines records for the labor charges.
4. Reviews the application of overhead to the asset.
5. Checks the clerical accuracy of the work orders and traces the total dollar amount for the asset to the property accounts.
6. Determines whether the asset life and salvage value as established by the company are reasonable.
7. For major construction, sometimes inspects the asset.

The auditor should review the company's policy regarding expensing asset acquisitions of small dollar amounts. As a matter of practicality and convenience, companies will often charge additions which are under a stated amount (e.g., $500) directly to expense. For instance, consider the inconvenience of depreciating a $10 wastebasket over 20 years. The cutoff point may be as small as $50 in a small company or as large as several thousand dollars in a very large company. This practice is an accepted one when the amounts involved are considered to be immaterial both individually and in total. The auditor should determine whether the policy is reasonable and test the accounting records to ascertain whether it is being followed consistently.

In addition to testing charges to fixed asset accounts, the auditor also should review the repair and maintenance accounts to ascertain whether all of the items included in these accounts represent proper charges to expense. Any charge which appears to be unusual or which may represent a capital expenditure should be noted and investigated.

The cost of all assets sold, traded, scrapped, or disposed of in any other manner should be removed from the asset accounts. The auditor should review the company's procedures regarding the sale, trade-in, abandonment, or other retirement of property, and should examine adequate support for significant disposals to determine whether these transactions have been recorded properly. To test a recorded disposal the following tests would normally be made:

1. Determine whether the disposal was authorized properly.
2. Determine whether the asset account has been relieved of the amount pertaining to the assets. In performing this test, the auditor should refer to the property records maintained by the company.
3. Substantiate the proceeds of the transaction by reference to evi-

dence such as remittance advices, correspondence, and the cash receipts journal.

4. Determine whether gains or losses on the disposals of assets are recorded properly (depreciation must be recorded up to the date of sale). If the client uses different methods of depreciation for tax and book purposes, the computation of both tax and book gain or loss should be tested.
5. Ascertain whether assets acquired in trade-ins have been recorded correctly.
6. Determine that the amount of investment credit and depreciation recapture, if any, has been computed properly.

If the company's controls over the disposal of assets are inadequate, there is a possibility that an asset may be disposed of without being removed from the accounts. The auditor should be alert for this possibility. Indications of this practice may be noted during the course of discussions with company personnel; by reviewing plant modifications, changes in product lines, changes in insurance coverage, and changes in tax bills; or by reviewing miscellaneous income and repair and maintenance accounts for clues of dismantling or other alterations.

Assets may be transferred from one account to another. The auditor should test the recording of these transfers. If assets are transferred into accounts having significantly different depreciation rates, an explanation for the use of the different rates should be obtained from the client and the auditor must be satisfied that the reason is proper.

The auditor must also be alert for any indications of the existence of unrecorded assets or evidence that the company does not hold title to any of its recorded property. Information of this nature may be obtained through discussions with management personnel and by inspecting tax bills, rent receipts, insurance policies, and similar documents. The auditor also should make inquiries concerning the existence of significant idle properties since these assets should be separately identified in the financial statements under a title such as "Land Held for Future Use" or "Assets Held for Sale."

Changes in Allowances for Depreciation. Balances in the allowance for depreciation accounts for property, plant, and equipment will change due to disposals, transfers, and the current year's provision for depreciation. The auditor should determine that the balances applicable to assets which have been disposed of were recorded up to the date of disposal and then removed from the accounts. For assets transferred, the computation of depreciation before and after the date of transfer should be tested, and the auditor must determine whether the transfer has been recorded properly in the accounts.

Various alternative methods are acceptable in providing for depreciation of property, plant, and equipment. The method used in a particular circumstance will depend on such factors as the nature of the assets and the accounting and tax philosophy of management. The auditor should determine whether the methods used by the company are both reasonable and are applied consistently. Any change in method should be noted and the effect of the change shown in the working papers. In testing provisions for depreciation, the auditor normally performs the following tests:

1. Determines whether the estimated useful lives and salvage values established by the company for depreciable assets are reasonable under the circumstances.
2. Determines whether the company's methods of computing depreciation on additions and disposals made during the year are reasonable and followed consistently. For example, many companies follow the practice of providing for a half year's depreciation on all assets acquired or disposed of during the year. If a major facility is placed into service during the last month of the year, this practice would normally be unacceptable because of the significance of the amount involved.
3. Tests the arithematical accuracy of the computations of depreciation.
4. Determines over what period leasehold improvements are being amortized. Leasehold improvements should be written off over the life of the lease or the life of the improvement, whichever is shorter.
5. Summarizes depreciation expense for both book and tax purposes, and reconciles the book total with the credits to the allowance for depreciation accounts.

On certain engagements, depreciation lapsing schedules are maintained by the client and carried forward each year. These schedules provide a convenient means of computing the provision for depreciation. A copy of the schedules may be retained in the auditor's permanent file of working papers. Lapsing schedules would normally include information concerning the class of asset; the useful life or depreciation rate; the amount of asset additions and deductions by years; the accumulated asset balance; the depreciation expense by years; and the additions to, deductions from, and balance of accumulated depreciation.

Summary of Transactions for the Year. The auditor normally obtains a summary of the beginning and ending balances in the asset and related allowance accounts and the intervening transactions from the client. (Figure 12–2 is an example of such a summary.) The items included on this schedule should be traced by the auditor as follows:

1. Beginning balances to the prior year's working papers.
2. Total asset additions and disposals to the detail working papers.
3. The depreciation provision to lapsing schedules or other supporting data, and depreciation deductions to the schedule of gains or losses on disposals.
4. Ending balances to the general ledger accounts.

A reconciliation of the differences in the amounts shown for book and tax purposes for fixed assets, allowances for depreciation, depreciation expenses, gains or losses on disposals of fixed assets, and the treatment of the investment tax credit should be prepared. The auditor also should test the provision for any deferred income taxes resulting from such differences.

PREPAID EXPENSES AND DEFERRED CHARGES

Prepaid expenses, such as insurance, interest, rents, taxes, royalties, advertising service paid for but not yet received, and operating supplies usually are classified as current assets. Prepaid expenses which are chargeable to the operations of several years, or deferred charges such as issue costs of debt or costs of rearrangement of factory layout or relocation expenses, generally should be classified separately as noncurrent assets. Effective internal control over prepaid expenses and deferred charges usually focuses on the existence of adequate records and documentation and the existence of proper authorization for transactions.

The auditor's objective in examining prepaid expenses and deferred charges is to determine that these items represent proper charges to future operations and that the amounts, and their allocation to costs and expenses, are reported in accordance with generally accepted accounting principles applied on a consistent basis. Audit procedures will vary with the nature of the item. To illustrate, the procedures associated with prepaid insurance will now be reviewed.

Usually, prepaid insurance is not a significant item nor does it normally represent a control problem. Thus, the auditor should only spend a limited amount of time in examining it. Ordinarily the auditor should obtain from the company a schedule of prepaid insurance, showing coverage, premiums, and prepaid premiums. Policies should be inspected on a test basis to learn the nature and amount of coverage, name of the insured, location covered, premium, premium period, and any coinsurance features. The loss payable clause, which

FIGURE 12-2
Summary of property, plant, and equipment

	NAME client Maier	DATE 2-23-81
	PREPARED	
	APPROVED Williams 2-23-81	

SUMMARY OF PROPERTY, PLANT AND EQUIPMENT
DOUGLAS MANUFACTURING
12-31-80

	Cost					Allowances				
	Balance 1-1-80	Additions	Disposals (Cr)	Other Dr (Dr)	Balance 12-31-80	Balance 1-1-80	Provision	Reduction	Other (Dr) Cr	Balance 12-31-80
Land	1562000 ✔	1020 00			858200 ✔	-0-				-0-
Buildings:										
New York:										
No. 1	410828.10 M	20120.62		40120.00	470887.72	2206835.00 M	172647.12		1024820	2481973.2
No. 2	3021020.00 M	45902.02		(40120.00)	3078840.2	178462.11 M	106021.20		(1024820)	1788355.11
Boiler house	1562000.0 ✔		1562000		-0-	6200.10.9	131010.40	741050		-0-
Baltimore:										
Warehouse	1403020.10 M	30000			1433020.10 / 922072.844	621624.84	72963.40			694588
Leasehold improvements:										
Chicago	1489100.02 M	20211.6			1502331.18	924743.04 M	7621.49		1024820	1002957.9
Los Angeles	2621107.0 M	124821.4			2633528.4	1421628.04 M	96441.50		(1024820)	1518043.0
St. Louis	812920.44 M				812920.4	921020 M	1389.62			104998.2
Atlanta	36189.20 M				36189.20	432040.9 M	3859.64			8180.04
					5310652.64					2707799.5 ✔

Machinery and equipment:

New York:									
Straight line	320200.00 M		3021060		289989.40	1202062.14 M	3246.821	2164531	13108531
Declining balance	260200.00 M	2126801			2814680.1	1042264.4 M	27103145		13195793
Baltimore:									
Straight line	162220.01 M		20200.00		1420201	937483.04 M	81216.0	1564530	8524460
Declining balance	2924446.05 M	4210120	1210.00		333233725	1394627.04 M	1128650	102012	1397239.08
					10446.1467 ✓				488006.92 ✓
Automotive equipment	36380413 M	821000	6421.20		381691231	20483134 M	748890	429430	2382291 ✓
Office furniture & equipment:									
New York	604180.90 M	221440.21	844020		761609	2926431.14 M	328430	262480	2992381
Baltimore	9380401 M	2628.66	620.00		1128906	1026204 M	52061	10210	144471
Chicago	186102.04 M				1861020	9621404 M	71020		1033160
Los Angeles	620420404 M	1527020	1120.00		6669060	2062140 M	624010	642090	20440.60
St. Louis	518943 M	921020			839963	584204 M	82139		140559
Atlanta	8088464 M	962.40			96508.6	3240121.4 M	289440		352252
					19080124 ✓				6707583 ✓
	2710408.44 F	98296.83 F	9394200 F	-0-	281474324 F	247503.22 F	1578403 F	5816333 F	13461739.2 F
	Ⓐ	Ⓐ	Ⓐ	Ⓐ	Ⓐ	Ⓐ	Ⓐ	Ⓐ	

Procedures Performed by Maier:

M = Traced to prior years W/P.
F = Total & crossfooted to total
Ⓐ = See detail schedule.
✓ = Traced to general ledger.

FIGURE 12-3
Prepaid insurance

PREPAID INSURANCE
THE ABBOTT CORP.
12-31-80

NAME client Chetman 1-19-81
APPROVED Emey 1-21-81

Policy No.	Insurer	Type of Coverage and Property Insured	Amount of Insurance	Effective date	Expiration	Prepaid Premium 1-1-80	Premium	Prepaid Premium 12-31-80	Expense
F11568 ✓	Hartford Insur. Co.	Fire and extended coverage - St. Louis plant, office building and contents	5000000	6-1-78	6-1-81	(A) 1067666	2153282	3499006	717760
511663 ✓	Do	Use and occupancy - St. Louis plant, office building and contents	2000000	6-1-78	6-1-81	1328865	2589600	3596065	8603200
101514 ✓	Continental Insur. Co.	Fire and extended coverage - Plants and offices in Memphis, Houston, Dallas, Wichita, and Kansas City	45000000	7-1-78	7-1-81	6050726	12101463	20116908	46983818
77015 ✓	Rhode Island Insur. Co.	Use and occupancy - Manufactured offices in Memphis, Houston, Dallas, Wichita and Kansas City	5250000	2-1-78	2-1-80	4094188	5895565	21889845	19651188

285	B	Wolverine Ins. Co.	Auto liab - property damage - 300,000	500,000 Pr
			auto liab - bodily injury - all	1,000,000
			autos owned or hired by company	
			Representations	

	8-1-92 8-1-91	-0- 196500	345381	2020556 R 196500	1443326 -0-

EBB2714	Missouri Surety Co.	Blanket liability bond. Covers all

officers and employees. Policy
expired 12-31-80. Renewed for 1981 per
invoice of 1-2-81 from insurance co.
1980 payment charged direct to expense.

12-31-79 12-31-80	100000 126318 90	50574 79 7949792	30000 30000 7949792
	G/L	G/L	

Procedures Performed by Chairman

✓ Traced to general ledger.
1. Examined policy, type and amount of coverage.
A. Traced amount to prior year's E&W workpapers.
R. Recomputed; amount is reasonable.

See attached letter from company's insurance agent
discussing adequacy of coverage and confirming
the in force status of all policies.

Insurance expense: A/c 2690 5690

6273081	94
16767111	G/L
7949792	

478

indicates to whom payment is to be made in the event of a loss, may furnish information as to any possible pledging of the insured asset. Any new endorsements, which are changes to the original policy, should be noted. These will often alter the coverage and the premiums. Because insurance contracts are often complex, the auditor may wish to discuss the adequacy of the coverage and related matters with the company's insurance agent. The auditor may review premiums paid, amounts charged to expense during the year, and amounts prepaid at year end. Usually these amounts are not significant and do not necessitate a detailed review.

Figure 12–3 is an example of a prepaid insurance schedule.

INTANGIBLE ASSETS

The auditor's objective in examining intangible assets is to determine whether such assets have value to the company and whether the accounting for them, including their amortization, is in conformity with generally accepted accounting principles consistently applied. Intangibles such as patents, licenses, and similar rights are usually carried in the accounts at cost and amortized over their estimated useful lives. The auditor should examine any documents supporting the existence of these types of intangible assets and test the calculation of the amortization for the period. Also, the auditor should inquire if there is any change in the estimated period to be benefited.

Goodwill arises from the acquisition of a business when the purchase price is in excess of the amounts assigned to the net assets acquired. Goodwill acquired after October 31, 1970 (the date established in APB Opinion 17) is amortized from the date of acquisition by systematic charges to income over the estimated period to be benefited. According to Opinion 17 this period should not exceed 40 years. The auditor should review annually the unamortized goodwill to determine whether there are any changes in the estimated period to be benefited. Goodwill acquired prior to November 1, 1970, need not be amortized as long as the auditor determines annually that the asset has a continuing value over an indeterminate future period. The amortization of goodwill is not deductible for tax purposes. The auditor should test the amount of the recorded goodwill and the calculation of the amortization for the period.

MISCELLANEOUS ASSETS

Other assets that are commonly found on financial statements include: sundry receivables; properties not used in operations; and cash surrender value of life insurance. The objectives in examining these assets are: (1) to become satisfied that the asset does, in fact, exist; (2) to determine the basis of the carrying amount; and (3) to determine whether the asset is fairly presented in the financial statements in accordance with generally accepted accounting principles applied on a consistent basis. Generally, the auditor will spend only a small portion of the total audit time in examining such assets.

Audit procedures will vary depending on the nature of the asset in question. For example, cash surrender value will be tested by inspecting the policy and requesting confirmations from the insurance company. For properties not used in operations the auditor will determine how the properties were acquired, the basis of the carrying amounts, proper depreciation, and the intended disposition of these assets.

AUDIT MEMORANDA

The auditor should prepare a memorandum or memoranda that clearly state(s) the audit objectives, the work performed in regard to these other assets, the findings of the work performed, and the auditor's opinion as to whether each of these assets is fairly stated in conformity with generally accepted accounting principles applied on a consistent basis.

GLOSSARY

Long-term investments   Securities which are held for either long-term capital appreciation or to influence or control another company.

Temporary investments   All securities that have a ready market and that management intends to convert to cash within a short period of time.

Marketable equity securities   See footnote on page 461.

QUESTIONS AND PROBLEMS

12-1.   What is the central issue when considering internal control over prepaid expenses and deferred charges?

12-2.   Define temporary investments.

12-3.   What is the auditor's objective in examining securities?

12-4.   Outline the general procedures an auditor uses while examining securities.

12-5.   What are the auditor's objectives in examining prepaid expenses and deferred charges?

12-6.   What are the auditor's objectives in examining intangible assets? Give some examples of intangible assets.

12-7.   What are the auditor's objectives in the examination of property, plant, and equipment?

480

12-8. Should the auditor physically examine individual items of property, plant, or equipment in every case? Discuss.

12-9. What are the more important controls a company should implement over its property, plant, and equipment?

12-10. How does examination of property, plant, and equipment differ from the examination of some of the other asset accounts?

12-11. Describe the steps normally taken by the auditor to:

a. Support an addition to property, plant, and equipment.
b. Test assets built by the company.
c. Test a recorded disposal.
d. Test provisions for depreciation.

12-12. List and discuss briefly the purpose of all audit procedures which might reasonably be taken by an auditor to determine that all fixed asset retirements have been recorded on the books.

(AICPA, adapted)

12-13. Select the *best* answer for each of the following items:

a. In order to avoid the misappropriation of company-owned securities, which of the following is the *best* course of action that can be taken by the management of a company with a large portfolio of securities?
   1. Require that one trustworthy and bonded employee be responsible for access to the safekeeping area, where securities are kept.
   2. Require that employees who enter and leave the safekeeping area sign and record in a log the exact reason for their access.
   3. Require that employees involved in the safekeeping function maintain a subsidiary control ledger for securities on a current basis.
   4. Require that the safekeeping function for securities be assigned to a bank, that will act as a custodial agent.

b. In violation of company policy, the Jefferson City Company erroneously capitalized the cost of painting its warehouse. The CPA examining Jefferson City's financial statements most likely would learn of this by
   1. Reviewing the listing of construction work orders for the year.
   2. Discussing capitalization policies with the company controller.
   3. Observing, during his physical inventory observation, that the warehouse had been painted.
   4. Examining in detail a sample of construction work orders.

c. A company has additional temporary funds to invest. The board of directors decided to purchase temporary investments and assigned the future purchase and sale decisions to a responsible financial executive. The best person(s) to make periodic reviews of the investment activity should be

      1. An investment committee of the board of directors.
      2. The chief operating officer.
      3. The corporate controller.
      4. The treasurer.
   d. Which of the following is a customary audit procedure for the verification of the legal ownership of real property?
      1. Examination of correspondence with the corporate counsel concerning acquisition matters.
      2. Examination of ownership documents registered and on file at a public hall of records.
      3. Examination of corporate minutes and resolutions concerning the approval to acquire property, plant, and equipment.
      4. Examination of deeds and title guaranty policies on hand.

                               (AICPA, adapted)

12-14. A manufacturing company whose records you are auditing has $1,000,000 of Buildings and $3,000,000 of Machinery on its books. During the year you are covering in your audit, additions amounted to $100,000 for Buildings and $500,000 for Machinery. All additions were made through construction orders controlled by a Construction Work in Progress account which had a balance of $20,000 at the close of last year and $55,000 at the close of this year. Some of the additions were purchased and a number were constructed by the company. You are to state in detail the audit procedures you would follow in verification of the fixed asset additions during the year. Assume that your firm made the audit for the prior year.

                               (AICPA, adapted)

12-15. Public accounting firms often develop and use a questionnaire to investigate and record their inquiries into the client's internal control system in order to determine whether there are weaknesses in internal control. Prepare an internal control questionnaire pertaining to securities held by a medium-sized manufacturing company. You may want to refer back to Chapter 5 in answering this question.

                               (AICPA, adapted)

12-16. Terra Land Development Corporation is a closely held family corporation engaged in the business of purchasing large tracts of land, subdividing the tracts, and installing paved streets and utilities. The corporation does not construct buildings for the buyers of the land and does not have any affiliated construction companies. Undeveloped land is usually leased for farming until the corporation is ready to begin developing it.

    The corporation finances its land acquisitions by mortgages; the mortgagees require audited financial statements. This is your first audit of the company and you have now begun the examination of the financial statements for the year ended December 31, 1981.

    Your preliminary review of the accounts has indicated that the corporation would have had a highly profitable year except that the president and vice president, his son, were reimbursed for exceptionally large travel and entertainment expenses.

Required:

The corporation has three tracts of land in various stages of development. List the audit procedures to be employed in the verification of the physical existence and title to the corporation's three landholdings.

(AICPA, adapted)

12-17. In connection with a recurring examination of the financial statements of the Louis Manufacturing Company for the year ended December 31, 1981, you have been assigned the audit of the Manufacturing Equipment, Manufacturing Equipment—Accumulated Depreciation, and Repairs to Manufacturing Equipment accounts. Your review of Louis's policies and procedures has disclosed the following pertinent information:

1. The Manufacturing Equipment account includes the net invoice price plus related freight and installation costs for all of the equipment in Louis's manufacturing plant.
2. The Manufacturing Equipment and Accumulated Depreciation accounts are supported by a subsidiary ledger which shows the cost and accumulated depreciation for each piece of equipment.
3. An annual budget for capital expenditures of $1,000 or more is prepared by the budget committee and approved by the board of directors. Capital expenditures over $1,000 which are not included in this budget must be approved by the board of directors and variations of 20 percent or more must be explained to the board. Approval by the supervisor of production is required for capital expenditures under $1,000.
4. Company employees handle installation, removal, repair, and rebuilding of the machinery. Work orders are prepared for these activities and are subject to the same budgetary control as other expenditures. Work orders are not required for external expenditures.

Required:

a. Cite the major objectives of your audit of the Manufacturing Equipment, Manufacturing Equipment—Accumulated Depreciation, and Repairs to Manufacturing Equipment accounts. Do not include in this listing the auditing procedures designed to accomplish these objectives.
b. Prepare the portion of your audit program applicable to the review of 1981 additions to the Manufacturing Equipment account.

(AICPA, adapted)

12-18. You are the senior accountant in the audit of the Paulsen Grain Corporation whose business primarily involves the purchase, storage, and sale of grain products. The corporation owns several elevators located along navigable water routes and transports its grain by barge and rail. Your assistant submitted the following analysis for your review.

PAULSEN GRAIN CORPORATION
Advances Paid on Barges under Construction—a/c 210
December 31, 1981

Advances made:	
1/15/81—Ck. no. 3463—Jones Barge Construction Co.	$100,000*
4/13/81—Ck. no. 4129—Jones Barge Construction Co.	25,000*
6/19/81—Ck. no. 5396—Jones Barge Construction Co.	63,000*
Total Payments	$188,000
Deduct cash received 9/1/81 from Eastern Life Insurance Co.	188,000†
Balance per general ledger—12/31/81	-0-

* Examined approved check request and canceled check and traced to cash disbursements record.
† Traced to cash receipts book and to duplicate deposit ticket.

Required:

a. In what respects is the analysis incomplete for report purposes? (Do not include any discussion of specific auditing procedures.)
b. What two different types of contractual arrangements may be inferred from your assistant's analysis?
c. What additional auditing procedures would you suggest that your assistant perform before you accept the working paper as being complete?

(AICPA, adapted)

12-19. While auditing an urban bus company in a city of 50,000 population, you encounter the following situation:

a. You have checked an authorization for the purchase of five engines to replace the engines in five buses.
b. The cost of the old engines was removed from property and that of the new engines properly capitalized. The work was done in the company garage.
c. You find no credits for salvage or for the sale of any scrap metal at any time during the year. You have been in the garage and did not see the old engines.
d. The accountant is also treasurer and office manager. He is an authorized check signer and has access to all cash receipts. Upon inquiry he says he does not recall the sale of the old engines nor of any scrap metal.

Assuming that the engines were sold as scrap, outline all steps that this fact would cause you to take in connection with your audit. Also mention steps beyond those related directly to this one item.

(AICPA, adapted)

12-20. The Irving Manufacturing Company uses a system of shop orders in its plant. This system includes a series of orders for construction and installation of fixed assets, another series for retirement of assets, and a third series for maintenance work. There are "standing order" numbers for minor repetitive maintenance items and special orders for unusual or major maintenance items.

In connection with a regular annual audit of the Irving Manufacturing Company, prepare a program for work to be done on the maintenance orders. Assume that there appears to be reasonable internal control in the company. Prepare the program to avoid doing any more work than is necessary to meet acceptable auditing standards and explain the purpose or objective of each of your proposed steps.

(AICPA, adapted)

12–21. In the audit of fixed assets an auditor has several problems. For example, the auditor must be satisfied that all of the owned assets are recorded. Also, the auditor must be satisfied that the amounts at which the assets are recorded are in accordance with generally accepted accounting principles.

In connection with the annual audit of the fixed assets of a medium-sized manufacturing company, state the general procedures by which the auditor can be satisfied *(a)* that all of the owned assets are recorded, and *(b)* that the recorded amounts are proper. Briefly explain how each procedure will help to satisfy the auditor and to which of the two problems it is applicable. Do not include depreciation provisions as a part of these problems.

(AICPA, adapted)

12–22. As a result of highly profitable operations over a number of years, Eastern Manufacturing Corporation accumulated a substantial temporary investment portfolio. In his examination of the financial statements for the year ended December 31, 1981, the following information came to the attention of the corporation's CPA:

1. The manufacturing operations of the corporation resulted in an operating loss for the year.
2. In 1981, the corporation placed the securities making up the temporary investment portfolio with a financial institution which will serve as custodian of the securities. Formerly the securities were kept in the corporation's safe-deposit box in the local bank.
3. On December 22, 1981, the corporation sold and then repurchased on the same day a number of securities that had appreciated greatly in value. Management stated that the purpose of the sale and repurchases was to establish a higher cost and book value for the securities and to avoid the reporting of a loss for the year.

Required:

a. List the objectives of the CPA's examination of the Temporary Investment account.

b. Under what conditions would the CPA accept a confirmation of

securities on hand from the custodian in lieu of inspecting and
counting the securities himself?

c. What disclosure, if any, of the sale and repurchase of the securities would the CPA recommend for the financial statements?
If the client accepts the CPA's recommendations for disclosure,
what effect, if any, would the sale and repurchase have upon the
CPA's opinion on the financial statements? Discuss.

(AICPA, adapted)

12-23. You are in charge of the audit of the financial statements of the Demot
Corporation for the year ended December 31, 1981. The corporation
has had the policy of investing its surplus funds in temporary investments. Its stock and bond certificates are kept in a safe-deposit box in
a local bank. Only the president or the treasurer of the corporation
has access to the box.

You were unable to obtain access to the safe-deposit box on December 31 because neither the president nor the treasurer was available. Arrangements were made for your assistant to accompany the
treasurer to the bank on January 11 to examine the securities. Your
assistant has never examined securities that were being kept in a
safe-deposit box and requires instructions. He should be able to inspect all securities on hand in an hour.

Required:

a. List the instructions that you would give your assistant regarding
the examination of the stock and bond certificates kept in the
safe-deposit box. Include in your instructions the details of the
securities to be examined and the reasons for examining these
details.

b. When he returned from the bank your assistant reported that the
treasurer had entered the box on January 4. The treasurer stated
that he had removed an old photograph of the corporation's original building. The photograph was loaned to the local chamber of
commerce for display purposes. List the additional audit procedures that are required because of the treasurer's action.

(AICPA, adapted)

12-24. You are engaged in the audit of the financial statements of the Sandy
Core Company for the year ended December 31, 1981. Sandy Core
Company sells lumber and building supplies at wholesale and retail;
it has total assets of $1 million and a stockholders' equity of $500,000.

The company's records show an investment of $100,000 for 100
shares of common stock of one of its customers, the Home Building
Corporation. You learn that Home Building Corporation is closely
held and that its capital stock, consisting of 1,000 shares of issued and
outstanding common stock, has no published or quoted market value.

Examination of your client's cash disbursements record reveals an
entry of a check for $100,000 drawn on January 23, 1981, to Mr. Felix

486

Wolfe, who is said to be the former holder of the 100 shares of stock. Mr. Wolfe is president of the Sandy Core Company. Sandy Core Company has no other investments.

Required:

List the auditing procedures you would employ in connection with the $100,000 investment of your client in the capital stock of the Home Building Corporation.

(AICPA, adapted)

12–25. In connection with his examination of the financial statements of Belasco Chemicals, Inc., Kenneth Mack, CPA, is considering the necessity of inspecting securities on the balance-sheet date, May 31, 1981, or at some other date. The securities held by Belasco include negotiable bearer bonds, which are kept in a safe in the treasurer's office, and miscellaneous stocks and bonds kept in a safe-deposit box at The Merchants Bank. Both the negotiable bearer bonds and the miscellaneous stocks and bonds are material to proper presentation of Belasco's financial position.

Required:

a. What are the factors that Mr. Mack should consider in determining the necessity for inspecting these securities on May 31, 1981 as opposed to other dates?

b. Assume that Mr. Mack plans to send a member of his staff to Belasco's offices and The Merchants Bank on May 31, 1981 to make the security inspection. What instructions should he give to this staff member as to the conduct of the inspection and the evidence to be included in the audit working papers? (Note: Do not discuss the valuation of securities; the income from securities; or the examination of information contained in the books and records of the company.)

c. Assume that Mr. Mack finds it impracticable to send a member of his staff to Belasco's offices and The Merchants Bank on May 31, 1981. What alternative procedures may he employ to assure himself that the company had physical possession of its securities on May 31, 1981 if the securities are inspected (1) May 28, 1981? (2) June 5, 1981?

(AICPA, adapted)

12–26. The cashier of a bank is also treasurer of a local charity. He is authorized to purchase $10,000 in U.S. bonds for the bank and a similar amount for the charity. He makes both purchases but misappropriates the bonds belonging to the charity. When an audit is made of the charity, the treasurer borrows the bonds from the bank and places them in the charity's safe-deposit box.

Required:

Discuss the internal controls you would recommend for the charity to prevent the occurrence of this manipulation.

(AICPA, adapted)

Learning Objectives

Study of the material in this chapter is designed to achieve several learning objectives. These include:

1. An understanding of the auditor's objectives in examining the various equity and income statement accounts including trade accounts payable; notes payable; accrued payables; long-term debt; loss contingencies; litigation, claims, and assessments; stockholders' equity; revenues; and expenses (including payrolls).
2. A knowledge of the essential elements of internal control over equity and income statement items.
3. An understanding of the necessary steps in the audit of equity and income statement items.
4. An understanding of the audit aspects of segment information.
5. An understanding of the need to be alert for related party transactions and to see that they are properly disclosed.
6. An understanding of the objectives and the procedures used when an accountant is engaged to review interim financial information.

13

Creditors' and Owners' Equities; Income Statement Accounts; and Other Matters

LIABILITIES

Chapters 9 through 12 have discussed the auditor's examination of assets. Since there is a tendency for assets to be overstated, the auditor normally is primarily concerned with detecting any overstatement. In the case of liabilities, the subject of this section, there is a tendency for them to be understated or omitted altogether. Thus, in the examination of liabilities, the auditor normally is more concerned with detecting any understatement or omission. The proper valuation of recorded liabilities usually is not difficult for the auditor to determine. However, it is often much more difficult for the auditor to detect an understatement or omission of a liability.

Internal Control over Liabilities

The internal control over liabilities is closely related to the internal control over cash receipts and cash disbursements. Many of the liabilities incurred by a business are the result of transactions that involve an inflow of cash. Examples of these types of transactions would include borrowing from a bank or issuing long-term bonds. Likewise, the payment (reduction) of a liability usually involves a cash disbursement. Thus, the portions of Chapter 9 that relate to internal control over receipts and disbursements also relate to the internal control over liabilities. Similarly, the purchase of inventory normally is a credit transaction. As a consequence, purchases often will result in the creation of a liability. Thus, the portions of Chapter 11 that relate to internal control over inventory also relate to the control of liabilities.

A strong system of internal control over liabilities requires that the

489

business specify in advance the individual(s) who are authorized to incur or renew each particular type of liability. Additionally, when liabilities are paid there should be a proper system of authorization and documentation of the payment.

Audit Procedures for Liabilities

Testing the Purchases Journal, Invoice Register, or Voucher Register. The procedures used by the auditor in testing purchases usually involve tests of the purchases journal, invoice register, or voucher register (whichever is used). These tests made on transactions selected by the auditor typically involve:

1. *Comparing Vouchers and Purchase Invoices with the Register or Journal.* As a part of this procedure, the auditor will test the accounting distribution of expenditures; inspect approvals for disbursements; examine authorization for the purchase and evidence of the receipt of goods; and test the arithmetical accuracy of the recorded amounts. The items selected for examination by the auditor should comprise a representative sample. From the information noted, the auditor will decide whether the distribution entered on the voucher or invoice represents the proper accounting treatment for the transaction. The auditor must be familiar with the company's current chart of accounts if this test is to be performed effectively. The accounting distribution shown on the vouchers (or invoices) tested should be traced to the postings in the register or journal.

2. *Checking the Footings of the Register or Journal and Tracing of Postings.* Footings of the register or journal should be checked and the resulting totals traced to the general and subsidiary ledgers (e.g., expense or inventory ledgers) to determine whether the vouchers or invoices were in fact entered in the accounts indicated in the distribution.

3. *Accounting for the Numerical Sequence of Documents.* The numerical sequence of the vouchers should be tested by the auditor.

Trade Accounts Payable. Trade accounts payable are usually numerous and significant in total amount. Thus, they require the careful scrutiny of the auditor. It is, of course, important that the auditor test the recorded amounts. It is even more important that a thorough search be made for amounts not recorded.

The failure to record all liabilities may be due to carelessness, or it may be a deliberate attempt on the part of the client to present false or misleading financial statements—referred to as "window dressing." This "window dressing" may be accomplished, for example, by holding the cash disbursements book open after year-end or by curtailing loans at the balance-sheet date and refinancing them shortly thereafter. The purpose of this manipulation is not to present an improved profit picture but to create an artificially high current ratio, thus giving the appearance of increased liquidity.

Some companies may, by their very nature, be somewhat conservative. In these cases, care should be taken to ascertain whether their liabilities are overstated rather than understated.

The procedures used by the auditor to examine trade accounts payable are determined by an evaluation of the effectiveness of the company's internal controls. As indicated earlier, it is important that the auditor investigate these controls thoroughly during the course of the examination. It may be determined that incoming invoices are promptly and properly recorded, in which case the auditor may justifiably decide that the scope of the search for unrecorded items may be reduced. Alternatively, it may be found that: (1) incoming invoices are not recorded at all; (2) invoices are routinely transferred between departments with the consequent risk of loss; or (3) other procedures are lax on the assumption that creditors will follow up on any unpaid debts sooner or later. In these situations, the auditor must make extensive tests for unrecorded liabilities. This discussion concerning the auditor's examination of trade accounts payable is divided into three sections: trial balance of accounts payable; vendors' statements; and the search for unrecorded liabilities.

Trial Balance of Accounts Payable. The auditor normally begins the tests of accounts payable by obtaining a trial balance of the trade accounts payable from the client. This trial balance may consist of a listing of open items in the voucher register, of the items in the open invoice file, of the open items in the accounts payable ledger, or of remittance advices. The form of the listing will, of course, vary from client to client. In some instances, the trial balance will simply be an adding machine tape of the items.

The auditor should test the arithmetic accuracy of the trial balance and reconcile the total to the general ledger control account. Ordinarily, the auditor will examine invoices or other supporting documents for selected items. This procedure, along with the examination of selected vendors' statements, helps the auditor ascertain whether the recorded amounts are fairly stated.

The auditor should also review the detail of the trial balance for possible items which are not properly classified as trade accounts payable, e.g., accounts with affiliates; amounts payable to officers, directors, stockholders or employees; wages; and taxes. Debit balances in vendors' accounts, if material, should be examined in the same way as accounts receivable, including written confirmation. If debit balances are substantial in amount, they should be removed from accounts payable and reclassified as an asset.

The auditor should review the trial balance for accounts payable which are past due. If there are only a few large past-due accounts, the reason frequently is that their amounts are in dispute. The auditor should investigate this possibility, remembering that the actual amounts payable may differ widely from those recorded. On the other hand, many past-due accounts usually indicate a shortage of working capital. These recorded amounts are less likely to differ from actual amounts, and they need not all be examined.

Vendors' Statements. The auditor's examination of trade accounts payable normally will involve the reconciliation of selected vendors' statements to the year-end accounts payable trial balance. This is accomplished by the auditor asking the client for copies of the vendors' statements that have been received by the company.

The auditor sometimes will confirm accounts payable directly with suppliers. Confirmation of accounts payable is not absolutely required as is the confirmation of accounts receivable. In confirming receivables the auditor is concerned with overstatement of the asset and is testing the value of the receivable. In contrast, with accounts payable the auditor is essentially concerned with possible understatement of the account. Consequently, confirmation would be of little value where the auditor is not aware of the existence of a particular supplier (whose account is not recorded).

In confirming payables, the auditor asks the client to request that the suppliers send statements directly to the auditor. Often confirmations are sent to principal suppliers (regardless of the size of the balance in the account). The number of suppliers to whom confirmation requests are sent will vary with each engagement. Where internal control is strong and the condition of the records is good, requests made to a limited number of major suppliers ordinarily are considered to be sufficient. If the records are unsatisfactory, if important accounts appear to be in error or in dispute, or if there is some other reason to believe that the accounts payable balance is misstated, a more extensive confirmation of payables may be necessary. These requests are handled in the same general manner and using the same controls as were described for the confirmation of receivables.

The auditor usually can obtain a current list of the major suppliers of the company from its purchasing department. Also the auditor may obtain indications of the identity of the major suppliers from compliance testing, from inventory pricing tests, from the prior year's working papers, and from discussions with the client's employees. Each request for vendors' statements (see Figure 13–1) should include the exact name of the company (including division and location if applicable), the date of the statement requested, and the auditor's business reply envelope. Vendors' statements should be requested by

FIGURE 13–1
Request for statement of account

REQUEST FOR STATEMENT OF ACCOUNT

Wolston Hardware Co.
105 Main Street
Los Angeles, California

Gentlemen:

Our auditors are making an examination of our financial statements and wish to obtain a complete statement of our account with you as of the date shown below. Please furnish them with details of our indebtedness to you on open account, notes, acceptances, loans, or contracts. If secured, state nature and extent of security.

Your prompt reply made directly to our auditors, Ernst & Whinney, will be appreciated. A reply envelope which requires no postage is enclosed for your convenience.

Very truly yours,
Acme Manufacturing Co.

John Davis

Accounts Payable Supervisor

Statement requested as of <u>December 31, 1980</u>

Please send statement to <u>Los Angeles, California</u> *Office of Ernst & Whinney*

---

the auditor at an early date so they will be received before the field work is completed. It usually is desirable to mail the requests on or prior to the balance-sheet date. If a vendor fails to reply to a request, a second request may be sent.

The auditor should reconcile any differences noted between the accounts payable trial balance and the vendors' statements—for both those statements received directly by the auditor and those obtained from the company. In some instances, client personnel may be asked to prepare the reconciliation under the general supervision of the auditor. Of course, statements received directly by the auditor must be under his or her control. The auditor will test the differences shown on the reconciliation by tracing payments in transit to the cash disbursements record, by examining correspondence and other supporting documents for debit memos which have not been processed by the vendor, and by obtaining explanations for any other differences.

Search for Unrecorded Liabilities. One of the greatest dangers in the audit of liabilities is that certain material amounts in existence will remain unrecorded. Thus, the auditor must be satisfied that the search for unrecorded liabilities will disclose all liabilities of a material amount.

A schedule of any unrecorded liabilities noted by the auditor during the examination should be prepared for inclusion in the working papers. This schedule should indicate the name of the vendor, the date of the invoice, the date goods or services were received, the amount, and the account to be charged. The balance sheet and income statement effect of the unrecorded liabilities listed on the schedule should be summarized at the bottom of the schedule. The auditor's search for unrecorded liabilities will normally include the following steps.

1. Reconcile vendors' statements to the accounts payable trial balance.
2. Review transactions recorded subsequent to the balance-sheet date to determine whether any significant transactions apply to the period under audit.
3. Review unprocessed invoices for items which should be included as liabilities in the period under audit; that is, where a commitment has been made and a liability exists as of the balance-sheet date.
4. Examine receiving reports for items received on or prior to the balance-sheet date but for which no payment has been made or any liability established.
5. Inquire of accounting and purchasing personnel as to whether they have any knowledge of any significant unrecorded liabilities.
6. Inquire about consignment sales. The records should be reviewed to ascertain whether the liability and related expense have been recorded in the proper period for all sales made from consigned stock.

The above procedures are concerned only with the search for unrecorded trade accounts payable. The search for all unrecorded liabilities is more extensive, and includes an investigation of such diverse sources of information as the corporate minutes, legal fees, and other related areas.

Notes Payable. The auditor's objective in examining notes payable is to determine whether the balance is fairly stated at the balance-sheet date. It is important to determine that all notes payable have been recorded on the books in accordance with generally accepted accounting principles applied on a consistent basis.

The audit procedures for notes payable may include the following:

1. Obtain a schedule of notes payable from the client. The schedule should show the details relating to the notes (dates, payees, amounts, interest rates, collateral, endorsers or guarantors, and accrued or prepaid interest).
2. Confirm the outstanding notes directly with the creditors. The information that should be confirmed includes: principal amount, maturity date, date to which interest is paid, collateral, and information as to noncompliance with the loan agreement.
3. Consider requesting confirmations from lenders from which the client borrowed money during the year but from whom there is presently no loan outstanding recorded on the books. Such a confirmation might uncover an unrecorded note payable.
4. Compare liabilities reported in the confirmations with the recorded book amounts. Any differences should be investigated.
5. Obtain and review copies of notes or loan agreements. The auditor should investigate compliance with any restrictive provisions affecting the financial statements that may appear in such agreements.
6. Test the computation of accrued or prepaid interest.

Accrued Payables. Accrued payables are generally those liabilities which have been incurred for which invoices normally are not received from creditors. They must be computed periodically from other sources. Examples of typical accrued payable items include payrolls, taxes, commissions and bonuses, interest, pension and profit-sharing plans, and sundry expenses.

The examination of accrued payables consists of two major categories of tests: (1) testing the recorded accruals for reasonableness, and (2) determining whether all accruals have been recorded. As is the case with most liabilities, the latter is generally the more difficult. The auditor may obtain indications of the existence of accrued payables during any phase of the audit examination. For example, a licensing agreement may require that an accrual for royalties be made; notes payable may require an accrual for interest; and a profit-sharing or pension plan may require an accrual for payment of future benefits to employees.

Often the auditor is able to obtain from the company the detailed computations of the accruals which have been made and recorded. The procedures used by the auditor to test the accruals depend on their nature, and may include such work as: testing the computations, examining underlying contracts or agreements, reviewing subsequent payments, and comparing the amounts accrued with those which were made at prior dates.

Federal, state, and foreign taxes have an important effect on both the income statement and the balance sheet. In auditing income taxes payable, the auditor should consider:

1. Obtaining an analysis of changes in the income tax liability accounts during the period under review.
    a. The auditor should reconcile additions to the accrual with the appropriate expense account.
    b. The auditor should examine the nature of payments and the year to which they apply. Paid checks or other evidence of payment should be examined.
2. Obtaining and testing data necessary for allocation of income to various states, possessions, or foreign countries. The auditor should investigate the possibility of liability for income or similar taxes for which returns have not been filed by the client.
3. Reviewing the computation of the provision for income taxes for the period under review.
4. Ascertaining the status of returns filed for prior years. The extent to which returns have been examined by taxing authorities should be noted. Information should be obtained on changes made by taxing authorities and the effect of any unsettled matters. The auditor should give consideration to questionable items that may be present in returns filed which have not been examined and also their effect on future years.

The auditor should also consider the need for, or proper use of, a deferred income tax account.

Long-Term Debt. The auditor's objective in the examination of long-term debt is to determine whether the amount of long-term indebtedness at the balance-sheet date is properly stated, to test that the accrual of interest thereon is fairly stated, to determine whether all of the provisions of the indenture or other agreement have been met, and to determine that adequate disclosure is made in the financial statements. The audit procedures generally employed to satisfy these objectives include the following:

1. Review changes which occurred in long-term debt during the period and test such changes by examining the related supporting documents.

2. Confirm the principal amount, maturity date, date to which interest is paid, collateral security, and other pertinent details of each long-term liability directly with the creditor or trustee and request information as to any known noncompliance with the loan agreement.

3. Read the bond indentures or other agreements, noting the principal provisions affecting the financial statements (particularly such features as sinking fund or redemption requirements), requirements as to current or other asset amounts and/or related ratios, dividend or surplus restrictions, pledge of assets and deposits of proceeds from disposition thereof, and insurance requirements. The auditor must determine if such requirements or restrictions have been met. Copies of all agreements normally are included in the auditor's working papers.

4. Inspect bonds redeemed, retired, or surrendered during the period, including those held by the company in the treasury. Obtain confirmation of bonds retired or held by the trustee in sinking funds or other funds.

5. Ascertain the amount of the long-term debt maturing within one year. Determine the amount, if any, that is required to be paid into sinking funds or other funds within one year.

6. Test the computation of interest expense for the period including the amortization of any premium or discount, and test the accrued interest at the end of the period.

7. Classify indebtedness as to secured and unsecured obligations and as to type or classification—such as to banks, affiliates, officers, and stockholders.

There are several nonroutine transactions and events that can affect a company's debt structure. Several of these transactions have been addressed by the Accounting Principles Board and the Financial Accounting Standards Board and have resulted in the following pronouncements: (1) *APB Opinion No. 26*, "Early Extinguishment of Debt"; (2) *FASB Statement No. 4*, "Reporting Gains and Losses from Extinguishment of Debt"; (3) *FASB Statement No. 6*, "Classification of Short-Term Obligations Expected to be Refinanced"; (4) *FASB Statement No. 15*, "Accounting by Debtors and Creditors for Troubled Debt Restructurings"; and (5) *FASB Interpretation No. 8*, "Classification of a Short-Term Obligation Repaid Prior to Being Replaced by a Long-Term Security." An in-depth discussion of these areas is beyond the scope of this book. However, the auditor should recognize circumstances when these pronouncements are applicable, and be able to research the accounting and auditing requirements for a specific situation.

498

Loss Contingencies. *FASB Statement No. 5* defines a contingency as:

> . . . an existing condition, situation, or set of circumstances involving uncertainty as to possible gain [gain contingency] . . . or loss [loss contingency] . . . to an enterprise that will ultimately be resolved when one or more future events occur or fail to occur.[1]

FASB Statement No. 5 was issued in recognition of the variety of accounting practices that had developed with respect to contingencies—primarily contingent liabilities. Contingent liabilities are loss contingencies that arise as the result of the occurrence of a liability. A loss contingency is a broader concept since in addition to contingent liabilities it also includes possible impairment of assets.[2]

Loss contingencies arise, for example, from endorsements on notes, guarantees of indebtedness, repurchase commitments, pending litigation, probable tax assessments, decisions to self-insure, threat of expropriation, and establishment of a warranty policy.

The auditor should be alert to the existence of loss contingencies during all phases of an audit. Bank confirmations may disclose that guarantees and endorsements of loans and open letters of credit exist. The review of contracts, lease agreements, sales and purchase commitments, and minutes of meetings may disclose loss contingencies.

FASB Statement No. 5 indicates that loss contingencies should be accrued only if both of the following exist:

a. Information available prior to issuance of the financial statements indicates that it is probable that an asset had been impaired or a liability had been incurred at the date of the financial statements. . . . It is implicit in this condition that it must be probable that one or more future events will occur confirming the fact of the loss.

b. The amount of the loss can be reasonably estimated. [par. 8]

Furthermore, if the above conditions are not met *FASB No. 5* indicates that ". . . disclosure of the contingency shall be made when there is at least a reasonable possibility that a loss or an additional loss may have been incurred. . . . " [par. 10]

The auditor should request a letter from the client's legal counsel setting forth all pertinent information regarding litigation, claims, and

[1]*Statement of Financial Accounting Standards No. 5*, "Accounting for Contingencies," Financial Accounting Standards Board, 1975. [par. 1] Copyright © by Financial Accounting Standards Board. High Ridge Park, Stamford, Connecticut 06905, U.S.A. Reprinted with permission. Copies of the complete document are available from the FASB.

[2]See Donald E. Kieso and Jerry J. Weygandt, *Intermediate Accounting*, 2d ed. (Wiley/Hamilton, 1977), p. 411.

assessments. The authoritative pronouncement on this subject is *SAS No. 12*, "Inquiry of a Client's Lawyer Concerning Litigation, Claims, and Assessments." In many cases, the nature, timing, and evaluation of the responses to these inquiries may prove to be an involved and complicated process. *SAS No. 12* is discussed in detail in the next section.

Litigation, Claims, and Assessments.[3] *SAS No. 12* states that with respect to litigation, claims, and assessments, the auditor should obtain evidential matter concerning the following:

    a. The existence of a condition, situation, or set of circumstances indicating an uncertainty as to the possible loss to an entity arising from litigation, claims, and assessments.

    b. The period in which the underlying cause for legal action occurred.

    c. The degree of probability of an unfavorable outcome.

    d. The amount or range of potential loss.

Management is the primary source of information about litigation, claims, and assessments. According to *SAS No. 12*, the audit procedures should include:

a. Questioning and discussing with management the policies and procedures ". . . for identifying, evaluating, and accounting for . . ." these items (litigation, claims, and assessments).

b. Obtaining from management a description and evaluation of such items ". . . that existed at the date of the balance sheet being reported on, and during the period from the balance sheet date to the date the information is furnished, including an identification of those matters referred to legal counsel, and obtain assurances from management, ordinarily in writing, that they have disclosed all such matters required to be disclosed by Statement of Financial Accounting Standards No. 5."

c. Examining all documents in the client's possession concerning such items, including correspondence and invoices sent by any attorney.[4]

d. Obtaining assurance from management (ordinarily in writing), that all unasserted claims have been disclosed ". . . that the lawyer has

---

[3]This section is based on *Statement on Auditing Standards No. 12*, "Inquiry of a Client's Lawyer Concerning Litigation, Claims, and Assessments," American Institute of Certified Public Accountants, 1976. Copyright © 1976 by the American Institute of Certified Public Accountants, Inc.

[4] According to *AICPA Professional Standards, Volume 1, AU Section 9337*, "Inquiry of a Client's Lawyer Concerning Litigation, Claims, and Assessments: Auditing Interpretations of AU Section 337," " . . . in recognition of the public interest in protecting the confidentiality of lawyer-client communications . . . [*SAS No. 12*] is not intended to require an auditor to examine documents that the client identifies as subject to the lawyer-client privilege." [Section 9337.09]

500

advised them are probable of assertion and must be disclosed in accordance with Statement of Financial Accounting Standards No. 5." With the client's permission, the auditor ". . . should inform the lawyer that the client has given the auditor this assurance."

e. Requesting management to send a letter of inquiry to any lawyer with whom management consulted regarding such items.

In addition, *SAS No. 12* suggests that audit procedures performed for other purposes may disclose litigation, claims, and assessments. Some of the examples of such procedures suggested by *SAS No. 12* include: (1) reading the minutes of meetings (e.g. board of directors, stockholders); (2) reading various client legal documents (e.g., contracts, lease agreements) and correspondence with government agencies; and (3) looking at bank confirmations for information concerning guarantees.

SAS No. 12 suggests that letters of inquiry to the client's lawyers ask the lawyers to provide corroboration of the information furnished by management concerning litigation, claims, and assessments. See Fig-

Figure 13–2
List of items that should appear in an inquiry of a client's lawyer

The matters that should be covered in a letter of audit inquiry include, but are not limited to, the following:

a. Identification of the company, including subsidiaries, and the date of the examination.

b. A list prepared by management (or a request by management that the lawyer prepare a list) that describes and evaluates pending or threatened litigation, claims, and assessments with respect to which the lawyer has been engaged and to which he has devoted substantive attention on behalf of the company in the form of legal consultation or representation.

c. A list prepared by management that describes and evaluates unasserted claims and assessments that management considers to be probable of assertion, and that, if asserted, would have at least a reasonable possibility of an unfavorable outcome, with respect to which the lawyer has been engaged and to which he has devoted substantive attention on behalf of the company in the form of legal consultation or representation.

d. As to each matter listed in item *b,* a request that the lawyer either furnish the following information or comment on those matters as to which his views may differ from those stated by management, as appropriate:

(1) A description of the nature of the matter, the progress of the case to date, and the action the company intends to take (for example, to contest the matter vigorously or to seek an out-of-court settlement).

Figure 13-2 (Continued)
List of items that should appear in an inquiry of a client's lawyer

---

    (2)   An evaluation of the likelihood of an unfavorable outcome and an estimate, if one can be made, of the amount or range of potential loss.

    (3)   With respect to a list prepared by management, an identification of the omission of any pending or threatened litigation, claims, and assessments or a statement that the list of such matters is complete.

  e. As to each matter listed in item *c*, a request that the lawyer comment on those matters as to which his views concerning the description or evaluation of the matter may differ from those stated by management.

  f. A statement by the client that the client understands that whenever, in the course of performing legal services for the client with respect to a matter recognized to involve an unasserted possible claim or assessment that may call for financial statement disclosure, the lawyer has formed a professional conclusion that the client should disclose or consider disclosure concerning such possible claim or assessment, the lawyer, as a matter of professional responsibility to the client, will so advise the client and will consult with the client concerning the question of such disclosure and the applicable requirements of Statement of Financial Accounting Standards No. 5.

  g. A request that the lawyer confirm whether the understanding described in item *f* is correct.

  h. A request that the lawyer specifically identify the nature of and reasons for any limitation on his response.

Inquiry need not be made concerning matters that are not considered material, provided the client and the auditor have reached an understanding on the limits of materiality for this purpose.

Source: This figure is quoted from *SAS No. 12*, "Inquiry of a Client's Lawyer Concerning Litigation, Claims, and Assessments." Copyright © 1976 by the American Institute of Certified Public Accountants, Inc.

ure 13-2 for a description of items that should appear in such a letter. *SAS No. 12* states that "a lawyer's refusal to furnish the information requested in an inquiry letter either in writing or orally . . . would be a limitation on the scope of the auditor's examination sufficient to preclude an unqualified opinion. . . ."

SAS No. 12 notes that "a lawyer may be unable to respond concerning the likelihood of an unfavorable outcome of litigation, claims, and assessments or the amount or range of potential loss, because of inherent uncertainties." In such a case, the auditor normally ". . . will conclude that the financial statements are affected by an uncertainty concerning the outcome of a future event which is not susceptible of reasonable estimation." *(SAS No. 12)* If material, the auditor normally will conclude that an unqualified opinion should not be rendered.

Items for Letter of Representation

The auditor should consider asking the client to include in a letter of representation matters concerning liabilities. The letter might contain statements asserting that:

1. The liabilities to be reported in the financial statements are at their proper amounts and there are no material unrecorded liabilities.
2. All loss contingencies have been identified.
3. All assets which have been pledged or assigned have been identified.

STOCKHOLDERS' EQUITY

Internal Control

Capital Stock. Effective internal control over capital stock (both common and preferred) usually will be present if a corporation utilizes an independent outside registrar (to see that the stock is properly issued) and an independent outside transfer agent (to maintain the records of the stock and handle stock transfers). If a corporation does not utilize such agencies, the stock recordkeeping and transfer functions should be assigned to a responsible designated officer or employee of the client. This individual should maintain detailed records that should be reconciled periodically to the general ledger control accounts. The certificates should be controlled carefully. Canceled certificates should be kept on file. The certificate books should be reconciled periodically to both the general ledger control accounts and the detailed records.

Dividends. Effective internal control over dividends usually will be present if a corporation utilizes an independent outside agency for the payment of dividends. In such an instance, the board of directors should notify this agent of the details of the dividend declaration and of the shareholders who are entitled to receive the dividends. If a company has a stock transfer agent, the use of the transfer agent to distribute dividends relieves the company of sending a stockholder list (the transfer agent maintains that list). The corporation should then send the agent the funds required to pay the dividends. If, on the other hand, the company handles the payment of dividends itself, a bank account which is separate from those normally used by the company may be used to isolate and facilitate control over these transactions.

Auditing Stockholders' Equity

The objectives of the auditor's examination of stockholders' equity include: (1) a determination of the propriety of the charges and credits to the accounts; (2) a determination of the propriety of the presentation of the accounts on the balance sheet; and (3) a determination that the client has complied with relevant legal requirements.

The audit procedures employed in examining stockholders' equity accounts include checking the exact nature and terms of each issue of capital stock and the number of shares authorized. This usually is accomplished by examining the articles of incorporation (and amendments thereto, if any). The auditor will determine the number of shares of capital stock issued and outstanding as of the balance-sheet date. Furthermore, the auditor will normally ask the registrar to confirm the number of shares issued. If the company has no independent registrar, the auditor must check a listing of stock certificate stubs or the stockholders' ledger to obtain this data.

The auditor also will account for all changes which have taken place in the capital accounts during the period under review. The minutes of the board of directors' and shareholders' meetings and any amendments to the charter or articles of incorporation should reveal any changes which have occurred in the capital structure of the company. The auditor should review the documents relating to all changes in the capital accounts. Data regarding changes in stock options and the information which is necessary in order to comply with the reporting requirements of stock exchanges and of the SEC should be obtained for the working papers.

The auditor will obtain pertinent information as to warrants outstanding and shares reserved for purposes such as future conversion of debt or preferred stock. The number of shares of treasury stock held as of the balance-sheet date should be accounted for by inspecting certificates or by requesting confirmation from the custodian or registrar. The auditor should examine the position of the company with respect to compliance with all stock provisions that are in effect.

It usually will be necessary for the auditor to prepare an analysis of the retained earnings account for the period under review, giving consideration to the propriety of charges and credits to this account.

The auditor also should determine if there are any dividend restrictions imposed by the provisions of a capital stock issue, loan agreement, or indenture and verify the amount of the dividend restriction at the balance-sheet date. Restrictions on retained earnings imposed by the existence of treasury stock also should be considered. The auditor will refer to minutes of the directors' meetings to see that all dividends paid were properly declared and to determine whether dividends declared have been either paid or included in liabilities. If a stock dividend was declared, the auditor should ascertain that the charge to retained earnings was at the proper amount. The auditor's knowledge of the applicable state law is important in all these matters.

OPERATIONS

The objective of the auditor's examination of operations is to determine whether the items of revenue and expense included in the income statement present fairly the results of operations for the period, in accordance with generally accepted accounting principles applied on a basis consistent with that of the preceding period. This objective involves determining that all revenues that have been earned for the period have been recorded and that all the revenues that have been recorded have, in fact, been earned. The auditor must also become satisfied that all the expenses which were incurred in earning the revenues have been recorded and properly matched with the related revenues. Finally, the auditor must ascertain that the classifications of the various items of revenue and expense are proper and have been followed consistently.

The auditor ordinarily does not subject every operating account to a detailed examination. In fact, it often may seem that only a small portion of the time spent on an audit engagement is devoted to the audit of the statement of income or that the examination of income and expense items does not receive as much attention as do balance-sheet items. This is not the case, however. The auditor devotes a considerable portion of time to the examination of income and expense items. Much of the work relating to the audit of operations, however, is completed during other phases of the examination. The auditor's tests of cash receipts, cash disbursements, and other compliance tests provide important evidence as to the fairness of operating accounts as well. In addition, many operating accounts come under the scrutiny of the auditor during the examination of the related balance-sheet accounts.

Compliance testing provides the auditor with information concerning operating accounts, the propriety of account classifications, and the accuracy of distributions to the income and expense accounts. For example:

1. Tests of sales and customer credits are made to determine whether all sales are being recorded accurately and whether the

credits for returns and allowances and discounts conform to the company's stated policies.

2. The tests of cash receipts help the auditor to determine the various sources of the client's revenue. This includes not only sales but also miscellaneous revenue.

3. Tests of payrolls are made to determine whether payroll disbursements have been computed properly and payroll expense is distributed properly (these various payroll tests are discussed at the end of this chapter).

4. Tests of cash disbursements are made to determine whether the disbursements have been made for goods and services actually received and whether these items have been charged to the proper accounts.

The examination of balance-sheet accounts provides the auditor with additional information and evidence with regard to matters relating to the income statement. For example:

1. The review of the allowance for uncollectible accounts includes tests of bad debts expense.

2. The examination of property, plant, and equipment includes tests of provisions for depreciation, gains and losses on disposals of assets, and repairs and maintenance of the property, plant, and equipment.

3. Insurance expense is tested in connection with the test of prepaid insurance.

4. Interest expense is tested in connection with the examination of notes payable, long-term debt, and accrued interest payable.

5. Dividend income and interest income are tested in connection with the tests of marketable securities.

6. The cutoff tests made in connection with the audit of asset accounts such as accounts receivable, inventories, and deferred items, and the audit of payables and other liability accounts, help the auditor to ascertain whether revenues and expenses are matched properly for the period.

Analysis of Operating Accounts

In addition to the audit work described above, the auditor usually will review certain selected operating accounts to supplement the information already obtained during compliance testing and the examination of balance-sheet accounts. Because of the wide variety of situations encountered in practice, there are no definite rules which can be stated as to which individual accounts should be reviewed or how extensive this review should be. It is the responsibility of the experienced auditor to make this decision.

Factors which are considered in making this decision include:

1. Any changes in the nature of the company's operations which affect the accounting records. Examples include changes in product line, compensation methods, or the level of production.
2. Comparisons of current-period amounts to both budgeted and prior-period amounts.
3. Comparisons of the dollar relationship among two or more accounts in the current period. Ratio analysis techniques might be used. Some auditors use regression analysis techniques for testing the reasonableness of account balances. Those which appear to be unreasonable are subjected to a more thorough investigation.
4. Economic conditions in general and the economic situation in the particular industry or line of business of the company being audited.

Once a particular operating account has been selected for detailed analysis, the auditor usually will follow the general guidelines listed below:

1. Understand completely the purpose of the particular analysis and the number and kinds of items to be checked.
2. Begin the analysis with a review of the general ledger account. In some instances it may contain all the information the auditor needs. However, if it contains only summary postings, the auditor may have to refer to the books of original entry.
3. Whenever possible have the client's employees prepare schedules of accounts selected for analysis by the auditor. Usually the purpose of the analysis may be satisfied by listing and supporting only larger entires and showing the remainder as a single figure. In other cases it may be adequate for the auditor to scan the entries in the account and summarize the findings in a memorandum. This is particularly true of those accounts in which recurring entries are made.
4. Compare the actual results of operations with last year's results and with budgeted amounts. Any unusual fluctuations noted are then investigated.
5. Examine supporting documents (e.g., invoices, contracts, agreements, paid checks) when appropriate.

In addition to the analyses of income and expense accounts for audit purposes, the detailed analyses of certain accounts also may be required in connection with the preparation of tax returns, SEC reports, and other reports. These analyses might include, for example, contributions, compensation of officers, and rent.

Other operating accounts may be tested in detail to satisfy other audit objectives. For example, professional fees (legal fees) may be reviewed to search for potential unrecorded or contingent liabilities and to see that requests for attorneys' letters have been sent to the appropriate attorneys retained by the client during the year.

Recognizing Management Problems

Expenses are incurred with the intention of benefiting the company. But effective control over expenses may be lost in some instances and unnecessary costs may be incurred. It is helpful to the auditor to compare prior years' expenses with those of the current year. A decrease in an expense is not always desirable, nor is an increase always undesirable. The important point to consider is what was achieved by the change or the lack of change in the expenditure.

The auditor always should remember that expenses behave in different ways—some are fixed with time, some vary with the level of operations, and yet others behave in more complex ways. Keeping these points in mind, the auditor should consider carefully the meaning of what is noted as operations are reviewed and analyzed.

The review of operations provides the auditor with an additional opportunity to consider the interrelationship between balance sheet and income statement accounts. For example, the auditor might investigate why accounts receivable increased 20 percent over the previous year while sales increased only 5 percent. Reporting the findings to management might be helpful, and management would probably appreciate the auditor's interest in its problems. For instance, if the auditor found in the review of sales returns that customers were dissatisfied with certain products, or in the review of sales allowances that some customers did not receive all items ordered because of "stockouts," such information might give valuable clues as to the causes of a deteriorating credit situation. Most companies welcome such observations from their auditors.

Financial Reporting and Changing Prices

In 1979, the FASB issued *Statement of Financial Accounting Standards No. 33*. The summary to the Statement (pp. i and ii) notes:

> This Statement applies to public enterprises that have either (1) inventories and property, plant, and equipment (before deducting accumulated depreciation) amounting to more than $125 million or (2) total

508

assets amounting to more than $1 billion (after deducting accumulated depreciation).

No changes are to be made in the primary financial statements; the information required by the Statement is to be presented as supplementary information in published annual reports.

For fiscal years ended on or after December 25, 1979, enterprises are required to report:

a. Income from continuing operations adjusted for the effects of general inflation
b. The purchasing power gain or loss on net monetary items.

For fiscal years ended on or after December 25, 1979, enterprises are also required to report:

a. Income from continuing operations on a current cost basis
b. The current cost amounts of inventory and property, plant, and equipment at the end of the fiscal year
c. Increases or decreases in current cost amounts of inventory and property, plant, and equipment, net of inflation.

* * * * *

Enterprises are required to present a five-year summary of selected financial data, including information on income, sales and other operating revenues, net assets, dividends per common share, and market price per share. In the computation of net assets, only inventory and property, plant, and equipment need be adjusted for the effects of changing prices.[5]

The auditor must be alert to these new requirements and must ensure that generally accepted accounting principles are applied in reporting this information. A more detailed description of the requirements of *FASB Statement No. 33* is beyond the scope of this text.

PAYROLLS

Payroll is a major expense for most companies and thus has a significant effect on the financial statements. The audit procedures used in the compliance testing of payrolls are designed primarily to assist the auditor in evaluating the effectiveness of the client's system of internal controls in this area.

Payrolls—Plant

The payroll procedures employed by a company often are tested by the auditor by examining the records of a representative number of

---

[5]*Statement of Financial Accounting Standards No. 33*, "Financial Reporting and Changing Prices," Financial Accounting Standards Board, 1979. Copyright © by Fi-

employees. Statistical sampling techniques may be used. The tests used by the auditor would include testing gross pay and deductions, comparing time cards with the payroll journal, and examining the authorization for wage rates. An auditor examining employee payroll records normally would employ the following procedures.

1. Check the recorded pay against the original record of hours worked or units produced.
2. Compare the rates paid with authorization forms, union contracts, or other pertinent source data.
3. Check the computation of payroll.
4. Check all deductions from gross pay.
5. Check the personnel records to ascertain whether the persons paid were actually employed during the pay period tested.
6. Examine the canceled employee payroll checks for propriety. If employees are paid in cash, examine receipts signed by the employees to determine that payments have in fact been made to the proper party.
7. Consider observing the actual paying of employees.
8. Trace the payroll tested to summaries, trace postings of summary totals to the general ledger and to subsidiary ledgers, and check the propriety of the accounting distribution.
9. Compare the total of the payroll tested with the appropriate recorded disbursements from the general bank account.
10. Review the payroll bank account reconciliation.
11. Investigate the company's method of handling unclaimed pay.

The following comments will assist the reader in understanding the auditor's objectives in performing the above tests.

Comparing the Recorded Pay against the Original Record of Hours Worked or Units Produced. The auditor compares the employee's name, clock number, department number, and recorded pay as shown on the original record (time card, time sheet, and so on) with the information included in the payroll journal. The auditor also should become satisfied that the hours worked or units produced have been properly approved. Generally, the employee's supervisor initials the time card or other record in order to indicate this approval. The auditor should test the controls relating to overtime hours and to the number of units produced under incentive compensation plans.

Comparing the Rates Paid with Authorization Forms, Union Contracts, or Other Pertinent Data. To determine whether employees are being paid at the proper rate, the auditor compares the rates paid

nancial Accounting Standards Board, High Ridge Park, Stamford, Connecticut 06905, U.S.A. Reprinted with permission. Copies of the complete document are available from the FASB.

with source documents, such as a union contract, which indicate the company's authorized rates of pay. Not all organizations are governed by union contract; and in those which are, not all classes of employees may be covered. Where applicable, however, a contract should be used as the source for testing wage rates. Other types of source documents include authorization forms, internal memos, and letters of employment agreement.

Checking the Computation of Payroll. The pay of plant employees usually is determined by either of two basic methods: (1) an hourly or daily rate plan; or (2) an incentive plan. The auditor should verify the calculations of the pay of the individuals selected for testing.

The arithmetical accuracy of the payroll journal is tested by the auditor in order to ascertain whether the client's system of internal control is functioning properly and to detect any errors in footings which could misstate payroll expense or conceal defalcations.

Checking Deductions from Gross Pay. Statutory provisions require the employer to maintain certain withholding authorization forms (such as federal government Form W-4 for income taxes), and sound administrative practice dictates maintaining authorizations for all other payroll deductions. Typically, either the payroll or personnel department maintains authorizations signed by employees for the withholding of income taxes, group insurance premiums, union dues, payroll advances, bond purchases, and credit union deposits. The auditor examines support for the amounts deducted from employees' pay and ascertains whether proper authorization for these deductions is maintained on file. For example, the amount of income tax and social security tax withheld should be verified by reference to withholding tables and to W-4 forms of individual employees.

In addition to examining authorizations, the auditor should test deductions by reference to invoices and other appropriate data. Group insurance charges may be traced to contracts or to invoices from the union. Payroll advances may be supported by memos or payroll advance forms which specify the details of repayment. Bond purchases and credit union deposits may be traced to transmittal sheets and to the amounts shown on the authorization forms.

Checking the Personnel Records. One of the purposes of this procedure is to enable the auditor to ascertain whether the persons paid were actually employed during the pay period tested. An obvious method for an employee to obtain funds by fraudulent means would be to falsify the time records for a fellow employee who has left the employ of the company and then misappropriate the pay. The auditor may test for this possibility by tracing selected names from the payroll records to employment records or other evidence maintained independently of the payroll department, noting the employee's name, clock number, hiring date, and, if applicable, termination date. The auditor also should obtain information for selected new and terminated employees from the personnel department and determine whether prompt action has been taken to add or remove their names on the payroll records.

Examining the Canceled Payroll Checks or, for Cash Payments, Examining Receipts Obtained from Employees. The purpose of this procedure is to enable the auditor to ascertain whether the proper employees received their pay and whether the amounts paid are in agreement with the payroll journal. The auditor should compare the check number, payee, and amount with the payroll journal. The payee's endorsement, the names of check signers (which must be the authorized signers), and the date the check cleared the bank should be examined for propriety.

The auditor is not expected to be a handwriting expert and could not reasonably be held responsible for failure to recognize a well-concealed forgery. However, if endorsements in different names on more than one check are apparently in the same handwriting, the auditor should investigate this situation. Checks which bear more than one endorsement, or those which lack an endorsement, may call for special consideration by the auditor. In many instances, the second endorsement may be that of a local business executive who cashes the checks as a convenience. This is usually a normal occurrence. If the second endorser is an individual associated with the company and, in particular, if this endorser is an employee associated with the preparation and distribution of the payroll, the auditor should note the item for further investigation and ascertain its propriety. In the case of paychecks which lack an endorsement and those which are noted for further investigation, the auditor should ascertain whether properly approved time records support the check and whether records show the payee of the check was employed during the period.

Being Present to Observe the Actual Paying of Employees. This procedure normally is used by the auditor when the client's system of internal control over payrolls is considered to be weak. Its purpose is to ascertain whether the proper employees did receive their pay as authorized. The auditor checks the identification of the employees being paid, compares the amount paid with the payroll journal, and observes the employee signing the receipt. Where checks are issued, the auditor compares the paychecks to the payroll journal. During such a test, the auditor should arrange to have a responsible official from the company present during the payoff in case any disputes arise.

Tracing the Payroll Tested to Summaries, Tracing Postings of Summary Totals to the General Ledger and to Subsidiary Ledgers, and Checking the Propriety of Distribution. The tests of the payroll journal are not complete until the auditor is satisfied that the details of the payroll have been summarized properly and the totals have been recorded properly in both the general and subsidiary ledgers.

In a manufacturing company, the subsidiary ledgers may be manufacturing expense ledgers or job cost ledgers. Financial information from these ledgers affects inventory valuation, profit determination, and managerial control. The auditor should compare the totals in the payroll journal for the pay period tested with the amounts on the summary sheets. The arithmetical accuracy of the summary sheets also should be tested and the totals should be traced to the general ledger and subsidiary ledger accounts. The distribution of payroll expense should be tested by the auditor by referring to the company's chart of accounts. The proper segregation of direct and indirect labor expenses and departmental breakdown of indirect labor is of particular interest to the auditor.

Comparing the Total of the Payroll Tested with the Appropriate Recorded Disbursements from the General Bank Account. Often imprest bank accounts are maintained for payrolls. The auditor should reconcile the amount transferred from the general account to the imprest fund with the applicable payroll. Examples of reconciling items normally encountered by the auditor in these circumstances include checks issued in advance, correction of previous reimbursements, and changes in the amount of the imprest balance. Although these items are normally not considered to be unusual, they must always be checked thoroughly by the auditor, who must be satisfied as to their propriety.

Reconciling the Payroll Bank Account. An imprest payroll bank account is reconciled in the same manner as any other bank account. However, the imprest bank account balance differs in that it is reconciled to a general ledger amount which does not change as payroll checks are written and as reimbursements are made to the payroll account. If checks are not issued simultaneously with the reimbursement of the payroll account, a reconciling item arises. The procedures used by the auditor in testing the payroll account reconciliation follow the same general pattern as those used for other bank accounts.

Investigating the Company's Method of Handling Unclaimed Pay. The procedures used by the client for handling unclaimed pay must be designed effectively and followed closely in order to reduce the possibility of misappropriation of funds. Unclaimed wages for the period under investigation should be listed by the auditor and the checks or pay envelopes turned over to a responsible, independent employee for subsequent distribution to the payees. The list should be checked periodically to determine the disposition that has been made of the items, and after a reasonable length of time they should be taken into income or recorded as a liability.

Payrolls—Office and Executive

Payroll tests for office and executive employees are similar to those for plant employees. In many instances, however, the internal controls over the office and executive payroll are not as strong as those over the plant payroll. For example, time clock cards usually are not required. Instead, department heads may verify the time worked by their employees on daily or weekly report sheets. Also, an attendance record usually is not maintained for executive employees. Companies often guard the security of office payroll information to such an extent that the same individual may prepare both the payroll and the payroll checks, sign the checks, distribute the checks, and reconcile the payroll bank accounts. Where internal controls are weak, as would be the case under the circumstances outlined above because of the lack of segregation of duties, the auditor will be required to expand the scope of the tests. The procedures used often will be the same as those for plant payrolls, but the number of employees included in the tests and the extent of testing may be increased.

Officers' salaries should be verified by reference to the minutes of board of directors' meetings, to employment agreements, or to other independent sources. In some cases, it may be desirable to verify salary amounts for the entire year.

AUDIT ASPECTS OF SEGMENT INFORMATION[6]

FASB Statement No. 14 requires that certain information concerning the client's operations in various industries, foreign operations, and export sales and major customers be included in the annual financial statements.[7] Independent auditors then must audit and report on segment information. The audit of segment information is presented here, while reporting on segment information is discussed in Chapter 14.

FASB Statement No. 14 requires the presentation of segment in-

---

[6]This section is based on *Statement of Auditing Standards No. 21*, "Segment Information," American Institute of Certified Public Accountants, 1977. Copyright © 1977 by the American Institute of Certified Public Accountants, Inc.

[7]*FASB Statement Nos. 18, 21*, and *24* amend *FASB Statement No. 14. Statement No. 21* suspended the requirements of *Statement No. 14* ". . . in the financial statements of nonpublic enterprises. . . ."

514

formation for the benefit of users of financial statements. *SAS No. 21* states that "the objective of auditing procedures applied to segment information is to provide the auditor with a reasonable basis for concluding whether the information is presented in conformity with *FASB Statement No. 14* in relation to the financial statements taken as a whole." *SAS No. 21* further states that the auditor "... is not required to apply auditing procedures that would be necessary to express a separate opinion on the segment information."

Materiality

SAS No. 21 indicates that materiality in considering segment information should be evaluated in terms of dollar magnitude of the information in relation "... to the financial statements taken as a whole." However, qualitative factors as well as quantitative factors should be considered in judging materiality. *SAS No. 21* notes the following qualitative factors that an auditor may want to consider:

[1] The significance of a matter to a particular entity (for example, a misstatement of the revenue and operating profit of a relatively small segment that is represented by management to be important to the future profitability of the entity),

[2] [T]he pervasiveness of a matter (for example, whether it affects the amounts and presentation of numerous items in the segment information), and

[3] [T]he impact of a matter (for example, whether it distorts the trends reflected in segment information). . . .

Modification of Regular Audit Procedures

SAS No. 21 states that "in planning his examination, it may be necessary for the auditor to modify or redirect selected audit tests to be applied to the financial statements taken as a whole. For example, the auditor may decide to select inventories for physical observation on the basis of industry segments or geographic areas." Examples of factors which should be considered in determining whether procedures should be modified or redirected include:

a. Internal accounting control and the degree of integration, centralization, and uniformity of the accounting records.

b. The nature, number, and relative size of industry segments and geographic areas.

c. The nature and number of subsidiaries or divisions in each industry segment and geographic area.

d. The accounting principles used for the industry segments and geographic areas. [*SAS No. 21*]

SAS No. 21 notes that ". . . the tests of underlying accounting records normally applied in an examination of financial statements should include a consideration of whether the entity's revenue, operating expenses, and identifiable assets are appropriately classified among industry segments and geographic areas."

Procedures Applied to Segment Information

SAS No. 21 suggests that the following procedures should be applied to segment information:

1. Discuss with management its method of determining segment information. Evaluate the reasonableness of the methods in relation to *FASB* statements relating to segment information.
2. "Inquire as to the bases of accounting for sales or transfers between industry segments and between geographic areas, and test, to the extent considered necessary, those sales or transfers for conformity with the bases of accounting disclosed."
3. "Test the disaggregation of the entity's financial statements into segment information."
4. "Inquire as to the methods of allocating expenses incurred and identifiable assets used jointly by two or more segments, evaluate whether those methods are reasonable, and test the allocations to the extent considered necessary."
5. "Determine whether the segment information has been presented consistently from period to period and, if not, whether the nature and effect of the inconsistency are disclosed and, if applicable, whether the information has been retroactively restated in conformity with paragraph 40 of FASB Statement No. 14."

RELATED PARTY TRANSACTIONS[8]

During the course of the audit examination, the auditor should be alert to the possibility of the existence of material related party[9] trans-

---

[8] This section is based on *Statement of Auditing Standards No. 6*, "Related Party Transactions," American Institute of Certified Public Accountants, 1975. Copyright © 1975 by the American Institute of Certified Public Accountants, Inc.

[9] Related parties include ". . . the reporting entity; its affiliates . . .; principal owners, management, and members of their immediate families . . .; entities for which investments are accounted for by the equity method; and any other party with which the reporting entity may deal when one party has the ability to significantly influence the management or operating policies of the other, to the extent that one of the transacting parties might be prevented from fully pursuing its own separate interests. Related parties also exist when another entity has the ability to significantly influence the management or operating policies of the transacting parties or when another entity has an ownership interest in one of the transacting parties and the ability to significantly influence the other, to the extent that one or more of the transacting parties might be prevented from fully pursuing its own separate interests." [*SAS No. 6*, paragraph 2]

516

actions that could have an effect on the financial statements. *SAS No. 6* indicates that the auditor must be satisfied "... as to the substance of and accounting for such transactions, including financial statement disclosure." The auditor should consider "... related party transactions within the framework of existing pronouncements, placing primary emphasis on the adequacy of disclosure of the existence of such transactions and their significance in the financial statements of the reporting entity."[10]

Audit Procedures

According to *SAS No. 6* the following specific audit procedures might be included to determine the existence of related parties:

a. Evaluate the company's procedures for identifying and properly accounting for related party transactions.
b. Inquire of appropriate management personnel as to the names of all related parties and whether there were any transactions with these parties during the period.
c. Review filings by the reporting entity with the Securities and Exchange Commission and other regulatory agencies for the names of related parties and for other businesses in which officers and directors occupy directorship or management positions.
d. Determine the names of all pension and other trusts established for the benefit of employees and the names of the officers and trustees thereof. ...
e. Review stockholder listings of closely held companies to identify principal stockholders.
f. Review prior years' work papers for the names of known related parties.
g. Inquire of predecessor, principal, or other auditors of related entities as to their knowledge of existing relationships and the extent of management involvement in material transactions.
h. Review material investment transactions during the period under examination to determine whether the nature and extent of investments during the period create related parties.

SAS No. 6 also contains recommended procedures for identifying transactions with related parties. Some of these include: providing audit personnel with the names of related parties; reviewing the minutes of meetings; reviewing proxy and other material filed with the SEC; reviewing "conflict-of-interests" statements that the company obtains from its management; reviewing the accounting records for very large, unusual, or nonrecurring transactions or balances (especially transactions occurring near the end of a reporting period); de-

---

[10] *SAS No. 6*, paragraph 6.

termining if transactions are not being given accounting recognition (e.g., the client receiving services at no charge); and reviewing invoices from law firms that have performed services for the client.

Once related party transactions have been identified, *SAS No. 6* suggests that additional audit procedures may be needed to determine " . . . the purpose, nature, and extent of these transactions and their effect on the financial statements." *SAS No. 6* suggests that the auditor should consider the following:

a. Obtain an understanding of the business purpose of the transaction. . . .

b. Examine invoices, executed copies of agreements, contracts, and other pertinent documents, such as receiving reports and shipping documents.

c. Determine whether the transaction has been approved by the board of directors or other appropriate officials.

d. Test for reasonableness the compilation of accounts to be disclosed, or considered for disclosure, in the financial statements.

e. Arrange for the audits of intercompany account balances to be performed as of concurrent dates, even if the fiscal years differ, and for the examination of specified, important, and representative related party transactions by the auditors for each of the parties, with an appropriate exchange of relevant information.

f. Inspect or confirm and obtain satisfaction as to the transferability and value of collateral.[11]

Disclosure

The auditor should be satisfied that material related party transactions are adequately disclosed in the financial statements. According to *SAS No. 6* disclosure should include:

a. The nature of the relationship(s).

b. A description of the transactions (summarized when appropriate) for the period reported on, including amounts, if any, and such other information as is deemed necessary to an understanding of the effects on the financial statements.

c. The dollar volume of transactions and the effects of any change in the method of establishing terms from that used in the preceding period.

d. Amounts due from or to related parties and, if not otherwise apparent, the terms and manner of settlement.

Sometimes the client includes a representation in the financial statements that a related party transaction was consummated on ap-

---

[11] *SAS No. 6* in paragraph 15 also suggests procedures that may be used to completely understand a certain transaction.

518

proximately the same terms as if the transaction had been with an unrelated party. If the auditor is unable to reach a conclusion as to the propriety of this representation, consideration should be given to including a comment to that effect in the audit report and expressing a qualified opinion or disclaiming an opinion. If the auditor believes the representation is misleading, a qualified or adverse opinion should be rendered (depending on materiality).

REVIEW OF INTERIM FINANCIAL INFORMATION[12]

This section discusses the objectives and procedures that an auditor should apply to interim financial information when engaged by a client to make a review of interim financial information. The review may be " . . . of interim financial information presented alone, including interim financial statements and summarized interim financial data, that purport to conform with the provisions of Accounting Principles Board Opinion No. 28, as amended, and that is contained in reports issued by a public entity to stockholders, boards of directors, or others, or filed with regulatory agencies." [SAS No. 24] Alternatively, the review may be of interim financial information that is included as a note to the audited financial statements of a public or nonpublic enterprise.

Objective of a Review

SAS No. 24 states:

The objective of a review of interim financial information is to provide the accountant, based on objectively applying his knowledge of financial reporting practices to significant accounting matters of which he becomes aware through inquiries and analytical review procedures, with a basis for reporting whether material modifications should be made for such information to conform with generally accepted accounting principles.

The review is not an audit in accordance with generally accepted auditing standards. While significant matters may come to the accountant's attention during a review, there is no assurance that all of such matters that would be disclosed by an audit will be disclosed by a review.

---

[12] This section is based on *Statement on Auditing Standards No. 24*, "Review of Interim Financial Information," American Institute of Certified Public Accountants, 1979. Copyright © 1979 by the American Institute of Certified Public Accountants, Inc.

Nature of Procedures for a Review

SAS No. 24 notes that the procedures used in "... a review of interim financial information consist primarily of inquiries and analytical review procedures concerning significant accounting matters. ..." Furthermore, *SAS No. 24* indicates that usually these procedures include:

a. "Inquiring concerning (1) the accounting system, to obtain an understanding of the manner in which transactions are recorded, classified, and summarized in the preparation of interim financial information and (2) any significant changes in the system of internal accounting control, to ascertain their potential effect on the preparation of interim financial information."

b. "Application of analytical review procedures to interim financial information to identify and provide a basis for inquiry about relationships and individual items that appear to be unusual. Analytical review procedures for purposes of this Statement [*No. 24*], consist of (1) comparison of the financial information with comparable information for the immediately preceding interim period and for corresponding previous period(s), (2) comparison of the financial information with anticipated results, and (3) study of the relationships of elements of financial information that would be expected to conform to a predictable pattern based on the entity's experience. In applying these procedures, the accountant should consider the types of matters that in the preceding year or quarters have required accounting adjustments."

c. "Reading the minutes of meetings of stockholders, board of directors, and committees of the board of directors to identify actions that may affect the interim financial information."

d. Reading the interim financial information coming to the accountant's attention to consider whether it conforms with generally accepted accounting principles.

e. "Obtaining reports from other accountants, if any, who have been engaged to make a review of the interim financial information of significant components of the reporting entity, its subsidiaries, or other investees."

f. Inquiring of management personnel responsible "... for financial and accounting matters concerning (1) whether the interim financial information has been prepared in conformity with generally accepted accounting principles consistently applied, (2) changes in the entity's business activities or accounting practices, (3) matters as to which questions have arisen in the course of applying the foregoing procedures, and (4) events subsequent to the date of the interim financial information that would have a material effect on the presentation of such information."

g. Obtaining written representations from management on matters the accountant feels are appropriate (e.g., subsequent events).

Timing and Extent of Procedures

The accountant should plan carefully the review of interim information. Consideration should be given to accomplishing some of the work before the end of the interim period.

SAS No. 24 indicates that the extent of the application of the procedures for a review is a function of a variety of factors. Examples of such factors include:

1. The accountant's knowledge of the client's accounting and financial reporting practices. This knowledge is a basis for various procedures used in a review.
2. The accountant's knowledge of the client's internal control system and any weaknesses in that system.
3. The accountant's knowledge of ". . . changes in the nature or volume of the client's business activities or accounting changes."
4. Questions raised during a review that may require the accountant to make additional inquiries or perform additional procedures.
5. The results of the procedures used in the regular audit of financial statements. Such procedures may result in the modification of the procedures used in the review of interim financial statements.

SAS No. 24 also discusses reporting on interim financial information. This is covered in Chapter 14.

AUDIT MEMORANDA

As in all major phases of the audit, the auditor should prepare a memorandum or memoranda for each of the major areas discussed in this chapter.

GLOSSARY

Letter of inquiry A letter from the client addressed to the client's lawyer asking the lawyer to provide to the auditor corroboration of the information furnished to the auditor by management regarding litigation, claims, and assessments. Figure 13-2, contains a list of items that should appear in such a letter. [*SAS No. 12*]

Related parties Include ". . . the reporting entity; its affiliates . . .; principal owners, management, and members of their immediate families . . .; entities for which investments are accounted for by the equity method; and any other party with which the reporting entity may deal when one party has the ability to significantly influence the management or operating policies of the other, to the extent that one of the transacting parties might be prevented from pursuing fully its own separate interests. Related parties also exist when another entity has the ability to significantly influence the management or operating policies of the transacting parties or when another entity has an ownership interest in one of the transacting parties and the ability to significantly influence the other, to the extent that one or more of the transacting parties might be prevented from fully pursuing its own separate interests." [*SAS No. 6*, paragraph 2.]

Segment information Information concerning a company's operations in various industries, foreign operations and export sales, and major customers. [*FASB Statement No. 14*]

QUESTIONS AND PROBLEMS

13-1. What is the objective of the auditor's examination of notes payable?

13-2. What two features should be included in an effective internal control system over liabilities?

13-3. What is "window dressing"? How may it be accomplished? How may it be discovered by the auditor?

13-4. Discuss three basic steps taken by an auditor when examining trade accounts payable.

13-5. How is a search for unrecorded trade accounts payable conducted by the auditor?

13-6. Define accrued payables. Give examples.

13-7. Into what segments may the audit of accrued commissions payables be broken down?

13-8. What are the objectives of auditing long-term debt?

13-9. On what matters must the auditor obtain evidence concerning litigation, claims, and assessments?

13-10. What are the procedures generally applied by the auditor during the examination of stockholders' equity?

13-11. What is the overall objective of the auditor's examination of operations? How is this accomplished by the auditor?

13-12. List the procedures typically used in testing employee payroll records.

13-13. What is the objective of the auditor in examining segment information?

13-14. Upon what should the auditor place primary emphasis regarding related party transactions?

13-15. The auditor should be satisfied that material related party transactions are adequately disclosed in the financial statements. Discuss items that should appear in such a disclosure.

13-16. What is the objective of the accountant in making a review of interim financial information for a client?

13–17. Select the *best* answer for each of the following questions.

    a. If a client is using a voucher system, the auditor who is examining accounts payable records should obtain a schedule of all unpaid vouchers at the balance-sheet date and

        1. Retrace voucher register items to the source indicated in the reference column of the register.

        2. Vouch items in the voucher register and examine related canceled checks.

        3. Confirm items on the schedule of unpaid vouchers and obtain satisfaction for all confirmation exceptions.

        4. Compare the items on the schedule with open vouchers and uncanceled entries in the voucher register and account for unmatched items.

    b. Under which of the following circumstances would it be advisable for the auditor to confirm accounts payable with creditors?

        1. Internal accounting control over accounts payable is adequate and there is sufficient evidence on hand to minimize the risk of a material misstatement.

        2. Confirmation response is expected to be favorable and accounts payable balances are of immaterial amounts.

        3. Creditor statements are *not* available and internal accounting control over accounts payable is unsatisfactory.

        4. The majority of accounts payable balances are with associated companies.

    c. Which of the following is the *most* efficient audit procedure for the detection of unrecorded liabilities?

        1. Compare cash disbursements in the subsequent period with the accounts payable trial balance at year-end.

        2. Confirm large accounts payable balances at the balance-sheet date.

        3. Examine purchase orders issued for several days prior to the close of the year.

        4. Obtain a "liability certificate" from the client.

    d. Which of the following audit procedures would be *least* effective for detecting contingent liabilities?

        1. Abstracting the minutes of the meetings of the board of directors.

        2. Reviewing the bank confirmation letters.

        3. Examining confirmation letters from customers.

        4. Confirming pending legal matters with the corporate attorney.

    e. During the course of an audit, a CPA observes that the recorded interest expense seems to be excessive in relation to the balance in the long-term debt *account*. This observation could lead the auditor to suspect that

        1. Long-term debt is understated.

        2. Discount on bonds payable is overstated.

    3. Long-term debt is overstated.

    4. Premium on bonds payable is understated.

f. The auditor's program for the examination of long-term debt should include steps that require the

    1. Verification of the existence of the bondholders.

    2. Examination of any bond trust indenture.

    3. Inspection of the accounts payable subsidiary ledger.

    4. Investigation of credits to the bond interest income account.

g. It would be appropriate for the payroll accounting department to be responsible for which of the following functions?

    1. Approval of employee time records.

    2. Maintenance of records of employment, discharges, and pay increases.

    3. Preparation of periodic governmental reports as to employees' earnings and withholding taxes.

    4. Distribution of paychecks to employees.

h. A surprise observation by an auditor of a client's regular distribution of paychecks is primarily designed to satisfy the auditor that

    1. All unclaimed payroll checks are properly returned to the cashier.

    2. The paymaster is *not* involved in the distribution of payroll checks.

    3. All employees have in their possession proper employee identification.

    4. Names on the company payroll are those of bona fide employees presently on the job.

i. If a company employs a capital stock registrar and/or transfer agent, the registrar or agent, or both, should be requested to confirm directly to the auditor the number of shares of each class of stock

    1. Surrendered and canceled during the year.

    2. Authorized at the balance-sheet date.

    3. Issued and outstanding at the balance-sheet date.

    4. Authorized, issued and outstanding during the year.

j. An audit program for the examination of the retained earnings account should include a step that requires verification of the

    1. Gain or loss resulting from disposition of treasury shares.

    2. Market value used to charge retained earnings to account for a two-for-one stock split.

    3. Authorization for both cash and stock dividends.

    4. Approval of the adjustment to the beginning balance as a result of a write-down of an account receivable.

k. The auditor generally gives most emphasis to ratio and trend analysis in the examination of the statement of

    1. Retained earnings.

    2. Income.

524

3. Financial position.
4. Changes in financial position.

(AICPA, adapted)

13-18. Describe the audit procedures that would generally be followed in establishing the propriety of the recorded liability for federal income taxes of an established corporation which you are auditing for the first time. Consideration should be given the status of *(a)* the liability for prior years and *(b)* the liability arising from the current year's income.

(AICPA, adapted)

13-19. You have been called upon by the ABC Corporation, a nationwide organization using the accrual method of accounting, to make a balance-sheet audit at December 31, 1981.
  a. Outline an audit program for the verification of state and federal social security and unemployment taxes.
  b. Why and for what purpose is an analysis needed?

(AICPA, adapted)

13-20. List and describe the procedures by which an auditor who is making a regular annual audit might discover unrecorded liabilities.

(AICPA, adapted)

13-21. You are making a regular annual audit of a small, but growing, manufacturing corporation. As a result of inadequate working capital, the corporation has borrowed from its bank on short-term notes and has occasionally given notes to suppliers for overdue accounts payable. Prepare an audit program for notes payable.

(AICPA, adapted)

13-22. *a.* In practice, confirmation of accounts payable is less common than confirmation of accounts receivable. Give reasons why this is so.
  b. Prepare a confirmation request for notes payable.

(AICPA, adapted)

13-23. In connection with various steps, other than those concerned directly with notes and mortgages payable in the usual annual audit, the auditor's verification work assists in determining that all notes and mortgages payable are properly recorded on the books of the client. List five of these procedures, stating the manner in which each procedure aids in determining that notes and mortgages payable are correctly recorded.

(AICPA, adapted)

13-24. You are assigned to the regular annual audit of a print shop with 20 employees. List the records, reports, or other data as to personnel and compensation that would be of interest to an auditor which you would expect to find in this business. Indicate the purposes for which these records, reports and data would be used on an audit.

(AICPA, adapted)

13-25. In most medium-sized and large audits, it is customary for the auditor to select for detailed examination a series of items entered in the voucher register. The selection is from a period other than at year end.

Required:

a.   What are the objectives or purposes of the vouching test?
b.   Name the items for which each voucher is to be examined by the auditor performing this test.

(AICPA)

13-26.   One of the auditor's primary means of verifying payroll transactions is by a detailed payroll test. You are making an annual examination of the Joplin Company, a medium-sized manufacturing company. You have selected a number of hourly employees for a detailed payroll test. The following work sheet outline has been prepared.

Column Number	*Column Heading*
1	Employee number
2	Employee name
3	Job classification
	Hours worked
4	Straight time
5	Premium time
6	Hourly rate
7	Gross earnings
	Deductions
8	F.I.C.A. withheld
9	F.I.T. withheld
10	Union dues
11	Hospitalization
12	Amount of check
13	Check and check number
14	Account number charged
15	Description of account

Required:

a.   Using the column numbers above as a reference, state the principal way(s) that the information in each column would be verified.
b.   In addition to the payroll test, the auditor employs a number of other audit procedures in the verification of payroll transactions. List five additional procedures which may be employed.

(AICPA, adapted)

13-27.   The Generous Loan Company has 100 branch loan offices. Each office has a manager and four or five subordinates who are employed by the manager. Branch managers prepare the weekly payroll, including their own salaries, and pay employees from cash on hand. The employee signs the payroll sheet signifying receipt of his salary. Hours worked by hourly personnel are inserted in the payroll sheet from time cards prepared by the employees and approved by the manager.

The weekly payroll sheets are sent to the home office along with other accounting statements and reports. The home office compiles employee earnings records and prepares all federal and state salary reports from the weekly payroll sheets.

Salaries are established by home office job-evaluation schedules. Salary adjustments, promotions, and transfers of full-time employees are approved by a home office salary committee based upon the recommendations of branch managers and area supervisors. Branch managers advise the salary committee of new full-time employees and terminations. Part-time and temporary employees are hired without referral to the salary committee.

Required:

a. Based upon your review of the payroll system, how might funds for payroll be diverted?

b. Prepare a payroll audit program to be used in the home office to audit the branch office payrolls of the Generous Loan Company.

(AICPA)

13-28. You were engaged on May 1, 1981, by a committee of stockholders to perform a special audit as of December 31, 1980, of the stockholders' equity of the Major Corporation, whose stock is actively traded on a stock exchange. The group of stockholders who engaged you believe that the information contained in the stockholders' equity section of the published annual report for the year ended December 31, 1980, is not correct. If your examination confirms their suspicions, they intend to use the report in a proxy fight.

Management agrees to permit your audit but refuses to permit any direct confirmation with stockholders. To secure cooperation in the audit, the committee of stockholders has agreed to this limitation and you have been instructed to limit your audit in this respect. You have been instructed also to exclude the audit of revenue and expense accounts for the year.

Required:

a. Prepare a general audit program for the usual examination of the stockholders' equity section of a corporation's balance sheet, assuming no limitation on the scope of your examination. Exclude the audit of revenue and expense accounts.

b. Describe any special auditing procedures you would undertake in view of the limitations and other special circumstances of your examination of the Major Corporation's stockholders' equity accounts.

c. Discuss the content of your auditor's report for the special engagement including comments on the opinion that you would render. Do not prepare your auditor's report.

(AICPA, adapted)

13-29. You are a CPA engaged in an examination of the financial statements of Pate Corporation for the year ended December 31, 1981. The financial statements and records of Pate Corporation have not been audited by a CPA in prior years.

The stockholders' equity section of Pate Corporation's balance sheet as of December 31, 1981, follows:

Stockholders' equity

Capital stock—10,000 shares of $10 par value authorized; 5,000 shares issued and outstanding	$ 50,000
Capital contributed in excess of par value of capital stock	32,580
Retained earnings	47,320
Total stockholders' equity	$129,900

Pate Corporation was founded in 1975. The corporation has ten stockholders and serves as its own registrar and transfer agent. There are no capital stock subscription contracts in effect.

Required:

a. Prepare the detailed audit program for the examination of the three accounts comprising the stockholders' equity section of Pate Corporation's balance sheet. (Do not include in the audit program the verification of the results of the current year's operations.)

b. After every other figure on the balance sheet has been audited by the CPA it might appear that the retained earnings figure is a balancing figure and requires no further verification. Why does the CPA verify retained earnings as he does other figures on the balance sheet? Discuss.

(AICPA, adapted)

13-30. You were in the final stages of your examination of the financial statements of Ozine Corporation for the year ended December 31, 1980, when you were consulted by the corporation's president who believes there is no point to your examining the 1981 voucher register and testing data in support of 1981 entries. He stated that (a) bills pertaining to 1980 which were received too late to be included in the December voucher register were recorded as of the year end by the corporation by journal entry, (b) the internal auditor made tests after the year end and (c) he would furnish you with a letter certifying that there were no unrecorded liabilities.

Required:

a. Should a CPA's test for unrecorded liabilities be affected by the fact that the client made a journal entry to record 1980 bills which were received late? Explain.

b. Should a CPA's test for unrecorded liabilities be affected by the fact that a letter is obtained in which a responsible management official certifies that to the best of his knowledge all liabilities have been recorded? Explain.

c. Should a CPA's test for unrecorded liabilities be eliminated or reduced because of the internal audit test? Explain.

    d. Assume that the corporation, which handled some government contracts, had no internal auditor but that an auditor for a federal agency spent three weeks auditing the records and was just completing his work at this time. How would the CPA's unrecorded liability test be affected by the work of the auditor for a federal agency?

    e. What sources in addition to the 1981 voucher register should the CPA consider to locate possible unrecorded liabilities?

(AICPA, adapted)

13–31. The Moss Company manufactures household appliances that are sold through independent franchised retail dealers. The electric motors in the appliances are guaranteed for five years from the date of sale of the appliances to the consumer. Under the guaranty defective motors are replaced by the dealers without charge.

    Inventories of replacement motors are kept in the dealers' stores and are carried at cost in The Moss Company's records. When the dealer replaces a defective motor, he notifies the factory and returns the defective motor to the factory for reconditioning. After the defective motor is received by the factory, the dealer's account is credited with an agreed fee for the replacement service.

    When the appliance is brought to the dealer after the guaranty period has elapsed, the dealer charges the owner for installing the new motor. The dealer notifies the factory of the installation and returns the replaced motor for reconditioning. The motor installed is then charged to the dealer's account at a price in excess of its inventory value. In this instance, to encourage the return of replaced motors, the dealer's account is credited with a nominal value for the returned motor.

    Dealers submit quarterly inventory reports of the motors on hand. The reports are later verified by factory salesmen. Dealers are billed for inventory shortages determined by comparison of the dealers' inventory reports and the factory's perpetual records of the dealers' inventories. The dealers order additional motors as they need them. One motor is used for all appliances in a given year, but the motors are changed in basic design each model year.

    The Moss Company has established an account, Estimated Liability for Product Guaranties, in connection with the guaranties. An amount representing the estimated guaranty cost prorated per sales unit is credited to the Estimated Liability account for each appliance sold and the debit is charged to a Provision account. The Estimated Liability account is debited for the service fees credited to the dealers' accounts and for the inventory cost of the motors installed under the guaranties.

    The engineering department keeps statistical records of the number of units of each model sold in each year and the replacements that were made. The effect of improvements in design and construction is under continuous study by the engineering department, and the estimated guaranty cost per unit is adjusted annually on the basis of experience and improvements in design. Experience shows that, for a given motor model, the number of guaranties made good varies widely from year to year during the guaranty period, but the total number of guaranties to be made good can be reliably predicted.

Required:

a. Prepare an audit program to satisfy yourself as to the propriety of the transactions recorded in the Estimated Liability for Product Guaranties account for the year ended December 31, 1981.

b. Prepare the work sheet format that would be used to test the adequacy of the balance in the Estimated Liability for Product Guaranties account. The work sheet column headings should describe clearly the data to be inserted in the columns.

(AICPA, adapted)

13-32. Mincin, CPA, is the auditor of the Raleigh Corporation. Mincin is considering the audit work to be performed in the accounts payable area for the current year's engagement.

The prior year's working papers show that confirmation requests were mailed to 100 of Raleigh's 1,000 suppliers. The selected suppliers were based on Mincin's sample that was designed to select accounts with large dollar balances. A substantial number of hours were spent by Raleigh and Mincin resolving relatively minor differences between the confirmation replies and Raleigh's accounting records. Alternate audit procedures were used for those suppliers who did not respond to the confirmation requests. ·

Required:

a. Identify the accounts payable audit objectives that Mincin must consider in determining the audit procedures to be followed.

b. Identify situations when Mincin should use accounts payable confirmations and discuss whether Mincin is required to use them.

c. Discuss why the use of large dollar balances as the basis for selecting accounts payable for confirmation might not be the most efficient approach and indicate what more efficient procedures could be followed when selecting accounts payable for confirmation.

(AICPA, adapted)

13-33. Arthur, CPA, is auditing the RCT Manufacturing Company as of February 28, 1982. As with all engagements, one of Arthur's initial procedures is to make overall checks of the client's financial data by reviewing significant ratios and trends so that he has a better understanding of the business and can determine where to concentrate his audit efforts.

The financial statements prepared by the client with audited 1981 figures and preliminary 1982 figures are presented below in condensed form.

RCT MANUFACTURING COMPANY
Condensed Balance Sheets
February 28, 1982 and 1981

Assets	1982	1981
Cash	$ 12,000	$ 15,000
Accounts receivable, net	93,000	50,000
Inventory	72,000	67,000
Other current assets	5,000	6,000
Plant and equipment, net of depreciation	60,000	80,000
	$242,000	$218,000

Equities		
Accounts payable..............	$ 38,000	$ 41,000
Federal income tax payable	30,000	14,400
Long-term liabilities	20,000	40,000
Common stock	70,000	70,000
Retained earnings	84,000	52,600
	$242,000	$218,000

RCT MANUFACTURING COMPANY
Condensed Income Statements
Years Ended February 28, 1982 and 1981

	1982	1981
Net sales	$1,684,000	$1,250,000
Cost of goods sold	927,000	710,000
Gross margin on sales	757,000	540,000
Selling and administrative expenses	682,000	504,000
Income before federal income taxes	75,000	36,000
Income tax expense	30,000	14,400
Net income	$ 45,000	$ 21,600

Additional information:
a. The company has only an insignificant amount of cash sales.
b. The end of year figures are comparable to the average for each respective year.

Required:

For each year compute the current ratio. Based on the ratio, identify and discuss audit procedures that should be included in Arthur's audit of accounts payable.

(AICPA, adapted)

part four

Auditors' Communications

Learning Objectives

Study of the material in this chapter is designed to achieve several learning objectives. Among these are an understanding of the:

1. Nature and form of the auditor's standard, nonstandard, and long-form reports.
2. Nature of the unqualified opinion, qualified opinion, adverse opinion, and disclaimer of opinion.
3. Situations in which each of the above types of opinions should be used.
4. Effect of "subsequent events," other information, and segment information on the auditor's report.
5. Applicability of "special reports" and the form that these reports commonly take.
6. Various other types of reports including interim financial information, forecasts, and reports on internal control.
7. Accountant's role and responsibilities when assisting in the preparation of unaudited statements.

14

The Auditor's Report

The audit report is the most important form of communication used by the auditor. It must clearly and concisely communicate the nature of the auditor's examination and the degree of responsibility being taken. The report may be a standard (short-form) report, a departure from a standard report, or a long-form report.

The standard report consists of a scope paragraph and an opinion paragraph. The scope paragraph is a representation of the work performed by the auditor. It specifically designates the statements and the period covered. The opinion paragraph gives the auditor's opinion on the statements.

Sometimes circumstances require that the auditor's report be a departure from a standard report. Such reports usually will contain three paragraphs. The scope of the auditor's examination is given in the first paragraph. An explanation of why the auditor is departing from a standard report is set forth in a middle paragraph. The auditor's opinion, or the reasons for disclaiming one, is included in the third paragraph.

A long-form report usually contains scope and opinion paragraphs. However, these reports also contain analyses that are useful to management or to creditors.

THE STANDARD REPORT

When the auditor has formed the opinion (on the basis of an examination made in accordance with generally accepted auditing standards) that the financial statements present fairly the financial position, results of operations, and changes in financial position in conformity with generally accepted accounting principles applied on the basis consistent with that of the preceding period, an unqualified opinion should be issued. The standard report was presented in Fig-

ure 1–3, Chapter 1. You should study Figure 1–3 carefully before
continuing with the remainder of this chapter.

Separate Financial Statements

If the auditor is not asked to examine all of the basic statements,
only those statements which were examined should be referred to in
the auditor's report. For example, when the examination includes only
the balance sheet, the following wording is suggested:

> We have examined the balance sheet of The National Co. as of De-
> cember 31, 1980. Our examination was made in accordance with gener-
> ally accepted auditing standards and, accordingly, included such tests of
> the accounting records and such other auditing procedures as we con-
> sidered necessary in the circumstances.
>
> In our opinion, the accompanying balance sheet presents fairly the
> financial position of The National Co. at December 31, 1980, in confor-
> mity with generally accepted accounting principles applied on a basis
> consistent with that of the preceding year.

When the examination covers only the income statement or the
statement of changes in financial position, a similarly worded report
referring to the income statement and results of operations or to the
statement of changes in financial position for the period should be
used.

Consolidated Statements

The following wording is suggested in accountants' reports which
accompany consolidated statements:

> We have examined the consolidated balance sheet of The United
> Corporation and subsidiaries (properly distinguished if there are uncon-
> solidated subsidiaries) as of December 31, 1980, and the related con-
> solidated statements of income, retained earnings, and changes in finan-
> cial position for the year then ended. Our examination was made in
> accordance with generally accepted auditing standards and, accord-
> ingly, included such tests of the accounting records and such other au-
> diting procedures as we considered necessary in the circumstances.
>
> In our opinion, the financial statements referred to above present
> fairly the consolidated financial position of The United Corporation and
> subsidiaries (properly distinguished, if necessary) at December 31,
> 1980, and the consolidated results of their operations and changes in
> their financial position for the year then ended, in conformity with gen-
> erally accepted accounting principles applied on a basis consistent with
> that of the preceding year.

It usually is not necessary to identify the subsidiaries by name. However, when it is necessary, the form could be *The Federal Company and consolidated subsidiaries, X Company and Y Company.*

If the consolidated subsidiaries can be concisely described to distinguish them from the unconsolidated subsidiaries, it is preferable to use such a description, both in the accountants' report and in the heading of the financial statements. Examples of such distinguishing descriptions include:

Wholly-owned subsidiaries.

Wholly-owned domestic subsidiaries.

Wholly-owned retail subsidiaries.

Manufacturing subsidiaries.

Domestic manufacturing subsidiaries.

Domestic subsidiaries.

U.S. and Canadian subsidiaries.

Care must be taken to select a description which is mutually exclusive and which is not equally applicable to one or more of the unconsolidated subsidiaries.

Parent Statements

Ordinarily, only the consolidated financial statements will be issued to present financial position and the results of operations and changes in financial position of a corporation and its subsidiaries, and the auditor's opinion will extend only to these statements. However, there will be instances where separate financial statements of the parent company also will be issued, as in the case of certain reports to be used for credit purposes and also for certain filings with the Securities and Exchange Commission.

The following wording is suggested in accountants' reports which accompany both parent company (unconsolidated) and consolidated statements:

> We have examined the balance sheets of The Eastern Company and of The Eastern Company and subsidiaries as of December 31, 1980, and the related statements of income, retained earnings, and changes in financial position for the year then ended. Our examination was made. . . .
>
> In our opinion, the aforementioned financial statements present fairly the financial position of The Eastern Company and the consolidated financial position of the Company and subsidiaries at December 31, 1980, and the respective results of their operations and changes in

their financial position for the year then ended, in conformity with generally accepted accounting principles applied on a basis consistent with that of the preceding year.

Comparative Statements[1]

If the audited financial statements include financial statements of one or more preceding year(s) for comparative purposes, reference to the prior year(s) statements should be made in the accountants' report. *SAS No. 15* notes that a continuing auditor (a current auditor who has examined one or more immediately preceding periods) should update (re-express the previous opinion or express a different opinion from the previous opinion) his or her report on the financial statements for prior period(s) when those financial statements are presented on a comparative basis with the current financial statements. Such an update need not be done ". . . if only summarized comparative information of the prior period(s) is presented." [*SAS No. 15*]

SAS No. 15 suggests the following example of an auditor's report on comparative statements for two periods:

We have examined the balance sheets of ABC Company as of [at] December 31, 19X2 and 19X1, and the related statements of income, retained earnings, and changes in financial position for the years then ended. Our examinations were made in accordance with generally accepted auditing standards and, accordingly, included such tests of the accounting records and such other auditing procedures as we considered necessary in the circumstances.

In our opinion, the financial statements referred to above present fairly the financial position of ABC Company as of [at] December 31, 19X2 and 19X1, and the results of its operations and the changes in its financial position for the years then ended, in conformity with generally accepted accounting principles applied on a consistent basis.[2]

SAS No. 15 suggests that during the audit of the current period, the auditor should be alert for anything that might relate to prior period statements that are presented with the current statements.

---

[1]This section is based on *Statement on Auditing Standards No. 15*, "Reports on Comparative Financial Statements", American Institute of Certified Public Accountants, 1976. Copyright © 1977 by the American Institute of Certified Public Accountants, Inc. Also, on *Exposure Draft: Proposed Statement on Auditing Standards*, "Association with Financial Statements," American Institute of Certified Public Accountants, May 31, 1979. At the time of this writing, the AICPA's Auditing Standards Board had not voted on the exposure draft. Due to the importance of the subject we will use and cite the exposure draft in this chapter. The reader is urged to review the *SAS* in its final form.

[2]Copyright © 1977 by the American Institute of Certified Public Accountants, Inc.

Different opinions. It is permissible to have different kinds of opinions for the different years for which statements are shown in comparative statements. The auditor should explain all substantive reasons for departures from an unqualified opinion in an explanatory paragraph(s). The explanatory paragraph is not needed, however, when the exception is due to a change in accounting principle.

Differing Updated Report. In the process of updating a report from a prior period, the auditor should consider anything that may affect the financial statements of that period. *SAS No. 15* notes that:

> An updated report on prior-period financial statements should be distinguished from a reissuance of a previous report . . . since in issuing an updated report the continuing auditor considers information that he has become aware of during his examination of the current-period financial statements . . . and because an updated report is issued in conjunction with the auditor's report on the current-period financial statements.

SAS No. 15 suggests that the following will likely cause a different opinion from that expressed in an earlier report (in a prior year):

1. If an uncertainty is resolved in a subsequent period, it may not be necessary to modify the opinion or disclaim an opinion with respect to the uncertainty.
2. During the current examination the auditor finds an uncertainty that affects the financial statements of a prior period.
3. In a situation in which the auditor has initially issued a modified opinion due to a departure from generally accepted accounting principles and then in a subsequent period the client restates the statement to conform to generally accepted accounting principles.

The auditor, in a separate explanatory paragraph(s) should explain the substantive reasons for the change in the report. This explanation is needed only when the updated opinion differs from the last opinion issued.

Predecessor Auditor. A predecessor may reissue a report on statements of a prior period at the request of a former client. Before doing so the predecessor auditor should determine if the report is still appropriate. This may be accomplished by:

1. Reading the current financial statements. The auditor should ". . . compare the prior-period financial statements that he reported on with the financial statements to be presented for comparative purposes. . . ."[*SAS No. 15*]
2. Obtaining a letter from the current auditor that comments on whether the current audit revealed anything that might have a

material effect on the financial statements reported on by the predecessor auditor. The predecessor auditor's report, however, should not mention the current auditor's work. The predecessor might want to consider the independence and professional standing of the current auditor. This may be done by employing techniques similar to those a principal auditor would use when part of an audit is conducted by another auditor (see page 543).

If the predecessor auditor becomes aware of something occurring subsequent to his or her report that affects that report, the predecessor auditor should make such inquiries and perform such procedures that are needed. The auditor should then decide if the report need be changed. (See *SAS No. 15* for a more detailed discussion of this entire topic.)

One Period Unaudited. The Exposure Draft on "Association with Financial Statements" indicates that unaudited financial statements presented in comparative form with audited statements in documents filed with the SEC should be marked "unaudited" but not referred to in the auditor's report. In other than documents filed with the SEC, the unaudited statements should be clearly labeled and either (1) the prior period report reissued or (2) the current period report should contain a separate paragraph describing the responsibility assumed for the prior period financial statements. The Exposure Draft gives the following example of a separate paragraph to be used in the current period report in a situation in which the prior period statements are audited and the current period is unaudited:

> The financial statements for the year ended December 31, 19X1, were examined by us (other accountants) and we (they) expressed an unqualified opinion on them in our (their) report dated March 1, 19X2, but we (they) have not performed any auditing procedures since that date.

Note that the paragraph indicated that (1) the statements for the year ended December 31, 19X1 had been previously examined, (2) the type of opinion expressed (unqualified), (3) the report was dated March 1, 19X2, and (4) that no audit procedures had been performed after the date of the previous report. If the prior report was other than unqualified, the reasons for the lack of an unqualified opinion should be noted in the paragraph. The Exposure Draft notes that in situations where the prior period statements are unaudited and the current report will contain a separate paragraph concerning the prior year, the paragraph should include:

1. A statement concerning the service performed in the prior period and the date of the report of that service.
2. A notation of any material modifications indicated in the prior period report.

3. An indication that the service was not an audit and consequently there is no basis for expressing an opinion on the financial statements as a whole.
4. If the client is a public entity there should be a disclaimer of opinion or a description of the review in the paragraph.[3]
5. If the client is a nonpublic entity and a compilation or review was done (later in this chapter we discuss compilation or reviews for nonpublic entities), the paragraph should include a description of the service performed.

The Exposure Draft gives the following example of a separate paragraph describing a review:

> The 19X1 financial statements were reviewed by us (other accountants) and our (their) report thereon, dated March 1, 19X2 stated we (they) were not aware of any material modifications that should be made to those statements for them to be in conformity with generally accepted accounting principles. However, a review is substantially less in scope than an audit and does not provide a basis for the expression of an opinion on the financial statements taken as a whole.

QUALIFICATIONS, ADVERSE OPINIONS, AND DISCLAIMERS

There will be occasions on which departures from the standard report will be required. This section of the chapter is devoted to a discussion of these departures and to presenting representative illustrations of the auditor's report in these circumstances.

Middle Paragraphs

As previously indicated, the standard auditor's report consists of two paragraphs. However, a middle paragraph or paragraphs should be included for the following matters:

a. To give reasons for a qualification of the opinion.
b. To emphasize a certain matter, even though an unqualified report is given. SAS No. 2[4] points out that the auditor may use such a paragraph to discuss a subsequent event or to discuss a matter

---

[3]The Exposure Draft notes that "in the rare circumstances when a public entity does not have its annual financial statements audited, an accountant may be requested to review its annual or interim financial statements. In those circumstances, an accountant may make a review and may look to the guidance in statements on Standards for Accounting and Review Services for the standards and procedures and form of report applicable to such an engagement."

[4]*Statement on Auditing Standards No. 2*, "Reports on Audited Financial Statements," American Institute of Certified Public Accountants, 1974.

affecting the comparability of the financial statements with those of the prior year.

c. To give reasons for a disclaimer of opinion or an adverse opinion.

A middle paragraph (or paragraphs) sometimes is (are) used to explain further the scope of the auditor's examination. But such explanations represent only an elaboration of the scope paragraph, which in itself, with qualifications where necessary, should constitute a complete statement of scope. Therefore, such a middle paragraph ordinarily should not be required in these circumstances. If the scope of the examination has been extended beyond what was required to express an opinion on the financial statements, the extended procedures may be made the subject of a separate letter to the client, but they should not be referred to in the accountants' report as *additional* procedures. An example of these circumstances might be where the testing of cash has been extended to search for possible fraud.

Qualified Opinion

SAS No. 2 notes that in the case of a qualified opinion, the auditor expresses certain reservations concerning the scope of the audit or the fairness of the presentation of the financial statements due to such factors as departures from generally accepted accounting principles, a material change in accounting principles or their application between periods, or the existence of uncertainties. In issuing a qualified opinion, the auditor should clearly explain the qualification. The reasons for the qualification and the effect, if any, on the financial statements should be noted in one or more middle paragraphs. If the effect cannot be determined, this fact should be noted. *SAS No. 2* states that "if such disclosures are made in a note to the financial statements, the explanatory paragraph(s) may be shortened by referring to it." Also, *SAS No. 2* suggests that the auditor should state in the middle paragraph whether the exception is due to an uncertain situation or a disagreement between the auditor and the client. Qualifications based on scope should be restricted to the auditor's report (not mentioned in the footnote to the financial statements). Such a qualification should be mentioned in an explanatory paragraph and referred to in the scope and opinion paragraphs. The explanatory paragraph is not required when the qualification is due to a change in accounting principle.

SAS No. 2 also recommends that ". . . a qualified opinion should include the word 'except' or 'exception' in a phrase such as 'except for' or 'with the exception of' unless the qualification arises because of an uncertainty affecting the financial statements; then the expression 'subject to' should be used."

Adverse Opinion

In an adverse opinion, the auditor (according to *SAS No. 2*) states that "In our opinion, because of matters discussed in the preceding paragraph, the financial statements referred to above do not present fairly, in conformity with generally accepted accounting principles, the financial position of X Company as of December 31, 19xx, or the results of its operations and changes in its financial position for the year then ended." The auditor thus is of the opinion that the financial statements as a whole are not presented fairly in conformity with generally accepted accounting principles (*SAS No. 2*). Furthermore, the auditor should have concluded that the exceptions are so material that a qualified opinion cannot be issued. The auditor should have definite evidence of lack of fair presentation.

SAS No. 2 notes that the auditor should, in one or more middle paragraphs, explain the reasons for the adverse opinion. Further, the auditor should discuss the effects of the exception on the financial statements. When such effects are not determinable this should be noted. Finally, since a reference to consistency in the opinion paragraph implies that generally accepted accounting principles have been used, an auditor should not refer to consistency in the opinion paragraph if an adverse opinion is given. If an auditor does have consistency exceptions, these reservations should, however, be noted in the report.

Disclaimer of Opinion

Sometimes an auditor is unable to form an opinion as to the fairness of the financial statements and thus disclaims an opinion. When disclaiming an opinion, *SAS No. 2* suggests that the auditor should state in an explanatory paragraph the reasons for the disclaimer. A disclaimer may be due to a limitation on the scope of the auditor's examination. Sometimes an unusual uncertainty is very material, and the auditor may wish to issue a disclaimer of opinion. Also a disclaimer should be given if an auditor is not independent.

SAS No. 2 gives the following example of a disclaimer when sufficient competent evidence is not obtained:

(Scope Paragraph)
... Except as set forth in the following paragraph, our examination was made in accordance with generally accepted auditing standards and accordingly included such tests of the accounting records and such other auditing procedures as we considered necessary in the circumstances.

542

(Separate Paragraph)

The Company did not take a physical inventory of merchandise, stated at $ . . . . . . in the accompanying financial statements as of December 31, 19XX, and at $ . . . . . as of December 31, 19X1. Further, evidence supporting the cost of property and equipment acquired prior to December 31, 19XX, is no longer available. The Company's records do not permit the application of adequate alternative procedures regarding the inventories or the cost of property and equipment.

(Disclaimer Paragraph)

Since the Company did not take physical inventories and we were unable to apply adequate alternative procedures regarding inventories and the cost of property and equipment, as noted in the preceding paragraph, the scope of our work was not sufficient to enable us to express, and we do not express, an opinion on the financial statements referred to above.[5]

REASONS FOR DEPARTURE FROM THE WORDING OF THE STANDARD REPORT

SAS No. 2 suggests seven principal reasons why an independent auditor may depart from the wording of the standard report. These are:

1. Limitations on the scope of the auditor's examination.
2. Reliance on the report of another auditor.
3. Lack of conformity with generally accepted accounting principles (GAAP).
4. A departure from an accounting principle set by the body designated to establish such principles.
5. Lack of consistency.
6. Uncertainties.
7. Emphasizing a matter.

Limitations of Scope

SAS No. 2 notes that the auditor, in order to express an unqualified opinion on the statements being examined, must use all audit procedures that are necessary in the circumstances. Limitations on the scope of the auditor's examination may result in a qualified opinion or a disclaimer of opinion. Such limitations may be due to restrictions imposed by the auditor's client or to circumstances (e.g., timing of the audit), lack of competent evidence, or poor accounting records.

SAS No. 2 notes that the decision to qualify or disclaim an opinion depends upon the importance of the omitted procedure(s) to the auditor's ". . . ability to form an opinion on the financial statements examined. This assessment will be affected by the nature and magnitude of the potential effects of the matters in question and by their significance to the financial statements. If the potential effects relate to many financial statement items, this significance is likely to be greater than if only a limited number of items is involved."

Other Auditors

Sometimes a part of an audit will be conducted by another independent auditing firm. For example, the principal auditor may not have an office in the city that contains a large subsidiary of a client. Under these circumstances, the subsidiary may be audited by another CPA firm.

The principal auditor has a choice as to whether and how to reference the other auditor in the (principal auditor's) report. First, the principal auditor may choose to make no reference to the other auditor. Under these circumstances, the principal auditor becomes responsible for the other auditor's work. SAS No. 1, section 543.05, suggests that the principal auditor usually will make no reference to the other auditor when:

1. The other auditor is: (a) associated with the principal auditor or (b) a correspondent to the principal auditor, or
2. The principal auditor hired, supervised, or guided the other auditor, or
3. The principal auditor becomes satisfied as to the other auditor's work, or
4. The work of the other auditor is not material in relation to the financial statements.

If no reference is made, SAS No. 1, section 543.12, suggests that the auditor should also possibly perform one or more of the following:

a. Visit the other auditor and discuss the audit procedures followed and results thereof.
b. Review the audit programs of the other auditor. In some cases, it may be appropriate to issue instructions to the other auditor as to the scope of his audit work.
c. Review the working papers of the other auditor, including his evaluation of internal control and his conclusions as to other significant aspects of the engagement.

Alternatively, the principal auditor may wish to make reference to the other auditor in the report. Then the report, in both the scope and opinion paragraphs, should refer to the other auditor and indicate the extent of the responsibility of the other auditor for the report. The principal auditor may name the other auditor only if (1) the other auditor has given permission and (2) the other auditor's report is also presented. Reference to the other auditor is a departure from the standard report, but is not a qualification of the auditor's opinion.

Whether or not reference is made to the other auditor, SAS No. 1, section 543.10, suggests the principal auditor should consider:

1. Inquiring of professional organizations, practitioners, bankers, and so on, as to the professionalism of the other auditor.
2. Obtaining a representation from the other auditor that he or she is independent.
3. Making sure that the other auditor is familiar with generally accepted auditing standards and the reporting requirements of regulatory agencies. Also making sure that the other auditor realizes that the work will be relied on by the principal auditor.
4. Coordinating the activities of the two auditors to facilitate the review of items that may affect the consolidation of the accounts.

If the principal auditor feels that the work of the other auditor cannot be relied upon, the principal auditor should qualify the opinion or disclaim an opinion. In such an event, the principal auditor should state the reasons for the exception (SAS No. 1, section 543.11).

Lack of Conformity with GAAP

SAS No. 2 notes that if the auditor believes that the financial statements materially depart from generally accepted accounting principles, the auditor should issue a qualified opinion or an adverse opinion. SAS No. 2 suggests that deciding whether the departure is "... sufficiently material to require either a qualified or an adverse opinion ..." will depend on the dollar size of the departure and qualitative factors such as the significance of the item to the client's business, whether the misstatement is pervasive, and how the misstatement affects the financial statements taken as a whole.

SAS No. 2 as amended by SAS No. 21 notes that "if the financial statements, including accompanying notes, fail to disclose information that is required by generally accepted accounting principles, the auditor should express a qualified or an adverse opinion because of the departure from those principles and should provide the information in his report, if practicable, unless its omission from the auditor's report is recognized as appropriate by a specific Statement on Auditing Standards."

Departure from a Promulgated Principle

In Chapter 2 it was noted that Rule 203 of the Code of Ethics states:

A member shall not express an opinion that financial statements are presented in conformity with generally accepted accounting principles if such statements contain any departure from an accounting principle promulgated by the body designated by Council to establish such principles which has a material effect on the statements taken as a whole, unless the member can demonstrate that due to unusual circumstances the financial statements would otherwise have been misleading. In such cases his report must describe the departure, the approximate effects thereof, if practicable, and the reasons why compliance with the principle would result in a misleading statement.

SAS No. 2 suggests that if the auditor believes that such unusual circumstances are present, an unqualified opinion can be given unless there is some other reason to modify the audit report. However, the departure and its effects must be described in a separate paragraph.

Consistency

SAS No. 1, section 546.01, notes that a change in accounting principle makes it necessary for an auditor to indicate the inconsistency in the audit report. The auditor should indicate agreement or lack thereof with the change. Failure to indicate agreement will mean that the auditor concurs with the change.

SAS No. 1, section 546.01, notes that "the form of modification of the opinion depends on the method of accounting for the effect of the change." If the change in accounting principle ". . . should be reported by restating financial statements of prior years, the appropriate reference to consistency is that the statements are consistent after giving retroactive effect to the change." (SAS No. 1, section 546.02.) An example of such an opinion covering one year is given in SAS No. 1, section 546.02:

> . . . applied on a basis consistent with that of the preceding year after giving retroactive effect to the change, with which we concur, in the method of accounting for long-term construction contracts as described in Note X to the financial statements.

SAS No. 1, section 546.03, gives an example (when the auditor is reporting only on the year in which the change takes place) of an opinion to use when the change in accounting principle should be reported by a means other than restating prior year statements. Specifically:

> . . . in conformity with generally accepted accounting principles which, except for the change, with which we concur, in the method of computing depreciation as described in Note X to the financial statements, have been applied on a basis consistent with that of the preceding year.

If the new accounting principle or the method of accounting for the

546

effect of the change are not in accordance with generally accepted accounting principles, a qualification or adverse opinion due to departure from generally accepted accounting principles may be in order. Also, if the auditor is not satisfied with management's reason for the change in accounting principles a qualification may be needed (*SAS No. 1*).

Uncertainties

SAS No. 2 in discussing uncertainties notes:

> In certain instances, the outcome of matters that may affect the financial statements or the disclosures required therein is not susceptible of reasonable estimation; such matters are to be regarded as uncertainties for purposes of this Statement. When such uncertainties exist, it cannot be detemined whether the financial statements should be adjusted or in what amounts.

Uncertainties include such examples as the result of lawsuits or the results of income tax adjustments. When material uncertainties exist the auditor should consider qualifying or disclaiming the opinion. A very material uncertainty might lead to a disclaimer of opinion. An uncertainty that is less material may result in a qualified opinion.

The following opinion paragraph is suggested by *SAS No. 2*, when a qualified opinion is to be used in these circumstances:

> In our opinion, subject to the effects, if any, on the financial statements of the ultimate resolution of the matter discussed in the preceding paragraph, the financial statements referred to above present fairly . . .

Note that the words "subject to " are used. Uncertainties are the only instances in which such a phrase may be used. In other types of qualifications, the phrase "except for" is usually proper. *SAS No. 2* indicates that the auditor need not modify the opinion because of the existence of an uncertainty when it is concluded ". . . that there is only a minimal likelihood that resolution of the uncertainty will have a material effect on the financial statements."

Emphasizing a Matter

SAS No. 2 points out that, in certain situations, an auditor may wish to emphasize a certain matter but still issue an unqualified opinion. Examples (per *SAS No. 2*) would be where the auditor wishes to:

1. ". . . point out that the entity is a component of a larger business enterprise. . . ."
2. ". . . call attention to an unusually important subsequent event or

to an accounting matter affecting the comparability of the financial statements with those of the preceding period."

Such information may be included in a separate paragraph in the report.

Independence

As stated earlier, *SAS No. 2* mentions seven reasons why an independent auditor might be required to depart from the wording of the standard report. An additional reason calling for a departure is where the auditor is *not* independent. The Exposure Draft on "Association with Financial Statements" states:

> When an accountant is not independent, any procedures he might perform would not be in accordance with generally accepted auditing standards, and he would be precluded from expressing an opinion, on such statements. Accordingly, he should disclaim an opinion with respect to the financial statements and should state specifically that he is not independent. In these circumstances, if the financial statements are those of a nonpublic entity, the accountant should look to the guidance in Statements on Standards for Accounting and Review Services.

(Standards for nonpublic entities will be discussed later.)

SUBSEQUENT EVENTS

The auditor's report on the usual examination of financial statements includes an opinion on financial position as of a given date and the results of operations and changes in financial position for a period ended on that date. Certain events and transactions occurring after the balance-sheet date may have an important impact on the financial statements and therefore require extension of the audit into the subsequent period. In certain instances, these events may require changes in the statements or in the footnotes thereto.

Generally the period of occurrence of the post–balance-sheet-date events extends from the date of the balance sheet to the date used in the auditor's report, which in most cases is the date of completion of the field work. When preparing registration statements for the SEC this period is extended to the date of the registration statement.

Types of Subsequent Events

There are two types of subsequent events which should be considered:

1. Events which affect the financial statements at the balance-sheet date and should be reflected therein. If subsequent information is acquired in time to permit its use, if the information provides a basis for more accurate estimates or provisions, and if the information would have been utilized had it been available at the balance-sheet date, appropriate adjustments should be made in the financial statements. Examples are collection or settlement of receivables or determination or settlement of liabilities on a substantially different basis than previously anticipated, or events which make worthless large portions of the inventory or investments in stock or plant assets.

2. Events that relate to occurrences that arose subsequent to the balance-sheet date. These are events which do not require adjustment of the financial statements but whose effect in the future may be such that disclosure is advisable. Examples are changes in short- and long-term debt and capital stock, restrictive covenants relating to dividends or other matters, mergers or acquisitions, disposal of a substantial portion of the productive assets, or serious losses from flood, fire, or other casualty. SAS No. 1, section 560.05, notes that "occasionally . . . an event may be so significant that disclosure can best be made by supplementing the historical financial statements with pro forma financial data giving effect to the event, as if it had occurred on the date of the balance sheet." Furthermore, SAS No. 1, section 560.09, notes that when such events are very material ". . . the auditor may want to include in his report an explanatory paragraph directing the reader's attention to the event and its effects. . . ."

Certain events do not require adjustment of the financial statements and usually do not require disclosure. Examples are war, strikes, unionization, management changes, marketing agreements, or loss of important customers. These events usually are not disclosed because (a) even if they had occurred before the balance-sheet date they would not be commented on in the financial statements and (b) disclosure of such events frequently creates doubt as to the reasons therefor, and the inferences drawn could be misleading as often as they are informative.

Auditing Procedures in the Subsequent Period

The auditor should search for the occurrence of subsequent events. Such a search may include the following steps (see SAS No. 1, section 560.12):

1. Test cutoff bank statements and returned checks and bank charges.
2. Review collections of accounts receivable.

3. Review credit memoranda issued for sales returns and allowances. Ascertain that there is no important time lag in issuing the credits.
4. Scan cash receipts book for evidence of proceeds of loans or significant sales of productive assets.
5. Scan cash disbursements book for unusual payments and payment of liabilities not recorded as of the balance-sheet date.
6. Review the various corporate minutes. Inquire about matters covered at meetings for which minutes are not yet available.
7. Review interim company financial statements.
8. Obtain management's representation concerning events which may have occurred.
9. "Inquire of client's legal counsel concerning litigation, claims, and assessments. . . . " [SAS No. 1, Section 560.12(d) as amended by SAS No. 12]
10. Review general journal entries.

Subsequent Discovery of Facts

The auditor's responsibility generally ends as of the date of the audit report. However, at a later date the auditor may discover facts which existed at the date of the audit report. The auditor's actions depend (according to SAS No. 1, section 561.05) on whether "(a) . . . [the auditor's] report would have been affected if the information had been known to him at the date of his report and had not been reflected in the financial statements and (b) he believes there are persons currently relying or likely to rely on the financial statements who would attach importance to the information." SAS No. 1, section 561, gives a detailed description of the procedures the auditor should follow in such a situation. Also, see the Yale Express case in Chapter 4.

OTHER INFORMATION AND THE AUDITOR[6]

Client entities often publish information along with financial statements. The information, while not the subject of the auditor's report, may relate to the audit examination or propriety of the auditor's report. Consequently, the auditor should read this "other information" and consider whether it is inconsistent with the information in or the presentation in the financial statements. SAS No. 8 notes that:

---

[6]The material in this section is based on Statement on Auditing Standards No. 8, "Other Information in Documents Containing Audited Financial Statements." Copyright © 1976 by the American Institute of Certified Public Accountants, Inc.

550

If the auditor concludes that there is a material inconsistency, he should determine whether the financial statements, his report, or both require revision. If he concludes that they do not require revision, he should request the client to revise the other information. If the other information is not revised to eliminate the material inconsistency, he should consider other actions such as revising his report to include an explanatory paragraph describing the material inconsistency, withholding the use of his report in the document, and withdrawing from the engagement.

If the auditor believes there is a material misstatement of fact, rather than an inconsistency, this should be discussed with the client. *SAS No. 8* notes that, if after discussing the matter with the client, " . . . the auditor concludes that a material misstatement of fact remains, the action he takes will depend on his judgment in the particular circumstances. He should consider steps such as notifying his client in writing of his views concerning the information and consulting his legal counsel as to further appropriate action in the circumstances."

REPORTING SEGMENT INFORMATION[7]

The auditor's standard report also covers segment information included in the financial statements covered by the report. *SAS No. 21* indicates that reference to segment information should be made only if the audit disclosed one of the following:

1. " . . . [A] misstatement or omission, or a change in an accounting principle, relating to the segment information that is material in relation to the financial statements as a whole . . ." *(SAS No. 21)*
2. A restriction on the scope of the examination.

Misstatement or Omission

A misstatement in segment information that is material in relation to the statements as a whole should cause the auditor to modify his or her opinion due to a departure from generally accepted accounting principles. *SAS No. 21* gives the following example of such a qualification:

(Explanatory Paragraph)
With respect to the segment information in Note X, $ . . . . . . of the operating expenses of Industry A were incurred jointly by Industries A and B. In our opinion, Statement No. 14 of the Financial Accounting Standards Board requires that those operating expenses be allocated

---

[7]This section is based on *Statement on Auditing Standards No. 21,* "Segment Information," American Institute of Certified Public Accountants, 1977. Copyright © 1977 by the American Institute of Certified Public Accountants, Inc.

between Industries A and B. The effect of the failure to allocate those operating expenses has been to understate the operating profit of Industry A and to overstate the operating profit of Industry B by an amount that has not been determined.

(Opinion Paragraph)
In our opinion, except for the effects of not allocating certain common operating expenses between Industries A and B, as discussed in the preceding paragraph, the financial statements referred to above present fairly. . . .[8]

If the client does not include all or part of the needed segment information, the auditor should modify his or her opinion due to inadequate disclosure. The auditor need not present the omitted information in his or her report, but should describe the kind of information omitted. *SAS No. 21* gives the following example of a report that might be used in such a situation:

(Explanatory Paragraph)
The Company declined to present segment information for the year ended December 31, 19XX. In our opinion, presentation of segment information concerning the Company's operations in different industries, its foreign operations and export sales, and its major customers is required by *Statement No. 14* of the Financial Accounting Standards Board. The omission of segment information results in an incomplete presentation of the Company's financial statements.

(Opinion Paragraph)
In our opinion, except for the omission of segment information, as discussed in the preceding paragraph, the financial statements referred to above present fairly. . . .[9]

Consistency

FASB Statement No. 14 requires that a change in the methods by which a client's segment information is prepared and presented should be disclosed in the period of change. *SAS No. 21* states that:

if the nature and effect of a change are not disclosed or, if applicable, the segment information is not retroactively restated, the auditor should modify his opinion because of the departure from generally accepted accounting principles. . . .
* * * * *
A modification of the auditor's report as to consistency is not required . . . except for a change in accounting principle that affects the financial statements taken as a whole. . . .

---

[8]Copyright © 1977 by the American Institute of Certified Public Accountants, Inc.
[9]Ibid.

552

Scope

If an auditor is not able to reach a conclusion as to whether the client need disclose segments as required by *FASB Statement No. 14* and the client refuses to develop information that would be needed to reach such a conclusion, *SAS No. 21* notes that the auditor should indicate this in the scope paragraph and then qualify the report. *SAS No. 21* provides the following example:

(Scope Paragraph)
. . . Except as explained in the following paragraph, our examination . . . and such other auditing procedures as we considered necessary in the circumstances.

(Explanatory Paragraph)
The Company has not developed the information we consider necessary to reach a conclusion as to whether the presentation of segment information concerning the Company's operations in different industries, its foreign operations and export sales, and its major customers is necessary to conform with *Statement No. 14* of the Financial Accounting Standards Board.

(Opinion Paragraph)
In our opinion, except for the possible omission of segment information, the financial statements referred to above present fairly. . . .[10]

If the auditor is not able to apply auditing procedures to the reported segment information that are deemed necessary, then a qualification for the statements as a whole is necessary. *SAS No. 21* gives the following example of such a report:

(Scope Paragraph)
. . . Except as explained in the following paragraph, our examination . . . and such other auditing procedures as we considered necessary in the circumstances.

(Explanatory Paragraph)
In accordance with the Company's request, our examination of the financial statements did not include the segment information presented in Note X concerning the Company's operations in different industries, its foreign operations and export sales, audits major customers.

(Opinion Paragraph)
In our opinion, except for the effects of such adjustments or disclosures, if any, as might have been determined to be necessary had we applied to the segment information the procedures we considered necessary in the circumstances, the financial statements referred to above present fairly. . . .[11]

[10]Ibid.
[11]Ibid.

Reporting Separately

SAS No. 21 indicates that the auditor may, if requested, report separately on segment information either: (1) as part of the report on the financial statements taken as a whole or (2) as a special report. SAS No. 21 states that "paragraphs 10–13 of SAS No. 14, 'Special Reports,' provide guidance that is applicable to reporting separately on segment information. However, since segment information is one of the disclosures required by generally accepted accounting principles, all of the generally accepted auditing standards are applicable to an engagement to report separately on segment information."

LONG-FORM REPORTS

Occasionally auditors issue long-form reports. These reports often consist of data and comments of both an accounting and nonaccounting nature in addition to the opinion on the basic financial statements. SAS No. 1, section 610.02, requires that since ". . . the usual short-form report [or standard report] covers only the basic financial statements, the auditor should clearly establish his position regarding the other [additional] data in the long-form report." So that the auditor's responsibility is explicit, a separate accountants' report on additional financial information should be included, or the basic report should be expanded. The following points should be considered in drafting the report:

a. Reference should be made to the source of the additional financial information; that is, to the accounting records which were tested by the auditor.

b. Care should be exercised to avoid any statement that the additional financial information is fairly presented in any absolute sense or in any broader sense, when the accounting records from which it was derived were subjected only to the usual tests applied as part of the auditing procedures followed. Rather, it should be stated that the information is fairly presented in all material respects in relation to the financial statements taken as a whole.

c. When the additional financial information includes nonaccounting information or additional data which is not susceptible to being tested by the auditor, an adequate and explicit disclaimer should be employed.

d. Distinction should be made between the basic financial statements and the additional financial information. This distinction should be made by a transitional comment whenever a separate report is presented; however, when a third paragraph is included in the basic accountant's report, no such comment will be required since the distinction is obvious.

e. It is desirable, but not essential, to state that the additional financial information is not necessary to a fair presentation of the financial statements.

Report on Additional Financial Information

When there is no nonaccounting information present which would lead to a disclaimer, the following wording of the report might be used:

> The audited financial statements of the Corporation and our report thereon are presented in the preceding section of this report. The financial information presented hereinafter was derived from the accounting records tested by us as part of the auditing procedures followed in our examination of the aforementioned financial statements, and in our opinion it is fairly presented in all material respects in relation to the financial statements taken as a whole; however, it is not necessary for a fair presentation of the financial position, results of operations, and changes in financial position of the Corporation.

When a schedule that does not involve information affecting the financial statements is included in the other financial information, the following wording is suggested:

> The audited financial statements of the Corporation and our report thereon are presented in the preceding section of this report. The financial information presented hereinafter, excepting the schedule of _____*, was derived from the accounting records tested by us as part of the auditing procedures followed in our examination of the aforementioned financial statements, and in our opinion it is fairly presented in all material respects in relation to the financial statements taken as a whole; however, it is not necessary for a fair presentation of the financial position, results of operations, and changes in financial position of the Corporation.
>
> The information shown in the schedule of _____* was prepared from the information furnished to us by the Corporation, but we did not make independent tests of the schedule as it does not involve information which enters into the financial statements.

If a schedule of additional data regarding the organization is included, a statement may be made similar to that included in the above example. Since the information included in this schedule obviously contains nonaccounting data, the schedule of organization data also may be shown on the contents page as nonfinancial information with no reference made to the schedule in the accountants' report on addi-

---

*Name of particular schedule included.

tional financial information. The contents page would be presented as:

Audited Financial Statements
  Accountants' Report
  Various Statements
Additional Financial Information
  Accountants' Report on Additional Financial Information
  Various Schedules
Organization Data

In instances where an opinion on the basic financial statements has been denied (or an adverse opinion given), reference to a fair presentation should be omitted.

In instances where the additional financial information consists only of one or two schedules, it may be appropriate to add a third paragraph to the basic accountants' report to clarify the auditor's position with respect to such schedules. This would eliminate the need for a separate accountant's report for these schedules.

Comments

Ordinarily, it should not be necessary to comment on the scope of the examination when reporting on "additional financial information." Many of the auditor's tests, particularly compliance tests, are directed primarily to determining whether the system of internal control is functioning effectively. Inasmuch as such testing is implicit in the representation made in the scope paragraph of the accountants' report, no further description of scope in that respect is necessary.

Recommendations for changes in accounting procedures, for improvements in internal control and so on, ordinarily should not be included in reports on financial statements. Rather, they should be made the subject of a management letter (as discussed in Chapter 15). It may be appropriate to refer to such a letter in the "additional financial information" section of the report. Such reference is appropriate when the accounting deficiencies cited in the letter were so pervasive as to have required a qualified opinion. Even in the absence of such a situation, the auditor may deem it desirable to refer to the existence of such a letter in the long-form report.

A Proposed Revision[12]

A new proposed SAS, if adopted, would supersede section 610 of SAS No. 1. It would redefine certain items comprising long-form re-

---

[12]This section is based on *Exposure Draft: Proposed Statement on Auditing Standards*, "The Effect on the Auditor's Report When Additional Information Is Presented," American Institute of Certified Public Accountants, 1979.

ports. The long-form report, itself, would be termed a *document*. "... [A]ny information presented that is not necessary for a fair presentation of financial position, results of operations, and changes in financial position in conformity with generally accepted accounting principles" would be termed *additional information*. According to this proposed SAS, when additional information is present the auditor would indicate the following in the report:

a.　His examination has been made for the purpose of forming an opinion on the basic financial statements taken as a whole.
b.　The additional information included in the document is presented for purposes of analysis and is not necessary for a fair presentation of the basic financial statements in conformity with generally accepted accounting principles.
c.　Whether the additional information has been subjected to the auditing procedures applied in the examination of the basic financial statements and whether he expresses an opinion on the information.

The proposed SAS states that "the auditor may either express an opinion that additional information is stated fairly in all material respects in relation to the basic financial statements taken as a whole or disclaim an opinion on it depending on whether the information has been subjected to the auditing procedures applied in the examination of the basic financial statements."

The proposed SAS notes that "the additional information should be presented as a separate section of the document and should be appropriately labeled as additional information." An example of the wording the auditor might use (in a separate paragraph of the standard report or with the additional information) would be as follows:

> Our examination was made for the purpose of forming an opinion on the basic financial statements taken as a whole. The additional information is presented for purposes of analysis and is not necessary for a fair presentation of the basic financial statements in conformity with generally accepted accounting principles. The additional information has been subjected to the auditing procedures applied in the examination of the basic financial statements and, in our opinion, the additional information is stated fairly in all material respects in relation to the basic financial statements taken as a whole. [per the proposed SAS]

In situations where appropriate, the last sentence of the report would read:

> The additional information has not been subjected to the auditing procedures applied in the examination of the basic financial statements and, accordingly, we express no opinion on it. [per the proposed SAS]

SPECIAL REPORTS[13]

This section of the chapter presents recommendations to be followed in those situations where the standard report (or one departing therefrom) and the related report on additional financial information are not suitable. In all instances involving special reports, the general standards and the standards of field work, when appropriate in relation to the nature of the audit, are applicable. The first standard of reporting (generally accepted accounting principles) does not apply to statements which do not claim to present the financial position, results of operations, and changes in financial position, as for example, statements prepared on the basis of cash receipts and disbursements. The second standard of reporting (consistency) is frequently appropriate, depending upon the nature of the matter being reported upon. The third and fourth reporting standards (adequacy of informative disclosures and expression of opinion) are clearly applicable to special reports.

Special reports should serve a useful purpose and should be prepared in a manner which is appropriate to the nature of the organization. For example, a statement of cash receipts and disbursements would serve a useful purpose and be appropriate in reporting the operations of a charitable organization, but it would not be suitable for reporting the operations of a manufacturing company.

Special reports are appropriate for:

a. Financial statements that are prepared in accordance with a comprehensive basis of accounting other than generally accepted accounting principles. . . .
b. Specified elements, accounts, or items of a financial statement. . . .
c. Compliance with aspects of contractual agreements or regulatory requirements related to audited financial statements. . . .
d. Financial information presented in prescribed forms or schedules that require a prescribed form of auditor's report. . . . [SAS No. 14]

Basis Other Than GAAP

SAS No. 14 indicates the following four are the only cases in which a comprehensive basis other than generally accepted accounting principles (GAAP) may be used:

a. A basis of accounting that the reporting entity uses to comply with the reporting requirements or financial reporting provisions of a

---

[13]This section is based on SAS No. 14, "Special Reports", American Institute of Certified Public Accountants, 1976. Copyright © 1977 by the American Institute of Certified Public Accountants, Inc.

government regulatory agency to whose jurisdiction the entity is subject. . . .

b. A basis of accounting that the reporting entity uses or expects to use to file its income tax return for the period covered by the financial statements.

c. The cash receipts and cash disbursements basis of accounting, and modifications of the cash basis having substantial support, such as recording depreciation on fixed assets or accruing income taxes.

d. A definite set of criteria having substantial support that is applied to all material items appearing in financial statements, such as the price-level basis of accounting described in Accounting Principles Board *Statement No. 3*.

SAS No. 14 indicates that an auditor's report in any of the above instances should include *all* of the following:

1. A scope paragraph.
2. An explanatory paragraph that *(a)* states (or refers to the note to the statements that states) the basis on which the statements are presented, *(b)* refers to the note that indicates how the basis differs from GAAP, and *(c)* states that the statements were not intended to be in conformity with GAAP.
3. An opinion paragraph that comments on *(a)* the consistency of current statements (on the basis used) with the prior period statement and *(b)* whether the current statements are fairly presented in conformity with the basis used. Any departure from an unqualified opinion should be explained in an additional explanatory paragraph.

SAS No. 14 indicates that "when reporting on financial statements prepared in accordance with the requirements or financial reporting provisions of a government regulatory agency . . . , the auditor may use the form of reporting . . . [noted in the preceding paragraph] only if the financial statements are intended solely for filing with a regulatory agency or if additional distribution is recognized as appropriate by an AICPA accounting or audit guide or auditing interpretation."

Terms such as "balance sheet" or "income statement" are generally understood to be associated with statements that are based on GAAP. Consequently, consideration should be given as to whether the financial statements have appropriate titles. *SAS No. 14*, paragraph 8, presents examples of reports that may be used when the basis of accounting is other than GAAP.

Reports on Specific Elements, Accounts Or Items

Expressing an Opinion. *SAS No. 14* indicates that an auditor may express an opinion on specific elements, accounts, or items in financial statements as either a separate engagement or as part of an examination of financial statements. However, in the later instance if an adverse opinion or disclaimer of opinion is given for the statements as a whole, the auditor should take care that the report on the specific elements, accounts, or items is not in essence a piecemeal opinion on the financial statements (the elements, accounts, or items reported on and the scope of the examination should not be intended to or should not encompass a major portion of the financial statements). Also, the report should not accompany the entire financial statements.

A report on specific elements, accounts, or items should:

    a. Identify the specified elements, accounts, or items examined.

    b. State whether the examination was made in accordance with generally accepted auditing standards and, if applicable, that it was made in conjunction with an examination of financial statements. (Also, if applicable, any modification of the auditor's standard report on those statements should be indicated.)

    c. Identify the basis on which the specified elements, accounts, or items are presented and, when applicable, any agreements specifying such basis.

    d. Describe and indicate the source of significant interpretations made by the client in the course of the engagement relating to the provisions of a relevant agreement.

    e. Indicate whether in his opinion the specified elements, accounts, or items are presented fairly on the basis indicated.

    f. If applicable, indicate whether in his opinion the disclosed basis has been applied in a manner consistent with that of the preceding period. [*SAS No. 14*]

Applying agreed-upon procedures. *SAS No. 14* indicates that CPAs can also report on ". . . the results of applying agreed-upon procedures to one or more specified elements, accounts, or items of a financial statement. . . ." Examples of such reports include a report in connection with a proposed acquisition or a report in connection with claims of creditors (to help a client evaluate the reasonableness of the claims). *SAS No. 14* notes that "acceptance of such an engagement is appropriate only if (a) the parties involved have a clear understanding of the procedures . . . to be performed, (b) distribution of the report is to be restricted to named parties involved, and (c) financial statements of the entity are not to accompany the report." See *SAS No. 14*, paragraphs 15 through 17, for a more complete discussion of this topic.

Reports on Compliance

Entities may be required by contracts (e.g., bond indentures) or regulatory agencies to provide compliance reports by independent auditors. The auditor can give negative assurance relative to the items in question "... in a separate report or in one or more paragraphs of the auditor's report accompanying the financial statements. Such assurance, however, should not be given unless the auditor has examined the financial statements to which the contractual agreements or regulatory requirements relate." [SAS No. 14]

SAS No. 14 also notes that the

> ... negative assurance should specify that it is being given in connection with an examination of the financial statements. The auditor may also wish to state that the examination was not directed primarily toward obtaining knowledge regarding compliance. A separate report giving negative assurance should contain a paragraph stating that the financial statements have been examined, the date of the report thereon, and whether the examination was made in accordance with generally accepted auditing standards.

See SAS No. 14, paragraph 19, for some examples of compliance reports.

Prescribed Forms

Some authorities may require that financial statements be prepared on printed forms that the independent auditor may believe results in a presentation that is not in conformity with reporting standards of the profession. The forms may specify report wording. SAS No. 14 points out that whenever printed forms would force the auditor to make an assertion which is believed to be unjustified in the circumstances, the auditor has no alternative but to reword that portion of the form or to submit a separate report on the matter.

OTHER TYPES OF REPORTS

Reports on Interim Financial Information Presented Other Than in a Note to Audited Financial Statements[14]

If an accountant conducts a review of interim financial data, he or she may issue a report that may be included in a written communication that sets forth interim financial information. The accountant's report should consist of:

> ...(a) a statement that the review ... was made in accordance with the standards for such reviews, (b) an identification of the interim finan-

---

[14]The next two sections are based on *Statement on Auditing Standards No. 24*, "Review of Interim Financial Information," American Institute of Certified Public Accountants, 1979. Copyright © 1979 by the American Institute of Certified Public Accountants, Inc.

cial information reviewed, *(c)* a description of the procedures for a review of interim financial information, *(d)* a statement that a review of interim financial information is substantially less in scope than an examination in accordance with generally accepted auditing standards, . . . and accordingly, no such opinion is expressed, and *(e)* a statement about whether the accountant is aware of any material modifications that should be made to the accompanying financial information so that it conforms with generally accepted accounting principles. [SAS No. 24]

The report should usually be dated as of the completion of the review and each page of the interim financial data should be marked "unaudited."

SAS No. 24 gives the following example of such a report.

> We have made a review of (describe the information or statements reviewed) of ABC Company and consolidated subsidiaries as of September 30, 19X1 and for the three-month and nine-month periods then ended, in accordance with standards established by the American Institute of Certified Public Accountants.
>
> A review of interim financial information consists principally of obtaining an understanding of the system for the preparation of interim financial information, applying analytical review procedures to financial data, and making inquiries of persons responsible for financial and accounting matters. It is substantially less in scope than an examination in accordance with generally accepted auditing standards, the objective of which is the expression of an opinion regarding the financial statements taken as a whole. Accordingly, we do not express such an opinion.
>
> Based on our review, we are not aware of any material modifications that should be made to the accompanying financial (information or statements) for them to be in conformity with generally accepted accounting principles.[15]

A modification of the accountant's report is needed if there is a departure from generally accepted accounting principles (including adequate disclosure). However, an uncertainty or lack of consistency in applying accounting information that affects interim financial information will not necessitate a modified report if there is disclosure of such matters. A change in principles that is not in conformity with generally accepted accounting principles would require disclosure in the report.

In the case of a departure from generally accepted accounting principles, the modification should describe the departure and if possible its effect on interim financial information. If a departure is due to inadequate disclosure, the report should, if possible, include the needed information.

---

[15]Copyright © 1979 by the American Institute of Certified Public Accountants, Inc.

562

SAS No. 24 gives the following example of a modified accountant's report (due to a departure from generally accepted accounting principles):

(Explanatory Third Paragraph)
Based on information furnished us by management, we believe that the Company has excluded from property and debt in the accompanying balance sheet certain lease obligations that should be capitalized in order to conform with generally accepted accounting principles. This information indicates that if these lease obligations were capitalized at September 30, 19X1, property would be increased by $ . . . . . . , and long-term debt by $ . . . . . . , and net income and earnings per share would be increased (decreased) by $ . . . . . . , $ . . . . . . , $ . . . . . . , and $ . . . . . . , respectively, for the three-month and nine-month periods then ended.

(Concluding Paragraph)
Based on our review, with the exception of the matter(s) described in the preceding paragraph(s), we are not aware of any material modifications that should be made to the accompanying financial (information or statements) for them to be in conformity with generally accepted accounting principles.[16]

The following is SAS No. 24's suggested modificaton due to inadequate disclosure:

(Explanatory Third Paragraph)
Management has informed us that the Company is presently contesting deficiencies in federal income taxes proposed by the Internal Revenue Service for the years 19XX through 19XX in the aggregate amount of approximately $ . . . . . . , and that the extent of the Company's liability, if any, and the effect on the accompanying (information or statements) are not determinable at this time. The (information or statements) fail to disclose these matters, which we believe are required to be disclosed in conformity with generally accepted accounting principles.

(Concluding Paragraph)
Based on our review, with the exception of the matter(s) described in the preceding paragraph(s), we are not aware of any material modifications that should be made to the accompanying financial (information or statements) for them to be in conformity with generally accepted accounting principles.[17]

---

[16]Ibid.
[17]Ibid.

Reporting on Interim Financial Information Presented in a Note to Audited Financial Statements

Some companies include a note on certain interim financial information in their audited financial statements. In such a case, the auditor will use the review procedures noted in Chapter 13. The auditor usually will not need to modify the audit report to make reference to either the review or the interim financial information. Furthermore, it is not necessary for the accountant's report on the review of the interim financial information to accompany the audited statements. There are, however, some circumstances that call for an expansion of the auditor's report. Examples include: (1) where the scope of the review of interim financial information was restricted; (2) where the interim financial information is not presented in conformity with generally accepted accounting principles; (3) where no review was conducted of the interim financial data (and this is not mentioned in the note); and (4) where the information included in the note is not marked "unaudited."

Forecasts

In 1975 the AICPA's Accounting Standards Executive Committee (the senior technical body of the AICPA relating to financial accounting and reporting, cost accounting and presentation of financial forecasts), issued *Statement of Position 75-4 (SOP 75-4)*, "Presentation and Disclosure of Financial Forecasts."[18] *SOP 75-4* makes the following distinction between financial forecasts, financial projections, and feasibility studies:

Financial forecast: "... an estimate of the most probable financial position, results of operations and changes in financial position for one or more future periods."

Financial projection: "... an estimate of financial results based on assumptions which are not necessarily the most likely."

Feasibility study: "... an analysis of a proposed investment or course of action. A feasibility study may involve the preparation of financial projections and/or a financial forecast."

SOP 75-4 provides presentation and disclosure guidance for entities issuing financial forecasts. However, the *SOP* notes that finan-

[18]*Statement of Position 75-4*, "Presentation and Disclosure of Financial Forecasts," American Institute of Certified Public Accountants, 1975. Copyright © 1975 by the American Insititute of Certified Public Accountants, Inc.

cial forecasts are not part of the basic financial statements. The reader should refer to the *SOP* for the details on the recommendations on presentation and disclosure. Briefly some of the major suggestions indicated by *SOP 75-4* include:

1. Presenting forecasts in historical financial statement format.
2. Preparing the forecasts on a basis consistent with generally accepted accounting principles that will likely be used in historical financial statements in the period forecasted.
3. Expressing forecasts ". . . in specific monetary amounts representing the single most probable forecasted result." This figure may be ". . . supplemented by ranges and probabilistic statements. . . ."
4. Disclosing important assumptions.

Sometimes CPAs are engaged to assist management in the preparation of financial forecasts and then are asked to issue a report. The content of a report on forecasts should be responsive to Rule 201E of the Code of Ethics which does not permit the auditor's name ". . . to be used in conjunction with any forecast of future transactions in a manner which may lead to the belief that the member vouches for the achievability of the forecast." Furthermore, Interpretation 201-2 indicates that, when an auditor is associated with a forecast, disclosure should be made of: (1) the source of the information used; (2) the important assumptions used; (3) the character of the work done by the auditor; and (4) the degree of responsibility the auditor is taking.[19]

At the time of this writing, the AICPA has under consideration a proposed exposure draft of a guide relating to an accountant's review of forecasts and reporting on such a review. The reader should be alert to future developments in this area.

Reports on Internal Control

SAS No. 1, section 640.01, notes that auditors may be asked to issue a report on their client's internal control. Such a request may originate with the client's management, a government agency, or various other sources. Sections 640 and 641 of *SAS No. 1* discuss reports on internal controls. More specifically, sections 640.12 and 640.13 give the suggested forms for reports on internal control. These sections which give the language to be used in an internal control report were amended as a result of the issuance of *SAS No. 20*. The wording de-

---

[19]*AICPA Professional Standards, Vol. 2*, Section 201.03.

scribes in reasonable detail the objective and limitations of internal accounting control and the auditor's evaluation of it.

Reporting on Required Supplemental Information[20]

A proposed SAS ". . . provides guidance to the independent auditor on the nature of procedures to be applied to supplemental information required by the FASB and the form and content of the auditor's reporting on such information."[21] In the future, the Auditing Standards Board (ASB) may propose additional SASs on specific FASB requirements of supplemental information. For example, as of this writing it appears likely that the ASB will issue an exposure draft on auditor involvement with the supplemental disclosure requirements of *FASB Statement No. 33.*

The general guidelines contained in the proposed SAS state that the auditor should apply the following procedures to required supplemental information:

  a. Inquire of management regarding the methods of preparing the information, including (1) whether it is measured and presented within guidelines prescribed by the FASB, (2) whether methods of measurement or presentation have been changed from those used in the prior period, and (3) the reasons for any such changes and any significant assumptions or interpretations underlying measurement or presentation.

  b. Compare the information for consistency with (1) audited financial statements, (2) other information obtained during the examination, and (3) management's responses to the foregoing inquiries.

  c. Consider whether representations on required supplemental information should be included in specific written representations obtained from management *(See SAS No. 19, Client Representations).*

  d. Apply additional procedures, if any, specified in other SASs for specific types of supplemental information.

  e. Make additional inquiries if application of the above procedures causes the auditor to believe the information has not been measured or presented within applicable guidelines.[22]

Suggested wording in the proposed SAS for reporting on the information (in a separate report or in an additional paragraph to the standard report) is as follows as per paragraph 6 of the proposed *SAS:*

---

[20]This section is based on *Exposure Draft: Proposed Statement on Auditing Standards,* "Reporting on Required Supplemental Information," American Institute of Certified Public Accountants, October 1, 1979.

[21]*Exposure Draft: Proposed Statement on Auditing Standards,* "Reporting on Required Supplemental Information," paragraph 1.

[22]Ibid., paragraph 5.

566

We have read the supplemental information on (specifically identify information subjected to prescribed procedures), inquired of management regarding the methods of presentation and measurement, and compared it with the audited financial statements. Such supplemental information is not part of the basic financial statements and, accordingly, we did not audit, and do not express an opinion on, such information. However, based on the procedures described above, we are not aware of any material modifications that should be made to the supplemental information identified above for it to conform with guidelines established by the Financial Accounting Standards Board.

UNAUDITED STATEMENTS: PUBLIC ENTITIES[23]

Public accountants often prepare or assist clients in the preparation of financial statements that are not audited. The nature of the public accountant's involvement with unaudited statements of public entities is discussed in the Exposure Draft on "Association with Financial Statements." Furthermore, the nature of the public accountant's involvement with unaudited financial statements or other unaudited financial information of a nonpublic entity is governed by a new AICPA senior technical committee—the Accounting and Review Services Committee (this committee will be discussed later in this chapter).

When an Accountant Is Associated with Financial Statements

The Exposure Draft on "Association with Financial Statements" specifies the conditions under which an accountant is considered to be associated with financial statements. It states that:

An accountant is associated with financial statements when he has consented to the use of his name in a report, document, or written communication containing the statements. . . . Also, when an accountant submits to his client or others financial statements that he has prepared or assisted in preparing, he is deemed to be associated even though the accountant does not append his name to the statements. Although the accountant may participate in the preparation of financial statements, the statements are representations of management, and the fairness of their presentation . . . is management's responsibility.

The Exposure Draft recognizes that an accountant may be associated with either audited or unaudited financial statements. Furthermore, the Exposure Draft indicates:

[23]This section is based on Exposure Draft: Proposed Statement on Auditing Standards, "Association with Financial Statements," American Institute of Certified Public Accountants, May 31, 1979. See footnote 1 in this chapter.

Financial statements are audited if the accountant has applied auditing procedures sufficient to permit him to report on them as described in . . . [*SAS No. 2*]. The unaudited interim financial statements (or financial information) of a public entity are reviewed when the accountant has applied procedures sufficient to permit him to report on them as described in . . . [*SAS No. 24*].

Disclaimer of Opinion

If a public accountant is associated with the financial statements of a public entity, but neither reviews nor audits such statements, the Exposure Draft on "Association with Financial Statements" suggests the following form of report:

The accompanying balance sheet of X Company as of December 31, 19X1, and the related statements of income and retained earnings and changes in financial position for the year then ended were not audited by us and accordingly we do not express an opinion on them.

(Signature and date)

The public accountant's report may be placed on the statements or it may accompany them. Each page of the financial statements should be labeled "unaudited."

As noted in footnote 3 of this chapter, the Exposure Draft on "Association with Financial Statements" indicates that ". . . when a public entity does not have its annual financial statements audited, an accountant may be requested to review its annual or interim financial statements. In those circumstances, an accountant may make a review and may look to the guidance in Statements on Standards for Accounting and Review Services for the standards and procedures and form of report applicable to such an engagement."

Modified Disclaimer

Even though a CPA prepares the statements without an audit, it may become obvious that the statements are not in accordance with generally accepted accounting principles. The Exposure Draft on "Association with Financial Statements" suggests that the CPA should ask the client to make the appropriate revisions. If the client does not comply, the CPA should explain the inadequacies in a disclaimer of opinion. Such an explanation should discuss the nature of the departure and, if practicable, its effect on the financial statements. The Exposure Draft notes that in some instances departures due to inadequate disclosure may be so substantial that it may not be practicable to include all omitted disclosures in the report. However, the accountant should describe this in the report (without including the actual disclosures.)

The Exposure Draft also suggests that if the client will not revise the report or will not accept a disclaimer of opinion, the accountant should withdraw from the engagement.

UNAUDITED STATEMENTS: NONPUBLIC ENTITIES[24]

The Accounting and Review Services Committee issues *Statements on Standards for Accounting and Review Services (SSARS)* to provide guidance in dealing with unaudited financial statements or unaudited financial information of nonpublic entities. As of this writing the committee has issued one statement *(SSARS No. 1)* entitled "Compilation and Review of Financial Statements." This statement defines a nonpublic entity as:

> Any entity other than one *(a)* whose securities trade in a public market either on a stock exchange (domestic or foreign) or in the over-the-counter market, including securities quoted only locally or regionally, or *(b)* that makes a filing with a regulatory agency in preparation for the sale of any class of its securities in a public market.

SSARS No. 1 provides the following additional definitions:

> **Financial Statement.** A presentation of financial data, including accompanying notes, derived from accounting records and intended to communicate an entity's economic resources or obligations at a point in time, or the changes therein for a period of time, in accordance with generally accepted accounting principles or a comprehensive basis of accounting other than generally accepted accounting principles.
>
> **Compilation of Financial Statements.** Presenting in the form of financial statements . . . information that is the representation of management (owners) without undertaking to express any assurance on the statements.
>
> **Review of Financial Statements.** Performing inquiry and analytical procedures that provide the accountant with a reasonable basis for expressing limited assurance that there are no material modifications that should be made to the statements in order for them to be in conformity with generally accepted accounting principles or, if applicable, with another comprehensive basis of accounting.

A review is not an audit in accordance with generally accepted auditing standards since a review would not include the study and

---

[24]This section is based on *Statement on Standards for Accounting and Review Services No. 1.*, "Compilation and Review of Financial Statements," American Institute of Certified Public Accountants, 1978. Copyright © 1979 by the American Institute of Certified Public Accountants, Inc.

evaluation of internal accounting control and the other aspects of an opinion audit. Consequently, a review may disclose certain important matters, but not necessarily all matters that would be disclosed by an audit.

Reporting Obligation

When an accountant compiles or reviews statements for a nonpublic client, he or she should issue an appropriate report. Should more than one service be performed (e.g., a review and an audit) for a client the report issued should be one that is appropriate for the highest level of service.

SSARS No. 1 indicates an accountant should not allow his or her name to appear on any document containing the unaudited financial statements of a nonpublic entity unless (1) the accountant has either compiled or reviewed the statements and a report accompanies the statements, or (2) there is an indication with the statements that the accountant has not done a compilation or review and is not assuming any responsibility for the statements. If the client uses the accountant's name improperly in a document (prepared by the client) containing unaudited financial statements, the accountant should (1) advise the client of the situation, and (2) consider taking other appropriate actions, including consulting an attorney.

SSARS No. 1 notes that an " . . . accountant should not submit unaudited financial statements of a nonpublic entity to his client or others unless, as a minimum, he complies with the provisions of this statement applicable to a compilation engagement. This precludes the accountant from merely typing or reproducing financial statements as an accommodation to his client."

Compilation

SSARS No. 1 sets forth a number of requirements for the accountant compiling financial statements. They include:

1. The requirement that the accountant have enough knowledge of accounting principles and practice of the client's industry so that he or she can compile appropriate financial statements.
2. The requirement that the accountant generally understand ". . . the nature of the entity's business transactions, the form of its accounting records, the stated qualifications of its accounting personnel, the accounting basis on which the financial statements are to be presented, and the form and content of the financial statements." [*SSARS No. 1*]
3. The requirement that if the accountant becomes aware that the

information supplied by the client is "... incorrect, incomplete, or otherwise unsatisfactory for the purpose of compiling financial statements ..." [*SSARS No. 1*], he or she should ask for revised or additional information. If the client does not comply, the accountant should withdraw from the engagement.
4. The requirement that before issuing a report, the accountant check the statements for appropriateness of form and obvious material errors.

Each page of the financial statements should include a notation such as "See Accountant's Compilation Report." The report should be dated as of the date of the completion of the compilation.

SSARS No. 1 suggests the following report form for a compilation:

> The accompanying balance sheet of XYZ Company as of December 31, 19XX, and the related statements of income, retained earnings, and changes in financial position for the year then ended have been compiled by me (us).
>
> A compilation is limited to presenting in the form of financial statements information that is the representation of management (owners). I (we) have not audited or reviewed the accompanying financial statements and, accordingly, do not express an opinion or any other form of assurance on them.[25]

If the client asks the accountant to compile financial statements that "... omit substantially all of the disclosures required by generally accepted accounting principles ..." [*SSARS No. 1*], the accountant may compile the financial statements if (1) the fact that disclosures normally required are omitted is noted in the report and (2) omission of those disclosures is not to the knowledge of the accountant done to mislead financial statement users. *SSARS No. 1* suggests the following report form for use in such a situation:

> The accompanying balance sheet of XYZ Company as of December 31, 19XX, and the related statements of income, retained earnings, and changes in financial position for the year then ended have been compiled by me (us).
>
> A compilation is limited to presenting in the form of financial statements information that is the representation of management (owners). I (we) have not audited or reviewed the accompanying financial statements and, accordingly, do not express an opinion or any other form of assurance on them.
>
> Management has elected to omit substantially all of the disclosures (and the statement of changes in financial position) required by generally accepted accounting principles. If the omitted disclosures were included in the financial statements, they might influence the user's

---

[25]Copyright © 1979 by the American Institute of Certified Public Accountants, Inc.

conclusions about the company's financial position, results of operations, and changes in financial position. Accordingly, these financial statements are not designed for those who are not informed about such matters.[26]

Finally, if an accountant is not independent, a report on his or her compilation is still possible. In such a situation *SSARS No. 1* suggests the following as the last paragraph of the report: "I am (we are) not independent with respect to XYZ Company."

Review of Financial Statements

The accountant should understand the accounting principles and practices in the client's industry and also understand the client's business. This knowledge along with inquiry and analytical procedures provide the accountant ". . . with a reasonable basis for expressing limited assurance that there are no material modifications that should be made to the financial statements in order for the statements to be in conformity with generally accepted accounting principles." [*SSARS No. 1*]

SSARS No. 1 indicates that an accountant's inquiry and analytical procedures should usually include:

a.   Inquiries concerning the entity's accounting principles and practices and the methods followed in applying them. . . .

b.   Inquiries concerning the entity's procedures for recording, classifying, and summarizing transactions, and accumulating information for disclosure in the financial statements. . . .

c.   Analytical procedures designed to identify relationships and individual items that appear to be unusual. For the purposes of this statement, analytical procedures consist of (1) comparison of the financial statements with statements for comparable prior period(s), (2) comparison of the financial statements with anticipated results, if available (for example, budgets and forecasts), and (3) study of the relationships of the elements of the financial statements that would be expected to conform to a predictable pattern based on the entity's experience. In applying these procedures, the accountant should consider the types of matters that required accounting adjustments in preceding periods. Examples of relationships of elements in financial statements that would be expected to conform to a predictable pattern may be the relationships between changes in sales and changes in accounts receivable and expense accounts that ordinarily fluctuate with sales, and between changes in property, plant, and equipment and changes in depreciation expense and other accounts that may be affected, such as maintenance and repairs.

---

[26]Ibid.

d. Inquiries concerning actions taken at meetings of stockholders, board of directors, committees of the board of directors, or comparable meetings that may affect the financial statements.

e. Reading the financial statements to consider, on the basis of information coming to the accountant's attention, whether the financial statements appear to conform with generally accepted accounting principles.

f. Obtaining reports from other accountants, if any, who have been engaged to audit or review the financial statements of significant components of the reporting entity, its subsidiaries, and other investees. . . .

g. Inquiries of persons having responsibility for financial and accounting matters concerning (1) whether the financial statements have been prepared in conformity with generally accepted accounting principles consistently applied, (2) changes in the entity's business activities or accounting principles and practices, (3) matters as to which questions have arisen in the course of applying the foregoing procedures, and (4) events subsequent to the date of the financial statements that would have a material effect on the financial statements.[27]

The accountant during his or her work may find the information received to be unsatisfactory. In such a case, additional procedures may be needed.

SSARS No. 1 notes that the financial statements should be accompanied by a report that is dated as of the completion of the accountant's inquiry and analytical procedures. Each page of the financial statements should include a notation such as "See Accountant's Review Report." The following standard report is suggested by SSARS No. 1:

I (we) have reviewed the accompanying balance sheet of XYZ Company as of December 31, 19XX, and the related statements of income, retained earnings, and changes in financial position for the year then ended, in accordance with standards established by the American Institute of Certified Public Accountants. All information included in these financial statements is the representation of the management (owners) of XYZ Company.

A review consists principally of inquiries of company personnel and analytical procedures applied to financial data. It is substantially less in scope than an examination in accordance with generally accepted auditing standards, the objective of which is the expression of an opinion regarding the financial statements taken as a whole. Accordingly, I (we) do not express such an opinion.

---

[27]Ibid. SSARS No. 1 also suggests that the accountant may want to obtain a letter of representation from an appropriate official of the client entity. SSARS No. 1 contains an example of such a letter.

> Based on my (our) review, I am (we are) not aware of any material modifications that should be made to the accompanying financial statements in order for them to be in conformity with generally accepted accounting principles.[28]

If the accountant is not able to perform the procedures that are needed to properly perform a review, a review report should not be issued. *SSARS No. 1* indicates that "in such a situation, the accountant should consider whether the circumstances resulting in an incomplete review also preclude him from issuing a compilation report on the entity's financial statements." (See *SSARS No. 1* for a further discussion of this point.) Additionally, the accountant should not issue a review report if he or she is not independent. However, *SSARS No. 1* states that "if the accountant is not independent, he may issue a compilation report provided he complies with compilation standards."

Departures from GAAP

During a compilation or review, the accountant may become aware of material departures from generally accepted accounting principles (including adequate disclosure) or the comprehensive basis of accounting in use by the entity. Earlier we noted the effect of omission of substantially all disclosures on a compilation. In other circumstances, assuming the client does not make any changes in the statements, a modified report may be needed. If the accountant believes that a modified report is not adequate in the circumstances, the accountant should consider withdrawing from the engagement.

When a modified report is given *SSARS No. 1* indicates that

> ... the departure should be disclosed in a separate paragraph of [the] report, including disclosure of the effects of the departure on the financial statements if such effects have been determined by management or are known as the result of the accountant's procedures. The accountant is not required to determine the effects of a departure if management has not done so, provided the accountant states in his report that such determination has not been made.

SSARS No. 1 suggests the following examples of compilation and review reports that disclose departures from generally accepted accounting principles:

Compilation Report

The accompanying balance sheet of XYZ Company as of December 31, 19XX, and the related statements of income, retained earnings, and

---

[28]Copyright © 1979 by the American Institute of Certified Public Accountants, Inc.

changes in financial position for the year then ended have been compiled by me (us).

A compilation is limited to presenting in the form of financial statements information that is the representation of management (owners). I (we) have not audited or reviewed the accompanying financial statements and, accordingly, do not express an opinion or any other form of assurance on them. However, I (we) did become aware of a departure (certain departures) from generally accepted accounting principles that is (are) described in the following paragraph(s).

(Separate Paragraph)

As disclosed in note X to the financial statements, generally accepted accounting principles require that land be stated at cost. Management has informed me (us) that the company has stated its land at appraised value and that, if generally accepted accounting principles had been followed, the land account and stockholders' equity would have decreased by $500,000.

or

A statement of changes in financial position for the year ended December 31, 19XX, has not been presented. Generally accepted accounting principles require that such a statement be presented when financial statements purport to present financial position and results of operations. [If the statement of changes in financial position is not presented, the first paragraph should be modified—see SSARS No. 1].

Review Report

I (we) have reviewed the accompanying balance sheet of XYZ Company as of December 31, 19XX, and the related statements of income, retained earnings, and changes in financial position for the year then ended, in accordance with standards established by the American Institute of Certified Public Accountants. All information included in these financial statements is the representation of the management (owners) of XYZ Company.

A review consists principally of inquiries of company personnel and analytical procedures applied to financial data. It is substantially less in scope than an examination in accordance with generally accepted auditing standards, the objective of which is the expression of an opinion regarding the financial statements taken as a whole. Accordingly, I (we) do not express such an opinion.

Based on my (our) review, with the exception of the matter(s) described in the following paragraph(s), I am (we are) not aware of any material modifications that should be made to the accompanying financial statements in order for them to be in conformity with generally accepted accounting principles.

(Separate Paragraph)

As disclosed in note X to the financial statements, generally accepted accounting principles require that inventory cost consist of material, labor, and overhead. Management has informed me (us) that the inventory of finished goods and work in process is stated in the accompanying financial statements at material and labor cost only, and that the effects of this departure from generally accepted accounting principles on financial position, results of operations, and changes in financial position have not been determined.

or

As disclosed in note X to the financial statements, the company has adopted (description of newly adopted method), whereas it previously used (description of previous method). Although the (description of newly adopted method) is in conformity with generally accepted accounting principles, the company does not appear to have reasonable justification for making a change as required by Opinion No. 20 of the Accounting Principles Board.[29]

GLOSSARY

Adverse opinion An opinion in which the auditors state that the financial statements do *not* present fairly the financial position, results of operations, and changes in financial position.

Compilation of financial statements "Presenting in the form of financial statements . . . information that is the representation of management (owners) without undertaking to express any assurance on the statements." [*SSARS No. 1*]

Disclaimer of opinion When the auditors state that they cannot give an opinion because of scope limitations or some other reason.

Opinion paragraph The paragraph of the auditor's report which gives the auditor's opinion as to the fairness of the presentation of the financial statements.

Qualified opinion An opinion in which the auditors express certain reservations concerning the scope of the audit and/or the financial statements.

Scope paragraph The paragraph of the auditor's report which describes the scope of the examination.

Segment information Information concerning a company's operations in various industries, foreign operations and export sales, and major customers. [*FASB Statement No. 14*]

Statement on Standards for Accounting and Review Services (SSARS) Statements issued by the AICPA's Accounting and Review Services Committee to provide guidance in dealing with unaudited financial statements or unaudited financial information of nonpublic entities. [*SSARS No. 1*]

---

[29]Ibid.

Subsequent events Events and transactions occurring a[t]
sheet date which may have an important impact on the f[i]
ments.

Uncertainties Where the outcome of matters that may affect the [i]
statements cannot reasonably be estimated. [*SAS No. 2*]

Unqualified opinion A "clean" opinion, meaning that the auditor[s]
that the financial statements present fairly the financial position, re[
operations, and changes in financial position.

QUESTIONS AND PROBLEMS

14-1. What is included in the scope and opinion paragraphs of the auditor's standard report?

14-2. For what reasons should an independent auditor depart from the wording of the auditor's standard report?

14-3. For what reasons would a middle paragraph be added to the auditor's standard report?

14-4. Under what circumstances should the following opinions be expressed by the auditor:

    a. Qualified.
    b. Adverse.
    c. Disclaimer.

14-5. Under what circumstances may the principal auditor be willing to assume responsibility for the work of another auditor?

14-6. Can an independent CPA rely on another independent CPA to audit a subsidiary of a client?

14-7. What is a long-form report?

14-8. List the procedures that an independent auditor might use in searching for the occurrence of subsequent events.

14-9. CPA X, who practices in Philadelphia, has a client located in Philadephia. The client has a large division in Georgia. Since CPA X does not have an office in Georgia he has another firm, ABC, do the audit of the division in Georgia. ABC, in fact does a lot of correspondent work for CPA X in the southeast area. Due to the long and close relationship between CPA X and ABC, X decides not to make reference to ABC in the audit report. Since X will make no reference to ABC, should X perform any additional procedures?

14-10. Discuss the function of the AICPA's Accounting and Review Services Committee.

14-11. Define each of the following as they relate to the preparation of unaudited financial statements for a nonpublic entity:

    a. compiliation of financial statements.
    b. review of financial statements

14-12. Discuss some of requirements expected of an accountant who is compiling financial statements for a nonpublic client.

14-13. Balsam Corporation is engaged in a hazardous trade and cannot obtain insurance coverage from any source. A material portion of the corporation's assets could be destroyed by a serious accident. The corporation has an excellent safety record and has never suffered a catastrophe. Assume that the audit examination was made in accordance with generally accepted auditing standards, that generally accepted accounting principles were applied on a consistent basis, and that disclosure was adequate.

Required:

What type of opinion should be rendered?

(AICPA, adapted)

14-14. Select the *best* answer for each of the following items:

a. The term "special reports" may include all of the following *except* reports on financial statements

1. Of an organization that has limited the scope of the auditor's examination.
2. Prepared for limited purposes such as a report that relates to only certain aspects of financial statements.
3. Of a not-for-profit organization which follows accounting practices differing in some respects from those followed by business enterprises organized for profit.
4. Prepared in accordance with a cash basis of accounting.

b. Whenever special reports, filed on a printed form designed by authorities, call upon the independent auditor to make an assertion that the auditor believes is *not* justified, the auditor should

1. Submit a short-form report with explanations.
2. Reword the form or attach a separate report.
3. Submit the form with questionable items clearly omitted.
4. Withdraw from the engagement.

c. In which of the following circumstances would an auditor be required to issue a qualified report with a separate explanatory paragraph?

1. The auditor satisfactorily performed alternative accounts receivable procedures because scope limitations prevented performance of normal procedures.
2. The financial statements reflect the effects of a change in accounting principles from one period to the next.
3. A particular note to the financial statements discloses a company accounting method which deviates from generally accepted accounting principles.
4. The financial statements of a significant subsidiary were examined by another auditor, and reference to the other auditor's report is to be made in the principal auditor's report.

(AICPA, adapted)

14-15. You were engaged to examine the financial statements of Barnes Corporation (a public entity) for the year just ended. The CPA firm previously engaged declined to make the examination because a son of one of the CPA firm's partners received a material amount of Barnes Corporation common stock in exchange for engineering services rendered to the corporation. The partner in the CPA firm advises his son in business affairs but does not own an interest in his son's engineering firm and had not participated in this examination in past years. Another of the CPA firm's 15 partners would have been in charge of this engagement.

This new client wants to receive three different reports from you. In the past the stockholders have considered and discussed the corporation's annual report containing the financial statements and the auditor's opinion at their annual meeting. Because of the shortage of time before the stockholders' meeting, corporation executives are willing to accept (a) your report containing unaudited statements to be used for the meeting and (b) your final report after your examination is complete. Thereafter, the client would like to receive (c) a report containing a forecast of the corporation's 1980–82 operations.

Required:

a. Should the CPA firm previously engaged by Barnes Corporation have declined the examination of the financial statements for the year just ended? Discuss the ethical issues involved.

b. Discuss the issues in the client's request that you render unaudited financial statements prior to rendering your final report.

c. What are the issues for a CPA in rendering a report containing a forecast of a client's future operations? Discuss.

(AICPA, adapted)

14-16. The auditor's report must contain an expression of opinion or a statement to the effect that an opinion cannot be expressed. Four types of opinions which meet these requirements are generally known as:

1. An unqualified opinion.
2. A qualified opinion.
3. An adverse opinion.
4. A disclaimer of opinion.

Required:

For each of the following situations indicate the type of opinion which you would render. Unless there is an implication to the contrary in the situation as stated, you may assume that the examination was made in accordance with generally accepted auditing standards, that the financial statements present fairly the financial position, results of operations, and changes in financial position in conformity with generally accepted accounting principles applied on a consistent basis, and that the statements include adequate informative disclosure necessary not to be misleading.

a. During the course of the examination, the CPA suspects that a material amount of the assets of the client, Ash Corporation, have been misappropriated through fraud. The corporation refuses to allow the auditor to expand the scope of the examination sufficiently to confirm these suspicions.

b. Dogwood Corporation owns properties which have substantially appreciated in value since the date of purchase. The properties were appraised and are reported in the balance sheet at the appraised values with full disclosure. The CPA believes that the values reported in the balance sheet are reasonable.

c. The CPA has examined Ginkgo Corporation's financial statements for many years. During the year just ended a service bureau was employed to process the corporation's financial data by computer. The CPA knows very little about computers and does not wish to conduct the audit for the year just ended. The CPA and the president of the corporation are old friends, however, and the president persuaded the CPA to not withdraw from the engagement. After glancing at the records and comparing the current year's statements with those of prior years, the CPA believes that the statements prepared by the service bureau are stated fairly.

d. Subsequent to the close of Holly Corporation's fiscal year a major debtor was declared bankrupt due to a rapid series of events. The debtor had confirmed the full amount due to Holly Corporation at the balance-sheet date. Since the account was good at the balance-sheet date, Holly Corporation refuses to disclose any information in relation to this subsequent event. The CPA believes that all accounts were stated fairly at the balance-sheet date.

e. Linden Corporation has material investments in stocks of subsidiary companies. Stocks of the subsidiary companies are not actively traded in the market, and the CPA's engagement does not extend to any subsidiary company. The CPA is able to become satisfied that all investments are carried at original cost, and has no reason to suspect that the amounts are not stated fairly.

f. Maple Corporation has large investments in stocks of subsidiary companies, but the investments are not material in relation to the financial position and results of operations of the corporation. Stocks of the subsidiary companies are not actively traded in the market, and the CPA's engagement does not extend to any subsidiary company. The CPA is able to become satisfied that all investments are carried at original cost and has no reason to suspect that the amounts are not fairly stated.

g. Pecan Corporation has material investments in stocks of subsidiary companies. Stocks of the subsidiary companies are actively traded in the market, but the CPA's engagement does not extend to any subsidiary company. Management insists that all investments shall be carried at original costs and the CPA is satisfied that the original costs are fairly stated. The CPA believes that the client will never ultimately realize a substantial portion of the investments, but there is no disclosure to this effect in the financial statements.

(AICPA, adapted)

14-17. The auditor's standard report usually contains a sentence like this: "Our examination was made in accordance with generally accepted auditing standards and, accordingly, included such tests of the accounting records and such other procedures which we considered necessary in the circumstances."

  a. Distinguish between auditing standards and auditing procedures.
  b. Quote or state in your own words *four* generally accepted auditing standards.

(AICPA, adapted)

14-18. At the beginning of your examination of the financial statements of the Efel Insurance Company, the president of the company requested that in the interest of efficiency you coordinate your audit procedures with the audit being conducted by the state insurance examiners for the same fiscal year. The state examiners audited the asset accounts of the company while you audited the accounts for liabilities, stockholders' equity, income, and expenses. In addition, you obtained confirmations of the accounts receivable and were satisfied with the results of your audit tests. Although you had no supervisory control over the state examiners, they allowed you to review and prepare extracts from their work papers and report. After reviewing the state examiners' work papers and report to your complete satisfaction, you are now preparing your standard report.

Required:

What effect, if any, would the above circumstances have on your auditor's standard report? Discuss.

(AICPA, adapted)

14-19. Following are the financial statements of the Young Manufacturing Corporation and the auditor's report of their examination for the year ended January 31, 1980. The examination was conducted by John Smith, an individual practitioner, who has examined the corporation's financial statements and reported on them for many years.

YOUNG MANUFACTURING CORPORATION
Statements of Condition
January 31, 1980 and 1979

Assets	*1980*	*1979*
Current Assets:		
Cash	$ 43,822	$ 51,862
Accounts receivable—pledged—less allowances for doubtful accounts of $3,800 in 1980 and $3,000 in 1979 (see note)	65,298	46,922
Inventories, pledged—at average cost, not in excess of replacement cost........................	148,910	118,264
Other current assets	6,280	5,192
Total Current Assets	$264,310	$222,240
Fixed Assets:		
Land—at cost......................................	$ 38,900	$ 62,300
Buildings—at cost, less accumulated depreciation of $50,800 in 1980 and $53,400 in 1979	174,400	150,200
Machinery and equipment—at cost, less accumulated depreciation of $30,500 in 1980 and $25,640 in 1979........................	98,540	78,560
Total Fixed Assets	$311,840	$291,060
Total Assets	$576,150	$513,300

Liabilities and Stockholders' Equity	*1980*	*1979*
Current Liabilities:		
Accounts payable	$ 27,926	$ 48,161
Other liabilities...................................	68,743	64,513
Current portion of long-term mortgage payable	3,600	3,600
Income taxes payable	46,840	30,866
Total Current Liabilities	$147,109	$147,140
Long-term Liabilities:		
Mortgage payable................................	90,400	94,000
Total Liabilities	$237,509	$241,140
Stockholders' Equity:		
Captital stock, par value $100, 1,000 shares authorized, issued and outstanding................	$100,000	$100,000
Retained earnings.................................	238,641	172,160
Total Stockholders' Equity	$338,641	$272,160
Total Liabilities and Stockholders' Equity .	$576,150	$513,300

Note: I did not confirm the balances of the accounts receivable but satisfied myself by other auditing procedures that the balances were correct.

YOUNG MANUFACTURING CORPORATION
Income Statements
For the Years Ended January 31, 1980 and 1979

	1980	1979
Income:		
Sales	$884,932	$682,131
Other income	3,872	2,851
Total	$888,804	$684,982
Costs and expenses:		
Cost of goods sold	$463,570	$353,842
Selling expenses	241,698	201,986
Administrative expenses	72,154	66,582
Provision for income taxes	45,876	19,940
Other expenses	12,582	13,649
Total	$835,880	$655,999
Net income	$ 52,924	$ 28,983

Mr. Paul Young, President   March 31, 1980
Young Manufacturing Corporation

I have examined the balance sheet of the Young Manufacturing Corporation and the related statement of income and retained earnings.

These statements present fairly the financial position and results of operations in conformity with consistent generally accepted principles of accounting. My examination was made in accordance with generally accepted auditing standards, and accordingly included such tests of the accounting records and such other auditing procedures as I considered necessary in the circumstances.

(Signed) John Smith

Required:

List and discuss the deficiencies of the auditor's report prepared by John Smith. Your discussion should include justifications that the matters you cited are deficiencies. (Do not check the addition of the statements. Assume that the addition is correct.)

(AICPA, adapted)

14-20. The complete opinion included in the annual report of The Modern Department Store for 1981 is reproduced below:

Auditor's Certificate
DOE & DOE
New City, New State

To whom it may concern:

In our opinion, the accompanying balance sheet and related
statements of income, retained earnings, and changes in financial position present fairly the financial position of The Modern
Department Store and the results of its operations and the
changes in its financial position. Our examination of these financial statements was made in accordance with generally accepted auditing standards and accordingly included such tests
of the accounting records and such other auditing procedures as
we considered necessary, except that we did not confirm accounts receivable, but instead accounted for subsequent collections in the accounts, and we did not observe the taking of
the physical inventory because it was taken prior to our appointment as auditors.

Required:

List and discuss the deficiencies of the "Auditor's Certificate" prepared by Doe & Doe.

(AICPA, adapted)

14-21. The president's salary has been increased substantially over the prior
year by action of the board of directors. His present salary is much
greater than salaries paid to presidents of companies of comparable
size and is clearly excessive. You determine that the method of computing the president's salary was changed for the year under audit. In
prior years the president's salary was consistently based on sales. In
the latest year, however, his salary was based on net income before
income taxes. The Claren Corporation is in a cyclical industry and
would have had an extremely profitable year except that the increase
in the president's salary siphoned off much of the income that would
have accrued to the stockholders. The president is a substantial
stockholder.

Required:

a. Discuss your responsibility for disclosing this situation.

b. Discuss the effect, if any, that the situation has upon your auditor's opinion as to

1. The fairness of the presentation of the financial statements.
2. The consistency of the application of accounting principles.

(AICPA, adapted)

14-22. About two years ago you were engaged to conduct an annual audit of Pierson Company. This was shortly after the majority stockholders assumed control of the company and discharged the president and several other corporate officers. A new president canceled a wholesaler's contract to distribute Pierson Company products. The wholesaler is a Pierson Company minority stockholder and was one of the discharged officers. Shortly after you commenced your initial audit, several lawsuits were filed against Pierson Company by the wholesaler. Pierson Company filed countersuits.

None of the suits have been decided. The principal litigation is over the canceled contract, and the other suits are claims against the company for salary, bonus, and pension fund contributions. Pierson Company is the plaintiff in suits totaling approximately $300,000 and defendants in suits totaling approximately $2 million. Both amounts are material in relation to net income and total assets. Pierson's legal counsel believes the outcome of the suits is uncertain and that all of the suits are likely to be "tied up in court" for an extended time.

You were instructed by the board of directors each year to issue an audit report only if it contained an unqualifed opinion. Pierson Company refuses to provide for an unfavorable settlement in the financial statements because legal counsel advised the board of directors that such a provision in the financial statements could be used against Pierson by the opposition in court. The pending litigation was fully disclosed in a footnote to the financial statements, however.

You did not issue a report on the completion of your audit one year ago and you have now completed your second annual audit. The scope of your audits was not restricted in any way and you would render unqualified opinions if there were no pending litigations. You have attended all meetings of the stockholders and the directors and answered all questions directed to you at these meetings. You were promptly paid for all work completed to the current date. The board of directors of Pierson Company invited you to deliver to them an audit report containing an unqualified opinion or to attend the annual meeting of the stockholders one week hence to answer questions concerning the results of your audit if you are unwilling to render an unqualified opinion.

Required:

a. Discuss the issues raised by the fact that the auditor attended the stockholders' and directors' meetings and answered various questions. Do not consider the propriety of the failure to issue a written audit report.

b. Should a CPA issue the audit report promptly after completing the examination? Why?

c. 1. What kind of auditor's opinion would you render on Pierson Company's financial statements for the year just ended? Why? (You need not write an auditor's opinion.)

2. Write the middle paragraph that you would include in your auditor's standard report for Pierson Company's financial statements for the year just ended.

(AICPA, adapted)

14-23. On April 6, 1981, fire completely destroyed the warehouse and all books and records of the Kramer Corporation, a wholesaler of office stationery. Kramer Corporation had a fire insurance policy on the inventory (in addition to insurance policies on other assets) which did not require the corporation to file a monthly inventory report. The Ecker Insurance Company retained you to audit the statement of the actual cash value of the inventory fire loss of $263,000 reported by Kramer Corporation.

The corporation began doing business on January 1, 1980, and the financial statements for 1980 were audited by the corporation's certified public accountant, who rendered an unqualified opinion. The CPA also prepared the corporation's income tax return for 1980 and, with the president's permission, has granted you access to his copy of the tax return as well as to his work papers relating to Kramer Corporation.

Required:

a. List the audit procedures you would apply to verify the amount of the inventory fire loss on April 6, 1981, claimed by the assured.

b. Assume that you are satisfied with the results of your examination and you are now preparing your report.

1. Which, if any, of the generally accepted auditing standards pertaining to reporting would apply to this report? Discuss.

2. Describe the topics relating to your examination to which you should refer in your report.

(AICPA, adapted)

14-24. In prior years your client, Noches, Inc., a manufacturing company, has used an accelerated depreciation method for its depreciable assets for both federal income taxes and financial reporting. At the beginning of 1981 the corporation changed to the straight-line method for financial reporting. As a result, depreciation expense for the year was $200,000 less for financial reporting than for income tax reporting, an amount which you consider to be material. The corporation did not use interperiod income tax allocation in 1981. Taxable income for 1981 was $600,000. Assume that the income tax rate was 48 percent and ignore the tax surcharge and state and local income taxes.

Required:

a. Financial statement presentation:
1. Describe the effects of the accounting change on Noches' 1981 balance sheet, income statement, and statement of changes in financial position.
2. Explain what disclosure of the accounting change should be made in Noches' 1981 financial statements.

b. Auditor's report:
1. Assuming that the financial statement disclosure is considered to be adequately informative, discuss the effects that the change in depreciation methods should have on the auditor's report.
2. Assuming that the financial statement disclosure of the change in depreciation methods is not considered to be adequately informative, discuss the effects on the auditor's report.
3. Discuss whether the auditor's report should indicate approval of the change in depreciation methods.
4. Discuss the effects on the auditor's report of the failure to use interperiod income tax allocation.

(AICPA, adapted)

14-25. The following draft of an auditor's report has been submitted for review:

To: Eric Jones, Chief Accountant
Sunshine Manufacturing Co.

We have examined the balance sheet of the Sunshine Manufacturing Co. for the year ended August 31, 1981, and the related statements of income, retained earnings, and changes in financial position. Our examination included such tests of the accounting records and such other auditing procedures as we considered necessary in the circumstances except that, in accordance with your instructions, we did not count the buyers' cash working fund.

In our opinion, subject to the limitation on our examination discussed above, the accompanying balance sheet and statements of income, earned surplus, and changes in financial position present fairly the financial position of the Sunshine Manufacturing Co. at August 31, 1981, and the results of its operations and changes in its financial position for the year then ended.

Frank George & Co.
August 31, 1981

It has been determined that:

1. Except for the omission of the count of the buyers' cash working

fund, there were no scope restrictions placed in the auditor's examination.

2. The Sunshine Manufacturing Co. has been in continuous operation since 1953; but its financial statements have not previously been audited.

Required:

a. Assuming that Frank George & Co. was able to perform alternative auditing procedures to satisfactorily substantiate the buyers' cash working fund and purchases through the fund, identify and discuss the deficiencies in the auditor's report.

b. Assuming that Frank George & Co. was unable to satisfactorily substantiate the buyers' cash working fund and purchases through the fund by alternative auditing procedures, discuss the appropriateness of the opinion qualification proposed by Frank George & Co's report.

c. Discuss the potential consequences to the CPA of issuing a substandard report or failing to adhere in the examination to generally accepted auditing standards.

(AICPA, adapted)

14-26. Charles Burke, CPA, has completed field work for his examination of the Williams Corporation for the year ended December 31, 1981, and now is in the process of determining whether to modify his report. Presented below are two independent, unrelated situations which have arisen.

Situation I

In September 1981, a lawsuit was filed against Williams to have the court order it to install pollution-control equipment in one of its older plants. Williams's legal counsel has informed Burke that it is not possible to forecast the outcome of this litigation; however, Williams's management has informed Burke that the cost of the pollution-control equipment is not economically feasible and that the plant will be closed if the case is lost. In addition, Burke has been told by management that the plant and its production equipment would have only minimal resale values and that the production that would be lost could not be recovered at other plants.

Situation II

During 1981, Williams purchased a franchise amounting to 20 percent of its assets for the exclusive right to produce and sell a newly patented product in the northeastern United States. There has been no production in marketable quantities of the product anywhere to date. Neither the franchisor nor any franchisee has conducted any market research with respect to the product.

Required:

In deciding the type-of-report modification, if any, Burke should take into account such considerations as follows:

Relative magnitude.

Uncertainty of outcome.

Likelihood of error.

Expertise of the auditor.

Pervasive impact on the financial statements.

Inherent importance of the item.

Discuss Burke's type-of-report decision for each situation in terms of the above and other appropriate considerations. Assume each situation is adequately disclosed in the notes to the financial statements. Each situation should be considered independently. In discussing each situation, ignore the other. It is not necessary for you to decide the type of report which should be issued.

(AICPA, adapted)

14-27. Presented below is an independent auditor's report. The corporation being reported on is profit oriented and publishes general-purpose financial statements for distribution to owners, creditors, potential investors, and the general public. The report contains deficiencies.

Auditor's Report

We have examined the consolidated balance sheet of Belasco Corporation and subsidiaries as of December 31, 1981, and the related consolidated statements of income and retained earnings and changes in financial position for the year then ended. Our examination was made in accordance with generally accepted auditing standards and accordingly included such tests of the accounting records and such other auditing procedures as we considered necessary in the circumstances. We did not examine the financial statements of Seidel Company, a major consolidated subsidiary. These statements were examined by other auditors whose report thereon has been furnished to us, and our opinion expressed herein, insofar as it relates to Seidel Company, is based solely upon the report of the other auditors.

In our opinion, except for the report of the other auditors, the accompanying consolidated balance sheet and consolidated statements of income and retained earnings and changes in financial position present fairly the financial position of Belasco Corporation and subsidiaries at December 31, 1981, and the results of its operations and the changes in its financial position for the year then ended, in conformity with generally accepted accounting principles applied on a basis consistent with that of the preceding year.

Required:

Describe the reporting deficiencies of the auditor's report, explain the reasons therefor, and briefly discuss how the report should be corrected. Do not discuss the addressee, signatures, and date. Also do not rewrite the auditor's report.

(AICPA, adapted)

14-28. Nancy Miller, CPA, has completed field work for her examination of the financial statements of Nickles Manufacturers, Inc., for the year ended March 31, 1981, and now is preparing her auditor's report. Presented below are two independent, unrelated assumptions concerning this examination:

Assumption 1

The CPA was engaged on April 15, 1981, to examine the financial statements for the year ended March 31, 1981, and was not present to observe the taking of the physical inventory on March 31, 1981. Her alternative procedures included examination of shipping and receiving documents with regard to transactions during the year under review as well as transactions since the year end; extensive review of the inventory-count sheets; and discussion of the physical inventory procedures with responsible company personnel. She has also satisfied herself as to inventory valuation and consistency in valuation method. Inventory quantities are determined solely by means of physical count. (Note: Asssume that the CPA is properly relying upon the examination of another auditor with respect to the beginning inventory.)

Assumption 2

As of April 1, 1981, Nickles has an unused balance of $1,378,000 of federal income tax net operating loss carryover that will expire at the end of the company's fiscal years as follows: $432,000 in 1982, $870,000 in 1983, and $76,000 in 1984. Nickles's management expects that the company will have enough taxable income to use the loss carryover before it expires.

Required:

For each assumption described above discuss:

a.   In detail, the appropriate disclosures, if any, in the financial statements and accompanying footnotes.
b.   The effect, if any, on the auditor's standard report. For this requirement assume that Nickles makes the appropriate disclosures, if any, recommended in (a).

Note: Complete your discussion (both [a] and [b]) of each assumption before beginning discussion of the next assumption. In considering each independent assumption assume that the other situation did not occur.

(AICPA, adapted)

14-29. Roscoe, CPA, has completed the examination of the financial statements of Excelsior Corporation as of and for the year ended December 31, 1980, Roscoe also examined and reported on the Excelsior financial statements for the prior year. Roscoe drafted the following report for 1980.

March 15, 1981

We have examined the balance sheet and statements of income and retained earnings of Excelsior Corporation as of December 31, 1980. Our examination was made in accordance with generally accepted accounting standards and accordingly included such tests of the accounting records as we considered necessary in the circumstances.

In our opinion, the above mentioned financial statements are accurately prepared and fairly presented in accordance with generally accepted accounting principles in effect at December 31, 1980.

Roscoe, CPA
(signed)

Other Information:

a. Excelsior is presenting comparative financial statements.

b. Excelsior does not wish to present a statement of changes in financial position for either year.

c. During 1980 Excelsior changed its method of accounting for long-term construction contracts and properly reflected the effect of the change in the current year's financial statements and restated the prior-year's statements. Roscoe is satisfied with Excelsior's justification for making the change. (The change was discussed in a footnote to the financial statements.)

d. Roscoe was unable to perform normal accounts receivable confirmation procedures but alternate procedures were used to satisfy Roscoe as to the validity of the receivables.

e. Excelsior Corporation is the defendant in a litigation, the outcome of which is highly uncertain. If the case is settled in favor of the plaintiff, Excelsior will be required to pay a substantial amount of cash which might require the sale of certain fixed assets. The litigation and the possible effects have been properly disclosed in a footnote to the financial statements.

f. Excelsior issued debentures on January 31, 1979, in the amount of $10 million. The funds obtained from the issuance were used to finance the expansion of plant facilities. The debenture agreement restricts the payment of future cash dividends to earnings after December 31, 1985. (Excelsior declined to disclose this essential data in the footnotes to the financial statements.)

Required:

Consider all facts given and rewrite the auditor's report in acceptable and complete format incorporating any necessary departures from the standard (short-form) report.

Do not discuss the draft of Roscoe's report but identify and explain any items included in *"Other Information"* that need not be part of the auditor's report.

(AICPA, adapted)

Learning Objectives

Study of the material in this chapter is designed to achieve several learning objectives. These include:

1. An understanding of the nature and purpose(s) of management letters.
2. An understanding of the nature of an audit committee.
3. An understanding of the types of subjects which are appropriate for inclusion in management letters, including safeguarding resources, accounting systems and procedures, administrative controls, change and obsolescence, and tax-related matters.
4. An appreciation of the importance of timeliness, planning, and follow-up regarding management letters.
5. An understanding of how to prepare management letters.

15

Management Letters

In connection with an audit engagement, many CPA firms send their client a letter referred to as a management letter. A management letter may be addressed to the board of directors (or its audit committee), to the chief executive officer, or to any official designated as an appropriate recipient. It contains suggestions and recommendations for improving procedures, operations, and controls in areas within the auditor's competence in accounting and auditing, tax, and management services matters. Such a letter is an important communication for many reasons. The letter demonstrates, in a very tangible manner, the CPA's continuing interest in the client's welfare, and in addition contributes to the quality of the CPA's services in the following ways:

1. It adds a constructive dimension to the CPA's services in bringing attention to matters of merit which were noted in the performance of the audit procedures.
2. Recommendations for improvement are an integral part of the services offered by the profession, and most clients generally expect to obtain benefits beyond the attest function from their independent accountants.
3. Prosperous, financially sound clients are the lifeblood of an auditor's continued growth. Ideas which contribute to the improvement of clients' operations or financial position serve to strengthen the auditor's relations with them.

To perform an audit in accordance with generally accepted auditing standards and express an opinion on the financial statements, the auditor must understand both the client's operations and the general business environment. The auditor is in a unique position to recognize and understand the client's important needs and problems because the auditor: (1) is not restricted to a single function such as finance, marketing, or production, but rather deals with the entire organization; (2) is involved, yet not completely immersed, in the company's day-to-day affairs; and (3) has a broad range of work experiences from which to draw ideas.

Although the auditor can make suggestions orally, a timely and well-written letter has several important advantages. It provides the client's executives with the auditor's carefully prepared analysis of the particular situation and recommendations for action. It can be referred to when necessary and passed along for action without the danger of distortion which is always possible in spoken communications. It is a record of what was said and a reminder of the services rendered by the auditor.

Comments in the management letter should not conflict with the auditor's opinion on the financial statements. In order to prepare the letter the auditor must: (1) identify existing and potential problem areas; (2) propose improvements; (3) assemble the information; and (4) present it in an understandable and usable format. To prepare a management letter which is both helpful and useful, the auditor should have knowledge of the major operating problems facing management (e.g., shortage of cash, rising production costs, personnel problems, and so on), and should recognize these issues in the comments made. The letter should identify situations which might become serious problems in the future as well as dealing with current problems.

The study and review of the system of internal control and accounting procedures usually identifies the particular subjects that merit comment in management letters. This is especially pertinent since during the past several years much public attention has been given to corporate accountability. There has been increasing pressure by the stock exchanges, Congress, and the SEC for corporate boards of directors and their audit committees to assume greater responsibility for corporate activities, especially for assuring the maintenance of an adequate system of internal control. The Foreign Corrupt Practices Act of 1977 requires, among other things, publicly held companies to devise and maintain a system of internal control sufficient to provide reasonable assurance that transactions are properly authorized and recorded. Furthermore, *SAS No. 20* requires the auditor to ". . . communicate to senior management and the board of directors or its audit committee material weaknesses in internal accounting control . . . that comes to his attention during an examination of financial statements made in accordance with generally accepted auditing standards."[1]

---

[1] *Statement on Auditing Standards No. 20*, "Required Communication of Material Weaknesses in Internal Accounting Control," American Institute of Certified Public Accountants, 1977. Copyright © 1977 by the American Institute of Certified Public Accountants, Inc.

SAS No. 1, section 320.68, defines a material weakness in internal accounting control as ". . . a condition in which the auditor believes the prescribed procedures or the degree of compliance with them does not provide reasonable assurance that errors or irregularities in amounts that would be material in the financial statements being audited would be prevented or detected within a timely period by employees in the normal course of performing their assigned functions."

SAS No. 20 indicates that it would be preferable for the auditor's findings to be ". . . communicated in a written report to reduce the possibility of misunderstanding. If the auditor's findings are communicated orally, he should document the communication by appropriate notations in his audit working papers." SAS No. 20 suggests the following as a possible written report form when reporting a material weakness in internal control:

> We have examined the financial statements of ABC Company for the year ended December 31, 19X1, and have issued our report thereon dated February 23, 19X2. . . . As a part of our examination, we made a study and evaluation of the Company's system of internal accounting control to the extent we considered necessary to evaluate the system as required by generally accepted auditing standards. Under these standards, the purposes of such evaluation are to establish a basis for reliance on the system of internal accounting control in determining the nature, timing, and extent of other auditing procedures that are necessary for expressing an opinion on the financial statements and to assist the auditor in planning and performing his examination of the financial statements. . . .
>
> Our examination of the financial statements made in accordance with generally accepted auditing standards, including the study and evaluation of the Company's system of internal accounting control for the year ended December 31, 19X1, that was made for the purposes set forth in the first paragraph above, would not necessarily disclose all weaknesses in the system because it was based on selective tests of accounting records and related data. However, such study and evaluation disclosed the following conditions that we believe to be material weaknesses, excluding those which were corrected before they came to our attention. (A description of the material weaknesses that have come to the auditor's attention would follow.)
>
> The foregoing conditions were considered in determining the nature, timing, and extent of audit tests to be applied in our examintion of the financial statements, and this report of such conditions does not modify our report dated February 23, 19X2, on such financial statements.[2]

The management letter will also be studied carefully by the audit committee of the board of directors. Since such audit committees are

---

[2] Ibid.

now very common, we need to explain their role in the communication process.

In March 1977, the Securities and Exchange Commission ". . . approved a rule proposed by the [New York Stock Exchange] that *requires all domestic companies listing common stock on the exchange to establish independent audit committees by July 1, 1978.*" (emphasis added)[3] An independent audit committee is one which is composed of members of the board of directors who are not members of management and have no other relationship with the company which could affect their independence.[4]

The duties of the audit committee differ from business to business. Traditionally, audit committees frequently have appointed (or recommended the appointment of) and have consulted with the outside auditor. Also, sometimes audit committees have had to dismiss the outside auditor when necessary. In recent years the committee has become more actively involved in the audit process.[5] Another of the important functions of the audit committee is to carefully review management letters and to see that recommendations made in the management letter have received consideration.[6]

APPROPRIATE SUBJECTS FOR INCLUSION IN A MANAGEMENT LETTER

The area of accounting and administrative controls includes an almost limitless number of more specific "subjects" which may be appropriate for inclusion in a management letter.[7] Among other areas that might be included in a management letter are tax related matters.

Safeguarding Resources

Recommendations for important improvement in accounting controls are a valuable service to a client. Such recommendations were subjects in the earliest management letters issued by independent accountants and remain frequent ones today.

During the audit, the auditor considers the adequacy of accounting controls and procedures including the appropriate segregation of

---

[3] Harold M. Williams, "Audit Committees—The Public Sector's View," *The Journal of Accountancy*, September 1977, p. 72.

[4] Ibid., p. 71.

[5] Ibid., p. 73.

[6] Ibid., p. 74.

[7] See the glossary for definitions of "accounting control" and "administrative control."

duties; internal audit activity (if any); deterrents against pilferage, fraud, and irregularities by employees, customers, vendors, and others; and adherence to management policies. Weaknesses affecting resources most susceptible to loss or misappropriation require careful attention. Such items often include cash and checks, securities, inventories (especially small, high-value items and consumer goods), office equipment and portable tools, contracts, agreements, and important papers.

Safeguarding resources includes protecting them against fire, disappearance, and vandalism as well as theft. The auditor should note such matters as the adequacy of the client's insurance coverage (types and amounts); safety deposit boxes; safes, vaults, and fire resistant files; backup records for information vital to the business; and background investigations of new, key employees.

When accounting and financial procedures are computerized, the auditor must review both the installation and the system to be satisfied that valuable items processed (checks, customer credits, and so on), vital computer programs, and data files are protected adequately. The auditor especially must be alert for weaknesses in controls concerned with the accumulation of source data, processing, "housekeeping," and the distribution of output data.

Accounting Systems and Procedures

For an organization to function successfully, systems and procedures must make the right information available to the appropriate person on a timely basis to enhance correct and timely decisions. Accounting has a central role in informing management. To determine whether the accounting system meets management's needs, the following kinds of questions should be considered:

1. Is the accounting system (whether computerized or hand-posted) primarily designed to provide management with the information most vital to the operations of the business? For example, a retailer needs to know how well specific fashion items are selling to reorder correctly; a cash-tight business needs accurate information on daily cash balances to be able to pay its employees and vendors; and to avoid serious losses a construction contractor needs to know immediately when costs begin to exceed estimates on fixed-fee contracts.
2. Are timely financial statements always available? Is supporting information for divisions, subsidiaries, or profit centers included when needed for decision making?
3. Are expenses classified in appropriate detail considering SEC re-

quirements, tax return needs, and management decision-making requirements?

4. Is a uniform, up-to-date chart of accounts in use throughout the organization?
5. Is the account numbering system as helpful as possible?
6. Should the fiscal year be changed to one more appropriate to the company's business cycle?

As the auditor investigates the general usefulness of the accounting information system, the efficiency and ecomony of data processing and clerical effort should be considered. Does it eliminate unnecessary work and duplication of effort, and does it utilize work-saving devices and techniques appropriate to the client's size and operations? Some accounting-related systems and procedures that frequently merit attention are:

Cash Management
    Shipping and billing (promptness).
    Receivable collection activities.
    Scrap sales and miscellaneous receipts.
    Deposits to banks (lockbox or daily).
    Bank transfer system (number of accounts and timing).
    Daily cash balance reporting.
    Temporary investment of excess cash.
    Vendor payments timing (discounts).
Sales and Receivables
    Appropriate detail for marketing needs (product lines or type of services).
    Returns and allowances procedures.
    Aging information (trends).
    Collateral for notes.
    Bad debts write-off and follow-up.
    Employee sales.
    Credit procedures.
Inventory and Costs
    Standard cost accounting system.
    Current standards (updated).
    Perpetual records for important items.
    Periodic test-checking of perpetual records.
    Slow-moving items reports.
    Procedures for salvaging "seconds."
    Physical inventory procedures (planning and efficiency).
Payroll and Personnel
    Time cards or other time approval procedures.
    Periodic review of pay rates (executive, office, and factory).
    Overtime, sick time, and vacation approval procedures.

Records Retention and Disposal Procedures
Consideration of tax laws, statutes of limitations, state laws, and space needs.
Coordination of the program with record protection needs (such as backup locations).

Administrative Controls

The effectiveness of administrative controls may be reviewed and evaluated within certain broad areas as follows:

1. Planning (corporate strategy, economic opportunities, policy objectives, forecasting).
2. Organizing (executive responsibilities and authorities, delegation, line versus staff relationships, management development).
3. Deciding (corporate tactics, leadership, consistency, maintenance of harmony within the organization, resolution of policy conflicts).
4. Communicating (dissemination of plans, decisions, programs, and results to all concerned parties by means of both oral and written methods and by example).
5. Controlling (determining that plans, decisions, etc., are carried out or that appropriate alternatives exist to handle exceptions).

The following two examples, which are taken from actual management letters issued by CPAs, illustrate comments which may be made concerning administrative control matters. Because they have been excerpted from actual management letters, as presented here they may lack appropriate background information.

An example of a general management suggestion:

Long-range planning:

The company is using a budget to control current operations, but there is no formal long-range planning. Long-range planning in which a company defines its objectives and formulates plans and policies for attaining those objectives is as essential a management tool as budgeting.

We suggest that management prepare a five-year forecast of sales and expenses. This project will require you (1) to establish goals, (2) to analyze current markets the company serves and try to recognize and adapt to expected changes in these markets, and (3) to identify attractive new markets. The five-year plan should also include research and development objectives, and estimates of expenditures and expected benefits for each objective.

A five-year cash flow forecast should be prepared in conjunction with the operating forecast of sales and expenses to plan borrowing requirements or investment of surplus cash.

Long-range planning is frequently overlooked by company managements because of the pressure of short-range matters. However, if a long-range plan is revised to reflect changes as they occur, and is properly used, it can be very helpful and productive in guiding a company's progress.

An example of an organization and personnel suggestion:

Organizational structure:

The organizational structure should be studied with the intent of modifying it to accommodate future growth and to reduce officers' involvement in routine matters. Such changes will allow officers time to define company goals and move toward attaining them. Job responsibilities and reporting channels should be defined for executives and supervisors.

Your present organization chart is outdated due to changes in employees and reassignment of duties and responsibilities. A new organization chart should be prepared to avoid (1) confusion, (2) overlapping of duties and responsibilities, and (3) duplication of effort.

Change and Obsolescence

Obsolescence in organizations is often an appropriate subject for inclusion in management letters, and it applies to all accounting and administrative controls. Organizations are changing continually. The scale of operations of many clients is growing, while that of others is declining. Few remain constant. Yesterday's procedures may be inappropriate for either today or tomorrow. Auditors often can recognize the impact of changing conditions on procedures or controls before the situation comes to management's attention.

The auditor should review the present adequacy of the client's accounting and administrative controls in view of recent events and conditions such as, but not limited to, the following:

General growth (present business lines).

New products or services.

Acquisition, liquidation, or sale of subsidiaries.

Industry trends.

Clients' technologies.

Competing technologies.

Going public.

Legal environment (including tax laws).

Financial position changes (i.e., liquid to tight).

Aging management.

Key personnel changes.

New foreign operations.

New computer installation.

Such events and conditions have a subtle but often far-reaching impact on the effectiveness of both operations and internal controls. The auditor should attempt to identify and predict the more important effects of such changes.

Tax-Related Matters

Certain tax matters are appropriately included in management letters. Auditors should draw on their tax experience to seek out tax-saving opportunities and indications of client practices that may lead to tax problems.

TIMELINESS, PLANNING, AND FOLLOW-UP

Timeliness

Prompt submission of the management letter to the client is important. Rarely will a client be favorably impressed with recommendations that are not made on a timely basis. A management letter ordinarily should be issued for each audit client shortly after the conclusion of the field work. In many instances, it also may be desirable to issue a letter upon the completion of interim audit procedures since this is often the time when attention will be devoted specifically to the study of internal control and accounting procedures. Frequently, more than one letter may be issued in connection with a single examination. For instance, a separate letter could be issued communicating any material weaknesses in internal control discovered during the audit.

Planning

Timeliness requires planning. Planning for the management letter should always be an integral part of planning the audit engagement. The audit program should include appropriate steps for gathering information and preparing the letter. Steps such as the following may be appropriate:

1. During the field work the auditor should be alert for client procedures, accounting controls, and administrative controls which may be improved. Specific situations, suitably documented, should be accumulated in writing in a separate management letter file as they are encountered.
2. The auditor should note action taken on the prior year's letter.

In most instances, it will not be practicable to extend tests in depth each year to all functional areas of the client's operations. In addition to the general review of accounting controls, particular emphasis may be directed to specific accounting and administrative controls each year so that over a period of a few years all control areas will have been reviewed by the auditor in detail. If a rotation of emphasis is used, it should be provided for in the audit program.

Follow-up

Previous management letters should be filed for reference and subsequent follow-up by the auditor. They represent a valuable history of service and experience with the client.

During the course of the audit examination, the auditor should determine the action taken on all important matters discussed in the prior year's management letter. The auditor should note in the working papers any action taken, or why action was not taken. Favorable comments on client improvements may be included in the current letter. If no action was taken on an important recommendation, the auditor may wish to repeat the comment. This reminds management and the audit committee that a problem situation still exists (which management and/or the audit committee may assume was corrected).

PREPARING THE LETTER

The objective of the management letter is to encourage management to *act* on the matters discussed. A clearly thought-out and well-written letter will help to attain this objective. The management letter is a flexible report. Since to meet its objective it must be tailored to the situation of a particular client, there are no rigid instructions for preparing it as there are for preparing tax returns, nor are there well-defined guidelines such as there are for preparing financial statements and SEC reports. However, as was noted earlier in the chapter, *SAS No. 20* does give some suggested wording for letters reporting material weaknesses in internal accounting control.

As stated earlier, the management letter may be addressed to the board of directors (or its audit committee), to the chief executive officer, or to any official designated as an appropriate recipient. When the material included in the letter relates solely to accounting matters, it may be directed to the chief financial officer of the client. In some instances, it may be desirable to direct separate letters to operating personnel with copies to the chief executive. Furthermore, in some instances, it may be appropriate to send a separate letter to the audit committee.

The auditor should know the reader(s). The reader's background should be considered as the letter is written. Throughout the letter, the auditor should describe facts and recommendations in terms that the reader will understand; the auditor should offer reasons or advantages that the reader will recognize as valid. A reader with an accounting background may accept a suggestion to hire an internal auditor, because the auditor indicates it will improve internal controls and procedures. Although a CPA might understand the real benefits inferred, a business executive wants the benefits described in understandable terms as in the following example:

> The salary, expenses, and clerical back-up costs [which the reader can estimate or ask about] for one experienced internal auditor performing frequent audits of equipment and construction materials at job sites might produce time and cost savings as well as "insurance-type" benefits. The internal auditor could suggest improved procedures to provide management with better information faster and to reduce accounting costs. That person could also perform certain audit tasks which, if coordinated with our work, could reduce our audit time [dollar benefits.]

Before beginning to write the body of the letter, the auditor should plan what is to be said. The notes prepared during the audit and the internal control working papers should be reviewed at this time. The auditor also may wish to review the financial statements and memoranda to put things in perspective and to recall possible additional topics. It may be helpful in preparing longer letters to organize the topics initially in a subject outline.

Presenting a Topic

The auditor should provide appropriate background information to place things in proper perspective for the reader. Distinction should be made between the following items:

Observed facts.
Real problems.
Recommendations.
Costs or disadvantages of recommendations.
Savings or advantages of recommendations.

Observed Facts. Observed facts are the easiest of these items to report. The auditor should know the frequency and dates of occurrence and report them in the letter whenever they will be useful to the reader (see example below).

> We noted numerous small differences between company perpetual inventory records at March 31, 1980, and counts by the Los Angeles, Tucson, and Seattle independent regional warehouses.

Problems. The real, or underlying problems may be the same as indicated by the observed facts (a large inventory shortage which *is* the problem, for example). On the other hand, the observed facts may be merely *symptoms* of a different and possibly larger problem (an excessive number of accounting errors which might indicate that better qualified accounting personnel are needed).

Recommendations. In certain situations, bringing the problem to management's attention is the real service of the letter. To say that "negotiable securities are kept in an unlocked file cabinet" alerts management to a problem they should recognize must be corrected promptly. In other situations the problem is obvious to management but the solution is not. The auditor's service then consists of proposing practical suggestions for solving the problem. Consider the following example:

> The company had a substantial book-to-physical inventory loss last year. We understand that the causes are not yet known. Accordingly we recommend that you review all procedures designed to safeguard inventory and correct any weaknesses, take an interim physical inventory during the current fiscal year to determine if shortages are still occurring, and also stress the importance to the receiving clerks of verifying the quantity and condition of goods as they are received.

An unnecessarily critical description of the problem can set a negative tone and anger the reader or others whose work is being criticized. Frequently, a situation can be described more effectively in terms of potential for improvement. Which of the following presentations of the same situation would you prefer to receive in a letter if you were the client?

> The EDP system is not adequately documented because the manager has a lack of experience. Errors can escape detection, personnel training is likely to be inadequate, and it is difficult for an outsider to check what is being done.

or

> In the past there has been little documentation in the EDP Department. Now the department processes more data, prepares more reports, and employs more people than ever before, and further documentation could improve daily operations. Insufficient EDP documentation of the required type can jeopardize otherwise acceptable federal income tax deductions.
>
> Documentation of EDP procedures and programs reduces errors by clarifying tasks, helps detect errors which do occur, and is valuable in training new operators. It can also assure continuity and avoid confusion should key employees leave the company. We recommend the following kinds of documentation for your most vital programs and their related operating procedures. . . .

The first example has a negative tone and is especially likely to anger the EDP manager. The second makes its point in terms of potential improvements.

There is an art to making recommendations. Part of the art is knowing when to make a definite recommendation and when to keep the suggestion flexible. The following example of a suggestion does not hedge.

> To ensure that officers and trustees of the Foundation are properly fulfilling their fiduciary trust, we recommend that a record be maintained by the Controller to clearly show the purpose and conditions of each restricted gift. . . .

In other situations, the recommendation should be made flexible because the auditor does not know management's intentions. The following proposes a choice. "We suggest that the college's policy of not registering students until their tuition has been paid either be uniformly enforced or rescinded, because it is frequently violated." Flexible wording should be used when recommending action which seems appropriate but is based on limited or ambiguous information. For example, "You may wish to consider using a student loan billing and collection service offered by some of the large banks. Under such a plan. . . ."

Another part of the art of making recommendations consists of effectively setting the stage by informing a reader of something that may not have been considered and describing the importance of the situation as follows:

> Approximately $875,000 or 65 percent of the hospital's expenses last year were for payroll. Accordingly, the controls and record keeping for payroll are of considerable importance. The following recommendations would strengthen those controls and simplify record keeping. . . .

Cost of Recommendations. The art of making recommendations frequently includes indentifying the costs or disadvantages of implementing the suggestions as well as the potential benefits. The reader may challenge the estimates, but the fact that costs have been considered is at least evident. When the auditor suggests adding personnel, an estimate of the costs should be made and compared to the potential benefits. Recognizing the costs helps to assure practical and imaginative recommendations. Consider the following recommendation made to a contractor:

> Our tests indicated different accounting procedures were in use at various job sites. We recommend that field accounting policies and procedures be stated in a manual. Such a manual would enhance the use of the same efficient procedures at each job site and would provide guid-

ance for new accounting employees. It should detail all important accounting procedures performed at the job sites.

We recognize that preparing a manual would require time and effort; probably one accountant for a month. However, the project would be an excellent method for familiarizing your new accounting assistant with field accounting procedures. We have consultants experienced in such work and would be pleased to participate in this project to any extent you desire.

Benefits of Recommendations. The art of making recommendations includes the effective presentation of expected benefits. Consider these three alternate presentations of a lockbox recommendation:

> To improve controls over customers' payments by segregating cash handling and recording functions, we recommend....

or

> To speed the flow of cash receipts into your commercial bank account, we recommend....

or

> We recommend that you consider using a lockbox for customer remittances. Cash would be credited to or be available for use in your commercial account an average of two days sooner. In 1980, a two-day speed-up would have freed $138,000 for business use. The method provides strong internal control over cash receipts by completely separating handling and accounting functions. Customers are instructed to send their payments to a post office box to which only your commercial bank has access. Your bank account is immediately credited for the day's receipts and the account balance can be obtained daily by telephone. The bank sends your accounting department copies of all checks, remittance advices, and correspondence the following day. Service charges by the bank for this additional service tend to be more than offset by the earnings of funds freed and reduction in clerical costs.

Note that the third example presents the major benefits to be expected and estimates the dollar savings to be realized.

Graphs, flowcharts, organization charts, sample forms, ratios, and data tables may provide effective presentation in some instances. A graph was used in a management letter to dramatically illustrate the following comment to the board of trustees of an educational institution.

During the fiscal year the operating deficit was substantially in excess of the approved budget. There is a definite need to exercise control over spending by the various departments (see Figure 15-1).

Including a sample form in a smaller client's management letter may improve the chances of having a particular recommendation adopted. It simplifies management's task of implementing the suggestion and effectively communicates what is meant.

FIGURE 15-1
Operating profit or deficit year-to-date

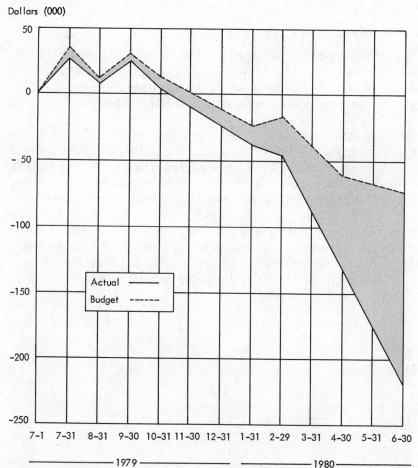

We recommend that you use a wage rate change authorization form such as the sample presented below.

Approval of Wage Rate Change

Employee _____

Job Title _____

Old Rate $ _____ Per _____ New Rate $ _____ Per _____

Effective Date of Change _____ 19 ____

Reasons or Comments:

Approved by _____ Date _____

Organizing the Topics

Comments should be arranged in a logical order and grouped under major headings. It is seldom appropriate to organize the letter in trial balance sequence; comments of the greatest significance should be presented first and various suggestions of minor significance may be grouped in a later paragraph.

Many management letters could be improved significantly by arranging the topics in a better sequence. The auditor should determine the most appropriate order of presentation when beginning to draft the letter. It often helps to outline the topics using descriptive titles. Working with brief titles on one page, topics will often "collect themselves" around more general subject headings and those headings (groups of topics) can then be presented in order of importance. Since too many suggestions of minor significance can detract from the letter, some editing is desirable after the initial draft has been completed.

The following *cover letter* illustrates several suggestions which have already been discussed:

J. J. JONES, CPA
1800 WEST ROAD
ATHENS, OHIO

Mr. Warren Kennedy
Vice President, Finance
Astute Manufacturing Company
Cleveland, Ohio

Dear Mr. Kennedy:

Our examination of the consolidated financial statements of Astute Manufacturing Company and subsidiaries for the year ended December 31, 1980, included a review of the system of internal control and the accounting procedures of the various accounting centers within your organization to the extent we considered necessary to evaluate the system as required by generally accepted auditing standards. Although our reviews disclosed no weaknesses which we consider material in relation to the consolidated financial statements, we would like to comment on some matters that came to our attention.

Our attached comments refer to specific accounting areas, the most important of which deals with suggestions which could measurably improve control over cash flows. The parent Company has accounting systems, procedures, and personnel which are generally adequate for present operations. In contrast, the subsidiaries are weaker in systems, procedures, and personnel. With respect to the subsidiaries, we identify broad problem areas that we feel should be given management attention and make suggestions for solving them. Solutions may require considerable effort by the Company to produce practical results, but the effect of these changes on operations should be important in the next several years.

This letter is organized so you can send the comments pertaining to any location to the responsible executive for his or her consideration and response.

Our comments are based upon conditions noted during our audit and are not intended to be all-inclusive. They are submitted as constructive suggestions to assist you in strengthening controls and procedures and are not intended to reflect on the honesty or integrity of any employee.

We appreciate the opportunity to present these comments and recommendations for your consideration, and are prepared to discuss them further at your convenience.

Very truly yours,

J. J. Jones, CPA

Athens, Ohio
March 31, 1981

610

The first paragraph is an introduction which bridges the gap from the audit to the letter and states plainly that there are no control or procedural weaknesses which are material in relation to the financial statements. The second is a summary paragraph which provides the necessary perspective to help the reader distinguish the relative importance of topics and characterizes the contents of the letter. The third paragraph indicates that each page relates to only one location or manager so that each section may be conveniently distributed by the client to the appropriate employees for comment and action. The purpose of the fourth paragraph is to avoid reflections on the integrity of the client's employees. In closing the letter, brevity and directness are appropriate. A closing similar to the last paragraph of the cover letter may be used.

PROCESSING THE LETTER

Before sending the letter, each situation to be discussed in the letter should be discussed with an appropriate representative of the client (e.g., one having knowledge of and responsibility for the area under discussion). Such discussions may help to determine whether the recommendations are practicable and also may lessen the chance of possible misrepresentation and/or resentment from executives concerned with the area under discussion.

In larger CPA firms, it also may be helpful to have management service and tax personnel review the supporting documents and the letter itself. This is especially desirable if these specialists are familiar with the client's affairs and have been involved with any of the areas pertaining to the recommendations in the letter.

A typed draft of the letter should be discussed in person with the recipient and other client executives appropriate in the circumstances. In most instances, a draft of the letter should be reviewed with the chief accounting officer of the client before its issuance. This will eliminate the element of surprise from the letter and may avoid embarrassment from making comments about items on which the auditor has not been fully informed.

GLOSSARY

Accounting control "... comprises the plan of organization and the procedures and records that are concerned with the safeguarding of assets and the reliability of financial records. ..." [SAS No. 1]

Administrative control "... the plan of organization and the procedures and records that are concerned with the decision processes leading to management's authorization of transactions. Such authorization is a management function directly associated with the responsibility for achieving the objectives of the organization and is the starting point for establishing accounting control of transactions." [SAS No. 1]

Audit committee   A committee of the board of directors (that usually is made up of individuals who are not part of management) which normally hires, communicates with, and sometimes fires the auditor. [see page 596]

Management letter   A letter addressed to the board of directors (or its audit committee), to the chief executive officer, or to any official designated as an appropriate recipient. It contains recommendations for improving accounting procedures, operations, and controls.

QUESTIONS AND PROBLEMS

15-1.   What is a management letter?

15-2.   Discuss the importance of a management letter.

15-3.   What advantages does a management letter have over suggestions made orally to management?

15-4.   What is an audit committee?

15-5.   List some general areas that may be the subject of management letters.

15-6.   "Management letters are only issued shortly after the conclusion of the field work." Comment.

15-7.   Should the costs of recommendations be included in management letters? Comment.

15-8.   The XYZ Corp. prepares sales forecasts in dollars only. Prepare a paragraph that might be included in a management letter stating that the forecasting should be in units, in dollars, and by product.

15-9.   The Large Co.'s scrap reporting procedures do not include the cause of scrapping. Prepare a paragraph that might be included in a management letter stating that the cause should be included in the reporting.

15-10.   The Small Co. rarely uses purchase orders. Prices on purchases are only approved when the office manager checks the invoices. Prepare a paragraph that might be included in a management letter suggesting improvements.

15-11.   During his audit of the Middle Co., J. Jones, CPA, is told by the Treasurer that Middle Co. has problems hiring and keeping production workers. The company is considering reviewing its compensation policies.

Required:

Prepare a paragraph for Mr. Jones that he might include in a management letter commenting on this situation.

15-12.   Below are some statistics that relate to the ABC Co.

ABC COMPANY

	Year Ended December 31			Industry Average
	1981	1980	1979	(1980)
Financial Position Relationships				
Total liabilities to tangible net worth	1.0	0.5	0.5	0.8
Current assets to current liabilities	2.5	2.2	2.3	2.0
Acid-test, quick assets to current liabilities	1.1	0.9	1.0	—
Inventory to net working capital	0.9	1.1	1.0	0.6
Operating Relationships				
Net income to tangible net worth	15.3%	10.4%	6.9%	5.6%
Net income per share of common stock	$13.10	$ 7.89	$ 4.87	—
Earnings retained (net income less dividends) to net income	77.2%	64.9%	46.9%	—
Number of days sales in receivables (accounts receivable to average daily sales)	24.9	26.8	29.3	—
Merchandise turnover (cost of sales to average inventory)	8.9	8.3	7.2	8.2
Gross profit to sales	10.3%	9.5%	9.1%	—
Net income to sales	2.2%	1.7%	1.3%	1.3%
Sales per payroll dollar	$ 9.58	$ 8.69	$ 8.40	—

Required:

Prepare some formal comments on the financial statistics of ABC Co. that could be included in a management letter that relates to the following topics:

a. Current assets to current liabilities. (ABC Co. has a long-term debt covenant that requires a minimum ratio of 1.5:1.)
b. Inventory to net working capital.
c. Net income to tangible net worth.
d. Net income per share of common stock.
e. Number of days sales in receivables.
f. Gross profit and net income to sales (sales in 1981 increased by 30 percent).

13. Read the following management letter which is designed to be issued to the partners of the law firm of Smart & Dumb. Keep in mind these questions and note your specific comments:

Is each topic presented effectively? Why?
Is the letter organized effectively? Why?
Could the writing be significantly improved? How?
Would you delete any topics? Which ones?
What are the letter's strong points? Why?

Do you believe you need more information to evaluate its effectiveness? If so, what information do you need and why is it necessary?

J. JONES, C.P.A.

April 12, 1980

The Partners of
Smart & Dumb

Gentlemen:

In connection with our examination of the balance sheet of Smart & Dumb as of December 31, 1979, we reviewed the accounting procedures and systems of internal control employed by the Partnership. We found no material weaknesses in internal accounting control. However, the attached comments and suggestions for improvements therein, are submitted for your consideration. They were derived from our examination of the records, general observations, and discussions with various partners and employees.

We wish to express our appreciation for the cooperation and courtesy extended to us by your partners and employees. We would be pleased to discuss any of these matters with you further and to assist in their implementation if you so desire.

Very truly yours,

J. J. Jones, C.P.A.

Cash Receipts

Cash receipts are manually and separately posted to the cash receipts journal and detail accounts receivable ledger cards. Pending further evaluation as to the desirability of mechanizing the entire accounting system, we recommend that a pegboard system, which would eliminate this double posting, be implemented as an immediate time-saving device.

To facilitate the daily posting of cash receipts and avoid incorrect postings, we recommend that unidentified receipts be posted initially to a suspense account. A listing of these unmatched receipts could be periodically circulated to the partners for proper identification. Requesting that clients return a copy of the invoice, or a detachable portion thereof, with their remittances would probably reduce the number of unidentified receipts.

Cash Disbursements

Approved invoices should be recorded by use of a pegboard system which would simultaneously prepare the checks.

Upon issuance of the checks, all supporting detail for the disbursement should be defaced to preclude the potential reuse thereof.

Signed checks should be mailed and bank accounts should be reconciled by individuals not connected with the preparation and recording of the respective disbursements.

Petty Cash

To improve internal control over petty cash, each disbursement should be evidenced by a prenumbered petty cash voucher. Applicable supporting detail should be attached thereto and, upon reimbursement, the voucher and supporting detail should be defaced to prevent potential reuse.

The petty cash custodian is frequently interrupted in performing her accounting duties to make change for the vending machines. Consideration should be given to maintaining a small change fund at the switchboard, possibly on an "honor" basis, for this purpose.

Accounts Receivable

Sixty-four accounts receivable confirmation requests were returned by the Post Office due to bad addresses, and 48 clients reported various differences in their account balances to us. These items were either satisfactorily resolved or were written off as uncollectible. Our review of the accounts and discussion thereof with the respective partners resulted in the write-off of accounts aggregating approximately $80,000 and the recording of allowances for additional doubtful accounts aggregating $40,000. We suggest that additional efforts be made to periodically furnish each partner with a listing of past-due accounts so that appropriate follow-up can be initiated on a timely basis.

A pegboard system which would provide simultaneous posting of the revenue journal and detail accounts receivable ledger cards should be instituted.

As a result of the additional effort expended, a reasonably accurate billing cutoff was achieved as of Dec. 31, 1979. Similar efforts should be made at future fiscal year ends and particularly at dates of admission, withdrawal, or retirement of partners, when cash payments are required to be calculated on the accrual basis net worth of the firm. However, accurate billing cutoffs are not essential at interim month ends; and to expedite the monthly closings, we suggest that the established twentieth of the following month cutoff date be strictly adhered to at these times.

Charges Reimbursable from Clients

Although it was impractical to make a complete reconcilement of this account as of Dec. 31, 1979, our review of these charges resulted in a write-off of approximately $18,000 to adjust this account to a reasonable estimate of charges recoverable from clients as of Dec. 31, 1979. To insure that all items are billed or that approved write-offs are recorded for unbilled items, the detail of this account, which consists of various charge slips in the billing folders, should be periodically reconciled to the general ledger control account.

Luncheon Club Billings

A time saving may be achieved by requesting that The Luncheon Club bill each attorney separately or group charge slips by attorney. Each attorney's secretary could then segregate the charge slips and furnish the accounting department with the aggregate personal amount (to be deducted from the monthly dividend) and detail billing memos for amounts chargeable to clients.

Telephone Charges

Switchboard and accounting personnel spend approximately 40 hours each month checking telephone charges and investigating unidentified calls. Consideration should be given to charging unidentified calls, which we were informed were large in number but minor in aggregate amount, to office expense. This policy could be instituted after emphasizing to the staff the importance of placing toll calls through the switchboard, where detail charge slips would be prepared, or obtaining time and charges on calls made after office hours.

The telephone company could be requested to review the overall effectiveness of the present phone system.

Duties of Accounting Manager

The accounting manager presently spends approximately three hours each day performing duties that could apparently be handled by an office boy. These duties include (1) changing light bulbs; (2) making bank deposits; (3) ordering, checking, unpacking, and distributing supplies; (4) dealing with taxicab companies and the Highway Express Agency, Inc.; (5) Post Office errands; (6) personal errands; and (7) obtaining signatures on checks. An office boy (perhaps a college student on a part-time basis) could be hired at a much lower wage rate to handle these miscellaneous jobs, thereby enabling the accounting manager to devote full time to accounting matters.

Partners' Dividends

Cash receipts on the day of calculation are presently included in the computation of the partners' monthly dividends. To faciliate the orderly preparation of these dividends, consideration should be given to including cash receipts only through the previous day.

Mechanization of Accounting System

As previously mentioned, implementation of pegboard systems should provide immediate time savings in several areas at a nominal cost. However, we believe that further consideration could be given to the desirability of utilizing an accounting machine to further reduce clerical time and provide additional management information on a more timely basis.

Time and Billing Controls

We recommend that further consideration be given to improving and standardizing time control and billing procedures. Procedures could be established to:

1. Ensure that all chargeable time is billed.
2. Facilitate more timely billing.
3. Provide comparison of actual fees billed with fees at standard billing rates.
4. Provide an inventory of jobs in process including appropriate detail of unbilled charges.
5. Provide, if desired, a summary of time devoted to clients, administration, civic activities, professional societies, or other categories.
6. Provide a summary of billings by partner.
7. Ease the work load on attorneys' secretaries.

If it is decided to mechanize the accounting system, as mentioned in the preceding section, a time control and billing system would be an ideal application.

15-14. It has been quite a year for Delta Corporation, a September 30 audit client. For years the company was operated as a family business by R. Founder, who is now 68 years old, manufacturing a line of traditional toys in a single plant. Delta toys had been sold through department stores ever since Mr. Founder built the first one in his basement while working at the local supermarket. About two years ago a combination of factors caught up with the company in the form of declining sales and profits, which dipped below the toy industry average for the first time in many years.

On October 1, 1979, Bob Founder, Jr. became president and treasurer. In the six years since earning his MBA, Bob has worked in the sales, production, and accounting areas of the company and showed promise as a business executive. His first task as president was to analyze the market. After analyzing the market, Bob decided to phase out toy guns, a major product line, over the next three years and press development of more sophisticated and expensive battery-operated toys. He believed their profit potential was greater, but he recognized such high-fashion toys presented a greater risk of obsolescence as there was little demand for last year's best seller.

Three months later, at a meeting, Bob met Ray Builder, who owned Alliance, another family-owned toy company with capabilities in the sophisticated toy field and a progressive marketing group which uses the company's computer to analyze sales. His sales outlets included the larger hardgood discount chains. Delta acquired Alliance as a subsidiary on April 1, 1980, with a combination of cash and stock, and in doing so incurred Delta's first bank loan in 30 years. Bob and Ray decided to work as a team with Ray managing Alliance's marketing and manufacturing operations at its two plants. All other activities will be handled at Delta's offices and key personnel from Alliance will transfer to Delta. They plan a secondary offering of part of the stock held by the two families after the audited financial statements are available for the year ended September 30, 1980.

You were the in-charge accountant on the September 30, 1979, audit which was completed in late December as the books were not closed until December 7. You recall that the company's accounting department was doing a satisfactory job with relatively few people. The only significant problem was the length of time needed to close the books. Delta's chief accountant told you several times that the IRS had never made an adjustment to the company's returns and that "after I make *my* audit, you auditors have it clean as a whistle." Internal controls were generally very good. Last year's management letter discussed receipts from scrap sales, the high number of past-due customers' accounts at year end (almost all paid before the report was issued), and several matters of lesser importance.

The partner on the engagement recently had lunch with Bob Founder, who enthusiastically described the events of the last year. Since you will be the senior on the September 30, 1980, examination of Delta's consolidated financial statements, the partner suggested that you begin planning for the engagement now.

The requirements of this case study are:

1. Describe the important events which have occurred since the last audit.
2. List the topics you plan to consider for possible management letter attention. Be as specific as possible.

Index

619

620

American Institute of Certified Public
Accountants—Cont.
Opinions of the Accounting Principles
Board No. 26, 497
Opinions of the Accounting Principles
Board No. 28, 518
Private Companies Practice Section,
13
SEC Practice Section, 12
Statement on Auditing Procedure No.
33, 96
Statement on Auditing Procedure No.
41, 137
Statement on Auditing Standards No.
1, 12, 25, 126, 162–66, 169–70,
172, 204, 221–23, 230, 232, 237,
249, 277–78, 293, 313–14, 323,
401–2, 429–30, 543–49, 553, 564,
595
Statement on Auditing Standards No.
2, 401, 430, 539–47, 567
Statement on Auditing Standards No.
3, 309, 331
Statement on Auditing Standards No.
4, 16, 18–21
Statement on Auditing Standards No.
5, 24
Statement on Auditing Standards No.
6, 515–17
Statement on Auditing Standards No.
7, 54
Statement on Auditing Standards No.
8, 549–50
Statement on Auditing Standards No.
9, 174–75
Statement on Auditing Standards No.
11, 228–29
Statement on Auditing Standards No.
12, 499–500, 549
Statement on Auditing Standards No.
14, 514, 553, 557–60
Statement on Auditing Standards No.
15, 536–38
Statement on Auditing Standards No.
16, 176–79, 204
Statement on Auditing Standards No.
17, 180–81, 204
Statement on Auditing Standards No.
18, 117–19
Statement on Auditing Standards No.
19, 226–27, 565
Statement on Auditing Standards No.
20, 167, 205, 564, 594–95, 602
Statement on Auditing Standards No.
21, 513–15, 550–53
Statement on Auditing Standards No.
22, 21, 27

American Institute of Certified Public
Accountants—Cont.
Statement on Auditing Standards No.
23, 225, 227
Statement on Auditing Standards No.
24, 518–20, 560–62, 567
Statement on Responsibilities in Tax
Practice, 57–59
Articles of incorporation, 503
Assembly sheets in working papers, 233
Assets, miscellaneous, 478
Attestation, defined, 4
Average cost, for inventories, 428
Audit
partial, by different firm, 543
performing audit work, 28
preliminary planning, 27–28
reporting the findings, 28
steps in an, 27
Audit contract, 81–86
Audit function, value added by, 5
Audit memoranda, 234
cash, 379
inventories, 447
other assets, 479
receivables, 414
Audit program
accounts payable, 495
accounts receivable, 397–414
deferred charges, 473, 478
defined, 175–76
example for tests of transactions,
200–203
intangible assets, 478
inventories, 429–47
long-term debt, 496–97
notes payable, 495
notes receivable, 413–14
operations, 404–5
payrolls, 508–13
prepaid expenses, 473, 478
property, plant and equipment, 468–73
securities, 463–64
shareholders' equity, 503–4
Audit (auditor's) report
additional financial information, report
on, 554–55
adverse opinion, 26, 541
basis other than GAAP, 557, 573
cash basis, 557–58
comments, 555
comparative statements, 536–39
compilation, 569–75
compliance reports, 559–60
consistency, 545–46
consolidated statements, 534–35
defined, 533

624

626

Opinion No. 18, 462
Opinion No. 26, 497
Opinion No. 28, 518
Opinions, auditor's
  adverse, 26, 541
  disclaimers, 26, 541–42, 567
  expression of, 25
  qualified, 25, 540
  unqualified, 25, 533
Organization
  of firms, 14
  within a firm, 15
Owners' equity; see Stockholders' equity

P

Partner, in a CPA firm, 15
Payrolls
  audit memorandum, 520
  audit program, 508–13
  auditor's objectives, 508
  canceled payroll checks, 511
  checking amounts, 512
  executive, 513
  internal control, 508, 513
  office, 513
  personnel records, 510
  plant, 508–13
  reconciling payroll bank account, 512
  testing, 508–13
  testing postings to ledgers, 512
  unclaimed paychecks, 512
Period of time analysis, 234
Perpetual inventory method, 429
Prepaid expenses
  audit memorandum, 479
  audit program, 473, 477–78
  auditor's objectives, 473
  defined, 473
  prepaid insurance, 476–78
  prepaid insurance schedule,
    illustrated, 476–77
Prepaid insurance, 476–78
Primary beneficiaries
  defined, 89
  liability of CPA to, 89–91
Private Companies Practice Section, 13
Procedures, auditing; see Auditing
  procedures
Program, audit; see Audit program
Property, plant, and equipment
  acquisitions, 467–68
  audit memorandum, 479
  audit program, 468–73
  auditor's objectives, 467
  capital budget, 467–68
  constructed versus purchased, 469–70
  depreciation, changes in allowance for,
    471–73

Property, plant, and equipment—Cont.
  expensing, 470
  idle properties, 471
  internal control over, 467
  investment tax credit, 471, 473
  physical inspection, 469
  repair and maintenance accounts, 468
  retirements, 468–70
  summary of property, plant, and
    equipment, illustrated, 474–75
  summary of transactions for year,
    472–73
  testing changes in accounts, 469–73
  testing depreciation, 471–72
  transfers, 471
  unrecorded property, 471
  working papers, 472
Property not used in operations, 478
Prospectuses, 116
Proxy, defined, 132
Proxy solicitations, 132
Public accountant, 8
Public accounting, as a profession, 9–12
Public accounting firms
  "Big Eight," 14
  organization, 14–15
  quality review, 29
Purchases journal, testing of, 490

Q

Qualified opinion, 25, 540
Quality review, 29
Questionnaires
  sample, 182–94
  in testing internal control, 168

R

Receivables, sundry, 478
Regulation S-X, 116–21
Related party transactions, 515–18
  audit procedures, 516–17
  disclosure, 517
Replacement cost information, 117–20
Reporting, standards of, 17, 22
Retained earnings, 503
Revenue accounts, audit of; see
  Operations
Review, (unaudited statements), 571–75
Rhode Island Hospital Trust National
  Bank v. Swartz, 95–96
Rusch Factors, Inc. v. Levin, 94–95

S

S-1 review, 128–29
Sales, test of transactions, 397–401
Sales cutoff, 412–13
Sampling
  in audit tests, 248–49